D1072060

THE BRUCE

John Barbour's origins are unknown, though it is likely that his father was barber to a prominent Scot. A clerk at Dunkeld cathedral in 1355, a year later he moved to what was to be his job for the rest of his life – the archdeaconry of Aberdeen. He studied at a university at some stage (in England or France) and became fluent in French, reading the popular *romans-histoires* of the time – fiction to us, but history to him. On their model, about 1375 he wrote his great poem, *The Bruce*, the story of Robert the Bruce and his loyal captain, James Douglas, their tribulations and successes, their chivalry and loyalty. It is a vivid picture of gallant men struggling for the freedom of their country without compromising the values of their society, the earliest work of literature in Scots and the finest written in the Middle Ages. Barbour took time off to serve King Robert II (Stewart) as an auditor, and wrote for him an account of the genealogy of the Stewarts, now lost. He died in 1395, probably at Aberdeen.

A. A. M. Duncan was born in Pitlochry in 1926, educated at George Heriot's School (where he first encountered *The Bruce*), and at Edinburgh and Oxford Universities. He became in 1962 Professor of Scottish History at Glasgow University, a chair he held till retiral in 1993. He has published a history of Scotland up to 1286, has edited all the charters and letters of King Robert I (Bruce), and written numerous articles on medieval Scottish history.

John Barbour

THE BRUCE

An edition with
translation and notes by

A. A. M. DUNCAN

CANONGATE
CLASSICS
78

This edition first published as a Canongate Classic in 1997 by Canongate Books Limited, 14 High Street, Edinburgh EH1 1TE.
Introduction, translation and notes copyright © A. A. M. Duncan, 1997. All rights reserved. The publishers gratefully acknowledge general subsidy from the Scottish Arts Council towards the Canongate Classics series and a specific grant towards the publication of this volume.
Set in 9½ Monotype Plantin by Carnegie Publishing Limited. Printed by Caledonian International Book Manufacturing, Bishopbriggs.

British Library Cataloguing in Publication Data
A catalogue record for this book is available from the British Library

ISBN 0 86241 681 7

Contents

Preface

When I was a schoolboy in 1940–44, the blackboard in our History classroom at George Heriot's School carried a permanent text which an imaginative teacher, William Gould, asked us to memorise, a text for the struggle against tyranny which later took the lives of some of my class-mates. The fifteen lines of poetry began:

A! Fredome is a noble thing

Sadly they had little to do with a History curriculum then laid down by the Scottish Education Department and blessed by the universities (sadly, too, I heard nothing of the poem when I was an undergradute later in the 1940s), but, amid the dictated notes on the Diplomatic Revolution, there was always the poem on the board to show another approach to the past, through the materials it has left to us. That is what prevails in the classroom today, and it is my hope that this poem, which tells us so much about chivalric society in Scotland, will become known there and to newer generations of young Scots.

Many people then despised, and some people still fear, the study of the literature and history of Scotland. How wrong they are is surely proved by the work of my contemporaries, G. W. S. Barrow and T. C. Smout. There are two great books about Robert Bruce, one written in the fourteenth century by John Barbour, the other in our time by G. W. S. Barrow: *Robert Bruce and the Community of the Realm of Scotland* (1988). I have cited it rarely because there is almost nothing in it which one could not cite and am assuming that every reader will know it, or be prepared to discover it.

On thing you may look for in this book (or indeed Professor Barrow's) and will not find there: the Bruce in a cave watching the trials of a spider seeking to spin its web across a gap and vowing that if the spider should succeed, he too would continue the struggle. It is one of the best known stories from Scotland's history, but unfortunately there is no authority for it earlier than the eighteenth century. It is a folk tale told of others and borrowed for Bruce because he did indeed try and try again; so it has its value for our understanding because it resonates with the tribulations of which we read in this, Barbour's more immediate and authentic account. This poem is a treasure as an historical source and a masterpiece of Scottish literature.

Over the years I have benefited from much critical help from Professor D. E. R. Watt, whose edition of Bower will stand when we are long gone. I wish to thank him and Dr Colm McNamee who kindly made available to me, in typescript, his *The Wars of the Bruces* which I found very helpful, and who saved me from errors in my notes on books 14–18. My colleague, Dr Graeme Small has been most patient in helping with the translation of Le Bel, and with other queries about French historiography, while Dr John Taylor of Leeds read the introduction and notes, gave me very helpful further light on English sources and spotted many spelling errors committed, of course, by my pc.

They will be understanding when I express as my greatest debt that to the University of Glasgow. First to my students there, who over twenty years put up with, sometimes shared, my enthusiasm for Barbour and who made me think about the poem week by week. Secondly to the University Library where I have enjoyed the privilege of a magnificent collection and a staff of sympathetic and helpful colleagues. Thirdly to the Scottish History Department, the Faculty of Arts and the University Court which have given me fellowship standing to make retirement less of a break from their congenial company.

Archie Duncan
March 1997

Introduction

I. THE READER

I hope that you have bought this book to read one of the masterpieces of Scottish literature, and an important account of the history of Robert the Bruce. It becomes a powerful narrative, alive with dramatic descriptions of travels by land and sea, escapes, single combats, sieges and battles; there is little about domestic or social life, much about the ethos and blood-spattered reality of chivalry. Above all, there is the invocation of freedom for our land which resonates so powerfully in the late twentieth century. The language is not easy, but neither is it difficult if you will persist with the initial problems, using the translation on the opposite page to discover what the words now out of use mean, and how Barbour arranges words to suit rhyme and metre. I have added a translation of the Declaration of Arbroath from Latin, another statement of the ideal of freedom, but contemporary with Bruce.

You need to know little other than Barbour's language to enjoy the poem, but conventionally some background is supposed to help the reader. Barbour lived from the 1330s to 1395. For most of his adult life he was archdeacon of Aberdeen and, as he tells us, he was writing this poem in 1375 under the first Stewart king, Robert II, son of Bruce's daughter. There is no significant piece of literature in Scots which is known to be earlier than *The Bruce*. It is written in that form of northern English known as early Scots, but, magré that, it also contains many borrowings from French. You may find his reminiscences of ancient Thebes and Rome and his digressions on necromancy and astrology strange irrelevancies in the biography of a great king, but they give an insight into the mind-set of Barbour and his readers which is still valuable.

I suggest that, unless you are familiar with the poem, you skip for now the studies in the rest of this introduction and betake yourself to the poem forthwith – and I mean the poem, not the translation! Afterwards you should find something of value and interest in the discussion which follows and in the notes, which seek to compare Barbour with other sources, not always to his advantage.

2. JOHN BARBOUR

[1] John Barbour died on 13 March, 1395 after a documented career of forty years. His family background is a mystery, though the trade name suggests an urban origin.[2] His most recent editor, McDiarmid, rejected the north-east for John's origins, because based only upon his ecclesiastical office. He suggested instead that the references in *The Bruce* to Ayrshire and Galloway placed him there, but the case is no stronger. His birth is usually placed about 1325, as much to give him a toehold in King Robert's reign as for anything his career tells us. He could well have been born as late as 1335, because he appears out of the blue, in 1356, when he gave up the precentorship of Dunkeld, held for scarcely a year,[3] on his promotion to the archdeaconry of Aberdeen; his advancement had been very rapid, since there is no sign of his having held a chaplainry, vicarage or parsonage, as steps toward higher church office; this suggests that he owed these offices to a special event, and that he may have been much younger than usual for such promotion. When he obtained the Dunkeld post in 1355, he was probably at the papal court at Avignon with the previous precentor.

Scotland in 1354 had at last negotiated the ransoming of King David from seven years of captivity in England; the Guardian (Regent), his nephew Robert Stewart, unenthusiastic at the prospect, tinkered with the prospect of French assistance, and so neglected the ransom negotiations that they fell through at the final stages. This politicking may have earned John Barbour his Dunkeld promotion for work in France, though in what way we cannot know. In 1356 he obtained the Aberdeen archdeaconry presumably from the same Stewart patronage; but King David came home in November 1357 for an even larger ransom, at which prospect John sought leave to study in England (August 1357). He had further English safe-conducts to leave Scotland when David II was an active king (1357–71), for study in England (1364), to visit St Denis, France (1365), and for study in France (1368); he may have studied at a French university 1368–71, but had already been to a university because in 1368 (and occasionally later) he is called 'Master'. The rarity of this description suggests that he had not graduated and was not entitled to it.

After 1356 he received no further advancement in his long life, certainly not the bishopric for which he was as well qualified as any of the bishops. Everything suggests that he was a known client of Robert Stewart, who, in 1371, at last ascended the throne. John Barbour, it seems, wrote *The Bruce* for this royal patron, whose father appears in a generous measure and light in its pages. When he began to write is a matter of judgment, but I do not see how the poem as it stands can have taken fewer than two years, and would not be surprised if it took five or six. I therefore suggest that composition began in 1372, and detained or brought John to court, as a result of which he was employed in February 1373 as one of the auditors at the exchequer (worth £40 per annum), acting for the second time in that office two years later. 1375 marks a change in his career because from now he appears in a north-eastern context; in 1378 the king granted him a pension of £1 annually from Aberdeen burgh's annual payment to the crown. This was paid till his death and (since the grant was perpetual, to assigns) from 1395 to his legatees, the cathedral chapter; in 1429 it was said to have been granted 'for the compilation of the book of the deeds of the late King Robert the Bruce'.

In the 1380s he did return to court, serving as auditor again in 1383, '84 and '85, had several one-off gifts of money from the king in 1382–86, and in 1388 an annual pension of £10 for life; this last, I suggest, means that he had satisfactorily completed a literary work, but was not to be given a bishopric. His patron, Robert II having died in 1390, he was at Aberdeen in 1391–92 and probably till his death. Aberdeen cathedral lists give the anniversary of his death on 13 and 14 March, and the transfer of his £1 pension shows that the year was 1395.

What did he write? Before 1449 the chroniclers Wyntoun and Bower had ascribed to him: *The Bruce*, sections and lines from which were silently borrowed by Wyntoun; *The Brut*; *The Stewartis Oryginalle;* and *The Stewartis Genealogy*. The last two are certainly identical, and if a mythical Trojan origin were suggested for the Stewarts, *The Brut* could be another title for the same. They surely confirm that Barbour devoted his literary talents pretty single-mindedly to one family, the Stewarts. And whether one or two works, they are lost.

A number of other works were once said to have come from Barbour's pen: *The Buik of Alexander*, with many silent borrowings from *The Bruce*, but ascribed to 1438 in the manuscript of its text; sections of a translation of Guido delle Colonne's Latin history of the taking of Troy; all or part of a translation of the Legends of the Saints. McDiarmid has given cogent reasons for rejecting all the ingenious hypotheses supporting these attributions.

3. *The Bruce* ANTECEDENTS

The poem was written in the 1370s (to anticipate later discussion) in the vernacular, in rhyming octosyllabic couplets (with frequent irregular lines including many with ten syllables) linking it to narrative poetry in both English and Anglo-Norman. There are over a thousand alliterative lines, showing that Barbour was familiar with the contemporary revival of alliterative English poetry, but the vocabulary is shot through with words borrowed from French, showing his familiarity with that language; it has been calculated that 52% of the words in the poem derive from Old English, 37% from French (though many would be old borrowings).[4] His *exempla*, drawn from French romances show that he was familiar with – I would not say steeped in – some of that literature, including the Troy book and the *Roman d'Alixandre*.[5]

The Bruce is unique, in being in verse, in English, and a romance-biography not a chronicle. There were chronicles in verse, notably that of Peter Langtoft (to 1307), written in northern England in French, and partly translated by Robert Manning in the 1330s into English in Barbour's metre, virulently anti-Scottish and populous in its view of Edward I's time, relegating chivalrous deeds to the distant past. Lives of kings, the Latin *Vita Edwardi Secundi* in England and Joinville's French life of St Louis from France, are in prose and tend to a strict chronology – indeed the former may have been written in contemporary sections; they are not chivalrous in tone.

In fact, from *c.* 1330 there was a rather thin tradition of writing recent or contemporary history in England, though prose text-book histories 'from the earliest times', the Latin *Polychronicon*, by Ranulph Higden (first version 1327), and the French *Brut* (to 1307) written not very far from 1310, appealed to the landed class by a sympathetic interest in chivalry. Both were translated into English some fifty years or more later, part of the efflorescence of literary English in the mid and late fourteenth century. But with one exception

Edward III's England produced no significant chivalrous account of his time, for a very good reason: events had moved to France. That historical writing followed the cavalry to entertain with chivalry is shown by the exception, the *Scala-cronica* of Sir Thomas Gray. Written by a northern English knight in French prose, it is 'chivalrous history at its best and most representative',[6] a chronicle from mythical times to his own, with graphic descriptions of the involvement of his father and himself in the Scottish wars, but with much emphasis on bold and brave deeds, and some interest in courtly love.

It is a work to be placed with that of the other great chroniclers of chivalry, Gray's contemporary Jean le Bel, canon of Liège, and the greatest (at least in volume of writings) of them all, Jean Froissart, Barbour's contemporary.[7] Le Bel served in and described the Northumberland campaign of Edward III in 1327, largely as an exhausting trudge through wind and rain in search of the enemy; in these reminiscences chivalry is not prominent. His narrative overlaps that of Barbour, but it also links the Scottish to the French wars, the preferred reading-matter of the chivalrous classes in England and France. He writes in prose, disdaining a 'big rhymed book, which I have seen and read ... the beginning of which is quite false and full of lies, up to the beginning of the war which [Edward III] undertook against King Philip [VI]' (i.e. to 1338); it is difficult to see what other subject this poem can have dealt with than the Scottish wars of 1327–37. Le Bel contrasts this poem with his own 'small book' – of 230 folios! The poem's size tells against identifying it with the 'old romance on thick and short paper, in bastard letters, one column and in verse, and it is about the wars of Scotland and England' in the library of Charles V of France and worth 4 sous.[8] These lost works show the stimulus given by a sustained war to chivalrous verse history and suggest that the Scottish war of 1306–27 would generate contemporary chronicling and encomium of the Scottish leaders in Scotland.

Froissart probably began his chronicles in verse,[9] but abandoned this work as tending to prolixity and exaggeration. To record a multitude of chivalric deeds by the knightly class, of which he was an assiduous collector, to suggest the gradation of achievement which appealed so strongly to that class, in short, to write 'true history' (*vraie histoire*) avoiding poetic fancy and fable, he thought prose necessary, but French prose, the language of immediate access, which was displacing Latin for chronicle and history as the language of 'truth'. But Froissart's pursuit of 'truth', often protested, produced a skeleton of fact – most but not all of the people mentioned did live – fleshed with exploits exaggerated in most detail and tricked out in sheer fiction.[10] Beware the proclaimed intention to write only the truth.

But France was to produce other verse histories: Guillaume de Machaut, who dined with David II in London in 1363, wrote on Peter I king of Cyprus (*La prise d'Alexandrie*) in octosyllabic couplets about 1372;[11] in the same metre the life of the Black Prince by Chandos Herald (who in his introduction claims that poets recording the deeds of good men are no longer esteemed), was written about 1380–85;[12] other surviving lives of Bertrand du Guesclin, of John IV duke of Brittany, and of Boucicault are of the 1390s or later.[13]

Thus, amid important prose chivalric chronicles of the Anglo-French wars, the verse chivalric biography revived in France, prompting the question whether there were other and earlier verse biographies of less prominent valiant knights written by domestic minstrel-heralds,[14] cherished by the family for a generation or two and then forgotten and lost. It is possible, but the verse literature known only from incidental references seems to have been romance or chronicle not biography. The culture which stimulated writing in biographical form had its roots in the French war which began in 1338, but the writings themselves belong to a later phase, of French recovery and uneasy truce from 1369 to *c.* 1410. Only the famous Machaut's work could have been known to, or served as model for, John Barbour – a distant possibility for which the texts provide no support.

In England, chivalrous history in Anglo-Norman verse had made a brief appearance from the pen of a minstrel-herald in *The Siege of Caerlaverock* (an event of 1300), but, although Anglo-Norman remained a language of use among the highest English nobility, it, and the demand for verse in it, died out among middling men. Neither in English nor in Anglo-Norman is there any model for *The Bruce* in what we would regard as history; the only models are in romance. Barbour's poem owes its metre to Middle English romances, but otherwise its inspiration was native to Scotland, the ethos and literature of the victorious war of 1306–27.

Barbour's choice of the medium of Scots reflects the accomplishments of the Scottish nobility in the fourteenth century;

if French remained a language of use among the highest
English nobility, it had ceased to be more than an esoteric
skill in Scotland,[15] where the king had treaties translated from
French into Latin in order that they might be understood.
The use of verse tells us that this poem was written for
declamation: 'Lordings! who chooses now to hear' (1.445) the
romance of gentle folk and their chivalry, a word which I have
not attempted to translate but which in Barbour means both
a group of knights (or at least of men-at-arms)[16] and knightly
acts in battle. The verse form appealed to a knightly audience
in Scotland for it was retained by Wyntoun for his *Chronicle*
and by Hary for his pseudo-biography, *the Wallace* (c. 1470);
the same appreciation is shown by translated romances such
as *the Buik of Alexander* (1438).

The address 'Listen, lordings!' is a commonplace of medi-
eval romances in English, usually at the very beginning, and
it may well be followed by occasional requests for silence and
breaks calling for the filling of cups. But Barbour's only
implication of noise in his audience is 'who *chooses* to hear',
and the poem is evidently addressed to a remarkably well-
behaved audience. It is not for market-place or tavern, but
belongs with those romances about what was thought to be
history, such as the Troy Book, which appealed to a sophisti-
cated public by claiming a serious didactic purpose, the
example of men of old.

Nonetheless, there are other uses of 'you hear', showing
that it was to be declaimed to an audience, a fact which the
division into books, first made by Pinkerton in 1790, does
much to obscure. That does not mean that it was without
divisions, for no man could recite (or read) 13,600 lines
without pause. In some romances there is explicit mention of
divisions (*passus* or 'fit'), but not in *The Bruce*. The manu-
scripts might indicate by a new paragraph where those breaks
were intended to fall, but since C has many more than E,
and since the new paragraph often opens by referring to the
preceding one as 'thus' or 'in this way' (which suggest con-
tinuation, not pause), it is better to accept the obvious changes
of subject matter in the poem as marking the pauses. In the
first five books obvious breaks occur at 1.445, 2.49, 4.1, 4.336,
5.123; almost certainly there were other pause-places, espe-
cially in book 3, but it may be that they are less clear because
the author wished to be able to choose between them for the
reading of the day.[17]

We have no evidence that this poem was read at the court of Robert II, but no other patron or place seems at all likely.

4. THE COMPOSITION OF THE POEM

The poem which Barbour set out to write about 1372, was outlined at 1.445–52,[18] as a 'truthful story' and a 'book' (1.13, 33), but at 1.445, in phrases whose substance is commonplace, he says the 'romance' now begins of men in distress – Robert Bruce and James Douglas – who rise to honour. That these were well-recognised overlapping genres is shown by their recurrence in Cuvelier's use of *chanson, livre, istoire, roman* for his account of du Guesclin; only 'song' is missing from *The Bruce*.[19] The same meaning of romance as 'distress to honour' occurs at 2.46, but more generally, at 9.496, a romance is about 'hey worschip and manheid', great valour and courage. This poem was an account of their rise from appalling adversity to triumph and to recover both their heritages at Bannockburn. It began with a necessary setting of the scene, a selective account of how the English came to take over Scotland, which identified Robert Bruce the Competitor with his grandson, the king, and gave no account of the wars against Edward I between 1296 and 1304 in which Bruce first opposed, then submitted to, that king. Instead Bruce is pictured as rightful king, moved by Comyn to take kingship – it is not explained how this was to happen – and then betrayed by him. Thus Bruce was justified in becoming king, and in killing Comyn.

The sacrilege of murder at the altar brought about Bruce's misfortunes in 1306–08, to which books 2–8 are devoted; there is no account of the years 1309–12.[20] Thereafter the wheel of Fortune turned and the king rose to his height in the great victory at Bannockburn, while the same half-turn cast Edward II down (13.636–70). A short passage deals with the exchange of prisoners which brought Marjory Bruce home to marry Walter Stewart and produce Robert Stewart who is 'now' king, the poem's happy outcome. The date of completion, rather than being written as a colophon, is then worked into the text in four different ways: regnal year, AD, age of Robert II, and years since the death of Robert I. There are problems about fitting these together but 1375–76 covers these and suffices here. This poem concludes, at 13.722 of *The Bruce*, with a prayer that the offspring of Bruce's offspring will rule as well as he did.

The work when completed was probably in some 8,800 lines, was expansive, with fairly frequent reference to other romances, and some heavy moralising; it consists of a series of episodes involving Bruce or Douglas or both, of varying length, each self-contained and loosely connected to those on either side, but often containing a comment on the moral significance of the action, either in words from the author, or in a set speech attributed to a participant. The structure of books, a modern imposition, obscures Barbour's method, his loose narrative and emphasis on the exemplary value of each incident.

But an exemplary value also informed the whole poem, one which has given it much of its appeal in the late twentieth century. For the poem is not only about the recovery of Bruce's right by his and Douglas's valour. At 1.225 Barbour identifies what had been lost by the English occupation of Scotland in his most famous lines, the encomium of freedom, and, in less appreciated lines, a lament at serfdom (-1.274). The quality is individual to 'man' and its loss leads to oppression of poor and rich, but the kingdom is not identified as what lacks freedom; that point is made only by comparing Bruce and Douglas to the Maccabees, who fought to deliver their country from serfdom, and 'delivered their land all free' (1.469-75). And even as the narrative develops and the English are expelled from e.g. Douglas, Forfar, Linlithgow, freedom does not figure as a benefit, nor is it mentioned in Robert's speech before the battle of Loudoun (8.235-57). The theme is picked up only in the extended account of Bannockburn, where the king's speech tells that his hearers 'might have lived in serfdom, but because you yearned to have freedom, you are gathered here with me', and that they they fight for 'our' lives, children, wives, freedom and land (12.245-47, 282-83). Even if, as seems likely, this speech was famous, in an episodic poem this version served to unite end to beginning by invoking an ideal achieved by chivalry, great valour and courage.

Freedom takes the place of courtly love, a motive in most romances – only the brief story of the letter to Sir John Webiton from his lady, that he must keep the adventurous and perilous castle of Douglas for a year (8.489-99), hints at courtly love as a feature of his sources. But like courtly love, this freedom was an ideal of chivalric society, appealing to those whom Barbour can call the 'good men' (2.398, 13.438), that is the men of social worth to whom his speeches are addressed. To them King Robert says: if we win you will have in your hands 'honour, reputation, riches, freedom, wealth and happiness' (12.274–76). Loss of freedom offends because men of property are oppressed, treated as serfs, afflicted with the most wicked injustice to which a bad ruler can descend – disinheritance.

In particular King Robert and James Douglas sought their rightful heritages, Robert's struggle being identified with the freeing of the country (2.100–08). Douglas's struggle for heritage is repeatedly emphasised as his motive in the early books, and has no such national garb; heritable right was an unvarying concern, even preoccupation, of the landed class, the basis of their power, and therefore of social order, under Robert II as under his grandfather. It occurs in the early books only, it is true, but is justification for the whole struggle which follows; from a rightful king and a rightful order come the freedom of the social group for whom the poem is written. The king won his heritage at Bannockburn; a central theme of the poem was complete at the end of book 13, though modern historians rightly see victory achieved only in 1328.

With this completion Barbour was able to leave the court and return to his archdeaconry, but the poem was clearly a success, for he was persuaded to continue it, and may indeed have revised the earlier text somewhat – we have no means of knowing.[21] Two interpretations of the record evidence are then possible. One possibility is that he completed *The Bruce* by 1378 and that his £1 pension was his reward; his return to court in the 1380s and more generous £10 pension would be for the writing of *the Stewartis Oryginalle*. The other possibility is that the 1378 pension was a *douceur* to persuade him to continue *The Bruce*, which he did at court between 1382 and 1386; the £10 pension was his final reward for its completion. While the latter seems rather more persuasive to me (because £1 per annum is small reward for so much labour), I know of no evidence to strengthen the case for one or other suggestion.

The final third of the poem, books 14–20,[22] while it sustains the exploration of episodes of valour and chivalry in some episodes, is marked by the absence of material from other romances.[23] There is a loss of focus in the Irish campaigns (10% of the whole poem) where the enemy is not the English, but 'the lords of that country', the native Irish, and Edward Bruce's rashness, and where every skirmish becomes a mighty battle.[24] There is a striking diminution in moralising, and comparisons from antiquity are reduced to one (20.531–71), followed by an apology for its intrusion (–20.574). Freedom is not again mentioned and the political peace of 1328 is narrated with two lines on the vital recognition of independence (20.48–49). In the Douglas episodes there is, perhaps, a greater willingness to retail the brutality of war.[25] The poem now concludes with the burial of Douglas, and of the king's heart and with Moray's death followed by a recapitulation of the earlier prayer to God (13.718–22), that these lords' offspring govern the land well.

The poem uses the word 'God' about a hundred times, but Barbour writes the deeds of men, and while there is a Christian providential God, each man accepts his *werd* (fate), and the *ure* (fate, destiny) God will send, with little sense that we sinners are here as a brief passage in the history of Christ's kingdom on earth, the church. In references to Fortune (one to the wheel), Barbour shows his adherence to the Boethian framework for his history, for fortune, the instrument of Divine Providence, brings about the rise and fall of men and empires (3.271, 4.640, 649, 7.300, 13.632, 659, 15.435, 19.615). In this framework, which has been called 'dynastic history', Barbour's cosmology was a pretty sceptical one, as is shown by his questioning of foretelling the future and of Edward I's familiar spirit and the necromancy of earl Ferrand (4.668ff, 4.219ff). It rained, the barons gathered, Douglas's men were armed, a plot was revealed, Bruce awoke suddenly, the king escaped, all by God's grace (3.234, 536, 4.455, 5.535, 7.204, 293, 495), Boethius' *beatitudo*, the highest good which man can receive. But while Douglas swears by St Bride (the patron of Douglas church) and once by St Mary (11.639), Bruce and Moray invoke no such protectors; Mary is otherwise mentioned only in a feast-date (17.335–37). This is not a world in which the saints are prayed to and secure from God the protection of their devotees, but a world in which men exercise their free wills as God timelessly ordains, and in which Fortune brings about 'what happens' – history.[26]

Men – even the bishop of St Andrews – behave in a secular spirit which does not even attempt to make the horrors of war acceptable on the ecclesiastically-approved grounds that it was 'just'. Their fight is chivalry, the ennobling of the spirit by contemplating deeds of bravery, valour, by men of birth. The simplest bravery is battle against overwhelming odds, and Barbour treats us to frequent instances of huge enemy forces overcome against absurd odds; lest we doubt, he cites a parallel from ancient Greece (6.181–280), from a romance which to him and his audience was entirely factual, but, as romance, was presented to emphasise chivalry. Of human qualities Barbour values loyalty most highly, as did his James Douglas; the most contemptible of vices is treason, that is betrayal especially of one's lord – a sentence which tells the poem's essence, and may explain why it is silent about the deals of Robert I with the 'traitor' English earls Thomas of Lancaster and Andrew Harcla (both of whom are mentioned in the poem). The necessary qualities which go to make up valour are explored, and Barbour stresses the importance of moderation, common sense, 'mesur', in exposing the fatal rashness of Edward Bruce. There is no explicit comparison with King Robert, and a contrast between the two is not a theme of the poem.[27]

In fact the depictions of the heroes, notably the king (8.381–86) and Moray (10.285–300), are the conventional ones for heroes of romance. Recognition of the hero's horn (4.496–507, 7.497–98) comes straight from romance and contrasts with another passage where the horn is not recognised (3.484–87); even so striking a passage as the combat with de Bohun is phrased in the language of romance (12.32–61).[28] There are many literary devices also found widely in romances – notably the use of irony – and the use of spring, irrespective of the true season, to mark the beginning of a new episode (5.1, 16.63) is strikingly inappropriate (to a modern eye) in a work which claims to be history.

Women scarcely appear in the poem, and only four are named: Dame Marjory, the king's daughter, Joan wife of David Bruce, and two Isabellas, Edward II's queen and Edward Bruce's wife; even Robert's queen is anonymous. The part of the countess of Buchan in sharing in enthroning the king, a story found only in English sources but surely known to Barbour's sources, and her punishment, are ignored. Equally missing is any element of the supernatural as part of the narrative; necromancy is discussed but in very sceptical terms. In both respects *The Bruce* differs from the romances which in other respects have influenced Barbour, and is more akin to earlier French epics. But in respect of women, the odd naming of the two Isabellas suggests that his silence may be that of his sources rather than by his choice.

Mingled with the claims of loyalty and the deeds of chivalry is the reality of war. There is little about ransoms, but booty, *pray* (2.448, 4.453, 9.535, 539, 10.108, 13.747, 14.130, 15.342, 345, 406, 481, 539, 17.891) sometimes saves the day for the Scots. The blackmail extracted from Lothian and England between 1311 and 1314 is wholly ignored, while the ravaging of Northumberland in late 1314 is dismissed because no chivalry was done (13.742–51). Truces have no place in Barbour's war till that of 1323, though those of 1308–10 and 1319–21 each lasted two years. In early days hardship, and, if caught, a dreadful death, are shown as the lot of the vanquished, but by the end prisoners are exchanged daily after each skirmish by armies (19.524–28). There are ruses which break solemn undertakings, but a challenge can be made and accepted to fight on a stated day and field. But it is in the fighting, the stabbing, slashing, and bashing, the shrieking of wounded men and neighing of frightened horses, weapons broken, armour spattered with brains, grass red with blood, basinets wet with sweat, lungs panting with exhaustion, that the reality of war sweeps aside the chivalry. Even so, in the battles it is the captains and generals to whom the eye is drawn in Barbour's canvasses.

This is a poem about war, and despite the rhetoric of freedom and country, patriotism is not its central theme. The late twentieth century finds that theme relevant and congenial, and lays emphasis upon it, sometimes as part of an argument that Scottish nationhood stretches back into the thirteenth or earlier centuries. Indeed it probably does, but, as in *The Bruce*, in the consciousness of a small section of society, those who fought for the right to rule 'their' land. Nor, to judge from the poem, was it the ideal which they valued most. This is a poem about chivalry, about valour and fidelity, about personal qualities which secure the repute of a man without validation by his fighting for a corporate political destiny. As with other fourteenth-century historical writings, the real enemy is not the other country or people, but cowardice and treachery.

The term 'community', once much employed for the political class speaking for all Scots, occurs only once (20.129), and now means the same as 'commons', those who are not lords. But Barbour has surprisingly little to say about such men, on the march or in battle. For the lower orders in the mass, yeomen, common folk, poveraill, he has little time (2.499–510). Sometimes they fight, as at Methven and Inverurie, but their courage fails, they are untrustworthy; sometimes, as at Loudoun and Bannockburn, they are herded

out of the army to an encampment. Presumably these latter
are men who came to serve 'naked' – unarmed – for many
of the infantry who fought must have been of much the same
standing, and indeed Umfraville describes the army as 'ye-
omanry', a word implying peasant standing (19.171–73). To
Barbour even these presented problems of discipline, against
which the king warned before Bannockburn, but vainly, for
Edward II escaped while the Scots stripped corpses (12.305–
11; 13.443–66); and at Berwick in 1318 the Scots' silent
penetration of the town became a rush for loot as though they
were mad (17.101–6). Yet Barbour gives due credit to indi-
vidual common men, Tom Dickson, Philip the forester,
Bunnok, Neil Fleming, all of the middling sort, and to Sym
of the Ledhouse and William Francis who seem to have been
humbler, raising the suspicion that in these attitudes he often
reflects his sources as much as his prejudices.

5. THE SOURCE QUESTION

There can be no doubt that Barbour wrote to please Robert
II, about the deeds of his grandfather, and for the same reason
said as much as he could to praise Walter Stewart, who,
however, remains a minor character. A poem about the Bruce,
assuming that sources were available, is understandable, but
why did Barbour wish to write 'the truth', in a poetic frame-
work, about the deeds of Bruce *and Douglas*? The head of the
Douglas family was important, powerful, in the 1370s, but
not the equal of Robert II, not able to demand a place for
his ancestor in this family work.[29] The double biography
required two narrative strands, alternating or interwoven, but
each affecting the other in some degree. To undertake the
complex task of writing the poem in this way, there must have
been the compelling reason of available sources with a strong
narrative line. Barbour had an account of James Douglas
which offered so much chivalric narrative that it could not be
ignored. Douglas was of minor importance before 1314 com-
pared with Edward Bruce and Moray, and even thereafter he
stood third behind the king and Moray in Scotland, yet
Barbour presents him always as second only to the king.

Barbour says nothing of such a source, naming an oral
source, Sir Alan Cathcart, once, and occasionally taking refuge
in 'as I heard tell' and similar phrases. These have been enough
for most commentators: Barbour knew and collected remi-
niscences (Cathcart), popular lays, traditions, and from these

he constructed a poem, whose occasional lapses from accuracy can be attributed to failing popular memory. The proposition that the patriotic war lived on in memories has an appeal which 'I heard tell' confirms, and of which he cites one example in young women's songs about the capture of Andrew Harcla (16.527-30); but other works not unlike Barbour's warn us that practice and convention allowed an author to validate his statements by just such claims, when the author was in fact using or even adding to a specific source. In the whole poem I have noted some 20 examples of 'I heard' or 'some say'. They can validate a number (2.230, 8.22, 9.416, 14.103), introduce an alternative version (2.39, 7.54), an extraordinary circumstance or one which might be doubted (3.672, 5.543, 12.398, 13.294), a name omitted (19.23), even a tale omitted (9.660). Some seem to be simply chevilles (line fillers) (5.411, 9.120, 10.603 (cf. 625), 19.264).

They are most likely to introduce a true oral report at 5.506, where 'I can't tell his name, but I have heard sundry men say he had one eye', and at 20.618, where old men reported on Moray's regency; the latter was probably a true report, the former Barbour's means of associating two distinct stories, like most other uses, a literary device to improve credibility. It is most frequent in books 2–9 about the king's adventures, occurs only twice in the account of Bannockburn (books 11–13) and only once in the Irish sections, where it might well be expected. This uneven distribution suggests that sometimes it represents a phrase not of Barbour's but of his source, an *ut dicitur*, or *si comme on disoit*, if the sources were in Latin or French; this seems particularly likely in books 1–9.[30]

I have never found in the least convincing the idea that the poem was largely produced from 'popular lays', or from the tales of old sweats for whom Barbour bought drinks in the inns of Ayr or Edinburgh. It fails to explain the generally sound chronology, something lays and tales do not retain, the omission of Harcla's capture *because* of songs about it, the peculiarity of naming only Cathcart, the narratives of campaigns in England (1319, 1322, 1327) which would have no Scottish locus, the general accuracy of names given, the precise dates which, as F. Brie long ago argued, must have come from written narrative, and the occasional error which is best explained by a misreading of a written source. Above all it fails to explain the detailed account of the life and deeds of James Douglas from boyhood to death, broken up in the poem

but surely taken from an earlier full narrative. I propose now
to examine the likely sources for some protagonists, under
the name of each.

6. KING ROBERT

Books 2–8 give an account of the king's hardships and advent-
ures from the death of Comyn to the battle of Inverurie,
1306–08. For some of these he was reputedly alone or with
men who were subsequently killed; in most he defeated
enemies against such overwhelming odds that mighty exag-
geration has been at work. There is clear repetition of episodes,
presumably unrecognised by Barbour; occasionally alternative
versions are given. There is also contamination by stories
drawn from non-Scottish episodes.[31] Whence did all this
come? In the first place from oral tradition, without a doubt.
But a collection of narratives much earlier than Barbour's
work is surely required. Jean le Bel, writing in the 1350s, had
certainly heard of one. He tells us that in 1333 the Scottish
lords held out in forests and wild places, where

> And one time, it is said, and it is found in [a] history (*en
> hystoire*) made by the said King Robert, the good King Edward
> [I] had him chased through these great forests for three or
> four days by dogs and leash-hounds to blood and train them ...
> but he could not be found.[32]

Le Bel goes on to say that after Edward had conquered and
garrisoned Scotland and returned to England, Robert recov-
ered the kingdom, a very unhistorical narrative, but like that
in *The Brut*.[33] Nonetheless, Le Bel knew of a written *hystoire*
narrating the king's early adventures, a work with a title like
Regis Roberti Historia, which persuaded him that it was royal
autobiography; as Brie pointed out long ago, this was surely
a misunderstanding, Le Bel having heard a little of the work
but not seen it.[34]

Gray, too, cites a story of Bruce in the mountains and isles,
often alone: 'as the chronicles of his deeds bear witness' he
once took passage from two boatmen who were Comyn's men
and hated Bruce; when he landed he revealed his identity.[35]
That this story does not figure in Barbour may mean that
Gray's collection was unknown to him, or that he knew it,
but omitted the story because it featured adherence to Comyn.
Barbour's alternative versions and his unrecognised duplicated
stories show that he knew a collection which had grown by

accretion, or two collections of tales, or that the collection he used was based on two prior collections – we have no means of knowing which.

Finally Fordun, writing before 1363, also knew much of Bruce's deeds, which he 'will forbear to describe ... because they would take up many leaves, and because, though they are undoubtedly true, the time and place wherein they happened ... are known to few in these days'.[36] He does not say that this was a written collection, but implies it by 'many leaves', and by 'undoubtedly true', an authorial reference to an unquestionable source, oral if for contemporary events, written if reporting a previous generation. It is striking that Fordun emphasises one characteristic of Barbour's version, the lack of time and place for such adventures, implying that they were something of a jumble, the very condition which would lead to unrecognised duplication.

The characteristics of these adventures in *The Bruce*, their inconsistencies, the companionship they depict, yet the individual bravery of an often-isolated king, do not feature after the king's departure from the south-west. The king's illness at Slioch and Inverurie is not part of a similar cycle dealing with his time in the north, a difference, incidentally, which tells against the survival of popular lays into Barbour's time as source for the archdeacon of Aberdeen. The period of greatest adversity, from the murder of Comyn to this departure seems to have formed the main body of tales; when it was collected can only be conjectured as probably before the disastrous wars of the 1330s,[37] but after the king had achieved the significant success of Bannockburn, which would make interest in his early travails relevant. Delay in collecting from 1307 to 1314 or later would allow for variants and the growth of legend. How many features of it found their way into Barbour's poem only a detailed analysis could suggest; the appearance of 'God's grace' in books 3–7 and only in those books may be another example of Barbour preserving a phrase from the collection.

Yet within this period a chronological narrative must also have been available. The accounts of Methven, describing the battle and listing the prisoners taken by the English (2.301–470), of the siege of Kildrummy with Osbarn's treachery by fire, but also naming the English leaders (4.59–183), and of Loudoun Hill, again describing the battle but preserving the exact location and date, 10 May (8.126–354), suggest that

Barbour had a vivid tale about each but also a more sober chronicle entry, the latter probably from an English source not known today. By contrast, the brief account of the taking of Loch Doon castle (4.16–26) seems to owe nothing to a chronicle, and Barbour also omits all mention of the siege and fall of Dunaverty – he takes Bruce there intending to over-winter yet has him depart after three days (3.385–87, 677).

There were available English narratives of the first two years of Robert's reign, themselves probably based on newsletters.[38] One, the *Flores Historiarum*, gives the names of prisoners at Methven; it is related to a Latin *passio*, a highly coloured version of events from February to August 1306 which includes a conversation between Bruce and Comyn which is the mirror image of Barbour's.[39] Guisborough, who wrongly places the taking of Neil Bruce in a Kintyre castle,[40] also mentions the fall of Loch Doon and, without name, the battle of Loudoun. Since he has detailed knowledge of where the Scots' ladies were secluded and how Edward I distributed the lands of the rebels, he must have had a good source, but his detail overlaps with Barbour's only in describing the ruse of the English in Perth before Methven.[41] Barbour did not use any of these, but his source was related to theirs and presumably continued at least up to Loudoun.

For later books and events Scottish sources must have been used by him, for we have no evidence of any knowledge in English narratives, of Slioch and Inverurie, the Argyll campaign, the taking of Perth, some of Bannockburn, the judgment of forfeiture in 1314 and the plot of 1320 – the main matters in the *Bruce* for 1307–23 in which Robert Bruce is the central figure. There is just one available Scottish narrative, Fordun's *Annals*, which was at least drafted by 1363, and which, with his *Chronica*, has been urged as a source for Barbour.[42] It is indeed striking that much in Fordun's narrative is parallelled in Barbour:[43] Perth a walled town; the wives following their husbands; a fight at Dalry; the queen taken in Ross; Neil Bruce and Kildrummy taken by treachery; the continued loyalty of Gilbert Hay and Lennox; the fight at a castle in Carrick – all before September 1307. Thereafter some Fordun items, famine and dearth, Gaveston's death, the cardinals in 1317, the king and the cardinals in 1320, are understandably not in Barbour; omitting these and putting other items not in Barbour [*thus*], Fordun notices the following:

the fight and the king's sickness at Slioch; the death of Edward I; the battle at Inverurie and ravaging of Buchan; Edward Bruce in Galloway; the defeat of Argyllsmen, siege of Dunstaffnage [*and departure of Alexander of Argyll*; *the king twice attacks England in 1311*]; the taking of Perth and punishment of those within; [*the taking of Buittle, Dumfries and Dalswinton*]; the taking of Roxburgh and Edinburgh; [*the king conquers Man*]; Bannockburn; Edward and Robert Bruce in Ireland; [*Moray attacks England in 1318*]; the taking of Berwick; the death of Edward Bruce; Edward II besieges Berwick; Moray attacks England as far as Boroughbridge; the plot against the king in 1320, those condemned [*and those acquitted; the trial of Roger Mowbray*; *Moray attacks England; in 1322 Robert attacks England by the west*]; Edward II's 1322 campaign to Edinburgh; [*destruction of monasteries on his retreat*]; Robert's campaign to Byland, defeat of Edward II and taking of Sully and Brittany; [*execution of Andrew Harcla in 1323*; *renewal of the French alliance in 1325*]; birth of David Bruce.

There are so few accounts of attacks on England in Barbour that it is fair to conclude that he decided to omit these unless there was 'chivalry' as in 1319, 1322 and 1327; similarly the taking of Man. In fact it is clear that Barbour had other and better sources for many of Fordun's events, especially where Fordun gives little more than the date, which interested Barbour little. The supposed use of Fordun can be investigated for only a few of these events, the most difficult to evaluate being those rhetorical passages in which Fordun describes the hardships undergone by Bruce. But where he says the king 'went barefoot',[44] Barbour says nothing of the king's feet, but that *his following* rent their shoes and had to make *others of hide* (2.513–14). This is not a 'telling detail'[45] showing borrowing by Barbour, but, like the rest of the passage, evidence that Fordun had a collection of tales of the king's adventures, quite possibly the same as that behind *The Bruce*.

It is more relevant that Fordun mentions as Bruce's last companions Gilbert Hay and Lennox, Barbour these two and Neil Campbell, that Fordun tells of Christiana of the Isles helping Bruce before he returned to Carrick, but Barbour knows her not, that Fordun tells of the immediate taking of a castle in Carrick, but Barbour (and Guisborough) describe the holing up of Percy in Turnberry.[46] These differences suggest that, while they may well have had a common source, Barbour did not use Fordun. There is no instance of Barbour following Fordun into error, and indeed his account of Alexander of Argyll's submission in 1308 is more correct than that of Fordun, which jumps straight to the expulsion of Alexander in 1309.

For events which Fordun does describe (as distinct from what he specifically omits) their common source seems to be Latin verses partly preserved in Bower, probably from two different collections but which I have called the Verse Chronicle; these lines give the date of the battle in Argyll as the feast of the Assumption, as does Fordun; indeed Fordun generally follows the date-form of the Verse Chronicle for the day-date;[47] his account of Edward Bruce in Galloway (1308) is a very obvious instance of his debt to the verses. But more tellingly, Fordun and the verses both put Slioch at Christmas while the verses put Inverurie at Ascension (23 May) in the words *in festo Domini quo scandit sidera celi*, 'in the feast of the Lord when he mounts the stars of heaven'. This phrase was so literary that it defeated Fordun who gives no date; but it was, I suggest, known to Barbour who misunderstood it as 'when the star mounts the heaven' i.e. the day before Christmas; having placed Inverurie then (9.205), he had to move Slioch back to the vague 'after Martinmas' (9.128). The verses describe the enemy as fleeing from Inverurie 'through the district of *Durum* to Fyvie';[48] Fordun has Fyvie, Barbour has rightly understood *Durum* as Old Meldrum. Barbour has not borrowed from Fordun; both knew the verses.

For the fall of Perth Fordun took little from the verses,[49] though he gives the date in the same form; Barbour says much that is also in the verses, but (as with Slioch and Inverurie but more markedly) he has additional matter, notably the comment of the French knight on Bruce's personal involvement, and the (erroneous) story of a six-week siege and week's withdrawal (9.360–79, 395–410); these must come from an independent source, but one which either was misled, or misled Barbour, over the siege's length. It probably reached at least as far as the battle of Bannockburn, for it was so worded that it caused Barbour to ascribe the siege of Stirling, and not just the final surrender arrangement, to Edward Bruce and to confuse that arrangement with the year's stay to give allegiance to the king (10.810–30, 13.736).

How much of the account of Bannockburn itself was in that source is uncertain. While the encounter with de Bohun is found in English narratives, the king's reaction afterwards suggests a Scottish source(12.27–93); so also for the pointless pots (11.371), found otherwise only in Baston's poem, the description of the English flight to the rock (13.428–59), and the surrender of Tweng (13.520–39). The address of Bruce to his men before Bannockburn is in the verses [50] and Barbour (12.210–327), but not in Fordun; however, it may have enjoyed currency in many ways. The account of the battle is vivid yet amounts to little: the four divisions were committed in turn – but it is doubtful if any commentator could have seen much more. The role of the cavalry in dispersing the English archers, and, of course, the final intervention of the baggage men, are evidence of more detailed knowledge. This came, I suggest, from a careful and knowledgeable but incompletely informed source, whose own narrative included the fall of Perth. It was probably a continuation of the collection of tales about 1306–07, may have used the Verse Chronicle but certainly had narratives collected from participants (whence the errors?); it was, effectively, 'chronicles' of King Robert, perhaps indeed that to which Gray referred.

7. EDWARD BRUCE

Edward Bruce plays a prominent role in the king's fortunes till 1314, and indeed may sometimes be credited by Barbour with a part played by his brother Thomas. For Edward's Galloway campaign of 1308 (9.477–676) Barbour ignored the Verse Chronicle to follow an account in which Ingram Umfraville was central, adding the one tale from a named oral source (Sir Alan Cathcart) in the whole poem, the triple charge of fifty men against 1,500. These events do not require a separate account of Edward Bruce, but they are curiously sandwiched in hints of other material: at 9.495–500 that there is ten times as much information from which many romances might be written, and at 9.660–665 that many more encounters happened, 'not written here', including the taking of thirteen castles and overcoming many men, whoever wishes to *reid* the truth about him. Now *reid* is ambiguous, with the sense of 'advise', hence 'tell' and finally 'read' (i.e. aloud), but the implication of these hints is surely that Barbour knows of much further information about Edward, which was highly coloured and (in modern eyes) improbable.

With the same reservations he hastened by Edward's taking of Nithsdale, Rutherglen (1308) and Dundee (1312) (10.797–809) with mere mentions, to reach the siege of Stirling and the agreement with Mowbray. The mentions of Nithsdale and Dundee again hint at an Umfraville source, for Ingram was in Nithsdale, and his friend Brechin probably at Dundee. At Bannockburn Edward engages in no striking act of chivalry (12.497–532), but Barbour brings in his dubious morals (13.488–94), while also commenting, in one of two places, on his bonds with male companions (13.478–80, 15.226–42).

He again comes into prominence with the accounts of the Irish campaigns, which cannot possibly have been recovered from anyone alive in 1370. They are detailed, with personal and place names, not in abundance, but sufficiently frequently to indicate a written source. They are also much given, however, to wild exaggeration, and are confused about the geography and uncomfortable with the chronology, features much more pronounced here than elsewhere in *The Bruce*. There is certainly one serious mix-up, events of the second expedition, of November 1315– February 1316, being mingled with those of the first in the summer of 1315. But all four expeditions are represented.

Should we, then, postulate a lost account of Edward Bruce? Barbour does not call Edward lord of Galloway, calls him earl of Carrick once and admits that Edward was acknowledged as king of Ireland belatedly and in an off-hand way (15.137, 160–61, 16.315); this is in marked contrast to his careful use of title for King Robert and Moray, and suggests that there was indeed a highly-coloured and none-too accurate account of the rash Edward (as he is depicted in agreement with Fordun and Gray). This account was perhaps not Barbour's immediate source, for reasons I shall explore, but was a minstrel product whose author we can perhaps identify in *The Bruce*.

Gib Harper the minstrel was killed at the final battle of Faughart in 1318 wearing a surcoat with Edward Bruce's arms (18.98, 165), that is he was the minstrel and herald of Edward Bruce,[51] named, I suggest, in his own work celebrating his lord's deeds with exaggeration and confusion in the committal to parchment (for composition would involve writing down) during the long stalemate of 1317–18. Obviously he cannot have written, sung or dictated the story of the last campaign, where Barbour relates his death, the cutting off of his head and the sending of it salted in a box to Edward II. But, again exceptionally, Barbour names the source (but not, as modern commentators claim, directly to *him* (18.147–49)) for the battle of Faughart, John Thomson, leader of the men of Carrick.

Why? Because John completed the main narrative by Gib (himself probably a Carrick man)? The story of the head is wild rumour turned into fact, but would round off the compositional efforts of Gib.

8. MORAY

At one point, the struggle between Moray and Clifford on the eve of Bannockburn, the existence of conflicting versions becomes clear. In one version, Douglas went to aid Moray but desisted lest Moray be deprived of due credit; this is from a Douglas source. In the other version the king refused Douglas permission to leave to save Moray (11.648-58). The latter belongs to an account of Moray, which described the king's generosity in lands to him, his appearance, and the siege of Edinburgh. But it is much less well represented in Barbour's poem than the career of Douglas, and we have no suggestion that, for instance, it described his youth, his rehabilitation in 1308-09, or his visits to France and the papal court in 1323-25. By any reckoning, except Barbour's, Moray was the most important noble at Robert's court and commander in his armies. King's lieutenant before Bannockburn, general in war, ambassador to England and France, recipient of an earldom even before the king's brother, designated regent should a minor succeed Robert I, he was probably sent to Ireland as the best commander among the Scots. In his only certain citation of a written source, Barbour states that Douglas strove to take Roxburgh at the time 'that the good earl Thomas besieged, *as the lettre sayis*, Edinburgh' (10.357-59). Elsewhere Barbour uses *lettre* and its plural for a missive [52] but the more general sense of a writing is not impossible and must surely be used here; but it does not specify a life.

Moray was reported present on the first three Irish expeditions. For the fourth, in 1318, Barbour places considerable emphasis upon Edward Bruce's failure to await the reinforcements which were on their way under a brother of a Stewart. But other sources show that the brother was Edward's, i.e. King Robert. And when Robert crossed, he would bring Moray with him as in 1317. Now there can be no doubt that in Barbour's version of the Irish campaigns, Moray (and in 1317, King Robert) is presented in a much more favourable light, and is often given greater prominence, than Edward Bruce. In other words, the Edward Bruce narrative was edited to give it a different slant, though its existence is further vouched for by the account of a relief of Carrickfergus castle in April 1316 (15.101–253), when Moray was not in Ireland. In July he was at Duns with the king and Sir John Stewart who had been in Ireland,[53] after which the king is thought to have gone there, perhaps with Moray, to help take Carrickfergus.[54] Barbour attributes this, in one line, to Edward Bruce (15.262), but this may be a guess, if the castle had in fact surrendered to King Robert. In September 1316 all three were at an assembly at Cupar Fife where Edward acknowledged Moray's right to his massive landed endowments.[55]

Was the Edward Bruce narrative edited to give greater prominence to Moray by Barbour, or in an intermediate stage, the *lettre* to which Barbour refers for 1314? There is scant evidence that this *lettre* covered the years after 1317, for Barbour has little on Moray thereafter. The accounts of the campaigns in England in 1319, 1322 and 1327 are written from Douglas's point of view; the marriage of David Bruce in 1328 and settlement of the regency in 1326 (a very confused passage, 20.82–152) put Moray and Douglas as equals, whereas Moray was more eminent. All this could have, and probably did, come from the life of Douglas. We are left seeking a source for the siege of Berwick in 1319, for Edward II's invasion in 1322, for the obituary of Walter Stewart, and for the king's last invasion of England and the peace of 1328. These alone show that narratives of the king, 'chronicles', continued into the 1320s, presumably with less chivalry than the life of Douglas, which Barbour preferred.

It is possible that the Edward Bruce narrative was edited for inclusion into these 'chronicles'; indeed I think that more likely than that Barbour had access to that narrative as a separate source. Again, although the existence of a life of Moray has been suggested by Professor Watt, it is more likely that the *lettre* which narrated his deeds and the 'chronicles' of King Robert were one and the same, that it included the revised version of the Irish campaigns and that it went on to deal with the 1320s and the end of the reign. There is enough error in Barbour to suggest that his source, the 'chronicles', was written a few years after the 1310s, and, if it was a compilation from other sources (as I am suggesting), that it was begun as a memorial after the king's death, commissioned by Moray when he was Guardian.

This may, indeed, explain the most puzzling fragment of narrative in *The Bruce*: the placing of the settlement of the succession and regency in 1326 and the coronation of David II (really in 1331) at a point which must be the autumn of 1328 (20.120–52). That coronation contrasts with the cursory account of Robert's inauguration 'set on the throne as was the way at that time' (2.180), for the king had secured the right to his own coronation in 1329. Unbeknown to John XXII, he had died when this was granted, and David II was the first beneficiary; only a narrative written after 1329 could have presented the concession as one sought by Robert *for his son*, who was duly crowned. That coronation Barbour has placed in Robert's reign; but his source (which was ambiguous enough to allow this) was written after November 1331. Professor Watt has suggested a lost life to explain the stories of Moray's judicial activities as Guardian (1329–32) in Bower and Wyntoun.[56] I suggest that a continuation of the 'chronicles' of King Robert is an alternative explanation, one which went on to narrate the supposed poisoning of Moray which is found in Bower and Wyntoun and is the last event in *The Bruce* (20.619–20).

To sum up, if this is correct, we seem to have behind Barbour a narrative, 'chronicles' of King Robert, which drew on a collection of the early adventures, then perhaps used the Verse Chronicle as skeleton for events from 1307, embarking on a fuller narrative of events from 1313 to which the Verse Chronicle may have contributed; recollections of participants would form an important source. A narrative of Edward Bruce written about 1317–18 was also laid under contribution for the Irish campaigns. Some prominence was given to Moray (whose death on 20 July, 1332 is the last event mentioned in *The Bruce*), but this was often lost to Douglas in the presentation of events by Barbour. These 'chronicles' may or may not have been the work referred to under that name by Gray.

9. JAMES DOUGLAS

Skilfully interwoven with the Bruce narrative is a second and quite distinct account, that of James Douglas. That a poem entitled *The Bruce* gives so powerful a place to James Douglas, telling of his youth but not of Bruce's, lauding his desperate struggle to recover his heritage, giving him an improbable command at Bannockburn and thereafter, the Irish sections excepted, thrusting Bruce into his shadow, indicates that a major source for the poem and the only source for Douglas's war, was a history of him which has not survived. It would be written after his death, but the detail is so vivid and so specific, that no great length of time can have passed between death and composition – a conclusion which rules out even William, first earl of Douglas (who came of age in 1348), and certainly James's son, Archibald, third earl (who paid for James's tomb), as sponsor and patron.

Whether this history was in verse or prose, in French, Latin or Scots, we cannot tell, though (for example) a greater preponderance of French borrowings in the Douglas sections of *The Bruce*, would be a hint. But those sections already tell us something about it. It cast an unrelenting spotlight upon Douglas, rarely mentioning his companions or associates. Tom Dickson, Bishop Lamberton, Sir Robert Boyd, Sym of Ledhouse, Sir William Sinclair and Sir William Keith of Galston, play but small parts. Boyd is named as being in Arran with Douglas, a man older than Douglas and with the king even before he was king – yet he drops from sight before the fight at Brodick. Barbour depicts Douglas as the king's second-in-command, a role accepted by modern accounts. Yet careful reading suggests that this is Barbour's attempt to weave his story into the king's, that Douglas was the freebooting leader of the men of Ettrick (and so Wallace's successor!) in 1307–08, in 1314 when he took Roxburgh, perhaps even in 1322 when he ambushed the English at Melrose, and that Bruce had as little to do with those episodes as with the fight at Lintalee or the brutal deaths of Caillou and Sir Robert Neville.

We know something of Douglas from other sources. He was at Loudoun when he tried to desert Bruce and make terms with the English. By March 1309 he figured immediately after Thomas Randolph among the magnates, but had not been rewarded with an office such as constable nor with a lordship, even one to be reconquered. In January 1316 he narrowly escaped with his life from an abortive attack on Berwick. He appears as baronial witness to royal charters from November 1314, following Walter Stewart and John Menteith, but was promoted to second place from 1318 and first place when Stewart died in 1327. Lands were given to him by the king, and he qualified with Moray and Stewart to have his grants entered on a separate chancery roll which shows how widely he was endowed in southern Scotland, and how careful he was to secure written title.[57] He sold three French knights taken prisoner at Byland to the king in return for some judicial revenues in perpetuity. All this helps to form a rounded picture of the man and his importance, but, except for the lands given to him, is not to be expected in a praise-life. That Barbour makes no mention of these landed rewards conferred by the king, is striking evidence that the life followed by Barbour left the king in Douglas's shadow.

One feature of the version in Barbour is noteworthy: the reports of the knighting of Douglas Stewart and others in 1314 (12.417–20), of William Keith of Galston in 1318 (17.149) and of William Erskine in 1327 (19.377). These and the reckoning of Douglas's defeats and victories (8.432–33) suggest that the chivalric interests of the author of the life were quite professional. Although Barbour mentions heralds only in the English host (12.371), Le Bel makes it clear that such protected messengers were also known among the Scots. The closest analogy must be the *Life of the Black Prince*, written a decade after the Prince's death in the interests of his brother Lancaster, and concentrating on a few episodes in his career; the author, Chandos Herald, names himself only in the last two lines. That Life was the unacknowledged source for the Prince's Spanish campaign in Froissart's Chronicles, a fact we would not know had not the Life survived in two manuscripts, one of which passed unnoticed until the mid-twentieth century. A life of Douglas by his herald,[58] kept by the head of the family in one of few copies in his book-chest until loaned to Barbour would have little chance of fame unless Barbour identified it, and, if returned, little chance of surviving the fall of the house of Douglas in 1455. That the encomium of the family written in 1446, *the Buik of the Howlat*, shows no awareness of it is an argument against its survival then.

Bower, writing at much the same time as the author of *the Howlat*, has a description of Douglas's death taken from Fordun and differing from Barbour's version, then refers us for his deeds to *The Bruce*. But he then quotes 37 lines of Latin verse by 'someone' (*quidam*), celebrating his deeds and character, an encomium with little fact, save at the end, Douglas's death on 25 August, 1330 at Teba castle; Fordun has 26 August and no place so is not the source. The poem goes on to urge Douglas's Christian credentials: 'he kept his heart fixed well on Christ, as a writer says, he lived as a knight like him' [Christ?]; lines on his valour follow.[59] The 'writer' (*scriptor*) can scarcely be Barbour who makes no such comparison, but could be the lost life. However Bower's note,

after the poem, that 'this James was overcome and defeated
in battle 13 times and won 57 victories' comes from 8.432–33.

It is likely that the taking of Randolph and his subsequent
confrontation with the king came from the Life. On the other
hand, other evidence gives Douglas a leading part in the taking
of Berwick in 1318, whereas Barbour at this point (17.16–260)
has his only frank recognition of rivalry between Douglas and
Moray and gives them a secondary role, after the king had
plotted with 'the marischal' (Keith), sheriff, and leader of the
men, of Lothian, to leave matters in Keith's hands. This
interesting variant may be explained by the one figure to whom
chivalry is ascribed: a new-made knight called Sir William of
Keith and of Galston to difference his surname (17.149–70),
i.e. from that of the marischal, his cousin, Sir Robert
Keith,[60] probably also named in Barbour's source. If Sir
William was the author's (?herald's) informant for the taking
of Berwick, as he probably was for the death of Douglas in
Spain, then these matters were being recorded before Sir
William's death in 1336.

The language and form of the lost life are unrecoverable;
to list its contents – all the episodes in *The Bruce* in which
Douglas figures – would fill space needlessly. Its existence is
demanded not by phrases in Bower but by the detailed account
of Douglas's life in Barbour's *Bruce*.

10. INGRAM D'UMFRAVILLE

A patriot driven by the murder of Comyn to reject Bruce and
fight with the English, Ingram plays an extraordinary role in
the poem. He is Polonius in the play, advising Valence on
how to trick and defeat Bruce at Methven, at Bannockburn
offering Edward II a ruse to break Scottish discipline, then
identifying Scottish determination, and later telling him how
to undermine Scottish war-capacity by a long truce. But he
also appears as a soldier, sending a man to kill the king, and
fighting a battle against Edward Bruce in Galloway then fleeing
to Buittle castle. His disgust at the execution of Sir David
Brechin in 1320 led to his authorised withdrawal to England
– though Barbour has not explained that he had been taken
prisoner at Bothwell in 1314 and had made some kind of
peace with Robert I.

It is likely that other episodes belong with this collection.
Sir David Brechin seems to have been close to Umfraville
both when they were patriots before 1304 and when they

served Edward I and II after 1306; the surrender of Brechin castle (9.286–94), and perhaps something about Slioch and Inverurie, where Brechin was present, may have come via this source. More difficult to place is the source for the Soules conspiracy (19.1–68). Barbour's account includes an impossible chivalric story of Soules having 360 squires (19.35–38), but otherwise is well supported by Fordun and Gray who are in agreement save over the name of the betrayer. All give first place to Soules, but only Barbour, seeking a motive, extends that to make Soules aim to become king; I do not think this distortion was in his source, because other authorities are silent about it. The link of this plot to the withdrawal of Umfraville, who was certainly planning to go to England before it was betrayed, is David Brechin, whose innocence is likely to have come from a pro-English source. For that reason I would make the Umfraville text a source of Barbour's knowledge of the conspiracy.

No other parliament of Robert I was commented on by narrative sources, even those in which other men were condemned (in 1316 and 1325). In view of the knowledge in Barbour, Gray and Fordun of the names of those involved, an account of the trials must have circulated, and that soon after the event. It was so silent about the nature of the treason that it must have been officially inspired, and may have taken the form of a royal letter to sheriffs outlining the king's version of events; some intimation would in any case be necessary for the forfeited lands to be taken into the sheriffs' hands. The naming of the betrayer of the plotters would not be in such a letter, but would circulate by rumour. Such information the Umfraville author developed in his version and Barbour embroidered by making Soules aspirant to the throne.

The Umfraville text may have told of the siege of Henry Percy and of the Northumbrian relieving force in 1307 (5.185–216), for Percy and Umfraville were co-heirs of Balliol of Redcastle – the English gave Umfraville's half to Percy and Robert I gave Percy's half to Umfraville. But it is the picture of 'Umfraville the wise' which stakes a claim for some pro-English account of his life having come to Barbour's hand. If Ingram retired in 1321 to France, as may have been the case, he may have sponsored a self-serving version of his life, to smooth away his many changes of allegiance; that would include his knowing a relative and enemy of Bruce, a figure whom Barbour identified with the one-eyed would-be

murderer of the story-collection (5.485–522). I certainly find
it difficult to see from what other source the various Umfraville
episodes can have come than one retailing the man's intimacy
with kings and the wise advice he offered them.

11. OTHER SOURCES

There are outstanding episodes which are not obviously
derived from any of the sources so far suggested: the taking
of Forfar in 1308 (9.311–24) and Linlithgow in 1313 (10.150–
252), vivid accounts of the repulse of the English naval attack
on Fife by Bishop Sinclair of Dunkeld (the king's 'own
bishop') in 1317 (16.545–682) and of the defence of Berwick
in 1319 (17.261–490). The Linlithgow assault is particularly
interesting because it is one place where the narrative, which
does not involve the king, seems to have been adulterated, by
similar events at Edinburgh three decades later. This is not
the only such instance, for the story of Bruce's flight from
Edward's parliament, and of Moray's chaplet of roses at
Bannockburn have close parallels in France of the 1340s; these
two are elaborations of stories whose main element is well
vouched for, and may be additions by Barbour or of his
generation. Similarly in the Linlithgow story either the name
Bunnock suggested the modus operandi, or, and this is more
probable, the modus suggested the name Bunnock.

The Fife episode, I suggest, came to Barbour from 'chroni-
cles' of King Robert. The defence of Berwick seems to use
two sources. One of these evidently dealt with the role of
Walter Stewart, and presumably gave Barbour his pursuit of
the English to York in 1322 (18.486–95) and the facts in his
obituary (19.205–28), passages which give the impression of
much made from very little, again probably from the 'chron-
icles'. Of the two accounts of the destruction of the sow at
the defence of Berwick (17.605 ff.), that with the anonymous
browbeaten engineer is probably later than Crab's (?brow-
beaten) change of sides in 1333, when he helped Edward III
take Berwick, and is a conventional description of artillery
range-finding. The other version, which names Crab as the
engineer who burned the sow, is more correct, and would
come from a Scottish source nearer in time to the actual event.
It is not impossible that Barbour, travelling to England, would
have access to a source within Berwick.

12. BARBOUR AT WORK

It has been usual to attribute the repetition of stories, errors and other features requiring explanation, to Barbour. But it is possible that many or all of these features were already there in his sources, and that, accepting the authority of the source, as most authors did, he repeated them in his particular literary form. Barbour is neutral about men who changed sides and who were represented by descendants in his day. The earl of Dunbar is depicted as English in 1314, but under another name leads a Scottish army in 1327 (13.616, 19.784); the earl of Fife, whose recent desertion to Bruce is not commented on, behaved pusillanimously in 1317 (16.560), and the late (1327) adherence of Mar to Bruce is also passed over in silence (19.243, 351). Barbour makes no mention of Murdoch of Menteith who adhered to Bruce about 1320, apparently betrayed the Soules conspiracy and was made earl. Thus magnates of the first rank did not win a place of any prominence unless they were in some way involved in chivalry, and even then the treatment could be perfunctory. Barbour was just following his sources.

There are, however, features which, I believe, are of Barbour's time and Barbour's composition. The attempt to give prominence to Walter Stewart, and particularly to his rather frenetic activity in defence of Berwick, would please Robert II. The prominence of Douglas is attributable to a life of him being available, and to the importance of the family in the later fourteenth century. On the other hand the Randolph family died out in the male line in 1346, when the earldom of Moray should have lapsed; the absence of a male Randolph in the 1370s does much to explain the subordination of Moray to Douglas in several episodes in the poem where they were both involved.

This is true in a different way of other episodes. Quite frequently Barbour describes the forming and the execution of a plan. The Douglas Lardner is a good example where the plan almost goes awry through premature action (5.255–345), but other examples are the taking of Linlithgow (10.150–86) and Francis' plan to take Edinburgh (10.543–82). This last, where one protagonist puts forward the plan to others, occurs several times, notably on the 1327 Weardale campaign (19.532–51, 635–755). A parallel editorial practice occurs when Barbour sets a scene by naming those present; the same or almost the same names then recur after the event as prisoners or escapees – as in the account of Methven (2.235-39, 408-13, 491-94). In these instances Barbour's source pretty certainly had no plan, and no list of those present; Barbour has read these back from information about the action and from the names of prisoners and escapees. Whether this is padding serving no artistic purpose, or a means of raising dramatic tension by the 'plan' and adding verisimilitude by the 'names', the reader must judge from his or her own reading. But he or she should be aware of the device.

13. THE TEXT AND EDITIONS

The poem was evidently widely known: it (or 1.37-2.336) was used by Wyntoun c. 1400, borrowed without acknowledgment in *the Buik of Alexander*, 1438, cited by Bower c. 1440, plagiarised in Blind Hary's *Wallace* c. 1470, all before the only surviving two manuscripts were written, Cambridge (C), which begins at 4.57, in 1487, and Edinburgh (E), the only complete MS, in 1489.[61] It was first printed (so far as we know) in 1571, early in the history of Scottish printing, apparently from a manuscript now lost; and again by Hart, basing himself on 1571, in 1616. Numerous other editions followed, but the first attempt to return to the manuscripts was made by Pinkerton in his 1790 edition, based on E. The major nineteenth century edition was Skeat's of 1894, based on C from 4.57, followed in 1907 by a prose translation by George Eyre-Todd and in 1909 by W. Mackay Mackenzie's handy one-volume edition, the first with thorough historical notes. Mackenzie was to prepare, for the Scottish Text Society, an edition with the two manuscripts on facing pages, but this never appeared.

These held the field when important work was done on the *Dictionary of the Older Scottish Tongue*, and by Klaus Bitterling in his valuable concordance. Then in 1980-85 M. P. McDiarmid and J. A. C. Stevenson, following linguistic work which established that E preserved earlier language-forms, returned, in a careful edition, to that manuscript.[62] They reproduced exactly the letter forms used (e.g. y for 'th' sound) and put all the expanded abbreviations in italics, so their text is a scholar's delight, but not for the general reader. The E text has many more irregular lines than C and the decision to rely on it has been criticised, but so far as I can tell they have much on their side, and I have in most cases followed their readings without comment.

When Skeat made his edition he followed the book and line numbering of Pinkerton; any additional lines accepted were given an asterisked number. References were to this system until the 1980–85 edition when lines were renumbered in most books to eliminate asterisks and admit more lines. Thus the references in *DOST* change from about 1980, and those in Bitterling have to be converted.

14. THIS EDITION

I have not made a new study of the manuscripts or language, but have accepted E's readings with the few emendations proposed in the 1980–85 edition. I have made some literal changes. The 'th' sound is represented by th; yogh (consonantal y) by y; where i represents a consonant it is printed as j; similarly with u and w, where v is meant; I have also reduced w to u in some places where that will help the reader. Sometimes I have printed final e as é to indicate a syllable.

The numbering of lines on the left hand side is that of the 1980–85 edition, and of Skeat's where it does not differ. Where a difference comes in, Skeat's numbering is given on the right hand side. It is thus possible to look up references in both the old and the new systems.

The translation and notes refer to the left-hand line numbering. In the translation I have sometimes omitted the cheville 'in hy', which, if taken literally, would have chivalric society in a lather of perpetual hurry. I have also broken up Barbour's long sentences into two or three, omitting 'and', or have treated 'he did this and then he did that' as 'he did that after doing this.' However, with the publisher I felt that the translation should always help the reader with the original text, and therefore, at the cost of some naturalness, I have tried, so far as reasonable, to retain the phrase or clause sequence of the original.

I have used [square brackets] to enclose words supplied by me or my own summary of part of a text.

The notes deal mainly with historical questions.

15. ABBREVIATIONS

To extend an already long work by a full bibliography is not possible. Most references will present no difficulty to anyone seeking to follow them up. The following are more cryptic:

ASR: *Anglo-Scottish Relations, 1174–1328, Some Selected Documents*, ed. E. L. G. Stones (1965, 1970).

B1894: The Bruce . . . by Master John Barbour, ed. W. W. Skeat, Scottish Text Society, ii (1894).

B1907: The Bruce, trans. G. Eyre-Todd (1907, reprint 1996).

B1909: The Bruce by John Barbour, ed. W. M. Mackenzie (1909).

B1985: Barbour's Bruce, ed. M. P. McDiarmid and J. A. C. Stevenson, Scottish Text Society, vol. i, Introduction and Notes (1985). (Vols ii and iii contain the text and were published in 1980–81).

Barrow, *Bruce*: G. W. S. Barrow, *Robert Bruce and the Community of the Realm of Scotland* (3rd edition, 1988).

Bitterling, *Wortschatz*: Klaus Bitterling, *Die Wortschatz von Barbours 'Bruce'* (1970).

Bower6, Bower7: Scotichronicon by Walter Bower, gen. ed. D. E. R. Watt, vols vi (1991) and vii (1996).

Brie, *Nationale Literatur*: Friedrich Brie, *Die Nationale Literatur Schottlands von den Anfängen bis zur Renaissance* (1937).

CDS2, CDS3, CDS5: Calendar of Documents relating to Scotland, ii (ed. J. Bain, 1884), iii (ed. J. Bain 1887), v (ed. G. G. Simpson and J. D. Galbraith, 1986). A reference in italic means the document of that number; in roman the page of that number.

Chron. le Bel: Chronique de Jean le Bel, ed. J. Viard & E. Déprez, Société de l'histoire de France, 2 vols (1904–05).

CP: Complete Peerage by G.E.C. revised edition (1910–59).

DOST: Dictionary of the Older Scottish Tongue, W. A. Craigie and others.

F1, F2: Johannis de Fordun Chronica Gentis Scotorum, ed. W. F. Skene, The Historians of Scotland (1871–72), vol. 1 (Latin text), vol. 2 (translation).

G. Chronicle of Walter of Guisborough, ed. Harry Rothwell, Camden Series LXXXIX (1957).

Goldstein, *Matter*: R. James Goldstein, *The Matter of Scotland* (1993).

Gray: *Scalacronica*. see *S* and *ST*.

L: Chronicon de Lanercost, ed. J. Stevenson, Maitland Club (1839).

LT: Chronicle of Lanercost, 1272–1346, trans. H Maxwell (1913).

Laud, Laud annals: *Chartularies of St Mary's Abbey, Dublin*, ed. J. T. Gilbert, Rolls Series, ii (1884), pp. 281–2, 296–302, 344–59. (I have not given page references in the notes; entries can be found under date.)

RotSci: Rotuli Scotiae, i (1814).

RRS5: The Acts of Robert I, King of Scots, 1306–1329, Regesta Regum Scottorum vol. v, ed. A. A. M. Duncan (1988). A reference in italic is to document number, in roman to page number.

S: Scalacronica, by Sir Thomas Gray of Heton, knight, ed. J Stevenson, Maitland Club (1836).

SP: J. Balfour Paul, *Scots Peerage* (1904–14).

ST: Scalacronica, the Reigns of Edward I, Edward II and Edward III, trans. H. Maxwell (1907).

VitaEd: Vita Edwardi Secundi, The Life of Edward the Second, ed. N. Denholm-Young (1957).

NOTES

1. This account is based on the documented biography in D. E. R. Watt, *Biographical Dictionary of Scottish Graduates to A.D. 1410* (1977), 28–9. I have not repeated the references which are all given in those pages.

2. In England in the 1320s, Barber was an occupation name. I have seen *Willelmus Barber barbitonsor comitis de X* in a Wardrobe book of Edward II; it is likely that Barbour's father was a barber, i.e. one who shaved and bled his patron and customers. The patron could have been a prelate, perhaps William Sinclair bishop of Dunkeld (16.582–682).

3. John Luce, precentor of Dunkeld was elected to the see of Dunkeld in 1355.

4. Bitterling, *Wortschatz*, 26.

5. Janet M. Smith, *The French Background of Middle Scots Literature* (1934), ch. 1 deals with this but unfortunately accepts, as did most commentators, Barbour's authorship of the *Buik of Alexander*, for which see R. L. Graeme Richie's edition of the *Buik*.

6. Taylor, *Eng. Hist. Lit.* 172. Gransden, *Historical Writing in England*, ii, 92–6. Gray wrote it from *c.* 1355 to *c.* 1360, and began it in Edinburgh castle using books there. Dr Gransden points out that these were presumably collected by the English before 1314. They would have to be tucked away when the castle was deserted from 1314 to at least 1322; Scots could neither write nor read thereafter, we must assume.

7. But Barbour may have been in France in 1365 when Froissart visited Scotland.

8. *Un viel rommant en papier gros et court, de lettre bastarde, a une coulombe et en ryme, et parle des guerres d'Escoce et d'Angleterre.* Douët d'Arcq, *Inventaire de la bibliothèque du roi Charles VI* (Paris, 1867), no. 196. See also L. Delisle, *le Cabinet de manuscrits de la bibliothèque impériale/nationale*, i (1868), 30; iii (1881), nos 1017, 1018, which shows that there were two such romances by the inventory of 1411.

9. After visiting Scotland in 1365 Froissart wrote Méliador, a very long verse romance largely based in Scotland (ed. A Lognon, 3vv. 1895, Société des anciens textes français).

10. The subject is well surveyed in *Froissart: Historian*, ed. J. J. N. Palmer (1981).

11. *La Prise d'Alexandrie par Guillaume de Machaut*, ed. M. L. de Mas Latrie (Société de l'Orient latin, Genève, 1877). This is a life of Peter, from his birth in 1329, watched over by Mars, Venus, Vesta and Saturn, to his death in 1369. It is almost 9,000 lines long and its editor thinks that it would take three or four years to compose, say 1369–72. Machaut is thought to have died in 1377.

12. *Life of the Black Prince by the Herald of Sir John Chandos*, ed. M. K. Pope and E. C. Lodge (1910), 135. A second MS was found and led to the edition (*La Vie du Prince Noir*) by Diana B. Tyson (1975), which has a valuable introduction. But the 1910 edition has a translation, where Chandos' introductory passage is comparable with the first 36 lines of *The Bruce*. The emphasis on 'truth-telling' is strikingly similar. For the date and Froissart's use of the poem,

see Palmer, *Froissart*, 31–3 and P. F. Ainsworth, *Jean Froissart and the Fabric of History* (1990), 221–2. There is an interesting discussion by Sumner Ferris, 'Chronicle, chivalric biography, family tradition in fourteenth-century England', in *Chivalric Literature*, ed. L. D Benson and J Leyerle (1980).

13. For surveys of this literature see Tyson, *La Vie du Prince Noir*, 24–5; Ainsworth, *Froissart and the Fabric of History*, ch. 1. There is a fine new edition of *La Chanson de Bertrand du Guesclin de Cuvelier*, by Jean-Claude Faucon (3 vols, 1990–91). This poem is in 24,346 Alexandrines, but is divided into 776 *laisses* each of 20 or more lines; within each *laisse* every line ends with the same rhyme, which makes for dreadful monotony.

14. On the role of the herald see M. Keen, 'Chivalry, Heralds and History', in *The Writing of History in the Middle Ages*, ed. R. H. C. Davis and J. M. Wallace-Hadrill (1981), 393–414.

15. There is some evidence that Robert I knew Anglo-Norman, and of course his son, who spent five years in Château Gaillard, would know French.

16. A man-at-arms was the least noble and least well equipped cavalry figure, below knights and esquires; but the name can also be used to include all three categories of mounted men.

17. These paragraphs owe much to the writings of A. C. Baugh, especially 'The Middle English Romance', *Speculum*, xlii (1967), 1–31.

18. Or to 1.476.

19. *Chanson de Bertrand du Guesclin*, ed. Faucon, iii, 40.

20. The same imbalance is found in Cuvelier's *Chanson de Bertrand du Guesclin*, 40% of which deals with campaigns in Spain, which took up about 7% of du Guesclin's life; and in Chandos Herald, *Vie du Prince Noir*, 50% of which deals with one year's Spanish campaigns, the rest with the Prince's other 30 years. *Chanson de Bertrand ...* ed. Faucon, 81.

21. It is possible that 13.723–41 figured a little earlier in the original version.

22. I had reached the conclusion that this marks the end of the poem as originally written before finding that Eyre-Todd had written of the two parts of the poem, noting that 'a very striking falling-off in style takes place in the poem after the description of Bannockburn. The subsequent narrative is marked by looseness of treatment in recording facts, and an inadequacy in the description of great events, in singular contrast with the vigour, fulness and general accuracy of the earlier books.' *B1907*, xiii*n*. I would not agree with 'looseness' or 'inadequacy', but the contrast is certainly there.

23. The tale of Fabricius and Pyrrhus, 20.531–571, came from Eutropius' *Breviarium* and not, so far as I know, from a romance.

24. 14.1–15.266; 16.1–334; 18.1–210.

25. e.g. Douglas turned over the fallen Richmond and stabbed him to death, 16.422.

26. In this paragraph I follow (or hope that I follow) ch. III, 'Fortune', in F. P. Pickering, *Literature & Art in the Middle Ages* (1970).

27. Lois A. Eben, 'John Barbour's *Bruce*: Poetry, History, and Propa-

ganda', *Studies in Scottish Literature*, ix (1972), 218–42, is an interes-
ting attempt to find in *The Bruce* 'an *exemplum* or mirror designed
to illustrate the importance of the ideals of freedom and loyalty for
the Scottish nation'. I doubt that Barbour addressed the Scottish
nation.

28. Cf. *Beves of Hamtoun*, M3047–48, A1001–5.
29. Stephen Boardman, *The Early Stewart Kings, Robert II and Robert III*
    (1996) is the only full treatment of this reign.
30. On this subject see Jeanette M. A. Beer, *Narrative Conventions of Truth
    in the Middle Ages* (1981).
31. e.g. the flight from Edward I's parliament, 1.589–2.18.
32. *Chron. le Bel*, i, 111; the full quotation will be found at the note to
    6.36.
33. *The Brut*, ed. Brie, 200–2.
34. Brie, *Nationale Literatur* 27.
35. *S,132*.
36. *F1,341; F2,334*. The comment on lack of date, a conspicuous feature
    of Barbour's chronological jumble of the early stories, suggests that
    Fordun knew a written collection.
37. This King Robert may have contributed to the Robin Hood legends.
    The 'rycht sturdy frer' at 18.300–17 recalls a companion of Robin
    Hood – but he comes in a Douglas episode.
38. Several newsletters survive from the period, including one describing
    events in the weeks after the murder of Comyn. They could be
    'popularised' by ballad-mongers, especially in London, but also the
    information in them could reach chroniclers.
39. *Flores Historiarum*, iii, 132–4; *Proc. Soc. Antiquaries Scot.* new series,
    vii (1884), 166–92.
40. Confusion of Kildrummy with Dunaverty.
41. *Chron. Guisborough*, 368–9, 378. Gray knew the same source.
42. *B1985*, 38–9 claims that Barbour 'certainly knew and partially used'
    Fordun, but late and with only a few revisions in its light. Dr Anne
    McKim ('Gret Price off Chewalry: Barbour's debt to Fordun', *Studies
    in Scottish Literature*, 24 (1989), 7–29) says (p. 11) that McDiarmid
    saw borrowing from Fordun, *Chronica*, I, ch. xvi, in 1.229–31, 3.220–
    31, 16.607; I can find only the first in *B1985* (p. 52). McKim makes
    a stronger claim for Barbour's use of Fordun.
43. In the following discussion I have not given page references to
    Fordun's discussion since it takes up few pages and the events
    discussed can readily be found there under the appropriate date.
44. *F1*, 343.
45. McKim, 18.
46. *G*, 370.
47. Fordun has far too many errors of date: for the king's inauguration
    (error also in Verse Chronicle), Methven, Edward I's death, the
    taking of Berwick (probably), Harcla's execution, all on the wrong
    day, and David Bruce's birth, postdated by two years. The Verse
    Chronicle correctly gives Edward I's death as the Translation of St
    Thomas, i.e. 7 July, i.e. non. Jul. Fordun gives 5 April, i.e. non. Apr.
48. *Bower6*, 328 (Slioch), 342 (Inverurie).

49. *Bower6*, 346–9.

50. *Bower6*, 362–5.

51. On this dual function see N. Denholm-Young, *Heralds and Heraldry, 1254 to 1310* (1965), 54–60.

52. Full references in Bitterling, *Wortschatz*, under *lettir*.

53. *Newbattle Registrum*, no. 123.

54. Laud annals. See note to 15.254.

55. *RRS5, 101*

56. *Bower7*, 193.

57. Discussed in *RRS5*, introduction.

58. In the early fourteenth century heralds were not yet the self-important caste they were to become. They were often minstrels and quite lowly in the social hierarchy; this would be especially true of the herald of a private lord.

59. *Bower7*, 68–71. The translation there takes 'like him' as 'like himself', meaning 'without compare'. This too is not a claim made by Barbour, who, for example, at 9.665–76, says that there was no one worthier than Edward Bruce except Robert, 'to whom there was none like in chivalry in his day'.

60. For their descent, *SP6*, 29–30.

61. St John's College, Cambridge, MS G23; National Library of Scotland, Advocates MS 19.2.2.

62. See *B1894,1*, p. lxvii–lxxxviii for the MSS and editions; *B1980*, p. xi for the language.

LIST OF MAPS

Map of principal Scottish places named

The Clyde river and estuary

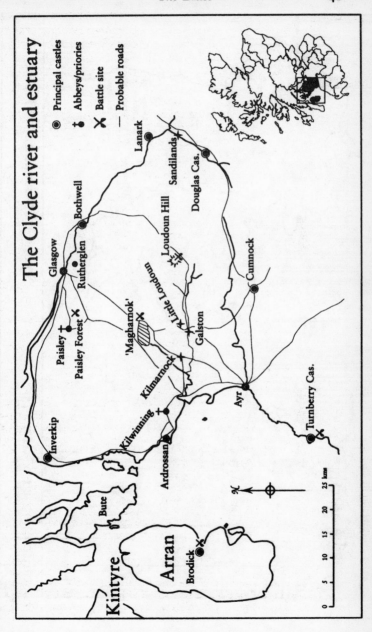

Principal castles
Abbeys/priories
Battle site
Probable roads

Lanark
Sandilands
Douglas Cas.
Bothwell
Glasgow
Rutherglen
Loudoun Hill
Cumnock
Little Loudoun
Paisley
Paisley Forest
'Magharnok'
Galston
Kilmarnock
Inverkip
Kilwinning
Ardrossan
Ayr
Turnberry Cas.

Bute
Kintyre
Arran
Brodick

0 5 10 15 20 25 kms

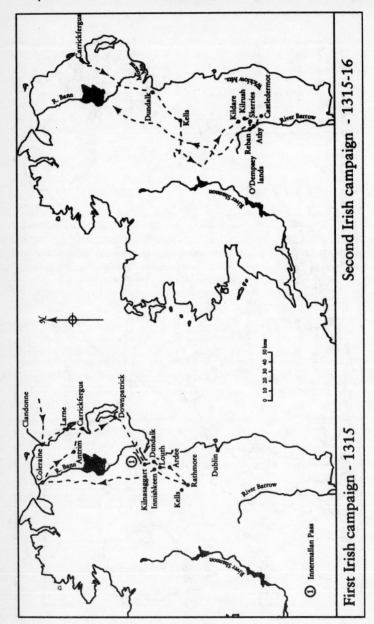

Second Irish campaign - 1315-16

First Irish campaign - 1315

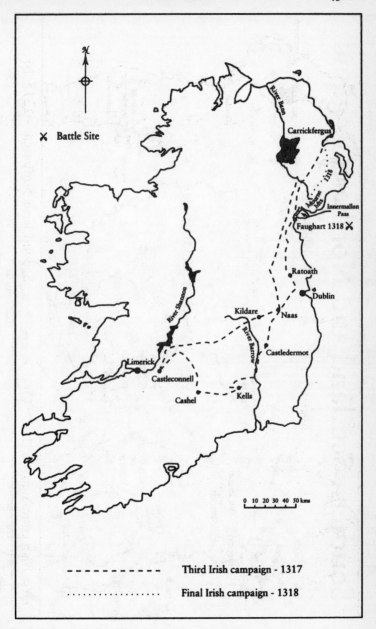

X Battle Site

Carrickfergus

1318

Innermallan
Pass

Faughart 1318 X

Ratoath

Dublin

Kildare

Naas

Castledermot

Limerick

Castleconnell

Cashel

Kells

River Shannon

River Barrow

River Bann

0 10 20 30 40 50 kms

– – – – – – – – – Third Irish campaign - 1317

. . . . Final Irish campaign - 1318

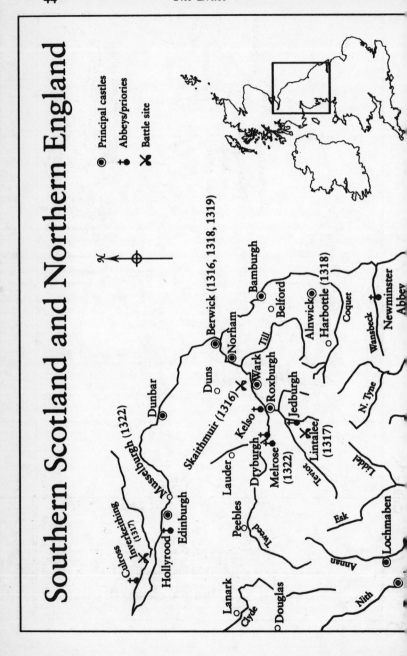

Southern Scotland and Northern England

- ◉ Principal castles
- ✝ Abbeys/priories
- ✗ Battle site

Musselburgh (1322)
Calross
Inverkeithing (1317)
Hollyrood
Edinburgh
Lanark
Clyde
Douglas
Peebles
Lauder
Dunbar
Skaithmuir (1316)
Duns
Dryburgh
Melrose (1322)
Kelso
Roxburgh
Jedburgh
Lintalee (1317)
Berwick (1316, 1318, 1319)
Norham
Wark
Till
Bamburgh
Belford
Alnwick
Harbottle (1318)
Coquet
Wansbeck
Newminster Abbey
N. Tyne
Liddel
Esk
Teviot
Tweed
Nith
Annan
Lochmaben

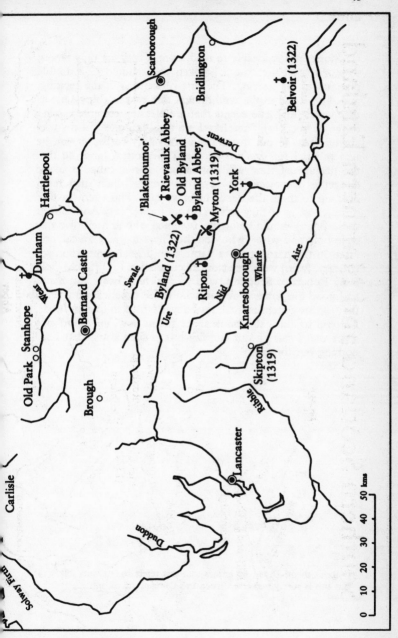

(1) Stories are enjoyable to read, even if they are only fables, so stories that are true, if spoken well, should give double pleasure in the hearing. The first pleasure is in the reciting, and the second in the truthfulness that reveals things just as they were, [for] true events that are pleasing are entertaining to the hearer. (11) Therefore I am firmly resolved, if my wits are up to it, to put in writing a true story so that it will be remembered for ever in [people's] memories, [and] so that the passage of time will not impair it, nor cause it to be altogether forgotten. (17) For old stories which men read, hold up to them the deeds of brave men who lived [in past times], just as if they were with us [now]. (21) And indeed those [men] should be highly esteemed who in their own day were bold and wise, [who] led their lives in great travail, and often in the hard press of battle won a great reputation for chivalry, [who] were free from all cowardice. (27) [Such] were King Robert of Scotland, who was brave in heart and hand, and good Sir James Douglas, who in his time was so worthy that for his generous qualities he was famed in distant lands. I intend to make this book about them; now, may God give grace that I carry it out and finish it in such a way that I say nothing but the truth!

---

33. about them. *B1985*, 67 argues that this refers to 'stalwart folk' (19) but this is surely perverse; Bruce and Douglas are meant.

BOOK I

[This book the true story of King Robert and Sir James Douglas]

	Storys to rede ar delatibill
	Suppos that thai be nocht bot fabill,
	Than suld storys that suthfast wer
	And thai war said on gud maner
5	Have doubill plesance in heryng.
	The first plesance is the carpyng,
	And the tother the suthfastnes
	That schawys the thing rycht as it wes,
	And suth thyngis that ar likand
10	Till mannys heryng ar plesand.
	Tharfor I wald fayne set my will
	Giff my wyt mycht suffice thartill
	To put in wryt a suthfast story
	That it lest ay furth in memory
15	Swa that na tyme of lenth it let
	Na ger it haly be foryet.
	For auld storys that men redys
	Representis to thaim the dedys
	Of stalwart folk that lyvyt ar
20	Rycht as thai than in presence war.
	And certis thai suld weill have prys
	That in thar tyme war wycht and wys
	And led thar lyff in gret travaill,
	And oft in hard stour off bataill
25	Wan gret price off chevalry
	And war voydyt off cowardy,
	As wes King Robert off Scotland
	That hardy wes off hart and hand,
	And gud Schir James off Douglas
30	That in his tyme sa worthy was
	That off hys price and hys bounte
	In ser landis renownyt wes he.
	Off thaim I thynk this buk to ma,
	Now God gyff grace that I may swa
35	Tret it and bryng till endyng
	That I say nocht bot suthfast thing.

(37) When Alexander the king, who had Scotland to govern and lead, had died, the land lay desolate after his time for six years and longer, until the baronage finally assembled together and tried hard to choose to govern their land a king, who in ancestry had come from kings who possessed that kingdom and had the best right to be their king. (47) But envy, that treacherous [foe], created dissension among them. For some would have the Balliol [for] king, since he was descended from the offspring of her who was the eldest sister. (52) And various others rejected that whole argument, and said that he should be their king who was in as near degree and was descended from the nearest male and in a collateral branch. (57) They said that succession to a kingdom was not like [that] to inferior feus, because there no female could succeed as long as a male could be found, descended, no matter how, in direct line; they contended quite otherwise, that the nearest descended of the seed, man or woman, should succeed. (65) For this reason all that party thought that the lord of Annandale, Robert Bruce, earl of Carrick, ought to succeed to the kingdom. The barons were in disagreement like this, [and] could in no way reach agreement, till eventually they all agreed that their whole debate should be [sent as] record to Sir Edward king of England, (74) and he should swear that, without dissembling, he would declare that decision [as to] which of those two that I told of previously should succeed to such an eminence,

---

57–64. This summarises the Bruce case, though the surviving pleadings of Bruce and Balliol do not allege that Balliol sought to apply the law of lower fiefs, i.e. fiefs which are less than a kingdom; the phrase implies that the kingdom was a superior fief, which was true in 1292, though 'fief' was rejected by Robert I later. Bruce certainly argued that 'there', i.e. for a kingdom, a female should not succeed if there was a collateral male; 'in lyne evyn descendand' translates *en la dreyte lyne descendaunt* found in Bruce's 1292 pleadings, though these were much more elaborate than Barbour's single point. For a discussion, see Goldstein, *Matter of Scotland*, 155–7, though Barbour is less 'garbled' than Goldstein suggests.

67. The claimant of 1291–2 was of course Robert Bruce lord of Annandale (and never earl of Carrick), grandfather of Robert I; Barbour must have known this and deliberately homologated the two, ignoring Robert Bruce who married Marjory Countess of Carrick and in 1292 passed on that earldom to his eldest son, later king.

75. arbitre disclar and 88. amicable compositor. The first indicates an arbitration, in which a third party is called in to decide between two contenders. The second is slightly different, for the compositors (often several in number) may decide to give something to each contender, and will seek the agreement of the contenders in the final 'deal', so that it cannot be upset.

[Alexander III's death; the dispute over the succession submitted to Edward I's arbitration]

    Quhen Alexander the king wes deid
    That Scotland haid to steyr and leid,
    The land sex yer and mayr perfay
40 Lay desolat eftyr hys day
    Till that the barnage at the last
    Assemblyt thaim and fayndyt fast
    To cheys a king thar land to ster
    That off auncestry cummyn wer
45 Off kingis that aucht that reawté
    And mayst had rycht thair king to be.
    Bot envy that is sa feloune
    Maid amang thaim gret discencioun,
    For sum wald haiff the Balleoll king
50 For he wes cummyn off the offspryng
    Off hyr that eldest syster was,
    And other sum nyt all that cas
    And said that he thair king suld be
    That war in als ner degre
55 And cummyn war of the neyst male
    And in branch collaterale.
    Thai said successioun of kyngrik
    Was nocht to lawer feys lik,
    For thar mycht succed na female
60 Quhill foundyn mycht be ony male
    How that in lyne evyn descendand.
    Thai bar all otherwayis on hand,
    For than the neyst cummyn off the seid
    Man or woman suld succeid.
65 Be this resoun that part thocht hale
    That the lord off Anandyrdale
    Robert the Bruys erle off Carryk
    Aucht to succeid to the kynryk.
    The barounys thus war at discord
70 That on na maner mycht accord
    Till at the last thai all concordyt
    That thar spek suld be recordyt
    Till Edward off Yngland king
    And he suld swer that but fenyeyng
75 He suld that arbytré disclar
    Off thir twa that I tauld off ar
    Quhilk succeid to sic a hycht,

and let him reign who had the right. (79) They thought this decision was the best, because at that time there was peace and quiet between England and Scotland, and they could not discern the harm that was approaching towards them. (84) Because the king of England had such friendship and companionship with their king, who was so worthy, they believed that he would have judged faithfully as a good neighbour and amicable compositor – but the game went quite another way. (91) Oh, blind folk, sunk in stupidity, if you had really considered the danger that threatened you, you would not have acted in that way. (95) If you had given heed [to] how that king, always, without hesitating, struggled to win lordship [over], and to occupy by his power, lands that bordered upon his, as did Wales and also Ireland, which he reduced to such serfdom that those who were of high birth had to go on foot like the rabble, whenever he sought to assault our people. (105) No Welshman dared ride in a host, nor yet stay after sunset inside a castle or walled town, [on pain of] losing life and limbs. In that kind of serfdom he kept those he overcame by his power. (111) You would see that he took by slight what he could not get by might. If you had paid attention to what serfdom was, and considered his practice of always taking without handing back, without his judgment you would have chosen a king for yourselves who would have maintained the land in justice.

---

84. The king of England. Several sources bear out Barbour's account, including Fordun who says firstly: 'the nobles ... sent messengers to Edward that in that case he should become supreme judge and declare the right of each, and by his power properly coerce according to the requirements of law, that party against whom he might promulgate judgment.' This is Barbour's 'arbitre'. Then, according to Fordun, in a second passage, Edward agreed, provided that there was no prejudice to Scotland and no right of lordship to Edward. 'For he was called to this not as superior lord or as judge of right, but as amicable arbiter and distinguished neighbour, to settle discord, by his wisdom and power, in the manner of an amicable compositor and by reason of his being a neighbour.' (*F1*, 312) This has generally been rejected in recent times in favour of Edward I's version which brings him and the Scots together in 1291 without any preliminaries. The matter is too large for discussion here, but I believe that Barbour is essentially correct.

105-9. Fordun has a similar passage on the conquest of Wales, including the prohibition of Welshmen from staying overnight in castle or town. About 1295 Edward made an ordinance 'that no Welshman should dwell in the walled towns nor hold burgages, but should be removed by the mayors and bailiffs of the said towns, and that no Welshman should carry arms within the walled or English towns ...' The exclusion from castles would be so obvious as not to require an ordinance.

And lat him ryng that had the rycht.
This ordynance thaim thocht the best,
80   For that tyme wes pes and rest
Betwyx Scotland and Ingland bath,
And thai couth nocht persave the skaith
That towart thaim wes apperand.
For that at the king off Ingland
85   Held swylk freyndschip and cumpany
To thar king that wes swa worthy,
Thai trowyt that he as gud nychtbur
And as freyndsome compositur
Wald have jugyt in lawté
90   But othir-wayis all yheid the gle.

[Edward I's ambitions]

A! Blind folk full off all foly,
Haid ye umbethocht you enkrely
Quhat perell to you mycht apper
Ye had nocht wrocht on that maner.
95   Haid ye tane keip how at that king
Alwayis foroutyn sojournyng
Travayllyt for to wyn senyhory
And throu his mycht till occupy
Landis that war till him marcheand
100   As Walis was and als Ireland,
That he put to swylk thrillage
That thai that war of hey parage
Suld ryn on fute as rebaldaill
Quhen he wald our folk assaill.
105   Durst nane of Walis in bataill ride
Na yhet fra evyn fell abyd
Castell or wallyt toune within
That he ne suld lyff and lymmys tyne,
Into swilk thrillage thaim held he
110   That he ourcome throu his powsté.
Ye mycht se he suld occupy
Throu slycht that he ne mycht throu maistri.
Had ye tane kep quhat was thrillag
And had consideryt his usage
115   That gryppyt ay but gayne-gevyng,
Ye suld foroutyn his demyng
Haiff chosyn you a king that mycht
Have haldyn weyle the land in rycht.

(119) Wales could have been an example to you if you had looked further. Wise men say that he is a happy man who corrects himself [from the mistakes] of others, because evil events can happen just as well tomorrow as yesterday. (125) But you put your trust in loyalty, like simple guileless folk, and knew not what would happen afterwards. For in this world, that is so wide, there is certainly no-one who knows what the future will bring, but God, who is omnipotent, reserved to His majesty the knowledge, in His prescience, of the pattern of eternity.

(135) The barons agreed in the way I told you of previously, and through the consent of all of them sent messengers to [King Edward] who was then in the Holy Land, to make war on Saracens. And when he heard what their business was, without hesitation he got ready, left the matter he was engaged on, and went back to England. (145) Then he sent word to Scotland that they should hold a meeting and he would forthwith come to act in every matter [just] as they had written to him. But he fully intended that, by their disagreement, he would cunningly find the way whereby he would obtain all the lordship through his great might. (153) So he said to Robert the Bruce, 'If you and your offspring will hold of me in chief in perpetuity, I shall so act that you will be king.' 'Sir,' said [Bruce], 'as God saves me, I do not hanker after the kingdom, unless it falls rightfully to me.

---

139. Edward I had returned from Palestine in 1274, and, though he undertook to return on crusade in 1291, he never did so. *B1985* suggests that Barbour wrote for 139: 'That was bound to the haly land,' but that would require a change in 140 also, 'warrayand' to 'to warray.'

Walys ensample mycht have bene
120 To you had ye it forow sene,
And wys men sayis he is happy
That be other will him chasty,
For unfayr thingis may fall perfay
Als weill to-morn as yhisterday.
125 Bot ye traistyt in lawté
As symple folk but mavyté,
And wyst nocht quhat suld efter tyd.
For in this warld that is sa wyde
Is nane determynat that sall
130 Knaw thingis that ar to fall,
But God that is off maist powesté
Reservyt till his majesté
For to knaw in his prescience
Off alkyn tyme the movence.

[Edward I offers Scotland to Robert Bruce; and to John Balliol]

135 On this maner assentyt war
The barounis as I said you ar,
And throuch thar aller hale assent
Messengeris till hym thai sent,
That was than in the Haly Land
140 On Saracenys warrayand.
And fra he wyst quhat charge thai had
He buskyt hym but mar abad
And left purpos that he had tane
And till Ingland agayne is gane,
145 And syne till Scotland word send he
That thai suld mak ane assemblé,
And he in hy suld cum to do
In all thing as thai wrayt him to.
Bot he thocht weile throuch thar debat
150 That he suld slely fynd the gate
How that he all the senyhoury
Throu his gret mycht suld occupy.
And to Robert the Bruys said he,
'Gyff thou will hald in cheyff off me
155 For evermar, and thine ofspryng,
I sall do swa thou sall be king.'
'Schyr,' said he, 'sa God me save
The kynryk yharn I nocht to have
Bot gyff it fall off rycht to me,

And if God will that it be so, I shall hold it as freely in all things as is proper to a king, or as my elders before me held it, in freeest royalty.' (165) The [king] grew angry, swore that he would never have it, and turned away in wrath. But Sir John Balliol, *perfay*, agreed with him [to do] all his will, as a result of which great misfortune occurred afterwards. (171) He was king for only a short time, and by great cunning and guile, for little or no reason, he was taken and arrested, and then degraded of [his] honour and dignity. Whether that was right or wrong, God knows, [for] he is omnipotent.

(179) When Sir Edward the mighty king had done what he wanted in this way with John Balliol, who was so speedily found wanting and deprived, he went speedily to Scotland and occupied the whole land, so completely that castles and towns were in his possession from Wick next Orkney to the Mull of Galloway, and [were] all filled with Englishmen. (190) He appointed sheriffs, bailies and various other officers necessary to govern the country; he appointed Englishmen who then became so cruel, so wicked and greedy, so haughty and arrogant, that Scotsmen could never do anything to please [them and meet] their wishes. (199) They would often arrogantly rape the [Scots'] wives and daughters,

---

159–169. This circumstantial story is found also in Fordun, but is certainly untrue.

189. stuffyt with Inglismen. It does not seem that Edward installed English garrisons in Scottish castles in 1296, with the possible exception of Berwick.

190. He appointed ... In 1296 Englishmen were appointed as Guardian (a man too lazy to take up duty), treasurer, chancellor, escheators and as sheriffs in Stirling and sheriffdoms between the Forth and the Border. Even in 1305 this restricted use of Englishmen as officials can be found, though English garrisons were much more widespread. But Gray attributes support for Bruce at his rising 'chiefly to bad government by the king's ministers, who ruled them [?Scots, ?lands] too harshly, for personal gain.' (*S*, 140, *ST*, 51)

199–218. Despite Gray's words in note to 190, it is difficult to find evidence to prove or disprove these allegations of oppression. It is probable that matters grew worse after 1302, but indiscriminate hangings are likely to be the stuff of rumour and myth.

160 And gyff God will that it sa be
I sall als frely in all thing
Hald it as it afferis to king,
Or as myn eldris forouth me
Held it in freyast reawté.'

165 The tother wreyth him and swar
That he suld have it never mar
And turnyt him in wreth away.
Bot Schyr Jhon the Balleoll perfay
Assentyt till him in all his will,

170 Quharthrouch fell efter mekill ill.
He was king bot a litill quhile
And throuch gret sutelté and ghyle
For litill enchesone or nane
He was arestyt syne and tane,

175 And degradyt syne wes he
Off honour and off dignité,
Quhether it wes throuch wrang or rycht
God wat it that is maist off mycht.

[*The miseries of English occupation*]

Quhen Schyr Edward the mychty king
180 Had on this wys done his likyng
Off Jhone the Balleoll, that swa sone
Was all defawtyt and undone,
To Scotland went he than in hy,
And all the land gan occupy

185 Sa hale that bath castell and toune
War intill his possessioune
Fra Weik anent Orknay
To Mullyr Snuk in Gallaway,
And stuffyt all with Inglismen.

190 Schyrreffys and bailyheys maid he then,
And alkyn other officeris
That for to govern land afferis
He maid off Inglis nation,
That worthyt than sa rycht fellone

195 And sa wykkyt and covatous
And swa hawtane and dispitous
That Scottismen mycht do na thing
That ever mycht pleys to thar liking.
Thar wyffis wald thai oft forly

200 And thar dochtrys dispitusly

and if anyone was incensed at this, they punished him with very great pains, for they would soon find an excuse to destroy him. (205) And if any man near them had anything of value, like a horse or hound or something else that pleased [and] was to their liking, rightly or wrongfully, they would have it. And if anyone objected, they would so act that he would lose either land or life, or live in hardship. For they judged [the Scots] at their will, paying no heed to right nor to the proprieties. (215) Ah! how wickedly they judged them! For good knights who were worthy, for little excuse, or even none, they hanged by the neck. Alas that a people who had always been free and accustomed to be in freedom, through their [own] great misfortune and folly were treated so badly then, [when] their enemies were their judges. What worse wretchedness can a man have?

[*Lines 225–242 are translated line for line*] (225) Ah! freedom is a noble thing/Freedom lets a man have pleasure,/Freedom all solace to man gives,/He lives at ease who freely lives./ (229) A noble heart will have no ease/Nor aught else that pleases him/If freedom fails, for free decision/Is longed for above all else./No, he who has always lived free/Cannot well know the properties,/The anger, no, the miserable fate,/That are coupled to foul thralldom./ (237) But, if he had experienced it/ Then he would know it perfectly/And would think freedom more to be prized/Than all the gold there is in this world./ (241) Thus opposites always are/

---

240. All the gold. Barbour probably recalled the moral added by Walter the Englishman, archbishop of Palermo at the end of the twelfth century to his translation of Phaedrus version of the fable of the wolf and the dog: 'I am not in such need that I should want to make myself a serf for the sake of my belly ... The serf does not own himself or his property, whereas a free man does. Freedom, the eminently sweet good, contains all other goods ... Freedom cannot be sold for all the gold in existence, this heavenly good excels earthly wealth.'

And gyff ony of thaim tharat war wrath
Thai watyt hym wele with gret scaith,
For thai suld fynd sone enchesone
To put hym to destruccione.

205   And gyff that ony man thaim by
Had ony thing that wes worthy,
As hors or hund or other thing
That war plesand to thar liking,
With rycht or wrang it have wald thai,

210   And gyf ony wald thaim withsay
Thai suld swa do that thai suld tyne
Othir land or lyff or leyff in pyne,
For thai dempt thaim efter thar will,
Takand na kep to rycht na skill.

215   A! Quhat thai dempt thaim felonly,
For gud knychtis that war worthy
For litill enchesoune or than nane
Thai hangyt be the nekbane.
Alas that folk that ever wes fre,

220   And in fredome wount for to be,
Throu thar gret myschance and foly
War tretyt than sa wykkytly
That thar fays thar jugis war,
Quhat wrechitnes may man have mar.

[*In praise of freedom; on the pains of thralldom*]

225   A! Fredome is a noble thing
Fredome mays man to haiff liking.
Fredome all solace to man giffis,
He levys at es that frely levys.
A noble hart may haiff nane es

230   Na ellys nocht that may him ples
Gyff fredome failyhe, for fre liking
Is yharnyt our all other thing.
Na he that ay has levyt fre
May nocht knaw weill the propyrté

235   The angyr na the wrechyt dome
That is couplyt to foule thyrldome,
Bot gyff he had assayit it.
Than all perquer he suld it wyt,
And suld think fredome mar to prys

240   Than all the gold in warld that is.
Thus contrar thingis evermar

Revealing one about the other./He that is a thrall has nothing;
all that he has is at the disposal of his lord, whoever he is.
(246) He does not even have as much free[dom] as free choice
to leave [alone], or to carry out, that which his heart inclines
him to. When they fall into a disputation, clerks may [debate
this] question: (251) if a man orders his thrall to do something,
and at the same time his wife comes to him and asks her due
of him, whether he should set aside his lord's need, pay first
what he owes [to his wife] and then do his lord's command,
or leave his wife's [debt] unpaid and do the things that were
commanded to him? (259) I leave the solution to those who
are more distinguished [than me]. But since they make such
a comparison between the duties of marriage and of a lord's
command to his thrall, you can see, even though no-one tells
you, how hard a thing thralldom is. (266) For men who are
wise can see quite well that marriage is the hardest bond that
any man can take on [himself] and thralldom is a good deal
worse than death; for while a thrall can live his life, it afflicts
him, body and bones, [while] death afflicts him only once.
To speak briefly, no-one can tell the whole condition of a
thrall.

(275) They lived in that way, in [just] such thralldom, the
poor and the well-born, for the [English] slew some of the
lords, hanged some, drew some and put some in harsh cap-
tivity, without cause or excuse. (281) And among others was
put in prison

243-74. Serfdom seems to be a well-understood and prevalent condition
for Barbour and his audience, but is generally thought to have disap-
peared by 1400. Its decay needs further study.

250-58. Disputation. These lines pose a *quaestio* as it would have been
put in a law faculty for debate by students; the issue of conjugal rights
was well known to canon lawyers.

Discoveryngis off the tother ar,
And he that thryll is has nocht his.
All that he has enbandounyt is
245   Till hys lord quhatever he be.
Yheyt has he nocht sa mekill fre
As fre wyll to leyve or do
That at his hart hym drawis to.
Than may clerkis questioun
250   Quhen thai fall in disputacioun
That gyff man bad his thryll owcht do,
And in the samyn tym come him to
His wyff and askyt him hyr det,
Quhether he his lordis neid suld let,
255   And pay fryst that he awcht, and syne
Do furth his lordis commandyne,
Or leve onpayit his wyff and do
Thai thingis that commaundyt is him to.
I leve all the solucioun
260   Till thaim that ar off mar renoun
Bot sen thai mak sic comperyng
Betwix the dettis off wedding
And lordis bidding till his threll,
Ye may weile se thoucht nane you tell
265   How hard a thing that threldome is.
For men may weile se that ar wys
That wedding is the hardest band
That ony man may tak on hand,
And thryldome is weill wer than deid,
270   For quhill a thryll his lyff may leid
It merrys him body and banys,
And dede anoyis him bot anys.
Schortly to say, is nane can tell
The halle condicioun off a threll.

[*The fate of Sir William Douglas; his son James goes as a boy to Paris*]

275   Thusgat levyt thai and in sic thrillage
Bath pur and thai off hey parag,
For off the lordis sum thai slew
And sum thai hangyt and sum thai drew,
And sum thai put in hard presoune
280   Foroutyn caus or enchesoun,
And amang other off Douglas

Sir William, lord and seigneur of Douglas; they made a martyr
of him. After they killed him in prison, they gave his lands,
which were fair enough, to the lord of Clifford. (288) [Dou-
glas] had a son, a small boy, who was then just a little page,
though later he was of great gallantry. He so avenged his
father's death that there was no-one alive in England, I guar-
antee, who did not fear him, for he cleft the skulls of so many
that none alive can tell of them. Marvellously difficult things
befel him before he arrived at [his high] position. (298) No
occurrence could daunt his heart, nor prevent him carrying
out whatever he was set on [doing], for he always thought
seriously about doing his deed prudently. (303) He thought
[that a person] was deserving of no good fortune who couldn't
put up with vexations; and also [he meant] to achieve great
things, hard struggles and combats, which should cause his
reputation to be doubled. (308) Therefore in his whole lifetime
he was at great effort and great endeavour, and would never
give up because of trouble but would persist right to the end,
and take the outcome that God would send. (313) His name
was James Douglas, and when he heard his father had been
put in prison so wickedly, and that all his lands had been
given to Clifford, he truly did not know what to do or say,
for he had nothing for expenses, nor was there anyone who
had ever known him who would do so much for him that he
would be sufficiently looked after. (323) Then he was com-
pletely at a loss, and suddenly took the notion

---

282. Sir William Douglas. Known as '*le hardi*', the bold, the tough, he
had a career of violence even before the patriotic rising of 1297, where
he joined first Wallace, then Carrick. Imprisoned in Berwick, where he
was 'very wild and abusive', he was transferred after Stirling Bridge to
the Tower of London, where he was in company with several taken
prisoner at the time of the battle of Dunbar. He died there, doubtless
of natural causes (cf. 285), on 9 November, 1298. (*SP3*, 138–40)

287. There is no confirmatory evidence that Douglas's lands were given
to Sir Robert Clifford, but this is probably correct.

288. a son, a small boy, that is James Douglas. His mother was a sister
of James Stewart, and seems to have died by 1289, when Sir William
forced his second wife into marriage. So James was born no later than
1288 and would be at least nine in 1297 when his father was imprisoned,
eighteen in 1306, and twenty-six when knighted at Bannockburn.

Put in presoun Schyr Wilyam was
That off Douglas was lord and syr,
Off him thai makyt a martyr.
285 Fra thai in presoune him sleuch
His land that is fayr inewch
Thai the lord off Clyffurd gave.
He had a sone, a litill knave,
That was than bot a litill page,
290 Bot syne he wes off gret vaslage.
Hys fadyr dede he vengyt sua
That in Ingland I underta
Wes nane off lyve that hym ne dred,
For he sa fele off harnys sched
295 That nane that lyvys thaim can tell.
Bot wonderly hard thing fell
Till him or he till state wes brocht.
Thair wes nane aventur that mocht
Stunay hys hart na ger him let
300 To do the thing that he wes on set,
For he thocht ay encrely
To do his deid avysily.
He thocht weill he was worth na seyle
That mycht of nane anoyis feyle,
305 And als for till escheve gret thingis
And hard travalys and barganyngis,
That suld ger his price doublyt be.
Quharfor in all hys lyvetyme he
Wes in gret payn and gret travaill,
310 And never wald for myscheiff faill
Bot dryve the thing rycht to the end
And tak the ure that God wald send.
His name wes James of Douglas,
And quhen he herd his fader was
315 Put in presoune so fellounly,
And at his landis halyly
War gevyn to the Clyffurd perfay
He wyst nocht quhat to do na say,
For he had na thing for to dispend
320 Na thar wes nane that ever him kend
Wald do sa mekill for him that he
Mycht sufficiantly fundyn be.
Than wes he wonder will off wane,
And sodanly in hart has tane

that he would travel overseas, be a while in Paris and suffer misfortune where no-one knew him, until God sent him some help. (329) He did just as he had thought, and soon went to Paris, living there quite simply. Nonetheless he was happy and fun-loving, was up to such dissolute behaviour as nature expects of youth and [was] sometimes in low company. (336) That may many a time be of help, for knowledge of many conditions can sometimes be useful in many ways, as happened to Robert the good count of Artois, in his [life-]time, for pretending to behave badly was often of great use to him. (343) Cato says to us, in his writings, that sometimes pretending folly is wisdom. He lived in Paris for nearly three years, and then came news over the sea that his father had been done to death; he was [full of] woe and at a loss, and decided that he would go home again, to see whether without any difficulty he could recover his heritage, and [take] his men out of thralldom.

(353) He went speedily to St Andrews where the bishop received him very courteously, and had him carry his knives before him, for cutting; [he] clad him right honourably and had [a place] designated where he could sleep. He remained there a fairly long time. (360) All men loved him for his generosity, for he was of really good conduct, wise, courteous and debonair, and also generous and affectionate; above everything he loved loyalty.

325–45. Douglas's three year stay in Paris is mentioned by no other source except *The Wallace*. It could have begun in 1299 and must have ended by 1304, when (409–12) he went to Edward I at Stirling. In view of his service as knife-bearer to the bishop of St Andrews (353–59), it seems likely that he went to Paris with the bishop either in the embassy of 1301–2, or, and this is more likely, in that of 1302–3; possibly Douglas was with both embassies, or may even have stayed in Paris between them. The bishop returned in 1304, to swear fealty to Edward I on 3 May, 1304, at Stirling; this is referred to in 427.

339–44. Robert count of Artois was a stormy petrel in French politics in the 1330s, who was said to have feigned madness. 344 is a translation of *Stultitiam similare loco prudentia summa est* from *Disticha Catonis*.

325   That he wald travaile our the se
    And a quhile in Parys be,
    And dre myscheiff quhar nane hym kend
    Til God sum succouris till hym send.
    And as he thocht he did rycht sua,
330   And sone to Parys can he ga
    And levyt thar full sympylly,
    The-quhether he glaid was and joly,
    And till swylk thowlesnes he yeid
    As the cours askis off youtheid,
335   And umquhill into rybbaldaill.
    And that may mony tyme availl,
    For knawlage off mony statis
    May quhile availye full mony gatis
    As to the gud erle off Artayis
340   Robert befell in his dayis
    For oft fenyeyng off rybbaldy
    Availyeit him and that gretly.
    And Catone sayis us in his wryt
    That to fenyhe foly quhile is wyt.
345   In Parys ner thre yer dwellyt he,
    And then come tythandis our the se
    That his fadyr wes done to ded.
    Then wes he wa and will of red,
    And thocht that he wald hame agayne
350   To luk gyff he throu ony payn
    Mycht wyn agayn his heritage
    And his men out off all thryllage.

[*Douglas returns to Scotland, to serve the bishop of St
Andrews; his appearance*]

    To Sanct Androws he come in hy,
    Quhar the byschop full curtasly
355   Resavyt him and gert him wer
    His knyvys forouth him to scher,
    And cled him rycht honorabilly
    And gert ordayn quhar he suld ly.
    A weile gret quhile thar dwellyt he.
360   All men lufyt him, for his bounté,
    For he wes off full fayr effer
    Wys curtais and deboner.
    Larg and luffand als wes he,
    And our all thing luffyt lawté.

(365) Loyalty is to love wholeheartedly, by loyalty men live righteously. With one [other] virtue and loyalty a man can still be adequate, but without loyalty he is worthless, even if he is valiant or wise, for where [loyalty] is lacking, no virtue is of [sufficient] price or value to make a man so good that he can be called simply 'a good man'. (375) He was loyal in all his actions, for he did not deign to have truck with treachery or with falseness. His heart was set on high honour, and he behaved in such a way that that all who were near him, loved him. But he was not so good-looking that we should say much of his beauty. His face was somewhat pale, and, as I heard it, he had black hair, but he was well made in his limbs, with strong bones and broad shoulders. (387) His body was well made and lean, as those who saw him told me. When he was cheerful he was engaging, quiet and gentle in company, but if you saw him in battle, he had quite another look [to him]. In speech he lisped a bit, but that suited him remarkably well. (395) He could be likened to good Hector of Troy in many respects. Hector had black hair, as he had, and strong well-made limbs, and lisped too, just like him; [Hector] was wholly endowed with loyalty, and was courteous, wise and courageous. (402) But in manliness and great energy I dare compare to Hector no-one in the world's inhabitants. Nonetheless, in his time [Douglas] did such [deeds] that he should be greatly praised.

395-404. Barbour is using the Latin *Historia Destructionis Troiae*, by Guido de Columnis, where all this may be found, though the black hair is attributed not to Hector but, a few lines earlier, to Telamon. Hair colour is the best explanation of 'the black Douglas' for black was not his heraldic colour.

365 Leawté to luff is gretumly,
    Throuch leawté liffis men rychtwisly.
    With a vertu and leawté
    A man may yeit sufficyand be,
    And but leawté may nane haiff price
370 Quether he be wycht or he be wys,
    For quhar it failyeys na vertu
    May be off price na off valu
    To mak a man sa gud that he
    May symply callyt gud man be.
375 He wes in all his dedis lele,
    For him dedeynyeit nocht to dele
    With trechery na with falset.
    His hart on hey honour wes set,
    And hym contenyt on sic maner
380 That all him luffyt that war him ner.
    Bot he wes nocht sa fayr that we
    Suld spek gretly off his beauté.
    In vysage wes he sumdeill gray
    And had blak har as Ic hard say,
385 Bot off lymmys he wes weill maid
    With banys gret and schuldrys braid,
    His body wes weyll maid and lenyé
    As thai that saw hym said to me.
    Quhen he wes blyth he wes lufly
390 And meyk and sweyt in cumpany,
    Bot quha in battaill mycht him se
    All othir contenance had he.
    And in spek wlispyt he sumdeill,
    Bot that sat him rycht wondre weill.
395 Till gud Ector of Troy mycht he
    In mony thingis liknyt be.
    Ector had blak har as he had
    And stark lymmys and rycht weill maid,
    And wlispyt alsua as did he,
400 And wes fullfillyt of leawté
    And wes curtais and wys and wycht
    Bot off manheid and mekill mycht
    Till Ector dar I nane comper
    Off all that ever in warldys wer.
405 The-quhethyr in his tyme sa wrocht he
    That he suld gretly lovyt be.

(407) He lived there until at one time King Edward, with great pride, came to Stirling with a great following, to hold an assembly there. Thither went many barons; Bishop William Lamberton rode there also, and with him was this squire, James Douglas. The bishop led him to the king, and said, (417) 'Sir, here I bring you this child, who lays claim to be your man, and begs you, *par charité,* that you would receive his homage here, and grant him his heritage.' 'What lands does he claim?' said the king.'Sir, if it please you, he claims the lordship of Douglas, for his father was lord of that.' (425) Then the king was absolutely furious, and said, 'Sir bishop, assuredly if you want to keep your fealty, you will make no such speech to me. His father was always an infamous enemy of mine, and died for that in my prison; he was [then] against my authority, and therefore I ought to be his heir. Let him go get land wherever he can, for he shall have none of that [lordship], I swear. (435) The Clifford shall have them, for he has always served me loyally.' The bishop heard him answer thus, and dared speak no more to him then, but hurried from his presence, for he dreaded [the king's] violent [temper] sorely, so dared speak no more on the matter. The king did the business he had come to do, and then went back to England, with many very powerful men.

409–14. Bishop Lamberton was with Edward I at Stirling, at least intermittently, in May–July 1304, to which this episode may be dated, even though Edward was engaged not in a parliament but in besieging Stirling castle. Alternatively, the place was St Andrews, where a parliament was held in March 1304. The bishop's intercession makes an association with Douglas in Paris the more likely.

[*Douglas asks Edward I for his lands*]

He dwellyt thar quhill on a tid
The King Edward with mekill prid
Come to Strevillyne with gret mengye
410 For till hald thar ane assemblé.
Thidderwart went mony baroune,
Byschop Wilyame off Lambyrtoun
Raid thiddyr als and with him was
This squyer James of Douglas.
415 The byschop led him to the king
And said, 'Schyr, heyr I to you bryng
This child that clemys your man to be,
And prays you par cheryté
That ye resave her his homage
420 And grantis him his heritage.'
'Quhat landis clemys he?' said the king.
'Schyr, giff that it be your liking
He clemys the lordschip off Douglas,
For lord tharoff hys fader was.'
425 The king then wrethyt him encrely
And said, 'Schyr byschop, sekyrly
Gyff thou wald kep thi fewté
Thoue maid nane sic speking to me.
His fadyr ay wes my fay feloune
430 And deyt tharfor in my presoun
And wes agayne my majesté
Tharfor hys ayr I aucht to be.
Ga purches land quharever he may
For tharoff haffys he nane, perfay.
435 The Clyffurd sall thaim haiff for he
Ay lely has servyt to me.'
The bischop hard him swa answer
And durst than spek till him na mar,
Bot fra his presence went in hy
440 For he dred sayr his felouny
Swa that he na mar spak tharto.
The king did that he com to do
And went till Ingland syn agayn
With mony man off mekill mayn.

(445) Lords, for whoever cares to listen, there now begins here the romance of men who were in great distress, and made mighty efforts, before they could come to their goal; (450) but then Our Lord sent them such grace that eventually, by their great valour, they came to great esteem and to honour, despite all their enemies, who were so numerous that they were pretty well a thousand to one [Scot]. But where God helps, what [earthly power] can withstand ? (457) But, if we tell the truth of it, they were sometimes more rather than less, but God, who is omnipotent, preserved them in his prescience to avenge the harm and frustration that that a numerous and cruel people did to a worthy simple folk, who could not help themselves. (465) Therefore they were like the Maccabees, who, as men see in the Bible, by their great courage and valour, fought in many a fierce battle to free their country, from people who unjustly held them and theirs in thralldom. (472) They achieved this by their bravery, so that with few men they won victory over mighty kings, as the story goes, and delivered their land to freedom; for that, their name should be honoured.

(477) The lord Bruce, of whom I spoke before, saw the whole kingdom so oppressed, and the people so troubled, that he felt great sorrow at it. But he did not reveal whatever sorrow he felt, until, one time as they came riding from Stirling,

---

445. Lordingis! Cf. 'Lordinges, herkneth to me tale!' *Beves of Hamtoun*, A1. Such an apostrophe was common in a romance.

458. That is, sometimes they were more than a thousand to one!

465. Like to the Maccabees. This refers to unnamed 'men' (448), presumably Scotsmen. Fordun at this point likens Bruce to Judas Maccabeus, and the same, fairly obvious, comparison was made in the Declaration of Arbroath. (*F1*, 337)

481. riding from Stirling. This points to the siege in the summer of 1304 as the date of an agreement between Comyn and Bruce.

[*The romance begins; the Scots and the Maccabees*]

445   Lordingis, quha likis for till her,
        The romanys now begynnys her
        Off men that war in gret distres
        And assayit full gret hardynes
        Or thai mycht cum till thar entent.
450   Bot syne our Lord sic grace thaim sent
        That thai syne throu thar gret valour
        Come till gret hycht and till honour,
        Magré thar fayis everilkane
        That war sa fele that ay till ane
455   Off thaim thai war weill a thousand,
        Bot quhar God helpys quhat may withstand.
        Bot and we say the suthfastnes
        Thai war sum tyme erar may then les,
        Bot God that maist is off all mycht
460   Preservyt thaim in his forsycht
        To veng the harme and the contrer
        At that fele folk and pautener
        Dyd till sympill folk and worthy
        That couth nocht help thaim self. For-thi
465   Thai war lik to the Machabeys
        That as men in the bibill seys
        Throw thar gret worschip and valour
        Faucht into mony stalwart stour
        For to delyver thar countre
470   Fra folk that throu iniquite
        Held thaim and thairis in thrillage.
        Thai wrocht sua throu thar vasselage
        That with few folk thai had victory
        Off mychty kingis as sayis the story,
475   And delyveryt thar land all fre,
        Quharfor thar name suld lovyt be.

[*Comyn's proposal to Bruce*]

        Thys lord the Bruys I spak of ayr
        Saw all the kynryk swa forfayr,
        And swa troublyt the folk saw he
480   That he tharoff had gret pitté.
        Bot quhat pite that ever he had
        Na contenance tharoff he maid,
        Till on a tym Schyr Jhone Cumyn

Sir John Comyn said to him, (485) 'Sir, can you not see how this country is governed ? They kill our people without [any] excuse, and hold this land against [all] reason, when you should be lord of it. If you will listen to me, you shall have yourself made its king, and I shall be your helper, provided that you give me all the land that you now have in your possession; (495) and if you won't do this, nor take this position for yourself, then all my land shall be yours, and allow me to take the position for myself and bring this land out of serfdom. (500) For there is neither man nor boy in all this land who does not yearn to make himself free.' The lord Bruce heard his discourse, and knew he spoke only the truth. (505) And because it agreed with his feelings he soon gave his assent to it and said, 'Since you want it so, I will cheerfully take upon myself the position, for I know that I have the right [to it], and right often makes the weak strong.

(511) The [two] barons agreed thus, and that very night their indentures were written and oaths sworn,

---

485–510. In the many versions of this conversation, e.g. by Fordun and Gray, Barbour alone has Comyn propose the pact, thereby placing the responsibility for betraying fealty to Edward I on his shoulders. The conversation is surely fiction, designed to place the indenture between the two men in the worst possible light. The granting of family lands by the successful contestant to the unsuccessful as a reward for support, had already been promised to a rival by the elder Bruce in 1292.

513. Indenture. This is a document written twice on a parchment, the two texts then cut apart on a wavy line. Each party would seal one text which would be kept by the other party. The existence of a written promise of treason (as here) is so improbable as to be ludicrous. But there is a persistent account, e.g. in Gray and Fordun, of an indenture of just the kind described by Barbour, so probably an account of a real indenture, found after the event, was inflated thus to explain the murder of Comyn. Because on 11 June, 1304, at Cambuskenneth, (near Stirling, at the time of the siege) Bruce and the bishop of St Andrews did make an indenture whereby

> conferring on future mutual dangers and wishing to avoid them as far as possible and to resist prudently the strivings of rivals, they entered a treaty of friendship in the following form, namely that they will faithfully consult mutually in whatsoever their business and dealings at whatever times and against whatever persons, and will bring aid or help by themselves and their men with all their strength for ever and without dissembling; that neither of them will try any difficult business without consulting the other and that each will forewarn or cause to be forewarned the other of imminent dangers as soon as he

As thai come ridand fra Strevillyn
485   Said till him, 'Schyr, will ye nocht se
How that governyt is this countré.
Thai sla our folk but enchesoune
And haldis this land agayne resoune,
And ye tharoff suld lord be.
490   And gyff that ye will trow to me
Ye sall ger mak you tharoff king,
And I sall be in your helping
With-thi ye giff me all the land
That ye haiff now intill your hand.
495   And gyff that ye will nocht do sua
Ne swylk a state upon you ta,
All hale my land sall youris be
And lat me ta the state on me
And bring this land out off thyrllage,
500   For thar is nother man na page
In all this land than thai sall be
Fayn to mak thaim selvyn fre.'
The lord the Bruis hard his carping
And wend he spak bot suthfast thing,
505   And for it likit till his will
He gave his assent sone thartill
And said, 'Sen ye will it be swa
I will blythly apon me ta
The state, for I wate that I have rycht,
510   And rycht mays oft the feble wycht.'

[*The dangers of treason*]

The barounys thus accordyt ar,
And that ilk nycht writyn war
Thair endenturis, and aythis maid

---

can consider them and will cause them to be impeded with all his
strength ... To observe all these things ... they have bound themselves
with mutual faith and an oath ... under pain of £10,000 to be applied
to the Holy Land ...

The only sinister feature of this is that it does not include a clause
'saving always our faith to the lord King Edward.' It is likely that Bruce
and Comyn made a similar indenture a month or so later. The aim
may have been to build up support for Bruce and to minimise opposition
to him in the event that he (peacefully) claimed the Scottish throne
after the death of Edward I who completed 65 years in June 1304.

to maintain what they had discussed. But beware of treachery
above all things! For there is neither duke nor baron, no earl,
no prince, no mighty king, be he never so wise or vigorous,
in wit, valour, esteem, or renown, who can ever guard himself
against treason. (521) Was not all Troy taken by treason after
ten years of warfare? Then many thousands were slain of those
outside by strength of hand, as Dares wrote in his book, and
Dictys [in his]; they knew the whole story. (527) [The Trojans]
might not have been taken by force, but treason took them
by [her] tricks. (529) And Alexander the conqueror, who
subdued Babylon's tower, and the length and breadth of this
world in twelve years, by his brave deeds, was eventually
destroyed by poison in his own house, by great treason. But
before he died he distributed his lands; to see his death was
a great sorrow. (537) Julius Caesar, another valiant man, won
Britain and France, Africa, Arabia, Egypt, Syria and the whole
of Europe, and because of his worthiness and valour was the
first to be made emperor of Rome; (543) then in his Capitol
he was killed by those of his inmost council, [stabbed] to
death with a dagger, and when he saw that there was no help
[for it], he closed his eyes with his hand, to die more hon-
ourably. (549) Next, Arthur, who by prowess made Britain
mistress and lady of twelve kingdoms which he won, and also,
as a great man, won all France completely, by battle; he
defeated Lucius Iber who was then emperor of Rome. (556)
Yet, despite all his great valour,

525–26. Barbour is using Guido de Columnis, a version of the accounts
of the siege of Troy based on those by Dares and Dictys, early medieval
fabrications.

529–36. This account is taken from *Le Roman d'Alixandre*. 533, 545, E
has both men killed by 'pusoune', but for Caesar 'punsoune', a
puncheon or pointed weapon, is meant.

537–48. A similar account of Caesar, repeating Suetonius' error of calling
him the first emperor, is found in Fordun, though the closing of the
eyes (547) is unique to Barbour.

549–60. For this, his sole allusion to Arthurian matter, Barbour is probably
using *The Brut* in one of its languages – French, English, Latin. 560
makes it unlikely that he used Geoffrey of Monmouth's *History* directly.

To hald that thai forspokyn haid.
515   Bot of all thing wa worth tresoun,
For thar is nother duk ne baroun
Na erle na prynce na king off mycht
Thocht he be never sa wys na wycht
For wyt worschip price na renoun,
520   That ever may wauch hym with tresoune.
Was nocht all Troy with tresoune tane
Quhen ten yeris off the wer wes gane?
Then slayn wes mony thousand
Off thaim without throu strenth of hand,
525   As Dares in his buke he wrate,
And Dytis that knew all thar state.
Thai mycht nocht haiff beyn tane throu mycht,
Bot tresoun tuk thaim throu hyr slycht.
And Alexander the conqueroure
530   That conqueryt Babilonys tour
And all this warld off lenth and breid
In twelf yher throu his douchty deid
Wes syne destroyit throu pusoune
In his awyne hous throu gret tresoun,
535   Bot or he deit his land delt he;
To se his dede wes gret pité.
Julius Cesar als, that wan
Bretane and Fraunce as douchty man,
Affryk, Arrabe, Egipt, Surry
540   And all Europe halyly,
And for his worschip and valour
Off Rome wes fryst made emperour,
Syne in his capitole wes he
Throu thaim of his consaill prevé
545   Slayne with punsoune rycht to the ded,
And quhen he saw thar wes na rede
Hys eyn with his hand closit he
For to dey with mar honesté.
Als Arthur that throu chevalry
550   Maid Bretane maistres and lady
Off twelf kinrikis that he wan,
And alsua as a noble man
He wan throu bataill Fraunce all fre,
And Lucius Yber vencusyt he
555   That then of Rome wes emperour,
Bot yeit for all his gret valour

his sister's son, Mordred, killed him and more than enough good men also, by treason and wickedness; the *Brut* bears witness to this. (561) That's what became of this agreement; for the Comyn rode to the king of England, and told the whole situation, though, not, I'm sure, all [exactly] as it was. But he gave him the indenture, that soon showed the double-dealing, and for that subsequently he suffered death, when he could find no way out of it.

(569) When the king saw the indenture, he was in a towering rage, and swore that he would take revenge on that Bruce, who had presumed thus to strive or rise against him, or to conspire in this way. (575) To Sir John Comyn he said that he would be rewarded for his loyalty, and well [at] that, and [Comyn] thanked him humbly. Then he meant to have the governing of all Scotland, without contradiction, when the Bruce had been put to death. (582) But a fool's plan often fails, and wise men's intentions don't always come to the conclusions which they think they will come to, because God knows well what will befall. It happened just like that with his intention, as I shall tell afterwards. (589) [Comyn] took his leave and went home; the king thereupon had a parliament arranged hastily, and summons to it speedily the barons of his kingdom. He sent to the lord Bruce, ordering him to come to that assembly, and he, who had no inkling of the treason and falsehood,

---

569. Fordun's account of these events is quite different and is referred to in the notes to book 2.

590. Parliament. A parliament was summoned for 15 September, 1305, and was opened in the king's absence. The next parliament met on 30 May, 1306. Thus Barbour's parliament must be dismissed along with his story of Edward showing the indenture and Bruce's escape. He was probably in Scotland during the winter 1305-6. But this whole episode surely derives from Philip VI of France submitting the claim of John de Montfort for the duchy of Brittany to the court of Peers. John was forbidden to leave Paris for 15 days, but in his chamber decided that things would go against him, that he would be arrested and forced to hand over castles and wealth. He fled to Brittany without the king's knowledge – everyone thought he was ensconced in his Paris house. (*Chron. le Bel*, i. 261-62). The story was obviously well known, and if placed in the parlement of Paris (a possible variant) the transfer is more readily understandable. In fact a commission of two bishops heard his claim.

Modreyt his syster son him slew,
And gud men als ma then inew
Throu tresoune and throu wikkitnes,
560 The Broite beris tharoff wytnes.
Sa fell of this conand-making,
For the Cumyn raid to the king
Off Ingland and tald all this cas
Bot I trow nocht all as it was
565 Bot the endentur till him gaf he
That soune schawyt the iniquité.
Quharfor syne he tholyt ded,
Than he couth set tharfor na rede.

[*Edward I confronts Bruce with the indenture in parliament*]

Quhen the king saw the endentur
570 He wes angry out of mesur,
And swour that he suld vengeance ta
Off that Bruys that presumyt swa
Aganys him to brawle or rys
Or to conspyr on sic a wys.
575 And to Schyr Jhon Cumyn said he
That he suld for his leawté
Be rewardyt and that hely,
And he him thankit humyly.
Than thocht he to have the leding
580 Off all Scotland but gane-saying
Fra at the Bruce to dede war brocht.
Bot oft failyeis the fulis thocht,
And wys mennys etling
Cummys nocht ay to that ending
585 That thai think it sall cum to,
For God wate weill quhat is to do.
Off hys etlyng rycht swa it fell
As I sall efterwartis tell.
He tuk his leve and hame is went,
590 And the king a parlyament
Gert set tharefter hastely
And thidder somounys he in hy
The barounys of his reawté,
And to the lord the Bruce send he
595 Bydding to cum to that gadryng.
And he that had na persavyng
Off the tresoun na the falset

rode without hesitation to the king. (599) He lodged himself in London on the first day of their meeting, then on the next day went to court. The king sat in parliament, called the lord Bruce before his privy council there and showed him the indenture. (606) He was in very real danger of losing his life, but God Almighty, not wanting him to die in those circumstances, preserved him for a higher destiny. The king offered him in that place the indenture, to look at the seal, and asked if he had sealed it? (613) He looked intently [at] the seal and answered [the king] circumspectly, saying, 'Because I am a man of little consequence my seal is not with me all the time; I have someone else to carry it. (618) So if it were you will, I ask you for an adjournment until tomorrow to look at this letter and be advised about it when you are sitting, and then without longer delay, I shall produce this letter here before all your plenary council. For that I offer as pledge all my heritage.' (627) The king thought he could be trusted enough, since he put his lands in pledge, and allowed him to go with the letter, to produce it as had been promised.

---

615. Bruce's claim of humble standing is presumably a literary flourish by Barbour.

616. Seal here means both the matrix with which an impression was made (which Bruce claimed not to have with him), and the impression. Ordinary men would normally have one seal-matrix which they kept on their persons. By the late thirteenth century nobles would usually have a large seal for use on legal documents (e.g. sales of land) and a private seal (*secretum*), much smaller, for use on letters; the former might well be kept by a clerk, the latter by the noble. The father and grandfather of Robert Bruce had both large seal (double faced) and small seal; for Robert himself only a small seal (single faced, about 2.4 cm. in diameter) seems to be known. When the Bruce-Lamberton indenture fell into English hands in 1306, the bishop was interrogated about it, and the first question was, 'Is that your seal and did you append it voluntarilly?' (Cf. 612)

Raid to the king but langer let,
And in Lundon hym herberyd he
600 The fyrst day off thar assemble,
Syne on the morn to court he went.
The king sat into parleament
And forouth hys consaile prevé
The lord the Bruce thar callyt he
605 And schawyt hym the endentur.
He wes in full gret aventur
To tyne his lyff, bot God of mycht
Preservyt him till hyer hycht,
That wald nocht that he swa war dede.
610 The king betaucht hym in that steid
The endentur the seile to se,
And askyt gyff it enselyt he?
He lukyt the seyle ententily
And answeryt till him humyly
615 And sayd, 'How that I sympill be
My seyle is nocht all tyme with me.
Ik have ane other it to ber.
Tharfor giff that your willis wer
Ic ask you respyt for to se
620 This letter and tharwith avysit be
Till tomorn that ye be set,
And then foroutyn langer let
This letter sall I entyr heyr
Befor all your consaill planer,
625 And thartill into borwch draw I
Myn herytage all halily.'
The king thocht he wes traist inewch
Sen he in bowrch hys landis drewch,
And let hym with the letter passe
630 Till entyr it as forspokin was.

(1) Bruce went quickly to his lodging, but, believe you me, he was very relieved that he had obtained that respite. Soon he called his marischal to him, and ordered him to make every endeavour to provide good cheer for his men, since he wanted to be a good long while in his chamber in private, with only one clerk with him. (10) The marischal went to the hall and did his lord's bidding. The lord Bruce, without hesitating, had two horses brought secretly. He and the clerk mounted unnoticed, without anyone else, and day and night, without stopping, rode until on the fifteenth day they came to Lochmaben. (19) They found his brother Edward there, who, I assure you, marvelled that they had come home so secretly; [Bruce] told his brother the whole [story], how he had been lured there, and how he had managed to escape.

(25) It so happened that at the same time Sir John Comyn was staying at Dumfries, near to [Lochmaben]. Bruce mounted up and rode there, meaning to repay him without further delay for his revelation [to the king]. (31) [So] he rode there at once

---

10. The clerk is a curiously redundant player; it is possible that he represents Bruce's brother, Alexander, dean of Glasgow, accompanying Robert to Lochmaben. It is possible that the two brothers did travel together from London at some point late in 1305.

17. It would take perhaps a week to reach Lochmaben, with only short stops for rest.

19. His brother Edward. Almost certainly this represents a mention in Barbour's source of Bruce's brothers, Neil and Thomas. Barbour cuts out the role which the brother(s) played as messengers to Comyn, for Edward has none here.

31–36. This account of the murder of Comyn on 10 February, 1306, is extraordinarily brief, laconic and distorted, though a fuller version of it is given by Fordun, who says that Bruce showed the indenture, accused Comyn, who gave him the lie and was stabbed by him. The earliest report is by Guisborough:

Bruce ... fearing Comyn, who was powerful amd faithful to the English king, and knowing he could be stopped by him [in his aspiring to be king] sent to him in deceit his two brothers Thomas and Neil, asking that he would please come to him at Dumfries to deal with certain business touching them both. The justiciars of the king of England were sitting on that day [10 February, 1306] in the castle. Comyn, suspecting nothing, came to him with a few men, and they gave each other a kiss (but not of peace) in the cloister of the Friars Minor. When they were speaking together in turn, with words which

[*Bruce escapes to Lochmaben*]

  The Bruys went till his innys swyth,
  Bot wyt ye weile he wes full blyth
  That he had gottyn that respyt.
  He callit his marschall till him tyt
5 And bad him luk on all maner
  That he ma till his men gud cher,
  For he wald in his chambre be
  A weile gret quhile in prevaté,
  With him a clerk foroutyn ma.
10 The marschell till the hall gan ga
  And did hys lordys commanding.
  The lord the Bruce but mar letting
  Gert prevely bryng stedys twa,
  He and the clerk foroutyn ma
15 Lap on foroutyn persavyng,
  And day and nycht but sojournyng
  Thai raid quhill on the fyften day
  Cummyn till Louchmaben ar thai.
  Hys broder Edward thar thai fand
20 That thocht ferly Ic tak on hand
  That thai come hame sa prevely.
  He tauld hys brodyr halyly
  How that he thar soucht was
  And how that he chapyt wes throu cas.

[*The killing of Comyn and his uncle*]

25 Sa fell it in the samyn tid
  That at Dumfres rycht thar besid
  Schir Jhone the Cumyn sojornyng maid.
  The Brus lap on and thidder raid
  And thocht foroutyn mar letting
30 For to quyt hym his discovering.
  Thidder he raid but langer let

seemed peaceful, suddenly, in a reversal and with different words, he [Bruce, presumably] began to accuse him of betrayal, in that he had accused him to the king of England and had worsened his position to his harm. When he [Comyn, presumably] spoke peaceably and excused himself, [Bruce] did not wish to hear his speech, but, as he had conspired, he struck him with foot and sword and went away and met with Sir John Comyn in the [Grey] Friars, at the high altar; in a mocking manner he showed him the indenture, and then with a knife took his life on that very spot. Sir Edmund Comyn also was killed, and many others of great importance. (39) Nonethless some men still say that that quarrel happened otherwise; but whatever caused the quarrel, he died because of it, I know for certain. He acted wrongly there, without doubt [for he did] not respect sanctuary at the altar. Because of it such great misfortune befel him that I have never heard tell in a romance of a man so hard beset as he was, who came afterwards to such good fortune. (49) Now let us go again to the king [of England], who on the following day sat with his barons

---

out. But [Bruce's] men followed [Comyn] and cast him down on the paving before the altar, leaving him for dead ... Robert Comyn his uncle ran to bring him help, but Christopher Seton (who had married Bruce's sister) met him, struck his head with a sword and he died. Bruce came out, saw John's fine charger and mounted it, and his men mounted with him. They went to the castle, and took it. When they told what had happened, the Scots ran to him. The fearful justices closed the doors of the hall in which they sat with a few English, and when he heard this he ordered fire to be applied unless they gave themselves up. They surrendered, stipulating for their lives and safe exit from the land, which he granted them. Then some evil folk told him that ... Comyn still lived, for the Friars had carried him down to the altar vestry, to treat him and for him to confess his sins. When he confessed and was repentant, by the tyrant's order he was pulled out of the vestry and killed on the steps of the high altar ...

Some of this, notably the justices' sitting, is confirmed by the charges Edward I brought against Scottish bishops later in 1306, and the absence of the indenture also gives it credibility. Bruce did not kill Comyn, but was responsible for his death. The subject of their conversation, reported verbatim by some colourful chronicles, is unlikely to have been overheard, and it is surely clear that the murder was unpremeditated, but there must be a suspicion that Comyn, who had shown himself a violent man, was provocative. Barbour depicts, on the contrary, a premeditated and sudden killing, excused by the treachery (which is probably a myth) of the indenture; for this God punished Bruce by many dangers and hardships. (*F1*, 332–33; *G*, 366–67)

And with Schyr Jhone the Cumyn met
In the Freris at the hye awter,
And schawyt him with lauchand cher
35 The endentur, syne with a knyff
Rycht in that sted hym reft the lyff.
Schyr Edmund Cumyn als wes slayn
And othir mony off mekill mayn.
Nocht-for-thi yeit sum men sayis
40 At that debat fell other-wayis,
Bot quhat-sa-evyr maid the debate
Thar-throuch he deyt weill I wat.
He mysdyd thar gretly but wer
That gave na gyrth to the awter,
45 Tharfor sa hard myscheiff him fell
That Ik herd never in romanys tell
Off man sa hard frayit as wes he
That efterwart com to sic bounté.

[*Edward hears of Bruce's flight; news of Comyn's death reaches the bishop of St Andrews*]

Now agayne to the king ga we
50 That on the morn with his barne
Sat intill his parleament,

37–38. Sir Edmund Comyn was laird of Kilbride, and was not present; John's uncle was Sir Robert Comyn. There do not seem to have been other deaths.

39–40. There were several highly coloured accounts of the murder. Gray knew an elaboration of that in Guisborough, whereby Bruce sent his brothers Thomas and Alexander to Comyn, but with instructions to kill him. He greeted them in such a friendly way that they could not bring themselves to do it. Bruce, brushing them aside as faint-hearted, met Comyn and offered that one should become king, while the other took his estates.

'Indeed,' Comyn said then, 'I shall never be false to my English lord in a matter which might be charged against me as treason, for I am bound to him by oath and homage.' 'No!' exclaimed Bruce, 'I had different hopes of you, by the promise of yourself and your friends. You have betrayed me to the king in your letters, so you cannot escape my will. You shall have your reward!' So saying, he struck him with his dagger, and the others cut him down in the middle of the church, before the altar. A knight, [Comyn's] uncle, who was present, struck the said Bruce with a sword in the chest, but he, being in armour, was not wounded; the uncle was slain immediately.

Like Guisborough this has no mention of the indenture, but it has elaborated the role of Bruce's two brothers, to blacken his character. (*S*, 129–30)

in parliament; he sent bold knights to his lodging for the lord Bruce. When he had been summoned several times, they asked his men about him, and they said that since yesterday he had remained all the time in his chamber, with only a clerk with him. (59) Then they knocked at his chamber [door] and when nobody was heard to answer, they broke down the door but found nothing, although they searched the whole room. [So] they told the king the whole business, and how he had escaped. (65) He was sore at this escape and swore very colourfully in anger that [Bruce] would be hanged and drawn. He threatened what he intended, but [Bruce] meant matters to go otherwise. (70) When, as you heard me say, he had killed Sir John in the kirk he went back to Lochmaben, and had men ride with his letters in every direction to friends who came to him with their followings; and he gathered his men too, and planned to make himself king. (78) Over all the land the word spread that the Bruce had killed the Comyn; and among others, letters went to the bishop of St Andrews, telling how that baron had been slain. (83) The letter told him the whole deed, and he read it to his men, saying to them afterwards, 'Assuredly I hope that the prophecy of Thomas of Ercildune will be fulfilled in him; for, as God helps me, I have a great hope that he will be king and have all this land to govern.'

81. The bishop of St Andrews. William Lamberton was a sworn member of Edward I's council for Scotland at Berwick, though the bishop may well not have been there. On 9 June, 1306 he wrote to Aymer de Valence denying involvement in the death of Comyn and in the beginning of the war. He was arrested and interrogated for Edward I, and revealed that he had been in contact with Bruce but had been too fearful to go to Scone to participate in the inauguration there; under Bruce's threats he went two days later to say mass for the new king on Palm Sunday. Before mid-June he sent his tenants to serve in Bruce's army.

86-90. No appropriate prophecy has been found in the work attributed to Thomas of Ercildoune. But there are contemporary reports that prophecies attributed to Merlin and foretelling the success of Bruce after the death of 'the covetous king' [Edward I], were circulating in 1307.

Sat intill his parleament,
And eftyr the lord the Bruys he sent
Rycht till his in with knychtis kene.
Quhen he oft-tyme had callit bene
55 And his men efter him askit thai,
Thai said that he sen yhysterday
Dwelt in his chambyr ythanly
With a clerk with him anerly.
Than knokyt thai at his chamur thar
60 And quhen thai hard nane mak answar
Thai brak the dur, bot thai fand nocht
The-quhethir the chambre hale thai socht.
Thai tald the king than hale the cas
And how that he eschapyt was.
65 He wes off his eschap sary
And swour in ire full stalwartly
That he suld drawyn and hangit be.
He manansyt as him thocht, bot he
Thoucht that suld pas ane other way
70 And, quhen he as ye herd me say
Intill the kyrk Schyr Jhone haid slain,
Till Louchmabane he went agayne
And gert men with his lettres ryd
To freyndis apon ilk sid
75 That come to hym with thar mengye,
And his men als assemblit he
And thocht that he wald mak him king.
Our all the land the word gan spryng
That the Bruce the Cumyn had slayn,
80 And amang other, lettres ar gayn
To the byschop off Androws towne
That tauld how slayn wes that baroun.
The letter tauld hym all the deid,
And he till his men gert reid
85 And sythyn said thaim, 'Sekyrly
I hop Thomas prophecy
Off Hersildoune sall veryfyd be
In him, for swa Our Lord help me
I haiff gret hop he sall be king
90 And haiff this land all in leding.'

(91) James Douglas who always and everywhere carved [the meat] before the bishop, had heard the whole letter read intently, and also took very good heed of what the bishop had said. When the boards were dismantled, they went speedily to a room and James Douglas privately (99) said to the bishop, 'Sir, you see how Englishmen disinherit me of my land by their might, and men have given you to understand that the earl of Carrick too claims to govern the kingdom. And because of that man whom he has killed, all Englishmen are against him, and would cheerfully disinherit him; for that reason I want to stick with him. (109) So, sir, if it is agreeable to you, I would take good and ill with him. Through him I mean to win my land, despite Clifford and his kin.' The bishop listened and had pity [on him]; he said, 'Sweet son, as God helps me, I would be delighted if you were there, as long as I am not blamed. (117) You should act in the following way. You shall take Ferrand, my palfrey because there is no horse in this land so nimble and so well-trained. Take him as if on your own impulse, as if I had not agreed to it, (123) and if his keeper refuses at all, make sure that you take him in spite of [the man]; that way I shall escape blame. Almighty God, in his power, grant that you and he to whom you are going, acquit [yourselves] so well at all times that you defend yourselves from your foes.' (130) He gave him silver for spending-money, then gave him 'Good day',

---

96. The boards. When the tables had been dismantled by lifting the boards from the trestles.

99–108. Disinheritance. The speech is doubtless Barbour's composition, but it must reflect his source in its emphasis upon the recovery of heritage by both Douglas and Bruce.

[Douglas leaves St Andrews on the bishop's horse and joins Bruce]

<pre>
        James off Douglas that ay-quhar
        Allwayis befor the byschop schar
        Had weill hard all the letter red,
        And he tuk alsua full gud hed
  95   To that the byschop had said.
        And quhen the burdys doun war laid
        Till chamyr went thai then in hy,
        And James off Douglas prevely
        Said to the byschop, 'Schyr, ye se
 100   How Inglismen throu thar powsté
        Dysherysys me off my land,
        And men has gert you understand
        Als that the erle off Carryk
        Clamys to gevern the kynryk,
 105   And for yon man that he has slayn
        All Inglismen ar him agayn
        And wald disherys hym blythly,
        The-quhether with hym dwell wald I.
        Tharfor, schir, giff it war your will
 110   I wald tak with him gud and ill.
        Throu hym I trow my land to wyn
        Magré the Cliffurd and his kyn.'
        The byschop hard and had pite
        And said, 'Swet son, sa God help me
 115   I wald blythly that thou war thar
        Bot at I nocht reprovyt war.
        On this maner weile wyrk thou may.
        Thou sall tak Ferrand my palfray,
        For thar is na hors in this land
 120   Sa swytht na yeit sa weill at hand.
        Tak him as off thine awyne hewid
        As I had gevyn tharto na reid,
        And gyff his yhemar oucht gruchys
        Luk that thou tak him magré his,
 125   Swa sall I weill assonyeit be.
        Mychty God for his powsté
        Graunt that he that thou pasis to
        And thou in all tyme sa weill to do
        That ye you fra your fayis defend.'
 130   He taucht him siluer to dispend
        And syne gaiff him gud day
</pre>

and bade him go forth on his way, for he would not speak [again] before he had gone. (134) The Douglas then took his way right to the horse, as [the bishop] had bidden him; the man who had charge of [the beast] hindered him with insults, but he became very angry and felled him with a sword-stroke. Then, without further delay, he hastily saddled the horse, mounted him with a leap, and departed without taking leave [of anyone]. (144) Dear God, who is king of heaven, preserve him, and shield him from his foes! All by himself he took the road towards the town of Lochmaben, and a little from the Arickstone met the Bruce with a large force, riding to Scone to be set on the king's throne and become king. (152) When Douglas saw him coming he rode [forward], greeted him swiftly and bowed courteously to him; he told him all about himself, who he was, and also how Clifford held his heritage and that he had come to do homage to him as to his rightful king; [also] that he was ready to take good and bad with him in everything. (162) When the Bruce had heard his wishes, he received him with great joy, and gave him men and arms. He expected that [Douglas] would be a fine [man], for all his ancestors were doughty. That's how they made each other's acquaintance, [men] who never afterwards disagreed for any reason, as long as they lived. (170) Their friendship increased more and more all the time, because [Douglas] always served loyally, and [Bruce], who was worthy, brave and wise, with a good will rewarded him well [for] his service.

---

139. Barbour passes by Douglas's ruthless killing of the stableman doing his duty without comment.

The episode may reflect the episode in which the earl of Atholl seized the horses of the earl of Buchan in mid-March 1306, to inhibit pursuit when taking the countess of Buchan to Scone for the inauguration.

146-151. Arickstone was at the head of Annandale, and Bruce would be on his way to Glasgow in early March, whence he travelled by Dumbarton to Scone. On 9 June 'James Douglas' was one of two valets of Sir Henry Sinclair and Sir Robert Keith receiving wine and grain at Linlithgow from the English commander, Piers Lubaud. The knights were Lothian men, and this James was surely James Douglas 'of Lothian' (ancestor of the earls of Morton), so called to distinguish him from Bruce's commander. (*CDS5*, 215b)

169. departyt, i.e. separated; but this is such an exaggeration that I have translated as 'disagreed'.

And bad him pas furth on his way,
For he ne wald spek till he war gane.
The Douglas then his way has taine
135 Rycht to the hors, as he him bad,
Bot he that him in yhemsell had
Than warnyt him dispitously,
Bot he that wreth him encrely
Fellyt hym with a swerdys dynt,
140 And syne foroutyn langer stynt
The hors he sadylt hastely,
And lap on hym delyverly
And passyt furth but leve-taking.
Der God that is off hevyn king
145 Sauff hym and scheld him fra his fayis.
All him alane the way he tais
Towart the towne off Louchmabane,
And a litill fra Aryk stane
The Bruce with a gret rout he met
150 That raid to Scone for to be set
In kingis stole and to be king.
And quhen Douglas saw hys cummyng
He raid and hailsyt hym in hy
And lowtyt him ffull curtasly,
155 And tauld him haly all his state
And quhat he was, and als how-gat
The Cliffurd held his heritage,
And that he come to mak homage
Till him as till his rychtwis king,
160 And at he boune wes in all thing
To tak with him the gud and ill.
And quhen the Bruce had herd his will
He resavyt him in gret daynté
And men and armys till him gaff he.
165 He thocht weile he suld be worthy
For all his eldris war douchty.
Thusgat maid thai thar aquentance
That never syne for nakyn chance
Departyt quhill thai lyffand war.
170 Thair frendschip woux ay mar and mar,
For he servyt ay lelely,
And the tother full wilfully
That was bath worthy wycht and wys
Rewardyt him weile his service.

(175) The lord Bruce rode to Glasgow, and sent [messages to those] thereabouts, until he had a great following of his friends. Then he rode swiftly to Scone, and without delay was made king; he was placed in the king's throne, as was the way at that time. (182) But about their high rank, [their] pomp, their service or their magnificence, you will hear nothing now from me except that he took homage from the baronage who had come there, and then went through all the land getting friends and friendship, in order to support what he had begun. (190) He knew that, before all the land would be won,

---

175-77. We are particularly well informed about this stay at Glasgow by a report from Berwick dated in March and based on intelligence from the west:

> The earl of Carrick has been at Glasgow and Rutherglen and thereabouts and has received the fealty of the people where he went and has ordered them to be ready to go with him with rations for nine days, whenever they receive twenty-four hours notice. The wicked bishop remains at Glasgow as his chief adviser and the earl comes often and takes ... [text defective; later in a postscript] On the day this letter was written, John of Menteith informed me that the earl of Carrick had crossed the sea [the Forth] with 60 men at arms. If the people on the other side are trustworthy, which I do not doubt, he will have but a short stay among them. The Saturday before this letter was written, the earl of Carrick came to Glasgow and the bishop gave him absolution fully for his sins, and made him swear that he would abide under the direction of the clergy of Scotland, and freed him to go to secure his heritage by all the means that he could. They had a meal together and then the earl left in the direction of Menteith to cross the River Forth, and when he came to Dumbarton he ordered Alexander Lindsay and Walter Logan to demand the surrender of the castle ... John [Menteith] replied that he held the castle by commission from the king ... and he would not surrender it except to the king, unless he had a letter under the king's great seal, so that he should be acquitted in the same way as he had been commissioned.

Robert Wishart, bishop of Glasgow, may have persuaded Bruce to take the throne without seeking a deal with Edward I. (*ASR, 34*)

179-81. The inauguration of Robert I. This took place on 25 March, 1306 at Scone. Despite the lazy habit of English sources of referring to this as a coronation, Barbour is right in describing it as a traditional inauguration, in which the king, wearing a crown, was enthroned and invested in royal robes. We do not know what was used for the 'king's seat' in 1306, but the countess of Buchan was brought to take part in that enthronement as representative of her family, the earls of Fife. In charges sent by Edward I to the pope it was said:

> when the earl by force of war wanted to make himself king, ... the bishop of Glasgow caused to be made and apparelled in his own wardrobe the robes and attire with which the said earl had himself vested and attired on the day on which he wished to have himself

[*Bruce becomes king; Edward I sends Aymer de Valence
against him; King Robert's force at Perth*]

175   The lord the Bruce to Glaskow raid
          And send about him quhill he haid
          Off his freyndis a gret menyhe,
          And syne to Scone in hy raid he
          And wes maid king but langer let,
180   And in the kingis stole wes set
          As in that tyme wes the maner.
          Bot off thar nobleis, gret affer,
          Thar service na thar realté
          Ye sall her na thing now for me,
185   Owtane that he off the barnage
          That thidder come tok homage
          And syne went our all the land
          Frendis and frendschip purchesand
          To maynteym that he had begunnyn.
190   He wyst or all the land war wonnyn

called king of Scotland, and he sent this attire together with the banner
of the late king of Scotland, which he had long before hidden in his
treasury, to the said earl at the abbey of Scone before the day when
he had himself called king of Scotland.

Robert I would have been crowned and annointed in 1329, had he not
died before the arrival of the papal bull conferring the privilege.

184. The abbots of Scone and probably Inchaffray were present, but no
bishop; the earls of Atholl, and possibly Menteith and Lennox were
present. The bishops of Glasgow and Moray came out for the king.

187. Many circumstantial details, such as the names of Robert's forfeited
supporters, and the persons taken in his camp at Methven, show that
he went north to Banff and spent some time at Aberdeen, between the
inauguration and the battle of Methven on 19 June, 1306. In March
1307 Edward I agreed to repair the fortifications of Perth, Dundee,
Forfar, Aboyne and Aberdeen; they can only have been damaged a year
earlier by Robert. Sir Richard Siward was taken prisoner at Tibbers
and released at Kildrummy where he had been imprisoned by 'the earl
of Carrick'. (*CDS2, 1911; CDS5, 472r*)

188. Robert undoubtedly attracted some supporters, but it should be
remembered that as king he could lawfully command men to serve in
the army. His efforts to get the earl of Strathearn to do so involved
arrest in breach of a safe-conduct, threats of being hanged, and finally
an attack on his manor house at St Fillans. The earl bowed to the
threats but reneged once he was released. Barbour does not dwell on
such blackmail, but shows it incidentally. He passes silently over the
royal expedition to raise support, north to the Moray Firth and Aber-
deen, in April–May 1306. The Aberdeen stay is transposed to 515–69,
after the defeat at Methven.

he would have a very hard struggle with him who was king
of England, for there was no-one alive so severe, so deadly,
or so cruel. (195) And when King Edward was told how the
Bruce, who was so bold, had finished off the Comyn, and
then had made himself king, he nearly went out of his mind.
(200) He called to him Sir Aymer de Valence, who was wise,
brave and a noble knight in his deeds, and ordered him to
take men at arms, [to] go to Scotland with all despatch, and
burn, kill and raise the dragon [banner]. (206) He promised
all Fife as a reward to whoever might either take or kill Robert
the Bruce, who was [Edward's] enemy. Sir Aymer did as he
had ordered him, taking great chivalry with him; Philip Mow-
bray was with him and Ingram Umfraville, who was both wise
and prudent, and very chivalrous; they had the greater part
of Scotland in their company, because then much of the land
was in Englishmen's hands. (219) They went then with an
army to Perth,

199. Edward I reacted to the murder of Comyn moderately, ordering the
suppression of 'dispeace', and (unspecifically) 'some Scots' who had
risen against him. Edward had no expectation that Bruce would take
the throne. Then on 5 April, clearly on receipt of the news of Robert's
inauguration, a flurry of orders against the rebellion of the earl of Carrick
shows that Edward was indeed infuriated by it.

200. Aymer de Valence was born about 1270, inheriting his father's
lordship of Montignac in Poitou in 1296; his mother, countess of
Pembroke, was daughter of a daughter of William Marshall, earl of
Pembroke (d. 1219), and on her death in September 1307 he became
earl of Pembroke, a title which Barbour never gives him. He had served
Edward I in Scotland when the king appointed him lieutenant south
of Forth in 1303. On the day news of Bruce's inauguration reached the
English court, 5 April, 1306, Valence was appointed lieutenant in the
north-east, between York and the Forth, to subdue the rebellion. There
is a good short account of him in *CPro*, 382–88, and a life by J. R. S.
Phillips (1972).

205. The dragon banner was raised as a sign that no quarter would be
given.

206. The promise of Fife is not confirmed by any source but the heir to
the earldom was a sixteen-year old boy in Edward's custody, and his
lands for the period of wardship would be worth about £500 annually.

211. [Sir] Philip Mowbray was certainly with Aymer de Valence at
Methven where his horse was killed; he was later constable of Kirkin-
tilloch castle (1309–10) and then of Stirling. He submitted to King
Robert, and served in Ireland. In 1336 he was the deceased lord of
Kirkmichael in Dumfriesshire and Alexander Mowbray was a close
relative. His connection with the Mowbrays of Barnbougle (near South
Queensferry) is uncertain. Sir John Mowbray of that family was active
in the English interest in March 1306, in conjunction with Umfraville.

He suld fynd full hard barganyng
With him that wes off Ingland king,
For thar wes nane off lyff sa fell
Sa pautener na sa cruell.

195 And quhen to King Edward wes tauld
How at the Bruys that wes sa bauld
Had brocht the Cumyn till ending,
And how he syne had maid him king,
Owt off his wyt he went weill ner,

200 And callit till him Schir Amer
The Vallang that wes wys and wycht
And off his hand a worthy knycht,
And bad him men off armys ta
And in hy till Scotland ga,

205 And byrn and slay and rais dragoun,
And hycht all Fyfe in warysoun
Till him that mycht other ta or sla
Robert the Bruce that wes his fa.
Schir Aymer did as he him bad,

210 Gret chevalry with him he had,
With him wes Philip the Mowbray,
And Ingram the Umfravill perfay
That wes bath wys and averty
And full off gret chevalry,

215 And off Scotland the maist party
Thai had intill thar cumpany,
For yheit then mekill off the land
Wes intill Inglismennys hand.
Till Perth then went thai in a rout,

He was associated with the murdered Comyn and was committed to
the Balliol cause. Perhaps Sir Philip and Sir John have been combined
here. (*ASR, 34; CDS5, 472p, 368. Knights of Edward I*, i. 223–24)

212. Ingram de Umfraville features prominently in the poem; he had
been a leading patriot, one of the Guardians from 1300, envoy to France,
and, on his submission to Edward I in 1304, recipient of the longest
period of exile imposed on any Scottish 'rebel' leader, though he was
in Scotland in 1306. His mother was probably a Balliol of Redcastle
(Angus), and he was committed to the Balliol cause. By 6 April, 1306
Sir John Mowbray and Umfraville had gone with a force to Carrick.
He is not named among those paid for having been with Valence at
Methven, and was probably in the south-west with Sir John Mowbray.
(*ASR, 34; CDS5, 419*)

214. Gret chevalry. We are fortunate in having the wages bill for this
army of some 50 knights, 210 esquires, 140 crossbowmen and 1,960
infantry / archers. (*CDS5, 492v–x*)

which was then completely walled with many towers and high battlements for defence if it was attacked. Sir Aymer remained there with all his great chivalry. (225) King Robert knew he was there, and what captains were with him, [so] gathered all his following. He had many of very great courage, but their enemies were more [numerous] than they [were] by fifteen hundred, as I heard said. Therefore [King Robert] had there, in that crisis, many who were valiant in action, and barons who were bold as boar. (234) There were two earls also with him, those of Lennox and Atholl. Edward Bruce was there too, Thomas Randolph, Hugh de le Hay, Sir David Barclay, Fraser, Somerville and Inchmartin. (240) James Douglas was there later, who was still of little significance, and many other folk, stout in fighting; good Christopher Seton too, and Robert Boyd of great fame, and many others of great might, but I can't say what they were called.

(247) Though they were few, they were bold, and full of great chivalry. They came before St Johnstoun [Perth] as a host in good array, and demanded that Sir Aymer come out to fight. He, trusting in the great power of those who were with him, ordered his men to arm themselves speedily. (255) But Sir Ingram Umfraville thought it was far too dangerous to advance on them in open formation, and while they were in such [good] battle-order; [so] he said then to Sir Aymer, 'Sir, if you will listen to me,

---

220. Perth and probably Berwick were walled, uniquely among Scottish towns.

229–30. Guisborough says that the Scots were more numerous.

235–40. This list differs from that of the prisoners taken, at 408–13, but the list of knights is very similar especially in not giving the first names of Inchmartin and Somerville. Fraser is later identified as Sir Alexander Fraser, not Simon, who seems to have operated for the king in Lothian-Selkirk. The late arrival of Douglas probably means that he had not been with the king between March and mid-June.

243–45. These lines are not in E, but in H. They fall awkwardly after the 'and others' of 242, a line virtually repeated in 245, which could explain why E lost them. For Christopher Seton see note to 421. Boyd was taken at Kildrummy which is not evidence that he was at Methven. These lines look suspect, but have won their place because it is difficult to see why H should invent them.

237. Randolph was lord of Stitchill (and not of Nithsdale), son of King Robert's half sister; for Hay see note to 412.

238. Barclay is identified in *B1985*, 71, as 'of Cairns'.

220	That then wes wallyt all about
	With feile towris rycht hey bataillyt
	To defend giff it war assaylit,
	Tharin dwellyt Schyr Amery
	With all his gret chevalry.
225	The King Robert wyst he wes thar
	And quhatkyn chyftanys with him war
	And assemblyt all his mengye.
	He had feyle off full gret bounte
	Bot thar fayis war may then thai
230	Be fyften hunder as Ik herd say,
	The-quhether he had thar at that ned
	Full feill that war douchty off deid
	And barounys that war bauld as bar.
	Twa erlis alsua with him war,
235	Off Levynax and Atholl war thai.
	Edward the Bruce wes thar alsua,
	Thomas Randell and Hew de le Hay
	And Schyr David the Berclay
	Fresale, Somerveile, and Inchmertyn.
240	James off Douglas thar wes syne
	That yheyt than wes bot litill off mycht,
	And othir fele folk forsye in fycht

	Als was gude Cristell of Setoun	243*
	And Robert Boyd of greit renoun,	244*
245	And uther feill of mekill micht	245*
	Bot I can nocht tell quhat thai hycht.	243

[At Perth; Umfraville's advice to Valence]

	Thocht thai war quheyn thai war worthy	
	And full off gret chevalry,	
	And in bataill in gud aray	
250	Befor Sanct Jhonystoun com thai	247
	And bad Schyr Amery isch to fycht,	
	And he that in the mekill mycht	
	Traistyt off thaim that wes him by	
	Bad his men arme thaim hastily.	
255	Bot Schir Ingram the Umfravill	252
	Thocht it war all to gret perill	
	In playne bataill to thaim to ga	
	Or-quhill thai war arayit sa,	
	And till Schyr Amer said he,	
260	'Schir, giff that ye will trow to me,	257

you will not go out to attack them while they are prepared in
battle-order. (263) For their commander is wise and prudent
and in his deeds a noble knight. He has in his company many
a good and worthy man, who will be hard to attack while they
are in such good order. (269) For it would require very great
force to put them to flight just now, since when folk are in
good array and well prepared for the battle, given that they
are all good men, they will be far more prudent, and far more
to be feared, than if they were in a state of some disorder.
(277) Therefore, sir, you could say to them that if they like
they can go to camp tonight, and sleep and rest, and that
tomorrow, without further delay, you will come out to [give]
battle and fight with them, unless they have left. So they will
troop to their camp and some will go to forage; those who
stay at the lodging, since they have come from travelling, will
shortly be disarmed. (288) Then we in our best manner, with
all our fair chivalry, may ride towards them right boldly; and
they, expecting to rest all night, when they see us, arrayed to
fight, coming upon them so suddenly, will be utterly terrified.
(295) And before they have come into a fighting-force, let us
hasten in such a way that we are ready for the engagement.
Some men who are bold when prepared, will shake with fear
when attacked suddenly.'

250–413. There is an early account of this battle in Guisborough:

> The new king ... gathered a copious army ... went to Perth ... where
> Aymer was ... with 300 men at arms and some infantry. The Scots
> were a great host. At the orders of their king all the men at arms on
> horses had a white coat over all their armour, so that they appeared
> to be in white shirts and you could not see who was who or what
> arms he bore. The king sent envoys that our men should come out
> and fight with him or should surrender. Seeing they were less
> numerous they replied cautiously that they would not come out but
> would fight with him tomorrow because it was a feast day. (It was
> Sunday after St John's Day [24 June].) Rather credulously the king
> withdrew at these words about a mile from the town and prepared a
> meal. Our men discussed this among themselves, saying, 'If we wait
> till tomorrow we shan't win, because he is stronger than us. But if
> we go out at vespers, we will win, because they are busy making food.'
> So they went out at vespers as agreed, found them lying peacefully,
> and before they could all get up, they attacked them fiercely, and
> when many had been killed the king fled with a few who still resisted.

The date is wrong – the battle was on 19 June – but this error is found
as early as the assize roll for the trial of prisoners sent from Scotland,
held at Newcastle on 4 August. Methven is about six miles from Perth.
There are elements in common with Barbour, who suppresses the white

Ye sall nocht ische thaim till assaile
Till thai ar purvayt in bataill,
For thar ledar is wys and wycht
And off his hand a noble knycht,
265 And he has in his cumpany   262
Mony a gud man and worthi
That sall be hard for till assay
Till thai ar in sa gud aray,
For it suld be full mekill mycht
270 That now suld put thaim to the flycht,   267
For quhen folk ar weill arayit
And for the bataill weill purvait
With-thi that thai all gud men be,
Thai sall fer mar be avisé
275 And weill mar for to dreid then thai   272
War sumdele out off aray.
Tharfor ye may, schyr, say thaim till
That thai may this nycht and thai will
Gang herbery thaim and slep and rest,
280 And to-morn but langer lest   277
Ye sall isch furth to the bataill,
And fecht with thaim bot gyf thai faile.
Sa till thar herbery went sall thai
And sum sall went to the forray,
285 And thai that dwellis at the logyng   282
Sen thai cum out off travelling
Sall in schort tyme unarmyt be.
Then on our best maner may we
With all our fayr chevalry
290 Ryd towart thaim rycht hardyly.   287
And thai that wenys to rest all nycht
Quhen thai se us arayit to fycht
Cummand on thaim sa sudanly,
Thai sall affrayit be gretumly,
295 And or thai cummyn in bataill be   292
We sall speid us swagat that we
Sall be all redy till assembill.
Sum man for erynes will trymbill
Quhen he assayit is sodanly
300 That with avisement is douchty.'   297

---

surcoats. These can only have been intended to conceal the identity of
the cavalrymen mustered before Perth. (*G*, 368)

(301) They did just as he advised; they sent [word] to those outside, bade them make camp for that night, and come to the fight in the morning. When [the Scots] saw that they could [achieve] no more, they went towards Methven and lodged themselves in the wood. A third part went foraging, and the remainder were soon disarmed, scattered to bivouac here and there. (311) Then Sir Aymer, not hesitating, came out in force, with all the folk he had with him, to the fight, and rode headlong and direct, [taking] the road straight towards Methven. (316) The king, who was then without armour, saw them coming so determinedly; then he shouted loudly to his men, 'To arms, at once, and get ready; here are our enemies at hand!' They [obeyed] right smartly, and mounted their horses speedily. (323) The king displayed his banner when his men had gathered, and said, 'Lords, you can see now that yon folk cunningly mean to do with a trick what they feared to do with force. Now I see that he who trusts his enemy will have cause to regret it. (331) Yet, although they are many, God may decide our fates well, for a multitude does not make a victory, as you'll have read in many a story, [where] the few have often defeated the many. Let us hope that we shall do just that. (337) Each of you is brave and worthy, full of great chivalry, and knows very well what honour is. Behave then, in such a way that your honour is always maintained.

---

333. From I Maccabees, 19.

[*The Scots go to Methven to camp; the English advance on them*]

As he avisyt have thai done,
And till thaim utouth send thai sone
And bade thaim herbery thaim that nycht
And on the morn cum to the fycht.

305   Quhen thai saw thai mycht no mar   302
Towart Meffayn then gan thai far
And in the woud thaim logyt thai.
The thrid part went to the forray,
And the lave sone unarmyt war

310   And skalyt to loge thaim her and thar   307
Schyr Amer then but mar abaid
With all the folk he with him haid
Ischyt inforcely to the fycht,
And raid intill a randoun rycht

315   The straucht way towart Meffen.   312
The king that wes unarmyt then
Saw thaim cum swa inforcely,
Then till his men gan hely cry,
'Till armys, swyth, and makis you yar,

320   Her at our hand our fayis ar.'   317
And thai did swa in full gret hy
And on thar hors lap hastily.
The king displayit his baner
Quhen that his folk assemblyt wer

325   And said, 'Lordingis now may ye se   322
That yone folk all throu sutelté
Schapis thaim to do with slycht
That at thai drede to do with mycht.
Now I persave he that will trew

330   His fa, it sall him sum-tyme rew.   327
And nocht-for-thi, thocht thai be fele
God may rycht weill our werdis dele
For multitud mais na victory,
As man has red in mony story

335   That few folk has oft vencusyt ma.   332
Trow we that we sall do rycht sua.
Ye ar ilkan wycht and worthy
And full of gret chevalry,
And wate rycht weill quhat honour is.

340   Wyrk yhe then apon swylk wys   337
That your honour be savyt ay.

One thing [more] I'll say to you: that he who dies for his
country shall dwell in heaven.' (345) When this had been said,
they saw their foes coming, riding near at hand, arrayed right
prudently, intent on doing chivalry.

(349) So they were prepared on both sides, and ready to do
battle. They levelled their spears on both sides and rode at
each other so fiercely that the spears were all smashed, and
many men [lay] dead or badly wounded; (355) the blood burst
out of their mail-coats, for the best and worthiest who were
determined to win honour plunged into the stalwart combat
and laid about them [with] fierce blows. (360) You could
have seen knights in that throng who were bold and valiant,
[lying] defiled under the feet of horses, some wounded, some
dead, [so that] the grass grew all red with blood. Those who
stayed on horseback swiftly [and] boldly drew their swords,
and gave and took so many hard blows that all the ground
around them shook. (369) The Bruce's folk hardily showed
their great chivalry, while he himself, even more than the
others, gave such hard and heavy blows, that wherever he
came, they gave way to him. (374) His men put themselves
under great pressure to decrease the great superiority of the
enemy, who had the better of the fight to such an extent that
they won more and more ground.

---

344. Received into heaven. The bishop of Moray in 1306 preached that
to fight against the English merited no less than fighting in the Holy
Land against Saracens. There was probably a lot of such preaching.
(B1985, 71)

250–443. Gray has a rather different account of the battle:
   Robert Bruce had gathered all the force of Scotland which was on
   his side, and some fierce young fellows, easily roused against the
   English, and came before the town of Perth in two great columns,
   offering battle to the said earl [Aymer] and to the English ... The
   earl kept quiet till their departure, when, by the advice of the Scottish
   lords who were with him in the town, friends of Comyn and adherents
   of the English, (Mowbray, Abernethy, Brechin and Gordon), he
   marched out in two columns. The Scottish enemy had decamped,
   sending their camp-makers to prepare a camp at Methven. They
   formed up as best they could and all on horseback attacked this sortie,
   but the Scots were beaten. John de Haliburton caught the reins of
   the said Robert Bruce, and let him escape as soon as he saw who it
   was, for Bruce had no coat armour, only a white shirt.
The resemblance to Guisborough and Barbour, particularly in men-
tioning a debate among the men in Perth, is striking, but Gray's version
has clearly been influenced by later events, e.g. in naming Valence 'earl
of Pembroke'. The records show the only waged Scottish knights in
Valence's army as Alexander Abernethy, Henry Inchmartin, and Adam

And a thing will I to you say,
That he that deis for his cuntre
Sall herbryit intill hevyn be.'

345 Quhen this wes said thai saw cumand 342
Thar fayis ridand ner at the hand
Arayit rycht avisely
Willfull to do chevalry.

[*The battle of Methven*]

On athir syd thus war thai yhar
350 And till assemble all redy war. 347
Thai straucht thar speris on athir syd
And swa ruydly gan samyn ryd
That speris al to-fruschyt war
And feyle men dede and woundyt sar,

355 The blud out at thar byrnys brest, 352
For the best and the worthiest
That wilfull war to wyn honour
Plungyt in the stalwart stour
And routis ruyd about thaim dang.

360 Man mycht haiff seyn into that thrang 357
Knychtis that wycht and hardy war
Under hors feyt defoulyt thar
Sum woundyt and sum all ded,
The gres woux off the blud all rede.

365 And thai that held on hors in hy 362
Swappyt out swerdis sturdyly
And sa fell strakys gave and tuk
That all the renk about thaim quouk.
The Bruysis folk full hardely

370 Schawyt thar gret chevalry 367
And he him selff atour the lave
Sa hard and sa hevy dyntis gave
That quhar he come thai maid him way.
His folk thaim put in hard assay

375 To stynt thar fais mekill mycht 372
That then so fayr had off the fycht
That thai wan feild ay mar and mar.

Gordon (no named esquires were Scots). Since Sir Philip Mowbray whose horse was killed in the battle, does not show up there, the record is clearly not a complete account of the army. But Haliburton (from Berwickshire) may well have been one of Adam Gordon's eight un-named esquires. (*S*, 130–31; *ST*, 31–32)

The king's lesser folk were nearly defeated, and when the king saw his men begin to lose ground, in utter fury he called his battle cry and rushed into the fray so boldly that the whole press [of men] shook. (384) He cut down all that he overtook, striking them as long as he could. To his men he shouted out loud, 'On them, on them, they are failing fast. This fight can't last much longer.' (389) And with those words he attacked so determinedly and so boldly that anyone seeing him in that fight would esteem him as a doughty knight. But though he was brave and hardy, and others of his company too, boldness did them no good there, for their lesser folk began to retreat, and fled, scattering here and there. (398) But the good [men], all hot with anger, stayed and kept up the struggle to win endless honour for themselves. When Sir Aymer saw the lesser folk fleeing together, and that so few stayed to fight, he rallied a good many knights to him and rushed into the fray with his chivalry so boldly that he drove all his enemies back. (408) Sir Thomas Randolph was taken there, still a young batcheler then, and Sir Alexander Fraser, Sir David Barclay, Inchmartin, Hugh de le Hay, Somerville, and many others; the king himself, too, was placed in really great danger by Sir Philip Mowbray who rode to him boldly, seized his reins and then called out, 'Help! help! I have the new-made king.' (420) With that Christopher Seton came directly, in a bee-line,

---

410-13. When appointed in April 1306, Valence was given authority to receive Scots into Edward's peace without referring each case to the king, and he exercised this after Methven. About 27 June Edward I ordered that all prisoners be executed, from which, on 28 June he exempted Bruce, Atholl and Simon Fraser. Valence must already have released some prisoners on bail (certainly Randolph and presumably Barclay and Fraser), and it cannot be shown that he executed any. He did send the countess of Buchan and Mary Bruce, eleven esquires, Sir David Inchmartin, Sir John Cambo and fourteen others of lesser standing (including John Somerville (of Carnwath) and a Cuthbert de Carrick), by ship to Berwick. See 468-70.

412. Hugh de la Hay is not named in English sources as a prisoner and may have died of wounds for he is not found again. He really cannot have been (as is usually said) brother of Sir Gilbert Hay of Errol, but may have been his uncle. (*Coupar Angus Chrs.* i, 137-8)

416-28. The story that Robert was almost captured occurs in a very different form in Gray, where John de Haliburton seized and then released him; see note to 250-443. Both could be true.

The kingis small folk ner vencusyt ar,
And quhen the king his folk has sene
380 Begouth to faile, for propyr tene 377
His assenyhe gan he cry
And in the stour sa hardyly
He ruschyt that all the semble schuk.
He all till-hewyt that he ourtuk
385 And dang on thaim quhill he mycht drey. 382
And till his folk he criyt hey,
'On thaim, on thaim, thai feble fast,
This bargane never may langer last.'
And with that word sa wilfully
390 He dang on and sa hardely 387
That quha had sene him in that fycht
Suld hald him for a douchty knycht.
But thocht he wes stout and hardy
And othir als off his cumpany,
395 Thar mycht na worschip thar availye 392
For thar small folk begouth to failye
And fled all skalyt her and thar.
Bot the gude at enchaufyt war
Off ire abade and held the stour
400 To conquyr thaim endles honour. 397
And quhen Schyr Amer has sene
The small folk fle all bedene
And sa few abid to fycht
He releyt to him mony a knycht
405 And in the stour sa hardyly 402
He ruschyt with hys chevalry
That he ruschyt his fayis ilkane.
Schyr Thomas Randell thar wes tane
That then wes a young bacheler
410 And Schyr Alexander Fraseyr 407
And Schyr David the Breklay
Inchmertyne and Hew de le Hay
And Somervell and other ma.
And the king him selff alsua
415 Wes set intill full hard assay 412
Throu Schyr Philip the Mowbray
That raid till him full hardyly
And hynt hys rengye and syne gan cry,
'Help! Help! I have the new-maid king.'
420 With that come gyrdand in a lyng 417

when he saw the king seized by his enemy like that; he struck
Philip such a blow, that he caused him to reel dizzily, although
he was [a man] of great strength; [Mowbray] would have
fallen straight to the ground had he not been propped up by
his steed. (428) Then the bridle slipped from his hand, and
the king called his battle cry, rallying the men who were near
him, [but] they were so few that they could not endure more
of the press of battle. (433) [So] they galloped then out of
the press and the king, who was angry because he saw his
men fleeing from him, said then, 'Lords, since luck runs
against us here, it would be wise to eschew the danger from
them until God sends us grace later; it could still happen that,
if they pursue us, we will repay them in kind.' (442) They all
agreed with this suggestion, and galloped further away from
the [enemy]. Their foes were weary too, so that none of them
gave chase, but they took their way back to the town with the
prisoners they had taken, mighty pleased and happy with their
booty. (449) All of them passed that night in the town; not
one among them all was of such great renown or so bold as
to lodge outside the wall, they so feared the return of Sir
Robert, the brave king. (455) To the king of England they
soon wrote about everything they had done, and he was
pleased at their news; from spite he ordered that all the
prisoners be hanged and drawn, despite their number. (460)
But Sir Aymer did not do so; to some he gave both life and
land to leave Bruce's fealty, serve the king of England,

---

421. Christopher Seton, who had married the king's sister; a northern
English knight. He is mentioned in a suspect passage, above 243, but
even if it is authentic, his name is probably Barbour's mistake. It is
difficult to see how Christopher could have reached Loch Doon castle
(which he defended in August) after Methven; he had probably been
there since March. Moreover, Sir Alexander Seton of East Lothian (no
relation) was taken as a prisoner to York, probably from Methven. (He
must have been released later.) Barbour has guessed wrongly from
'Seton' in his source. (*CDS5, 471f*)

440–54. This account is very improbable; Bruce's force was clearly
defeated and the English would be anxious to take knightly prisoners
for ransom and for reward by Edward I. Robert was surely pursued.
An English contingent which included Sir Giles d'Argentan, must have
pursued the fugitives up the Tay valley, for it fought in a second 'battle
of Loch Tay'. The loss of horses at this battle is recorded, but the battle
does not appear in any of the narrative accounts, Scottish (Fordun) or
English (Gray, Guisborough).

Crystall off Seytoun quhen he swa
Saw the king sesyt with his fa,
And to Philip sic rout he raucht
That thocht he wes of mekill maucht

425 He gert him galay disyly,   422
And haid till erd gane fullyly
Ne war he hynt him by his sted,
Then off his hand the brydill yhed.
And the king his enssenye gan cry,

430 Releyt his men that war him by   427
That war sa few that thai na mycht
Endur the fors mar off the fycht.
Thai prikyt then out off the pres,
And the king that angry wes

435 For he his men saw fle him fra   432
Said then, 'Lordingis, sen it is swa
That ure rynnys agane us her,
Gud is we pas of thar daunger
Till God us send eft-sonys grace.

440 And yeyt may fall giff thai will chace   437
Quyt thaim corn-but sumdele we sall.'
To this word thai assentyt all
And fra thaim walopyt ovyr-mar.
Thar fayis alsua wery war

445 That off thaim all thar chassyt nane,   442
Bot with presoneris that thai had tane
Rycht to the toune thai held thar way,
Rycht glaid and joyfull off thar pray.
That nycht thai lay all in the toun,

450 Thar wes nane off sa gret renoun   447
Na yeit sa hardy off thaim all
That durst herbery with-out the wall,
Sa dred thai sar the gayne-cummyng
Off Schyr Robert the douchty king.

455 And to the king off Ingland sone   452
Thai wrate haly as thai haid done,
And he wes blyth off that tithing
And for dispyte bad draw and hing
All the presonneris thocht thai war ma.

460 Bot Schyr Amery did nocht sua   457
To sum bath land and lyff gaiff he
To leve the Bruysis fewté
And serve the king off Ingland

hold their lands of him and make war on Bruce as their enemy.
(466) Thomas Randolph was one of those who became their
subject [in return] for his life. Of the others who were taken,
they ransomed some, killed some, hanged some and drew
some.

(471) In this way the Bruce was driven back, greatly mourning
those of his men who were taken or slain. He was so completely
at a loss, too, that he trusted nobody for sure, except those
of his company; they were so few that they could have been
about five hundred in the whole following. (479) His brother,
Sir Edward, who was so hardy, was always with him, and
with him was a bold baron, Sir William Burradon; the earl
of Atholl was also there. (484) But ever since they had been
defeated the earl of Lennox was away, and was put in really
great danger before he met with the king again, although, as
a powerful man, he always conducted himself manfully. The
king also had in his company James Douglas, who was bold,
wise and prudent, (493) Sir Gilbert de le Hay also, Sir Neil
Campbell and others as well whose names I can't give; [they]
spent many days as outlaws, suffering hardship in the Mounth,
eating flesh and drinking water.

466–67. See on 410–413. On 24 July Edward ordered that Randolph be
    imprisoned at Inverkip castle in the keeping of Sir Adam Gordon, and
    on no account be given bail. The date of his release is unknown, but
    on 14 September, 1307 he lost his horse when with a strong English
    force pursuing Douglas in Paisley Forest. (*CDS2, 1807; CDS5, 565*)

468–70. Sixteen prisoners sent to Berwick were tried and executed after
    trial at Newcastle in August; eleven disappeared to an unknown fate at
    York. (*CDS5, 472e, 492; CDS2, 1811*)

482. Sir William Burradon. Note the curious way in which this name is
    linked to Edward Bruce. This family held lands mainly in Northum-
    berland but also in Roxburghshire, and a Walter was sheriff of Lanark
    and took charge of Selkirk for Edward I in March 1306. As 'of North-
    umberland' he went surety for William Oliphant in May 1308. No
    William is found in Scottish or English record, and he is probably a
    mistaken expansion of the initial W for 'Walter'; I suggest he was not
    a supporter of Bruce, but a prisoner taken by Edward Bruce at Methven.
    (*ASR, 132; CDS3, 45*)

493. Sir Gilbert Hay of Errol had received favours from Edward I but
    was an early supporter of Robert and on 19 June, 1306 Edward ordered
    that his lands be ravaged. By March 1309 he had been appointed King
    Robert's constable. (*CDS2, 1787*)

494. Sir Neil Campbell. The Campbells were kin of the earls of Carrick.
    He had joined Robert before Methven, and married his sister Mary
    either before 1306 or more probably after her release about 1312. (*SP1,
    322–25*)

And off him for to hald the land
465 And werray the Brus as thar fa. 462
Thomas Randell wes ane off tha
That for his lyff become thar man.
Off other that war takyn than
Sum thai ransounyt, sum thai slew
470 And sum thai hangyt and sum thai drew. 467

[*The king goes to the Mounth as a refugee*]

In this maner rebutyt was
The Bruys that mekill murnyn mais
For his men that war slayne and tane,
And he wes als sa will off wane
475 That he trowit in nane sekyrly 472
Outane thaim off his cumpany,
That war sa few that thai mycht be
Fyve hunder ner off all mengye.
His broder alwayis wes him by
480 Schyr Edward that wes sa hardy, 477
And with him wes a bauld baroun
Schyr Wilyam the Boroundoun.
The erle off Athole als wes thar,
Bot ay syn thai discomfyt war
485 The erle off the Levenax wes away 482
And wes put to full hard assay
Or he met with the king agayn,
Bot always as a man off mayn
He mayntemyt him full manlyly.
490 The king had in his cumpany 487
James alsua of Douglas
That wycht wys and averty was,
Schyr Gilbert de le Hay alsua
Schir Nele Cambell and other ma
495 That I thar namys can nocht say, 492
As utelawys went mony day
Dreand in the Month thar pyne,
Eyte flesch and drank water syne.

496–98. Hardship in the Mounth. This is rather vague but presumably
refers to mountains between Tay and Dee. The king would scarcely
have done this had Aberdeen been available to him.

He dared not go to the open [country] since all the commons rejected him; to [save] their lives they felt compelled to pass to the English peace again. (503) It's often like that – no-one can trust the commons except the person who can be their protector. That's how they treated him then, for he could not protect them from their enemies; they turned to the other side. But serfdom, which they had to suffer, made them yearn that things would go well with him.

(511) He lived like that in the hills till the greater part of his following was tattered and torn; they had no shoes, except those they made of hide. So they went to Aberdeen, where Neil Bruce and the queen with other fair and comely ladies [came], each for love of their husbands, a true love and loyalty, wanting to share their sufferings. (521) They chose rather to take suffering and pain with them, than to be away from them. For love is of such great strength that it makes light of all suffering, and often gives such strength and such power to easy-going men that they can endure great tribulations and not give up, come what may, provided that they can sustain their lives thereby. (531) You read about the taking of Thebes, [that] when the men of King Adrastus who attacked the city were killed, the women of his country, came to fetch him home again when they heard all his folk were slain, where King Capaneus, with the help of Menesteus,

---

515. They went to Aberdeen. This episode is certainly misplaced from before the battle of Methven, April–May 1306; Aberdeen was taken by Robert before Methven, but would not be a safe refuge thereafter. Valence was there by 3 August 1306.

516. Neil Bruce was perhaps the oldest of Robert's brothers. The statement that he was here with the queen will relate to April–May and not to July.

514. Shoes of hides, that is untanned and with a short wearing-life.

530. Liffys. *B1909* reads 'luffys.' This has no MS support but it is perhaps better sense.

531–50. Thebes. The account of the Thebes story given here and in 6.181–270 is derived from the twelfth century *Roman de Thèbes*, possibly through a later prose version in French. The names are misspelt (for Capaneus and Adrastus, but this may have happened in transmission of *The Bruce*) and Menesteus who appears earlier in the *Roman*, should be Theseus at 538.

He durst nocht to the planys ga
500 For all the commounys went him fra 497
That for thar liffis war full fayn
To pas to the Inglis pes agayn.
Sa fayris ay commounly,
In commounys may nane affy
505 Bot he that may thar warand be. 502
Sa fur thai then with him, for he
Thaim fra thar fais mycht nocht warand
Thai turnyt to the tother hand,
Bot threldome that men gert thaim fele
510 Gert thaim ay yarne that he fur wele. 507

[*The king goes to Aberdeen; the queen joins him; a Theban
analogy; they ride to the hills and live rough*]

Thus in the hyllis levyt he
Till the mast part off his menye
Wes revyn and rent, na schoyn thai had
Bot as thai thaim off hydis mad.
515 Thar for thai went till Aberdeyne 512
Quhar Nele the Bruys come and the queyn
And other ladyis fayr and farand
Ilkane for luff off thar husband
That for leyle luff and leawté
520 Wald partenerys off thar paynys be. 517
Thai chesyt tyttar with thaim to ta
Angyr and payne na be thaim fra,
For luff is off sa mekill mycht
That it all paynys makis lycht,
525 And mony tyme mais tender wychtis 522
Off swilk strenthtis and swilk mychtis
That thai may mekill paynys endur
And forsakis nane aventur
That evyr may fall, with-thi that thai
530 Tharthrou succur thair liffys may. 527
Men redys, quhen Thebes wes tane
And Kyng Aristas men war slane
That assailyt the cité,
That the wemen off his cuntré
535 Come for to fech him hame agayne 532
Quhen thai hard all his folk wes slayne,
Quhar the King Campaneus
Throu the help off Menesteus

who happened to come riding by with a company of three
hundred, attacked at the king's request, but had still failed to
take the town. (543) Then the wives attacked the walls with
picks [so that] all the attackers entered and destroyed the
tower, slaying the people without mercy. Then when the duke
had gone on his way, and all the king's men were killed, the
wives took him to their country where there was no living
man but he. (551) Great comfort and all kinds of solace lies
in women. So it was here, for their arrival greatly heartened
the king [Robert] although each night he himself stayed awake,
resting during the daytime. (557) He stayed there for a good
while, cheering up his men wonderfully, until the English
heard news that he stayed there with his following, at ease
and in security. They gathered their army swiftly, believing
they would surprise him there. (564) But he, wise in his deeds,
knew that they had mustered and where, and knew that they
were so numerous that he could not fight against them. He
had his men array themselves quickly, ready to ride from the
town; the ladies rode right by his side. Then they rode [on]
their way to the hills, where they had a terrible shortage of
food. (573) But worthy James Douglas was always active and
busy finding food for the ladies, getting it in many [different]
ways. Sometimes he brought them venison, sometimes setting
traps with his hands to catch pike and salmon, trout, eels or
[even] minnows; sometimes they went hunting.

---

557. A good while. This suggests that Robert spent a week or two at
Aberdeen in April–May 1306.

That come percas ridand tharby
540 With thre hunder in cumpany 537
That throu the kingis prayer assailyt
That yeit to tak the toun had failyeit.
Then war the wiffys thyrland the wall
With pikkis, quhar the assailyeis all
545 Entryt and dystroyit the tour 542
And slew the pupill but recour.
Syn quhen the duk his way wes gayne
And all the kingis men war slayne
The wiffis had him till his cuntré
550 Quhar wes na man leiffand bot he. 547
In wemen mekill comfort lyis
And gret solace on mony wis,
Sa fell yt her, for thar cummyng
Rejosyt rycht gretumly the king.
555 The-quhether ilk nycht himselvyn wouk 552
And rest apon daiis touk.
A gud quhile thar he sojournyt then
And esyt wonder weill his men
Till that the Inglis-men herd say
560 That he thar with his menye lay 557
All at ese and sekyrly.
Assemblit thai thar ost in hy
And thar him trowit to suppris
Bot he that in his deid wes wys
565 Wyst thai assemblyt war and quhar, 562
And wyst that thei sa mony war
That he mycht nocht agayne thaim fycht.
His men in hy he gert be dycht
And buskyt of the toun to ryd,
570 The ladyis raid rycht by his syd. 567
Then to the hill thai raid thar way,
Quhar gret defaut off mete had thai.
Bot worthy James off Douglas
Ay travailland and besy was
575 For to purches the ladyis mete 572
And it on mony wis wald get,
For quhile he venesoun thaim brocht,
And with his handys quhile he wrocht
Gynnys to tak geddis and salmonys
580 Trowtis elys and als menounys, 577
And quhill thai went to the forray,

(582) That's how they forraged, each man struggling to pro-
cure and gather whatever they could eat. But of all those who
were there at all, there was not one among them who did
more for the ladies than James Douglas. (589) The king, too,
was often comforted by his wisdom and his activity. In this
way they managed [to live] till they came to the head of Tay.

And swa thar purchesyng maid thai.
Ilk man traveillyt for to get
And purches thaim that thai mycht ete.
585 Bot off all that ever thai war 582
Thar wes nocht ane amang thaim thar
That to the ladyis profyt was
Mar then James of Douglas,
And the king oft comfort wes
590 Throu his wyt and his besynes. 587
On this maner thaim governyt thai
Till thai come to the hed off Tay.

The lord of Lorn dwelt near there, who was the king's great enemy because of his uncle, John Comyn, and [who] meant to take vengeance in a cruel way. (6) When he knew the king was so near, he gathered his men in haste, having also in his company the barons of Argyll. They were a good thousand or more [in number] and came to surprise the king, who was well aware of their approach. (13) But he had all too few [men] with him, although he waited boldly for them, and very many at their first encounter were laid to earth without recovery. The king's men carried themselves very well, killing, felling and seriously wounding. (19) But the men on the other side fought so fiercely with axes (for they were each and all on foot), that they slew many of [Bruce's] horse, or gave great wounds to some. (24) James Douglas and also Sir Gilbert de le Hay were hurt at that time. The king saw his men frightened, shouted his battle-cry and rode among them with great force, pushing them all back, and causing many of them to fall. (31) But when he saw they were so numerous and saw them dealing such mighty blows, he feared losing his force, so called his men back to him and said, 'Lords, it would be folly for us to fight on, for they have killed many of our horses, and if we fight against them we shall lose [more] of our small following

---

1. The lord of Lorn dwelt near there. This is manifest exaggeration, for the Tay rises east of the watershed and Lorn is entirely to the west. But the whole episode is highly problematic. Barbour nowhere gives this lord a name. He is identified with John of Lorn 'because of his eym (uncle), John Comyn' in 3, the same phrase being used of John of Lorn in 6.505. Later 'eym' could be used of a near relative, but in the fourteenth century it seems always to be 'uncle'. But Wyntoun, who gives a full account of the Comyns, marries a daughter of 'John the red Comyn' who died between 1273 and 1281 to Alexander of Argyll. Thus Alexander of Argyll's wife was aunt, John of Lorn's cousin, to the John Comyn killed in 1306, grandson of 'the red John'; John of Lorn's uncle was the John Comyn who was Guardian in 1286 and who died about 1299. The mistake is understandable, but it is clearly Barbour's mistake, and shows that it was he who added this identification to his source.

7–9. His men and the barons of Argyll also. But Lorn's men were Argyllsmen.

BOOK 3

[The lord of Lorn attacks the king's men]

The lord off Lorne wonnyt thar-by
That wes capitale ennymy
To the king for his emys sak
Jhon Comyn, and thocht for to tak
5   Vengeance apon cruell maner.
Quhen he the king wyst wes sa ner
He assemblyt his men in hy,
And had intill his cumpany
The barounys off Argyle alsua.
10   Thai war a thousand weill or ma
And come for to suppris the king
That weill wes war of thar cummyng.
Bot all to few with him he had
The-quhethir he bauldly thaim abaid,
15   And weill ost at thar fryst metyng
War layd at erd but recoveryng.
The kingis folk full weill thaim bar
And slew and fellyt and woundyt sar,
Bot the folk off the tother party
20   Faucht with axys sa fellyly,
For thai on fute war everilkane,
That thai feile off thar hors has slayne,
And till sum gaiff thai woundis wid.
James off Douglas wes hurt that tyd
25   And als Schyr Gilbert de le Hay.
The king his men saw in affray
And his ensenye can he cry
And amang thaim rycht hardyly
He rad that he thaim ruschyt all
30   And fele off thaim thar gert he fall.
Bot quhen he saw thai war sa feill
And saw thaim swa gret dyntis deill
He dred to tyne his folk, forthi
His men till him he gan rely
35   And said, 'Lordyngis, foly it war
Tyll us for till assembill mar,
For thai fele off our hors has slayn,
And giff yhe fecht with thaim agayn
We sall tyne off our small mengye

and be in danger ourselves. (41) So I think it would be most
appropriate for us to withdraw, defending ourselves till we
get out of danger from them, because our strong-point is near
at hand.' (45) Then they withdrew altogether, but not in a
cowardly way, for they held together in a group and the king
always risked himself to defend behind his following. By his
valour he achieved so much that he rescued all those who
were fleeing, and so held up the pursuers that none [of them]
dared rush out from their formation, since he was always
there. (55) He defended his men so well that anyone seeing
him then proving his bold courage, turning his face so often,
would say he ought indeed to be king of a great kingdom.

(61) When the lord of Lorn saw his his men stand back from
[Bruce] in such fear that they dared not follow in pursuit, he
was very angry in his heart; and astonished that he could hold
them up like that, himself alone, without anyone else, he said,
'I'm thinking that Marjorie's son, just as Goll mac Morna
succeeded in taking all his following from Finn, in just the
same way has taken all his from us.' (71) He gave a middling
example like that, yet he could have likened him more appro-
priately to Gadifer of Laris, when the great Duke Betis
attacked the forrayers in Gadres, and when the king came to
their help Duke Betis took to flight, unwilling to stay and fight
any longer. (79) But worthy Gadifer

15–45, the battle. This battle is recorded by Fordun:
> The same year [1306], while this king was fleeing from his foes and
> lurking with his men in the borders of Atholl and Argyll, he was again
> defeated and put to flight on 3 id. August [14 August], at a place
> called Dalry; but there also he did not lose many of his men, though
> they were all filled with fear and were dispersed and scattered through-
> out various places. (*F1*, 342; *F2*, 334)

Dalry near Tyndrum is close to the source of the Dochart, the source
of Loch Tay. Moreover later Robert I began the establishment of a
small priory near Tyndrum at Glendochart, clearly as thanks for a very
significant deliverance. But Fordun does not say who defeated the king,
and it is possible that Barbour using the same source, conjured Lorn
and Argyllsmen out of 'the borders of Atholl and Argyll'. The true
enemy would then have been a 'lord who dwelt near there'.

72–87. This comes from the *Roman d'Alixandre*. At 85 E has 'Coneus',
probably miscopying of Corineus. (*B1985*, 73; *B1909*, 397)

40   And our selff sall in perill be.
       Tharfor me thynk maist avenand
       To withdraw us us defendand
       Till we cum out off thar daunger,
       For our strenth at our hand is ner.'
45   Then thai withdrew thaim halely
       Bot that wes nocht full cowartly
       For samyn intill a sop held thai
       And the king him abandonyt ay
       To defend behind his mengye,
50   And throu his worschip sa wrouch he
       That he reskewyt all the flearis
       And styntyt swagat the chassaris
       That nane durst out off batall chas,
       For alwayis at thar hand he was.
55   Sa weile defendyt he his men
       That quha-sa-ever had seyne him then
       Prove sa worthely vasselage
       And turn sa oft-sythis the visage
       He suld say he aucht weill to be
60   A king off a gret reawté.

[Comparisons from Celtic and classical legends with the king's defence of his men]

       Quhen that the lord off Lorne saw
       His men stand off him ane sik aw
       That thai durst nocht folow the chase
       Rycht angry in his hart he was,
65   And for wondyr that he suld swa
       Stot thaim him ane but ma
       He said, 'Me think Marthokys sone
       Rycht as Golmakmorn was wone
       To haiff fra Fyn all his mengne,
70   Rycht swa all his fra us has he.'
       He set ensample thus mydlike,
       The-quhethir he mycht mar manerlik
       Lyknyt hym to Gaudifer de Larys
       Quhen that the mychty Duk Betys
75   Assailyeit in Gadyrris the forrayours,
       And quhen the king thaim maid rescours
       Duk Betys tuk on him the flycht
       That wald ne mar abid to fycht.
       Bot Gaudifer the worthi

threw himself in so worthily to rescue all those who fled and
to hold up the pursuers, that he drove to the ground Alexan-
der, Tholimar, good Corineus, Danclins and others as well.
(87) But finally he was slain there – the analogy ends on that
point. For the king very chivalrously defended all his company,
placing himself in great danger yet escaping sound and fit.

(93) There were two brothers in that land who were the
hardest men who lived in that whole country; they had sworn
that if they could see the Bruce where they could overcome
him, they would die or slay him then. (99) Their surname
was Mac na Dorsair, which is as much as saying here 'the
doorward's sons', *perfay*. They had a third in their gang, who
was right strong, wicked and fierce. (104) When they saw the
king of good renown riding thus behind his company, and
saw him come back so many times, they waited till he had
gone into a narrow place between the side of a loch and a
brae, [a place] so narrow, I promise you, that he could not
turn his mount. (112) Then with a will they went to him, and
one seized him by the bridle, but [Bruce] struck him such a
blow that his arm and shoulder dropped from him. With that
another took him by the leg and thrust his hand between the
stirrup and his foot; when the king felt his hand there,

99. The doorward's son. The family would be doorkeeper to a great
chief, perhaps the Argyll (Macdougall) family, and are unlikely to be
connected with the Durward family prominent in thirteenth-century
Scotland. The episode in 99–146 is really unrelated to the 'Lorn'
episodes and is probably another version of the 'three attackers' story
for which see note to 5. 495.

108–9. A narrow place. This may have been a little broader than Barbour's
poetic description, but even so it can scarcely have been the side of
Loch Dochart or Loch Iubhair, both to the east of Dalry and quite
gentle. In fact the nearest appropriate site is the northern shore of Loch
Awe, well to the west. It would seem that on 14 August the king had
been seeking to break through from the west to the east, perhaps to
reach Kildrummy. Note that there is no hint of the presence of the
women at the time of this battle.

80   Abandonyt him so worthyly
      For to reskew all the fleieris
      And for to stonay the chasseris
      That Alysander to erth he bar
      And alsua did he Tholimar
85   And gud Coneus alsua
      Danklyne alsua and othir ma,
      Bot at the last thar slayne he wes.
      In that failyeit the liklynes,
      For the king full chevalrusly
90   Defendyt all his cumpany
      And wes set in full gret danger
      And yeit eschapyt haile and fer.

[*The king kills the two Mac na Dorsair brothers and their
fellow*]

      Twa brethir war in that land
      That war the hardiest off hand
95   That war intill all that cuntré,
      And thai had sworn iff thai mycht se
      The Bruys quhar thai mycht him our-ta
      That thai suld dey or then hym sla.
      Thar surname wes Makyne Drosser,
100   That is al-so mekill to say her
      As the Durwarth sonnys perfay.
      Off thar covyne the thrid had thai
      That wes rycht stout ill and feloune.
      Quhen thai the king off gud renoune
105   Saw sua behind his mengne rid
      And saw him torne sa mony tid,
      Thai abaid till that he was
      Entryt in ane narow place
      Betwix a louch-sid and a bra
110   That wes sa strait Ik underta
      That he mycht nocht weill turn in his sted.
      Then with a will till him thai yede
      And ane him by the bridill hynt,
      Bot he raucht till him sic a dynt
115   That arme and schuldyr flaw him fra.
      With that ane other gan him ta
      Be the lege and his hand gan schute
      Betwix the sterap and his fute,
      And quhen the king feld thar his hand

he stood hard in his stirrups and swiftly struck the horse with spurs. (122) [The horse] lept forward suddenly so that the other [man] lost his footing, yet nevertheless his hand was still under the stirrup, in spite of himself. At this the third [man] very swiftly went right [up] to the brae-side and rose up behind him on his steed. (129) The king was then in very great danger, though he intended that like [a man] who was prudent in all his actions, he would do an outstanding feat. So [the man] who was behind him, against his will he lifted from behind him, in spite of what [the man] had sworn, [and] laid him flat before him. (137) Then with a sword he struck such a blow that he split his skull to the brains. He dropped down, all red and bloody, as that moment he fell down dead. (141) Then the king, very swiftly, struck vigorously at the other whom he was dragging after his stirrup, so that he killed him at the first blow. In this way he freed himself from all three savage foes.

(147) When [the men] of Lorn saw the king give himself such great help, and defend himself so manfully, none of them was so bold as to dare attack him further in fight, they were so afraid of his great strength. (153) There was a baron, Macnaughton, who paid great heed in his heart to the king's chivalry, and esteemed him greatly in his heart. He said to the lord of Lorn, 'Assuredly, you can now see the heaviest trespass-payment taken that you ever saw taken [in] your lifetime.

136–39. It is difficult to see how 'laid evyn him beforn' could then 'rouschit doun' with blood. Line 139 is repeated at 5.647.

146. This episode is often linked, without authority, to the story of the brooch of Lorn, snatched from Bruce's cloak as he escaped from John of Lorn. The story is not found in Barbour, and the brooch is of sixteenth century manufacture.

153. Macnaughton. 'Alexander mac Neachten' witnesses a charter of Christina Mac Ruairidh to Arthur son of Sir Arthur Campbell, along with Sir John Menteith and Sir Donald Campbell, about 1310–20; presumably the same man, he had changed sides. The family held lands in Cowal and on Lochawe-side in the later fourteenth century. (Original charter with Faculty of Procurators, Glasgow.)

120   In his sterapys stythly gan he stand
    And strak with spuris the stede in hy,
    And he lansyt furth delyverly
    Swa that the tother failyeit fete,
    And nocht-for-thi his hand wes yeit
125   Undyr the sterap magré his.
    The thrid with full gret hy with this
    Rycht till the bra-syd he yeid
    And stert behynd hym on his sted.
    The king wes then in full gret pres,
130   The-quhether he thocht as he that wes
    In all hys dedys avisé
    To do ane outrageous bounte,
    And syne hyme that behynd him was
    All magré his will him gan he ras
135   Fra behynd him, thocht he had sworn,
    He laid hym evyn him beforn,
    Syne with the swerd sic dynt hym gave
    That he the heid till the harnys clave.
    He rouschit doun off blud all rede
140   As he that stound feld off dede.
    And then the king in full gret hy
    Strak at the tothir vigorusly
    That he efter his sterap drew
    That at the fyrst strak he him slew.
145   On this wis him delyverit he
    Off all thai felloun fayis thre.

[Mac Nachtan praises the king]

    Quhen thai of Lorne has sene the king
    Set in hym selff sa gret helping
    And defendyt him sa manlely,
150   Wes nane amang thaim sa hardy
    That durst assailye him mar in fycht,
    Sa dred thai for his mekill mycht.
    Thar wes a baroune Maknauchtan
    That in his hart gret kep has tane
155   To the kingis chevalry
    And prisyt him in hert gretly,
    And to the lord off Lorne said he,
    'Sekyrly now may ye se
    Be tane the starkest pundelan
160   That evyr your lyfftyme ye saw tane,

(161) For yon knight, by his bold deed and by his superhuman qualities, in a short time has killed three men of great pride. [He has] discomfitted all our company so [much] that no man dare go after him, and he turns his horse so often that he seems to have no fear of us.' (169) Then the lord of Lorn said, 'You seem to be pleased, *perfay*, that he kills our men like that.' 'Sir,' he said, 'as God is my witness, saving your presence, it's not like that. But whosoever wins the prize in chivalry, be he friend or foe, men should speak faithfully of it. And assuredly, in all my life, I never heard tell, in song or verse, of a man who achieved great chivalry so vigorously.' (180) That's how they spoke of the king [as] he rode after his force and led them into safety where he had no fear of his foes. And [the men] of Lorn went back, bemoaning the injuries that they have taken.

(187) The king set his watches that night, and gave orders that they could eat; he bade them be comforted and make merry as best they could. 'For being discouraged,' as he said then, 'is the worst thing possible. (193) For through great discouragement men often fall into despair, and when a man is in despair, then he is utterly beaten. If the spirit is discouraged, the body is not worth a jot. Therefore,' he said, 'above all keep yourselves from despair,

---

174. 'He'; so 1571. E has 'yhe', but 'ye' = you scarcely makes sense.
    Perhaps the 'y' was a false start, whose deletion was omitted, for 'thai'.
187–266. This account of Bruce's heartening of his men may be compared
    with Fordun, writing of his struggle in general:

> Not only did he lift his hand against the king of England ... but he
> also launched out into a struggle with all and sundry of the kingdom
> of Scotland except a few well-wishers of his who, if one looked at the
> hosts of those pitted against them, were as one drop of water compared
> with the waves of the sea ... His mishaps, flights and dangers,
> hardships and weariness, hunger and thirst, watchings and fastings,
> nakedness and cold, snares and banishment, the seizing, imprisoning,
> slaughter and downfall of his near ones, and, even worse, dear ones
> (for all this he had to put up with when overcome and routed at the
> beginning of his war) no one now living, I think, remembers or is
> equal to narrate ... Indeed he is said to have said to his knights one
> day when worn out by such ... hardships and dangers,
>
> 'Were I not moved by Scotland's freedom still,
> For rule of the world I would not bear this ill.'
>
> (*F1*, 340–41; *F2*, 333)

For yone knycht throu his douchti deid
And thro his outrageous manheid
Has fellyt intill litill tyd
Thre men off mekill prid,
165   And stonayit all our mengye swa
That eftyr him dar na man ga,
And tournys sa mony tyme his stede
That semys off us he had na dred.'
Then gane the lord off Lorn say,
170   'It semys it likis ye perfay
That he slayis yongat our mengye.'
'Schyr,' said he, 'sa Our Lord me se,
To sauff your presence it is nocht swa,
Bot quhether-sa he be freynd or fa
175   That wynnys prys off chevalry
Men suld spek tharoff lelyly,
And sekyrly in all my tyme
Ik hard never in sang na ryme
Tell off a man that swa smertly
180   Eschevyt swa gret chevalry.'
Sic speking off the king thai maid,
And he eftyr his mengye raid
And intill saufté thaim led
Quhar he his fayis na-thing dred,
185   And thai off Lorne agayn ar gayn
Menand the scaith that thai haiff tayn.

[*The king comforts his men with the example of the recovery of
Rome from Hannibal*]

The king that nycht his wachis set
And gert ordayne that thai mycht et,
And bad conford to thaim tak
190   And at thar mychtis mery mak.
For disconford, as then said he,
Is the werst thing that may be,
For throu mekill disconforting
Men fallis oft into disparing,
195   And fra a man disparyt be
Then utraly vencusyt is he,
And fra the hart be discumfyt
The body is nocht worth a myt.
'Tharfor,' he said, 'atour all thing
200   Kepys you fra disparyng,

and remember that, though we now feel injuries, God may yet relieve us well. (203) You can read about many men who were far worse placed than we are now, and then Our Lord gave them such grace that they well achieved their aims. (207) For Rome was once so badly placed when Hannibal had defeated them, that he sent three bolls of rings with rich stones taken from the fingers of knights to Carthage, and then set out to Rome to destroy all the city there. (214) Those within, both great and unimportant would have fled when they saw him approaching, had not the king been Scipio, who would have killed them before they fled, and in that way turned them back. Then, to defend the city, he made servants and serfs free, creating each of them knight. And next he took from the temple the arms which their ancestors had borne, offered there in the name of victory. (225) When they were armed and equipped, who were stalwart and bold fellows and who saw that they were free too, they decided that they would rather accept death than let the town be taken. (230) With common consent, as one, they went out of the town to fight where Hannibal's great host were arrayed against them. But, through the power of God's grace, it rained so hard and heavy that no-one was so determined as to dare stay in that place, but hurried to ride [off] hastily, one side to their tents, the other side going into the town. (241) Thus the rain prevented [any] fighting, and did so twice again after that. When Hannibal saw this marvel,

---

207–48. This story about the Punic wars is taken from a thirteenth-century compilation, Martinus Polonus, *Chronicon de Gestis Romanorum.* (*B1985*, 73)

211. The boll was a measure of capacity, varying in time and place, but perhaps generally of twelve gallons.

216. Scipio Africanus of course was not a king, and even in Barbour's source, Martinus, he is called 'Tribune'.

And think thouch we now harmys fele
That God may yeit releve us weill.
Men redys off mony men that war
Fer harder stad then we yhet ar
205 And syne Our Lord sic grace thaim lent
That thai come weill till thar entent.
For Rome quhilum sa hard wes stad
Quhen Hanniball thaim vencusyt had
That off ryngis with rich stane
210 That war off knychtis fyngeris tane
He send thre bollis to Cartage,
And syne to Rome tuk his viage
Thar to distroye the cité all.
And thai within bath gret and small
215 Had fled quhen thai saw his cummyng
Had nocht bene Scipio the king,
That or thai fled wald thaim haiff slayn,
And swagat turnyt he thaim agayn.
Syne for to defend the cité
220 Bath servandis and threllis mad he fre,
And maid thaim knychtis everilkane,
And syne has off the templis tane
The armys that thar eldrys bar,
In name off victory offeryt thar.
225 And quhen thai armyt war and dycht
That stalwart karlis war and wycht
And saw that thai war fre alsua,
Thaim thocht that thai had lever ta
The dede na lat the toun be tane,
230 And with commoune assent as ane
Thai ischit off the toune to fycht
Quhar Hannyball his mekill mycht
Aganys thaim arayit was.
Bot throu mycht off Goddis grace
235 It ranyt sa hard and hevyly
That thar wes nane sa hardy
That durst into that place abid,
Bot sped thaim intill hy to rid,
The ta part to thar pailyounys,
240 The tother part went in the toune is.
The rayne thus lettyt the fechtyn,
Sa did it twys tharefter syne.
Quhen Hanibal saw this ferly

he left the town with all his great chivalry, journeying on, and was put to such trials by the power of that city that he lost his life and his land. (249) From these few, who so worthily overcame such a mighty king, you can well see by example that no-one should be despairing, nor let his spirit be wholly vanquished, no matter what ill-fortune may befall, for we do not know in what short time God will sometimes send his grace. (257) If they had fled and gone their [various] ways, their enemies would have taken the town smartly. So men who make war should always set their sights on resisting the enemy's strength, sometimes head on, sometimes by guile, always intending to succeed, and if they had no other choice but to die or else to live a coward's life, they should prefer to die chivalrously.'

(267) The king comforted them in that way, and to encourage them he cited ancient stories of men who were placed in various difficult circumstances, whom fortune opposed strongly, but who in the end won through. So he said that those who would maintain their spirits undefeated should always persist in intending to bring their enterprises to a successful conclusion, (277) as once the worthy Caesar did, always struggling so actively with all his strength to make efforts to conclude what he had resolved upon. He thought he had not done his duty as long as there was something left for him to do. So he achieved great things, as you can see in his history.

281–82. From Lucan, *De Bello Civili*, ii, 657, *Nil actum credens si quid superesset agendum.*

With all his gret chevalry
245 He left the toune and held his way,
And syne wes put to sik assay
Throu the power off that cite
That his lyff and his land tynt he.
Be thir quheyne that sa worthily
250 Wane sik a king and sa mychty,
Ye may weill be ensampill se
That na man suld disparyt be,
Na lat his hart be vencusyt all
For na myscheiff that ever may fall,
255 For nane wate in how litill space
That God umquhile will send grace.
Had thai fled and thar wayis gane
Thar fayis swith the toune had tane.
Tharfor men that werrayand war
260 Suld set thar etlyng ever-mar
To stand agayne thar fayis mycht
Umquhile with strenth and quhile with slycht,
And ay thynk to cum to purpos,
And giff that thaim war set in chos
265 To dey or to leyff cowartly,
Thai suld erar dey chevalrusly.'

[*The king cites the example of Caesar*]

Thusgat thaim comfort the king
And to comfort thaim gan inbryng
Auld storys off men that wer
270 Set intyll hard assayis ser
And that fortoun contraryit fast,
And come to purpos at the last.
Tharfor he said that thai that wald
Thar hartis undiscumfyt hald
275 Suld ay thynk ententily to bryng
All thar enpres to gud ending,
As quhile did Cesar the worthy
That traveillyt ay so besyly
With all his mycht folowing to mak
280 To end the purpos that he wald tak,
That hym thocht he had doyne rycht nocht
Ay quhill to do him levyt ocht.
Forthi gret thingis eschevyt he
As men may in his story se.

(285) You can see from his persistent determination, if it is also accompanied by discretion, that [anyone] who forms a firm intention and then follows it attentively, without weakening nor [yielding to] temptation, provided that it is suitable, unless he is very unlucky he will achieve it in part. (293) And if he lives long enough, it may well be that he will achieve it all. Therefore no-one should despair of achieving some really great end, for if it happens that he fails in that, the fault could be in his exertions.

(299) He preached to them in this way, and pretended to be more cheerful than he had reason to be by far, for his cause went from bad to worse. They were always in this dreadful hardship, till the ladies began to weaken, unable to suffer their troubles any more; others who were there were the same. (307) Earl John of Atholl was one of these, who, when he saw the king defeated twice, so many folk rising against him, and life [passed] in such hardship and uncertainty, his spirits began to fail altogether. (313) He said to the king one day, 'If I dare say [this] to you, we live in such great fear, often have such want of food, and are always in such hardship with cold, hunger and wakefulness, that I am so tired myself that my life is not worth a straw. (321) I can no longer endure these afflictions, for even if I die for it, I must stop wherever it be. So leave me, for the love [of God].'

307–8. John earl of Atholl. He had fought at Dunbar, was imprisoned by Edward I, released, and drifted back to serve the patriots as sheriff of Aberdeen by 1300. He resubmitted to Edward in late 1303, and by September 1304 had been appointed 'Warden and justiciar of Scotland from Forth to Orkney'. In May 1305 he was appointed Guardian between Forth and Spey, Ross being given beyond Spey; but he was in the south, for early in March 1306 the English at Berwick reported that

'the earl of Buchan [a Comyn] and the earl of Atholl are agreed and sworn together to live in acccord and are preparing to ride when they can with Sir Alexander Abernethy and Sir David [Brechin?] ... [against Bruce].'

Yet he was already, or soon, in deep conspiracy with Bruce, for he snatched the countess of Buchan from her husband (along with his horses to inhibit pursuit), and took her to Scone where they both played a leading part in the royal inauguration. English sources comment fiercely on this, but Barbour first introduces him as one of those who were with Robert after Methven (2.483). The exhaustion ascribed to him by Barbour is the latter's device to explain how he separated from the king, and is unfair to the earl. (*CDS2, 1592, 1669; ASR, 34; SP1, 426–27*)

285   Men may se be his ythen will,
       And it suld als accord to skill
       That quha tais purpos sekyrly
       And folowis it syne ententily
       Forout fayntice or yheit faynding,
290   With-thi it be conabill thing,
       Bot he the mar be unhappy
       He sall eschev it in party,
       And haiff he lyff-dayis weill may fall
       That he sall eschev it all.
295   For-thi suld nane haff disparing
       For till eschev a full gret thing,
       For giff it fall he tharoff failye
       The fawt may be in his travailye.

[Atholl asks to be left; the king sends him, Neil Bruce and the ladies to Kildrummy]

       He prechyt thaim on this maner
300   And fenyeit to mak better cher
       Then he had mater to be fer,
       For his caus yeid fra ill to wer,
       Thai war ay in sa hard travaill,
       Till the ladyis began to fayle
305   That mycht the travaill drey na mar,
       Sa did other als that thar war.
       The Erle Jhone wes ane off tha
       Off Athole that quhen he saw sua
       The king be discumfyt twys,
310   And sa feile folk agayne him rys,
       And lyff in sic travaill and dout,
       His hart begane to faile all-out
       And to the king apon a day
       He said, 'Gyff I durst you say,
315   We lyff into sa mekill dreid,
       And haffis oftsys off met sic ned,
       And is ay in sic travailling
       With cauld and hunger and waking,
       That I am sad off my selvyn sua
320   That I count nocht my liff a stra.
       Thir angrys may I ne mar drey,
       For thoucht me tharfor worthit dey
       I mon sojourne, quharever it be.
       Levys me tharfor par cheryte.'

The king saw that he was so weak and that he was utterly
worn-out too. (327) He said, 'Sir earl, we shall quickly consider
and decide what is for the best. Wherever you may be, may
Our Lord send you grace to protect you from your enemies!'
With that, he called to himself those who were closest to him.
Then among them they thought it best, and ordered as most
appropriate, that the queen, and also the earl, with the ladies,
should go speedily to Kildrummy with Neil Bruce. (338) For
they thought that they could stay there in security, as long as
they were well victualled, for the castle was so strong that it
would be difficult to take by force as long as there were men
and food inside. They did quickly what [the advisors] had
ordained; the queen and her whole company mounted on
their horses and set out. (346) If you had been there you
would have seen the ladies weeping at leave-taking, and mak-
ing their faces wet with tears, [while] knights sighed, wept
and mourned for the sake of their loves; they kissed their
loved ones at parting. The king decided on one thing: that
from then on he would travel on foot, and take good and ill
on foot, having no mounted men with him. (356) So he gave
all of his horses to the ladies who had need [of them]. The
queen rode forth on her way and came safely to the castle,
where her party was well received, and made comfortable with
meat and drink. (362) But no [amount of] comfort could
prevent her from thinking about the king, who was so sorely
pressed that he had only two hundred with him,

335-37. The earl, the queen, Neil Bruce. Although generally accepted,
this narrative is quite impossible. First we may contrast Fordun, who
has no role for Atholl:

> [After Dalry on 14 August] the queen fled to St Duthac [of Tain] in
> Ross, from where she was taken by William earl of Ross and brought
> to the king of England ... Neil Bruce, one of the king's brothers fled
> with many ladies and damsels to Kildrummy castle and was there
> welcomed with his companions. But the same year the castle was
> taken by the English ... (*F1*, 342; *F2*, 334-35)

The queen was not taken with other women at Methven, and even
Barbour believed she was not there; but he was wrong in believing that
she and Neil joined the king at Aberdeen after Methven (2.516); I
conclude that she and Neil had been left in Kildrummy before Methven,
though Fordun supports Barbour in sending Neil (but not the queen)
from Dalry to Kildrummy. There would be no point whatever in sending
her to Kildrummy after 14 August. She and Neil were still there and
Dalry was perhaps Robert's attempt to break through to join them.

325   The king saw that he sa wes failyt
       And that he ik wes for-travaillyt.
       He said, 'Schyr erle, we sall sone se
       And ordayne how it best may be.
       Quharever ye be, Our Lord you send
330   Grace fra your fais you to defend.'
       With that in hy to him callyt he
       Thaim that till him war mast prevé.
       Then amang thaim thai thocht it best
       And ordanyt for the liklyest
335   That the queyne and the erle alsua
       And the ladyis in hy suld ga
       With Nele the Bruce till Kildromy,
       For thaim thocht thai mycht sekyrly
       Dwell thar quhill thai war vittaillit weile,
340   For swa stalwart wes the castell
       That it with strenth war hard to get
       Quhill that tharin war men and mete.
       As thai ordanyt thai did in hy,
       The queyne and all hyr cumpany
345   Lap on thar hors and furth thai far.
       Men mycht haiff sene quha had bene thar
       At leve-takyng the ladyis gret
       And mak thar face with teris wet,
       And knychtis for thar luffis sak
350   Bath sich and wep and murnyng mak,
       Thai kyssyt thar luffis at thar partyng.
       The king umbethocht him off a thing,
       That he fra thine on fute wald ga
       And tak on fute bath weill and wa,
355   And wald na hors-men with him haiff,
       Tharfor his hors all haile he gaiff
       To the ladyis that myster had.
       The queyn furth on hyr wayis rade
       And sawffly come to the castell
360   Quhar hyr folk war ressavyt weill
       And esyt weill with meyt and drynk,
       Bot mycht nane eys let hyr to think
       On the king that wes sa sar stad
       That bot twa hunder with him had,

When it failed he sent Atholl, to whom he gave all his horses for speed
of movement (352–57), to take the queen from Kildrummy to the 'safety'
of St Duthac's sanctuary.

although he always consoled them well. May God, who is omnipotent, help him!

(367) The queen stayed thus in Kildrummy, and the king and his company, no more than two hundred in number after they had sent their horses away, wandered among the high mountains, where he and his often suffered privations. For it was nearly winter and there were so many enemies around him that all the country made war on [the king's men]. (376) Such dreadful misfortunes tested them then, like hunger, cold and cutting rain, that no-one alive can tell it all. The king saw how his folk were placed, and what afflictions they suffered; [he] saw winter was nearly upon them and that in no way could he risk lying in the cold, or waking for the long nights, in the hills. (385) He thought he would go to Kintyre, make as long a stay there [as necessary] until winter weather had passed, and then he meant to arrive in the mainland, without more delay, and pursue his fate to the end. (391) Because Kintyre lies in the sea, he sent Sir Neil Campbell ahead to get food and ships for him. He fixed a certain time when he would meet him at the sea. Sir Neil Campbell with his company went on his way, without more hindrance, leaving his brother with the king. In twelve days he travelled [far] enough to get plenty of ships, and victuals in great abundance; he made noble provision thus, for his kinsmen lived near there

---

372–73. The sufferings in the mountains may have been real enough, but the time was mid to late August, not nearly winter.

386–87. Sojournyng. This is an intention which was not carried out (677).

391. Kintyre lies in the sea. It was commonly called the isle of Kintyre, for, though a peninsula, its southern reaches were most easily approached by sea.

392. Sir Neil Campbell, see note to 2.494. His brother (398) would be Donald. (*SP1*, 320)

365   The-quhethir thaim weill comfortyt he ay.
           God help him that all mychtis may.

[*The king plans to go to Kintyre; Neil Campbell sent to find ships; the king and his men cross Loch Lomond; he reads a romance to them*]

           The queyne dwelt thus in Kyldromy,
           And the king and his cumpany
           That war twa hunder and na ma
370   Fra thai had send thar hors thaim fra
           Wandryt emang the hey montanys,
           Quhar he and his oft tholyt paynys,
           For it wes to the wynter ner,
           And sa feile fayis about him wer
375   That all the countre thaim werrayit.
           Sa hard anoy thaim then assayit
           Off hunger cauld with schowris snell
           That nane that levys can weill it tell.
           The king saw how his folk wes stad
380   And quhat anoyis that thai had,
           And saw wynter wes cummand ner,
           And that he mycht on na maner
           Dre in the hillys the cauld lying
           Na the long nychtis waking.
385   He thocht he to Kyntyr wald ga
           And swa lang sojournyng thar ma
           Till wynter wedder war away,
           And then he thocht but mar delay
           Into the manland till aryve
390   And till the end his werdis dryv.
           And for Kyntyr lyis in the se
           Schyr Nele Cambel befor send he
           For to get him navyn and meite,
           And certane tyme till him he sete
395   Quhen he suld meite him at the se.
           Schir Nele Cambell with his mengye
           Went his way but mar letting
           And left his brother with the king,
           And in twelf dayis sua traveillit he
400   That he gat schippyne gud plenté
           And vittalis in gret aboundance.
           Sa maid he nobill chevisance
           For his sibmen wonnyt tharby

and helped him with a will. (405) After he had gone, the king took the way to Loch Lomond, coming near to it on the third day. But they found no boat thereabouts to carry them over the water. Then they were very cast-down indeed, for it was a long way to go round [the loch]. They were also in fear that they would meet their enemies, who were widespread. (414) For that reason they searched assiduously and quickly along their side of the loch, until finally James Douglas found a little submerged boat and drew it to the land hot-foot. But it was so tiny that it would only carry three people over the water. (421) They sent word of it to the king, who was very pleased at that discovery. He went first into the boat, Douglas with him, and the third was a man who rowed them over speedily, setting them on dry land; he rowed to and fro, always fetching [men] two by two, so often that in a night and day they [all] came over the loch. (431) For some of them could swim very well, bearing a pack on their backs. So, with swimming and with rowing, they got themselves over with all their kit. (435) Meanwhile the king read cheerfully to those who were with him the romance of worthy Fierabras, who was honourably beaten by the right doughty Oliver; and how the duke-peers were besieged in Aigremore, where King Lavan lay before them with more thousands [of men] than I can say. (444) There were only eleven inside and a woman, and they were so placed that they had no food inside

---

406. To Loch Lomond. The king cannot have approached the loch from the north, since he would not then have to cross it, but could choose either shore. It is generally thought that he approached from the east to cross westwards towards Loch Long; but this would mean he had been a refugee around Loch Katrine and the Trossachs, not far from the Lennox. I suggest that he had been at the head of Loch Awe and travelled south to the head of Loch Fyne, where he separated from Neil Campbell, then by Glenkinglass to Arrochar and Tarbet or further south, where he crossed Loch Lomond eastwards to find the earl of Lennox; see note to 472.

435–62. The romance of Fierabras, part of the matter of Charlemagne, compiled in the late twelfth century. Bruce could scarcely have the manuscript with him, but could have remembered the story of the crossing of Flagot. The forms Ferumbrace and Lavyne (for Balant) suggest that Barbour was using an English translation of the romance. (B1985, 74)

That helpyt him full wilfully.
405 The king efter that he wes gane
To Louch Lomond the way has tane
And come on the thrid day,
Bot tharabout na bait fand thai
That mycht thaim our the water ber.
410 Than war thai wa on gret maner
For it wes fer about to ga,
And thai war into dout alsua
To meyt thar fayis that spred war wyd.
Tharfor endlang the louchhis syd
415 Sa besyly thai socht and fast
Tyll James of Douglas at the last
Fand a litill sonkyn bate
And to the land it drew fut-hate,
Bot it sa litill wes that it
420 Mycht our the watter but a thresum flyt.
Thai send tharoff word to the king
That wes joyfull off that fynding
And fyrst into the bate is gane,
With him Douglas, the thrid wes ane
425 That rowyt thaim our deliverly
And set thaim on the land all dry,
And rowyt sa oftsys to and fra
Fechand ay our twa and twa
That in a nycht and in a day
430 Cummyn out-our the louch ar thai,
For sum off thaim couth swome full weill
And on his bak ber a fardele.
Swa with swymmyng and with rowyng
Thai brocht thaim our and all thar thing.
435 The king the quhilis meryly
Red to thaim that war him by
Romanys off worthi Ferambrace
That worthily our-cummyn was
Throu the rycht douchty Olyver,
440 And how the duk-peris wer
Assegyt intill Egrymor
Quhar King Lavyne lay thaim befor
With may thousandis then I can say,
And bot ellevyn within war thai
445 And a woman, and war sa stad
That thai na mete thar-within had

except such as they captured from their enemies. Yet, they behaved in such a way then that they held the tower manfully, till Richard of Normandy, despite his enemies, warned the king, who was joyful at his news, for he believed they had all been killed. (454) For that reason he turned swiftly back, won [the bridge of] Mantrible, crossed the Flagot [river], and finally decisively defeated Lavan and his whole fleet, setting his men free; the nails, the spear, the crown that Jesus wore and a great part of the [true] cross he won by his chivalry. (463) The good king [Robert] in this way cheered those who were with him, diverting and amusing them until his folk had all crossed.

(467) When they had crossed the broad waters, although they had plenty of enemies they joked and were cheerful. Nonetheless many times they had a great want of food, and so split into two parties to get venison. (474) The king himself was in one party and Sir James Douglas in the other. They went up into the hills, hunting for a long while of that day, combing the woods and setting snares – but they got little to eat. (481) It happened by chance at that time that the earl of Lennox was nearby among the hills, and when he heard this blowing [of horns] and shouting, he wondered what it could be; [but] he asked around in such a way that he learned it was the king.

---

440. Duke-peers is a corruption of douze-pairs, the twelve peers supposedly of Charlemagne. It is not clear whether Barbour or a copyist made this error.

472. To get venison (478), they hunted. The forest (i.e. hunting ground) of the earl of Lennox lay roughly between Balfron and Drymen on the south and Aberfoyle on the north, i.e. to the east of Ben Lomond and Loch Lomond. (*RRS5, 194*)

482. The earl of Lennox. He had succeeded to the earldom about 1303, and had played no part in the patriotic cause before that. Barbour names him among the king's earliest supporters (2.235, 485) and certainly Edward I forfeited his earldom and gave it to Sir John Menteith in 1306. Despite the risks he took, he played little part later in the reign and was not rewarded by the king.

Bot as thai fra thar fayis wan.
Yheyte sua contenyt thai thaim than
That thai the tour held manlily
450 Till that Rychard off Normandy
Magré his fayis warnyt the king
That wes joyfull off this tithing,
For he wend thai had all beyne slayne.
Tharfor he turnyt in hy agayne
455 And wan Mantrybill and passit Flagot,
And syne Lavyne and all his flot
Dispitusly discumfyt he,
And deliveryt his men all fre
And wan the naylis and the sper
460 And the crowne that Jhesu couth ber,
And off the croice a gret party
He wan throu his chevalry.
The gud king apon this maner
Comfort thaim that war him ner
465 And maid thaim gamyn and solace
Till that his folk all passyt was.

[Lennox joins the king; a reflection on weeping]

Quhen thai war passit the water brad
Suppos thai fele off fayis had
Thai maid thaim mery and war blyth.
470 Nocht-for-thi full fele syth
Thai had full gret defaut of mete,
And tharfor venesoun to get
In twa partys ar thai gayne.
The king himselff wes intill ane
475 And Schyr James off Douglas
Into the tother party was.
Then to the hycht thai held thar way
And huntyt lang quhill off the day
And soucht schawys and setis set
480 Bot thai gat litill for till ete.
Then hapnyt at that tyme percas
That the erle of the Levenax was
Amang the hillis ner tharby,
And quhen he hard sa blaw and cry
485 He had wonder quhat it mycht be,
And on sic maner spyryt he
That he knew that it wes the king,

(488) Then without hesitation he went speedily to the king with all those of his company, so happy and cheerful that there was no way he could have been more pleased, for he had believed the king was dead. (494) He was also at a loss, so that he dared not remain anywhere, nor since the king had been defeated at Methven had he ever heard anything that was definite about the king. So with a great deal of pleasure he greeted the king very humbly, and [the king] welcomed him very cheerfully, and questioned him very gently. (503) All the lords who were there were right joyful at their meeting, and kissed [the earl] with real pleasure. (506) It was really moving to see how they wept for joy and [with] great sympathy when they met with their comrade, who, they had believed, was dead; for that [reason] they welcomed him the more sincerely. He too, who was never so glad of a meeting, wept out of compassion. (513) Although I say that they wept, truthfully it wasn't real crying, because I firmly believe that weeping comes to men with misgiving, and that no-one can cry without grief, except women who can wet their cheeks with tears whenever they like, even though very often nothing is hurting them. (521) But I'm not lying when I say I know that whatever men say about such weeping, that great joy or pity can cause men to be so moved that water will rise from the heart wetting the eyes in such a way that it is like weeping but is not the same in all respects. (529) For when men cry properly, the heart is sorrowful or distressed.

---

502. Askyt tenderly. So in E, which I have retained, though tender questioning is an odd concept. 1571 has 'kissit' possibly dittography from 505, possibly the correct reading.

And then foroutyn mar duelling
With all thaim off his cumpany
490   He went rycht till the king in hy,
Sa blyth and sa joyfull that he
Mycht on na maner blyther be
For he the king wend had bene ded,
And he wes alsua will off red
495   That he durst nocht rest into na place,
Na sen the king discumfyt was
At Meffan he herd never thing
That ever wes certane off the king.
Tharfor into full gret daynte
500   The king full humyly haylist he,
And he him welcummyt rycht blythly
And askyt him full tenderly,
And all the lordis that war thar
Rycht joyfull off thar meting war,
505   And kyssyt him in gret daynte.
It wes gret pite for til se
How thai for joy and pite gret
Quhen that thai with thar falow met
That thai wend had bene dede, forthi
510   Thai welcummyt him mar hartfully,
And he for pité gret agayne
That never off metyng wes sa fayne.
Thocht I say that thai gret sothly
It wes na greting propyrly,
515   For I trow traistly that gretyng
Cummys to men for mysliking,
And that nane may but angyr gret
Bot it be wemen, that can wet
Thair chekys quhenever thaim list with teris,
520   The-quhethir weill oft thaim na thing deris,
But I wate weill but lesyng
Quhatever men say off sic greting
That mekill joy or yeit peté
May ger men sua amovyt be
525   That water fra the hart will rys
And weyt the eyne on sic a wys
That is lik to be greting,
Thocht it be nocht sua in all thing,
For quhen men gretis enkrely
530   The hart is sorowful or angry,

But with pity, I believe, weeping is nothing but an opening of the heart, showing the tenderness of compassion that is enclosed in it. (535) The barons in this way were gathered by the grace of God. The earl had food and plenty of it, and gave it to them with a glad heart, [so] they ate it with a good will, seeking no other sauce for it than the appetite which often takes a man – for their stomachs were completely empty. (543) They ate and drank whatever they had, and then gave praise to the Lord, thanking him with great cheer that they had met [up] in that way. The king then asked them eagerly how they had fared since he had seen them; and very sadly they told him the adventures, great dangers and deprivation that had befallen them. (552) The king was greatly moved at that, and in return, [arousing] sympathy, told them of the trouble, struggle and suffering that he had suffered since he had seen them. There was not one among them, [of] high or low [degree], but had compassion and pleasure when he heard recollections of the dangers that had passed. (560) But when men are at all at ease, telling of sufferings in the past is wonderfully pleasing to the hearing. To recall their former discomfort often gives them comfort and relief, provided that there follows from it no blame, dishonour, disrepute or shame. (567) After food, the king soon rose when he had finished his questions, got himself ready with his company and went in haste towards the sea, where Sir Neil Campbell met them,

---

561-2. Tell of pains. An echo of Vergil, *Aeneid*, I, 203.

570-71. Toward the sea where Neil Campbell met them. Whichever part of Lennox Bruce was in, this meeting would be in Loch Long, perhaps at the mouth of the Gare Loch.

Bot for pite I trow gretyng
Be na thing bot ane opynnyng
Off hart that schawis the tendernys
Off rewth that in it closyt is.
535   The barounys apon this maner
Throu Goddis grace assemblyt wer.
The erle had mete and that plenté
And with glad hart it thaim gaiff he,
And thai eyt it with full gud will
540   That soucht na nother sals thar-till
Bot appetyt, that oft men takys,
For rycht weill scowryt war thar stomakys.
Thai eit and drank sic as thai had
And till Our Lord syne lovyng maid,
545   And thankit him with full gud cher
That thai war mete on that maner.
The king then at thaim speryt yarne
How thai sen he thaim seyne had farne,
And thai full petwysly gan tell
550   Aventuris that thaim befell
And gret anoyis and poverté.
The king tharat had gret pité
And tauld thaim petwisly agayne
The noy, the travaill and the payne
555   That he had tholyt sen he thaim saw.
Wes nane amang thaim hey na law
That he ne had pite and plesaunce
Quhen that he herd mak remembrance
Off the perellys that passyt war,
560   Bot quhen men oucht at liking ar
To tell off paynys passyt by
Plesys to heryng petuisly,
And to rehers thar auld disese
Dois thaim oftsys comfort and ese,
565   With-thi tharto folow na blame
Dishonour wikytnes na schame.

[*They row past Bute; Lennox's boat escapes pursuers*]

Efter the mete sone rais the king
Quhen he had levyt hys speryng,
And buskyt him with his mengye
570   And went in hy towart the se
Quhar Schyr Nele Cambell thaim mete

with both ships and food, sails, oars and other things that were useful for their passage. (575) Then they boarded, not delaying; some went to steer and some to row, and they rowed by the isle of Bute. You could see many a handsome youngster looking along the coast there as they rose rowing on their oars, and fists that were stalwart and broad, used to grasping great spears, grasped the oars such that you could often see skin left on the wood. (585) For all were at it, knight and boy, [and] none could have any relief from steering and rowing [that] helped them in their passage. (589) But at the same time that they were sailing, as you heard me say, for reasons which I can't tell you, the earl of Lennox was left behind with his galley, till the king was far ahead. (595) When those of his country knew that he remained behind like that, they went after him by sea with ships, and he, seeing that he was not strong enough to fight with those traitors and that he had no help nearer than the king's fleet, sped after them in haste. (603) But the traitors so followed him than they came close to overtaking him. Despite all that he could do, they kept coming nearer and nearer to him. When he saw that they were so close that he could well hear their threats, and still saw them coming closer and closer, then he said to his followers, (611) 'Unless we find some stratagem we shall soon be completely overhauled. So I suggest that without any delay we throw everything except our arms [and armour]

591–658. The pursuit of the earl of Lennox. This vivid story makes it clear that Bruce and Lennox sailed down Loch Long and the Firth of Clyde fairly close to Dumbarton, since the pursuers were men of Lennox (595) and former vassals of the earl (640). The only place which would yield a significant pursuing fleet would be Dumbarton, where Sir John Menteith had been in command of the castle as sheriff and had now been made earl of Lennox by Edward I. In September 1306 he was in Kintyre with the besieging force at Dunaverty (*CDS5*, *471g*). He never appears in *The Bruce*, though stories about him certainly circulated. He had joined Bruce by March 1309.

Bath with schippis and with meyte
Saylys ayris and other thing
That wes spedfull to thar passyng.
575 Then schippyt thai foroutyn mar
Sum went till ster and sum till ar,
And rowyt be the ile of But.
Men mycht se mony frely fute
About the cost, thar lukand
580 As thai on ayris rais rowand,
And nevys that stalwart war and squar,
That wont to spayn gret speris war,
Swa spaynyt aris that men mycht se
Full oft the hyde leve on the tre.
585 For all war doand, knycht and knave,
Wes nane that ever disport mycht have
Fra steryng and fra rowyng
To furthyr thaim off thar fleting.
Bot in the samyn tyme at thai
590 War in schipping, as ye hard me say,
The erle off the Levenax was,
I can nocht tell you throu quhat cas
Levyt behynd with his galay
Till the king wes fer on his way.
595 Quhen that thai off his cuntré
Wyst that so duelt behynd wes he
Be se with schippys thai him socht,
And he that saw that he wes nocht
Off pith to fecht with thai traytouris
600 And that he had na ner socouris
Then the kingis flote, forthi
He sped him efter thaim in hy,
Bot the tratouris hym folowyt sua
That thai weill ner hym gan ourta
605 For all the mycht that he mycht do.
Ay ner and ner thai come him to,
And quhen he saw thai war sa ner
That he mycht weill thar manance her
And saw thaim ner and ner cum ay,
610 Then till his mengye gan he say,
'Bot giff we fynd sum sutelté
Ourtane all sone sall we be.
Tharfor I rede but mar letting
That outakyn our armyng

into the sea, and thus, when our ship is lightened we shall row, and [make] such [good] speed that we shall escape well from them, (619) because they will stop on the sea to pick up our things and we shall row on without resting until we have escaped [well] away.' As he planned, so they did; they lightened their ship soon and then rowed with all their might. (626) She, lightened in that way, scudded [forward] sliding through the waves. When their foes saw them always further and further ahead of them, they took the things that were floating there, and then turned back, so throwing away all their efforts.

(633) When the earl and his following had escaped in this way, he hurried after the king who had then arrived in Kintyre with all his company. The earl told him all that had passed, how he had been chased on the sea by those who should have been his own [men] (641) and how he would certainly have been taken had he not thrown overboard all that he had, to lighten his [boat]; thus they escaped from [the pursuers]. 'Sir earl,' said the king, '*perfay,* since you have escaped away [from them], [let's] not complain about the loss. But I will say one thing to you, that great harm will befall you [if you] depart often from my company. (651) For many times when you are away, you are placed in great danger, so I think it best for you [if you] stay always close to me.'

645–58. Lennox. This exchange is very curious, since Lennox had been with the king at Methven, which certainly put him 'intill hard assay' (652); and in the poem he is never again with the king. It is possible that in the source Bruce had concluded from Lennox's non-appearance that he had deserted to the enemy; hence 'hald the alwayis ner by me'. The shift to Angus of Islay is very abrupt.

615 We kast our thing all in the se,
    And fra our schip swa lychtyt be
    We sall row and speid us sua
    That we sall weill eschaip thaim fra,
    With that thai sall mak duelling
620 Apon the se to tak our thing
    And we sall row but resting ay
    Till we eschapyt be away.'
    As he divisyt thai have done
    And thar schip thai lychtyt sone
625 And rowyt syne with all thar mycht,
    And scho that swa wes maid lycht
    Raykyt slidand throu the se.
    And quhen thar fayis gan thaim se
    Forouth thaim alwayis mar and mar,
630 The thingis that thar fletand war
    Thai tuk and turnyt syne agayne,
    And leyt thai lesyt all thar payne.

[*Arrival in Kintyre; Angus of Islay submits at Dunaverty; they
sail for Rathlin*]

    Quhen that the erle on this maner
    And his mengye eschapyt wer,
635 Eftyr the king he gan him hy
    That then with all his cumpany
    Into Kyntyr aryvyt was.
    The erle tauld him all his cas,
    How he wes chasyt on the se
640 With thaim that suld his awyn be,
    And how he had bene tane but dout
    Na war it that he warpyt out
    All that he had him lycht to ma
    And swa eschapyt thaim fra.
645 'Schyr erle,' said the king, 'perfay,
    Syn thou eschapyt is away
    Off the tynsell is na plenyeing.
    Bot I will say the weile a thing,
    That thar will fall the gret foly
650 To pas oft fra my cumpany,
    For fele sys quhen thou art away
    Thou art set intill hard assay,
    Tharfor me thynk best to the
    To hald the alwayis ner by me.'

'Sir,' said the earl, 'it shall be so. I shan't go far from you for any reason until God gives grace that we are powerful enough to maintain our resolve against our enemies.' 659) Angus of Islay at that time was seigneur, lord and leader of Kintyre. He received the king very well, and undertook to be his man, and placed him and his at [the king's] service in different ways. (665) For greater assurance he then gave him his castle of Dunaverty, at his disposal to stay in. The king thanked him very warmly, and accepted his service. (670) Nonetheless, in many ways he feared for treason all the time, and therefore, as I heard men say, he trusted in nobody completely until he knew him through and through. But whatever fear he had [of people] he presented a smiling face to them. (677) He stayed then in Dunaverty for three days, no more. Then he had his followers get ready to go by sea towards Rathlin;

659–78. The Dunaverty episode. Dunaverty castle had been a bone of contention between Malcolm Mac Quillan and the Macdonalds of Islay, under their chief, Alastair, a supporter of the Bruces in 1296. But in March 1306 the English reported that Robert

> has had his castle of Loch Doon in Carrick and the castle of Dunaverty in Kintyre victualled for a long period. This castle of Dunaverty belongs to the king [Edward I] and to his crown, but the king, as a result of treacherous advice, granted it without inquest to a certain Malcolm [Mac] Quillan and this Malcolm has exchanged it with the earl [of Carrick] for another.

Malcolm was sent to Ireland, returning in February 1307 with the king's brothers to Galloway, where they were captured and executed. But Dunaverty was in Bruce's hands in August 1306. The English sent a force under Henry Percy, and including three earls, through Galloway, where it took Loch Doon castle about 14 August, then went, probably by Girvan, to Kintyre besieging Dunaverty from the very end of August (because Edward I was writing to the besiegers there as early as 2 September). From the nature of the force sent, the castle was seen by the English as key, with Loch Doon and Kildrummy still held for King Robert. It cannot have been in the possession of a Macdonald, and this surrender to Bruce belongs to some other location. (*CDS5, 472b,d,p,u–z*)

677. He stayed in Dunaverty for three days. At 385–87 he went to Kintyre to spend the winter, but Barbour offers no explanation for the change of plan. It is not known when Bruce left Dunaverty, but the fairly numerous English references to the siege speak of the castle and not of 'the earl of Carrick in the castle'. Thus on 25 September Edward I wrote to Sir John Menteith saying that he understood that 'the inhabitants of the isle of Kintyre who have come to his will to be at law' do

655   'Schyr,' said the erle, 'it sall be swa.
       I sall na wys pas fer you fra
       Till God giff grace we be off mycht
       Agayne our fayis to hald our stycht.'
       Angus off Ile that tyme wes syr
660   And lord and ledar off Kyntyr,
       The king rycht weill resavyt he
       And undertuk his man to be,
       And him and his on mony wys
       He abandounyt till his service,
665   And for mar sekyrnes gaiff him syne
       His castell off Donavardyne
       To duell tharin at his liking.
       Full gretumly thankyt him the king
       And resavyt his service.
670   Nocht-forthi on mony wys
       He wes dredand for tresoun ay,
       And tharfor, as Ik hard men say,
       He traistyt in nane sekyrly
       Till that he knew him utraly.
675   Boy quhatkin dred that ever he had
       Fayr contenance to thaim he maid,
       And in Donavardyne dayis thre
       Foroutyne mar then duellyt he.
       Syne gert he his mengye mak thaim yar
680   Towart Rauchryne be se to far

---

not supply his men besieging Dunaverty with provisions and necessities, as they should. (*CDS2, 1834*, revised from the original.) It is likely that Robert slipped away as soon as the English force landed in Kintyre. The castle fell at the end of September, as it was reported by Thomas earl of Lancaster from Irvine on 5 October. (*CDS5, 457*) Little remains of the castle, which is on a promontory surrounded by the sea on three sides.

670–74. This coded account of the king's distrust of Macdonald is noteworthy.

680. To go to Rathlin. It is highly unlikely that the king had any such intention, for Rathlin is much too close to the Irish mainland to have provided a refuge in the king's desperate circumstances. He sailed for the Scottish isles and was taken by current and wind (689–720) to Rathlin. Such weather would be characteristic of the equinox, 22 September, and may be reason for placing Robert's escape from Dunaverty rather later than I have suggested.

it is an island in the sea set midway between Kintyre and Ireland, where also swift currents run, as perilous to sail through on a voyage, or more [so], as is the Raz of Britanny or the strait of Morocco in Spain.

(689) They put their ships to sea, and without delay made ready anchors, ropes, sails and oars, and everything needed for a voyage. When they were ready they prepared to sail; the wind was just what they wanted. (695) They hoisted sail and set forth, soon passing by the Mull and entering the race where the current was so strong that strong waves, which were breakers, rose like hills here and there. The ships glided over the waves, for they had a wind blowing fair. (703) Nonetheless anyone who had been there would have seen a great shifting of ships, for sometimes some would be atop the waves, as if on a hill-top, and some would slide from top to bottom, as if bound for hell, then rise up suddenly on the wave, and other ships that were nearby swiftly sank into the trough. (712) It took great skill to keep their tackle in such danger, and with such waves, for from time to time the waves deprived them of sight of land. (716) When they were quite near to the land, and when the ships were sailing close, the sea would rise in such a way that the soaring height of the waves would often deprive them of sight of [land] (721) Nonetheless in Rathlin

---

695–720. The stormy crossing may owe something to an account of a sea voyage in the *Historia Destructionis Troiae*. Behind both (esp. 705–7) may be Vergil, *Aeneid*, I, 106–7, 'Hi summo in fluctu pendent, his unda dehiscens/Terram inter fluctus aperit.'

That is ane ile in the se,
And may weill in mydwart be
Betuix Kyntyr and Irland,
Quhar als gret stremys ar rynnand
685   And als peralous and mar
Till our-saile thaim into schipfair
As is the rais of Bretangye
Or Strait off Marrok into Spanye.

[*The stormy crossing; the panic and the submission of Rathlin*]

Thair schippys to the se thai set,
690   And maid redy but langer let
Ankyrs rapys bath saile and ar
And all that nedyt to schipfar.
Quhen thai war boune to saile thai went,
The wynd wes wele to thar talent.
695   Thai raysyt saile and furth thai far,
And by the Mole thai passyt yar
And entryt sone into the rase
Quhar that the stremys sa sturdy was
That wavys wyd wycht brakand war
700   Weltryt as hillys her and thar.
The schippys our the wavys slayd
For wynd at poynt blawand thai had,
Bot nocht-forthi quha had thar bene
A gret stertling he mycht haiff seyne
705   Off schippys, for quhilum sum wald be
Rycht on the wavys as on a mounté
And sum wald slyd fra heycht to law
Rycht as thai doune till hell wald draw,
Syne on the wav stert sodanly,
710   And other schippys that war tharby
Deliverly drew to the depe.
It wes gret cunnanes to kep
Thar takill intill sic a thrang
And wyth sic wavis, for ay amang
715   The wavys reft thar sycht of land
Quhen thai the land wes rycht ner-hand,
And quhen schippys war sailand ner
The se wald rys on sic maner
That off the wavys the weltrand hycht
720   Wald refe thaim oft off thar sycht.
Bot into Rauchryne nocht-forthi

they all arrived safely, pleased and happy that they had thus escaped the terrifying waves. They reached Rathlin, and went on land without delay, armed as best they could. (728) When the folk who lived there saw men-at-arms arriving in such numbers in their country, they fled with their cattle hastily towards a right strong castle that was nearby in that land. You could hear women crying aloud and fleeing with cattle here and there. (736) But the king's men, who were fleet of foot, overtook them, stopped them hastily and brought back to the king, none of them being slain. (741) The king then negotiated with them so that, to meet his demands, they all became his men and solemnly undertook to him that they and theirs, come what may, would be at his will in all things. (747) And while he chose to stay there they would send him every day victuals for three hundred men; they would acknowledge him as lord, but their possessions would be their own, free from all his men. (753) The agreement was made in these terms, and on the following day, without more delay, all Rathlin, both man and boy, knelt and did homage to the king, swearing fealty as well, to serve him always with loyalty. (759) They kept their agreement right well, for while he dwelt in that land they found food for his company, and served him very humbly.

725–62. The submission of Rathlin. This too is improbable; Bruce would leave so vulnerable a place quickly for the safety of the Scottish isles. The first major isle he would reach sailing north would be Islay, where the people fled in terror to the castle (731–33), that is of Dunyvaig. Macdonald of Islay then made terms, surrendering this castle, not Dunaverty, and reluctantly promising food for Robert's men; but the king did not trust him (670–74). Whether the Macdonald was in fact Angus is a matter of some doubt; his older brother, Donald, seems to have been chieftain at this time, but Barbour would be anxious to present Angus, father of John (the chieftain under Robert II), in a favourable light.

Fordun tells us where King Robert went for the early part of winter, though wrongly makes his hardships last for nearly a year, when 'aided by the help and power of a certain noble lady, Christina of the Isles, who wished him well, he, after endless toils, pain and distress, got back by a round-about way, to the earldom of Carrick.' (*F1*, 343; *F2*, 335) Christina Mac Ruairidh, lady of Garmoran, resided at Castle Tioram on the south shore of Loch Moidart, a beautiful site, with the castle-walls still standing. Dunyvaig can also be visited, but much less remains.

Thai aryvyt ilkane sawffly,
Blyth and glaid that thai war sua
Eschapyt thai hidwys wavis fra.
725 In Rauchryne thai aryvyt ar
And to the land thai went but mar
Armyt apon thar best maner.
Quhen the folk that thar wonnand wer
Saw men off armys in that cuntré
730 Aryve into sic quantité
Thai fled in hy with thar catell
Towart a rycht stalwart castell
That in the land wes tharby.
Men mycht her wemen hely cry
735 And fle with cataill her and thar.
Bot the kingis folk that war
Deliver of fute thaim gan our-hy
And thaim arestyt hastely
And brocht thaim to the king agayne
740 Swa that nane off thaim all wes slayne.
Then with thaim tretyt swa the king
That thai to fulfill his yarnyng
Become his men everilkane,
And has him trewly undertane
745 That thai and tharis loud and still
Suld be in all thing at his will,
And quhill him likit thar to leynd
Everilk day thai suld him send
Vittalis for thre hunder men,
750 And thai as lord suld him ken,
Bot at thar possessioune suld be
For all his men thar awyn fre.
The cunnand on this wys was maid,
And on the morn but langer baid
755 Off all Rauchryne bath man and page
Knelyt and maid the king homage,
And tharwith swour him fewté
To serve him ay in lawté,
And held him rycht weill cunnand,
760 For quhill he duelt into the land
Thai fand meit till his cumpany
And servyt him full humely.

(1) Let us leave the king now, resting in Rathlin without [any] struggle, and speak about his enemies for a while. Through their might and their power [they] made such a hard, difficult and harsh persecution of those who were well-disposed to him, or [were] kin or any kind of friend, that it is dreadful to hear [about]. (10) For they spared no-one who, they thought, was his friend, whatever his standing, ecclesiastic or lay. Both Robert, bishop of Glasgow and Mark, bishop of Man they violently imprisoned in fetters and in prison. (16) Worthy Christopher Seton was betrayed in Loch Doon [castle] by a disciple of Judas, a false traitor [called] Macnab, who had been continually, night and day, in his house, to whom [Seton] was a good companion. It was far worse than treason to betray such a noble person, of such reputation. (26) But he had no pity in doing so. Let him be condemned to hell! For when he had betrayed [Seton] the Englishmen quickly rode right with him into England, to the king, who had him drawn, beheaded and hanged, without compassion or mercy.

13–14. Robert Wishart, bishop of Glasgow, was a strong patriot who encouraged Robert to become king (though he was not himself at Scone), and after Methven was imprisoned by Edward I at Winchester. He was handed over to the Pope in 1308, must have been at the Council of Vienne, was returned to England and in January 1315 to Scotland. Mark was bishop of the Isles or Sodor, whose cathedral was on Man and had been imprisoned by Edward I about 1298–99 with Bishop Robert Wishart, an episode known to Barbour and which he wrongly assumed to be the same as Wishart's 1306 imprisonment; possibly his source was the story of William Douglas's imprisonment and death in 1298. Mark died probably in 1303 so is quite wrongly placed here. The other bishop who was imprisoned in 1306 was William Lamberton, bishop of St Andrews, named at 1.412 but otherwise ignored in the whole poem, although he held the see till 20 May, 1328. For Wishart and Lamberton see D. E. R. Watt, *Biographical Dictionary of Scottish Graduates*, 585–90, 318–25.

16–19. E has 'Loudon', but H correctly preserves 'Lochdon'. The octagonal Loch Doon castle was on an island but has now been rebuilt on the shore of the loch. It was a principal seat of the earls of Carrick, and one of the three places Bruce tried to hold in 1306. Besieged by Henry Percy from early August, 1306 it fell on or about 14 August. According to a later charter of Robert I the castle was surrendered and Seton betrayed by Arthur, nephew of Sir Gilbert Carrick. Of Macnab there is no other trace, and the name is an unlikely one for a member

BOOK 4

[*English harshness to prisoners*]

In Rawchryne leve we now the king
In rest foroutyn barganyng,
And off his fayis a quhile speke we
That throu thar mycht and thar powsté

5   Maid sic a persecucioune
Sa hard, sa strayt and sa feloune
On thaim that till hym luffand wer
Or kyn or freynd on ony maner
That at till her is gret pité.

10   For thai sparyt off na degré
Thaim that thai trowit his freynd wer
Nother off the kyrk na seculer,
For off Glaskow Byschop Robert
And Marcus off Man thai stythly speryt

15   Bath in fetrys and in presoune,
And worthy Crystoll off Seytoun
Into Loudoun betresyt was
Throu a discipill off Judas
Maknab, a fals tratour that ay

20   Wes off his dwelling nycht and day
Quhom to he maid gud cumpany.
It wes fer wer than tratoury
For to betreys sic a persoune
So nobill and off sic renoune,

25   Bot tharoff had he na pite,
In hell condampnyt mocht he be.
For quhen he him betrasyt had
The Inglismen rycht with him rad
In hy in Ingland to the king,

30   That gert draw him and hede and hing
Foroutyn peté or mercy.

---

of the household of Christopher Seton, an English knight. For Seton's earlier appearance in the poem see note to 2.421. (*B1985*.75; PRO E101/369/11, 51r–v; *CDS5*, 203a)

29. To England to the king. This may be true, but if so Seton was then sent to Dumfries, the scene of his crime, where he was hanged and where Robert I later founded a chapel for masses for his soul. His two brothers were also executed.

(32) Assuredly it was a [matter of] great sorrow that so worthy a person as him should be hanged in that way; that's how his nobility was extinguished. Also Sir Reginald Crawford and Sir Brice Blair were hanged in a barn in Ayr.

(39) The queen and also her daughter Dame Marjory, who was later worthily joined in God's union with Walter Steward of Scotland, were not prepared to stay any longer in the castle of Kildrummy, awaiting a siege, [and] rode promptly with both knights and squires through Ross right to the sanctuary of Tain. (48) But they made that journey in vain, for the men of Ross who would accept neither blame nor danger on their account, took them all out of sanctuary, and sent them all to England, to the king, who had all the men drawn and hanged, and put the ladies in prison,

---

36–38. Sir Reginald Crawford and Sir Bryce Blair, hanged in a barn in Ayr. This is the closest Barbour comes to a mention of two of Robert's brothers. Fordun says: Thomas and Alexander Bruce, hastening toward Carrick by another road, were taken at Loch Ryan and beheaded at Carlisle (*F1*, 342; *F2*, 335). Lanercost is fuller:

> On [9 February, 1307] Thomas and Alexander, and Sir Reginald Crawford, desiring to avenge themselves upon the people of Galloway, invaded their country with eighteen ships and galleys, having with them a certain kinglet of Ireland, the lord of Kintyre and other large following ... Dougal Macdouel a chief among the Galwegians ... defeated them and captured all but a few who escaped in two galleys. He ordered the Irish kinglet and the lord of Kintyre to be beheaded and their heads to be carried to the king ... at Lanercost. Thomas ... Alexander and Sir Reginald ... who had been severely wounded in their capture ... he likewise took alive to the king, who sentenced them, causing Thomas to be drawn at the tails of horses in Carlisle on Friday [17 February, 1307] and then to be hanged and afterwards beheaded. Also he commanded the other two to be hanged on the same day and afterwards beheaded. (*L*, 205–6; *LT*, 179–80)

The 'lord of Kintyre' here must be Malcolm Mac Quillan, and the force came from Ireland. The execution at Carlisle, including that of Crawford, is confirmed by record (*CDS5*, 216a), though Lanercost correctly says 'hanged and beheaded' – Barbour's 'beheaded and hanged' would be difficult! The fate of Sir Bryce Blair was evidently quite separate. It seems that Percy's force which took Dunaverty castle in late September 1306 reoccupied a badly damaged Ayr on its return; the English garrison there was paid from 6 October, 1306. Sir Bryce was certainly on King Robert's side, and was probably hanged in a barn there (the castle being in ruins) early in October 1306. His fate would be associated with that of Crawford, who had been sheriff of Ayr, if it was they who took (and slighted) Ayr for Robert in February 1306. (*B1985*, 75–76; *CDS4*, 391)

It wes gret sorow sekyrly
That so worthy a persoune as he
Suld on sic maner hangyt be,
35 Thusgat endyt his worthynes.
Off Crauford als Schyr Ranald wes
And Schyr Bryce als the Blar
Hangyt intill a berne in Ar.
The queyn and als Dame Marjory,
40 Hyr dochter that syne worthily
Wes coupillyt into Goddis band
With Walter Stewart off Scotland,
That wald on na wys langar ly
In the castell off Kyldromy
45 To byd a sege, ar ridin raith
With knychtis and squyeris bath
Throu Ros rycht to the gyrth off Tayne.
Bot that travaill thai maid in vayne,
For thai off Ros that wald nocht ber
50 For thaim na blayme na yeit danger
Out off the gyrth thame all has tayne
And syne has send thaim everilkane
Rycht intill Ingland to the king,
That gert draw all the men and hing,
55 And put the ladyis in presoune

39–40. The queen was not the mother of Marjory, who was the daughter of Robert's first, Mar, wife.

44–47. Sanctuary at Tain. The date of the ladies' flight from Kildrummy would be before the siege began there in the last week of August 1306; at 3.335 I have argued that they had been at Kildrummy with Neil Bruce since May 1306. They were certainly taken from there by John earl of Atholl, for Robert I later made the earl of Ross pay the crown £20 annually to pay for six chaplains at Tain saying masses for earlier kings and for Earl John. The earl tried to escape from Ross by sea, but was driven ashore in Moray, and captured about 20–25 August; the sanctuary may have been violated by (presumably) the earl of Ross when Valence was at Inverness in the second half of September. Edward I sent the queen from Lanercost only on 10 October. (*CDS*5, 203a, 205b)

55–56. The queen and Marjory were not put in castle or donjon (i.e. a tower, not a dungeon), though initially Marjory was to be put in a cage in the Tower of London; Edward relented and gave her and Christina, widow of Christopher Seton to the keeping of Percy. The queen was detained at the manor of Burstwick (Lincs.) but given servants who were forbidden to smile! She and Marjory returned to Scotland early in 1315.

some in a castle, some in a donjon. (57) It was very sad to hear of people being oppressed in this way.

(59) At that time Sir Neil Bruce was in Kildrummy with bold and hardy men, and I know well that the earl of Atholl was there. They victualled the castle well, procuring food and fuel, and so reinforcing the castle that they thought no force could take it. (67) When the king of England was told how they meant to hold that castle, he was extremely angry and quickly called his eldest son and heir apparent to him, a fine young batchelor called Sir Edward of Caernarvon; he was the strongest man of any that you could find in any country, [and] at that time was Prince of Wales. (77) He had summoned also two earls (they were Gloucester and Hereford), and ordered them travel to Scotland and set siege with a firm hand to the castle of Kildrummy. And [the king] ordered [that] all the garrison should be altogether destroyed without ransom, or brought to him in prison. (85) When they had received all the orders, they assembled an army immediately, and went to the castle forthwith, besieging it vigorously, and attacking it often [and] strongly; but still they failed to take it. For those within were very worthy and defended themselves doughtily, counter-attacking their enemies often, [so that] some [were] struck [and] wounded, some slain. (95) Many a time they would come out and have a fight at the outworks,

---

57. The C MS begins here.
62. The earl of Atholl. But Barbour has nothing further to say of him, ignoring his capture further north while the castle was still besieged.
83–84. C and E have 'in presoune' which is awkward since it does not really mean 'as prisoners'. It may represent 'in persoun' which accords better with Barbour's view of the treatment of some prisoners; see under 176, 314–15.

Sum intill castell sum in dongeoun.
It wes gret pite for till her
The folk be troublyt on this maner.

[*The siege of Kildrummy castle*]

That tyme wes in Kyldromy
60 Wyth men that wycht and hardy
Schyr Neile the Bruce and I wate weile
That thar the erle was off Adheill.
The castell weill vittalyt thai
And mete and fuell gan purvay
65 And enforcyt the castell sua
That thaim thocht na strenth mycht it ta.
And quhen it to the king was tauld
Off Ingland how thai schup till hauld
That castell, he wes all angry
70 And callyt his sone till hym in hy
The eldest and aperand ayr
A young bacheler and stark and fayr
Schyr Edward callyt off Carnauerane,
That wes the sterkast man of ane
75 That men fynd mycht in ony countre
Prynce of Walys that tyme wes he.
And he gert als call erlys twa
Glosyster and Harfurd war tha
And bad thaim wend into Scotland
80 And set a sege with stalwart hand
To the castell off Kyldromy.
And all the halderis halyly
He bad distroy for-owtyn ransoun
Or bryng thaim till him in presoune.
85 Quhen thai the commaundment had tane
Thai assemblyt ane ost onane
And to the castell went in hy
And it assegyt vigorusly
And mony tyme full hard assaylyt.
90 Bot for to tak it yeit thai failyt
For thai within war rycht worthy
And thaim defendyt douchtely
And ruschyt thair fayis oft agayne
Sum beft sum woundyt sum alslayne
95 And mony tymys ische thai wald
And bargane at the barrais hald

often wounding and killing their foes. In brief, they conducted themselves so [bravely] that those outside despaired and meant to go to England, for they saw the castle [was] so strong, knew that it was well provisioned and saw the men [inside] defending themselves so [well], that they had no hope of taking them. (105) They would have achieved nothing at that time, had there not been false treachery there, for there was a traitor inside. A false wretch, a betrayer, Osbern by name, committed the treason, for what reason I know not, nor with whom he made that agreement, (112) but, as those who were inside said, he took a coulter, glowing hot, that was still in a burning fire, went into the great hall, that was filled full then with corn, and threw it high up on a heap – but it wasn't hidden there for very long. (119) For men often say that you cannot hide fire or pride without discovery, for pomp often displays the pride, or else the great bragging that blows [about] it. Nor can you so cover fire that flame or smoke won't reveal it. (125) That's how it happened here, for obvious fire soon appeared through the roofing-boards, first like a star, then like a moon, and then much more widespread, the fire finally burst blazing out, the smoke rising amazingly fast. (131) The fire spread all over the castle, and no force of men could put it out. Then those inside went to the wall, which at that time was all embattled, both within as well as [on the] outside. That embattlement without doubt saved their lives, for it broke the flames that would have overcome them. (139) When their foes saw the damage

---

134. Embattlement. Barbour seems to mean that the wall walk had battlements on the courtyard side as well as the outside, which is most unlikely. It is more probable that a timber defensive hoarding with walkway had been erected around the outside of the wall-top.

And wound thar fayis oft and sla.
Schortly thai thaim contenyt sua
That thai withoute disparyt war
100 And thocht till Ingland for to far
For thai sa styth saw the castell
And with that it wes warnyst weill
And saw the men defend thaim sua
That thai nane hop had thaim to ta,
105 Nane had thai done all that sesoune
Gyff it ne had bene fals tresoun
For thar with thaim wes a tratour.
A fals lourdane a losyngeour
Hosbarne to name maid the tresoun,
110 I wate nocht for quhat enchesoun
Na quham with he maid that conwyn
Bot as thai said that war within
He tuk a culter hate glowand
That yeit wes in a fyr brynnand
115 And went him to the mekill hall
That then with corn wes fyllyt all
And heych up in a mow it did,
Bot it full lang wes nocht thar hid
For men sayis oft that fyr na prid
120 But discovering may na man hid,
For the pomp oft the prid furth schawis
Or ellis the gret boist that it blawis,
Na thar may na man fyr sa covyr
Than low or rek sall it discovyr.
125 Sa fell it her, for fyr all cler
Son throu the thak-burd gan apper
Fyrst as a stern syne as a mone
And weill bradder tharefter sone
The fyr out syne in bles brast
130 And the rek rais rycht wondre fast.
The fyr our all the castell spred
That mycht na force of man it red.
Than thai within drew to the wall
That at that tyme wes bataillit all
135 Within rycht as it wes withoute
That bataillyne withoutyn dout
Savit thar lyvis, for it brak
Bles that thaim wald ourtak.
And quhen thar fayis the myscheiff saw

they went to arms in a short time, and assaulted the castle
hard, where the fire's blast allowed them to approach. But
those inside, who were in [such] need, made such a strong
and bold defence that they drove back their enemies many
times, for they avoided no dangers [but] struggled to save
their lives. (148) But fate, which always drives worldly affairs
to a conclusion, so troubled them, that they were assaulted
on two sides, within by fire burning them, outside by folk so
assailing them that, in spite of the [defenders], they burned
the door; but [the English] dared not enter there quickly
because of the fire, which was so hot. (156) For that reason
they pulled back their folk and went to rest (for it was night)
till daylight in the morning. (159) Those within were in such
misfortune, as you hear tell, although they had always
defended themselves worthily and conducted themselves so
manfully, that before day[break] they had build up the en-
trance again. But in the morning, when the day was light and
the sun had risen, shining bright, those outside in one forma-
tion came armed, ready to attack. (169) Those inside, who
were so placed that [they] had no victual nor fuel wherewith
they might hold the castle, negotiated first, then surrendered
to be in the will of the king, who was then bitter against Scots,
as was soon thereafter well known, for they were all hanged
and drawn. (177) When this agreement had been negotiated
so, and affirmed with sureties, they soon took those of the
castle, and in a short time did sufficient

---

172. Treated then surrendered. Barbour somewhat unusually gives no
indication of the duration of the siege which began in late August 1306;
the castle fell on or very close to 10 September. The shortness of the
siege suggests that the fire did happen. By convention or laws of war,
a garrison which surrendered when a siege was set was entitled to life
and limb; resistence nullified that right. Hence this garrison was at the
king's will to deal with as he wished.

176. All hanged and drawn. But at 112 some of those within were able
to tell later of Osbern's treason! Summary execution may have been
done on some of the garrison troops, but a mass execution would
perhaps have caused more comment than we find in the sources. Sir
Robert Boyd and Sir Alexander Lindsay were reported to have been
taken when Kildrummy fell; if that report is accurate, they were released
and soon rejoined King Robert. (*CDS2, 1829*) For those taken south
to execution see 314–15.

140 Till armys went thai in a thraw
And assaylyt the castell fast
Quhar thai durst come for fyris blast,
Bot thai within that myster had
Sa gret defence and worthy mad
145 That thai full oft thar fayis rusit
For thai nakyn perall refusyt,
Thai travaillyt for to sauff thar lyffis
Bot werd that till the end ay dryvis
The warldis thingis sua thaim travaillyt
150 That thai on twa halfys war assailyt,
In with fyr that thaim sua broilyit
And utouth with folk that thaim sua toilyit
That thai brynt magré thaim the yat
That, for the fyre that wes sua hate
155 Thai durst nocht entyr sua in hy,
Tharfor thar folk thai gan rely
And went to rest for it wes nycht
Till on the morn that day wes lycht.

[*The surrender of Kildrummy and the death of Edward I*]

At sik myscheiff as ye her say
160 War thai within, the-quhethyr ay
Thai thaim defendyt douchtely
And contenyt thaim sa manlily
That or day throu mekill payn
Thai had muryt up thar yat agayn.
165 But on the morn quhen day wes lycht
And sone wes ryssyn schynand brycht
Thai without in hale bataill
Come purvayt redy till assaill,
Bot thai within that sua war stad
170 That thai vitaill na fewell had
Quhar-with thai mycht the castell hald
Tretyt fyrst and syne thaim yauld
To be in-till the kingis will,
Bot that to Scottis men wes ill
175 As sone eftyr weill wes knawin
For thai war hangyt all and drawyn.
Quhen this cunnand thus tretyt wes
And affermyt with sekyrnes
Thai tuk thaim of the castell sone
180 And in-till schort tyme has done

that they knocked a whole quarter of Snowdon down to the ground, then took their way to England. (184) But when King Edward heard news of how Neil Bruce had held Kildrummy so valiantly against his son, he gathered a great [force of] chivalry, and went towards Scotland speedily. (189) And as he was riding with his great army in Northumberland, illness overtook him en route, and put him in such a bad way that he could neither walk nor ride. (194) In spite of himself, he had to stay in a hamlet near thereby, a humble little village; they brought him there with great difficulty. He was so [ill] that he could not draw breath except with great difficulty, nor speak except in a very low [voice]. (201) Nonetheless he told them to tell him what village it was that he lay in. 'Sir,' they said, 'men of this country call this village Burgh by Sands.' 'Do they call it Burgh? Alas!' he said, 'My hope is now destroyed. (207) For I expected never to suffer the pains of death until I had taken the burgh of Jerusalem, with mighty efforts; I meant to end my life there. I knew well that I would die in Burgh, but I was neither clever nor cunning [enough] to pay heed to other burghs. Now there's no way I can go any further.' (215) Thus he bemoaned his folly, as indeed he had reason to do when he coveted certainty where no-one can be certain. (219) However, men said that he had a spirit, kept in hiding, which gave him answers to matters that he would enquire [about]. But he was without doubt a fool to give credence to that creature,

---

181. Snowdon has been attributed on this evidence as the name of the donjon at Kildrummy. But Barbour clearly means the whole castle, of which a part was demolished.

184. King Edward. He came north in July–August 1306, settling at Carlisle, and then in October at Lanercost priory close by. He was disabled by the illness which killed him on 7 July, 1307, and not as here (by implication) in September 1306. Barbour has altered the sequence in order to stress the king's lack of remorse on his deathbed.

209. The quirk of death in a 'Jerusalem' was told of Pope Sylvester II (in the church of Jerusalem in Rome) and of Henry IV of England (in the Jerusalem chamber).

That all a quarter of Snawdoun
Rycht till the erd thai tummyllyt doun
Syne towart Ingland went thar way.
Bot quhen the king Edward hard say
185   How Neill the Bruce held Kildromy
Agayne his sone sa stalwartly,
He gadryt gret chevalry
And towart Scotland went in hy,
And as in-till Northummyrland
190   He wes with his gret rout ridand
A sekness tuk him in the way
And put him to sa hard assay
That he mycht nocht ga na ryd.
Him worthit magre his abid
195   In-till ane hamillet tharby
A litill toun and unworthy,
With gret payne thidder thai him brocht.
He wes sa stad that he ne mocht
His aynd bot with gret paynys draw
200   Na spek bot giff it war weill law
The-quhether he bad thai suld him say
Quhat toun wes that that he in lay.
'Schyr,' thai said, 'Burch-in-the-sand
Men callis this toun in-till this land.'
205   'Call thai it Burch, als,' said he.
My hop is now fordone to me
For I wend never to thole the payne
Of deid till I throu mekill mayn
The burch of Jerusalem had tane,
210   My lyff wend I thar suld be gayne.
In burch I wyst weill I suld de
Bot I wes nother wys na sle
Till other burch kep to ta.
Now may I na wis forther ga.'
215   Thus pleynyeit he off his foly,
As he had mater sekyrly
Quhen he covyt certanté
Off that at nane may certan be,
The-quhether men said enclosit he had
220   A spyryt that him answer maid
Off thingis that he wald inquer.
Bot he fulyt foroutyn wer
That gaiff throuth till that creatur,

for evil spirits are of such a nature that they are envious of mankind, (226) for they know well and with certainty that those who live well here will achieve the throne [of grace] from which they were cast down because of their great pride. For that reason it will often happen that when evil spirits are forced to appear and to make answer by power of a conjuring-up, they are so false and wicked that they always give their answer with a double meaning, in order to deceive those who believe in them. (238) I will give an example here now of a war I heard about which occurred between France and the Flemings.

Count Ferrand's mother was a necromancer who raised Satan, asking him then what would be the outcome of the fighting between the French king and her son. He, as he was accustomed [to do] all the time, gave a deceitful answer, saying the following three lines: (249) *Rex ... caterva.* These were the words he spoke, in truth, which are to say in English: (254) 'The king will fall in the fighting, and will lack the honour of burial; thy Ferrand, my dear Minerva, will go to Paris, without doubt, followed by a great company of noble and worthy men.' This is the meaning of the saying that he made known to her in Latin. (262) He called her his 'Minerva' because Minerva was always wont to serve him while she was alive. Because she did this same service he called her his Minerva;

238–306. This long story, complete with familiar spirit, of the early thirteenth-century Count Ferrand of Flanders and Philip II of France comes from the Latin chronicle of Guillaume le Breton, and the Latin verse (249–51) is Barbour's composition from Guillaume's prose. Barbour also supplied the name Minerva, to rhyme with *caterva.* (*B1985*, 76–77)

For feyndys ar off sic natur
225 That thai to mankind has invy
For thai wate weill and witterly
That thai that weill ar liffand her
Sall wyn the sege quharoff thai wer
Tumblyt throuch thar mekill prid.
230 Quharthrou oft-tymys will betid
That quhen feyndys distrenyeit ar
For till aper and mak answar
Throu force of conjuracioun
That thai sa fals ar and feloun
235 That thai mak ay thar answering
Into doubill understanding
To dissaiff thaim that will thaim trow.
Insample will I set her now
Off a wer as I herd tell
240 Betwix Fraunce and the Flemyngis fell.
The erle Ferandis modyr was
Nygramansour, and Sathanas
Scho rasyt and him askyt syne
Quhat suld worth off the fechtyn
245 Betwix the Fraunce king and hyr sone,
And he, as all tyme he wes wone,
Into dissayt maid his answer
And said till hyr thir thre vers her,
   '*Rex ruet in bello tumilique carebit honore*
250 *Ferrandus comitissa tuus mea cara Minerva*
   Parisius veniet magna comitante caterva.'
This wes the spek he maid perfay
And is in Inglis toung to say,
   'The king sall fall in the fechting
255 And sall faile honour off erding,
And thi Ferand Mynerve my der
Sall rycht to Parys went but wer,
Folowand him gret cumpany
Off nobill men and off worthy.'
260 This is the sentence off this saw
That the Latyn gan hyr schaw.
He callyt hyr his Mynerve
For Mynerve ay wes wont to serve
Him, till scho leffyt, at his divis
265 And for scho maid the samyn service
His Mynerve hyr callyt he,

also he called her 'dear' by great cunning, to deceive her so
that she would the more readily take from his saying the sense
that was most to her liking. (272) His ambiguous saying so
deceived her that many came to death through her, because
she was pleased at his answer, quickly telling it to her son
and bidding him speed to the battle, as he would have victory
without fail. (278) He, who heard her words, hurried swiftly
to the fight; there he was defeated, put to shame, taken
[prisoner] and sent to Paris. But in the fighting, nonetheless,
the king by his chivalry was both knocked to the ground and
humiliated, although his men helped him pretty quickly. (286)
When Ferrand's mother heard how her son had fared in the
battle, and that he had been defeated thus, she swiftly raised
the evil spirit and asked why he had lied in the answer that
he had made her. And he said that all he had said was the
truth. (293) 'I said that the king would fall in the battle, and
he did just that, lacking burial as men can see. And I said
your son would go to Paris and he did just that; following
such a company that he never in his lifetime had such a
company under his leadership. Now you can see that I told
no lie.' (302) The woman was confused indeed, and dared
say no more to him. In that way, by ambiguity, that battle
came to such a conclusion that one side was deceived. (307)
It happened just like that in this case; he thought that he
would be buried in the burgh, [that is] at Jerusalem,

---

284. Humiliation. This corresponds to the promised 'lack honour' of
255.
298. Folowand a mengye. But the translation in 258 says 'folowand him
gret cumpany', i.e. puts him at its head. The Latin merely says *comitante*,
'accompanying'.

And als throu his sutelté
He callyt hyr der hyr till dissaiff
That scho the tyttar suld consaiff
270 Off his spek the undyrstanding
That mast plesyt till hyr liking.
This doubill spek sua hyr dissavit
That throu hyr feill the ded ressavit,
For scho wes off hyr answer blyth
275 And till hyr sone scho tald it swyth,
And bad him till the batell sped
For suld victory haiff but dred.
And he that herd hyr sermonuyng
Sped him in hy to the fechting
280 Quhar he discomfyt wes and schent
And takin and to Paris sent,
Bot in the fechting nocht-forthi
The king, throu his chevalry,
Wes laid at erd and lawit bath,
285 Bot his men helpyt him weill rath.
And quhen Ferandis moder herd
How hyr sone in the bataill ferd
And at he wes sua discomfyt,
Scho rasyt the ill spyryt als tyt
290 And askyt quhy he gabyt had
Off the answer that he hyr mad,
And he said he had said suth all.
'I said ye that the king suld fall
In the bataill, and say did he,
295 And failyeid erding, as men may se.
And I said that thi sone suld ga
To Paris, and he did rycht sua,
Folowand sic a mengye
That never in his lyff-tyme he
300 Had sic a mengye in leding.
Now seis thou I maid na gabbing.'
The wyff confusyt wes perfay
And durst no mar than till him say
Thusgat throu doubill understanding
305 That bargane come till sic ending
That the ta part dissavyt was.
Rycht sagat fell yt in this cas.
At Jerusalem trowit he
Gravyn in the burch to be,

but at Burgh by Sands he died in his very own land. And when he was near to death, the folk who had been at Kildrummy came with the prisoners that they had taken, and went later to the king. (316) To comfort him they told how [the prisoners] surrendered the castle to them, and how they were brought to his will, asking what they should do with them. Then he looked bitterly at them, and snarling, said, 'Hang and draw [them].' (323) It was very remarkable that in such words he, who was near to death, should answer in this way, without a hint of mercy. How could he safely call on Him who judges all things in truth to have mercy on the calling of one who, through his wickedness, had no mercy at this extremity? (332) His men did all his commands, and he died soon thereafter and then was brought to be buried; his son was then king after [him].

(336) Let us go to King Robert again, who lay at Rathlin with his company till winter had almost passed, taking his food from that island. James Douglas was fed up that they were lying idle for so long, and said to Sir Robert Boyd, 'The poor folk of this land are very heavily burdened by us lying here idle. (346) I hear it said that in Arran in a strong stone castle [there] are Englishmen who hold the lordship of the land with a firm hand. Let us go there and it could well be

---

314-15. They came with the prisoners and then went to the king. Neil Bruce, Alan Durward and Alexander Moray, knights, and a clerk were brought from Kildrummy to Berwick, tried before the Prince of Wales and executed on (or just after) 14 October, 1306. (*CDS*5.475; 213a) Presumably they had surrendered to the king's will, and could have been tried and executed at Kildrummy, but were brought south to discover the king's will. Edward I's role here is therefore correct. Barbour's 'syne' suggests the two stages of bringing south to Berwick and consulting the king at Lanercost.

340-42. Douglas and Boyd. For Boyd, who had joined the king even before the inauguration, see the note on 176, which suggests that he may have been in Kildrummy. Whether there or not, he presumably came to his lands in Ayrshire. We can safely reject Barbour's placing these two on Rathlin with Bruce. They are much more likely to have crossed to Arran from Ayrshire. Did Douglas push Boyd to rebel against Edward I yet again?

310   The-quhethyr at Burch-into-the-sand
    He swelt rycht in his awn land.
    And quhen he to the ded wes ner
    The folk that at Kildromy wer
    Come with presoneris that thai had tane,
315   And syne to the king ar gane
    And for to comfort him thai tald
    How thai the castell to thaim yauld
    And how thai till his will war brocht,
    To do off thame quhatever he thocht,
320   And askyt quhat men suld off thaim do.
    Than lukyt he angyrly thaim to
    And said grynnand, 'Hangis and drawys.'
    That wes wonder off sik sawis,
    That he that to the ded wes ner
325   Suld answer apon sic maner
    Foroutyn menyng and mercy.
    How mycht he traist on Hym to cry
    That suthfastly demys all thing
    To haiff mercy, for his criying,
330   Off him that throu his felony
    Into sic point had na mercy.
    His men his maundment has done
    And he deyt thatefter sone
    And syne wes brocht till berynes.
335   His sone syne king efter wes.

[Douglas and Boyd go from Rathlin to Arran]

    To the King Robert agayne ga we
    That in Rauchryne with his menye
    Lay till wynter ner wes gane
    And off that ile his mete has tane
340   James off Douglas wes angry
    That thai langar suld ydill ly
    And to Schyr Robert Boid said he,
    'The pure folk off thys countre
    Ar chargit apon gret maner
345   Off us that idill lyis her,
    And ik her say that in Arane
    Intill a styth castell off stane
    Ar Inglis men that with strang hand
    Haldys the lordschip off the land
350   Ga we thidder, and weill may fall

that we shall harrass them somehow.' Sir Robert said, 'I agree with that. Lying here any longer would not be right. (354) So let us go to Arran, for I know that country very well; also I know the castle. We will go there so secretly that they will have neither sight nor knowledge of our arrival. And we shall lie nearby in ambush where we can see their coming [and going]. In that way it can't happen that we [fail to] do damage to them in some way.'

(364) With that they got ready at once, took leave of the king, and then went forth on their way. They soon came to Kintyre, then rowed always down the coast till night had nearly fallen. (370) Then they went [across] to Arran, arriving there safely and drawing their galley into a glen, they then concealed it well enough. They hid their tackle, oars and rudder in exactly the same way, and journeyed right through the night so that before day had broken bright they were in ambush near the castle, armed in best manner. (380) Though they were wet, weary and hungry from long fasting, they meant to keep themselves all concealed until they could see a good opportunity.

(384) At that time Sir John Hastings with knights of great distinction, squires and yeomanry, in a pretty large company, was in the castle of Brodick. Often, when it pleased him, he went to hunt with his company,

---

384. Sir John Hastings of Abergavenny was a competitor in 1291–2, and had been Steward of Gascony in 1302–4. On 22 May, 1306 he was granted the earldom of Menteith and other lands of its earl; these would include Arran, and he is found in Scotland later in 1307.

388. Brodick castle. The castle lies about a third of a mile, half a kilometre, from Brodick bay, above the 100 foot contour. Although the castle is mostly of much later construction, the gateway mentioned here (431) can still be seen from outside and inside.

Anoy thaim in sum thing we sall.'
Schir Robert said, 'I grant thar-till,
Till her mar ly war litill skill.
Tharfor till Aran pas will we,
355   For I knaw rycht weill the countre
And the castell rycht sua knaw I
We sall cum thar sua prevely
That thai sall haiff na persavyng
Na yeit witting off our cummyng,
360   And we sall ner enbuschyt be
Quhar we thar outecome may se.
Sa sall it on na maner fall
Na scaith thaim on sum wis we sall.'
With that thai buskyt thaim on-ane
365   And at the king thar leiff has tane
And went thaim furth syne on thar way.
Into Kyntyr sone cummyn ar thai,
Syne rowyt alwayis by the land
Till that the nycht wes ner on hand,
370   Than till Arane thai went thar way
And saufly thar aryvyt thai,
And in a glen thar galay drewch
And syne it helyt weill ineuch.
Thar takyll ayris and thar ster
375   Thai hyde all on the samyn maner
And held thar way rycht in the nycht
Sua that or day wes dawyn lycht
Thai war enbuschyt the castell ner
Armyt apon thair best maner
380   And thoucht thai wate war and wery
And for lang fastyng all hungry
Thai thocht to hald thaim all prevé
Till that thai weill thar poynt mycht se.

[*Douglas plunders the provisions being brought to Brodick castle*]

Schir John the Hastingis at that tid
385   With knychtis off full mekill prid
And squyeris and yemanry,
And that a weill gret cumpany,
Wes in the castell off Brathwik
And oftsys quhen it wald him lik
390   He went huntyng with his menye

and so subdued the land that no-one dared refuse to do his will. (393) He was still in the castle when James Douglas was in ambush, as I have told [you]. (396) It happened by chance at that time that the underwarden had arrived, the day before in the evening, with victuals, provisions, clothes and arms in three boats, quite near the place where the folk I spoke about previously were lying secretly in ambush. (404) They soon saw thirty or more Englishmen leave the boats, laden with all sorts of things. Some carried wine, some arms, and the rest were all loaded up with different things; various others walked by them, as if they were the bosses, noncholantly. (412) Those who were in ambush saw them, and without fear or qualms, burst out of their ambush upon them, slaying all whom they could overcome. (416) The shouts rose hideously loud, for they, fearing they would die, roared and shouted like animals. [The Scots] killed them without mercy, so that there were almost forty [lying] dead in that place. (422) When those who were in the castle heard folk shouting and crying like that they came out to the fight, but when Douglas saw they were coming, he called his men back to him and went swiftly to meet them. (428)When [the men] of the castle saw him come on without fear, they fled without more resistence and [the Scots] followed them to the entrance, killing [some] of them as they went in. But they barred the entrance fast

---

405. Thirty or more. At 421 the number of dead is nearly forty. There may have been a misreading of roman numerals. This attack does not show up in the English records, but Brodick was a private castle, not a royal responsibility.

And sua the land abandounyt he
That durst nane warne to do his will.
He wes into the castell still
The tyme that James off Douglas
395   As Ik haiff tald enbuschit was.
Sa hapnyt that tyme throu chance
That with vittalis and purvyaunce
And with clething and with armyng
The day befor in the evynning
400   The undyr-wardane arivyt was
With thre batis weill ner the place
Quhar that the folk I spak off ar
Prevely enbuschyt war.
Syne fra tha batis saw thai ga
405   Off Inglismen thretty and ma
Chargit all with syndry thingis.
Sum bar wyne and sum armyngis,
The remanant all chargit wer
With thingis off syndry maner,
410   And other syndry yeid thaim by
As thai war maistrys ydilly.
Thai that enbuschyt war that saw
All foroutyn dreid or aw
Thar buschement on thaim thai brak
415   And slew all that thai mycht ourtak.
The cry rais hidwysly and hey
For thai that dredand war to dey
Rycht as bestis gan rar and cry.
Thai slew thaim foroutyn mercy.
420   Sua that into the samyne sted
Weill ner fourty thar war dede.
Quhen thai that in the castell war
Hard the folk sa cry and rar
Thai ischyt furth to the fechting,
425   Bot quhen the Douglas saw thar cummyng
His men till him he gan rely
And went till meit thaim hastily.
And quhen thai off the castell saw
Him cum on thaim foroutyn aw
430   Thai fled foroutyne mar debate
And thai thaim folowit to the yate
And slew of thaim as thai in past,
Bot thai thair yate barryt fast

so that they could no longer get at them. (435) For that reason
[the Scots] left them all there and turned to the sea again
where the men had been slain before. When those who were
in the boats saw them coming, and learned how they had
defeated their company, they put to sea in a hurry, rowing
fast with all their might. (443) But the wind was against them,
causing the surf to rise so high that they couldn't make way
[on] the sea at all and dared not come to land, but held
themselves bobbing about there for so long that two out of
three boats sank. When Douglas saw that's how things were,
he took the arms and clothing, victuals, wine and other things
that they found there, and [they] went their way, overjoyed
and jubilant at their booty.

(454) In this way James Douglas and his company, by God's
grace, were well helped with arms, with victuals and also with
clothing; then they went their way to a strong place and always
behaved very manfully, till on the tenth day, the king with all
that were in his following arrived in that country, with thirty
three small galleys. (464) The king arrived in Arran and then
went inland taking lodging in a village; he asked then particu-
larly if anyone had news of any strangers in that land. (470)
'Yes,' said a woman, 'Sir, indeed, I can tell you about strangers
who came into this country and a short while ago, by their
boldness discomfitted our warden,

---

463. Thirty-three small galleys. Even if the number be exaggerated, the
  sudden appearance of many galleys confirms that the king had received
  help on the western seaboard of Scotland.

464. The king arrived in Arran. I doubt this itinerary and suggest that
  as Guisborough says the king returned directly through Kintyre to
  Carrick. His meeting with Douglas on Arran is Barbour's invention.
  The English court at Lanercost heard of Bruce's return to the Clyde
  estuary on 27 January, 1307, sending out a flurry of letters 27–31 January
  in which he is 'lurking in the islands in the sea on the coast of Scotland',
  and ships were ordered so that 'he should not return to his boats
  (*batellos*)'. He was still thought to be there up to mid-February, Valence
  at Ayr gathering fifteen ships to be 'in the parts of the island next to
  Ayr'[?Ailsa Craig]. All of which suggests that Bruce was in Kintyre, or
  Arran if Barbour is correct, from about 25 January. (*CDS5, 512, 215a;
  CDS2, 1888*) For his departure see 5.14.

467–517. This account of Bruce's meeting with Douglas and Boyd,
  especially 508–12, is more like a rendezvous of two groups long parted,
  as suggested above on 340–42, than a meeting after ten days' separation.

That thai mycht do at thame na mar.
435 Tharfor thai left thaim ilkane thar
And turnyt to the se agayne
Quhar that the men war forouth slayn.
And quhen thai that war in the batis
Saw thar cummyng and wyst howgatis
440 Thai had discumfyt thar menye
In hy thai put thaim to the se
And rowyt fast with all thar mayne,
Bot the wynd wes thaim agayne
That sua hey gert the land-bryst rys
445 That thai moucht weld the se na wis.
Then thai durst nocht cum to the land,
Bot held thaim thar sa lang hobland
That off the thre batis drownyt twa
And quhen the Douglas saw it wes sua
450 He tuk armyng and cleything
Vittalis wyne and other thing
That thai fand thar and held thar way
Rycht glaid and joyfull off thar pray.

[*The king comes to Arran and is joined by Douglas and Boyd*]

Quhen this James off Douglas
455 And his menye throu Goddis grace
War relevyt with armyng
And with vittaill and clething
Syne till a strenth thai held thar way
And thaim full manly governyt ay
460 Till on the tend day that the king
With all that war in his leding
Aryvyt into that countre
With thretty small galayis and thre.
The king aryvyt in Arane
465 And syne to the land is gane
And in a toune tuk his herbery,
And speryt syne specially
Gyff ony man couth tell tithand
Off ony strang man in that land.
470 'Yhis,' said a woman, 'Schyr perfay
Off strang men I kan you say
That ar cummyn in this countre,
And schort quhile syne throu thar bounte
Thai haff discomfyt our wardane

killing many of his men. All their company are staying in a strong place near here.' (478) 'Lady,' said the king, 'if you would guide me to that place where their refuge is, I will reward you truly for they are all of my following; I would be truly pleased to see them, and I know that they would equally [be glad to see] me.' (484) 'Yes,' she said, 'Sir I will gladly go with you and your company until I show you their refuge.' 'Good enough, my fair sister, now lead the way,' said the king. (489) Then they went forth without delay, following her as she led them, till eventually she showed a place to the king, in a wooded glen and said, 'Sir, I saw the men that you were asking for make camp here. This, I'm sure, is their refuge.' (496) The king then quickly blew his horn, and had the men who were with him keep still and hidden; then he blew his horn again. James Douglas heard him blow, and he soon knew the sound; he said, 'In truth, yon is the king, I've known his call for a long time.' (504) At that [the king] blew a third time, and then Sir Robert Boyd recognised it and said, 'Yon is the king without a doubt, let's go more speedily to him.' Then they went quickly to the king, and saluted him courteously; the king, who was delighted at their meeting[-up], welcomed them cheerfully and kissed them, then asked how they had fared in their expedition. They told him everything truthfully, then praised God for their meeting[-up]. Then they went with the king to his lodging, thankful and glad.

475 And mony off his men has slane,
     Intill a stalwart place her-by
     Reparis all thar cumpany.'
     'Dame,' said the king, 'wald thou me wis
     To that place quhar thar repair is
480 I sall reward the but lesing,
     For thai ar all off my dwelling
     And I rycht blythly wald thaim se
     And sua trow I that thai wald me.'
     'Yhis,' said scho, 'Schir I will blythly
485 Ga with you and your cumpany
     Till that I schaw you thar repair.'
     'That is ineuch my sister fayr,
     Now ga we forth-wart,' said the king.
     Than went thai furth but mar letting
490 Folowand hyr as scho thaim led
     Till at the last scho schawyt a sted
     To the king in a wode glen
     And said, 'Schir, her saw I the men
     That yhe sper after mak logyng.
495 Her I trow be thar reparyng.'
     The king then blew his horn in hy
     And gert the men that wer him by
     Hald thaim still and all preve
     And syne agayn his horn blew he.
500 James off Douglas herd him blaw
     And he the blast alsone gan knaw
     And said, 'Sothly yon is the king,
     I knaw lang quhill syne his blawyng.'
     The thrid tym thar-with-all he blew
505 And then Schir Robert Boid it knew
     And said, 'Yone is the king but dreid
     Ga we furth till him better speid.'
     Than went thai till the king in hy
     And him inclynyt curtasly,
510 And blythly welcummyt thaim the kimg
     And wes joyfull of thar meting
     And kissit thaim and speryt syne
     How thai had farne in thar outyne,
     And thai him tauld all but lesing.
515 Syne lovyt thai God off thar meting,
     Syne with the king till his herbery
     Went bath joyfull and joly.

(518) On the next day the king said to his close advisers, 'You know full well, and you can see, how we are banished from our country by the might of the English, and how by their superiority they keep what should of right be ours; they would also destroy us all without mercy if they could. (527) But God forbade that it should turn out for us as they threaten, for then there would be no remedy [whereas] mankind bids us that we busy ourselves with taking revenge. For you can see that we have three things admonishing us to be worthy, wise and bold, and to harrass them with [all] our strength. (536) One is the safety of our lives, which couldn't be saved in any way if they had us at their mercy. The second that gives us encouragement is that they keep our possessions by force against reason. The third is the joy that awaits us if it happens, as it well may, that we have victory and strength to overcome their wickedness. (546) Therefore, let us lift up our hearts so that no trouble discourages us, and act always towards that conclusion which has honour and praise too. Therefore, lords, if you think among you that it is advisable, I will send a man to Carrick, to spy [out] and ask how the kingdom is governed, and [who is] friend or foe. (555) And if he sees that we could take land, he could make a fire on Turnbery Head on a certain day, and [so] give us a message that we could arrive there safely.

518. The king's return to the mainland is described quite differently at the end of Guisborough's chronicle. The passage is quoted and discussed under 5.89.

556. Turnberry Snook. This is either Turnberry Point where the lighthouse stands beside the few ruins of the castle, or a point 300 metres to the south. In either case the suggestion shows that Bruce did not know the castle was occupied by an English garrison, making it impossible for Cuthbert to light a beacon there.

[*The king sends a man to Carrick to see if he might land there*]

The king apon the tother day
Gan till his preve menye say,
520   'Ye knaw all weill and ye may se
How we are out off our cuntre
Banyst throu Inglismennys mycht
And that that suld be ouris of rycht
Throu thar maistrys thai occupy,
525   And wald alsua foroutyne mercy
Giff thai haid mycht destroy us all.
Bot God forbeid it suld sa fall
Till us as thai mak manassyng
For than war thar na recoveryng,
530   And mankind biddis us that we
To procur vengeance besy be.
For ye may se we haiff thre thingis
That makis us oft monestingis
For to be worthi wis and wycht
535   And till anoy thaim at our mycht.
Ane is our lyffis saufté
That on na wys suld sauft be
Gyff thai had us at thar liking
The tother that makys us eggyng
540   Is that thai our possessioune
Haldis strenthly agayn resoun.
The thrid is the joy that we abid
Giff that it happyn as weill may tid
That we wyn victour and maistry,
545   Till ourcum thar felony.
Therfor we suld our hartis rais
Sua that na myscheyff us abais
And schaip us alwayis to that ending
That beris in it mensk and loving.
550   And tharfor lordingis gyff ye se
Amang you giff that it speidfull be
I will send a man in Carrik
To spy and sper our kynrik
How it is led and freynd and fa.
555   And giff he seis we land may ta
On Turnberys snuke he may
Mak a fyr on a certane day
And mak takynnyng till us that we
May thar aryve in saufte.

And if he sees that we could not [do] so, take care that he in no way makes the fire. In that way we could have information, whether to cross or stay [here].' (564) They all agreed with this suggestion, and then the king immediately called to him one who was close, and [born] in his country, Carrick; he charged him in exactly the way you heard me describe previously, and set him a certain day to make the fire if he saw that [things] went such that it was possible for them to maintain themselves in that country. (574) And he, who was truly anxious to carry out his lord's desire, like a worthy and loyal man who could keep secrest well concealed, said he was ready to carry out his commands in all respects; he said he would do so wisely, so that there could be no reproaches afterwards. Then he took his leave from the king and went forth on his way.

(584) Now the messenger goes on his way – I heard that he was called Cuthbert – [and] soon arrived in Carrick, passing through all the country. But in truth he found few there who had a good [word] to say of his master, (590) for many of them dared not [do so] out of fear, and some others were deadly enemies of the noble king, who later regretted their opposition. (594) High and low, the land was then occupied wholly by the English, who scorned, above all else, Robert the Bruce, the doughty king. Carrick was then given altogether to Sir Henry, the lord Percy,

---

585. Cuthbert. A Cuthbert of Carrick was among the esquires or valets taken prisoner at Methven and executed at Newcastle on 4 August, 1306. The name is an unusual one in the context of Carrick, and one Cuthbert may have been son of the other. (*CDS2, 1811*)

560 And giff he seis we may nocht sua,
Luk on na wys the fyr he ma.
Sua may we thar-throu haiff wittring
Off our passage or our dwelling.'
To this spek all assentyt ar,
565 And than the king withoutyn mar
Callyt ane that wes till him prevé
And off Carrik his countré,
And chargyt him in les and mar
As ye hard me divis it ar
570 And set him certane day to mai
The fyr giff he saw it war sua
That thai had possibilité
To maynteyme wer in that cuntré.
And he that wes rycht weill in will
575 His lordis yharnyng to fullfill
As he that worthy wes and leile
And couth secreis rycht weill conseil
Sad he wes boune intill all thing
For to fulfill his commaunding,
580 And said he suld do sa wisely
That na repruff suld efter ly
Syne at the king his leiff has tane
And furth apon his way is gane.

[*Cuthbert the spy discovers that Percy, in Turnberry castle,
controls Carrick*]

Now gais the messynger his way
585 That hat Cuthbert as I herd say.
In Carrik sone aryvyt he
And passyt throu all the countre,
Bot he fand few tharin perfay
That gud wald off his maister say,
590 For fele off thaim durst nocht for dreid,
And other sum rycht into deid
War fayis to the nobill king,
That rewyt syne thar barganyng.
Baith hey and law the land wes then
595 All occupyit with Inglismen
That dispytyt atour all thing
Robert the Bruce the douchty king.
Carrik wes giffyn then halyly
To Schir Henry the lord Persy

who was in Turnberry castle at that time, with nearly three hundred men; he so dominated all the land that everyone was obedient to him. (604) This Cuthbert saw their wickedness, and saw the people, rich and poor, become so wholly [pro-] English that he dared not disclose himself to anybody. He meant to leave the fire unmade then go to his master without delay and tell him all their condition which was so grievously distressing.

(612) When the day came that the king, staying on Arran, had fixed with his messenger, as I explained to you long ago, looked hard for the fire, and as soon as noon was past, he was sure that he saw a fire burning very brightly by Turnbery; he showed it to his followers. (621) Each man was sure that he saw it. Then with a cheerful spirit the men cried, 'Good king, hurry at once so that we arrive early in the evening without being seen.' 'I agree,' he said, 'now get ready. May God help us in our journey!' (628) Then in a short time men could see them launch all their galleys on the sea, taking to sea both oars and rudder, and other things that were necessary. (632) As the king was going up and down on the sand, waiting for his following to be ready, his hostess came right to him there. And when she had greeted him, she spoke confidentially to him, saying, 'Pay attention to what I have to say;

---

635. His hostess. This is presumably the 'woman' in 470 who took Bruce to Douglas though Barbour makes no such an identification. Nonetheless the hostess's speech (638–67) introduces a sequence which is duplicated later. It has long been noted that a woman giving her two sons to the king occurs here and again at 7.238–68, where a housewife tells a stranger that he is welcome for the sake of Bruce, not knowing that he is Bruce; she (in effect now his hostess) gives him her two sons. But there is more to the coincidence than this, for, if the story of Cuthbert and the crossing is abstracted, in both cases the episode of the woman is followed by a night attack by Bruce upon that part – a third – of an English army, which lay in a 'toun', with breaking down of doors and the flight of the surprised third to join the main force (5.75–114 and 7.309–54). It seems that, using one version of the sequence, Barbour decided to place this attack at Turnberry castle; the woman therefore had to come earlier and was placed by Barbour on Arran.

600	That in Turnberyis castell then
	Was with weill ner three hunder men,
	And dauntyt sagat all the land
	That all wes till him obeysand.
	This Cuthbert saw thar felony,
605	And saw the folk sa halely
	Be worthyn Inglis baith rich and pur
	That he to nane durst him discur,
	But thocht to leve the fyr unmaid,
	Syne till his maister went but baid
610	And all thar convyne till him tell,
	That wes sa angry and sa fell.

[The king thinks he sees a fire; he prepares to cross to Carrick; his hostess predicts his ultimate success, and gives him her two sons]

	The king that intill Arane lay
	Quhen that cummyn wes the day
	That he set till his messinger
615	As Ik divisit you lang er
	Eftyr the fyr he lokyt fast
	And als sone as the none wes past
	Him thocht weill he saw a fyr
	Be Turnbery byrnand weill schyr,
620	And till his menye it gan schaw.
	Ilk man thocht weill that he it saw,
	Then with blyth hart the folk gan cry,
	'Gud king, speid you deliverly
	Sua that we sone in the evynnyng
625	Aryve foroutyn persayving.'
	'I grant,' said he. 'Now mak you yar,
	God furthyr us intill our far.'
	Then in schort time men mycht thaim se
	Schute all thar galayis to the se
630	And ber to se baith ayr and ster
	And other thingis that myster wer,
	And as the king apon the sand
	Wes gangand up and doun, bidand
	Till that his menye redy war,
635	His ost come rycht till him thar,
	And quhen that scho him halyst had
	A preve spek till him scho made
	And said, 'Takis gud kep till my saw,

for before you leave I shall tell you a great part of your fortune. (641) Before anything else, I shall give you a special knowledge of the conclusion that your plans will reach. For in this land there is truly no-one who knows what is to come as well as I [do]. You are setting out now on your journey to avenge the harm and injury that Englishmen have done to you; but you do not know what fortune you must bear in your war-making. (651) Know well that, for a certainty, after you reach land now, none so mighty, nor so strong in combat will cause you to leave your country until all is given up to you. (656) In a short time you will be king, having the land at your disposal, overcoming all your enemies, but you will suffer many adversities before you bring your plans to a conclusion, though you will overcome them all. So that you will be assured of this, I shall send my two sons with you to share in your troubles, for I know well that they will not fail to be rewarded properly [and] well, when you are raised to the height of your [power].' (668) The king who had listened to her whole speech, thanked her a great deal, for she comforted him somewhat, although he didn't altogether trust her word. (672) For he wondered greatly how she could know this for sure, as it was wonderful, *perfay*, how any man's perception can know for sure things that are to come, all or part, unless he was inspired by Him who, in his foreknowledge, sees everything to eternity,

---

656. Ye sall be king. This line and 774 raise another problem, for Robert was already king. The story of the hostess and her sons might, in its original version, have belonged to the period between Comyn's murder and the king's inauguration, and become attached later to the successful attack on the force in the toun, which must surely be post-Methven.

For or ye pas I sall you schaw
640   Off your fortoun a gret party,
Bot our all specially
A wyttring her I sall you ma
Quhat end that your purpos sall ta,
For in this land is nane trewly
645   Wate thingis to cum sa weill as I.
Ye pas now furth on your viage
To venge the harme and the outrag
That Inglismen has to you done,
Bot ye wat nocht quhat-kyne forton
650   Ye mon drey in your werraying.
Bot wyt ye weill withoutyn lesing
That fra ye now haiff takyn land
Nane sa mychty na sa strenththi of hand
Sal ger you pas out off your countré
655   Till all to you abandounyt be.
Within schort tyme ye sall be king
And haiff the land at your liking
And ourcum your fayis all,
Bot fele anoyis thole ye sall
660   Or that your purpos end haiff tane,
Bot ye sall thaim ourdryve ilkane.
And that ye trowis this sekyrly
My twa sonnys with you sall I
Send to tak part of your travaill,
665   For I wate weill thai sall nocht faill
To be rewardyt weill at rycht
Quhen ye are heyit to your mycht.'

[*A discourse on prophecy*]

The king that herd all hyr carping
Thankit hyr in mekill thing,
670   For scho confort him sumdeill,
The-quhethir he trowyt nocht full weill
Hyr spek, for he had gret ferly
How scho suld wyt it sekyrly,
As it wes wounderfull perfay
675   How ony mannys science may
Knaw thingis that ar to cum
Determinabilly, all or sum,
Bot giff that he inspyrit war
Off Him that all thing evermar

as if it was always in the present. (682) David was [so inspired],
and Jeremiah, Samuel, Joel and Isaiah, [men] who, by His
holy grace [fore]told many things that happened later. But
those prophets are sown so thinly that none is now known on
the earth. (688) But many folk are so curious, so anxious to
know things, that they either by their great knowledge or else
by their devilry, make an attempt to get knowledge of things
to come in the [following] two ways. (694) One of them is
astrology, by which clerks who are skilled can know the
conjunction of the planets and whether their course sets them
in a favourable or an unfavourable mansion; (699) also how
the complete disposition of the heavens can have an effect on
things down here, on parts of heaven, or on parts of earth;
[it] doesn't work everywhere in the same way, but in some
places more, in others less, according as their rays are emitted
evenly or awry. (707) But I think that it would be a great
achievement for any astrologer to say, 'this will happen at this
place on this day.' For though a man studies astrology for his
whole life, so that he cracks his head on the stars, the wise
man says that he couldn't make three firm prognostications
in his lifetime, but he would always [be in] doubt until he
saw how [the matter] was concluded. (717) So there is no
certain[ty in] forecasting. Or if those men who want to study
the craft of astrology, know all men's birth[-dates] and also
the constellation that gives them innate

---

706. Evenly or awry: directly or at an angle? I am no master of astrology;
   I take it that the rays are those of heaven.
713. The wise man, Solomon in Ecclesiastes (8.17), a book attributed to
   him.

680	Seys in his presciens	
	As it war ay in presens,	680*
	As was David and Jeremy	681
	Samuell, Joell and Ysai,	
	That throu His haly grace gan tell	
685	Fele thingis that efter fell,	684
	Bot the prophetis sa thyn ar sawyn	
	That nane in erd now is knawin.	
	Bot fele folk ar sa curyous	
	And to wyt thingis covatous	
690	That thai, throu thar gret clergy	689
	Or ellys throu thar devilry,	
	On thir twa maneris makis fanding	
	Off thingis to cum to haiff knawing.	
	Ane of thaim is astrologi,	
695	Quhar-throu clerkys that ar witty	694
	May knaw conjunctiones of planetis,	
	And quhethir that thar cours thaim settis	
	In soft segis or in angry,	
	And off the hevyn all halyly	
700	How that the dispositioun	699
	Suld apon thingis wyrk her doun	
	On regiones or on climatis,	
	That wyrkys nocht ay-quhar agatis	
	Bot sumquhar les and sumquhar mar	
705	Eftyr as thar bemys strekyt ar	704
	Othir all evyn or on wry.	
	Bot me think it war gud maistri	
	Till ony astrolog to say	
	'This sall fall her and on this day.'	
710	For thoucht a man his lyff haly	709
	Studyit sua in astrology	
	That on sternys his hewid he brak,	
	The wys man sayis he suld nocht mak	
	All his lyff certane dayis thre,	
715	And yeit suld he ay doute quhill he	714
	Saw how that it come till ending.	
	Than is that na certane demyng.	
	Or gyff thai men that will study	
	In the craft off astrology	
720	Knaw all mennys nacioun	719
	And knew the constellacioun	
	That kyndlik maneris gyfis thaim till	

inclinations to bring about good or ill, so that through skill [and] learning or through skill in astrology they could tell whatever danger appears to those who have innate inclinations, I believe that they would fail to tell the things that could happen to them. (730) For whether a man is inclined to virtue or to vice, he can restrain his inclination, either by nurture or by discretion, and turn his [inclination] completely to the opposite. (735) Men have seen it happen many times that men innately given to evil, by their great intelligence have driven away their evil and become of great good fame, despite the constellation. (740) [Thus] Aristotle, if, as men read, he had followed his innate actions, would have been false and greedy, but his intelligence made him virtuous. And since in this kind of way men can react against that course which is the main cause of [the astrologers'] judgment, I think their prognosis is not at all a certainty. (748) Necromancy is the second thing that teaches men by strong spells and exorcisms to cause spirits to appear to them in various ways, and to give various answers. Once the Pythoness did [that], for, when Saul had been defeated by the might of the Philistines, [she] quickly raised the spirit of Samuel by her great skill, or in his place the evil spirit, which gave a very prompt answer to her. (761) But by herself she knew nothing. Man is always in fear of things that he has heard tell of, and especially of things to come, until he has the certainty of the outcome.

740. Aristotle confesses in the *Roman d'Alixandre* that his innately vicious nature had been modified by the study of virtue.

745. That course, presumably of the stars and planets.

754. The Pythoness. Refers to the witch of Endor, I Samuel, 28.

For till inclyne to gud or ill,
How that thai throu science of clergi
725 Or throu slycht off astrology 724
Couth tell quhatkyn perell apperis
To thaim that haldys kyndlik maneris,
I trow that thai suld faile to say
The thingis that thaim happyn may.
730 For quhethir-sa men inclynyt be 729
To vertu or to mavyté,
He may rycht weill refreynye his will
Othir throu nurtur or thru skill
And to the contrar turne him all.
735 And men has mony tyme sene fall 734
That men kyndly till ivill gevyn
Throu thar gret wit away has drevyn
Thar ill and worthin off gret renoun
Magré the constellacioun,
740 As Arestotill, giff as men redis 739
He had folowyt his kyndly dedis,
He had bene fals and covatous
Bot his wyt maid him vertuous.
And sen men may on this kyn wys
745 Wyrk agayne that cours that is 744
Principaill caus off thar demyng
Me think thar dome na certane thing.
Nygromancy the tother is
That kennys men on syndry wys
750 Throu stalwart conjuracionys 749
And throu exorcizacionys
To ger spyritis to thaim apper
And giff answeris on ser maner,
As quhilum did the Phitones
755 That quhen Saul abaysyt wes 754
Off the Felystynys mycht,
Raysyt throu hyr mekill slycht
Samuelis spyrite als tite,
Or in his sted the ivill spyrite
760 That gaiff rycht graith answer hyr to, 759
Bot off hyr selff rycht nocht wyst scho.
And man is into dreding ay
Off thingis that he has herd say,
Namly off thingis to cum, quhill he
765 Knaw off the end the certante. 764

And since they are in such doubt without the certainty of knowing, I think that he who says he knows things to come, is telling great lies. (770) But whether she who told the king how his plans would come to a conclusion, had doubts or absolute certainty, it all happened afterwards as she had said, for he was later king and of very great reputation.

And sen thai ar in sic wenyng
Foroutyne certante off witting,
Me think quha sayis he knawis thingis
To cum he makys gret gabingis.
770 Bot quhether scho that tauld the king 769
How his purpos suld tak ending
Wenyt or wist it witterly,
It fell efter halyly
As scho said, for syne king wes he
775 And off full mekill renommé 774

This was in spring when winter time, with its long and dreadful storms was at an end, and tiny birds like the thrush and the nightingale began to sing right merrily, making sweet notes in their songs, various tunes, music pleasing to the ears. (9) The trees began to sprout buds and bright blooms too, to recover the covering of their heads which wicked winter had reft [them of], and all the grasses began to blossom. (14) At that time the noble king, with his fleet and a small company – I believe they may well have been three hundred – went to sea from Arran a little before nightfall. (19) They rowed hard, with all their might, until night fell upon them, getting very dark indeed, so that they did not know where they were, for they had neither needle nor stone, but rowed always in one [direction], aiming always towards the fire which they saw burning strong and bright. (27) It was only chance which guided them, and they so exerted themselves for a short time that they arrived at the fire and went to land without further delay. (31) Cuthbert, who saw the fire, was filled with anger and rage, because he dared not get rid of it; also he was always fearful that his lord would put to sea. For that reason he awaited their coming, and met them on their arrival. (38) He was rapidly brought to the king who asked him how he had got on.

1–13. The conventional poetic account of spring, used, as often in romances, to mark an abrupt change of action. There is a very similar passage with the same purpose at 16.63.

14. At that time. Bruce crossed to the mainland about 10 February, because on 12 February at Lanercost, orders were issued for a strike force of 25 knights with esquires to set out against him from Carlisle. (*CDS5*, 220b; *CDS2*, *1897*, *1923*)

23. They had neither lodestone nor magnetised needle.

BOOK 5

[The king goes to Carrick; he upbraids Cuthbert]

     Thys wes in ver quhen wynter tid
     With his blastis hidwys to bid
     Was ourdryvyn and byrdis smale
     As turturis and the nychtyngale
5   Begouth rycht sariely to syng
     And for to mak in thar singyng
     Swete notis and sounys ser
     And melodys plesand to her
     And the treis begouth to ma
10   Burgeans and brycht blomys alsua
     To wyn the helynd of thar hevid
     That wykkyt wynter had thaim revid,
     And all gressys beguth to spryng.
     Into that tyme the nobill king
15   With his flote and a few mengye
     Thre hunder I trow thai mycht be,
     Is to the se oute off Arane
     A litill forouth evyn gane.
     Thai rowit fast with all thar mycht
20   Till that apon thaim fell the nycht
     That woux myrk apon gret maner
     Sua that thai wyst nocht quhar thai wer
     For thai na nedill had na stane,
     Bot rowyt alwayis intill ane
25   Sterand all tyme apon the fyr
     That thai saw brynnand lycht and schyr.
     It wes bot aventur thaim led
     And thai in schort tyme sa thaim sped
     That at the fyr aryvyt thai
30   And went to land but mair delay.
     And Cuthbert that has sene the fyr
     Was full of angyr and off ire,
     For he durst nocht do it away
     And wes alsua doutand ay
35   That his lord suld pas to se.
     Tharfor thar cummyng waytit he
     And met thaim at thar aryving.
     He wes wele sone brocht to the kimg
     That speryt at him how he had done,

[Cuthbert] with a heavy heart soon told him how he had
found that no-one wished [him] well, but that all he en-
countered were [the king's] enemies; and that the lord Percy
with a company of almost three hundred was in the castle by
there, filled with hatred and pride. (47) But more than two-
thirds of his force was lodged in the village outside [the castle],
'and, Sir King, they detest you more than any man can detest
anything.' The the king, very angry indeed, said, 'Traitor!
then why did you make the fire?' (53) 'Ah, sir,' said he, 'as
God sees me, that fire was never made for me, nor did I know
[about it] before the night; but as soon as I knew of it I
realised that you and all your following would put to sea at
once. So I came to meet you here, to warn of the dangers
that could lie ahead.'

---

43. Henry Percy had been very active in Scotland for Edward I since
1296. He had been given the earldom of Buchan about 1298, and
Ingram Umfraville's share of Ingram Balliol's lands in 1299. He would
lose these in 1304–5, and was given the earldom of Carrick and the
castles and manors thereof 'of our enemy and rebel Robert Bruce which
he held in Carrick on the day on which he seditiously killed John Comyn
and rose against us hostilely'. The date is not recorded, but Annandale
was given to the earl of Hereford on 10 April, 1306, the earldoms of
Menteith and Lennox to Hastings and John Menteith on 22 May and
1 June. The grant of Carrick probably belongs to April; Percy is never
called earl of Buchan or of Carrick, but the other recipients of Scottish
earldoms are similarly always untitled. Having been appointed royal
lieutenant in the north-western English and south-western Scottish
'counties' (5 April, 1306), he commanded the forces which took Loch
Doon and Dunaverty castles in August–October 1306. He could have
returned to Ayrshire no earlier than the end of September 1306, went
to Carlisle in November 1306, was at or near Ayr on 11 February and
at Dumfries on 17 May, 1307. There is no English record evidence
about Turnberry castle about this time, but Barbour is surely right in
placing Percy there in what would be February 1307. (*Percy Chartulary*,
452–53; *CDS2, 1895–96, 1930; CDS3, 52*)

89. The encounter at Turnberry occurs in (a) Guisborough and (b)
Fordun:
    (a) About St Michael's feast [29 September] the new king returned
    from the islands of Scotland, to which he had fled with many Irish
    and Scots, and stayed in Kintyre sending some of his men to Carrick
    and they levied there his rents for Martinmas [11 November]. Hearing
    this the lord Henry de Percy descended there and the new king,
    coming by surprise, attacked Henry by night, killed a few of his
    following, took his chargers and silver plate and besieged him in the
    castle of the same place until ... the king of England freed him.
    (b) [Bruce returned from the Isles] by a roundabout way to the
    earldom of Carrick. As soon as he had reached that place, he sought

40 And he with sar hart tauld him sone
  How that he fand nane weill luffand
  Bot all war fayis that he fand,
  And that the lord the Persy
  With ner thre hunder in cumpany
45 Was in the castell thar besid
  Fullfillyt of dispyt and prid
  Bot ma than twa partis off his rowt
  War herberyt in the toune without,
  'And dyspytyt you mar, schyr king,
50 Than men may dispyt ony thing.'
  Than said the king in full gret ire,
  'Tratour, quhy maid thou than the fyr?'
  'A schyr,' said he, 'Sa God me se
  The fyr wes nevyr maid for me,
55 Na or the nycht I wyst it nocht,
  Bot fra I wyst it weill I thocht
  That ye and haly your menye
  On hy suld put you to the se,
  For-thi I come to mete you her
60 To tell perellys that may aper.'

---

out one of his castles, slew the inmates thereof, destroyed the castle and shared the arms and other spoils among his men ... (*G*, 370; *F1*, 343; *F2*, 335)

The date in Guisborough must be a mistake, Michael for Matthias, whose feast is on 24 February, Bruce thus collecting rents in arrears, not (improbably) in advance. The castle must be Turnberry and the sources disagree over whether Bruce took it; Guisborough is certainly wrong in telling of a relief by the English king, but Barbour does describe a relief of Percy, cowering in Turnberry, by men of Northumberland (185–216). I suggest that the accounts tell different parts of the truth: Bruce came to Carrick; Percy, sent against him by King Edward, was surprised by Bruce, who plundered his train; Percy withdrew to Turnberry, pursued by Bruce, sent for help and was evacuated by a relieving force; Bruce slighted Turnberry to make it untenable. The date seems to be the spring of 1306.

89–122. This account of the attack on two-thirds (47) of Percy's force, billetted in a village, is replicated at 7.327 51, and properly belongs to this later period, as the name of the escapee Macdowall (104) shows. He is entirely out of place in Percy's force. Barbour or his source has filled out what little he was told of the attack on Percy, including the booty taken (117 18), by borrowing from a different surprise attack.

(61) The king was annoyed by what he said, and at once asked his close advisors what they thought was the best thing to do. Sir Edward, his brother, who was so bold, [was] the first to answer, saying, 'I tell you for sure, there are no possible dangers that could drive me back on to the sea. I'll take my chances here, for good or ill.' (71) 'Brother,' said [the king], 'since you are determined, it is good that we take together trouble or a quiet life, pain or pleasure, whatever God will ordain. (75) And since men say that the Percy will occupy my heritage, and his force which detests us so much lies so near us, let's take revenge for some of that hatred. We could have that done very quickly, for they lie confidently, without [any] fear of us or of our coming here. (83) And even if we killed them all when sleeping, no man would reproach us for it. For a warrior should not bother whether he can overcome his enemy by might or by guile, so long as good faith is always maintained.' (89) When this had been said they went [on] their way, and soon came to the village, so secretly, without making a noise, that no-one noticed their arrival. They spread through the village quickly, broke down doors sturdily, and killed all whom they could overcome; (96) they, being defenceless, shouted and cried very pitifully, [but] they killed them mercilessly, like [men] who were determined to avenge the cruelty and ill which [the defenders] and their [men] had done to them.

[*The king decides to stay to attack Percy's men in a village by Turnberry*]

The king wes off his spek angry
And askyt his pryve men in hy
Quhat at thaim thocht wes best to do.
Schyr Edward fryst answert tharto
65 His brodyr that wes sua hardy,
And said, 'I say you sekyrly
Thar sall na perell that may be
Dryve me eftsonys to the se.
Myne aventur her tak will I
70 Quhethir it be esfull or angry.'
'Brother,' he said, 'sen thou will sua
It is gud that we samyn ta
Dissese or ese or payne or play
Eftyr as God will us purvay.
75 And sen men sayis that the Persy
Myn heritage will occupy,
And his menye sa ner us lyis
That us dispytis mony wys,
Ga we and venge sum off the dispyte,
80 And that may we haiff done als tite
For thai ly traistly but dreding
Off us or off our her-cummyng,
And thocht we slepand slew thaim all
Repruff tharoff na man sall
85 For werrayour na fors suld ma
Quhether he mycht ourcum his fa
Throu strenth or throu sutelté,
Bot that gud faith ay haldyn be.'
Quhen this wes said thai went thar way,
90 And to the toune sone cummyn ar thai
Sa prevely but noyis making
That nane persavyt thar cummyng.
Thai skalyt throu the toun in hy
And brak up duris sturdely
95 And slew all that thai mycht ourtak,
And thai that na defence mocht mak
Full petously gan rar and cry,
And thai slew thaim dispitously
As thai that war in full gud will
100 To venge the angyr and the ill
That thai and thairis had thaim wrocht.

(102) They sought them out with such grim determination that they killed every one of them, apart from Macdowall alone, who escaped by great guile, and because of the darkness of the night. (107) In the castle the lord Percy heard clearly the noise and shouts, as did the men who were inside, and, pretty frightened, put on their gear. But none of them was so bold that he would go out to the noise. They stayed that night frightened like that, till daylight on the following day, when the noise, slaughter and crying diminished in part. (117) Then the king had all the booty divided up among his men, and remained there for a further three days. That's the greeting that he gave to the folk at the very first beginning, [when he had] newly arrived.

(123) When the king and his men had arrived, as I told you before, he stayed in Carrick for a time to see who would be [his] friend or foe. But he found little warmth [of support], for although the people were partly inclined to his [side], Englishmen governed them so determinedly with power and intimidation, that they dared not show him any friendship. (133) But a lady of that country who was in a close degree of relationship to him, was greatly cheered at his arrival, and forthwith hurried to him in great haste accompanied by forty men [whom] she gave to the king to help him in his campaigning. (141) He accepted them gratefully and thanked her very warmly,

---

125–84. The king had no support because the inhabitants feared the English (125–32), but he often ravaged the land, seizing booty (181–84). The latter is unlikely to have remedied the former! These passages are separated by the mysterious kinswoman who gave the king forty men. She has been dubbed Christiana because in 1328–9 the king paid an annual allowance of 40s. to Christian of Carrick, probably but not certainly a woman. But the same Christian has been identified with 'Christian Bruce, the king's daughter', noted as recipient of a royal charter; the other summaries of this lost charter call her Christina de Cairns and Christina Flemyng and make no mention of 'the king's daughter'. I am sceptical that the king had an illegitimate daughter called Christiana, but if he did, the same references cannot be to her mother as Christiana, who would have to be the king's mistress. Neil Bruce alias Neil of Carrick, a supposed bastard of the king, is likely to have been the son of Neil brother of Robert I, not of the king and 'Christiana of Carrick'. I fear we have to leave Barbour's lady still anonymous, her virtue intact.

Thai with sa feloun will thaim soucht
That thai slew thaim everilkan
Owtane Makdowell him allan
105 That eschapyt throu gret slycht
And throu the myrknes off the nycht.
In the castell the lord the Persy
Hard weill the noyis and the cry,
Sa did the men that within wer
110 And full effraytly gat thar ger,
Bot off thaim wes nane sa hardy
That ever ischyt fourth to the cry.
In sic effray thai baid that nycht
Till on the morn that day wes lycht,
115 And than cesyt into party
The noyis the slauchtyr and the cry.
The king gert be departyt then
All hale the reff amang the men
And dwellyt all still thar dayis thre.
120 Syk hansell to that fokk gaiff he
Rycht in the fyrst begynnyng
Newlingis at his aryvyng.

[*A kinswoman gives him news and forty men*]

Quhen that the king and his folk war
Aryvyt as I tauld you ar,
125 A quhile in Karryk leyndyt he
To se quha freynde or fa wald be,
Bot he fand litill tendyrnes,
And nocht-forthi the puple wes
Enclynyt till him in party,
130 Bot Inglismen sa angrely
Led thaim with daunger and with aw
That thai na freyndschip durst him schaw.
Bot a lady off that cuntre
That wes till him in ner degré
135 Of cosynage wes wonder blyth
Off his aryvyng and alswyth
Sped hyr till him in full gret hy
With fourty men in cumpany
And betaucht thaim all to the king
140 Till help him in his werraying,
And he resavyt thaim in daynté
And hyr full gretly thankit he,

asking [for] news of the queen and of his friends whom he had left all together in that country when he had taken to the sea. (147) She told him, with sighs of great [sorrow] how his brother had been taken in the castle of Kildrummy, and then so vilely killed, and about the earl of Atholl also; [she told him] how the queen and various others who had supported his cause, had been taken, led into England and put in dreadful imprisonment. (156) Weeping she told the king how Christopher Seton had been executed, [and he] was moved at that news, saying, when he had reflected for a moment, the following words which I report: 'Alas!' he said, 'because of their love for me and their great loyalty these noble and worthy men have been vilely destroyed. (165) But if I live [to reach] full power their death will be right well avenged. The king of England, moreover, thought that the kingdom of Scotland was too small for [both] them and me, therefore he will make it all mine. (171) But it is a [great] sadness that good Christopher Seton, who was of such noble reputation, should die other than where reputation could be proved.'

(175) Sighing thus the king mourned, and the lady took her leave, going home to her dwelling. Many times she comforted the king, both with money and with food such as she could get in the land. (181) He often ravaged the whole land, making everything he found his, thus increasing his strength

151. Atholl. This is Barbour's only reference to his fate; he was taken to London, tried and (7 November 1306) hanged especially high because his mother was descended from an illegitimate daughter of John king of England.

170. I have accepted and translated E for this line, but C's 'I will it all myn be' makes better sense.

And speryt tythandis off the queyne
And off his freyndis all bedene
145   That he had left in that countre
Quhen that he put him to the se.
And scho him tauld sichand full sar
How that his brothyr takyn war
In the castell off Kyldromy
150   And destroyit sa velanysly
And the erle off Athall alsua
And how the queyn and other ma
That till his party war heldand
War tane and led in Ingland
155   And put in feloun presoune,
And how that Cristole off Setoun
Wes slayn, gretand scho tauld the king,
That sorowful wes off that tithing
And said quhen he had thocht a thraw
160   Thir wordis that I sall you schaw.
'Allace,' he said, 'For luff off me
And for thar mekill lawté
Thai nobill men and thai worthy
Ar destroyit sa velanysly,
165   Bot and I leyff in lege-powysté
Thar deid rycht weill sall vengit be.
The king the-quhether off Ingland
Thocht that the kynrik off Scotland
Was to litill to thaim and me
170   Tharfor he will it myn all be.
Bot off gud Cristole off Setoun
That wes off sa nobill renoun
That he suld dey war gret pite
Bot quhar worschip mycht provyt be.'

[Percy is rescued from Turnberry castle]

175   The king sichand thus maid his mayn
And the lady hyr leyff has tayn
And went hyr hame till hyr wonnyng
And fele sys confort the king
Bath with silver and with mete
180   Sic as scho in the land mycht get.
And he oft ryot all the land
And maid all his that ever he fand
And syne drew him till the hycht

the better to destroy the great power of his enemies. At that time the Percy was residing in Turnberry castle with a fairly small company, so afraid of King Robert that he dared not come out to travel from there to Ayr castle which was then full of Englishmen; (192) he lay hiding as if in a lair until the men of Northumberland should come armed and with a strong force to convoy him to his country. For he sent his messenger to them to deliver him, and they quickly gathered then more than a thousand men, I believe, and asked among them for advice [as to] whether they should stay or go. (201) But they were remarkably, [indeed] terribly, fearful about going so far into Scotland. For a knight, Sir Walter Lisle, said it was far too dangerous to go so close to those brigands. His speech so upset them all that they would have given up the whole journey had there not been a knight of great courage, called Sir Roger of St John who comforted them with all his might, and spoke such words to them that all together they held their way to Turnberry, where Percy mounted and went speedily with them to England, to his castle, without hindrance or difficulty.

(217) Percy is in England now, where I'm sure he will stay awhile before he contemplates going to make war any more [in] Carrick. Because he knew that he had no right [there], and also he feared the might of the king, who was exerting himself in Carrick in the best strongpoint of the land.

---

196. for his saynde. Other editions give 'saynde' as meaning 'messenger', but another meaning (*DOST*) is 'deliverance', and this is surely required by 'for his'.

203–09. Walter Lisle, Roger de St John. In November 1308 Walter de Insula had a protection to go to Scotland; I have found no other mention of him. Sir Roger of St John occurs only once in a Scottish context, when he was marshal of the force which fought in April 1307 with King Robert in Glentrool, so his role here is credible. (*RotSc1*, 59a; *CDS5*, 490)

To stynt better his fayis mycht.
185 In all that tym wes the Persy
With a full sympill cumpany
In Turnberys castell lyand,
For the King Robert sua dredand
That he durst nocht isch furth to fayr
190 Fra thine to the castell off Ayr
That wes then full off Inglismen,
Bot lay lurkand as in a den
Tyll the men off Northummyrland
Suld cum armyt and with strang hand
195 Convoy him till his cuntré.
For his saynd till thaim send he,
And thai in hy assemblyt then
Passand I weyne a thousand men
And askyt avisement thaim amang
200 Quhether that thai suld dwell or gang,
Bot thai war skownrand wonder sar
Sa fer into Scotland for to far,
For a knycht, Schyr Gawter the Lile
Said it wes all to gret perile
205 Sua ner thai schavalduris to ga.
His spek discomfort thaim sua
That thai had left all thar vyage
Na war a knycht off gret corage
That Schyr Roger off Sanct Jhon hycht
210 That thaim confort with all his mycht,
And sic wordis to thaim gan say
That thai all samyn held thar way
Till Turnbery, quhar the Persy
Lap on and went with thaim in hy
215 In Ingland his castell till
Foroutyn distroublyne or ill.

[*Douglas decides to visit his lands*]

Now in Ingland is the Persy
Quhar I trow he a quhile sall ly
Or that he schap hym for to fayr
220 To werray Carryk ony mar,
For he wyst he had na rycht
And als he dreid the kyngys mycht
That in Carrik wes travailland
In the maist strenth off the land,

(224) There James Douglas came one day to the king and said to him, 'Sir, with your leave I want to go and see how they are getting on in my country, and how my men are treated. (230) Because it troubles me very sorely that Clifford enjoys and holds so peacefully the lordship which by rights should be mine. But while I live and can have strength to lead a yeoman or a peasant, he shall not enjoy it unchallenged.' (237) The king said, 'Indeed I cannot see how you can yet be safe to go to that country, where Englishmen are so powerful, and you don't know who is your friend.' [Douglas] said, 'Sir, I will go out of necessity and take what chance sends, whether it is to live or die.' (245) The king said, 'Since it is the case that you have such a yearning to go, you will pass forth with my blessing. And if anything happens to you which is distressful or hurtful, I pray you, hurry quickly to me and we will take together whatever may befall.' 'I agree,' he said, and with that he bowed, took his leave and went towards his country.

(255) Now James takes his way towards Douglas, his heritage, with two yeomen, no more. That was [indeed] a basic company to take to win a land or castle, but he yearned to begin the achievement of his purpose, for there is some advantage in a good beginning. (263) For a bold and good start, if it is cleverly followed [up], can often cause an unpromising course

---

225–462. This vivid account of the taking of Douglas castle is so detailed and convincing that it must have had a written source. But it is also certainly misplaced, for it was so ruthless that it can only have followed, not preceded, the attack when Douglas took the castle and sent the garrison to Clifford in 8.437 514. Since it is precisely dated to Palm Sunday, it must be placed on 7 April, 1308, when the king had gone north leaving Douglas in the south.

262. There are too many syllables in this line, and C has: For God helpit his begynnyng. There is much to be said for this reading; the repetition of 'For gude' at the beginnings of two consecutive lines is suspicious.

225 Quhar Jamys off Douglas on a day
      Come to the king and gan him say,
      'Schyr, with your leyve I wald ga se
      How that thai do in my contre
      And how my men demanyt ar,
230 For it anoyis me wonder sar
      That the Clyffurd sa pesabylly
      Brukys and haldys the senyoury
      That suld be myn with alkyn rycht
      Bot quhile I lyff and may haiff mycht
235 To lede a yowman or a swayne
      He sall nocht bruk it but bargayne.'
      The king said, 'Certis I can nocht se
      How that thou yeit may sekyr be
      Into that countre for to far
240 Quhar Inglismen sa mychty ar
      And thou wate nocht quha is thi freynd.'
      He said, 'Schyr, nedways I will wend
      And tak that aventur will giff
      Quhether-sa it be to dey or lyff.'
245 The king said, 'Sen it is sua
      That thou sic yarning has to ga
      Thou sall pas furth with my blyssing,
      And giff the hapnys ony thing
      That anoyis or scaithfull be
250 I pray the sped the sone to me
      And tak we samyn quhatever may fall.'
      'I grante,' he said and thar-with-all
      He lowtyt and his leve has tane
      And towart his countre is he gane.

[*Douglas meets Tom Dickson; he acquires a following*]

255 Now takis James his viage
      Towart Douglas his heritage
      With twa yemen foroutyn ma.
      That wes a symple stuff to ta
      A land or castell to wyn,
260 The-quhether he yarnyt to begyn
      Till bring purpos till ending
      For gud help is in gud begynnyng
      For gud begynnyng and hardy
      Gyff it be folowit wittily
265 May ger oftsys unlikly thing

to come to quite a successful conclusion. It did that here; for he was clever and saw that in no way could he fight his enemies with an equal force, and so he meant to act with cunning. (271) He entered his own country, Douglasdale, one evening. [There was] a man who dwelt near there, who was very well provided with friends and rich in goods and cattle, who had been loyal to his father and had done many a useful service to himself in his youth. (279) His name, *perfay*, was Tom Dickson. [Douglas] sent to him and begged him to come by himself to speak confidentially with him, and [Dickson] went to him without reluctance. (284) But when [Douglas] told him who he was, he wept for joy and from compassion, and took him right to his house, where he kept him and his company in secret in a room, so that no-one could see them. They had plenty of food and drink and anything else [needed] to make them comfortable. (292) Then [Dickson] acted with such artfulness that all the true men of the land who had adhered to [Douglas's] father this good man caused to come, one by one, each one to do him homage; [Dickson] himself did homage first. (298) Douglas's spirits were greatly cheered that the good men of his country were willing to be bound to him in this way. He asked [about] the condition of the country, and who had charge of the castle. (303) They told him everything and then decided among themselves in confidence that he should still remain in hiding and in secret, until Palm Sunday, which fell close at hand, on the third following day.

---

279. Thom Dicson. The number and size of the rooms in his house bear out the description of him as 'rich' (275) and a 'gud' i.e. important, man (295). He was presumably the Thomas son of Richard (not a knight) who had a charter of the barony of Symington (Lanarkshire) from Robert I; this could have been a new title to his heritage, not necessarily a new gift. It is 17 kilometres from Douglas and could well have been the place where the attack on Douglas castle was planned. By the spring of 1308 Douglas would have a following of sorts from Ettrick Forest. (*B1985*, 78)

Cum to full conabill ending.
Sua did it her, bot he wes wys
And saw he mycht on nakyn wys
Werray his fa with evyn mycht
270   Tharfor he thocht to wyrk with slycht,
And in Douglasdaile his countré
Apon ane evynnyng entryt he.
And than a man wonnyt tharby,
That wes off freyndis weill mychty
275   And ryche off mobleis and off cateill
And had bene till his fadyr leyll,
And till himselff in his youthed
He haid done mony a thankfull deid,
Thom Dicson wes his name perfay.
280   Till him he send and gan him pray
That he wald cum all anerly
For to spek with him prevely,
And he but daunger till him gais.
Bot fra he tauld him quhat he wais
285   He gret for joy and for pite
And him rycht till his hous had he,
Quhar in a chambre prevely
He held him and his cumpany,
That nane of him had persaving.
290   Off mete and drynk and other thing
That mycht thaim eys thai had plenté.
Sa wrocht he throu sutelté
That all the lele men off that land
That with his fadyr war dwelland
295   This gud man gert cum ane and ane
And mak him manrent everilkane,
And he himselff fyrst homage maid.
Douglas in hart gret glaidschip haid
That the gud men off his cuntré
300   Wald suagate till him bundyn be.
He speryt the convyne off the land
And quha the castell had in hand
And thai him tauld all halily,
And syne amang thaim prevely
305   Thai ordanyt that he still suld be
In hiddillis and in preveté
Till Palme Sonday that wes ner-hand
The thrid day efter folowand

(309) For then the folk of that district would be gathered at the kirk and those who were in the castle would also be there to carry their palms, like men with no fear of ill, because they thought everything was under their control. (315) Then he would come with his two men, but so that no-one would know him he would wear an old, worn, mantle, and [carry] a flail as if he was a thrasher. Under the mantle, nonetheless, he would be secretly armed and when the men of his country, who would all be prepared before him, could hear him shout his rallying cry, then in full force they would assail the Englishmen right in the middle of the kirk with a strong attack, so that none could escape from them; for they planned by this to take the castle that was nearby. (330) When what I have just told you had been planned and agreed, each man went to his house and kept the discussion secret till the day of their encounter.

(335) On the Sunday the people held their way to St Bride's kirk, and those who were in the castle, great and small (apart from a cook and a porter), issued out and went to carry their palms. James Douglas had knowledge of their approach and of who they were, and sped hastily to the kirk. (344) But before he arrived, one of his men shouted prematurely, 'Douglas! Douglas!'. Tom Dickson, who was nearest to those who came from the castle, who were all inside the chancel,

336. St Bride's Kirk is in the village of Douglas; the chancel survives in the keeping of the state and may sometimes be visited. The castle, of which scarcely a trace remains, was a good 1 kilometre to the north-east.

For than the folk off that countre
310   Assemblyt at the kyrk wald be,
And thai that in the castell wer
Wald als be thar thar palmys to ber
As folk that had na dreid off ill
For thai thocht that all was at thar will.
315   Than suld he cum with his twa men,
Bot for that men suld nocht him ken
He suld ane mantill have auld and bar
And a flaill as he a thresscher war.
Under the mantill nocht-forthi
320   He suld be armyt prevely,
And quhen the men off his countre
That suld all boune befor him be
His ensenye mycht her hym cry,
Then suld thai full enforcely
325   Rycht ymyddys the kirk assaill
The Inglismen with hard bataill
Sua that nane mycht eschap thaim fra,
For thar-throuch trowyt thai to ta
The castell that besid wes ner.
330   And quhen this that I tell you her
Wes divisyt and undertane
Ilkane till his hous hame is gane
And held this spek in preveté
Till the day off thar assemblé.

[*The garrison are attacked and many slain in kirk; the castle is taken; the Douglas Lardner; slighting of the castle*]

335   The folk apon the Sonounday
Held to Saynct Bridis kyrk thar way,
And thai that in the castell war
Ischyt out bath less and mar
And went thar palmys for to ber,
340   Outane a cuk and a portere.
James off Douglas off thar cummyng
And quhat thai war had witting,
And sped him till the kyrk in hy,
Bot or he come, to hastily
345   Ane of his cryit, 'Douglas, Douglas.'
Thomas Dikson, that nerrest was
Till thaim that war off the castell
That war all innouth the chancell,

when he heard 'Douglas!' shouted so loud, drew out his sword
and without regard rushed among them here and there. (352)
Only one or two, no more, were speedily left lying then, until
Douglas came right to hand and reinforced the assault on
them. But they held the chancel very strongly and defended
themselves well until a number of their men were killed. (359)
But the Douglas bore himself so well that all the men who
were with him were inspired by his prowess, while he spared
himself no effort but so proved his strength in fighting that
by his valour and his courage he helped his men so boldly
then that they won the chancel for themselves. (367) They
laid into them then so fiercely that in a short time you could
see two thirds [of the English] lying dead or dying. The rest
were taken prisoner so that none of the thirty was left who
had not been killed there or taken – one and all. (373) When
this was over, James Douglas took the prisoners at once and
with those of his company went in haste towards the castle,
before any noise or cry could arise. (378) And because he
wanted to surprise quickly those who had been left in the
castle, who numbered no more than two, he sent five or six
men ahead who found the entry completely open, entered
and took the porter just at the gate and then the cook. (385)
With that Douglas came to the gate, went in without resistance
and found the food all ready prepared, with boards set and
cloths laid. He had them bar the gates and sit and eat at their
leisure. Then they bundled up all the goods

388. Boards set: tables would usually be trestles set up with boards laid
on top.

Quhen he 'Douglas' sua hey hard cry
350 Drew out his swerd and felloly
Ruschyt amang thame to and fra,
Bot ane or twa foroutin ma
Than in hy war left lyand,
Quhill Douglas come rycht at hand
355 And then enforcyt on thaim the cry,
Bot thai the chansell sturdely
Held and thaim defendyt wele
Till off thar men war slayne sumdell.
Bot the Douglace sa weill him bar
360 That all the men that with him war
Had confort off his wele-doyng,
And he him sparyt nakyn thing
Bot provyt sua his force in fycht
That throu his woschip and his mycht
365 His men sa keynly helpyt than
That thai the chansell on thaim wan.
Than dang thai on sua hardyly
That in schort tyme men mycht se ly
The twa part dede or then deand,
370 The lave war sesyt sone in hand
Sua that off thretty levyt nane
That thaine war slayne ilkan or tane.
James off Douglas quhen this wes done
The presoneris has he tane alsone
375 And with thaim off his cumpany
Towart the castell went in hy
Or noyis or cry suld rys,
And for he wald thaim sone suppris
That levyt in the castell war
380 That war bot twa foroutyn mar,
Fyve men or sex befor send he
That fand all opyn the entre
And entryt and the porter tuk
Rycht at the yate and syne the cuk.
385 With that the Douglas come to the yat
And entryt in foroutyn debate
And fand the mete all redy graid
And burdys set and claithis laid
The yhattis then he gert sper
390 And sat and eyt all at layser,
Syne all the gudis turssyt thai

that they thought they could take away, especially weapons and armour, silver, treasure and clothing. (395) Victuals, which couldn't be packed, he destroyed in the following way. All the victuals, apart from salt, [things] like wheat and flour and meal and malt, he had brought to the wine-cellar and thrown all together on the floor. (401) [Then] he had the prisoners whom he had taken beheaded there every one; then he struck the heads off the barrels [of wine]. He made a foul concoction there, for meal and malt and blood and wine all ran together into a mush that was disgusting to see. Therefore the men of that country, because so many things were mixed there, called it 'the Douglas Larder.' (411) Afterwards he took salt, as I heard tell, and dead horses and polluted the well, then burned everything apart from stonework, and went forth with his company to his [place of] shelter. (415) For he really believed that if he had held the castle it would quickly have been besieged, which he thought too great a danger, because he had no hope of relief. (420) It is too dangerous a thing to be besieged in a castle where there these three things are lacking: victuals, or men with their arms, or good hope of being rescued. (425) And because he feared these things would be lacking, he chose to journey on where he could be at large and so pursue his destiny.

(429) The castle was taken in this way, and all therein were slain. The Douglas then caused all his company to be split up in different places,

That thaim thocht thai mycht haiff away,
And namly wapnys and armyng
Silver and tresour and clethyng.
395 Vittalis that mycht nocht tursyt be
On this maner destroyit he,
All the vittalis outane salt
Als quheyt and flour and meill and malt
In the wyne-sellar gert he bring
400 And samyn on the flur all flyng
And the presonaris that he had tane
Rycht tharin gert he heid ilkane,
Syne off the tounnys the hedis outstrak.
A foul melle thar gane he mak,
405 For meile and malt and blud and wyne
Rane all togidder in a mellyne
That was unsemly for to se.
Tharfor the men off that countré
For sua fele thar mellyt wer
410 Callit it 'the Douglas lardner.'
Syne tuk he salt as Ic hard tell
And ded hors and fordid the well,
And brynt all outakyn stane,
And is furth with his menye gayne
415 Till his resett, for him thocht weill
Giff he had haldyn the castell
It had bene assegyt raith
And that him thocht to mekill waith,
For he had na hop of reskewyng.
420 And it is to peralous thing
In castell assegyt to be
Quhar want is off thir thingis thre,
Vittaill or men with thar armyng
Or than gud hop off rescuyng,
425 And for he dred thir thingis suld faile
He chesyt furthwart to travaill
Quhar he mycht at his larges be
And sua dryve furth his destané.

[*Douglas withdraws; Clifford repairs the castle*]

On this wise wes the castell tan
430 And slayne that war tharin ilkan.
The Douglas syne all his menye
Gert in ser placis departyt be,

for men would be worse informed where those were who had been split up here and there. (435) He had those who were wounded lie secretly in hiding places and had good leeches brought to them while they were convalescing. He himself, with a small following, sometimes one, sometimes two, sometimes three, and sometimes all by himself, went to hiding places throughout the land. (443) He so feared the might of the Englishmen that he dared not come into the open for at that time they were omnipotent, like complete lords over the whole land. (447) But news, which soon travels, of this deed done by Douglas quickly came to Clifford's ear, who was sad at his loss and mourned his men whom they had slain; then he formed the intention to build up the castle again. (454) For that, as a man of great power, he gathered a large company, went swiftly to Douglas, built up the castle speedily, made it very strong and secure and put men and victuals in it. He left behind him then as captain one of the Thirlwalls and then went again to England.

(463) The king was still in Carrick with a very basic following – he had no more than two hundred men. But Sir Edward, his brother, was then in Galloway quite close thereby [and] with him another company which kept the strongpoints of the land, for they dared not yet undertake to ride openly through the land. (472) For Sir Aymer de Valence was lying at Edinburgh;

447-59. Clifford repairs the castle. This certainly happened after the first attack upon it, and Clifford received a total of £100 from Edward I for this work, on 30 May and 26 June, 1307, plus the services of 21 masons for nine days (at 7s. 2d. per day), 28 June–7 July. Thus the first attack (described at 8.437–514) took place before 30 May, 1307.

460. Thirlwalls. The name is introduced here to provide a link with the next account of an attack on a force from Douglas castle, at 6.385.

463-74. There is no known period when the king was in Carrick, Edward Bruce in Galloway and Valence in Edinburgh; in particular, Valence seems to have been based in the west, on Bothwell, after the king's return. If this is meant to be in late February–March 1307, then it clashes with the detail given in 489.

For men suld les wyt quhar thai war
That yeid departyt her and thar.
435 Thaim that war woundyt gert he ly
Intill hiddillis all prevely,
And gert gud lechis till thaim bring
Quhill that thai war intill heling,
And himselff with a few menye
440 Quhile ane quhile twa and quhilis thre
And umquhill all him allane
In hiddillis throu the land is gane.
Sa dred he Inglismennys mycht
That he durst nocht wele cum in sycht
445 For thai war that tyme all-weldand
As maist lordis our all the land.
Bot tithandis that scalis sone
Off this deid that Douglas has done
Come to the Cliffurd his ere in hy,
450 That for his tynsaill wes sary
And menyt his men that thai had slane,
And syne has to his purpos tane
To big the castell up agayne.
Tharfor as man off mekill mayne
455 He assemblit gret cumpany,
And till Douglas he went in hy
And biggyt up the castell swyth
And maid it rycht stalwart and styth
And put tharin vittalis and men.
460 Ane of the Thyrlwallys then
He left behind him capitane
And syne till Ingland went agayne.

[*Umfraville finds a kinsman of the king willing to slay him*]

Into Carrik lyis the king
With a full symple gadryng,
465 He passyt nocht twa hunder men.
Bot Schyr Edward his broder then
Wes in Galloway weill ner him by,
With him ane other cumpany
That held the strenthis off the land,
470 For thai durst nocht yeit tak on hand
Till our-rid the land planly.
For off Valence Schyr Amery
Was intill Edynburgh lyand

he was still warden of the land beneath the English king,.
(476) When he heard of the arrival of King Robert and his
following in Carrick, and how he had killed men of the Percy,
he called together his advisers, and with consent of his council,
he sent to Ayr to attack [Bruce], Sir Ingram Umfraville, who
was a valiant [man], and with him a large company. (485)
When Ingram had arrived there, he thought it was not ap-
propriate to attack [Bruce] in the hills. Therefore he planned
to act with stealthiness, and lay quietly in the castle then (490)
until he got information about a man of Carrick, who was
cunning and clever, and also a man of great strength [who]
among the men of that country was closest to King Robert,
as one who was his close kinsman, (496) and, when he wanted,
could go without risk to the king's presence. Nonetheless he
and his two sons were still dwelling in the country, for they
did not want it to be remarked that they were close to the
king. (502) Many a time they gave him warning when they
could [fore]see his loss, [and] therefore he trusted in them. I
can't tell [the man's] name, *perfay,* but I have heard various
men say as a fact that he had lost an eye; but he was so sturdy
and stout that he was the most redoubtable man then living
in Carrick. (511) When Sir Ingram got to know that in truth
this was no exaggeration, he sent for [the man] in haste, and
he came at his command.

---

489. The castle of Ayr. The sheriff of Ayr was Sir John Hastings, the
constable of the castle Sir Robert Leybourn, from October 1306 to
February 1307 and later (e.g. *CDS5,* 220b). On 18 May, 1307, after the
battle of Loudoun, orders were issued for stores at Ayr to be given to
Umfraville and Sir William Felton for Cumnock castle. On 21 May
Felton was about to go there, and on 23 May they were said to have
been put in charge with a force of 30 men-at-arms and
100 infantry. Strictly this places this episode just before mid-May 1307,
but it is doubtful that Umfraville was at Ayr long enough for the delays
implied in the story. Perhaps the castle was really that of Cumnock,
and the date after mid-May. (*CDS2, 1931, 1933; CDS4, 1829*)

495. It is extraordinary that a one-eyed (507) close relative of Robert I
who frequented his refuge to warn him of dangers (501–3), should be
of unknown name. But Skeat long ago (*B1894,* 2, 249) listed the episodes
where three men planned to kill the king: 7.111–232, three men carrying
a wether spend the night in a house with Bruce and his foster-brother,
attack them and are killed, along with the foster-brother; 7.404–94, the
king in Carrick (cf 5.463, 491), hunting with his two hounds, is attacked
by three men with bows and swords. There are points in common
between the present episode and the second of these, and they probably

That yeyt was wardane of the land
475 Underneyth the Inglis king,
And quhen he herd off the cummyng
Off King Robert and his menye
Into Carryk and how that he
Had slain off the Persyis men
480 His consaile he assemblit then,
And with assent off his consaill
He sent till Ar him till assaill
Schyr Ingrame the Umfravill that wes hardy
And with him a gret cumpany.
485 And quhen Schyr Ingram cummyn wes thar
Him thocht nocht speidfull for till far
Till assaile him into the hycht,
Tharfor he thocht to wyrk with slycht
And lay still in the castell than
490 Till he gat speryng that a man
Off Carrik, that wes sley and wycht
And a man als off mekill mycht
As off the men off that cuntré,
Wes to the King Robert mast prevé
495 As he that wes his sibman ner,
And quhen he wald foroutyn danger
Mycht to the kingis presence ga,
The-quhether he and his sonnys twa
War wonnand still in the cuntre
500 For thai wald nocht persayvit be
That thai war speciall to the king.
Thai maid him mony tyme warnyng
Quhen that thai his tynsaill mycht se,
Forthi in thaim affyit he.
505 His name can I nocht tell perfay,
Bot Ik haiff herd syndry men say
Forsuth that his ane e wes out   506*
Bot he sa sturdy wes and stout   507*
That he wes the maist doutit man   507
510 That in Carrik lyvyt than.   508
And quhen Schyr Ingrame gat wittering
Forsuth this wes na gabbing,
Efter him in hy he sent
And he come at his commandment.

have their origin in one attack which in the present version became
attached to the Bruce kin whom Umfraville suborned.

Sir Ingram, who was cunning and clever, bargained with him then in such terms that he gave a solemn undertaking to kill the king treacherously, (519) and that if he carried out their plan, he would have for his service a good forty pounds' worth of land, for him and his heirs in perpetuity.

(523) The treachery was undertaken thus, and [the man] went back home to his house, waiting an opportunity to carry out his wickedness. The king was in great danger then, knowing nothing of his treason, for he in whom he trusted most of all, had falsely undertaken [the king's] death and no-one deceives more quickly than he in whose loyalty a man trusts. (533) The king trusted in him, [and] therefore he would have carried out his felony had not the king, by God's grace, got complete [fore]knowledge of his intention, and of how, and for how much land, he had taken this assassination on hand. (539) I don't know who gave the warning, but throughout his time he had such luck that when men meant to betray him, he always got knowledge of it, many a time, as I heard said, from women with whom he was sleeping, who would tell all that they heard; it may have been that it happened like that here. (547) But however it happened, I'm sure he will indeed be more wary. Nonetheless, this traitor always had in his thoughts, by day and night, how he could bring his treasonable undertaking to a conclusion, till eventually he remembered: he recollecteded in his heart that it was always the king's custom

---

527–38. The clumsy repetition excuses the lame failure to explain how the king got to know of this treachery, for which the loose women are an unconvincing suggestion.

550 54. The search for an opportunity. Cf. 7.428 9, 'wachyt him by-syly/To se quhen thai vengeance mycht tak.'

515   Schyr Ingrame that was sley and wis   513
            Tretyt with him than on sic wys
            That he maid sekyr undertaking
            In tresoun for to slay the king,
            And he suld haiff for his service
520   Gyff he fullfillyt thar divice   518
            Weill fourty pundis worth off land
            Till him and till his ayris ay lestand.

[*The traitor and his sons seek to kill the king but are killed*]

            The tresoun thus is undertane,
            And he hame till his hous is gane
525   And wattyt opertunyté   523
            For to fulfill his mavyté.
            In gret perell than was the king
            That off this tresoun wyst na thing,
            For he that he traistit maist of ane
530   His ded falsly has undertane,   528
            And nane may betreys tyttar than he
            That man in trowis leawté.
            The king in him traistyt, forthi
            He had fullfillyt his felony
535   Ne war the king throu Goddis grace   533
            Gat hale witting of his purchace,
            And how and for how mekill land
            He tuk his slauchter apon hand.
            I wate nocht quha the warnyng maid,
540   Bot on all tym sic hap he had   538
            That quhen men schup thaim to betrais
            He gat witting tharoff allwayis
            And mony tyme as I herd say
            Throu wemen that he wyth wald play
545   That wald tell all that thai mycht her,   543
            And sua myvht happyn that it fell her,
            Bot how that ever it fell perdé
            I trow he sall the warrer be.
            Nocht-forthi the tratour ay
550   Had in his thocht bath nycht and day   548
            How he mycht best bring till ending
            His tresonabill undretaking,
            Till he umbethinkand him at the last
            Intill his hart gan umbecast
555   That the king had in custome ay   553

to rise early every day, go a good way away from his following when he wanted to go to the privy, and seek a concealed place by himself, or at most have one [man] with him. (561) With his two sons [the traitor] meant to surprise the king, kill [him] and then take their way to the wood; but they failed in their plan, despite [the fact that] all three of them came to a covert that was secluded, where the king often used to go to fulfill his private needs. (569) They hid themselves there till he should come. And the king, in the morning, got up when he felt like it, and went straight towards the covert where the three traitors were waiting, to do his business there. (575) He had no thought of treason then, but he was accustomed, wherever he went, to wear his sword about his neck, and that served him well there. For if God, ruling everything, had not put help into his own hand, he would without doubt have been a dead [man]. (582) A chamber page went with him, and so, without any more followers he went towards the covert. Now, unless God helps the noble king, he is very close to his last [hour]! (587) For that covert to which he was going was on the other side of a hill [so] that none of his men could see it. He and his page went towards it, and when he had come into the thicket, he saw all those three coming in a line against him very sturdily. (594) Then he said quickly to his boy, 'Those men will kill us if they can. What weapon have you [got]?' 'Ah, sir, in truth I have only a [cross]bow and a bolt.' 'Give them both to me, at once.' 'Ah, sir,

---

559, 572. A covert for his private needs. Cf. 7.411, 'By a woud-syd to sett is gane.'

563. Traitors hide in a wood. Cf. 7.415, 'fra the woud cummand/Thre men.'

577. His sword about his neck. Cf. 7.413, 'Bot he his swerd ay with him bar'. In both cases his only personal weapon.

For to rys arly ilk day
And pas weill fer fra his menye
Quhen he wald pas to the prevé,
And sek a covert him allane
560   Or at the maist with him ane.   558
Thar thocht he with his sonnys twa
For to supprise the king and sla
And syne went to the wod thar way,
Bot yeit off purpos failit thai,
565   And nocht-forthi thai come all thre   563
In a covert that wes prevé
Quhar the king oft wes wont to ga
His preve nedys for to ma.
Thair hid thai thaim till his cumming,
570   And the king into the mornyng   568
Rais quhen that his liking was
And rycht towart that covert gais
Quhar lyand war the tratouris thre
For to do thar his prevete.
575   To tresoun tuk he then na heid   573
Bot he wes wont quharever he yeid
His swerd about his hals to ber
And that availlyt him gretli ther
For had nocht God all thing weldand
580   Set help intill his awine hand   578
He had bene ded withoutyn dreid.
A chamber page thar with him yeid,
And sua foroutyn falowis ma
Towart the covert gan he ga.
585   Now bot God help the noble king   583
He is ner-hand till his ending,
For that covert that he yeid till
Wes on the tother sid a hill
That nane of his men mycht it se.
590   Thiddirwart went this page and he   588
And quhen he cummyn wes in the schaw
He saw thai thre cum all on raw
Aganys him full sturdely.
Than till his boy he said in hy,
595   'Yon men will slay us and thai may.   593
Quhat wapyn has thou?' 'Ha, Schyr, perfay
Ik haiff bot a bow and a wyr.'
'Giff thaim me smertly bath.' 'A, Schyr

what do you want me to do, then?' 'Stand [well] away and watch us. If you see me get the upper hand, you will have weapons a-plenty, and if I die, clear out at once.' (604) With those words, without delay he snatched the bow out of his hand, for the traitors were approaching close. The father had only a sword, the second carried both sword and hand-axe and the third had a sword and a spear. (610) The king discerned from their appearance that everything men had told him was true. 'Traitor', he said, 'You have sold me. Come no further, but stay there. I order you to come no further.' 'Ah! sir, remember' he said, 'how close to you I should be; who should be near to you but me?' (618) The king said, 'I order firmly that at this time you don't come near; you can say what you want from afar.' But he, with false [and] insincere words, was still coming [on] with his sons. (623) When the king saw that he would not desist, but still came on with deceit [and] falseness, he aimed the bolt and let it fly, hitting the father in the eye until it went right into the brain, and he fell down backwards right then. (629) The brother who had the hand-axe, seeing his father lying there, aimed a blow right at the king, and struck at him with the axe. But [the king] who had his sword aloft struck him such a blow, tremendously forceful, [so] that he split his head to the brain, and felled him to the earth, dead. (637) The other brother who carried the spear, seeing his brother fallen there like that, ran at the king with his spear in a rush like a madman. But the king, somewhat afraid of him,

---

607-9. All three had swords (with other weapons). Cf. 7.447, 'with your swerdis till assay' (bows cast aside).

612. The first challenge comes from the king; similarly in 7.443.

615-17. The whole encounter should also be read in the light of these words. It is entirely possible that three innocent men approached the edgy king, who fearfully threatened the first, then killed him from a distance; not surprisingly the other two then attacked the king. After their deaths it became convenient to impute treason to them.

625-28. The first killed outright by a crossbow-bolt. Cf. 7.456-57, the first killed outright by a sword-stroke. Both 'fell down' dead. The deaths of the other two are quite different.

Howgaite will ye that I do?'
'Stand on fer and behald us to.   598
Giff thou seis me abovyn be
Thou sall haiff wapynnys gret plente,
And giff I dey, withdraw the sone.'
With thai wordis foroutyn hone
He tyte the bow out off his hand,   603
For the tratouris war ner cummand.
The fader had a swerd but mar,
The tother bath swerd and hand-ax bar,
The thrid a swerd had and a sper.
The king persavt be thar affer   608
That all wes as men had him tauld.
'Tratour,' he said, 'thou has me sauld.
Cum na forthyr bot hald the thar.
I will thou cum na forthermar.'
'A, Schyr, umbethinkis you,' said he,   613
How ner that I suld to you be.
Quha suld cum ner you bot I?'
The king said, 'I will sekirly
That thou at this tyme cum nocht ner.
Thou may say quhat thou will on fer.'   618
Bot he with fals wordis flechand
Was with his twa sonnys cummand.
Quhen the king saw he wald nocht let
Bot ay come on fenyeand falset
He taisyt the wyre and leit it fley,   623
And hyt the fader in the ey
Till it rycht in the harnys ran
And he bakwart fell doun rycht than.
The brother that the hand-ax bar
Sua saw his fader liand thar,   628
A gyrd rycht to the king he couth maik
And with the ax hym our-straik,
Bot he that had his sword on hycht
Roucht him sic rout in randoun rycht
That he the hede till the harnys claiff   633
And dede downe till the erd him draiff.
The tother broder that bar the sper
Saw his brodyr fallin ther
And with the sper as angry man
With a rais till the king he ran.   638
Bot the king that him dred sumthing

600

605

610

615

620

625

630

635

640

waited for the spear to come and with a swipe struck the head off, and before the other had time to take his sword, the king gave him such a blow that he split his head to the brain; he gushed red blood. (647) And when the king saw they were all three lying dead, he wiped his weapon. With that his boy came running fast, and said, 'Our Lord should be praised for granting you strength and power to cut down the felony and pride of these three in such a short time.' (655) The king said, 'As our Lord sees me, they would all three have been good men if they had not been full of treason; but that was their undoing.'

655–58. Good men ruined by their treason. Cf. 7.493–94, 'Thar tresoun combryt thaim perfay / For rycht wycht men all thre war thai.' There are obvious differences between the story here and that in 7.404–94, in the faithful companion (page or dogs), in the weaponry employed, in the role of the dogs. But the similarities are not phrases of Barbour's composition, point to a common origin and instruct us in the transformation of legends.

Waytyt the sper in the cummyng
And with a wysk the hed off strak,
And or the tother had toyme to tak
645 His swerd the king sic swak him gaiff 643
That he the hede till the harnys claiff,
He ruschyt down off blud all reid.
And quhen the king saw thai war all ded
All thre lyand he wipit his brand,
650 With that his boy come fast rynnand 648
And said, 'Our Lord mot lovyt be
That grantyt you mycht and powsté
To fell the felny and the prid
Off thir thre in sua litill tid.'
655 The king said, 'Sa our Lord me se 653
Thai had bene worthi men all thre
Had thai nocht bene full off tresoun,
Bot that maid thar confusioun.'

The king went to his lodging, and news of his deed soon came to Sir Ingram Umfraville, who realised [that] his cunning and guile had all failed in that place. (6) For that reason he was so angry that he took the road again to Lothian, to Sir Aymer, telling the whole event to him, who was utterly amazed by it – that any man could so suddenly do such great chivalry as the king did when he took revenge on three traitors by himself. (15) He said, 'Indeed I can well see it is very certain that fate always helps courageous men, as you can tell by this deed. If he had not been outstandingly brave he would not have seen his advantage dauntlessly [and] so quickly. (22) I fear that his great nobility and his exertions could bring to an end what men at one time scarcely imagined.' He spoke thus about the king, who travelled continually in Carrick, here and there, without tarrying. (28) His men were so dispersed from him to get their necessities and also to protect the country, that they left not sixty [men] with him. And when the Galloway-men knew for a fact that he was with a small company, they made a secret muster of a good two hundred men and more; (36) they took a tracker-dog with them for they planned to surprise him and, if he fled in any direction,

---

4. E and C have 'That thocht with sutelte ...' I have followed Skeat in accepting H, 'his' for 'with'.

32. Galloway men. This episode is not attributed to any English inspiration or command. It could have occurred in any month between March and September (but not August) 1307.

BOOK 6

[Sir Ingram Umfraville praises the king; the men of Galloway pursue him with a tracker dog]

	The king is went till his logyng
	And off this deid sone come tithing
	Till Schyr Ingrame the Umfravill
	That thocht his sutelte and gyle
5	Haid al failyeit in that place.
	Tharfor anoyit sua he was
	That he agayne to Lothyane
	Till Schyr Amer his gate has tane
	And till him tauld all hale the cas,
10	That tharoff all forwonderyt was
	How ony man sa sodanly
	Mycht do so gret chevalry
	As did the king that him allane
	Vengeance off thre traytouris has tane,
15	And said, 'Certis, I may weill se
	That it is all certanté
	That ure helpys hardy men
	As be this deid we may ken.
	War he nocht outrageous hardy
20	He had nocht unabasytly
	Sa smertly sene his avantage.
	I drede that his gret vassalag
	And his travaill may bring till end
	That at men quhile full litill wend.'
25	Sik speking maid he off the king
	That ay foroutyn sojournyng
	Travaillit in Carrik her and thar.
	His men fra him sa scalit war
	To purches thar necessité
30	And als the countre for to se
	That thai left nocht with him sexty.
	And quhen the Gallowais wyst suthli
	That he wes with sa few mengye
	Thai maid a preve assemblé
35	Off wele twa hunder men and ma,
	And slewth-hundis with thaim gan ta,
	For thai thocht him for to suppris
	And giff he fled on ony wys

to follow him with the hound so that he shouldn't escape
from them.

(41) They intended to surprise the king suddenly one evening,
and took there way straight to him. But he, who always had
his watches [set] on every side, knew of their coming long
before they arrived, and [also] how many they might be. (48)
For that reason he planned to withdraw from the place with
his following, because night had nearly fallen, and he thought
that because of the night, they would not be able to see to
take the way that he had passed with his following. (54) He
did just as he had planned, going down to a marsh, over a
flowing burn, and in the bog found a pretty narrow place that
was a good two arrow-flights from the burn they had crossed.
(60) He said, 'You can stay here, rest for a while and lie
[down]. I will go [and] watch secretly, [to see] if I hear
anything of them coming; and if I do hear anything, I shall
have you warned, so that we always have the advantage.'
(67) The king now takes his way to go, taking with him two
serjeants. He left Sir Gilbert Hay there

36, 39. Tracker dog. In C this is singular, but in E 'hundis', plural. In
view of the development of the story, a single hound seems preferable.
The story of pursuit by a hound recurs at 6.471–7.78, where there are
alternative endings. These stories were internationally famous, for Jean
le Bel, writing 1350–58 and describing Edward III's invasion of Scotland
in 1333, recalled

> In these forests and wild places where the Scottish lords kept them-
> selves, King Robert many a time took refuge when the good king
> Edward [I] had defeated him and driven him off, and several times
> was so harassed and chased that he could scarcely find anyone in his
> kingdom willing or daring to give him shelter in castle or strong-point,
> for fear of King Edward, who had so conquered Scotland that there
> was not town, castle or strong-point which was not obedient to him.
> And one time, one says and finds it in a story made by the said king
> Robert (*Aucune fois, ce dit on, et le treuve on en hystoire faitte par le dit
> roy Robert*) the good King Edward had him chased through these great
> forests for the space of three or four days, by dogs and leash-hounds
> to blood and train them, but he could never find him nor, whatever
> the miseries he endured, would he obey this good King Edward, and
> so, as soon as this King Edward had conquered all Scotland and put
> garrisons and guards in the towns and castles throughout the country,
> and had gone back to England, this King Robert gathered men-at-
> arms, as many as he could find, and recovered everything as far as
> Berwick, some parts by force, some by love. When ... Edward [I]
> knew this he was furious and quickly gathered his host, not ceasing
> till he had conquered again and defeated this brave King Robert ...
> [who] recovered his kingdom five times ... [They] were the two

To folow him with the hundis sua
40 That he suld nocht eschaip thaim fra.
Thai schup thaim in ane evynnyng
To suppris sodanly the king
And till him held thai straucht thar way,
Bot he, that had his wachis ay
45 On ilk sid, off thar cummyng
Lang or thai come had wyttering
And how fele that thai mycht be,
Tharfor he thocht with his menye
To withdraw him out off the place,
50 For the nycht weill fallyn was
And for the nycht he thocht that thai
Suld nocht haiff sycht to hald the way
That he war passyt with his menye.
And as he thocht rycht sua did he
55 And went him down till a morras
Our a watter that rynnand was,
And in the bog he fand a place
Weill strait that weill twa bow-draucht was
Fra the watter thai passit haid.
60 He said, 'Her may ye mak abaid
And rest you all a quhile and ly,
I will ga wach all prevely.
Giff Ik her oucht off thar cummyng
And giff I may her onything
65 I sall ger warn you sa that we
Sall ay at our avantage be.'

[*The king alone defends the ford*]

The king now takys his gate to ga
And with him tuk he sergandis twa
And Schyr Gilbert de le Hay left he

---

bravest kings in the world until King Edward died at Berwick and
his body was taken to London. (*Chron. le Bel*, i. 111)
Barbour echoes the comment on Bruce's inability to find supporters
(4.521; 5.41) and the leash-hound (*limier*).
68. A serjeant was a well-armed infantryman; C has servants.
69. Sir Gilbert Hay, already mentioned as a supporter of the king (2.493;
3.25), he plays no part in this adventure. It is possible that in a version
of the story known to Barbour upon which he embarked only to change
the conclusion, Hay failed to bring timeous help to the king. This may
explain the ambiguity (85–93; 108a–f) about the king sending for help.
But Hay became the king's constable, an office held heritably by his

to rest with his followers. He quickly came to the burn and listened very intently [to see] if he heard any [sign] of their coming, but he could still hear nothing then. (75) He went along the burn a great distance on either side, and saw the braes rising high, the water running deep through mud, and found no ford where men could cross, except where he himself had crossed over. (81) The ascent was so narrow that two men could not squeeze together, nor in any way press themselves together so that they could take [dry] land. (85) He then ordered his two men to go quickly to their companions to rest and lie [down] for he would watch to see their arrival. 'Sir', said they, 'Who will be with you?' 'Only God.' he said, 'Carry on, for these are my orders.' They did as he had ordered them, and he remained there all alone. (93) When he had stayed there for a time, he listened and heard what sounded like a hound's baying in the distance, always coming nearer and nearer to him. He stood still to hear better, and always the longer he was there the nearer and nearer he heard it coming; (100) but he thought he would stand still there until he heard more evidence. He did not want to waken his company, and so he would stay and see what people they were and whether they held the direct way toward him, or passed by another, distant, way. (108) The moon was shining very clearly; (108a) he stood so long that he could hear the noise of those who were coming. Then he sent his two men quickly to warn and waken his following,

family in 1375 and today. In the Tydeus story, the force which attacked the hero, Tydeus, was led by the constable of Ethiocles (203, and see 265 below). This uncomfortable coincidence may have led Barbour to strike out the role of Hay. It is possible that the story is a hybrid of an encounter with Galwegians with an episode north of the Tay (where Hay is more likely to be found). The latter strand could be the battle of Loch Tay against an English force in late June 1306.

85–92. These lines are found only in C. Part of their sense is repeated in E and H in 108a-f. I have included both passages in this text to make the problem plain. Since the king's men do not come to his aid, lines 85–92 have generally been preferred.

108a-f. These lines have been denounced as corrupt, but it is possible that they represent one strand in a hybrid story from an earlier version of the text, altered when Barbour saw the drift of the whole episode. See 85–92.

70	Thar for to rest with his menye.	
	To the watter he come in hy	
	And lysnyt full ententily	
	Giff he herd oucht off thar cummyng	
	Bot yeit then mocht he her na thing.	
75	Endlang the watter then yeid he	
	On ather syd a gret quantité	
	And saw the brayis hey standand,	
	The watter holl throu slik rynnand	
	And fand na furd that men mycht pas	
80	Bot quhar himselvyn passit was,	
	And sua strait wes the up-cumming	
	That twa men mycht nocht samyn thring	
	Na on na maner pres thaim sua	
	That thai togidder mycht land ta.	
85	His twa men bad he than in hy	*85
	Ga to thair feris to rest and ly	*86
	For he wald wach thar com to se.	*87
	'Schyr,' said thai, 'Quha sall with you be?'	*88
	'God,' he said, 'forouten ma	*89
90	Pas on, for I will it be sua.'	*90
	Thai did as he thame biddin had	*91
	And he thar all allane abaid,	*92
	And quhen he a lang quhile had bene thar	85
	He herknyt and herd as it war	
95	A hundis questyng on fer	87
	That ay come till him ner and ner.	
	He stud still for till herkyn mar	
	And ay the langer he wes thar	
	He herd it ner and ner cummand,	
100	Bot he thocht he thar still wald stand	92
	Tyll that he herd mar takynnyng.	
	Than for ane hundis questyng	
	He wald nocht wakyn his menye,	
	Tharfor he wald abid and se	
105	Quhat folk thai war and quhethir thai	97
	Held towart him the rycht way	
	Or passyt ane other way fer by.	
	The moyne wes schynand clerly,	100
108a	Sa lang he stude that he mycht her	101
108b	The noyis off thaim that cummand wer	102
108c	Than his twa men in hy send he	103
108d	To warn and wakyn and walkyn his menye	104

and they went forth on their way; he was left there all by himself. (109) He stood so long listening, till he saw come at hand the whole force, at very great speed. Then he quickly realised that if he went towards his company, the [enemy] would all have crossed the ford before he could get back. (116) So then he had one of two choices, either to flee or to die. But his heart which was stout and strong advised him to stay alone, keep them at the side of the ford and defend the ascent well; since he was protected in armour he did not need to fear their arrows. (124) And if he was of good courage, he could discomfit them all, since they could only come one at a time. He did just what his heart told him. He had great – outstanding – courage when by himself [and] with [only] a slight advantage of position, he so stoutly undertook to fight with two hundred and more. (132) At that he went to the ford, and those on the opposing side, seeing him standing there alone, rode in a crowd into the water, for they had little fear of him and rode at him full tilt. (138) He smote the first so hard with his spear, which cut mighty sharp, that he knocked him down to the ground. The rest came on impetuously, but the horse of [the man] knocked down prevented them from taking [to] the ascent. (144) When the king saw how things were, he stabbed the horse which reared and then fell at the ascent. The rest came on at that with a shout, and he, stalwart and brave, met them right stoutly at the brae,

---

114. Reparyt. I have translated as 'get back' but it is possible that 'reach' [his company] is meant.

135–80. The defence at the ford. At 135 the force becomes a cavalry one. But the Galwegians who made it up would produce very few mounted men at arms; the leading horseman and his mount killed at 140–42 was probably the leader of an expedition of footmen, but persuaded Barbour to envisage a cavalry force, without explaining how Bruce could escape enemy blows which would have come from above. His figure of 200 must be exaggerated – we are asked to believe that more than 186 men fled after he had killed fourteen of their number (315). If the number is scaled down to 20-30 footmen led by a mounted man at arms, the achievement is still impressive. It remains likely that the men fled because reinforcements were approaching.

108e	And thai ar furth thar wayis gane	105
108f	And he left thar all hym allane	106
109	And sua stude he herknand	107
110	Till that he saw cum at his hand	108
	The hale rout intill full gret hy.	
	Then he umbethocht him hastily	
	Giff he held towart his menye	
	That or he mycht reparyt be	
115	Thai suld be passit the furd ilkan,	113
	And then behuffyt him ches ane	
	Off thir twa, other to fley or dey.	
	Bot his hart that wes stout and hey	
	Consaillyt hym allane to bid	
120	And kepe thaim at the furd syde	118
	And defend weill the upcummyng	
	Sen he wes warnyst of armyng	
	That thar arowys thurth nocht dreid,	
	And gyff he war off gret manheid	
125	He mycht stunay thaim everilkane	123
	Sen thai ne mycht cum bot ane and ane,	
	And did rycht as hys hart hym bad.	
	Strang utrageous curage he had	
	Quhen he sa stoutly him allane	
130	For litill strenth off erd has tane	128
	To fecht with twa hunder and ma.	
	Tharwith he to the furd gan ga,	
	And thai apon the tother party	
	That saw him stand thar anyrly	
135	Thringand intill the water rad	133
	For off him litill dout thai had	
	And raid till him in full gret hy.	
	He smate the fyrst sua vygorusly	
	With his sper that rycht scharp schar	
140	Till he doun till the erd him bar.	138
	The lave come then intill a randoun,	
	Bot his hors that wes born doun	
	Combryt thaim the upgang to ta,	
	And quhen the king saw it wes sua	
145	He stekyt the hors and he gan flyng	143
	And syne fell at the upcummyng.	
	The layff with that come with a schout,	
	And he that stalwart wes and stout	
	Met thaim rycht stoutly at the bra	

making them such good payment that he killed a fivesome in the ford. (152) The rest, fearing his mightily grievous blows, then withdrew a bit, for he didn't stint the [blows] at all. (155) Then one said, 'In truth, we are to blame. What shall we say when we go home, when one man fights against us all? Who ever knew men to fail so miserably as we [will have done] if we leave like this?' With that they gave a yell all together, shouting, 'On him, he can't last.' (162) Then they pressed him so hard that if he had not been the better [man], he would have been dead, without a doubt. But he made so strong a defence that where he struck even one blow, nothing could withstand [it]. (168) In a short while he left so many lying [dead] that the ascent was then blocked by dead horses and men, so that his enemies could not reach the ascent because of that obstruction. (173) Ah! Dear God! Anyone [passing] by, seeing how he stood up so bravely against them all, I'm sure would call him the best who lived in his time. And if I am to tell you the truth, I never heard of anyone stop so many all by himself, in any past time.

(181) It's true [that] when Tydeus was sent as a messenger to Ethiocles from his brother Polynices, to ask the whole heritage of Thebes to be held for a year, because they were twins from one birth, they contested, because each wanted to be king. (188) But the baronage of their country got them to agree in the following manner,

---

181–270. The story of Tydeus is told in Statius' *Thebaid*, mediated to Barbour through the *Roman de Thèbes*. Barbour, however, does not make the obvious comparison of Ethiocles with the English king, unwilling to grant the other his rights. Both Tydeus and Bruce were sought by their enemies to be killed, yet the Theban story occurs before the rescue of Bruce and the number he held up, 'stinted', is compared with the number killed by Tydeus (271 86).

150 And sa gud payment gan thaim ma   148
That fyvesum in the furd he slew.
The lave then sumdell thaim withdrew
That dred his strakys wondre sar
For he in na thing thaim forbar

155 Then said ane, 'Certis we ar to blame.   153
Quhat sall we say quhen we cum ham
Quhen a man fechtis agane us all.
Quha wyst ever men sa foully fall
As us gyff that we thusgat leve.'

160 With that all haile a schoute thai geve   158
And cryit, 'On him, he may nocht last.'
With that thai pressyt him sa fast
That had he nocht the better bene
He had bene dede withoutyn wen,

165 Bot he sa gret defence gan mak   163
That quhar he hyt evyn a strak
Thar mycht nathing agane-stand.
In litill space he left liand
Sa fele that the upcummyng wes then

170 Dyttyt with slayn hors and men   168
Sua that his fayis for that stopping
Mycht nocht cum to the upcummyng.
A! Der God, quha had then bene by
And sene howe he sa hardyly

175 Adressyt hym agane thaim all   173
I wate weile that thai suld him call
The best that levyt in his day,
And giff I the suth sall say
I herd never in na tym gane

180 Ane stynt sa mony him allane.   178

[The story of Tydeus of Thebes]

Suth is, quhen till Ethiocles
Fra his brother Polnices
Wes send Thedeus in message
To ask haly the heritage

185 Off Thebes till hald for a yer,   183
For thai twynnys off a byrth wer,
Thai strave, for ather king wald be.
Bot the barnage off thar cuntre
Gert thaim assent on this maner,

that one should be king for a year, [during which] the other and his following should not be found in the country while the first brother was reigning. (194) Then the other should reign for a year and then the first should leave the land while the second was reigning. Thus always one should reign for a year [while] the other was absent for a year from there. (199) Tydeus was sent to Thebes to ask [for] keeping of this agreement, and spoke so for Polynices that Ethiocles of Thebes ordered his constable to take well-armed men with him, go forth to meet Thedeus on the road and kill him without further delay. (207) The constable went on his way taking forty-nine [men] with him, so that with them he made fifty. In the evening, secretly, they laid an ambush by the road where Thedeus had to go, between a high rock and the sea. (214) He, knowing nothing of their wickedness, took his way and went again towards Greece. As he rode in the night, he saw, in the light of the moon, the reflection of a great many shields, and wondered what it might be. (221) With that, all together, they gave a shout, and he, who heard this very sudden noise, was rather frightened; but in a short time he revived his spirits very boldly, for his gentle and noble heart reassured him in that need. (228) Then he struck his steed with his spurs and rushed in among them all. The first he met he caused to fall, then he drew his sword and struck many a blow around him,

190	That the tane suld be king a yer,	188
	And then the tother and his mengye	
	Suld nocht be fundyn in the countre	
	Quhill the fyrst brother regnand wer,	
	Syne suld the tother renge a yer	
195	And then the fyrst suld leve the land	193
	Quhill that the tother war regnand.	
	Thus ay a yer suld regne the tane,	
	The tother a yer fra that war gane.	
	To ask haldyn off this assent	
200	Wes Thedeus to Thebes sent,	198
	And sua spake for Polnices	
	That off Thebes Ethiocles	
	Bad his constabill with him ta	
	Men armyt weill and forouth ga	
205	To mete Thedeus in the way	203
	And slay him but langer delay.	
	The constable his way is gane	
	And nyne and fourty with him tane	
	Sua that he with thaim maid fyfty.	
210	Intill the evynnyng prevely	208
	Thai set enbuschement in the way	
	Quhar Thedeus behovyt away	
	Betuix ane hey crag and the se,	
	And he that off thar mavyté	
215	Wyst na thing his way has tane	213
	And towart Grece agane is gane.	
	And as he raid into the nycht	
	Sa saw he with the monys lycht	
	Schynyng off scheldys gret plenté,	
220	And had wondre quhat it mycht be.	218
	With that all hale thai gaiff a cry	
	And he that hard sa suddanly	
	Sic noyis sumdele affrayit was,	
	Bot in schort time he till him tais	
225	His spyritis full hardely,	223
	For his gentill hart and worthy	
	Assuryt hym into that nede.	
	Then with te spuris he strak the sted	
	And ruschyt in amang thaim all.	
230	The fyrst he met he gert him fall,	228
	And syne his sword he swapyt out	
	And roucht about him mony rout	

killing six very quickly, and more – then they kill his horse under him, and he fell. (235) But he quickly got up and, slashing, made space about him, slaying a number of them, though he was wounded very sorely. (239) With that he found a little path running up toward the crag. He went thither in great haste, defending himself valiantly, till he had climbed a little on the rock and found a well-enclosed place where only one [person] could attack him. (246) He stood there and gave them battle, while they all attacked and often fell. When he killed one, as he fell down to the ground he would knock down a good four or five. He stood there defending like that till he had killed more than half of them. (253) Then he saw a huge stone near him, which from long being there was detached, ready to fall; when he saw them all coming he tumbled the stone down on them, killing eight men with it and so dumbfounding the rest that they were almost ready to give up. (261) Then he would stay confined no longer but ran on them with naked sword and cut and killed with all his main till he had slain forty-nine. Then he took the constable [prisoner] and had him swear that he would go to King Ethiocles and tell [him] the events that had befallen them. (269) Tydeus bore himself doughtily in overcoming fifty by himself. You who read this, judge which should be more esteemed: the king, who deliberately undertook such a bold deed as to rebuff entirely on his own,

---

265. The constable. In the *Roman* Tydeus sends one of his enemies, not identified as the constable.

And slew sexsum swill sone and ma.
Then undre him his hors thai sla
235   And he fell, bot he smertly ras   233
And strykand rowm about him mas
And slew off thaim a quantite
Bot woundyt wondre sar wes he.
With that a litill rod he fand
240   Up towart the crag strekand.   238
Thidder went he in full gret hy
Defendand him full douchtely
Till in the crag he clam sumdell
And fand a place enclosyt weill
245   Quhar nane bot ane mycht him assail,   243
Thar stud he and gaiff thaim bataill
And thai assaylyt everilkane
And oft fell quhen that he slew ane
As he doun to the erd wald dryve
250   He wald ber doun weill four or fyve.   248
Thar stud he and defendyt sua
Till he had slayne thaim halff and ma.
A gret stane then by him saw he
That throu the gret anciente
255   Wes lowsyt redy for to fall,   253
And quhen he saw thaim cummand all
He tumblyt doun on thaim the stane,
And aucht men thar with it has slayn
And sua stonayit the remanand
260   That thai war weile ner recreand.   258
Then wald he presone hald no mar
Bot on thaim ran with swerd all bar
And hewyt and slew with all his mayn
Till he has nyne and fourty slayne.
265   The constabill syne gan he ta   263
And gert him swer that he suld ga
Till King Ethiocles and tell
The aventur that thaim befell.
Thedeus bar him douchtely
270   That him allane ourcome fyfty.   268
Ye that this redys, cheys yhe
Quhether that mar suld prysit be
The king, that with avisement
Undertuk sic hardyment
275   As for to stynt him ane but fer   273

those folk who were a good two hundred, (277) or Thedeus who unexpectedly, after they had raised a shout against him, by finding his courage, defeated fifty men by himself. They both did their deed in night-time, both fought by the moon's light, but the king defeated more while Thedeus slew more. (285) Now judge whether Tydeus should have more praise or the king!

(287) In this way that I have narrated, the king, who was strong and brave, fought beside the ford, giving and taking violent blows, until he made such slaughter there that he had completely blocked the ford, [so] that none of them could ride to him. (294) Then they thought it was folly to stay, and all together took to flight, going homewards whence they came from. For the king's men, wakened by the noise came in a great panic to seek their lord, the king. The Galloway-men heard their coming and, not daring to stay any longer, fled. (302) The king's men who feared for their lord['s safety] came to the ford at top speed, and soon found the king sitting alone, having taken off his basnet to take the air, because he was hot. (308) Then they asked him how he was, and he told them the whole story, the way he had been attacked, and how God helped him so that he altogether escaped from them. Then they looked [to see] how many were dead, and they found lying in that place fourteen whom he had killed by his hand. (316) Then they diligently praised Almighty God

---

290–99. The sudden arrival of the king's men is very curiously placed. The enemy all fled (295) for the king's men were awakened by 'the cry' (297), which either means 'all the noise' or refers to the cry narrated at 159, before the Theban story; they wakened in trepidation (298), and the noise of their approach caused the enemy to flee (301). It seems to me that the Theban story has been added in revision, and that originally Bruce sent his two men for help (108a-f), which came in some way possibly involving Gilbert Hay, arriving after the Galwegians had fled (295). The Theban story made it desirable that Bruce, like Tydeus, be without a companion to send for help (85–92), though he was rescued when the fortunate arrival of his men scared off his enemies.

291. Martyrdom. Fourteen were killed (315).

306. Bassynet. The basnet or bassinet was a simple helmet.

The folk that twa hunder wer,
Or Thedeus, that suddanly
For thai had raysyt on him the cry
Throu hardyment that he had tane
280 Wane fyfty men all him allane. 278
Thai did thar deid bath on the nycht
And faucht bath with the mone-lycht,
Bot the king discomfyt ma
And Thedeus then ma gan sla.
285 Now demys quhether mar loving 283
Suld Thedeus haiff or the king?

[His men find the king]

On this maner that Ik haiff tauld
The king that stout wes and bauld
Wes fechtand on the furd syd
290 Giffand and takand rowtis rid 288
Till he sic martyrdom thar has maid
That he the ford all stoppyt haid
That nane of thaim mycht till him rid.
Thaim thocht than foly for to byd
295 And halely the flycht gan ta 293
And went hamewartis quhar thai come fra,
For the kingis men with the cry
Walknyt full effrayitly
And com to sek thar lord the king.
300 The Galloway men hard thar cummyng 298
And fled and durst abid no mar.
The kingis men that dredand war
For thar lord full spedyly
Come to the furd and sone in hy
305 Thai fand the king syttand allane, 303
That off his bassynet has tane
Till avent him for he wes hate.
Than speryt thai at him off his state
And he tauld thaim all hale the case
310 Howgate that he assailyt was 308
And how that God him helpyt sua
That he eschapyt hale thaim fra.
Than lukyt thai how fele war ded,
And thai fand lyand in that sted
315 Fourtene that war slayne with his hand. 313
Than lovyt thai God fast all-weildand

that they found their lord hale and hearty, and said they should in no way fear their foes since their chieftain was of such spirit and strength that he had undertaken to fight alone for them against so many men.

(323) They said things like this about the king, marvelling at his great undertaking, and, always used to being with him, yearned to protect him. Ah! How valour is valued! For it causes men to be praised if it is consistently pursued. (330) For the prize of valour is nonetheless hard to win, for great effort, often defending, often attacking, and wisdom in their deeds, [these] cause men to win the prize of valour. No man can have that honour unless he knows how to control his actions and see what is to be left, [what] taken. (338) Valour has two extremes: foolhardiness is the foremost, and the other is cowardice; they are both to be avoided. Foolhardiness will try everything, things to be left [undone] as well as [to be] done. But cowardice does nothing like that, but abandons everything utterly; that was a more costly [thing] to occur than lack of discretion would be. (348) For the reason [that] valour has such fame is that it is the mean between these two, does what is to be undertaken, leaves what is to be left, for it has such a great endowment of sense that it saw well all dangers and all possible advantages. (355) I would stick entirely to brave deeds, provided that there was no rashness, for bravery with rashness is a fault.

346-47. Derer for to fal/na war faute of discretioune. The meaning of this is by no means clear to me. *B1907*, 100 translates: It were a marvel if this last fell out well, any more than want of discretion. (!)

That thai thar lord fand hale and fer,
And said thaim byrd on na maner
Drede thar fayis sen thar chyftane
320   Wes off sic hart and off sic mayn   318
That he for thaim had undretan
With sua fele for to fecht him ane.

[*A comment on valour*]

Syk wordis spak thai of the king,
And for his hey undretaking
325   Farlyit and yarnyt hym for to se   323
That with hym ay wes wont to be.
A! Quhat worschip is prisit thing,
For it mays men till haiff loving
Gyff it be folowit ythenly,
330   For pryce off worschip nocht-forthi   328
Is hard to wyn, for gret travaill
Offt to defend and oft assaill
And to be in thar dedis wys
Gerris men off worschip wyn the price,
335   And may na man haiff worthyhed   333
Bot he haiff wyt to ster his deid
And se quhat ys to leve or ta.
Worschip extremyteys has twa,
Fule-hardyment the formast is
340   And the tother is cowartys,   338
And thai ar bath for to forsak.
Fule-hardyment all will undertak,
Als weill thingis to leve as ta,
Bot cowardys dois na thing sua
345   But uttrely forsakis all,   343
Bot that war derer for to fal
Na war faute of discretioun.
Forthi has worschip sic renoun,
That it is mene betuix tha twa
350   And takys that is till underta   348
And levys that is to leve, for it
Has sa gret warnysing of wyt
That it all perellis weile gan se
And all avantagis that may be.
355   I wald till hardyment heyld haly   353
With-thi away war the foly
For hardyment with foly is vice

But bravery that is mixed with intelligence is always valour, *per dé*, for without intelligence there can't be valour. (361) This noble king of whom we speak always mingled intelligence with bravery, as you can see by this mellee. His intelligence showed him the narrow entry to the ford, and also the exit which, as he thought, would be difficult to take from a man who was bold. (368) Therefore his courage quickly realised that [the defence] could be undertaken, since only one could attack at one time. Thus courage ruled by intelligence, which he always sought to knit together, caused him to have the prize of valour and frequently overcome his enemies.

(375) The king still stayed in Carrick; when his men, who were travelling in the land, heard news of this deed, they gathered fast to him for they meant to take their lot with him if he was attacked like that afterwards. (381) But James Douglas was still travelling in Douglasdale or else near thereby, somewhat secretly in hiding-places. He wanted to see the control [exercised] by him who had the castle in [his] keeping, and caused make many a feint to see whether he would come out easily. (389) When [Douglas] saw readily that he would issue carelessly with his following, he secretly gathered those who were on his side, who were so numerous that they dared to fight with Thirlwall and the whole strength of those who were in the castle. (396) He got ready to go in the night to Sandilands and near thereby he lay in secret ambush.

385-86. His governyng that had the castell in keping. The keeper would be the constable of the castle, a term Barbour seems reluctant to use; at 394 he implies that this was Thirlwall, who, he had said, was made 'captain', implying keepership (5.461). But at 433 he calls Thirlwall the captain of the men who rode out, the correct use of captain.

388, 390. Blithly, usually 'cheerfully', but here surely with the sense of 'carelessly'.

394. Thirlwall. At 5.460 he was 'one of the Thirlwalls', and Barbour is ignorant of his first name. English records show a John Thirlwall as a valet of Sir Adam Swinburn (not with Clifford as in *B1985*, 78), going in pursuit of Bruce in Glen Trool in April 1307; such a man, or his brother, could have entered Clifford's service to become captain of the men-at-arms, probably around a dozen in number, in Douglas castle. (*CDS2, 1923*) The date of this episode is unknown. I do not think it is a doublet of that in 8.437–514.

397. Sandilands is 5 miles, 8 kilometres north-east of Douglas. The distance seems very great to lay such an ambush, for men on horseback who rode out so swiftly that they were incompletely armed would catch cattle within a mile or two. Perhaps James Douglas was at Sandilands when he plotted the ruse much nearer to Douglas castle.

Bot hardyment that mellyt is
With wyt is worschip ay perdé,
360   For but wyt worschip may nocht be.   358
This nobile king that we off red
Mellyt all tyme with wit manheid,
That may men by this melle se.
His wyt schawyt him the strait entre
365   Off the furd and the uschyng alsua   363
That as him thocht war hard to ta
Apon a man that war worthy,
Tharfor his hardyment hastily
Thocht it mycht be weill undretan
370   Sen at anys mycht assail bot ane.   368
Thus hardyment governyt with wyt
That he all tyme wald samyn knyt
Gert him off worschip haiff the price
And oft ourcum his ennymyis.

[*Douglas attacks Thirlwall at Douglas castle*]

375   The king in Carrik dwellyt ay still,   373
Hys men assemblyt fast him till
That in the land war travailland
Quhen thai off this deid herd tithand
For thai thar ure wald with him ta
380   Gyff that he eft war assaylyt sua.   378
Bot yeit than James of Douglas
In Douglas daile travailland was
Or ellysweill ner-hand tharby
In hydillys sumdeill prevely,
385   For he wald se his governyng   383
That had the castell in keping,
And gert mak mony juperty
To se quhether he wald ische blythly.
And quhen he persavyt that he
390   Wald blythly ische with his menye,   388
He maid a gadring prevely
Of thaim that war on his party,
That war sa fele that thai durst fycht
With Thyrwall and all the mycht
395   Of thaim that in the castell war.   393
He schupe him in the nycht to far
To Sandylandis, and ner tharby
He him enbuschyt prevely

He sent a few [men] to make a decoy; early in the morning they took cattle which were near the castle and then drove them away hurriedly towards those who were lying in ambush. (404) Then Thirlwall at once had his men arm [themselves] without delay, came out with all the men he had and followed fast after the cattle. He was suitably armed, completely except that his head was bare. (410) With the men who were with him he followed the cattle at speed, like a man with no fear, till he got sight of them. Then they galloped with all their might, chasing them in disorder, while [Douglas's men] hurried in flight until they had all passed by the ambush; Thirlwall still chased fast after [them]. (419) Then those who were lying in ambush, of high and low station, came out towards him, raising suddenly the [war-]cry, and those [English] who so unexpectedly saw those [Scots] come galloping so fiercely between them and their base, were in very great fear. (426) And because they were in disorder, some of them fled and some stayed, while Douglas, who had a big following there with him, attacked them fiercely, scattering them rapidly, and in a short time so overwhelmed them that almost no-one escaped from them. (433) Thirlwall, who was their captain, was killed there in the fight, along with the greater part of his men; the rest fled in terror. Douglas's following quickly gave chase and those fleeing took their way to the castle with great speed. (440) The foremost entered speedily, but the pursuers pressed so fast

---

401. Beasts. In 1346 the seneschal de Beaucaire gathered a force to take the town of 'Antenis' from the English. He drew the garrison out by driving by 60–80 stolen beasts; the garrison sallied out and followed to where a force lay waiting. There was a battle, many of the garrison were killed and the town was taken. All according to Jean le Bel. (*Chron. Le Bel*, ii, 50–52)

And send a few a trane to ma,
400 That sone in the mornyng gan ta 398
Catell that wes the castell by
And syne withdrew thaim hastily
Towart thaim that enbuschit war.
Than Thyrwall foroutyn mar
405 Gert arme his men foroutyn baid 403
And ischyt with all the men he haid
And folowyt fast efter the ky.
He wes armyt at poynt clenly
Outane his hede wes bar.
410 Than with the men that with him war 408
The catell folowit he gud speid
Rycht as a man that had na dreid
Till that he gat off thaim a sycht.
Than prekyt thai with all thar mycht
415 Folowand thaim out off aray, 413
And thai sped thaim fleand quhill thai
Fer by thar buschement war past,
And Thyrwall ay chassyt fast.
And than thai that enbuschyt war
420 Ischyt till him bath les and mar 418
And rayssyt sudanly the cry,
And thai that saw sa sudandly
That folk come egyrly prekand
Rycht betwix thaim and thar warand,
425 Thai war into full gret effray 423
And for thai war out off aray
Sum off thaim fled and sum abad,
And the Douglas that thar with him had
A gret mengye full egrely
430 Assaylyt and scalyt thaim hastyly 428
And in schort tyme ourraid thaim sua
That weile nane eschapyyt thaim fra.
Thyrwall that wes thar capitane
Wes thar in the bargane slane
435 And off his men the mast party, 433
The lave fled full effraytly.
Douglas his menye fast gan chas,
And the flearis thar wayis tays
Till the castell in full gret hy.
440 The formast entryt spedyly 438
Bot the chaseris sped thaim sa fast

that they overtook some at the back and killed them merci-
lessly. When those in the castle saw them killing [some] of
their men nearby like that, they barred the gates hastily and
ran quickly to the walls. (448) James Douglas's followers then
hastily seized to themselves what they found around the castle,
and then went to their shelter. That's how Thirlwall came
out that day.

(453) When Thirlwall had come out in the way that I've told
you here, James Douglas and his men readied themselves all
together, and went their way towards the king in great haste,
(458) for they heard news that Sir Aymer de Valence, with a
very large chivalry of both Englishmen and Scotsmen, were
prepared [and] mustered then to seek with great ruthlessness
the king, who was at that time at Cumnock with his force,
where it was narrowest. (466) Thither went James Douglas
who was very welcome to the king. When he had told this
news, how Sir Aymer was coming to hunt him out of the land
with hound and horn, just as if he were a wolf, a thief or
thief's accomplice, (473) then the king said, 'It could well
happen that even if he and all his might come, we shall remain
in this country, and if he comes, we shall see him.' (477) The
king spoke in these terms, and Sir Aymer de Valence gathered
a great company of noble and valiant men from England and
from Lothian.

---

465. Cumnock quhair it straitast was. Cumnock castle belonged to the
earl of Dunbar but was 'borrowed' for Edward I, by the Treasurer of
England who, on 15 May, 1307 ordered the payment of the garrisons
at Ayr, Lanark and Cumnock; Ingram Umfraville and William Felton
were put in charge and on 18 May were given provisions for the castle
to which Felton was about to go on 21 May; and the composition of
the garrison of 30 men-at-arms and 100 infantry became a matter of
concern. These moves show that, from mid-May 1307, immediately
after the battle of Loudoun, the castle was thought to be a critical place.
The castle cannot have been taken by King Robert, for it was not
slighted. Cumnock does lie in the narrow valley of the Lugar Water,
and Barbour's use of 'straitast' suggests tactics, a reference to a skirmish
which he does not report. But the meeting of Bruce and Douglas there
(466–67) would fit with a time just before Loudoun, to which they
went by way of Galston (8.123). (*CDS2, 1928, 1931, 1933; CDS4, 1829;
CDS5, 485, 503*)

That thai ourtuk sum of the last
And thaim foroutyn mercy gan sla.
And quhen thai off the castell sua
445   Saw thaim sla off thar men thaim by   443
Thai sparyt the yattis hastily
And in hy to the wallis rane.
James off Douglas his menye than
Sesyt weile hastily in hand
450   That thai about the castell fand   448
To thair resett, syne went thar way.
Thus ischyt Thyrwall that day.

[*The king is pursued by John of Lorn and his tracker-dog; he and his foster brother kill five men*]

Quhen Thyrwall on this maner
Had ischit as I tell you her,
455   James off Douglas and his men   453
Buskit thaim all samyn then
And went thar way towart the king
In gret hy, for thai herd tything
That off Valence Schyr Amery
460   With full gret chevalry   458
Bath off Scottis and Inglis men
With gret felny war redy then
Assemblyt for to sek the king,
That wes that tyme with his gadring
465   In Cumnok quhair it straitast was.   463
Thidder went James of Douglas
And wes rycht welcum to the king
And quhen he had tauld that tithing,
How that schyr Amer wes cummand
470   For till hunt him out off the land   468
With hund and horne rycht as he war
A woulff, a theyff, or theyffis fer,
Than said the king, 'It may weill fall
Thocht he cum and his power all
475   We sall abid in this countre,   473
And gyff he cummys we sall him se.'
The king spake apon this maner,
And of Valence Schyr Amer
Assemblyt a gret cumpany
480   Off noble men and off worthy   478
Off Ingland and of Lowthiane,

He also took with him John of Lorn and all his might, who had eight hundred valiant and bold men with him. (486) He had a tracker-dog with him there too, so good that nothing would put him off. Some men say still that the king had trained him in the chase and always made so much of him that he would feed him with his [own] hand. (492) The dog followed him wherever he went, [and] loved him so that he would in no way be parted from him. But how John of Lorn had him I never heard mention be made, (497) but men say that it was certainly true that he had him in his possession and meant to take the king by him, because he knew he loved him, so that once he got the king's scent he wouldn't leave it for anything. (504) This John of Lorn hated the king for the sake of Sir John Comyn, his uncle; if he could either kill or capture him, [the king] would not value his life a straw, provided that he could take revenge on him. (509) Sir Aymer, then the warden, in company with John of Lorn, and also others of good reputation – one of them was Thomas Randolph – came to Cumnock to seek the king, who was well aware of their arrival, and was then up in the strongholds, a good four hundred men with him.

---

483. This is the first mention in the poem of John of Argyll, whom Barbour calls 'of Lorn'. In his surviving letter to Edward II and almost always in English records, he figures as 'of Argyll' even when his father lived, but on two occasions he is 'of Lorn' (*CDS5*, 198a, 223a); the name implies that he had been infeft in Lorn by his father or had been born there. He lost all the family possessions, but his descendants were restored to some and were known as 'of Lorn'.

485. Eight hundred men. This figure is, quite remarkably, correct, because a letter of Valence of 19 July, 1307 shows that John was then guarding Ayr with 22 men-at-arms and 800 infantry. Barbour's source here must have had accurate knowledge, including the mention of Randolph at 512. By mid-August, when he wrote to Edward II, John was back in Argyll. There is no evidence that he and Valence went seeking Bruce together and indeed Valence's letter says that John was left behind to guard Ayr and district; in July 1307 Valence was at Glasgow (12), Ayr (18), Dalmilling (by Ayr, 17–19), Glenken (24, when he still did not know of Edward I's death on 7 July), Skeldon (6m. SE of Ayr, 31). He may have been driving Bruce towards Edward I but turned back on news of the latter's death. (*CDS2*, 1952–1959; *CDS5*, 223a) Grafted on to this expedition by Valence is a pursuit of Robert I by John of Lorn with hounds. This story could – probably does – belong to quite another time, possibly a year earlier in Argyll or Atholl. Barbour makes no mention of Edward II's invasion of the south-west during the whole of August 1307; he reached Cumnock, while his forces scoured for Bruce.

487. Strecour in C, a dog for the chase. E has 'traytour' which scarcely

And he has alsua with him tane
Jhone off Lorn and all his mycht
That had off worthi men and wycht
485 With him aucht hunder men and ma 483
A sleuth-hund had he thar alsua
Sa gud that wald chang for na thing,
And sum men sayis yeit that the king
As a strecour him noryst had
490 And sa mekill off him he maid 488
That hys awyn handis wald him feid.
He folowyt him quharever he yeid
Sa that the hund him lovit sua
That he wald part na wys him fra.
495 Bot how that Jhon of Lorn him had 493
Ik herd never mencioun be mad,
Bot men sayis it wes certane thing
That he had him in his sesyng
And throu him thocht the king to ta,
500 For he wyst he him luffyt sua 498
That fra that he mycht anys fele
The kingis sent he wyst rycht weill
That he wald chaung it for na thing.
This Jhon off Lorne hattyt the king
505 For Jhon Cumyn his emys sak, 503
Mycht he him other sla or tak
He wald nocht prys his liff a stra
Sa that he vengeance of him mycht ta.
The wardane than Schyr Amery
510 With this Jhone in cumpany 508
And other off gud renoun alsua,
Thomas Randell was ane off tha,
Come intill Cumnok to sek the king
That wes weill war off that cummyng
515 And wes up in the strenthis then 513
And with him weill four hunder men.

---

makes sense. Here the tracker dog plays a greater role than in the earlier
episode (36–102).
513. Cumnock is probably introduced here because Barbour has placed
it after the meeting of Douglas and the king at that place. The abortive
search for the king and attempt to encircle him is not mentioned in
any other source, but it would fit with July 1307.
513. Strenthis, a word used quite frequently by Barbour of the strong-
points at which King Robert took refuge. Here it must mean natural
eminences, hilltops, and that is probably its usual sense.

(517) His brother was with him at that time as well as James Douglas. He saw Sir Aymer's host which kept to the open low country, and always rode in one force. (522) The king, who had no idea that they were more [numerous] than those he [could] see, acting unwisely, kept [his] eye on them and nowhere else. (526) For John of Lorn, very deviously, meant to surprise the king's rear [and] therefore held the way, with all his force, round a hill, keeping himself always under cover, until he came so near to the king before [the latter] perceived his arrival, that he was well-nigh on top of him. (534) The other host and Sir Aymer pressed [him] on the other side. The king, was in great jeopardy, being beset from both sides by enemies threatening to kill him, the lesser of the two [forces] being far stronger – and more – than him. (541) When he saw them press upon him, he thought quickly [about] what was to be done, and said, 'Lords, we have no strength to stand and fight at this time. Therefore, let us split into three; thus all will not be attacked, and [we can] hold our way in three parties.' Then he said to those in his confidence, among them, in private, at what place their rendez-vous should be. (551) With that all went their way, taking the road in three parties. Then John of Lorn came to the place from which the king had left and set the hound on his tracks, which then, without any hesitation, held exactly the way after the king, just as if he recognised him, leaving the two other parties

---

541–674. The account of the chase, which now ignores Valence's force is not very convincing, since the pursuers seem to be in sight of the king, yet are not so, since they use the hounds. And if the pursuit was close, why detach five men to catch up on the king? He has time to fight and kill them and escape before John of Lorn appears on the scene.

His broder that tym with him was
And alsua James off Douglas.
Schyr Ameryys rowte he saw
That held the plane ay and the law
And in hale battaill alwayis raid.
The king that na supposyn had
That thai wer may then he saw thar
Till thaim and nother ellisquhar
Had ey and wrocht unwittily,
For Jhon off Lorn full sutelly
Behind thocht to supprys the king.
Tharfor with all his gadring
About ane hill he held the way
And held him into covert ay
Till he sa ner come to the king
Or he persavyt his cummyng
That he wes cummyn on him weill ner.
The tother ost and Schyr Amer
Pressyt apon the tother party.
The king wes in gret juperty
That wes on ather sid umbeset
With fayis that to sla him thret,
And the leyst party off the twa
Was starkar than he and ma.
And quhen he saw thaim pres him to
He thocht in hy quhat was to do
And said, 'Lordis we haiff na mycht
As at this tyme to stand and fycht,
Tharfor departis us in thre,
All sall nocht sa assailyt be,
And in thre partis hald our way.'
Syne till his preve folk gan he say
Betwix thaim into prevete
In quhat sted thar repayr suld be.
With that thar gate all ar thai gane
And in thre partis thar way has tane.
Jhone of Lorne come to the place
Fra quhar the king departyt was
And in his trace the hund he set
That then foroutyn langer let
Held even the way efter the king
Rycht as he had off him knawing,
And left the tother partys twa

518

523

528

533

538

543

548

553

520

525

530

535

540

545

550

555

as if he would pay no attention to them. (561) When the king saw him coming in a line after his force, he realised that they knew it was him, so he ordered his followers split into three [groups] quickly, [which] they did without delay, holding their way in three parties. The hound then showed such skill that, without losing [the scent], he kept after the force where the king was.

(571) When the king saw them take the way after him thus all in one force, and not follow his men, he had a clear intuition then that they recognised him; therefore at once he ordered his men to scatter quickly, each man to hold his way all by himself, and they did just that. (579) Each man went a different way, and the king took with him his foster-brother, no-one else, and those two took their way together. The hound always followed the king, not losing [the scent] for any parting, but always followed the king's tracks as he had passed [by], without diverging. (587) When John of Lorn saw the hound strain so hard after him, following straight after those two, he knew the king was one of them, and ordered five of his company who were very strong and bold men and also the fleetest of foot among all who were there in that force, to run after [the king], overtake him, and in no wise let him get away from them. (597) After they had heard their orders, they held the way after the king, following him so rapidly that they very quickly overtook him. (601) The king, who saw them coming close, was greatly vexed

560 As he na kep to thaim wald ta.   558
And quhen the king saw his cummyng
Efter hys route intill a ling
He thocht thai knew that it wes he,
Tharfor he bad till his menye
565 Yeit then in thre depart thaim sone,   563
And thai did sua foroutyn hone
And held thar way in thre partys.
The hund did thar sa gret maistrys
That held ay foroutyn changing
570 Eftre the rowt quhar wes the king.   568
And quhen the king had sene thaim sua
All in a rowt efter him ga
The way and folow nocht his men
He had a gret persaving then
575 That thai knew him, forthi in hy   573
He bad his men rycht hastily
Scaile and ilkan hald his way
All himselff, and sua did thai.
Ilk man a syndry gate is gane
580 And the king with him has tane   578
His foster broder foroutyn ma
And samyn held thar gate thai twa.
The hund folowyt alwayis the king
And changyt for na departing
585 Bot ay folowit the kingis trace   583
But waveryng as he passyt was
And quhen Jhon off Lorn saw
The hund sa hard eftre him draw
And folow strak after thai twa
590 He knew the king wes ane of tha,   588
And bad fyve off his cumpany
That war rycht wycht men and hardy
And als off fute spediast war
Off all that in thair rowt war
595 Ryn eftre him and him ourta   593
And lat him na wys pas thaim fra,
And fra thai had herd the bydding
Thai held thar way efter the king
And folowyt him sa spedely
600 That thai him weill sone gan ourhy.   598
The king that saw thaim cummand ner
Wes anoyit on gret maner,

for he thought [that] if they were worthy they could trouble
and delay him, holding him tarrying thus till the rest could
catch up. But had he feared only those five, I'm very sure he
would have had no great fear. (610) He said to his companion
as he went, 'Yon five are coming quickly; they are almost
upon us. So will you help at all, for we shall be attacked pretty
soon?' 'Yes, sir,' he said, 'all that I can.' (616) 'You say well
indeed,' said the king. 'I see them coming close to us. I'm
going no further but will stay right here, while I [still] have
breath, to see what strength they can muster.'

(621) The king then stood very sturdily, and the five-some
came very quickly, with a lot of threats and menaces. Three
of them went at the king, and the other two went sword in
hand, stoutly, to his man. (627) The king met those who tried
[to reach] him, and struck such a blow at the first that he
sliced his ear and cheek down to the neck, and also [some]
of [his] shoulder; he tumbled down dizzily. (632) The two
who saw their companion fall suddenly, were scared and
retreated a little backwards. The king at that looked aside and
saw the two-some making a great scrimmage against his man.
(636) At that he left his own two [opponents] and leapt lightly
to those who fought with his man, striking the head off one
of the two. Then he went to face his own [foes]. (643) They
came against him very strongly, [and] he met the first so
quickly that he took the arm from his body with his sharply-
cutting sword.

For he thocht giff thai war worthi
Thai mycht hi, travaile and tary
605 And hald him swagate tariand   603
Till the remanand com at hand,
Bot had he dred bot anerly
Thai fyve I trow all sekyrly
He suld have had na mekill dred.
610 And till his falow as he yeid   608
He said, 'Thir fyve ar fast cummand
Thai ar weill ner now at our hand,
Sa is thar ony help at the
For we sall sone assailyt be.'
615 'Ya, schyr,' he said, 'all that I may.'   613
'Thou sayis weill,' said the king. 'Perfay
I see thaim cummand till us ner.
I will na forthyr bot rycht her
I will byd quhill Ic am in aynd
620 And se quhat force that thai can faynd.'   618
The king than stud full sturdely
And the fyvesum in full gret hy
Come with gret schor and manassing.
Then thre off thaim went to the king,
625 And till his man the tother twa   623
With swerd in hand gan stoutly ga.
The king met thaim that till him socht
And to the fyrst sic rowt he roucht
That er and chek downe in the hals
630 He scharnand off the schuldir als,   628
He ruschyt down all disyly.
The twa that saw sa sudanly
Thar falow fall effrayit war
And stert a litill ovyrmar.
635 The king with that blenkit him by   633
And saw the twasome sturdely
Agane his man gret melle ma.
With that he left his awin twa
And till thaim that faucht with his man
640 A loup rycht lychtly maid he than   638
And smate the hed off the tane,
To mete his awne syne is he gane.
Thai come on him full sturdely,
He met the fyrst sa egrely
645 That with the swerd that scharply schar   643

I can't say what strokes they struck, but [things] went so well for the king that, although he had trouble and difficulty, he killed four of his enemies. His foster-brother soon after ended the days of the fifth. (653) When the king saw that all five had lost their lives in this way, he said to his companion, 'You have helped well indeed.' 'It's good of you to say so,' said [the other], 'but you took the greater part upon yourself, slaying four out of the five by yourself.' (660) The king said, 'As the game went I was able to do better than you, because I had more time for it. For the two fellows who were dealing with you, when they saw me attacked by three, had no worries about me, because they believed I was tightly engaged. (667) And because they didn't fear me, I could hurt them far more readily.' With that the king looked around and saw the company of Lorn close by, coming fast with their tracker-dog; then he went in haste to a wood that was nearby, with his companion. May God, in his great mercy, save them.

The arme fra the body he bar.
Quhat strakys thai gaiff I can nocht tell,
Bot to the king sa fayr befell
That thocht he travaill had and payne
650 He off his fa-men four has slayn, 648
His foster broder tharefter sone
The fyft out of dawys has done.
And quhen the king saw that all fyve
War on that wys broucht out off lyve
655 Till hys falow than gan he say, 653
'Thou has helpyt weile perfay.'
'It likys you to say sua,' said he,
'Bot the gret part to you tuk ye
That slew four off the fyve you ane.'
660 The king said, 'As the glew is gane 658
Better than thou I mycht it do
For Ik had mar layser tharto,
For the twa falowys that delt with the
Quhen thai saw me assailyt with thre
665 Off me rycht nakyn dout thai had 663
For thai wend I sa straytly war stad,
And forthi that thai dred me noucht
Noy thaim fer out the mar I moucht.'
With that the king lokyt him by
670 And saw off Lorn the company 668
Weill ner with thar sleuth-hund cummand.
Than till a wod that wes ner-hand
He went with his falow in hy.
God sayff thaim for his gret mercy.

The king went towards the wood, sweating, weary, and at a loss. He quickly entered the wood and went downwards towards a glen where a stream ran through the wood. (6) He went there in great haste then, and began to rest himself there, saying that he could go no further. His man said, 'Sir, that isn't possible; if you stay here, you'll soon see five hundred [men] out to kill you – and that's a lot against two [of us]. Since we can't very well cope with numbers, let's see how we can help with cunning.' (15) The king said, 'If that's what you want, you do it and I'll go along with you. But I've often heard it said that whoever wades down a stream for [the length of] an arrow-shot makes both the tracker-dog and his master lose the scent men had made him take. (22) Let's prove now whether it will do so, for if yon devil's hound were not there, I wouldn't worry at all about the rest.' They did just what he had suggested, and soon went into the burn, continuing along the stream and then to the land, resuming their journey as they had gone before. (30) John of Lorn with a great display [of force] came with his men right to the place where his five men had been killed. He bemoaned them when he saw them, and said after a little while that he would quickly avenge their blood, though the game turned out differently. (37) He decided to stay there no longer but quickly followed on after the king; they went right to the burn,

BOOK 7

[The king escapes from the hound]

The king towart the wod is gane
Wery forswayt and will of wane
Intill the wod sone entryt he
And held doun towart a vale
5   Quhar throu the woid a watter ran.
Thidder in gret hy wend he than
And begouth for to rest him thar
And said he mycht no forthirmar.
His man said, 'Schyr, it may nocht be.
10   Abyd ye her ye sall son se
Fyve hunder yarnand you to sla,
And thai ar fele aganys us twa.
And sen we may nocht dele with mycht
Help us all that we may with slycht.'
15   The king said, 'Sen that thou will sua,
Ga furth, and I sall with the ga.
Bot Ik haiff herd oftymys say
That quha endlang a watter ay
Wald waid a bow-draucht he suld ger
20   Bathe the slouth-hund and his leder
Tyne the sleuth men gert him ta.
Prove we giff it will now do sa,
For war yone devillis hund away
I roucht nocht off the lave perfay.'
25   As he dyvisyt thai haiff doyn
And entryt in the watter sone
And held down endlang thar way,
And syne to the land yeid thai
And held thar way as thai did er.
30   And Jhone off Lorn with gret affer
Come with hys rout rycht to the place
Quhar that his fyve men slane was.
He menyt thaim quhen he thaim saw
And said eftre a litill thraw
35   That he suld veng thar bloude,
Bot otherwayis the gamyn youde.
Thar wald he mak na mar dwelling
Bot furth in hy folowit the king.
Rycht to the burn thai passyt war,

but the tracker-dog hesitated there and for a long time wandered to and fro as though he couldn't go by any clear way, until eventually John of Lorn realised that the dog had lost the scent. (45) He said, 'We've lost this round. Going on will do no good, for the wood is both long and broad, and by now he is far away, so I think we should turn back and waste no more effort in a vain [endeavour].' With that he rallied his following and took his way to the army.

(53) The noble king escaped like that. But some men say that this escape occurred in a different way than by the wading, for they tell how the king had a good archer, who, when he saw his lord so placed that he was left alone like that, ran on foot always near him until he had gone into the wood. Then he said to himself alone that he would stop just there and see if he could kill the hound. (65) For if the hound could stay alive he knew full well that they would follow the king's tracks till they took him; he knew well they would kill him then. Because he wanted to support his lord, he put his life at risk, and stood hiding in a bush until the hound came [close] at hand, and with an arrow quickly killed him, then withdrew through the wood. (75) But whether the escape happened as I first told [it] or as I now tell, I'm quite sure, and not romancing: the king escaped at that burn.

---

47. Literally, the wood is both broad and wide.
56. This alternative ending shows how widespread the story of pursuit by dogs was. Presumably the archer in this version was the foster-brother in the earlier one.
87. After the death of Edward I Valence was commissioned by Edward II to remain as lieutenant in Scotland with a retinue of 60 men-at-arms, made up of 18 knights and 42 esquires. Among these were Sir Thomas Randolph and Patrick Dunbar (esq.), both of whom were among the many who lost horses pursuing Douglas in Paisley Forest on 14 September, 1307. It is not known when Randolph joined Valence, but it could have been in the spring of 1307 or even earlier. (*CDS5*, 655)

40   Bot the sleuth-hund maid styntyn thar
        And waveryt lang tyme to and fra
        That he na certane gate couth ga,
        Till at the last that Jhon of Lorn
        Persavyt the hund the slouth had lorn
45   And said, 'We haiff tynt this travaill.
        To pas forthyr may nocht availe
        For the void is bath braid and wid
        And he is weill fer be this tid,
        Tharfor is gud we turn agayn
50   And waist no mar travaill in vayne.'
        With that relyit he his mengye
        And his way to the ost tuk he.

[*An alternative account of the escape*]

        Thus eschapyt the nobill king,
        Bot sum men sayis this eschaping
55   Apon ane other maner fell
        Than throu the wading, for thai tell
        That the king a gud archer had,
        And quhen he saw his lord sua stad
        That he wes left sa anerly
60   He ran on sid alwayis him by
        Till he into the woude wes gane.
        Than said he till him selff allane
        That he arest rycht thar wald ma
        To luk giff he the hund mycht sla,
65   For giff the hund mycht lest in lyve
        He wyst rycht weile that thai wald dryve
        The kingis trace till thai him ta,
        Than wyst he weile thai wald him sla.
        And for he wald his lord succur
70   He put his liff in aventur,
        And stud intill a busk lurkand
        Till that the hund come at his hand
        And with ane arow sone him slew
        And throu the woud syne him withdrew.
75   Bot quhether this eschaping fell
        As I tauld fyrst or I now tell,
        I wate weill without lesing
        That at the burn eschapyt the king.

(79) The king went forth on his way and John of Lorn went back to Sir Aymer, who had returned from the pursuit with his men; they prospered little in their pursuing, for although they made a great effort very eagerly, they captured only a few; their foes nearly all escaped. (87) Men say that Sir Thomas Randolph captured the king's banner in the pursuit, and thereby had very great honour and praise with the king in England. When the pursuers had rallied and John of Lorn had met them there, he told Sir Aymer all the circumstances of the king's escape and how he slew [John's] five men and then withdrew to the wood. (97) When Sir Aymer heard this, he crossed himself at the wonder, and said, 'He is much to be admired, for I know of no-one who is alive who helped him thus in misfortune. I'm sure he would be hard to kill if he were properly equipped.' That's how Sir Aymer spoke. (105) The good king kept always on his way, he and his man, until they had passed through the forest, and then they entered on the moor which was both high and long and broad; before they had half passed [across] it, they saw three men coming from [one] side, [looking] like poor vagabonds. (113) They had swords and also axes, and one of them carried a big roped-up wether on his neck. They met the king, greeted him there and the king returned their greeting and asked them where they were going. (119) They said [that] they were seeking Robert the Bruce,

---

88. The king's banner. The presence of this symbol of command suggests that the Scottish force was indeed of some size, and therefore around the time of the battle of Loudoun. If Randolph was praised by Edward I or II for taking it, there is no trace of a reward.

103. Evynly means 'equally', i.e. as well as us. Skeat suggests 'If he were attacked (or challenged to fight) on equal terms.'

112. Licht men and waverand. *DOST* suggests 'frivolous' for 'licht' here; I had thought 'nimble' was the sense, but on reflection, 'waverand' seems to have the sense of vagabond, and 'licht men' must mean 'men unencumbered by possessions', hence 'poor'.

[*Three men with a wether try to kill the king and kill his foster-brother*]

The king has furth his wayis tane,
80 And Jhon of Lorn agayne is gane
To Schyr Aymer that fra the chace
With his men repayryt was
That sped lytill in thar chassyng
Thoucht at thai maid gret folowing
85 Full egrely thai wan bot small,
Thar fayis ner eschapyt all.
Men sayis Schyr Thomas Randell than
Chassand the kingis baner wan,
Quharthrou in Ingland with the king
90 He had rycht gret price and loving.
Quhen the chasseris relyit war
And Jhon of Lorn had met thaim thar
He tauld Schyr Aymer all the cas,
How that the king eschapyt was
95 And how that he his fyve men slew
And syne to the wode him drew.
Quhen Schyr Aymer herd this, in hy
He sanyt him for the ferly
And said, 'He is gretly to prys,
100 For I knaw nane that liffand is
That at myscheyff gan help him sua.
I trow he suld be hard to sla
And he war bodyn evynly.'
On this wis spak Schyr Aymery,
105 And the gud king held furth his way
Betwix him and his man quhill thai
Passyt out throu the forest war.
Syne in the more thai entryt ar
That wes bathe hey and lang and braid,
110 And or thai halff it passyt had
Thai saw on syd the men cummand
Lik to lycht men and waverand,
Swerdis thai had and axys als
And ane off thaim apon his hals
115 A mekill boundyn wether bar.
Thai met the king and halist him thar,
And the king tthaim thar hailsing yauld
And askyt thaim quhether thai wauld.
Thai said Robert the Bruys thai socht,

to meet with him, if they could; they wanted to stay with him. The king said, 'If that's what you want, come along with me, and I shall let you see him soon.' (125) They realised from his speech that he was the self-same King Robert. They changed countenance and demeanour and didn't keep their previous attitude, for they were enemies of the king, meant to come by stealth and stay with him until they saw their opportunity and then end his days. (133) They agreed with what he said therefore, but the king, who was clever, well understood from their bearing that they liked him not a whit, and said, 'Fellows, until we are better acquainted, you must, all three of you, go in front all by yourselves, and we two will follow you in the same way quite close behind.' (142) Said they, 'Sir, there is no need to believe any ill of us.' 'Nor do I,' said he, 'but I want you to go in front of us until we are better known to each other.' 'Alright,' they said, 'if that's what you want.' [So] they went forth on their way. (149) They went like that till night was near, and then the foremost came to a deserted husbandman's house, where they killed the wether they carried; they kindled fire to roast their meat and asked the king if he wanted to eat, resting himself until the meat was ready. (156) The king, who was hungry I'm sure, agreed at once to their offer, but said that he and his man wanted to be together alone at one fire, and [that] they should all three make another fire at the end of the house, which they did.

---

125. By his speech. It is not clear whether they guessed from the content, manner or accent of the 'speking' that he was King Robert. At 220 the king was wearing armour, which would surely indicate his social class.

120 For mete with him giff that thai moucht
Thar dwelling with him wauld thai ma.
The king said, 'Giff that ye will sua,
Haldys furth your way with me
And I sall ger you sone him se.'
125 Thai persavyt be his speking
That he wes the selvyn Robert king,
And chaungyt contenance and late
And held nocht in the fyrst state,
For thai war fayis to the king
130 And thocht to cum into sculking
And dwell with him quhill that thai saw
Thar poynt, and bryng him than off daw.
Thai grantyt till his spek forthi,
Bot the king that wes witty
135 Persavyt weill be thar having
That thai luffyt him nathing
And said, 'Falowis, ye mon all thre,
Forthir aquent till that we be,
All be yourselvyn forrouth ga,
140 And on the samyn wys we twa
Sall folow behind weill ner.'
Quod thai, 'Schyr, it is na myster
To trow in us ony ill.'
'Nane do I,' said he, 'bot I will
145 That yhe ga forrourth thus quhill we
Better with othyr knawin be.'
'We grant,' thai said, 'sen ye will sua.'
And furth apon thar gate gan ga.
Thus yeid thai till the nycht wes ner,
150 And than the formast cummyn wer
Till a waist husbandis hous, and thar
Thai slew the wethir that thai bar
And slew fyr for to rost thar mete,
And askyt the king giff he wald ete
155 And rest him till the mete war dycht.
The king that hungry was, Ik hycht,
Assentyt till thar spek in hy,
Bot he said he wald anerly
Betwix him and his fallow be
160 At a fyr, and thai all thre
In the end off the hous suld ma
Ane other fyr, and thai did sua.

(163) They withdrew to the end of the house, sending half the wether to him and [the king and his man] roasted their their meat hastily, falling to eating right eagerly. (167) For the king had fasted for a long time, and had had a great many exertions so he ate with a will. When he had eaten hastily, he had such a desire to sleep, that he couldn't overcome it, for when the veins are full, the body grows ever heavier, and heaviness leads to sleep. (176) The king, who was all worn out, felt that of necessity it behoved him to sleep. He says to his foster-brother, 'While I take a short nap, can I trust you to waken me?' 'Yes, sir,' he said, 'while I can hold out.' (182) The king then dozed for a short while, not sleeping at all deeply, but often glancing up suddenly, for he was afraid of those three men who were at the other fire then. He knew that they were his enemies, so he slept like a fowl on its perch. (189) The king slept but little then, when such a drowsiness overcame his man that he could not keep his eyes open; he fell asleep snoring loudly. Now the king is in great peril, for if he sleeps thus for a little while, he'll be dead, without a doubt. (196) For the three traitors took good care that he and his man were asleep, then got up with great speed, drawing their swords hastily, and went quickly towards the king, when they saw that he slept like that; they thought that they would kill him while asleep. (203) They went full tilt to him, but in that time, by God's grace, the king looked up quickly,

Thai drew thaim in the hous end
And halff the wethir till him send.
165 And thai rostyt in hy thar mete
And fell rycht freschly for till ete,
For the king weill lang fastyt had
And had rycht mekill travaill mad,
Tharfor he eyt full egrely
170 And quhen he had etyn hastily
He had to slep sa mekill will
That he mocht set na let thartill,
For quhen the vanys fillyt ar
Men worthys hevy evermar
175 And to slepe drawys hevynes.
The king that all fortravaillyt wes
Saw that him worthyt slep nedwayis.
Till his foser-broder he sayis,
'May I traist in the me to waik
180 Till Ik a litill sleping tak.'
'Ya, schyr,' he said, 'till I may dre.'
The king then wynkyt a litill wey,
And slepyt nocht full encrely
Bot gliffnyt up oft sodanly,
185 For he had dreid of thai thre men
That at the tother fyr war then.
That thai his fais war he wyst,
Tharfor he slepyt as foule on twyst.
The king slepyt bot a litill than
190 Quhen sic slep fell on his man
That he mycht nocht hald up his ey,
Bot fell in slep and rowtyt hey.
Now is the king in gret perile
For slep he sua a litill quhile
195 He sall be ded fotoutyn dreid,
For the thre tratouris tuk gud heid
That he on slep wes and his man.
In full gret hy thai rais up than
And drew thar swerdis hastily
200 And went towart the king in hy
Quhen that thai saw him sleip sua,
And slepand thocht thai wald him sla.
Till him thai yeid a full gret pas,   203*
Bot in that tym throu Goddis grace   204*
205 The king up blenkit hastily   203

saw his man sleeping near him and saw the three traitors coming [at him]. Quickly he sprang to his feet, drew his sword out and met them. (210) As he went, he put his foot firmly upon his man. He wakened and got up muzzily, for the sleep had so overcome him that before he got up one of those who came to kill the king gave him a stroke as he rose, so that he couldn't help [the king] any more. (218) The king was placed in such straits there, that he had never been so [badly] placed before, and but for the armour that he wore, he would have been dead, without a doubt. But nonetheless he defended himself in such a way in that struggle that he killed those three traitors, by the grace of God and by his own courage. (226) His foster-brother was dead there [and] he was seriously overcome when he saw that he was alone. He grieved for his foster-brother, cursed all the other three, and then took his way by himself, going directly toward his tryst.

(233) The king went forth, sad and angry, grieving tenderly over his man, holding his way by himself and going directly toward the house where he had made a tryst to meet his men. It was pretty late at night by then. (239) He came soon to the house and found

---

239–351. This is another telling of the meeting of the king with the woman sympathiser who gives him her two sons (4.635–667) followed by the night attack on a force in a village (5.89–119). The earlier telling is associated, wrongly, with Percy in Turnberry, but Macdowall alone escapes. This gives us our best clue to the nature of this attack: it was upon a force of native Galwegians led by (probably Dungal) Macdowall. He had been responsible for the taking of Alexander and Thomas Bruce at Loch Ryan in February 1307, and therefore for their execution. The men of Galloway were protected by the nearby English headquarters at Carlisle till Edward I died in July 1307. On 31 July, 1307, before even seeking a coronation, Edward II entered Scotland staying at Dumfries, Tibbers, Sanquhar and (19–28 August) Cumnock. He returned to Carlisle on 1 September. His men were searching unsuccessfully for Bruce, who must have kept a very low profile. After Edward's departure there was a renewed assault on Galloway, so that men of the province fled to England with their livestock by 25 September, and their leaders, Dungal Macdowall and Dungal Maccan wrote to Edward II about the devastation made there by Bruce who 'was procuring and compelling the men of those parts and parts adjacent to rise against' the English. (*Foedera2*, 8; *CDS3*, *14*, *15*)

The Lanercost chronicle gives a version which is unspecific as to month:

Robert Bruce, with Edward his brother and many other adherents of his, notwithstanding the English keepers, wandered in Scotland wherever he wanted, and especially in Galloway; he took tribute from that land, on condition that it should be left in peace. Because of the great

And saw his man slepand him by
And saw cummand the tother thre.
Deliverly on fut gat he
And drew his swerd out and thaim mete,
210 And as he yude his fute he set 208
Apon his man weill hevily.
He waknyt and rais disily,
For the slep maistryt hym sway
That or he gat up ane off thai
215 That com for to sla the king 213
Gaiff hym a strak in his rysing
Sua that he mycht help him no mar.
The king sa straitly stad wes thar
That he wes never yeit sa stad,
220 Ne war the armyng that he had 218
He had bene dede foroutyn wer.
Bot nocht-forthi on sic maner
He helpyt him in that bargane
That thai thre tratouris he has slan
225 Throu Goddis grace and his manheid. 223
Hys fostyr brother thar wes dede,
Then wes he wondre will of wayn
Quhen he saw him left allane.
His foster broder meny he
230 And waryit all the tother thre, 228
And syne his way tuk him allane
And rycht towart his tryst is gane.

[*The king goes to a house, where the goodwife gives him her two sons; he meets his companions and they take an enemy force in a village by surprise*]

The king went furth way and angri
Menand his man full tenderly
235 And held his way all him allane, 233
And rycht towart the hous is gan
Quhar he set tryst to meit his men.
It wes weill inwyth nycht be then,
He come sone in the hous and fand

---

number of people who then adhered to him, they could not resist him. (*L*, 210; *LT*, 185)

This blackmail agreement is likely to have been made after the September attacks. I believe that one of these was Barbour's attack on the force under Macdowall which was lodged in a village separated from the main force.

the good-wife sitting on the bench. She immediately asked him who he was, whence he came and whither he went. 'A travelling man, lady,' said he, 'who journeys here through the country.' (245) She said, 'All who are on the road are welcome here for the sake of one [man].' The king said, 'Good lady, who is he who makes you have such feelings for men who travel?' 'Sir,' said the good-wife, 'I'll tell you: good King Robert the Bruce is [the man] who is rightful lord of this country. (253) His enemies now have him surrounded, but I expect to see him, before long, lord and king over the whole country, [so] that no enemies will withstand him.' 'Lady, do you love him as much as that?' said he. 'Yes, sir,' she said, 'as God sees me!' 'Lady,' said he, 'he's near you, for I am he.' (260) 'Is that true?' – 'Yes indeed, lady.' – 'And where have your men gone, when you are alone like this?' 'At this time, lady, I have no more.' She said, 'It can't be like that. I have two sons, strong and hardy; they shall become your men at once.' (267) They did what she expected, [and] became his sworn men soon. The wife had him sit and eat soon, but he had sat at the food for only a short while when he heard a great stamping around the house; then, without hesitation, they started up to defend the house, but soon after the king recognised James Douglas. (275) Then he was pleased, and ordered the doors to be opened quickly, and they came, all of them. Sir Edward Bruce was there, also James Douglas, who had escaped from the pursuit and met [up] with the king's brother.

240   The houswyff on the benk sittand   238
       That askit him quhat he was
       And quhen he come and quethir he gais.
       'A travailland man, dame,' said he,
       'That travaillys throu the contre.'
245   Scho said, 'All that travailland er   243
       For ane his sak ar welcum her.'
       The king said, 'Gud dame, quhat is he
       That gerris you haiff sik specialté
       To men that travaillis?' 'Schyr, perfay,'
250   Quod the gud-wyff, 'I sall you say,   248
       The King Robert the Bruys is he,
       That is rycht lord off this countre.
       His fayis now haldis him in thrang,
       Bot I think to se or ocht lang
255   Him lord and king our all the land   253
       That na fayis sall him withstand.'
       'Dame, luffis thou him sa weil,' said he.
       'Ya, schyr,' said scho, 'sa God me se.'
       'Dame,' said he, 'hym her the by,
260   For Ik am he, I say the soithly,   258
       Yha certis, dame.' 'And quhar ar gane
       Your men quhen ye ar thus allane?'
       'At this tyme, dame, Ik haiff no ma.'
       Scho said, 'It may na wys be swa.
265   Ik haiff twa sonnys wycht and hardy,   263
       Thai sall becum your men in hy.'
       As scho divisyt thai haiff done,
       His sworn men become thai sone.
       The wyff syn gert him syt and ete,
270   Bot he has schort quhile at the mete   268
       Syttyn quhen he hard gret stamping
       About the hous, then but letting
       Thai stert up the hous for to defende,
       Bot sone eftre the king has kend
275   James off Douglas. Than wes he blyth   273
       And bad oppyn the durris swyth
       And thai come in all that thar war.
       Schyr Edward the Bruce wes thar,
       And James alsua off Douglas
280   That wes eschapyt fra the chace   278
       And with the kingis brother met,
       Syn to the tryst that thaim wes set

Then with their company (which was a hundred and fifty) they had hurried to the tryst arranged with them.

(285) When they saw the king they were joyful at the meeting-up, asking how he had escaped, and he told them all the circumstances. (289) How the five men pressed him fast, how he went through the burn, how he met the three thieves, how he would have been killed asleep when he wakened through God's grace, and how his foster-brother was killed; he told them all this. (296) Then together they all praised God for their lord's escape in those ways. Then they chatted to and fro, till at last the king said, 'Fortune has troubled us today, scattering us so suddenly. (302) Our foes will lie feeling secure tonight, because they believe that we are so scattered, fleeing aimlessly here and there, that we shall not be gathered together for [another] three days. So tonight they will lie securely, without watchmen, taking their ease. (309) Therefore anyone knowing their lodging-place and coming against them suddenly would quickly damage them with a small company, and yet escape without harm.' '*Perfay*,' said James Douglas, 'As I came here, by chance I came so near their lodging place that I can take you [to] where they lie. (317) If you hurry up, before daybreak we may still do more harm to them than they have done to us all day, for they lie scattered wherever they chose.' Then they all felt it would be best to press on to [the enemy] hastily. (324) They did that in a real hurry, coming upon them at the dawn,

Thai sped thaim with thar cumpany
That wer ane hunder and weile fyfty.
And quhen that thai haiff sene the king
Thai war joyfull of thar meting
And askyt how that he eschapyt was,
And he thaim tauld all hale the cas.
How the fyve men him pressyt fast,
And how he throu the water past,
And how he met the thevis thre
And how he slepand slane suld be
Quhen he waknyt throu Goddis grace
And how his foster brodyr was
Slayne he tauld thaim all haly.
Than lovyt thai God commounly
That thar lord wes eschapyt sua,
Than spak thai wordis to and fra
Till at the last the king gan say
'Fortoun us travaillyt fast today
That scalyt us sa sodanly.
Our fayis tonycht sall ly traistly
For thai trow we so scalit ar
And fled to-waverand her and thar
That we sall nocht thir dayis thre
All togiddir assemblit be.
Tharfor this nycht thai sall trastly
But wachys tak thar ese and ly.
Quharfor quha knew thar herbery
And wald cum on thaim sodanly
With few mengye mycht thaim scaith
And eschape foroutyn waith.'
'Perfay,' quod James of Douglas,
'As I come hyddyrwart per cas
I come sa ner thar herbery
That I can bring you quhar thai ly,
And wald ye speid you yeit or day
It may sua happin that we may
Do thaim a gretar scaith weile sone
Than thai us all day has done,
For thai ly scalyt as thaim lest.'
Than thocht thaim all it wes the best
To sped thaim to thaim hastily,
And thai did sua in full gret hy
And come on thaim in the dawing

285
290
295
300
305
310
315
320
325

283
288
293
298
301*
302*
303*
304*
305*
301*
303
308
313
318

just as daylight began to break. (327) It happened that a company had taken up lodging in a village, a good mile or more from the host – men said that [the company numbered] two hundred. The noble king attacked there, and, soon after their engagement, those who had been attacked [while] sleeping shouted and roared with a dreadful noise, (335) and some others who heard the shouting ran out so terrified that some of them were entirely unarmed, fleeing here and there all over the place; some dragged their arms with them and [Bruce's men] slew them mercilessly. (341) They took such a harsh revenge that more than two thirds of [the company] were killed in that very place; the rest fled to their army. The army, which heard the noise and shouting and saw their men come so wretchedly naked, fleeing here and there, some unharmed, some badly wounded, arose in real fright and each man goes to his banner, so that the host was all astir. (352) The king and those who were with him, when they saw the host astir like that, went toward their refuge and came to safety there. And when Sir Aymer heard how the king had slain their men, and how they had got away again, he said, (359) 'Now we can clearly see that, wherever it is, a noble heart is difficult to overcome by strength. For where a heart is really bold, it is always stout against stoutness; and in my opinion no doubt can cause it to be completely defeated as long as [the] body is alive and free, as you can see from this encounter. (368) We thought that Robert the Bruce had been

---

330. C gives 'twa thousand', perhaps because the syntax allows this line to describe the host rather than, as Barbour must have intended, the company which is the victim in the story. E's 200 is to be preferred.

334. A repetition of the line 5.98.

342. Two thirds were slain. Cf. 5.47-48, where two thirds of Percy's force was in the village.

Rycht as the day begouth to spryng.
Sa fell it that a cumpany
Had in a toun tane thar herbery
Weile fra the ost a myle or mar,
330 Men said that thai twa hunder war. 323
Thar assemblyt the nobill king,
And sone eftre thar assembling
Thai that slepand assaylyt war
Rycht hidwysly gan cry and rar,
335 And other sum that herd the cry 328
Ras sa rycht effrayitly
That sum of thaim nakit war
Fleand to warand her and thar,
And sum his armys with him drew,
340 And thai foroutyn mercy thaim slew 333
And sa evyll vengeance can ta
That the twa partis of thaim and ma
War slayn rycht in that ilk sted,
Till thar oist the remanand fled.
345 The oyst that hard the noyis and cry 338
And saw thar men sua wrechytly
Sum nakit fleand her and thar,
Sum all hale, sum woundyt sar,
Into full gret effray thai rais
350 And ilk man till his baner gays 343
Sua that the oyst wes all on ster.
The king and thai that with him wer
Quhen on ster the oyst saw sua
Towart thar warand gan thai ga,
355 And thar in saveté com thai 348
And quhen Schyr Aymer herd say
How that the king thar men had slayn
And how that thai turnyt war agayn
He said, 'Now may we clerly se
360 That nobill hart quharever it be 353
It is hard till ourcum throu maystri,
For quhar ane hart is rycht worthy
Agayne stoutnes it is ay stoute,
Na as I trow thar may na doute
365 Ger it all-out discumfyt be 358
Quhill body levand is and fre,
As be this melle may be sene.
We wend Robert the Bruce had bene

so defeated that in good discretion he would have had neither
heart nor will to undertake such an exploit. For he was so
overwhelmed that he was left all by himself, and all his folk
had gone from him; (375) he was so exhausted by dealing
with those who assailed him, that tonight he should have
longed for a rest above everthing else. But his heart is filled
with courage, so that it can't be defeated.'

(381) Sir Aymer spoke to this effect, and when those of his
company saw how they had struggled in vain and how the
king had killed their men and was now at large and quite free,
they thought it would be folly to stay there any longer, since
they could not harass the king; (389) they said that to Sir
Aymer, who hastily decided that he would go then to Carlisle,
spend some time there and keep his spies on the king to keep
in continual touch with his bearing. (395) For when he could
see his opportunity, he meant to move rapidly against him
with a large following. Therefore he took the way to England
with all his company. and each man went home. (401) He
went in haste to Carlisle and meant to be there till he saw his
opportunity with the king who was then with all his assembled
[men] in Carrick, where he would sometimes go with his men
to hunt. (407) It so happened that one day he went to hunt,
to try [to find out]

373-74. All him allane, and all his folk war fra him gayn. This speech
by Valence is obviously Barbour's invention, but it is curious that he
commits this error: in both versions of the story Bruce had a companion,
his foster-brother or an archer. Perhaps we should read '[virtually]
alone'!

391. Carlisle. Barbour sends Valence out of Scotland three times, but
the record evidence is that he remained within Scotland from the
outbreak of Bruce's rising until 12 October, 1307 when he left by royal
leave. He had been replaced as keeper of Scotland by the earl of
Richmond on 13 September, 1307. Barbour is therefore correct in
placing his departure to Carlisle after the assault on the men of Galloway
in mid-September. But when he makes Valence stay at Carlisle, lying
in wait for Bruce (401-3) he is creating a link with a following story,
the attack on Glen Trool.

Sua discomfyt that be gud skill
370 He suld nother haiff haid hart ne will 363
Swilk juperty till undreta
For he put was at undre sua
That he wes left all him allane
And all his folk war fra him gayn,
375 And he sagat fortravaillyt 368
To put thaim off that him assaylit
That he suld haiff yarnyt resting
This nycht atour all other thing.
Bot his hart fillyt is off bounte
380 Sua that it vencusyt may nocht be.' 373

*[The king goes hunting and is attacked by three men beside a
wood]*

On this wys spak Schyr Aymery,
And quhen thai off his cumpany
Saw how thai travaillit had in vayn
And how the king thar men had slayn
385 And that his wes gane all fre, 378
Thaim thocht it wes a niceté
For to mak thar langer dwelling
Sen thai mycht nocht anoy the king,
And said that to Schyr Amery,
390 That umbethocht him hastily 383
That he to Carlele wald ga
And a quhill tharin sojourn ma
And haff his spyis on the king
To knaw alwayis his contenyng,
395 And quhen that he his poynt mycht se 388
He thocht that with a gret menye
He suld schute apon him sudanly.
Tharfor with all his cumpany
Till Ingland he the way has tane,
400 And ilk man till his hous is gane. 393
In hy till Carlele went is he
And tharin thinkys for till be
Till he his poynt saw off the king,
That then with all his gaderring
405 Wes in Carryk quhar umbestount 398
He wald went with his men til hunt.
Sa happynyt that on a day
He went till hunt for till assay

what game there was in that country. By chance on that day
he went to sit by a wood-side, by himself with two hounds,
but always wearing his sword. He had sat there for only a
little while when he saw three men coming from the wood
with bows in their hands, who approached him speedily; (418)
he quickly realised from their bearing and their manner that
they loved him not one bit. He got up, drew his leash towards
him, and let his dogs go free. God help the king now with
His might! For unless he is clever and bold now he'll be under
great pressure. (426) For these three – no fewer – men were
utterly his enemies and watched him so carefully to see when
they could take revenge on the king for John Comyn's sake,
that they thought they had [plenty of] time then. (432) Since
he was situated alone, they thought they could kill him quickly;
and if they could achieve that, that after they had killed the
king, they might get back into the wood again; his men, they
believed, they need not fear. (438) They went quickly towards
the king, bending their bows when they were near, and he,
who had a great fear of their arrows because he was without
armour, quickly made an overture to them, saying, 'You ought
to be ashamed to shoot at me from afar, *perdé*, for I am one
and you are three. (446) But if you have the courage to come
close to attack me with your swords, defeating me in this way
if you can, you will be all the more esteemed.' 'Indeed,' said
one of the three, 'no man is going to say that we fear you so
much

410–494. The attack by three men by the wood. This story is another
version of that given at 5.490–658, for reasons which I have given at
that passage. In the present version, one who viewed the action from
a distance would see three travellers approach the king, throw away
their bows as a friendly gesture and be subjected to a savage attack;
the earlier version could also be read in this sense.

411. 'Sett' seems to mean 'sit' in the light of line 414, but where C has
it, E had a blank, suggesting uncertainty. And 'went to sit' seems
long-winded, when no purpose for the sitting is suggested. I suspect,
therefore, that 'sett' means 'trap' or 'lie in wait'.

430. For John Comyn's sake. This attempt to explain the malevolence
of the three travellers is more convincing than that in the book 5 version,
where they are Bruce's kin suborned by Umfraville. Comyn of Badenoch
was a Galloway landowner – Dalswinton castle was chief place of his
lands – so would have had Galwegian followers.

443. Here, as at 5.612, it is the king who challenges the approaching
travellers.

Quhat gamyn was in that countre,
And sua hapnyt that day that he 403
By a woud-syd to sett is gane
With his twa hundys him allane,
Bot his swerd ay with him bar.
He had bot schort quhile syttyn thar
Quhen he saw fra the woud cummand 408
Thre men with bowys in thar hand
That towart him come spedely,
And he that persayvyt in hy
Be thar affer and thar having
That thai luffyt him nakyn thing, 413
He rais and his leysche till him drew he
And leyte hys hundis gang all fre.
God help the king now for his mycht,
For bot he now be wys and wycht
He sall be set in mekill pres, 418
For thai thre men foroutyn les
War his fayis all utrely,
And wachyt him sa bysyly
To se quhen thai vengeance mycht tak
Off the king for Jhon Comyn his sak 423
That thai thocht than thai layser had.
And sen he hym allane wes stad
In hy thai thocht thai suld him sla,
And gyff that thai mycht chevys sua
Fra that thai the king had slayn 428
That thai mycht wyn the woud agayn,
His men thaim thocht thai suld nocht dred.
In hy towart the king thai yeid
And bent thar bowys quhen thai war ner,
And he that dred on gret maner 433
Thar arowys, for he nakyt was,
In hy a speking to thaim mais
And said, 'You aucht to schame perdé
Sen ik am ane and ye ar thre
For to schute at me apon fer. 438
Bot had ye hardyment to cum ner
And with your swerdis till assay,
Wyn me apon sic wys giff ye may,
Ye sall wele oute mar prisyt be.'
'Perfay,' quod ane than off the thre 443
'Sall na man say we dred the sua

that we will kill you with arrows.' (453) With that they threw
away their bows, and came on fast without more delay. The
king met them very bravely and smote the first so hard that
he fell down dead on the grass. (458) And when the king's
hound saw those men attacking his master like that, he leapt
at one and seized him very strongly right by the neck, until
he made him lie, top over tail. The king who had his sword
raised, saw that he had given him a lot of help. (465) Before
[the man] who had fallen could get up, [the king] attacked
him in such a way that he split his back precisely in two. The
third, who saw his fellows killed like that without remedy,
took his way to the wood again. (471) But the king followed
speedily, and also the hound which was beside him, when he
saw the man fleeing from him, rushed quickly to him, took
him right by the neck and pulled [him] to him; as he rose,
the king, who was near enough, gave him such a clout that
fell down to the earth, stone dead. (479) The king's men who
were then near, when they saw the king attacked so suddenly
like that, hurried to him quickly and asked how that had
happened? He told them the whole [business], how all three
had attacked him. (486) 'Indeed,' they said, 'we can well see
that it is hard to undertake such a scrimmage with you, who
has so briskly despatched those three, without [getting] hurt.'
'Well,' said he, 'I killed only one, no more. God and my
hound killed the [other] two. Their treason ruined them, in
truth, for all three were really strong men.'

That we with arowys sall the sla.'
With that thar bowys away thai kest
And come on fast but langer frest.
455 The king thaim met full hardyly 448
And smate the fyrst sa vygorusly
That he fell dede doun on the gren.
And quhen the kingis hund has sene
Thai men assailye his maister sua
460 He lap till ane and gan him ta 453
Rycht be the nek full sturdyly.
Till top our tale he gert him ly,
And the king that his swerd out had
Saw he sa fayr succour him maid.
465 Or he that fallyn wes mycht rys 458
He him assayllyt on sic wys
That he the bak strak evyn in twa.
The thrid that saw his falowis sua
Foroutyn recoveryng be slayne
470 Tok to the wod his way agane, 463
Bot the king folowit spedyly,
And als the hund that wes him by
Quhen he the man saw fle him fra
Schot till him sone and gan him ta
475 Rycht be the nek and till him dreuch 468
And the king that wes ner yneucht
In his ryssing sik rowt him gaff
That stane-dede to the erd he draff.
The kingis men that wer than ner
480 Quhen that thai saw on sic maner 473
The king assailyt sa sodanly
Thai sped towart him in hy
And askyt how that cas befell,
And he all haly gan thaim tell
485 How thai assaillyt him all thre 478
'Perfay,' quod thai, 'we may wele se
That it is hard till undretak
Sic melling with you to mak
That sua smertly has slayn thir thre
490 Foroutyn hurt.' 'Perfay,' said he, 483
I slew bot ane forouten ma
God and my hund has slayn the twa.
Thar tresoun combryt thaim perfay
For rycht wycht men all thre war thai.'

(495) When the king had escaped like this, by God's grace, he blew his horn and then his good men rallied to him in haste; he got ready to go homewards, meaning to hunt no more that day. He stayed in Glentrool for a time, going very often to hunt and relax, to get venison for themselves, for the deer were in season. (505) For all that time Sir Aymer lay in Carlisle with noble men in [his] company, awaiting his opportunity. When he heard for certain that the king was in Glentrool and engaged in hunting and relaxing, he decided to come upon him then suddenly with his chivalry, riding from Carlisle by night, and keeping cover by day. (515) He intended that he would surprise the king in that way and with that stratagem. Then he assembled a great company

---

502. Glen Trool. On the edge of Carrick and of Galloway but also allowing movement to the east.

The record evidence discussed under 509 shows that this remote upland glen was a refuge for Bruce on two occasions; there may have been others of which the records do not know.

507. Carlisle. See note to 391.

509. Glen Trool. When the king landed in February 1307, a strike force under Botetourt of 15 knights, some 30 esquires and 12 serjeants was sent against him, paid till 4 March; some 460 archers were sent to Valence (probably in Ayrshire) for the same purpose, paid till 10 and 15 March. By then the king was known to be in Nithsdale, for on 5 March a strike force of 20 knights with 50 esquires under Botetourt were in pursuit of the king, paid till 23 April; 180 archers were sent a few days later but served for shorter periods. On 12 March a number of horses were lost, so there may have been a skirmish on that day. This Nithsdale episode, which is unmentioned in Barbour, seems too late to have been an attempt by the king to rescue his brothers, taken prisoner at Loch Ryan in early February and executed at the middle of that month. But it stirred the English government to more action, because on 19 March the northern counties were ordered to levy 2,500 footmen to be at Carlisle on 15 April 'to pursue Robert Bruce and his accomplices who are lurking in the moors and marshes of Scotland'. Then on 17–18 April a smaller force, evidently scraped together, of 10 knights and 23 esquires was sent to Glen Trool 'riding in search of' Bruce till 30 April, while 300 archers levied in Tyndale after the orders of 13 March were sent to Carrick and Glen Trool from 10 April to 3 May. (*CDS2, 1923*) This has generally been taken as the occasion of the Glen Trool attack recorded in Barbour; in the glen a tablet in stone records the attack as taking place in March.

But there is another and more likely possibility. On 7–8 June, 1307 two men were sent from the English court on a foray to Galloway against Bruce which lasted some 16 days (to 23 June); they were clearly to join some larger force already in Scotland. In a separate valuation of horses, such as was usual at the beginning of an expedition, at Kirkpatrick in Galloway on 30 May, the names of 23 men-at-arms, including the three

[*The king goes to Glen Trool; Valence follows him there*]

495	Quhen that the king throu Goddis grace	488
	On this maner eschapyt was	
	He blew his horn and then in hy	
	His gud men till him gan rely,	
	Then hamwartis buskyt he to far	
500	For that day wald he hunt no mar.	493
	In Glentruell all a quhile he lay,	
	And went weyle oft to hunt and play	
	For to purches thaim venesoun,	
	For than der war in sesoun.	
505	In all that tyme Schyr Aymery	498
	With nobill men in cumpany	
	Lay in Carlele hys poynt to se,	
	And quhen he hard the certanté	
	That in Glentrewle wes the king	
510	And went till hunt and till playing,	503
	He thocht with hys chevalry	
	To cum apon him sodanly	
	And fra Carlele on nychtys ryd	
	And in covert on dayis bid,	
515	And swagate with sic tranonting	508
	He thocht he suld suppris the king.	
	He assemblyt a gret mengne	

St John brothers (one of whom was marshall of that army), are given, with the value of their mounts; this foray had been planned as early as 17 May. Another hand has added at the foot of the valuation, 'these were killed in the pursuit (*chacea*) of Robert Bruce between Glen Trool and "Glenheur" on the last day of the army in Galloway.' This is the expedition joined by the two from court. Now on 1 June, from Bothwell, Valence wrote that the English Treasurer had agreed that Ayr should have the protection of 300 infantry (an agreement which must have been made around 10 May), and he pressed for their payment. In an undated letter Valence reports that he had sent 6 men-at-arms and 300 archers to Ayr, to secure the country around while he is on his foray towards Carrick and Glen Trool; they are to be paid. The only possible group of 300 was that sent to Carrick and Glen Trool 10 April–3 May, who, we can take it, were then sent on to Ayr. Valence was himself at Ayr on 11 June. The date of his expedition to Glen Trool, joining the men-at-arms from Kirkpatrick, depends on the dating of the letter in which he mentions it; other matters in the letter suggest that he has recently been at Ayr, and it should therefore be placed after 11 June. The fight at Glen Trool can be placed 12–23 June, 1307. It resulted in losses by the English in forcing the withdrawal of Bruce to 'Glenheur', a chase of some 25 miles, 40 kilometres, if Heur is Urr. (*CDS2,1929, 1935, 1938, 1942*; *CDS5, 490, 220b*)

of folk of very high reputation, both Scots and Englishmen. (520) Then they all held their way together, riding so secretly at night till they came to a wood near by Glentrool, where the king was lodged; he did not know of their arrival. He is now in great danger, for, unless God by his great power saves him, he will be taken or killed; for they were six where he had one [man].

(529) When Sir Aymer, who was stout and bold came, as I told you, so near the king that they were only a mile away from him, he took advice from his men as to what they should do next. For he told them that the king was lodged in so narrow a place that horsemen couldn't attack him, and if foot-men gave him battle, he would be hard to defeat if he were warned of their coming. (541) 'Therefore I advise, all secretly, that we send a woman, poorly clad, to spy on him. She can ask for food as charity and see all their condition, and in what way they are disposed; meantime we and our company can be coming through the wood on foot, all armed as we are. (550) If we can do that, so that we come there upon them before they have a hint of our coming, we'll get no opposition from them.'

(553) They thought this advice was for the best, [and] sent forward withou longer delay the woman who was to be their spy. She held her way in haste, right to the lodging where the king,

---

542. A woman spy. This curious decision may be fiction, but it serves no obvious purpose, and I am inclined to accept it; it suggests that the force involved here was small. See under 625.

Off folk off full gud renomme
Bath off Scottis and Inglis-men.
520 Thar way all samyn held thai then 513
And raid on nycht sa prevely
Till thai come in a wod ner by
Glentruele, quhar logyt wes the king
That wyst rycht nocht off thar cummyng.
525 Into gret perile now is he, 518
For bot God throu his gret powsté
Save him he sall be slayne or tane,
For thai war sex quhar he wes ane.

[Valence sends a woman ahead to spy, but she is discovered;
Valence attacks and is discomfited; his captains quarrel]

Quhen Schyr Amery, as Ik haiff tauld
530 With his men that war stout and bauld 523
Wes cummyn sa ner the king that thai
War bot a myle fra him away
He tuk avisement with his men
On quhat maner thai suld do then.
535 For he said thaim that the king was 528
Logyt into sa strayt a place
That horsmen mycht nocht him assaile
And giff futemen gaiff him bataile
He suld be hard to wyn giff he
540 Off thar cummyng may wytteryt be. 533
'Tharfor I rede all prevely
We send a woman him to spy
That pouerly arrayit be.
Scho may ask mete per cherite
545 And se thar convyn halily 538
And apon quhat maner thai ly,
The quhilis we and our menye
Cumand out-throu the wode may be
On fute all armyt as we ar.
550 May we do sua that we cum thar 543
On thaim or thai wyt our cummyng
We sall fynd in thaim na sturting.'
This consaill thocht thaim wes to best,
Then send thai furth but langer frest
555 The woman that suld be thar spy, 548
And scho hyr way gan hald in hy
Rycht to the logis quhar the king

in no fear of [being] surprised, went unarmed, cheerful and happy. (560) He saw the woman quickly, saw she was uncouth and therefore looked more closely at her; by her face he realised that she had come for no good. Then he had [his] men seize her quickly, and she, fearing that the men would kill her, told how Sir Aymer, with Clifford in company, and the flower of Northumberland were nearby, coming upon them.

(571) When the king heard that news, he put on his armour without [any] more delay, as did all those who were there, and then they gathered in one body. I'm sure they were nearly three hundred, and when they had gathered, the king had his banner unfurled and put his men in good order. (579) They had stood for only a moment, when they saw, right [close] at hand, their enemies coming through the wood, armed on foot, with spears in their hands, [and] hurrying very determinedly. (584) The noise and shouting soon arose for the good king, who was in the front, went stoutly towards his foes, seizing out of the hand of a man who was going beside him, a bow and a broad arrow, [with which he] hit the foremost in the neck, until his windpipe and gullet split in two, and he fell down to the ground.

(593) The rest came to a stop at that, and then the noble king took his banner from his standard-bearer, and said, 'Upon them! For they are all beaten,' and with that word, he swiftly drew his sword and ran on them so boldly that all [the men] of his company

---

568. Clifford. Sir John Wigton was sent beyond the Cree to be in Clifford's company, 23 February–16 March, 1307. On 17 April he was one of those sent from Carlisle to Glen Trool to pursue Bruce – without mention of Clifford. Nonetheless if Clifford was 'beyond the Cree' in February, he would very probably be involved in any action in Glen Trool in June. (*CDS2, 1902*)

That had na drede of supprising
Yheid unarmyt mery and blyth.
560 The woman has he sene alswyth, 553
He saw hyr uncouth and forthi
He beheld hyr mar encrely,
And be hyr contenance him thocht
That for gud cummyn was scho nocht.
565 Then gert he men in hy hyr ta, 558
And scho that dred men suld hyr sla
Tauld how that Schyr Amery
With the Cliffurd in cumpany
With the flour off Northummyrland
570 War cummand on thaim at thar hand. 563
Quhen that the king herd that tithing
He armyt him but mar dwelling,
Sa did thai all that ever wes thar,
Syne in a sop assemblyt ar,
575 I trow thai war thre hunder ner. 568
And quhen thai all assemblit wer
The king his baner gert display
And set his men in gud aray,
Bot thai had standyn bot a thraw
580 Rycht at thar hand quhen that thai saw 573
Thar fayis throu the wod cummand
Armyt on fute with sper in hand
That sped thaim full enforcely.
The noyis begouth sone and the cry,
585 For the gud king that formast was 578
Stoutly towart his fayis gays,
And hynt out off a mannys hand
That ner besyd him wes gangand
A bow and a braid arow als,
590 And hyt the formast in the hals 583
Till thropill and wesand yeid in twa
And doun till the erd gan ga.
The laiff with that maid a stopping,
Than but mar bad the nobill king
595 Hynt fra his baneour his banar 588
And said, 'Apon thaim, for thai ar
Discumfyt all.' With that word
He swappyt swiftly out his sword
And on thaim ran sa hardely
600 That all thai off his cumpany 593

took courage from his good deed. (602) For some who had previously gone their way, came back quickly to the fight, meeting their foes so vigorously that all the foremost were driven [back]. And when those who were behind saw that the front [line] was leaving the field, they turned their backs and fled, withdrawing out of the wood. (610) The king killed a few of these men, for they got away very quickly. They were all so discouraged because the king and his followers were all armed [and ready] to defend that place, which they thought they would take by their subterfuge without fighting, that they were suddenly frightened. (618) He sought them so angrily that they ran back out of the wood into the open in a great hurry. Because they failed in their intention, they were so badly put to shame that fifteen hundred men and more had been driven off by fewer, that they withdrew themselves in shame. (626) For that reason there arose suddenly among them great debate and disagreement, each one with the others, about their misfortune. Clifford and Vaux had a fight, in which Clifford fetched him a blow and each then called on his following. But Sir Aymer, who was wise, separated them with great difficulty, and went home to England again. (635) He knew that when strife rose among them, he would not hold them together for long without quarrels and fighting, and so he turned to England, with more shame than he set out, when so many [men] of such renown saw so few men offer them battle, where they had not been strong [enough] to attack.

---

625. They withdrew. This contradicts the record evidence of a pursuit, but would be understandable if Barbour describes a preliminary probe by Valence before he was joined by St John's force. A further assault on Glen Trool and the expulsion of Bruce is simply ignored.

629. Waus. This was perhaps the Northumberland knight, Sir John Vaus or Vaux (de Vallibus) who had been named a justice beyond the Mounth in 1305, but was more probably his namesake the lord of Dirleton, who was among the Scots capitulating at Strathord in February 1304. About August–September 1306 he had gone in the company of Sir John Mowbray 'towards the Isles' (possibly only in the Firth of Clyde), when Edward I ordered the seizure of his castle and lands, while he was to be arrested and sent to the king; evidently he was suspected of having aided Bruce. On 11 June, 1307 a man of this name was with Mowbray at Ayr in English service, and after the flight of some Galwegians in September 1307 he was among those called on to aid the new keeper of Scotland, an order repeated in December. On both occasions he is named among Scots and was surely the laird of Dirleton. Was his quarrel with Clifford an example of ethnic tension in the pro-English party? (Palgrave, *DHS*, 356; *CDS2*, 1706, 1741, 1938; *CDS3*, 15, 29)

Tuk hardyment off his gud deid,
For sum that fryst thar wayis yeid
Agayne come to the fycht in hy
And met thair fayis vigorusly
605 That all the formast ruschyt war, 598
And quhen thai that war hendermar
Saw that the formast left the sted
Thai tornyt sone the bak and fled
And out off the wod thaim withdrew.
610 The king a few men off thaim slew 603
For thai rycht sone thar gat gan ga.
It discomfortyt thaim all sua
That the king with his mengne was
All armyt to defend that place
615 That thai wend throu thar tranonting 608
Till haiff wonnyn foroutyn fechtin
That thai effrayit war sodanly,
And he thaim soucht sa angyrly
That thai in full gret hy agane
620 Out off the wod rane to the plane 613
For thaim faillyt off thar entent.
Thai war that tyme sa foully schent
That fyften hunder men and ma
With a few mengne war reboytyt sua
625 That thai withdrew thaim schamfully. 618
Tharfor amang thaim sodanly
Thar rais debate and gret distance,
Ilkan wytt other off thar myschance.
Cliffurd and Waus maid a melle
630 Quhar Cliffurd raucht him a cole 623
And athir syne drew till partys,
Bot Schyr Aymer that wes wys
Departyt thaim with mekill payn,
And went till Ingland hame again.
635 He wyst fra stryff ras thaim amang 628
He suld thaim nocht hals samyn lang
Foroutyn debate or melle,
Tharfor till Ingland turnyt he
With mar schame then he went of ton,
640 Quhen sa mony off sic renone 633
Saw sa few men bid thaim battaill
Quhair thai ne war hardy till assaile.

---

634. The second return of Valence to England.

The king, when Sir Aymer had gone, gathered every one of his company and left both woods and mountains, holding his way straight to the plains. He was anxious to make an end of what he had begun, and he well knew that he could not bring it to a good conclusion without travelling. (9) He went first to Kyle and made all that land obedient to himself; the men for the most part came to his peace. Then afterwards, before he stopped, he had the greater part of Cunningham held to his lordship. (15) In Bothwell then was Sir Aymer, who had great anger in his heart because [the folk] of Cunningham and Kyle, who had recently been obedient to him, left Englishmen's fealty. (20) He was determined to be avenged for that, and sent Sir Philip Mowbray with, as I heard said, a thousand men who were in his following, to Kyle to make war on the king. (25) But James Douglas who all that time had spies out on every side, knew that they were coming, and that they would travel down Magharnok's way. He took with him, secretly, those who were in his company, who were forty [in number] – no more. (32) Then he went to a narrow place in Magharnok's way, which is called the Edirford, *perfay*.

---

8. 'But travalyng' perhaps means 'without a struggle' here.

9. Kyle. The central third of Ayrshire, north of Carrick.

13. Cunningham. The most northerly third of Ayrshire.

15. Bothwell. Valence had been given Bothwell, a castle and lordship of the Moray family, by Edward I in 1301. (*CDS2, 1214*)

20–106. The encounter at Edirford. If Valence sent Mowbray, then the date is before Valence's giving up the Guardianship and leaving Scotland in October 1307. The present encounter was probably the aftermath to an expedition in mid-September when Valence, Philip Mowbray and others lost several horses while pursuing Douglas in Paisley forest, which lay to the south of Paisley; on this occasion, probably, occurred the burning at Paisley abbey recorded by Bower. Mowbray was perhaps cleaning up after the pursuit with an inadequate force, lacking men-at-arms, followed Douglas south and was trapped by him at Edirford. It is noticeable that Barbour (unusually) mentions no horses killed at a site where they would be very vulnerable. (*CDS5, 655*)

28. Magharnok's way. Probably a district name (plain of Arnoc), this lost name is shown on Bleau's and General Roy's maps; a moor of this name lay to the north, part of Glenouther Moor. Magharnok Water is now Kingswell Burn, NS5149–4846, NNE of Fenwick. The way would be the A77. The site is 11 miles, 17 kilometres due south of Paisley.

34. Edirford from C and 1571. In E the name appears as 'Nethirford',

BOOK 8

The king fra Schyr Aymer wes gane
Gadryt his menye everilkan
And left bath woddis and montanys
And held hys way strak till the planys
5   For he wald fayne that end war maid
Off that that he begunnyn had,
And he wyst weill he mycht nocht bring
It to gud end but travalling.
To Kyle went he fryst and that land
10 He maid all till him obeysand,
The men maist force come till his pes.
Syne efterwart or he wald ses
Of Conyngayme the maist party
He gert held till his senyoury.
15 In Bothweill then Schyr Aymer was
That in hys hart gret angre has
For thai off Cunyngame and Kile
That war obeysand till him quhile
Left Inglismennys fewté.
20 Tharoff fayne vengyt wald he be,
And send Philip the Mowbray
With a thousand as Ik herd say
Off men that war in his leding
To Kile for to werray the king.

[Douglas defeats Sir Philip Mowbray at Edirford]

25 Bot James of Douglas that all tid
Had spyis out on ilka sid
Wyst off thar cummyng and that thai
Wald hald doune Makyrnokis way.
He tuk with him all prevely
30 Thaim that war off his cumpany
That war fourty withoutyn ma,
Syne till a strait place gan he ga
That is in Makyrnokis way,
The Edirford it hat perfay,

and H uses both forms. The ford has never been identified, but was
evidently known to Barbour (40).

It lies between two marshes where no horse can go and live. On the south side, where James was, is an ascent, a narrow pass, on the north side is the track, as difficult as it appears today. (41) Douglas made an ambush with those he had with him, waiting [for Mowbray's men]. He could see them coming far away, but they could see nothing of him. They stayed in ambush all night, and when the sun was shining bright, they saw in company order coming arrayed the vanguard, with banner displayed; then, soon [after] they saw the rest coming quite close behind. (51) Then they kept themselves motionless and hidden, till the foremost of the [enemy] company had entered the ford near them, when they rushed at them with a shout; with weapons that cut sharp they pushed some backward in the ford, and with broad-barbed arrows made such a slaughter of others, that they withdrew to give up the place. (60) But behind them the way was so blocked that they could not flee with any speed, which caused the death of many of them, because they couldn't get away in any direction except as they had come, [or] unless they forced their way through their enemies – a way they realised was all too hot. (69) Their foes met them so sturdily, and continued the fight so fiercely, that they became so frightened that those who could flee first fled away first. And when the rear saw them repulsed like that and clearing out, they fled afar and kept going.

(74) But Sir Philip Mowbray who was riding with the foremost who had entered the place,

---

38. 'pas' in E, 'plas', place, in C. I have accepted the former though both E and C give 'place' in 59, 'place' (E) 'plas' (C) in 76. The same variation occurs elsewhere in the poem.

42–50. This is a good description of a straggling infantry force led by one or a few horsemen.

35   It lyis betwix marrais twa
       Quhar that na hors on lyve may ga.
       On the south halff quhar James was
       Is ane upgang, a narow pas,
       And on the north halff is the way
40   Sa ill as it apperis today.
       Douglas with thaim he with him had
       Enbuschyt him and thaim abaid,
       He mycht weile fer se thar cummyng
       Bot thai mycht se of hym na thing.
45   Thai baid in buschement all the nycht,
       And quhen the sone was schynand brycht
       Thai saw in bataillyng cum arayit
       The vaward with baner displayit,
       And syne sone the remanand
50   Thai saw weile ner behind cummand.
       Then held thai thaim still and preve
       Till the formast off that mengye
       War entryt in the ford thaim by,
       Then schot thai on thaim with a cry
55   And with wapnys that scharply schar
       Sum in the ford thai bakwart bar,
       And sum with arowis barblyt braid
       Sa gret martyrdome on thaim has maid
       That thai gan draw to voyd the place,
60   Bot byhynd thaim sa stoppyt was
       The way that thai fast mycht nocht fle,
       And that gert mony off thaim de,
       For thai on na wys mycht away
       Bot as thai come bot giff that thai
65   Wald throu thar fayis hald the gat,
       Bot that way thocht thaim all to hat.
       Thar fayis met thaim sa sturdely
       And contenyt the fycht sa hardily
       That thai sa dredand war that thai
70   That fyrst mycht fle fyrst fled away,
       And quhen the rerward saw thaim sua
       Discumfyt and thar wayis ga
       Thai fled on fer and held thar way.

[The flight of Sir Philip Mowbray to Inverkip]

       Bot Schyr Philip the Mowbray
75   That with the formast ridand was

when he saw how he was placed, with the great valour that he had, struck his champion steed with spurs, and despite all his enemies, rode through the thickest of them. (82) He would have escaped without challenge if someone had not caught him by the sword, but the good steed which would not halt, galloped on unstoppably. But the other [man] held [on] so firmly that the sword-belt burst leaving sword and belt in his hand. (89) [Mowbray] rode on his way without a sword, well beyond [Douglas's men], and stopped there watching how his company fled, and how his enemies cleared the ground that was between him and his men. (94) So then he took the roads to Kilmarnock and Kilwinning, then afterwards to Ardrossan. Then he went by himself through the Largs to Inverkip, right to the castle which was then garrisoned by Englishmen, who received him with great joy. (102) After they learned how he had ridden so far by himself, through [folk] who were all his foes, they cherished him greatly and praised mightily his chivalry.

(107) Sir Philip escaped like that, and Douglas was now in the place where he had killed sixty and more. The rest like cowards took their way and fled home again to Bothwell, where Sir Aymer was not a bit glad to hear in what way his company had been beaten. (115) But when King Robert was told how the good Douglas, who was bold,

---

95–98. This journey is quite extraordinary, for Mowbray, having fled south to Kilmarnock, eschewed the obvious refuge of Ayr, with its substantial English garrison, to turn north-west for the coast at Ardrossan, a slightly greater distance. From there Ayr is still considerably nearer than Inverkip. In making for this last Mowbray must surely have been determined to join up with a larger force in Renfrewshire, which would fit with the English force there in mid-September 1307.

That entryt wes in the place,
Quhen that he saw how he wes stad
Throu the gret worschip that he had
With spuris he strak the steid off pryce
80   And magre all his ennymys
Throu the thikkest off thaim he raid,
And but challance eschapyt had
Ne war ane hynt him by the brand,
Bot he the gud steid that wald nocht stand
85   Lansyt furth deliverly.
Bot the tother sa stalwartly
Held that the belt braist off the brand
And swerd and belt left in hys hand,
And he but swerd his wayis raid
90   Weill otouth thaim and thair abaid,
And beheld how that his menye fled
And how his fayis clengyt the steid
That war betwix him and his men.
Tharfor furth the wayis tuk he then
95   To Kylmarnok and Kilwynnyne
And till Ardrossane eftre syne,
Syne throu the Largis him allane
Till Ennirkyp the way has tane
Rycht to the castell that wes then
100   Stuffyt all with Inglismen
That him resaiffyt in daynte,
And fra thai wyst howgat that he
Sa fer had rydin him allane
Throu thaim that war his fayis ilkan
105   Thai prisyt him full gretumly
And lovyt fast his chevalry.

[*The reactions of Valence and King Robert*]

Schyr Philip thus eschapyt was,
And Douglas yet wes in the place
Quhar he sexty has slayne and ma,
110   The layff fouly thar gat gan ga
And fled to Bothwell hame agayne
Quhar Schyr Aymer wes na thing fayn
Quhen he herd tell on that maner
That his mengne discumfyt wer.
115   Bot quhen to King Robert wes tauld
How that the Douglas that wes bauld

defeated so many with few followers, he was truly joyful in his heart, and all his men were cheered, for, both high and low-born, they felt strongly that they should fear their enemies less since their cause had prospered thus.

(123) The king lay in Galston, which is just close to Loudoun, and took the country to his peace. When Sir Aymer and his followers heard how he harried the whole land and how none dared withstand him, he was angry in his heart, (130) and sent [the king] word by one of his company, saying that if he dared see him in the open [country], he should on the tenth of May come under Loudoun Hill; (135) and if he would meet him here,

---

122. Literally 'since their enterprise went with them so'.

123–24. Galston. At 6.465 I suggested that after fleeing Glentrool in April 1307, the king moved to Cumnock where he was joined by Douglas; they now moved to Galston which lies 14 miles, 22 kilometres north-east of Ayr and 7 miles, 11 kilometres west of Loudoun Hill. It is only a mile from 'Little Loudoun' (note to 202).

127. 'rewlit' in C, 'ryotit' in E. I have hesitantly accepted the latter since Robert I is described as bringing to his peace by fear, and there was doubtless ravaging by the way.

131. Sent word. Valence's challenge is most improbable and should be regarded as Barbour's chivalric embellishment on information that Bruce knew the battle-site in advance and prepared it. It looks as though Barbour has brought Edirford and Loudoun together because they were fought within a few miles of each other.

Barbour's statement that Valence was at Bothwell (15, 110) is made in the context of Mowbray's defeat at Edirford, but he takes Valence back to Bothwell after the battle of Loudoun (357). The critical questions are: whence did Valence set out towards Loudoun, and why?

An account of the battle was known to a source used by (a) Guisborough and (b) Grey in Scalacronica:

(a) [Edward I appointed Percy, Valence and Gloucester as Guardians in Scotland, each with a force.] The new king [Robert] met the brigade of ... Valence and put it to flight though few were killed, then within three days met the brigade of Gloucester, killed many, drove him off and besieged him in Ayr castle until freed by armies sent by the king. (*G*, 378)

(b) Bruce had assembled his adherents in Carrick; hearing of this ... Valence marched against him, when ... Bruce met ... Valence at Loudoun and defeated him, and pursued him to the castle of Ayr; on the third day after Bruce defeated ... Gloucester ... and pursued him too to Ayr castle and there besieged him till the English army came to his rescue. (*S*,132; *ST*, 34–35)

There are grave problems with the second part of each account, for the countess of Gloucester died on 23 April, 1307; her husband held the title only by courtesy, and would probably be at her burial in Suffolk on 26 April. Thereafter he lost the title. Ayr castle was certainly not

Vencussyt sa fele with fewe menye
Rycht joyfull in his hart wes he,
And all his menye confortyt war
120 For thaim thocht weille bath les and mar
That thai suld less thar fayis dreid
Sen thar purpos sa with thaim yeid.

[Valence challenges the king to open battle at Loudoun hill]

The king lay in Galliston
That is evyn rycht anent Loudoun
125 And till his pes tuk the cuntre.
Quhen Schyr Aymer and his menye
Hard how he ryotyt the land
And how that nane durst him withstand
He wes intill his hart angry,
130 And with ane off his cumpany
He send him word and said giff he
Durst him into the planys se
He suld the tend day of May
Cum under Loudoun hill away,
135 And giff that he wald meyt him thar

---

attacked by Bruce in May 1307, nor relieved by a royal army then; on
17 May it was a busy English garrison town shipping supplies from
Dumfries and Ireland. This confusion of an episode of 1301 with
Loudoun in 1307 has arisen because the English general in both retreated
to Ayr, from a Scottish force at Loudoun. Valence had set out from
Ayr.

He did so because Walter bishop of Lichfield, Treasurer of England,
had set out on a tour of garrisons from Carlisle. He was at Ayr (where
he borrowed Cumnock for Edward I) on 8 May, and he sought to cross
to Bothwell, which he reached on 13 May, returning by Lanark and
Dumfries to Carlisle on 18 May. I suggest that he was accompanied
from Ayr to Bothwell by Valence, to protect the money-bags, and it
was those same bags which interested King Robert. He first awaited
the English at Galston but prepared at Loudoun a site where he might
entrap them, to which he withdrew. The battle was a success for Bruce,
but the check to the Treasurer and Valence was a very temporary one;
they got through to Bothwell in days. (*CDS2, 1979, 1768, 1774, 1928,
1931; CDS4, 1829* (all of 1307))

133. Tenth of May. It is generally agreed that this was the date of the
battle of Loudoun. It is one of the few dates given in the poem, one
of still fewer which seem to be correct, and unique in the form in which
it is given. No source confirms it directly – Valence's costs from 8 July
1307 are preserved, but not those up to 7 July – but there is indirect
confirmation in the letter quoted below on 271.

his reputation would be greater, and more one of nobility, if he won it out in the open, with hard blows in a fair fight, than by doing a lot more while skulking. (141) The king, who heard [Aymer's] messenger, felt no little scorn that Sir Aymer spoke so haughtily, so he answered angrily saying to the messenger, 'Say to your lord that if I am alive he shall see me that day very close, if he dares to hold the way that he has named, for, rest assured, I shall meet him by Loudoun Hill.' (151) Without more ado the messenger rode on his way to his master, and quickly told him [the king's] answer; he was glad and cheered by that, for he intended by his superior force, if the king dared come to fight, that by the great chivalry that would be in his company he would so overcome the king that there would be no recovery.

(161) The king, on the other hand, who was always prudent and careful, rode to survey and choose the place [for the encounter]; [he] saw that the high road lay over a fair field, flat and dry, but upon either side of it there was a great moss, long and broad, (168) almost an arrow-shot on either side of the way where men rode, and he thought that place was far too wide to wait for men who were on horseback. Therefore he cut three ditches at right angles [to the road] from both the mosses to the way, [each] so far from the other that they were an arrow-shot and more apart. (176) The ditches were so deep and high

---

136–37. I wonder if the text here should not be read 'his worschip suld be mar and mar be turnyt ...', 'his reputation would, by more and more, be turned [to one] of nobility.'

140. To do fer mar. That is by continuing hit and run tactics.

163. The place. The site was probably to the north and west of the steading of Allanton Plains. (NS6137)

172. Thre dykys. Ditches, but the upcast would form a rampart. Robert's intention and Barbour's understanding are worth examination. According to Barbour there were gaps (number unstated) in these ditches at both sides of the road to allow the enemy to ride through in controlled groups of 500 (179–81) where they would be fought (184, 249). Because of these he had no fear of flank attacks. Then he had three ditches dug 'there', apparently in front of his position (189–94). But these must be the same as the three in 172, not an additional three. The king's position was at the gap in the foremost ditch (273–74); his resistance caused the enemy's horses in the van to throw their riders who were scattered in gaps (326). The ditches would make it difficult for the English to retreat once they were lured through the gaps.

He said his worschip suld be mar,
And mar be turnyt in nobillay,
To wyn him in the playne away
With hard dintis in evyn fechtyng
140   Then to do fer mar with skulking.
The king that hard his messynger
Had dispyt apon gret maner
That Schyr Aymer spak sa heyly,
Tharfor he answeryt irusly
145   And to the messynger said he,
'Say to thi lord giff that I be
In lyfe he sall me se that day
Weyle ner giff he dar hald the way
That he has said, for sekyrly
150   Be Loudoun hill mete him sall I.'
The messinger but mare abaid
Till his maistre the wayis raid
And his answer him tauld alswith
Quharof he wes bath glaid and blyth,
155   For he thocht throu his mekill mycht
Gyff the king durst cum to fycht
That throu the gret chevalry
That suld be in his cumpany
He suld sua ourcum the king
160   That thar suld be na recovering.

[*The king chooses and prepares a battle field*]

And the king on the tother party
That was all wis and averty
Raid for to se and cheis the place,
And saw the hey gat liand was
165   Apon a fayr feild evyn and dry,
Bot apon athir sid tharby
Wes a gret mos mekill and braid
That fra the way wes quhar men raid
A bow-draucht weile on ather sid,
170   And that place thocht him all to wyd
Till abyd men that horsyt war.
Tharfor thre dykys our-thwort he schar
Fra baith the mossis to the way
That war sa fer fra other that thai
175   War ytwyn a bow-draucht or mar.
So holl and hey the dykys war

that men could not pass them without great difficulty, even
with nobody against them. But he left gaps in the way, so
large and so numerous that five hundred could ride together
in at the gaps, side by side. (183) He meant to stay to fight
there and resist them, for he had no fear that they would
attack from the flank, nor yet give battle from behind, and he
was well aware that in front he should be defended from their
power. (189) He had three deep ditches made there, for if he
could not well prevail when meeting them at the first, he
would have the second under his control, or finally the third,
if so be that they had passed the other two. (195) He made
his dispositions like this, then assembled his force, which
contained six hundred fighting men, apart from the rabble
who were with him then, who were as numerous as [the
fighting men] or more. (200) He went with all that force, the
evening before the battle was due, to Little Loudoun, where
he would wait to see them coming, then with the men under
his command he meant to hasten so that he would be at the
ditch before them.

(207) Sir Aymer, on the other hand, gathered so great a
chivalry that he might have had nearly three thousand, armed
and equipped in goodly fashion; then, like a man of great
nobility, he held his way toward his tryst. (213) When the day
fixed had arrived, he hurried fast towards the place he had
named for the fight. The sun had risen, shining bright, which
flashed on the broad shields.

---

202. Little Loudoun. 'O[ver] Loudoun' on the Bleau map of Cunning-
ham, quite close to Loudoun castle, north of Galston. This is 5 miles,
9 kilometres, west of Loudoun hill. Since the king watched Valence
approach from here and then moved to Loudoun hill, the English must
have come from Ayr.

That men mycht nocht but mekill pane
Pas thaim thocht nane war thaim agan,
Bot sloppys in the way left he
180 Sa large and off sic quantite
That fyve hunder mycht samyn rid
In at the sloppis sid be sid.
Thar thocht he bataile for to bid
And bargane thaim, for he na drede
185 Had that thai suld on sid assaile
Na yeit behind giff thaim battaile,
And befor thocht him weill that he
Suld fra thar mycht defendyt be.
Thre dep dykys he gert thar ma,
190 For gyff he mycht nocht weill ourta
To mete thaim at the fyrst, that he
Suld have the tother on his pousté,
Be than the thrid gyff it war sua
That thai had passyt the tother twa.
195 On this wys him ordanys he,
And syne assemblit his mengne
That war sex hunder fechtand men,
But rangale that wes with him then
That war als fele as thai or ma.
200 With all that mengne gan he ga
The evyn or that the bataill suld be
Till litill Loudoun quhar that he
Wald abid to se thar cummyng,
Syne with the men of his leding
205 He thocht to sped him sua that he
Suld at the dyk befor thaim be.

[*The armies before the battle of Loudoun*]

Schyr Aymer on the tother party
Gadryt sua gret chevalry
That he mycht be thre thousand ner
210 Armyt and dycht on gud maner,
Than as man off gret noblay
He held towart his trist his way
Quhen the set day cummyn was.
He sped him fast towart the place
215 That he nemmyt for to fycht,
The sone wes ryssyn schynand brycht
That schawyt on the scheldis brade

He had drawn up the folk in his command in two squadrons. (220) The king saw their first squadron coming quite early in the morning, well arrayed in ranks, and behind them, somewhat close at hand, he saw the other following. (225) Their basnets were all burnished bright, gleaming in the sun's light; their spears, their pennons and their shields lit up all the fields with light. Their best, bright-embroidered, banners, horse of many hues, coats of armour of diverse colours, and hauberks which were as white as flour, made them glitter as though they were like to angels from the kingdom of Heaven. (235) The king said, 'Lords, now ye see how yon men would, if they can fulfil their intention, kill us by their great power and make every show of [doing so]. Since we know their ill-intent, let us go and meet them bravely, so that the stoutest of their company is discouraged by our encounter. (243) For if the foremost be met fiercely, you will quickly see the hindmost be discouraged. Although they are more [numerous] than us, that should cause us little discouragement, for when we come to the fighting no more [men] than we [are] can meet us. (250) Therefore, lords, each [of us] should be of courage and great valour to maintain our high reputation. Think what gladness awaits us if we can win a victory over our foes here, as may happen for us! For there would be none then, far or near in all this land, who would doubt us.' (258) Then said all those who stood about, 'Sir, if God wills, we shall do what will bring no reproof.'

---

230. Horse. I am not clear whether Barbour refers here to the horses or to the coats thrown over them.

In twa eschelis ordanyt he had
The folk that he had in leding.
220 The king weile sone in the mornyng
Saw fyrst cummand thar fyrst eschele
Arrayit sarraly and weile,
And at thar bak sumdeill ner-hand
He saw the tother folowand,
225 Thar bassynettis burnyst all brycht
Agayne the son glemand off lycht,
Thar speris pennonys and thar scheldis
Off lycht enlumynyt all the feldis,
Thar best and browdyn brycht baneris
230 And hors hewyt on ser maneris
And cot-armouris off ser colour
And hawbrekis that war quhyt as flour
Maid thaim gleterand as thai war lyk
Till angelys hey off hevynnys ryk.
235 The king said, 'Lordis now ye se
How yon men throu thar gret powesté
Wald, and thai mycht fulfill thar will,
Sla us, and makys sembland thartill,
And sen we knaw thar felny
240 Ga we mete thaim sa hardily
That the stoutest of thar mengye
Off our meting abaysit be,
For gyff the formast egrely
Be met ye sall se sodanly
245 The henmaist sall abaysit be.
And thoucht that thai be ma than we
That suld abays us litill thing,
For quhen we cum to the fechting
Thar may mete us no ma than we.
250 Tharfor lordingis, ilkan suld be
Off us worthi off gret valour
For to maynteyme her our honour.
Thynkis quhat glaidschip us abidis
Gyff that we may as weile betidis
255 Haff victour off our fayis her,
For thar is nane than fer na ner
In all thys land that us thar doute.'
Then said thai all that stud about,
'Schyr gyff God will we sall sa do
260 That na reprov sall fall tharto.'

'Then let us go forth now,' said the king, 'and may He who made everything of nothing lead us, save us by his might, and help us to maintain our right.' (265) With that they held their way in haste, a good six hundred in company, stalward and bold, worthy and brave; but I think they were all too few to stand against so many in battle, were it not for their outstanding valour.

(271) Now the noble king goes on his way, right boldly and in good order, and is gone to the foremost ditch, and took the field by the gap. The carriage men and poor folk who were not of value in the battle he left behind him, standing all still together on the hill. Sir Aymer saw the king coming with his brisk and bold men down from the hill to the plain, as seemed to [Aymer] fully prepared to defend or attack if any would offer him battle. (285) Therefore he comforted his men, bidding them be brave and worthy, for if they could capture the king and have victory in the fighting, they would be right well rewarded and greatly increase their reputation. (291) Because they were quite near the king, he gave up his speech-making and had the call to battle sounded, and the foremost of his company grasped their broad shields and rode in close order together;

---

271. There is a simple contemporary comment on the battle in a letter written from Carlisle on 15 May, 1307 by a member of the English court:

The king and queen ... are in good health, but the king had been much enraged because [Valence] the Guardian of Scotland and the other folk had retreated before King Hobbe without doing any exploit, so he has been intending to go to Dumfries himself, and is so still, and he wants to go further forward. We doubt this if he hears no other news. But this will not be until after [24 June]. For that business he has sent to London to seek all his tents. The bishop of [Litchfield] went towards Ayr, on [8 May] to ordain about victuals and other things, and Sir Edmund Maulay went with him to be constable of the castle there. [Arrangements for victualling Ayr from Ireland and England.] David of Atholl has come to the peace, in what form we do not know. James Douglas sent and asked (*pria*) that he might be received and then, when he saw that our folk were retreating, he was no longer willing to parley (*tenir parlance*). Some folk say that there is bad behaviour by some of our folk who are conspiring with the king's enemies. [Describes a parade of troops]. Sir, please don't think ill of me that I do not send you more news, for what we hear one day to be true, another day we hear the reverse. (*Nat. MSS Sc*, ii, *12*)

This represents the news of Loudoun as presented in a favourable light to Edward I, but it is nonetheless illuminating in that it shows Valence

'Now ga we furth than,' said the king,
'Quhar He that maid off nocht all thing
Lede us and saiff us for his mycht
And help us for till hald our rycht.'
265 With that thai held thar way in hy
Weill sex hunder in cumpany
Stalwart and stout, worthi and wycht
Bot thai war all to few Ik hycht
Agayne sa fele to stand in stour
270 Ne war thar utrageous valour.

[The battle at Loudoun]

Now gais the nobill king his way
Rycht stoutly and in gud aray,
And to the formast dyk is gane
And in the slop the feld has tane.
275 The cariage and the povyrall
That war nocht worth in the bataill
Behynd him levyt he all still
Syttand all samyn on the hyll.
Schyr Aymer the king has sene
280 With his men that war cant and kene
Come to the playne doune fra the hill
As him thocht in full gud will
For to defend or to assaile
Gyff ony wald him bid bataill.
285 Tharfor his men confortit he
And bad thaim wycht and worthi be,
For gyff that thai mycht wyne the king
And haiff victour off his fechting
Thai suld rycht weile rewardyt be
290 And ek gretly thar renommé.
With that thai war weill ner the king
And he left his amonesting
And gert trump to the assemblé,
And the formest off his mengne
295 Enbrasyt with the scheldis braid
And rycht sarraly togydder raid

---

retreating after a skirmish from which he pulled out. David, son of John
earl of Atholl deserted King Robert, who must have kept him in his
company since Methven. And before the battle Douglas was dickering
to desert, a move which ties in with his having sought favour by sending
the garrison of Douglas castle back to Clifford (510-12).

(297) with heads bowed and spears straight they pressed their way right to the king, who met them with such great vigour that the best and most valorous were thrown to the ground at their encounter. (302) [T]here men could hear such a breaking of spears that were smashed, and the wounded shouting and bawling so [loud] that it was horrible to hear, for those who were at the battle-face thrust and fought very sturdily. The noise and shouting began then.

(309) Ah! Almighty God! [Anyone] who had been there and had seen the valour of the king and of his brother beside him, who discomfited [the enemy] so bravely that their bold deeds and their courage gave great encouragement to their followers, [who had seen] how Douglas so manfully encouraged those who were by him, they could well have said that they had determination to win honour and achieved it. (319) The king's men were so sterling that they impaled both men and horses with spears that sheared sharply, till red blood soon ran from the wounds. The horses that were wounded reared and in their rearing drove back men, so that those who were at the front were scattered in gaps here and there. (327) The king, who saw them driven back like that and saw them reeling to and fro, ran against them so fiercely and assaulted them so hardily [that] he felled many of his foes. (332) The field was pretty well all covered by both dead horses and [dead] men, for the good king followed them then with five hundred bearing weapons who were unsparing of their enemies. They laid into them so hardily

---

275–78. The carriage men and poor folk. As at Bannockburn these were kept out of the battle, presumably because ill-armed and of uncertain morale and discipline ('nocht worth'). Unlike Bannockburn, there is no opportunity for them to plunder the enemy.

295. Shields. These would hang by a thong around the neck until taken on the arm, and the grip on the back grasped by the hand.

299–344. The battle. A first encounter with the king, his brother and Douglas (310–15) made the enemy reel, whereupon the king attacked them (329) killing many. Seeing this, the king and 500 'followed then' slaying more and causing a retreat. This is not wholly coherent, but nowhere does it suggest that the enemy went behind the second ditch; on the contrary, it implies an early English withdrawal. In this sense, though not in the number of slain, it agrees with English sources.

With heid stoupand and speris straucht
Rycht to the king thar wayis raucht,
That met thaim with sa gret vigour
300   That the best and off maist valour
War laid at erd at thar meting
Quhar men mycht her sic a breking
Off speris that to-fruschyt war
And the woundyt sa cry and rar
305   That it anoyus wes to her
For thai that fyrst assemblyt wer
Fwyngyt and faucht full sturdely.
The noyis begouth then and the cry.

[*The victory of King Robert*]

A! mychty God quha thar had bene
310   And had the kingis worschip sene
And his brodyr that waine him by
That stonayit thaim sa hardely
That thair gud deid and thair bounté
Gaiff gret confort to thar mengye,
315   And how Douglas sa manlily
Confortyt thaim that war him by,
He suld weile say that thai had will
To wyn honour and cum thar-till.
The kingis men sa worthi war
320   That with speris that scharply schar
Thai stekit men and stedis baith
Till rede blud ran off woundis raith.
The hors that woundyt war gan fling
And ruschyt thar folk in thar flynging
325   Sua that thai that the formast war
War skalyt in soppys her and thar.
The king that saw thaim ruschyt sua
And saw thaim reland to and fra
Ran apon thaim sa egrely
330   And dang on thaim sa hardely
That fele gart off his fayis fall.
The feild wes ner coveryt all
Bath with the slane hors and with men,
For the gud king thar folowit then
335   With fyve hunder that wapnys bar
That wald thar fayis na thing spar.
Thai dang on thaim sa hardely

that in a short time men could see a hundred and a good few
more lying on the ground. (340) The remainder were weak-
ened [and] then they began to pull back; when those at the
rear saw their vanguard being so repulsed, they fled without
waiting any longer. (345) And when Sir Aymer saw his men
all fleeing together, you can be sure he was very upset; but
he could not rebuke [his men] so that any would turn back
for him. (350) When he saw his effort was in vain, he turned
his bridle and went. (352) For the good king pressed them
so, that some were dead, some taken, and the rest went on
their way.

(355) The folk fled in this way without stopping, and Sir
Aymer went again to Bothwell, bemoaning the loss that he
had suffered, so ashamed at being beaten that he went in
haste to England, right to the king, and in ignominy gave up
his guardianship. (363) Thereafter he never came to make
war on Scotland for any reason, unless he came with the king
himself. So badly he felt that the king, with a few folk like
rabble, in a set battle defeated him with a great following that
was famed for its good courage. (371) Sir Aymer had that
tribulation, and King Robert, who was bold, stayed still in
the place until his men gave up the whole pursuit and then
with the prisoners they had taken they went to their lodgings,
praising God diligently for their success. (378) Anyone who
had been there could have seen

355-65. Valence did not withdraw to Bothwell but to Ayr, achieving
    Bothwell a few days later; he resigned the Guardianship in September
    and left in October 1307; it is not quite true that he came back as earl
    of Pembroke only with Edward II – he was at Bannockburn (1314) and
    the siege of Berwick (1319) but he also came without the king to Berwick
    to complete the truce of Christmas 1319.

368. A quhone lik to pouerall. Barbour adopts English chivalric contempt
    for Robert's muster of peasantry.

372. The defeat bemoaned by Valence here was followed in fact by the
    successful passage of the Treasurer to Bothwell, and by the retreat of
    Bruce to the fastness of Glen Trool, not by the adherence of 'many
    who dwelt around then' (388). In July he was hounded by John of Lorn
    and in August lay low while Edward II searched for him. In September
    his adherents were scattered and in danger.

That in schort tyme men mycht se ly
At erd ane hunder and wele mar.
340 The remanand sa fleyit war
That thai begouth thaim to withdraw,
And quhen thai off the rerward saw
Thar vaward be sa discumfyt
Thai fled foroutyn mar respyt
345 And quhen Schyr Aymer has sene
His men fleand haly beden
Wyt ye weile him wes full way
Bot he moucht nocht ammonys sway
That ony for him walde torne agane,
350 And quhen he saw he tynt his payn
He turnyt his bridill and to-ga,
For the gud king thaim presit sua
That sum war dede and sum war tane
And the laiff thar gat ar gane

[*Valence resigns his keepership and returns to England*]

355 The folk fled apon this maner
Forout arest and Schir Aymer
Agane to Boithweill is gane
Menand the scaith that he has tane
Sa schamfull that he vencusit wais
360 That till Ingland in hy he gais
Rycht to the king and schamfully
He gaff up thar his wardanry,
Na nevyr syne for nakyn thing
Bot giff he come rycht with the king
365 Come he to werray Scotland,
Sa hevyly he tuk on hand
That the king into set battaill
With a quhone lik to poverall
Vencusyt him with a gret menye
370 That war renonyt off gret bounté.
Sic anoy had Schyr Amery,
And King Robert that wes hardy
Abaid rycht still into the place
Till that his men had left the chace,
375 Syne with presonaris that thai had tane
Thai ar towart thar innys gane
Fast lovand God off thar weilfar.
He mycht haiff sene that had bene thar

people who were happy and pleased at their victory, and also because they had a lord so sweet and debonair, so courteous and of such fine bearing, so blith too and so much fun, standing so firm in battle, so prudent and so wise too, that they had good reason to be cheerful. (387) They were blith thus, without a doubt, because many who dwelt around them, when they saw the king defend himself thus, did homage to him.

(391) Then his power grew more and more, and he thought that he would go over the Mounth with his followers, to see who was willing to be his friend. He trusted Sir Alexander Fraser, for they were cousins, [as was] his brother Simon, the two of them. (398) He had good need of more, for he had many an enemy; Sir John Comyn, Earl of Buchan, and Sir John Mowbray as well, and good Sir David Brechin, with all the folk under their command, were enemies to the noble king. (405) And because he knew they were his foes, he took his journey towards them, for he wanted to see what kind of conclusion they would make of their enmity. (409) The king prepared and made himself ready to go northwards with his men. He took his brother with him and also Sir Gilbert Hay.

---

392. Over the Mounth. He went north not in triumph but in search of more support. The date of this cannot be fixed more closely than September 1307. On 1, 4, 6, October there was sudden activity by Edward II's administration at Nottingham, including the appointment of John of Argyll as sheriff and keeper of the western seaboard. Allowing time for the news to have travelled, King Robert had probably passed northward in mid-September. See note to 413.

395–97. Sir Alexander Fraser, his brother Simon. Distantly related to Simon Fraser of Oliver castle who was executed in 1306 for his support of Bruce. It is not certain that this was the Sir Alexander Fraser who was taken prisoner at Methven (2.239, 410), and the cousinhood was, at best, distant, since Alexander married the king's sister Mary. He also became chamberlain. Simon went on to become a laird in and sheriff of the Mearns. (*SP7*, 425–28)

400. John Comyn, earl of Buchan, had taken the patriotic side from 1298 to 1304, but was active on the English side from 1306. He seems to have gone north to his earldom after Methven.

401. Sir John Mowbray, son of Sir Geoffrey, apparently of Barnbougle and Dalmeny. He had guardianship of the lands of the murdered John Comyn, but is not known to have had lands of his own in the north. Nonetheless he was Guardian of Scotland north of the Mounth before 1306 and asked Edward I to renew this after the Bruce revolt. Edward does not seem to have done so but his son gave this post to Mowbray on 26 August, 1307, with a retinue of 30 men-at-arms. (*CDS2, 1726; CDS5*, 221a)

A folk that mery wes and glaid
380   For thar victour, and als thai haid
A lord that sa swete wes and deboner
Sa curtais and off sa fayr effer
Sa blyth and als weill bourdand
And in bataill sa styth to stand
385   Sua wys and rycht sua avisé
That thai had gret cause blyth to be.
Sua war thai blyth withoutyn dout,
For fele that wynnyt thaim about
Fra thai the king saw help him sua
390   Till him thar homage gan thai ma.

[The king decides to go north across the Mounth]

Than woux his power mar and mar,
And he thoucht weile that he wald far
Oute-our the Mounth with his menye
To luk quha that his frend wald be.
395   Into Schyr Alexander Fraser
He traistyt for thai cosyngis wer
And his broder Symon, thai twa.
He had mystre weile of ma
For he had fayis mony ane.
400   Schir Jhon Cumyn erle off Bouchquhane
And Schyr Jhon the Mowbray syne
And gud Schyr David off Brechyne
With all the folk off thar leding
War fayis to the noble king,
405   And for he wyst thai war his fayis
His viage thidderwart he tais,
For he wald se quhatkyn ending
Thai wald set on thar manassing.
The king buskyt and maid him yar
410   Northwartis with his folk to far,
His brodyr gan he with him ta
And Schyr Gilbert de le Hay alsua,

---

402. Sir David Brechin, a descendant of an illegitimate son of David,
earl of Huntingdon, had fought on the patriotic side till 1304. He was
at Ayr in, probably, July 1307, and probably went north some time after
the king did so. Barbour has here guessed at his earlier presence from
the taking of Brechin castle (9.286–94). The use of 'good' is striking,
suggesting that Barbour had a source sympathetic to him.

The earl of Lennox was there also, who went everywhere with the king, [and] Sir Robert Boyd and various others.

(416) The king took his way forth and left behind Sir James Douglas with all the folk who were with him, to see if he could recover his country. (421) He left him in great danger, but afterwards, in a short time he did so much by his great valour that he brought to the king's peace the whole of Selkirk Forest, as he also did Douglasdale and also Jedworth Forest. (428) Whoever could fairly take on himself to tell his bold deeds one by one would find lots of them. Because in his time, as men told me, he was beaten thirteen times and won victory fifty seven. He never seemed to lie idle for long; apart from his labours he had no concerns; I think men should justly praise him. (437) This James secretly took his men after the king had gone, and went to Douglasdale again, making a trap clandestinely for those who were in the castle. (442) He cunningly laid an ambush there and had fourteen or more of his men, [just] as they were, take sacks filled with grass, then lay them upon their horses and take their way just as if they wanted [to go] to Lanark fair, past where the ambush was.

---

413. The earl of Lennox is not known to have been with Bruce in either Ayrshire or the north, and this mention suggests that he helped the king to make his way through Lennox to the north, avoiding hostile Macdougall territory.

435. *Be his travaill he had na will.* The translation I have offered is a free one, and I am not confident that it is correct. I wonder if 'be' (in both C and E) is a transcription error for 'but', i.e. without.

437–520. The ruse at Douglas castle. This is the second taking of Douglas castle in the poem, but I have argued that it must precede, not follow, the Douglas Lardner in 5.225–462, which belongs to 7 April, 1308. This attack would precede the grants of money by Edward I to Clifford for the repair of the castle made between 30 May and 7 July, 1307, and I suggest that it occurred shortly before the battle of Loudoun. Barbour presumably found the attacks in the correct order in his source, but he has inverted them to heighten the 'romantic' peril of Webiton in serving at Douglas castle after the Lardner.

447. *As thai wald to Lanark far.* Mackenzie (*B1909*, 416) takes this as Lanark fair, and I have followed him, though 'wald ... far' (C, 'fair') could mean 'wanted to go', and so the scribe of E probably understood it. But there is little point in the mention of Lanark unless the fodder was going there to be sold, i.e. to the fair, and that is what Barbour, it seems to me, must have written. By the sixteenth century Lanark had four fairs annually, of which the oldest would be that beginning at Whitsun. In 1307 this fell on 14 May, placing the attack on Douglas perhaps a week earlier, in time for James to join the king before the battle of Loudoun.

The erle off Levenax als wes thar
That with the king was our-all-quhar,
415   Schyr Robert Boyd and other ma.

[Douglas returns to Douglasdale, to trick the garrison of Douglas castle]

     The king gan furth his wayis ta,
And left James off Douglas
With all the folk that with him was
Behind him for to luk giff he
420   Mycht recover his countré.
He left into full gret perill,
Bot eftre in a litill quhile
Throu his gret worschip sa he wrocht
That to the kingis pes he brocht
425   The forest of Selcrik all hale,
And alsua did he Douglasdale
And Jedworthis forest alsua.
And quha-sa weile on hand couth ta
To tell his worschippis ane and ane
430   He suld fynd off thaim mony ane,
For in his tyme as men said me
Thretten tymys vencusyt wes he
And had victouris sevin and fyfty.
Hym semyt nocht lang ydill to ly,
435   Be his travaill he had na will,
Me think men suld him love with skill.
This James quhen the king wes gane
All prevely his men has tane
And went to Douglas daile agane,
440   And maid all prevely a trane
Till thaim that in the castell war.
A buschement slely maid he thar,
And off his men fourtene or ma
He gert as thai war sekkis ta
445   Fyllyt with gres, and syne thaim lay
Apon thar hors and hald thar way
Rycht as thai wald to Lanark far
Outouth quhar thai enbuschyt war.

(449) When those in the castle saw so many loads going in a line, they were very pleased at the sight and told of it to their captain, called Sir John Webiton. (454) He was both young, brave and ruthless, cheerful too and flighty, and because he was a loving [person], he would go out much more cheerfully. He had his men get all their kit, and went out to get that victual, for their provisions were failing fast. (461) They came out impetuously, and galloped on determinedly to seize the loads which they saw going by, until Douglas and his men were all between them and the castle. The load-men, who were watching carefully, threw down their loads hurriedly, cast off swiftly the cloaks that concealed them, (470) mounted their horses in great haste and rode against them sturdily; [they] met their foes with a shout, who were astonished when they saw [men] who had recently been moving so quietly come against them so hardily; they suddenly grew dismayed and wanted to get to the castle. (478) When they saw Douglas burst [out from] his ambush on the other side, going against them robustly, they didn't know what to do or say. (482) They saw their foes at hand striking them without sparing, and couldn't help themselves a whit but fled to safety wherever they could; [Douglas's men] attacked them so fiercely that of them all not one escaped.

---

453. Sir John Webiton is not found in published English records. There is a Webton in Herefordshire.

470. Hint, seized. But I have here translated as 'mounted' which the sense seems to require.

474. 'Lurkand sa law'. Usually in the sense of lurking, lying low. But these men were the decoy, not the ambush, and I have translated, therefore as 'moving so quietly'.

[*The garrison comes out*]

And quhen thai off the castell saw
450 Sa fele ladys gang on raw
Off that sycht thai war wonder fayn
And tald it to thar capitane
That hate Schyr Jhone of Webetoun.
He wes baith yong stoute and felloun
455 Joly alsua and valageous,
And for that he wes amorous
He wald isch fer the blythlyar.
He gert his men tak all thar ger
And isch to get thaim vittaille,
460 For thar vittaile gan fast thaim faile.
Thai ischyt all abandounly
And prykkyt furth sa wilfully
To wyn the ladys that thai saw pas
Quhill that Douglas with his was
465 All betwix thaim and the castell.
The laid-men that persavyt weill,
Thai kest thar ladys doun in hy,
And thar gownys deliverly
That heylyt thaim thai kest away,
470 And in gret hy thar hors hint thai
And stert apon thaim sturdely
And met thar fayis with a cry
That had gret wonder quhen thai saw
Thaim that war er lurkand sa law
475 Cum apon thaim sa hardely.
Thai woux abaysit sodanly
And at the castell wald haiff bene,
Quhen thai on other halff has sene
Douglas brak his enbuschement
480 That agayne thaim rycht stoutly went.
Thai wyst nocht quhat to do na say,
Thar fayis on athir sid saw thai
That strak on thaim foroutyn sparing,
And thai mycht help thaim selvyn na thing
485 Bot fled to warrand quhar thai mocht,
And thai sa angryly thaim socht
That off thaim all eschapyt nane.

(488) Sir John Webiton was killed there, and when he was dead, as you are hearing, they found in his purse a letter sent to him by a lady whom he loved [and would] serve. The letter was in the following terms, saying that when he had guarded for a year in war, as a good bachelor, the hazardous castle of Douglas, which was so dangerous to keep, and had managed [it] well, in every way, then he could ask a lady for her love and her service.

(499) The letter said these things. And when they had been killed in this way, Douglas rode right to the castle, and there he made such a strong effort that he got into the castle. I don't know all the facts, whether it was by force or a trick, (506) but he acted in such a way by his great strength that he took the constable and all the rest who were inside, man and boy, gave them expenses-money, and sent them home without more harm to Clifford in their [own] country. (512) Then he acted so energetically that he knocked down the wall and destroyed all the houses, then took his way to the Forest, where he had many a hard encounter, and many a gallant feat of war took place. (518) If anyone should go through, and narrate, them all, he would say that his name should last for ever with immortal fame.

---

492. per drowry. 'drowry' is 'love service'.

492a, 494a. These lines are not in EH, but come from C. However 492a is the same line as 499, and could well have been repeated in error in C. It would then require an additional line to preserve the rhyme scheme.

494. Bachiller. A young knight. Found only here and at 2.409 and 4.72.

[The letter of Webiton, the taking of the castle and the freeing of its garrison]

Schyr Jhoun Webetoun thar wes slane,
And quhen he dede wes as ye her
490   Thai fand intill his coffeir
A lettyr that him send a lady
That he luffyt per drouery,
492a   The letter spak on this maner   493*
That said quhen he had yemyt a yer
In wer as a gud bachiller
494a   And governit weill in all maner   495*
495   The aventuris castell off Douglas   495
That to kepe sa peralus was
Than mycht he weile ask a lady
Hyr amouris and hyr drouery,
The lettyr spak on this maner.
500   And quhen thai slayne on this wyse wer
Douglas rycht to the castell raid
And thar sa gret debate he maid
That in the castell entryt he,
I wate nocht all the certanté
505   Quhethyr it was throu strenth or slycht,
Bot he wrocht sua with mekill mycht
That the constabill and all the laiff
That war tharin, bath man and knav
He tuk and gaiff thaim dispending
510   And sent thaim hame but mar greving
To the Cliffurd in thar countre.
And syne sa besily wrocht he
That he tumblyt doun all the wall
And destroyit the housis all,
515   Syne till the Forest held his way
Quhar he had mony ane hard assay
And mony fayr poynt off wer befell.
Quha couth thaim all rehers or tell
He suld say that his name suld be
520   Lestand into full gret renoune.

Now [let] us leave, in the Forest, Douglas, who will have little
rest till the country is freed of Englishmen and their power,
and turn to the noble king, who, with folk who followed him,
has taken the road to the Mounth boldly in good order; (9)
Alexander Fraser met him there, and his brother too, called
Simon, and all the good folk they had with them. The king
was affable with them, very pleased at their arrival. They told
the king all the plans of John Comyn, earl of Buchan, who
had taken with him to help him Sir John Mowbray, Sir David
Brechin and others as well, with all their followings, (20) 'and
they are yearning to take revenge on you, Sir King, more than
anything, for the sake of Sir John Comyn, who was killed a
while ago in Dumfries.' (24) The king said, 'Lord save me,
I had good reason to kill him. And since they want to take
on board because of him to make war on me, I shall put up
with it for a time, and see how they show their might. (30)
And if it turns out that they want to fight, if they attack, we
must defend [ourselves], [and] then afterwards let God's will
prevail.' After this talk, the king took the way straight to
Inverurie

---

1. The Forest. Ettrick Forest.
5. The king goes north. For this period we now have good information
   in a letter written in April 1308 to Edward II by Duncan of Frendraught,
   his sheriff of Banff, telling all the events of the previous six months. It
   is in poor condition, especially towards the end, but is given here as
   'Duncan's letter'. Helpful too is a letter from the earl of Ross, undated,
   but perhaps of October–November 1307. He told Edward:

   > We heard of the coming of ... Bruce towards ... Ross with a great
   > force, so that we had no power against him, but nonetheless we had
   > our men called out and were stationed for a fortnight with 3,000 men
   > at our own cost on the borders of our earldom and in ... Sutherland
   > and Caithness. He would have destroyed them completely if we had
   > not made a truce with him, at the request of good men, clergy and
   > others, till Whitsun [2 June, 1308] [Pleads for help]. And know, dear
   > lord, that we would on no account have made a truce with him if the
   > keeper of Moray had not been absent from the country, and the men
   > of his province would not respond to us without his orders, in order
   > to attack our enemies, so that we have no help except from our own
   > men. [Send your instructions].

9–18. For these persons see the notes to 8.393–402.
34. Inverurie. 16 miles, 25 kilometres NW of Aberdeen. That the king
    fell ill there was known to Barbour, who erroneously concluded that
    he made a round trip, Inverurie to Slioch and back. (a) Duncan's letter

BOOK 9

[The king goes to Inverurie and falls ill]

        Now leve we intill the Forest
        Douglas that sall bot litill rest
        Till the countre deliveryt be
        Off Inglis folk and thar powste,
5   And turne we till the noble king
        That with the folk off his leding
        Towart the Month has tane his wai
        Rycht stoutly and intill gud array,
        Quhar Alysander Frayser him met
10   And als his broder Symonet
        With all the folk thai with thaim had.
        The king gud contenance thaim made
        That wes rycht blyth off thar cummyne.
        Thai tauld the king off the convyne
15   Off Jhone Cumyn erle of Bouchane
        That till help him had with him tane
        Schyr Jhon Mowbray and other ma,
        Schyr David off Brechyn alsua,
        With all the folk off thar leding,
20   'And yarnys mar na ony thing
        Vengeance off you, schyr king, to tak
        For Schyr Jhone the Cumyn his sak
        That quhylum in Drumfres wes slayn.'
        The king said, 'Sa our Lord me sayn,
25   Ik had gret caus him for to sla,
        And sen that thai on hand will ta
        Becaus off him to werray me
        I sall thole a quhile and se
        On quhat wys that thai pruve thar mycht,
30   And giff it fall that thai will fycht
        Giff thai assaile we sall defend,
        Syne fall eftre quhat God will send.'
        Eftre this spek the king in hy
        Held straucht his way till Enrowry,

---

and (b) Fordun, report the true sequence, showing that the king was near Inverness and on the Moray Firth coast, but not at Inverurie:

(a) On the feast of [St Catherine] the virgin [25 November] ... Bruce with his force came to the castle of Inverlochy, and caused that castle to be handed over to him by the deceit and treason of the men of

in haste, and there he took such an illness as put him in very
real danger. He gave up eating and drinking. (38) His men
could get no medicine which would do the king any good.
His strength failed him so completely that he could neither
ride nor walk. (42) Then, believe you me, his men were cast
down, for there was no-one in that company who would have
been half so sorry to have seen his [own] brother lying dead
before him in that place as they all were at his illness; for all
their comfort was in him. (49) But good and worthy Sir
Edward, [the king's] brother, who was so bold, wise and
strong, went to great trouble to comfort them with all his
strength, (53) and when the lords that were there saw that
the illness more and more troubled the king, they quickly
concluded that it was unwise to stay there; for the country
there was all open, and they were but a small company to
stay without strength in the open. (60) Therefore till their
chieftain had recovered from his serious illness, they decided
to go soon to some strongholds.

(63) For folk without a chieftain, unless they are the better
men, would not be so bold in their actions as [they would be
if] they had a lord to lead them who dared put himself at risk,
without shirking, to take the outcome that God sends; (69)
for when he is of such determination and such stout heart
that he dares put himself at risk, his folk will always take his
bold deeds and stout heart as an example

---

the castle. Then he began damnable [?attacks in] the kingdom. Sir
Gilbert Glencairnie senior [*a very obscure passage, probably meaning*
surrendered Inverness castle] because of lack of water and because
the earl of Ross would not include him in his truce. Your [castle of
Inverness] is then altogether destroyed to the foundations, the castle
of Invernairn is burned by the same Robert by night and the castle
of Urquhart lost for want of keeping ... Moreover the said ... Bruce
with his force besieged and strongly assaulted the castle of Elgin where
Sir Gilbert Glencairnie junior was [but they made a truce]. When
this truce was made with Sir Gilbert, he betook himself to the castle
of Banff, when he fell into sickness of the body, and stayed in a certain
manor of mine, Concarn, for two nights, burned the manor and all
my grain with some of your carts, and hearing of the arrival of the
earls of Buchan, Atholl and John Mowbray ... with all his force he
moved towards Slioch ... [continued at note to 108].

(b) [*From Ayrshire*] he got together his men, who had been scattered
... and, crossing the hills with them in a body, he got as far as
Inverness, took the castle there ... slew its garrison and levelled it to
the ground. In the same way he dealt with the other castles ... in the
north, as well as with their inmates, until he got with his army as far
as Slioch.

35 And thar him tuk sik a seknes
That put him to full hard distress.
He forbar bath drynk and mete,
His men na medicyne couth get
That ever mycht to the king availe,
40 His force gan him halyly faile
That he mycht nother rid na ga.
Then wyt ye that his men war wa,
For nane wes in that cumpany
That wald haiff bene halff sa sary
45 For till haiff sene his broder ded
Lyand befor him in that steid
As thai war for his seknes,
For all thar confort in him wes.
Bot gud Schyr Edward the worthy
50 His broder that wes sa hardy
And wys and wycht set mekill payn
To comfort thaim with all his mayn,
And quhen the lordis that thar war
Saw that the ill ay mar and mar
55 Travaillyt the king, thaim thocht in hy
It war nocht spedfull thar to ly,
For thar all playne wes the countre
And thai war bot a few menye
To ly but strenth into the playne.
60 Forthi till that thar capitane
War coveryt off his mekill ill
Thai thocht to wend sum strenthis till.

[*A reflection on leadership; the king goes to Slioch*]

For folk foroutyn capitane
Bot thai the better be apayn
65 Sall nocht be all sa gud in deid
As thai a lord had thaim to leid
That dar put him in aventur
But abaysing to tak the ure
That God will send, for quhen that he
70 Off sic will is and sic bounté
That he dar put him till assay
His folk sall tak ensample ay

48, 52. Comfort. This is not a biblical quotation, but it echoes 2 Corinthians, 1.3

[so] that one of them will be worth three of those who have a bad chieftain; (76) his wretchedness so permeates them that they will lose their manliness, through the cowardice of his outlook. For when the lord who should be leading them does nothing, as [if] he were dead, or flees away, [leaving] his men, don't you agree then that they will be beaten in their hearts? (84) Yes, they will, by God, as I believe, unless their hearts are so strong, that they will not flee because of their valour. And though some are of such stout heart, when they see the lord and his company flee yet they will nevertheless flee, for all men willingly fly from death. (91) See what he does who so disgracefully runs away like that out of cowardice; he is defeated, both he and his, and gives superiority to his enemies. But he who, from his great nobility, subjects himself always to great dangers, to encourage his following, causes them to be of such stout heart that many a time they bring an unpromising business to a really successful conclusion. (101) This king of whom I tell did [just] that, and by his extreme valour comforted his men in such a way that none had fear where he was. (105) They were unwilling to fight while he was lying in such sickness, so they placed him in a litter and took the way to the Slioch, expecting to stay there in that stronghold until his illness had passed.

---

108. Slioch, near Huntly in the Garioch (NJ5638). (a) Duncan's letter and (b) Fordun continue, and (c) the Verse Chronicle narrates:

(a) with all his force [Bruce] moved towards Slioch, left the plains ... we saw his force situated in a certain wooded marsh near Slioch on Christmas Day ... we were unwilling to fight with him on that day ... [*something,* ? trees] preventing us from making out his force, but, having changed our minds, [? we decided to fetch] a force of footsoldiers ... on the following Sunday [31 December, 1307] we returned to him after collecting a sufficient infantry force and on the same night he moved with his force towards [?Strathbogie] ... [continued at note to 189]

(b) John Comyn, earl of Buchan, with many nobles both English and Scots, hearing that King Robert was, with his army, at Slioch, marched forward to meet him and give battle. But when they saw the king over against them with his men, ready for the fight, they halted and on Christmas Day, overwhelmed with shame and confusion, they retired and asked for a truce, which the king granted. Afterwards ... the king stayed there without fear for a week, and he there fell into a sickness so severe that he was born on a litter wherever he had occasion to be moved.

(c) In 1307/on Christmas Day the English side overcome by shame/retired from Slioch and asked a truce from the king/which

Off his gud deid and his bounte,
And ane off thaim sall be worth thre
75   Off thaim that wikkyt chifftane hais,
His wrechytnes sa in thaim gais
That thai thar manlynes sall tyn
Throu wrechitnes of his convyn.
For quhen the lord that thaim suld leid
80   May do nocht bot as he that war ded
Or fra his folk haldis his way
Fleand, trow ye nocht than that thai
Sall vencusyt in thar hartis be.
Yis sall thai, as I trow per de,
85   Bot giff thar hartis be sa hey
That thai na will for thar worschip flei,
And thocht sum be of sic bounte
Quhen thai the lord and his menye
Seys fley, yeit sall thai fley apayn
90   For all men fleis the deid rycht fayne.
Se quhat he dois that sua foully
Fleys thus for his cowardy,
Bath him and his vencusys he
And gerris his fayis aboune be.
95   Bot he that throu his gret noblay
Till perallis him abandounys ay
To recomfort his menye
Gerris thame be off sa gret bounte
That mony tyme unlikly thing
100 Tha bring rycht weill to gud ending.
Sa did this king that Ik off reid,
And for his utrageous manheid
Confortyt his on sic maner
That nane had radnes quhar he wer.
105 Thai wald nocht fecht till that he wes   105*
Liand intill his seknes,   105
Tharfor in litter thai him lay
And till the Slevauch hald thar way
And thocht thar in that strenth to ly
110 Till passyt war his malady.   109

---

the king granted and then withdrew / though he bravely remained there
for a week. (*Bower*6, 328)
Fordun's truce may well have been discreetly omitted from Duncan's
letter; the Verse Chronicle is the source of Fordun who adds only the
illness and litter, omitting the withdrawal.

(111) But when the earl of Buchan knew that they had gone there, and that the king was so sick that men doubted he would get better, he sent for his men in a hurry, and gathered a large company. (117) For all his own men were there, and with him also his friends, namely Sir John Mowbray and his brother (so I heard), and Sir David Brechin too, with many folk in their followings. And when they had all mustered, in haste they took their way to go to the Slioch, with all their men, to attack the king, who was then lying sick. (128) This was after Martinmas, when snow had covered all the land. They came near to the Slioch, armed in their best array, and then the king's men, who were aware of their coming, kitted up to defend themselves if they were attacked. But nonetheless their enemies were still two for each of those [king's men] who were there. (137) The earl's men were coming near, [blowing] trumpets and making a great display, and made knights when they were near. And those who were in the side of the wood stood in arms in close order, expecting to wait there bravely for the arrival of their enemies. (144) In no way would they come out to attack them by fighting, until the noble king had recovered, but if the other [side] wanted to attack them, they would defend, come what may. (149) And when the earl's company saw that they organised [themselves] so wisely that they intended to defend their strong-point, [the earl's men] sent archers out to them,

---

120. His brother. It is not certain that John and Philip Mowbray were related, and the identity of this brother is uncertain. (*Knights of Edward I*, iii, 223–24)

128–29. Martinmas is 11 November. Robert was at Slioch, Christmas-Hogmanay 1307, which is a long time 'after' Martinmas. See the Introduction sec. 6. for an explanation of the errors of date for Slioch and Inverurie.

139. Made knights. This was appropriate before a battle which was to be important. It did not materialise.

[*The skirmishing at Slioch*]

Bot fra the erle of Buchane
Wyst that thai war thidder gane
And wyst that sa sek wes the king
That men doutyt off his covering,
115   He sent eftre his men in hy   114
And assemblyt a gret cumpany,
For all his awine men war thar
And all his frendis with him war,
That wes Schir Jhonne the Mowbray
120   And his brodyr as Ik hard say   119
And Schyr David off Brechynge
With fele folk in thar ledyng.
And quhen thai all assemblit war
In hy thai tuk thar way to far
125   To the Slevauch with all thar men   124
For till assaile the king that then
Wes liand intill his seknes.
This wes eftyr the Martymes
Quhen snaw had helyt all the land.
130   To the Slevauch thai come ner-hand   129
Arayit on thar best maner
And thane the kingis men that wer
War off thar come thaim apparaylyt
To defend giff thai thaim assaylyt
135   And nocht-forthi thar fayis war   134
Ay twa for ane that thai war thar.
The erlys men ner cummand war
Trumpand and makand mekill far
And maid knychtis quhen thai war ner,
140   And thai that in the woddis sid wer   139
Stud in aray rycht sarraly
And thocht to byd thar hardyly
The cummyng off thar ennymys,
Bot thai wald apon nakyn wys
145   Ische till assaile thaim in fechting   144
Till coveryt war the nobill king,
Bot and othir wald thaim assailye
Thai wald defend vailye que vailye.
And quhen the erlis cumpany
150   Saw that thai wrocht sa wisely   149
That thai thar strenth schupe to defend,
Thar archeris furth to thaim thai send

to skirmish with them, and strongly [armed] men. And [the
king's men] sent archers against them, who skirmished with
them boldly until those of the earl's party withdrew into their
force. (158) Three days they lay there like this, and skirmished
every day, but [the earl's] bowmen always got the worst of
it. And when the king's company saw their enemies lying
before them, growing more and more [numerous] each day,
(164)while they were few and so placed that they had nothing
to eat unless they laboured to get it, therefore they took counsel
in haste that they would not lie there any longer, but would
hold there way to where they could get for themselves and
their men victuals and food.

(171) They laid the king in a litter, got themselves ready and
took the way where all their foes could see them. Each man
according to his station readied himself to fight if they were
attacked. The carried the king in their midst, going close
around him, and not hurrying themselves very much. (179)
[When] the earl and those with him saw that they readied
themselves to travel, and saw how they jouneyed with the king
with so little fear, ready to fight anyone who might attack,
their spirits began to fail, they let them pass on their way in
peace, and went home to their houses.

(187) The earl took his way to Buchan, and Sir Edward Bruce
went to Strathbogie with the king,

---

158. Three days. The week of Duncan's letter and the Verse Chronicle
is clearly correct, but all three sources give differing accounts of how
this time was passed.

185. In peace. This may be Barbour's acknowledgment of the truce
mentioned by the Verse Chronicle.

189. Strathbogie. The period between Slioch and Inverurie is passed over by
Barbour and Fordun. The earlier part of it is covered in Duncan's letter:
When [Bruce] had crossed the mountains in flight, Sir John Mowbray
[placed] some serjeants in the castle of Coull [to protect] the land of
Mar ... [*the pro-English leaders*] crossed towards the earl of Ross who
... answered that he would not break [his truce]. Sir John Mowbray
[?seized, ?harried] all freeholders and others whom he knew to be of
ill repute ... when the magnates crossed the Mounth towards the lord
chief Guardian they sent their sheep and lambs into northern parts
... Bruce [negotiated a truce with] Mowbray which he accepted about
the beginning of Lent [3 March, 1308]. Then he crossed towards the
castle of Mortlach [*i.e. Balvenie*] and utterly destroyed that castle with
the land ... which belongs to Sir Reginald Cheyne, flames sweeping
right through it. Then he moved towards the castle of Tarradale [*in
the Black Isle*] ... the land nearby which belonged to Sir Alexander
Comyn was destroyed. The earl of Ross withdrew from him and
Henry ... and he left Ross undestroyed as we understand. William

To bykkyr thaim and men off mayn,
And thai send archeris thaim agayne
155 That bykkyrryt thaim sa sturdely 154
Till thai off the erlis party
Intill thar bataill dryvyn war.
Thre dayis on this wys lay thai thar
And bykkyryt thaim everilk day
160 Bot thar bowmen the war had ay. 159
And quhen the kingis cumpany
Saw thar fayis befor thaim ly
That ilk day wox ma and ma,
And thai war quhone and stad war sua
165 That thai had na thing for till eyt 164
Bot giff thai travaillit it to get,
Tharfor thai tuk consale into hy
That thar wald thai na langer ly
Bot hald thar way quhar thai mycht get
170 To thaim and tharis vittaillis and mete. 169

[*The king withdraws from Slioch*]

In a littar the king thai lay
And redyit thaim and held thar way
That all thar fayis mycht thaim se,
Ilk man buskyt him in his degre
175 To fycht giff thai assaillyt war. 174
In myddis thaim the king thai bar
And yeid about him sarraly
And nocht full gretly thaim gan hy.
The erle and thai that with him war
180 Saw that thai buskit thaim to far, 179
And saw how with sa litill effray
Thai held furth with the king thar way
Redy to fycht quha wald assaile.
Thar hartis begouth all to faile
185 And in pes lete thaim pas thar way 184
And till thar housis hame went thai.

[*The king goes to Strathbogie then to Inverurie*]

The erle his way tuk to Bouchane,
And Schyr Edward the Bruce is gane

Wiseman [?took] the castle of Skelbo on Palm Sunday [7 April] ...
he came to the castle of Elgin and besieged it ... [*the rest is lost*]

and made a long enough stay there till he began to recover and walk; then they took their ways straight to Inverurie again, intending to lie in the open for the winter season, since victuals would not fail them in the plain. (197) The earl knew that they were there, and gathered his following here and there. Brechin and Mowbray and their men all gathered to the earl then, and were a really large company of finely armed men. They took the way to Old Meldrum, and lodged there with their men no more than one night before Christmas Eve; I'm sure they numbered a thousand. (207) They all stayed there that night, and in the morning, when daylight came, Sir David, lord of Brechin, went towards Inverurie to see if he could do harm to his enemies in any way. (214) He came riding into the edge of Inverurie so suddenly that he slew some of the king's men, and others withdrew and fled towards the king, who was then lying with most of his force on the further side of the Don.

On 1 May, 1308 John Mowbray told Edward II that he had relieved Elgin castle, defended by Duncan of Frendraught; Bruce had withdrawn as he approached. It is clear from this narrative that Bruce had largely recovered from the illness which afflicted him at Slioch. Barbour acknowledges this in 191.

193. Inverurie. Fordun's account places Mowbray as occupant of the town:

> In 1308 [Comyn and Mowbray] with a great many Scots and English were assembled at Inverurie. But when King Robert heard of this, though he had not got rid of his serious illness yet, he arose from his litter ... and ordered his men to arm him and set him on horseback. When this was done, he too, with a cheerful countenance, hastened with his host against the enemy, to the battle-ground, although by reason of his great weakness, he could not go upright, except with the help of two men to prop him up. When the opposition saw him and his ready for battle, at the mere sight of him they were scared stiff and put to flight; they were pursued as far as Fyvie, twelve leagues away. (*F1*, 344; *F2*, 337)

205. Yhule evyn. Barbour has ascribed the arrival at Slioch to Inverurie. Fordun's '1308' would mean 'after 25 March, 1308'. The full date is preserved in the Verse Chronicle:

> In 1308/on the feast of our Lord when he mounts the stars of Heaven/the English side fled on seeing Robert as a king/but the king's infantry are borne, rushing, against the enemy/routing the earl of Buchan and John Mowbray./From Inverurie the flight lasted through the places of *Duri*/as far as Fyvie, nearly twelve leagues without a break. (*Bower6*, 342)

This gives Thursday, 23 May, 1308. Fordun (see note to 193) has assumed from this source that Mowbray occupied Inverurie, but Barbour is surely to be preferred. The Verse Chronicle extract does not

	Rycht to Strabolghy with the king	
190	And sua lang thar maid sojorning	189
	Till he begouth to covyr and ga,	
	And syne thar wayis gan thai ta	
	Till Innerroury straucht agane	
	For thai wald ly into the plane,	
195	The wynter sesone, for vittaile	194
	Intill the plane mycht thaim nocht faile.	
	The erle wyst that thai war thar	
	And gaderyt a mengne her and thar.	
	Brechyne and Mowbray and thar men	
200	All till the erle assemblyt then	199
	And war a full gret cumpany	
	Off men arayit jolyly.	
	Till Auld Meldrum thai yeid the way	
	And thar with thar men logit thai	
205	Befoir Yhule evyn a nycht but mar,	204
	A thousand trow I weile thai war.	
	Thai logyt thaim all thar that nycht	
	And on the morn quhen day wes lycht	
	The lord off Brechyn Schyr Davy	
210	Is went towart Innerroury	209
	To luk gyff he on ony wys	
	Mycht do skaith till his ennymys,	
	And till the end off Innerroury	
	Come ridand sa sodanly	
215	That off the kingis men he slew	214
	A part, and other sum thaim withdrew	
	And fled thar way towart the king	
	That with the maist off his gadryng	
	On the yond half Doun wes than lyand.	

refer to the king's illness (Barbour and Fordun) and being supported on his horse (Fordun and in the literature of chivalry). Inverurie must have been a stop by the king on the way to another target, perhaps Aberdeen, and the king's camp there does suggest that he had fallen ill again. That he was reported to have fallen ill at Inverurie would explain why Barbour wrongly took him there before fighting Slioch as a sick man (34–41). For Duri see note to 243.

219. McDiarmid in *B1985*, 83 argues, surely correctly, that 'Doun' here is the Don, not 'down'. It seems that Brechin crossed the river to the northern edge of Inverurie, and that Bruce's main force was further downstream across the river, on the same side as Old Meldrum which lies about 5 miles, 8 kilometres to the north. Barbour may have underplayed this encounter, which is the only battle at Inverurie described by him.

(220) And when men told him the news of how Sir David had killed his men, he called for his horse then in haste, and ordered his men to get ready with great speed, for he meant to go to fight against his enemies. (226) With that he prepared to get up, although not completely recovered then. Then said some of his close [attendants], 'What are you thinking of, going to fight like that, and you not better [yet]?' (231) 'Yes,' said the king, 'without doubt their insolence has made me hail and sound, for no medicine could have made me recover as quickly as they have done. So, as God is my witness, I shall either have them or they me!' (237) And when his men heard the king show himself so determined for the fight, they were all cheered up at his recovery and got themselves ready for the battle.

(241) The noble king and his company, probably about seven hundred [in number], took the way towards Old Meldrum where the earl and his following lay. The scouts saw them coming with banners waving in the wind, and hastily went to their lord, who had his men arm themselves in haste and arrayed them for battle. (250) They set their rabble behind them, and made a good show for the fight. The king came on with great strength, and they waited, making a great display, till they were nearly at impact. (255) But when they saw the noble king come bravely on without hesitation, they withdrew a little 'on bridle', and the king who well knew

---

243. Old Meldrum. At 203–4 Mowbray's force is lodged there. Although the Fordun–Bower tradition is for a battle of Inverurie, the Verse Chronicle seems to be their source and speaks of a flight from Inverurie to Fyvie, which is much what Barbour describes, but with the main encounter at Old Meldrum. In the Verse Chronicle in Bower, the flight through the places of Duri is *per loca Duri*, where the name probably represents *Durum*, a poetic attempt at [Mel]drum.

[*Preparation for battle*]

220 And quhen men tauld him tithand 219
How Schyr Davy had slayn his men
His hors in hy he askyt then
And bad his men all mak thaim yar
Into gret hy, for he wald far
225 To bargane with his ennymys. 224
With that he buskyt for to rys
That wes nocht all weill coveryt then.
Then said sum off his preve men,
'Quhat think ye thusgat to far
230 To fycht and nocht yeit coveryt ar.' 229
'Yhis,' said the king, 'withoutyn wer,
Thar bost has maid me haile and fer,
For suld na medicyne sa sone
Haiff coveryt me as thai haiff done.
235 Tharfor, sa God himself me se, 234
I sall othir haiff thaim or thai me.'
And quhen his men has hard the king
Set him sa hale for the fechting,
Off his coveryng all blyth thai war
240 And maid thaim for the battaill yar. 239

[*The battle of Old Meldrum*]

The nobill king and his mengye
That mycht weile ner sevin hunder be
Towart Auld Meldrum tuk the way
Quhar the erle and his menye lay.
245 The discurrouris saw thaim cummand 244
With baneris to the wynd wavand
And yeid to thar lord in hy
That gert arme hys men hastely
And thaim arayit for battaile,
250 Behind thaim set thai thar merdale 249
And maid gud sembland for to fycht.
The king come on with mekill mycht
And thai abaid makand gret fayr
Till thai ner at assembling wayr,
255 Bot quhen thai saw the nobill king 254
Cum stoutly on foroutyn fenyeing
A litill on bridill thai thaim withdrew,
And the king that rycht weill knew

that they were all close to defeat, pressed on them with his banner, [so that] they retreated more and more. (262) And when the small folk they had there saw their lords pull back like that, they turned tail and went, and fled, scattering here and there. The lords who were still together, [who] saw that their small folk were fleeing, and saw the king bravely coming, were each so dismayed that they turned tail and went. (271) They kept together for a short while, then each man took his own way. There was never so miserable an outcome after such a sturdy display. For when the king's company saw that they fled so disorderly, they chased them with all their might, took some and killed others. (279) The rest kept on fleeing – [the man] with the good horse got away best ! The earl of Buchan fled to England, Sir John Mowbray going with him, and [they] were given refuge by the king. But that lasted only a short while, for they died soon after that. (286) And Sir David Brechin fled to his own castle of Brechin, and provisioned it favourably and well. But David, the earl of Atholl, son of him who was in Kildrummy, came next and besieged him there. (292) And he who wanted no more of war, nor to fight with the noble king, became his man then, in a good deal.

(295) Now let us go to the king again, who was well pleased at his victory, and had his men burn all Buchan

---

262. The small folk are presumably the rabble of 250.

280. Barbour does not name Fyvie as the end of the chase. It lies a good 7 miles, 12 kilometres north of Old Meldrum. The pursuit must have been by cavalry.

281–85. Buchan and Mowbray fled to England, and were appointed keepers of Galloway and Annandale; but Buchan died before the end of 1308, childless.

286–94. Sir David Brechin. Brechin seems to have been a fairly strong castle, and the occasion on which it was taken by an earl of Atholl was probably April–May 1306, by Earl John, for his son Earl David was a supporter of Edward II till 1312. Sir David Brechin does not seem to have been caught then, as he was thanked by Edward II in May 1308. He is not named in the round-up of Bruce adherents at the St Andrews parliament of March 1309 and in July 1308 or 1309 – probably the former – he had a gift of wine from Edward II. He was taken at Brechin probably after the fall of Forfar at Christmas 1308, for on 15 June, 1310 Edward II gave Sir Alexander Abernethy power to receive Brechin to that king's peace. Between 1311 and 3 May, 1312 he was at Berwick, latterly as keeper, but that is the last mention of him in Edward's service; it is likely that he had sailed with a relief fleet to Dundee and was taken there. His wife, Margaret received money to help with his ransom,

That thai war all discumfyt ner
260   Pressyt on thaim with his baner   259
And thai withdrew mar and mar.
And quhen the small folk thai had thar
Saw thar lordis withdraw them sua
Thai turnyt the bak all and to-ga
265   And fled all scalyt her and thar.   264
The lordis that yeyt togydder war
Saw that thar small folk war fleand
And saw the king stoutly cummand,
Thai war ilkane abaysit swa
270   That thai the bak gave and to-ga,   269
A litill stound samyn held thai
And syne ilk man has tane his way.
Fell never men sa foule myschance
Eftre sa sturdy contenance
275   For quhen the kingis cumpany   274
Saw that thai fled sa foulyly
Thai chasyt thaim with all thair mayn
And sum thai tuk and sum has slayn.
The remanand war fleand ay,
280   Quha had gud hors gat best away.   279
Till Ingland fled the erle of Bouchquhane
Shyr Jhon Mowbray is with him gane
And war resett with the king,
Bot thai had bath bot schort lesting
285   For thai deyt sone eftre syne.   284
And Schyr David off Brechyne
Fled till Brechyne his awine castell
And warnyst it bath fayr and weill,
Bot the erle of Atholl, Davy,
290   His sone that wes in Kildromy   289
Come syne and him assegyt thar,
And he that wald hald were ne mar
Na bargane with the nobile king
Come syne his man with gud treting.

[*The ravaging of Buchan; the taking of Forfar castle*]

295   Now ga we to the king agayne   294
That off his victory wes rycht fayn,
And gert his men bryn all Bowchane

---

apparently in 1313. Altogether he seems no strong adherent of King
Robert. See note to 19.59. (*SP2*, 218–19)

from end to end, sparing none. He harried them in such a way that a good fifty years afterwards people bemoaned the devastation of Buchan. (302) The king then took to his peace the north country, which obeyed his lordship humbly, so that north of the Mounth there were none who were not his subjects, one and all. (307) His lordship spread always more and more. He went toward Angus then, and expected that he would soon make free everything north of the Firth of Forth. The castle of Forfar was then garrisoned by Englishmen. (313) But Philip the forester of Platan took some of his friends with him, and hurried to the castle with ladders, secretly, climbed over the stone wall and took the castle thus, by the failure of the guard, with little difficulty. (320) Then he killed all that he found [therein] and handed the castle over to the king, who gave him a very good reward. The [the king] had the castle wall broken down, and destroyed the well and the whole castle.

(325) When the castle of Forfar and all its towers had been cast down to the ground, as I've narrated, the wise, strong and bold king, who expected to make everything north of the Firth of Forth free, went to Perth with all his army, surrounded the town and soon set siege to it. (334) But as long as it could have men and food, it could not be taken without a great effort, for the walls were all of stone,

297–301. The Verse Chronicle describes the herschip of Buchan as directly following the advance to Fyvie: 'the king set up camp for his people in a wood there / and advancing from there consumed Buchan with fire / he punished some people, brought some to his peace. / He scattered his enemies and so came away from there as victor.' (*Bower6*, 342) The herschip must have occurred before about 31 July because on 11 August the English government postponed an expedition, appointed Buchan and Mowbray [having fled] as keepers in the south-west, and urged local keepers to take truces with Bruce. The news which prompted this was probably the herschip of Buchan and the fall of Aberdeen, besieged since late June. The herschip can be dated to June 1308. See note on 10.9.

311–24. Almost unknown, the motte of Forfar castle still exists in the middle of the town, though without trace of stone walls. It fell on Christmas night, 1308, according to the Holyrood chronicle. The Platan was a forest (hunting ground) nearby.

325. At this point four years disappear almost without trace, for Barbour goes on to the siege of Perth in January 1313. The link was probably a failed threat when the king was at Perth on 14 October, 1308, the date of an early royal charter (*RRS5*, 4)

336. The walls of stone. Although there was later work on the defences of Perth, there is reason to accept Barbour's claim that the town was

Fra end till end and sparyt nane,
And heryit thaim on sic maner
300 That eftre weile fyfty yer   299
Men menyt the herschip off Bouchane.
The king than till his pes has tane
The north cuntreys that humbly
Obeysyt till his senyoury
305 Sua that benorth the Month war nane   304
Then thai his men war everilkan,
His lordschip wox ay mar and mar.
Towart Angus syne gan he far
And thocht sone to mak all fre
310 That wes on the north halff the Scottis se. 309
The castell off Forfayr wes then
Stuffyt all with Inglismen,
Bot Philip the Forestar of Platane
Has off his freyndis with him tane
315 And with leddrys all prevely   314
Till the castell he gan him hy
And clam up our the wall off stane
And swagate has the castell tane
Throu faute off wach with litill pane,
320 And syne all that he fand has slayne   319
Syne yauld the castell to the king
That maid him rycht gud rewarding,
And syne gert brek doun the wall
And fordyd well and castell all.

[*The king goes to Perth and besieges it*]

325 Quhen that the castell off Forfar   324
And all the towris tumblyt war
Down till the erd as Ik haiff tauld
The king that wycht wes wys and bauld
That thocht that he wald mak all fre
330 Apon the northhalff the Scottis se   329
Till Perth is went with all his rout
And umbeset the toun about
And till it a sege has set.
Bot quhill it mycht haiff men and met
335 It mycht nocht but gret payne be tane   334
For all the wall wes then of stane

---

defended thus. There had been no castle at Perth since the flood of
1209. In 1311 Edward II had tried to strengthen Perth and Dundee,

with thick[-walled] high-standing towers. At that time there
stayed in it Muschet and also Oliphant; those two had the
keeping of the town. (341) The earl of Strathearn was also
there, but his son and [some] of his men were outside in the
king's force. There was often stout and fierce skirmishing,
and men [were] killed on either side. (346) But the king, who
was prudent in all his doings, saw the strong stone walls, the
defence that they provided, and how the town was difficult
to take by open attack, force or assault, so he decided to use
[some] cunning. (353) All the time that he lay there he
watched, and quietly had trials [to find] where the ditch was
shallowest, until finally he found a place where men could
wade [across] up to their shoulders. (358) And when he had
found that place, he had his men each get ready; when six
weeks of the siege had passed,

---

sending Piers Gaveston there with a force; on 8 July, 1311 120 men (of
this force?) including a few knights, had their horses valued there. But
the 1313 garrison is unlikely to have been as strong as this suggests.

339-41. Muschet, Olifard, Strathearn. Muschet was listed in the Perth
garrison in 1311, but was in command at Dundee before Easter 1312
when that town was besieged and surrendered to Bruce; the garrison
was allowed to leave. Olifard had been the valiant defender of Stirling
in 1304, and was imprisoned in the Tower of London till 1308; his
employment as keeper of Perth shows Edward II's difficulty in finding
reliable commanders in Scotland. In October 1313 a William Oliphant
had an English protection to go to Scotland. He was not a knight, so
probably son of the keeper of Perth. The Sir William Olphant who had
several charters from King Robert could have been either; see Lanercost
and Gray on Sir William in note to 360. Strathearn, on the other hand,
had defied Bruce in March 1306, submitting only when threatened with
death, and refusing to send men to his army. His oath of loyalty (to
Edward I), he said, was not 'fragile like glass'. He paid for this with
his earldom (441-42).

342. McDiarmid wrongly questions Barbour's account of the younger
Malise's adherence to Bruce. Certainly he was with his father in Eng-
land, between 1309 and July 1311, but the document recording his
allowance on 28 January, '1313' is of 1310. Barbour's account is trust-
worthy. The supposed report of the senior Earl Malise's death in 1312
is worthless. (B1985, 83)

355. The ditch. It is still possible to see the ditch of Perth from the road
near the Marshall Gallery and Museum. The water is now scarcely a
foot deep.

360. Six weeks. This is certainly wrong, because Lanercost describing
the invasion of England and the levying of tribute in the summer of
1312, goes on:

Seeing that he had the whole of England under tribute, [Robert]
applied all his efforts to getting possession of the town of Berwick ...
Coming unexpectedly to the castle on [6 December, 1312] he laid

And wycht towris and hey-standand,
And that tyme war tharin dwelland
Muschet and als Olyfard,
340   Thai twa the toun had all in ward   339
And off Straitherne als the erle wes thar,
Bot his sone and off his men war
Without intill the kingis rowt.
Thar wes oft bekering styth and stout
345   And men slayne apon ilk party,   344
Bot the gud king that all wytty
Wes in his dedis everilkane
Saw the wallis sa styth off stane
And saw defens that thai gan ma
350   And how the toun wes hard to ta   349
With opyn sawt strenth or mycht.
Tharfor he thocht to wyrk with slycht,
And in all tyme that he thar lay
He spyit and slely gert assay
355   Quhar at the dyk schaldest was,   354
Till at the last he fand a place
That men mycht till thar schuldris wad.
And quhen he that place fundyn had
He gert his men busk ilkane
360   Quhen sex woukis off the sege war gane,   359

---

ladders against the walls and began to scale them, and had not a dog
betrayed the approach of the Scots by loud barking, it is believed he
would quickly have taken the castle and in consequence the town ...
Having failed in his attempt on Berwick, Robert marched with his
army to the town of St John [Perth] ... and laid siege to it; on Monday
[8 January, 1313] it was taken by the Scots who scaled the walls by
night with ladders and entered the town through the negligence of
the sentries and guards. Next day Robert caused those citizens of the
better sort who were of the Scottish nation to be killed but the English
were allowed to go free ... Oliphant was bound and sent far away to
the Isles. (*L*, 220–21; *LT*, 200–1)

Thus the siege must have been much shorter than Barbour claims. It
is also incredible that an army sat through a prolonged siege in a Scottish
December. In 1318 Berwick castle held out against Bruce for about 11
weeks, but Barbour gives six days (17.198).

    Gray gives a unique version of the taking of Perth. Explaining how
Bannockburn came about, he claims that 'the chronicles explain that
after the earl of Atholl had captured [Perth] for the use of Robert Bruce,
from William Oliphant captain of it for the king of England, being at
that time an adherent of [Edward], although shortly after he deserted
him' [Bruce marched to Stirling]. (*S*,140–41; *ST*, 52) The name of the

they packed all their gear, and openly left the siege, departing
with all his folk as if to do nothing more [in the business].
(365) And those who were inside the town, when they saw
him ready to go like that they bawled at him with derision;
and he rode forth on his way, as if he had no will to turn
back, nor to stay beside them.

(371) But in eight days, nonetheless, he had ladders made
secretly which would be sufficient for his purpose, and on a
dark night went toward the town with his company. (376)
But he left all horses and valets far from the town, and then
[they] took their ladders and went on foot secretly towards
the town. (380) They heard no watches speaking or shouting,
for those within, maybe, were all asleep like men with no fear.
They had no fear then of the king, for they had had no news
of him for three days and more before, so they were relaxed
and trusting. (387) And when the king heard them not stirring,
he was extremely pleased, and took his ladder in his hand, to
show an example to his men. Well armed in all his gear,

---

keeper is correct, and Atholl had indeed joined Bruce in 1312. Since
he was to desert again in 1314 and become a non-person in Scotland,
Bruce historiography would minimise or ignore any role he had in the
taking of Perth. But other sources are unanimous that the commander
at the assault was King Robert.

374–454. The taking of the town. Fordun's account is brief:

> On 8 January, 1313 the town of Perth was taken with a strong hand
> by ... King Robert; and the disloyal people, both Scots and English,
> were taken, dragged and slain with the sword, and so, being lost, they
> drank of the gall they had prepared before. He spared the people by
> royal clemency and granted mercy to [any]one who asked it; he
> destroyed walls and ditches and burned the rest with fire. (*F1*, 346;
> *F2*, 338)

There is a long account in the Verse Chronicle, which Fordun used,
but which introduces a different element: that the king first asked for
tribute or blackmail. It describes the town as defended by ditches on
three sides and by fortified gates:

> the bitter and proud men of the city refused the royal gifts which he
> asked for without legal right ... [Then] / the king asked his men to
> cut timber, prepare and transport it; and he encouraged the bearer-
> s; / 'Let us choose the time of darkness and concealment / to seek and
> approach the defences of the town' / ... His folk took ladders and
> planks (*alas*) and lo! suddenly they crossed the deep waters and muddy
> ditches of the town. / The king and his followers soon brought the
> heavy timbers, lifted them and crossed to defeat the citizens. / A ladder
> collapsed, the company rushed [back] at the omen. / The king, with
> renewed strength, struggled to carry / at least ladders; / his men sought
> the defences with planks. / After this Robert had broken the black
> gratings [?portcullis] / and the way was opened for the troop by the

And tursyt thar harnes halyly
And left the sege all opynly
And furth with all his folk gan fayr
As he wald do tharto no mayr.

365 And thai tha war within the toun   364
Quhen thai to fayr sa saw him boun
Thai schoutit him and skornyn mad,
And he furth on his wayis rad
As he ne had will agayne to turn

370 Na besyd thaim mak sojourn.   369

[The assault on Perth]

Bot in aucht dayis nocht-forthi
He gert mak leddrys prevely
That mycht suffice till his enent,
And in a myrk nycht syne is went

375 Toward the toun with his menye   374*
Bath hors and knafis all left he   375*
Fer fra the toun, and syne has tane   376*
Thair ledderis and on fut ar gane   377*
Towart the toun all prevely.   374

380 Thai hard na wachys spek na cry   375
For thai war within may-fall
As men that dred nocht slepand all.
Thai haid na dreid then off the king
For thai off him herd na thing

385 All thai thre dayis befor or mar,   380
Thairfor sekyr and traist thai war.
And quhen the king thaim hard nocht ster
He was blyth on gret maner,
And his ledder in hand gan ta

390 Ensample till his men to ma,   385
Arayit weill in all his ger

---

bold prince. / The columns also crossed the streams by bridges. / Entering, raising standards, they thundered on. / They took those holding and guarding the defences. / Defeated thus, destroyed thus, there perished then / those who used to dominate and despoil the town wickedly. / Now defeated and despoiled are those in the town / who refused terms when offered, / so they deserved and received their losses. / The king asks money, the town refuses; he offers favour, it despises [that]; / he profits in silence, it lies annihilated. / After cockcrow William Elephant / lost honour, city, wealth, by night. / On 8 January the proud and wicked citizens / 1312 [i.e. 1313] / had lost a position dear to an ingrate. (*Bower6*, 348)

[he] plunged into the ditch, and with his spear tested as he waded over, but the water reached up to his throat. (395) At that time there was in his company a knight of France, a strong and bold [man]; and when he saw the king go into the water thus, and take his ladder with him without hesitation, he crossed himself at the wonder, (401) and said, 'Ah, Lord, what shall we say of our French lords, always stuffing their bellies with good food, willing only to eat, drink and dance, when such a knight, so noble as this one, by his chivalry has put himself in such danger, to win a wretched hamlet.' With that he ran to the ditch, and made it over after the king. (411) And when the king's company saw their lord cross over, in a crowd they crossed the ditch, and without more hindrance, set their ladders to the wall, and hastened to climb up fast. (416) But the good king, as I heard tell, was the second man who took the wall, and waited there till all his company had come over with all speed.

(420) Still then neither noise nor cry rose. But soon after those who first saw them made a noise, so that the cry arose through the town. (424) But he, who was ready to attack with his men, went to the town, and sent most of his company scattered through the town, while he stayed with a great company, so that he was always prepared for defence, if he were attacked. (431) But those whom he sent through the town, put into such confusion

Schot in the dik and with his sper
Taistyt till he it our-woud,
Bot till his throt the watyr stud.

395 That tyme wes in his cumpany   390
A knycht off France wycht and hardy,
And quhen he in the watyr sua
Saw the king pas and with him ta
His ledder unabasytly,

400 He saynyt him for the ferly   395
And said, 'A, lord, quhat sall we say
Off our lordis off Fraunce that thai
With gud morsellis fayrcis thar pawnce
And will bot ete and drink and dawnce

405 Quhen sic a knycht and sa worthy   400
As this throu his chevalry
Into sic perell has him set
To win a wrechyt hamillet.'
With that word to the dik he ran

410 And our efter the king he wan,   405
And quhen the kingis menye saw
Thar lord out-our intill a thraw
Thai passyt the dik and but mar let
Thar leddrys to the wall thai set

415 And to clymb up fast pressyt thai,   410
Bot the gud king as I herd say
Was the secund man tuk the wall
And bad thar till his mengye all
War cummyn up in full gret hy.

[*The king takes Perth; his treatment of the townsfolk*]

420 Yeit than rais nother noyis na cry,   415
Bot sone efter thai noyis maid
That off thaim fyrst persaving had
Swa that the cry rais throu the toun,
Bot he that with his men wes boun

425 Till assaill to the toun is went   420
And the maist off his menye sent
All scalyt throu the toun, bot he
Held with himselvyn a gret mengne
Sa that he moucht be ay purvayit

430 To defend giff he war assayit.   425
Bot thai that he send throu the toun
Put to sa gret confusioun

their foes, who were abed or scattered, fleeing here and there, that before sunrise, they had taken their enemies or defeated each one. (437) Both the wardens were taken therein, and Malise of Strathearn went to his father, Earl Malise, and then took him by force, with all his [men]; then, for his sake, the noble king gave him his [land] to rule. (443) The rest, who ran through the town, grabbed for themselves men armour and merchandise in great profusion, and other goods of various kinds, until they, who had been poor and needy before, became rich and mighty with that loot. (449) But few were slain, for the king had issued commands to them, under great penalty, that they should kill no-one who could be taken without a big fight. He knew that they were kin to the country, and had pity on them.

(455) The town was taken like that, and then he had cast down each and all the towers and the walls. He left not a tower, stone or wall standing around that town, but had them all entirely destroyed. The prisoners which he took there he sent to where they could be held, and took the whole land to his peace. (464) There was no-one who dared withstand him on the north side of the Firth of Forth; all obeyed his majesty, apart from the lord of Lorn and those of Argyll who would side with him. (469) He always stood against the king and hated him above everything else. But yet, before all the game is played, I know well that the king will take revenge for his great cruelty,

---

449. Few were slain. Compare the other accounts; this is one of the few occasions where the king's treatment of ordinary citizens is discussed in the sources. As a tailpiece to the Perth story, the Wardrobe book for 1322–23 shows that John Hastard, William Kinfauns, Geoffrey Scarburgh, William Errol, Stephen Andreston and John Milne were prisoners at Norwich until November–December 1322 when they were brought to Edward II, who freed them to Sir William Oliphant, a Scot, giving them 4s. each for their expenses on their way to Scotland. (Stowe MS 553, fos. 29v, 68r) These men must have been Scottish Perth burgesses (a Scarburgh was a burgess there in 1240), possibly caught in England and imprisoned at its fall in 1313, and now released by Oliphant's efforts.

Thar fayis that in beddis war
Or scalyt fleand her and thar
That or the sone rais thai had tane
Thar fayis or discumfyt ilkane.
The wardanys bath tharin war tane,
And Malice off Straithern is gane
Till his fadyr the Erle Malice
And with strenth tuk him and his,
Syne for his sak the noble king
Gave him his in governyng.
The lave that ran out-throu the toun
Sesyt to thaim into gret fusoun
Men and armyng and marchandis
And other gud on syndry wys,
Quhill thai that er war pour and bar
Off that gud rych and mychty war,
Bot thar wes few slayne for the king,
That thaim had gevyn in commanding
On gret payne that thai suld slay nane
That but gret bargane mycht be tane.
That thai war kynd to the countré
He wyst and off thaim had pité.

[The king controls Scotland north of the Forth]

On this maner the toun wes tane
And syne towris everilkane
And wallis gert he tumble down.
He levyt nocht about that town
Towr standand na stane na wall
That ne haly gert stroy thaim all,
And presonerys that thar tuk he
He send quhar thai mycht haldyn be,
And till his pes tuk all the land.
Wes nane that durst him than withstand
Apon northhalff the Scottis se,
All obeysyt till his majeste
Outane the lord of Lorn and thai
Off Arghile that wald with him ga.
He held him ay agayne the king
And hatyt him atour all thing,
Bot yete or all the gamyn ga
I trow weill that the king sall ta
Vengeance off his gret cruelté,

and that he will repent sorely that he continually opposed the king, perhaps when he cannot remedy it.

(477) When the town was taken thus, and knocked down, the king's brother, Sir Edward, who was so worthy, took a great company with him, and took the road to Galloway. (482) For with his men he meant to try whether he could recover that land, and win it from the hands of the English. This Sir Edward, forsooth, I dare say, was in his actions a noble knight, sweetly and cheerfully amiable, but he was extraordinarilly bold, and of such enterprise that he had never been defeated by a multitude of men; (491) because he usually defeated many with a few, therefore he was renowned above his peers. Whoever would recount all the acts of his great valour and courage would [enable] men to make a long romance. (498) Although I mean to undertake to say something about him, [it will] not [be] the tenth part of his struggles. (501) This good knight of whom I speak here, with all the folk with him, came soon to Galloway; he made his all that he found, and ravaged the land greatly.

---

479. Edward Bruce seeks to subdue Galloway. (a) Lanercost and (b) The Verse Chronicle (source for Fordun's account) have an account of such an expedition in 1308:

> (a) Meanwhile, taking advantage of the quarrels between the king of England and the barons, Edward Bruce ... Alexander Lindsay, Robert Boyd and James Douglas, knights, with their following which they had from the outer isles of Scotland, attacked the people of Galloway, disregarding the tribute which they took from them, and in one day slew many of the gentry of Galloway, and made nearly all that region subject to them. Those Galwegians who could escape came to England to find refuge.
>
> (b) In 1308/on the feast of Peter and Paul [29 June]/Edward Bruce and Donald from Islay/defeated the mighty Galwegian people./For an army of English gathered at the River Dee./They joined battle, the force of the lances struck down the cavalry./The crowd of infantry fled and their leader too./The noble knight Roland fell shamefully by the sword/and many others known by name./A little later .../an island always hostile to the Scots was burned/and handed over to Edward, when Donald Mac Can was taken. (*Bower*6, 344)

Edward II agreed in May 1308 to the exile of Piers Gaveston, the source of friction between him and the baronage, and Gaveston left England on 25 June, after which Edward achieved a short-lived reconciliation with his opponents. The invasion of Galloway is thus placed before the end of June by Lanercost, agreeing with the Verse Chronicle.

The Verse Chronicle might be saying that after Edward Bruce defeated the Galwegians he defeated an English force on the Dee, but it is more probable that one battle is described, the English forming the

And that him sar repent sall he
475 That he the king contraryit ay, 470
May-fall quhen he it mend na may.

[*Edward Bruce's reputation; he goes to Galloway*]

The kingis broder, quhen the toun
Wes takyn thus and dongyn doun,
Schyr Edward that wes sa worthy
480 Tuk with him a gret cumpany 475
And tuk his gayt till Galloway,
For with his men he wald assay
Giff he mycht recover that land
And wyn it fra Inglismennys hand.
485 This Schyr Edward forsuth Ik hycht 480
Wes off his hand a noble knycht
And in blythnes suete and joly,
Bot he wes outrageous hardy
And of sa hey undretaking
490 That he haid never yeit abaysyng 485
Off multitud off men, forthi
He discumfyt commounly
Mony with quhone, tharfor had he
Out-over his peris renomme.
495 And quha wald rehers all the deid 490
Off his hey worschip and manheid
Men mycht a mekill romanys mak,
And nocht-forthi I think to tak
On hand off him to say sum thing
500 Bot nocht tende part his travalyn. 495
This gud knycht that I spek off her
With all the folk that with him wer
Weill sone to Galloway cummyn is,
All that he fand he makyt his
505 And ryotyt gretly the land. 500

---

cavalry, the Galwegians the infantry. The problem about this battle is
the absence of any reaction in English records in July 1308, probably
because the effects of the defeat at Inverurie and of the herschip of
Buchan were more serious. The best suggestion about the anonymous
island is that it was Mac Can's chief place, Thrieve Island, NX7462.
*Bower*6, 444–45 has important notes on these sources.
495–97. A long romance. Gray comments that Edward Bruce's exploits
in Ireland 'would form a splendid romance, if it were all recounted'.
One might comment that by implication Barbour and Gray were familiar
with other romances recounting the chivalry of the Anglo-Scottish wars.

But at that time there dwelt in Galloway Sir Ingram Umfra-
ville, who was famed for such great prowess, that he passed
the rest in reputation; (510) for that reason he always had
carried about a red bonnet upon a spear, as a sign that he
was set at the apex of chivalry. Sir Aymer de St John also
[dwelt there].

(515) These two had the land to govern, and when they heard
of the arrival of Sir Edward, who rode over the land so openly,
then in great haste they assembled all their following; I'm sure
they would be twelve hundred [in number]. (521) But he met
them with fewer folk beside the Cree, and pressed them so
hard, with stiff fighting in a hard battle, that he put them all
to flight, and slew a good two hundred or more. (526) And
the chieftains in haste took their way to Buittle, to be taken
into safety. And Sir Edward chased them fast, but Sir Ingram
and Sir Aymer got to the castle finally, leaving behind them
the best of their company, dead on the [battle-] field. (534)
And when Sir Edward saw the pursuit had failed, he had the
booty seized, and took away so many cattle that it was re-
markable to see.

---

507. Sir Ingram Umfraville. See note to 2.212. He was appointed keeper
of Carrick on 11 August, 1308, having been in the south-west since
1306; the keeper of Galloway was to be the earl of Buchan, but he may
have been mortally ill; on 20 August Umfraville, John de St John and
Richard Siward were put in charge of Galloway. (*CDS3*, 47; *RotSc1*,
56–57) The bonnet on a spear (511–13) shows an Umfraville source
which has given Barbour this Galloway campaign, and would explain
why he ignores the Dee battle.

514. John de St John had a brother Aymer, but his name is unlikely to
have persisted in any Scottish account of this campaign; again an
Umfraville source is indicated.

522. Cree. There has been much debate over the 'conflict' between this
and the Dee of the Verse Chronicle and Fordun. They were, I believe,
quite different, and Barbour's explanation that Umfraville responded
rapidly to Edward Bruce's invasion (516–19) is an exaggeration. The
English lost control over western Galloway after the Dee battle; Um-
fraville and St John set out to restore it, and, by the Cree, far from
base, were heavily defeated, fleeing to Buittle, whence the latter went
to England and, returning, presumably to relieve Umfraville at Buittle,
was attacked by Edward Bruce (582–633). This second battle would
be to the east of Buittle, and that suits neither Dee nor Cree; my former
suggestion that Barbour has transferred 'Cree' from this to the earlier
battle does not hold water (*Bower6*, 445). It now seems likely to me
that, as Barbour was using an Umfraville source, he found the name
there, and, since it was less usual than 'Dee', it is likely to be correct.
The distance from Buittle, some 25 direct miles, 40 kilometres, is

Bot than in Galloway war wonnand
Schyr Ingrahame the Umfravill that wes
Renommyt off sa hey prowes
That he off worschippassyt the rowt,
510   Tharfor he gert ay ber about   505
Apon a sper a rede bonet
Into takyn that he wes set
Into the hycht off chevalry,
And off Saynct Jhone als Schyr Aymry.

[The battle by the Cree]

515   Thir twa the land had in stering,   510
And quhen thai hard off the cummyng
Off Schyr Edward that sa playnly
Oure-raid the land, thare in gret hy
Thai assemblyt all thar mengne,
520   I trow tuelf hunder thai mycht be.   515
Bot he with fewar folk thaim met
Besyd Cre and sa hard thaim set
With hard battaill and stalwart fycht
That he thaim all put to the flycht
525   And slew twa hunder well and ma,   520
And the chyftanys in hy gan ta
Thar way to Buttill for to be
Thar resavyt to sawfté,
And Schyr Edward thaim chasit fast,
530   Bot till the castell at the last   525
Gat Schyr Ingrahame and Schyr Amery,
Bot the best off thar cumpany
Left ded behind thaim in the place.
And quhen Schyr Edward saw the chace
535   Wes falyt he gert seys the pray   530
And sua gret cattell had away
That it war wonder for to se.

---

considerable, but inescapable if there was already no safe refuge in
western Galloway. These two battles took place before about 7 September, since, I suggest, they explain why on 21 September, 1308 the
English government was in a panic about a Bruce threat to the Marches;
this can only have come from a Bruce success in Galloway. (*RotSc1*, 57)
527. Buittle. On the river Urr near Dalbeattie, NX8161. This had been
the chief place of the Balliol lordship of Galloway; the stone walls have
almost all gone to build the later tower house, but the outline and that
of the large bailey are still clear.

From Buittle they saw how he had his men drive their prey with him, but they couldn't prevent him [doing] it. (541) Through his active chivalry Galloway was greatly disturbed, and feared him for his valour. Some of the men of the country came to his peace and swore an oath to him. (546) But Sir Aymer, who had the worse of the fight that I spoke about before, rode to England, and obtained there a great company of armed men, to avenge for himself the ill-turn that the noble knight, Sir Edward, did him in the fight by the Cree. (553) He gathered there a good fifteen hundred or more good men., who were of good reputation. He took the road with all those folk, and very secretly entered the land with that chivalry, expecting to surprise Sir Edward if he could at all, for he hoped that, if at all possible, he would attack him, before [Edward] left, in open battle.

(563) Now you will hear something remarkable, of truly high chivalry. For Sir Edward [who] was in the country very near at hand with his company, very early in the morning heard the countrymen shouting, and had knowledge of their coming. (570) Then he got ready without delay, and mounted his horse speedily. He had fifty men in his squad then, armed well [and] upon good horses. He had his small folk, each group, withdraw to a nearby glen and he rode forth with his fifty. (577) A knight who was in his squad,

---

556. His way. See note to 522.

Out of Buttill thai saw how he
Gert his men dryve with him thar pray
540   Bot na let tharin mycht thai.   535
Throu his chevalrous chevalry
Galloway wes stonayit gretumly
And he dowtyt for his bounté.
Sum off the men off the countré
545   Cum till his pes and maid him aith.   540
Bot Schyr Amery that had the skaith
Off the bargane I tauld off er,
Raid till Ingland till purches ther
Off armyt men gret cumpany
550   To veng him off the velany   545
That Schyr Edward that noble knycht
Him did by Cre into the fycht.
Off gud men he assemblit thar
Weill fyften hunder men and mar
555   That war rycht of gud renowne.   550
His way with all that folk tuk he,
And in the land all prevely
Entryt with tha chevalry
Thynkand Schyr Edward to suppris
560   Giff that he moucht on ony wis   555
For he thocht he wald him assaile
Or that he left in playn bataill.

*[In a second encounter Edward Bruce defeats a much larger
force]*

Now may ye her off gret ferly
And off rycht hey chevalry,
565   For Schyr Edward into the land   560
Wes with his mengne rycht ner-hand,
And in the mornyng rycht arly
Herd the countre men mak cry
And had wyttryng off thar cummyng.
570   Than buskyt he him but delaying   565
And lapp on hors deliverly,
He had than in route fyfty
All apon gud hors armyt weill,
His small folk gert he ilk-deill
575   Withdraw thaim till a strait thar-by,   570
And he raid furth with his fyfty.
A knycht that then was in his rowt

bold, brave, stalwart, stout, courteous, gentle and of good
repute, Sir Alan Cathcart by name, told me this tale which I
shall tell. A great mist fell that morning, so that they could
not see near them for mist for more than an arrow's flight. It
so happened that they found traces where the army of their
enemies, riding forth, had passed. (588) Sir Edward, who had
a great desire to do [deeds of] chivalry always, with all his
squad at great speed followed the traces of where they had
gone, and, before mid-morning of the day, the mist lifted
clear quite suddenly; then he and all his company were scarcely
an arrow's flight from the army. (596) Then they rushed on
them with a shout, becuse they knew that if they fled, scarcely
a fourth part of them would get away, so he put himself at
risk of death rather than flee. And when the English company
saw these folk coming so suddenly upon them without hesi-
tating, they were dismayed from fear. (605) And the others,
without hesitating, rode among them so fiercely, that they
bore many of them [down] to the ground. They were so
greatly confounded then by the force of that first assault, that
they were in great fear, and supposed that [the Scots] had
been far more [in number] because they were attacked thus.
(613) When they had broken right through them, Sir Edward's
company turned their horses' heads [and charged] again, and
in that charge [there] were borne down and slain a great part
of their enemies, who then were very frightened because they
were badly scattered. (620) And when Sir Edward and his
men

---

580. Sir Alan Cathcart. A Sir William Cathcart was in English service as
late as 1309; he is thought to be the father of Sir Alan, laird of Cathcart
by Glasgow, who made a gift to the Blackfriars of Glasgow in 1336.
Curiously a branch of this family, of Killochan, until recently owned a
charter of Robert I confirming one by Edward [Bruce] king of Ireland
to John de Carlton. (*RRS5, 235; SP2*, 504–6)

581. Told me this tale. Despite several persons supposed to be tellers of
tales to Barbour, this is the only occasion on which he plainly names
someone as informant. 'This tale' was the pursuit in the mist and the
three-fold attack (582–637).

Worthi and wycht stalwart and stout
Curtais and fayr and off gud fame
Schyr Alane off Catkert be name 575
Tauld me this taile as I sall tell.
Gret myst into the mornyng fell
Sa thai mycht nocht se thaim by
For myst a bow-draucht fullely.
Sa hapnyt that thai fand the trais 580
Quhar at the rowt furth passyt wais
Off thair fayis that forouth raid.
Schyr Edward that gret yarnyn had
All tymys to do chevalry
With all his rout in full gret hy 585
Folowyt the trais quhar gane war thai,
And befor mydmorne off the day
The myst wox cler all sodanly
And than he and his cumpany
War nocht a bowdraucht fra the rout. 590
Than schot thai on thaim with a schout,
For gyff thai fled thai wyst that thai
Suld nocht weill feyrd part get away,
Tharfor in aventur to dey
He wald him put or he wald fle. 595
And quhen the Inglis cumpany
Saw on thaim cum sa sodanly
Sik folk foroutyn abaysyng
Thai war stonayt for effrayng,
And the tother but mar abaid 600
Swa hardely amang thaim raid
That fele off thaim till erd thai bar.
Stonayit sa gretly than thai war
Throu the force off that fyrst assay
That thai war intill gret effray, 605
And wend be fer thai had bene ma
For that thai war assailit sua.
Quhen thai had thyrlyt thaim hastily
Than Schyr Edwardis cumpany
Set stoutly in the heid agayne, 610
And at that cours borne doune and slayn
War off thar fayis a gret party
That thai effrayit war sa gretly
That thai war scalyt gretly then.
And quhen Schyr Edward and his men 615

saw them in such poor order, they galloped on them for a third time. And they, seeing [the Scots] come on them so boldly, were terrified so that all their army, men and officers, fled [at a] gallop, scattered here and there. (627) None among them was brave enough to stay, but one and all they fled to safety, and [Edward] gave chase, determined to destroy them, for some he took [prisoner] and some were slain; but Sir Aymer escaped with great difficulty, and went his way. All his men were defeated, some taken, some slain, some got away. That was truly a glorious deed!

(637) Look how boldness, shown without hesitation and driven ruthlessly to a conclusion, can often cause an unlikely situation to come to a right fair and good conclusion, just as befell in this case here. (642) For doubtless boldness defeated fifteen hundred by fifty, Though there were thirty to one, and two men are one man's master; but fate led them in such a way that they were one and all defeated. (648) Sir Aymer went his way home again, pleased that he got away like that. I'm sure that for many a day he'll have no will to make war on that country, provided that Sir Edward is there! And [the latter] remained after in [that] land, making war on those who were rebels, and in a year he made war such that he wholly won that country to the peace of his brother, the king. (658) But that was not without hard fighting, for in that period there happened to him many a fine scrap, as I heard tell, which are not written [about] here.

653–76. Edward Bruce in Galloway. By March 1309 he had received the style of lord of Galloway, and it is likely that the English hold had been largely destroyed; in December 1309 they still held castles in Nithsdale, but to the west only Buittle and Ayr; I can find no trace of a keeper of Galloway, and Ingram Umfraville was constable of Caerlaverock castle. By October 1310 there was a keeper of 'the parts of Dumfries', while the Isle of Man was threatened by Bruce, suggesting that he now held Ayr, the key to Galloway from the north. The thirteen castles (663), if correct, must have included a number of mottes.

Saw thaim intill sa evill aray
The thrid tyme on thaim prekyt thai,
And thai that saw thaim sa stouly
Come on dred thaim sa gretumly
625 That all thar rowt bath les and mar 620
Fled prekand scalyt her and thar.
Wes nane amang thaim sa hardy
To bid, bot all comonaly
Fled to warand, and he gan chas
630 That wilfull to distroy thaim was 625
And sum he tuk and sum war slayn,
Bot Schyr Amery with mekill payn
Eschapyt and his gat in gayn.
His men discumfyt war ilkane,
635 Sum tane, sum slayne, sum gat away, 630
It wes a rycht fayr poynt perfay.

[*A comment on Edward Bruce in Galloway*]

Lo! how hardyment tane sa sudandly
And drevyn to the end scharply
May ger oftsys unlikly thingis
640 Cum to rycht fayr and gud endingis 635
As it fell into this cas her.
For hardyment withoutyn wer
Wan fyften hunder with fyfty
Quhar ay for ane thar wes thretty,
645 And twa men ar a mannys her, 640
Bot ure thaim led on swilk maner
That thai discumfyt war ilkane.
Schyr Amery hame his gat is gane
Rycht blyth that he swa gat away,
650 I trow he sall nocht mony day 645
Haiff will to werray that countré,
With-thi Schyr Edward tharin be.
And he dwelt furth into the land
Thaim that rebell war werrayand,
655 And in a yer sa werrayit he 650
That he wane quyt that countré
Till his broderys pes the king.
Bot that wes nocht but hard fechting,
For in that tyme thar him befell
660 Mony fayr poynt as Ik herd tell 655
The quhilk that ar nocht writyn her,

But I know well that in that year he won thirteen castles by force, and overcame many a proud man. (664) Whoever wants to tell the truth about him, he had moderation in his deeds; I believe that a worthier [man] than he could not be found in his time, apart only from his brother, to whom, in chivalry, none was equal in his day. (672) Because [the king] always behaved with moderation, and, with great wisdom, governed his chivalry so worthily that he often brought an unpromising situation right well to a good conclusion.

(677) All this time James Douglas was fighting in the Forest [of Ettrick] and, by boldness and cunning, occupied it in spite of the power of his enemies, even though they often tried him sorely. But through wisdom and spirit he brought his purpose to a good conclusion. (685) At that time it happened by chance that one night as he was travelling, he thought he would take his rest in a house on the Water of Lyne. And as he came with his company near to the house he listened and heard all their conversation, and easily understood from that, that those who had lodged there that night were strangers. (695) And it was [just] as he thought, by chance, for the lord of Bunkle was there, named Alexander Stewart, with two others of great spirit, Thomas Randolph of great reputation, and also Adam Gordon, (701) who had come there with a great company,

---

688. A house by the Water of Lyne. House may have the meaning of fortified place here, but that would be unusual. The Lyne is a tributary of the Tweed, to the west and north of Peebles.

690-91 He listened and heard their conversation. But a few lines later (707) the story changes – after he heard of the strange men in the house he hurried there, which is much more probable. Barbour's source was perhaps ambiguous.

696-700. This episode is earlier than March 1309, and not in August 1308 when Douglas was in Argyll. It probably belongs to the early summer of 1308. Alexander Stewart of Bonkle was son of Sir John Stewart killed at Falkirk, 1298; John's sister married Sir William Douglas, and James was their son. Alexander must have been ransomed after his capture here, and again served Edward II; he deserted the English a month before Bannockburn. His son became earl of Angus about 1327. Thomas Randolph was son of a Roxburghshire laird of the same name who married a daughter of Marjory, countess of Carrick by her first husband, Adam de Kilconquhar; this daughter was King Robert's half sister. Thomas had served the English since his release after Methven into the custody of Sir Adam Gordon. The latter took his name from a Berwickshire village, and was a knight of the earl of Dunbar, deserting to Bruce with his lord after Bannockburn. He was the knight who took the declaration of Arbroath to Avignon.

Bot I wate weile that in that yer
Thretten castellis with strenth he wan
And ourcome mony a mody man.
Quha-sa off him the south will reid, 660
665 Had he had mesure in his deid
I trow that worthyar then he
Mycht nocht in his tym fundyn be
Outakyn his broder anerly,
670 To quham into chevalry 665
Lyk wes nane in his day,
For he led him with mesur ay,
And with wyt his chevalry
He governyt sa worthily
675 That he oft full unlikly thing 670
Broucht rycht weill to gud ending.

[Douglas in the Forest surrounds and takes enemy Scots in a house]

In all this tyme James of Douglas
In the Forest travaland was,
And it throu hardiment and slycht
680 Occupyit all magre the mycht 675
Off his fell fayis, the-quhether thai
Set him full oft in full hard assay,
Bot oft throu wyt and throu bounté
His purpos to gud end brocht he.
685 Intill that tyme him fell throu cas 680
On ane nycht as he travaland was
And thocht till haiff tane resting
In ane hous on the watyr off Lyne
And as he come with his mengne
690 Ner-hand the hous sua lysnyt he 685
And herd thair sawis ilke deill,
And be that he persavyt weill
That thai war strang men that thar
That nycht tharin herbryd war.
695 And as he thocht it fell per cas, 690
For off Bonkle the lord thar was
Alexander Stewart hat he
With other twa off gret bounté,
Thomas Randell off gret renowne
700 And Adam alsua off Gordoune, 695
That thar come with gret cumpany

expecting to lie in the Forest, occupying it through their great power, with both effort and stalwart fighting, and to chase Douglas out of that country. But the game went in a different direction. (707) For when James got wind that strangers had taken up lodgings in the place where he had intended to lie, he went hastily to the house and surrounded it. When those within heard such a force around the house, they got up in a hurry and took their gear quickly, rushing forth when they were kitted up. (716) Their enemies met them with drawn weapons and attacked right boldly, and they defended [themselves] doughtily with all their might, till eventually their foes pressed them so hard that their men all gave way. (722) Thomas Randolph was taken there, and Alexander Stewart was also wounded in one or two places. Adam Gordon escaped from the fight, either by cunning or by might, and many of their men; but those who were seized then were very cast down at being taken, as indeed it behoved them to be.

(731) That night the good lord of Douglas was very affable with Sir Alexander, who was his uncle's son; and he did the same, doubtless, to Sir Thomas Randolph, because he was closely related to the king by blood, for [the king's] sister bore him. (738) And in the morning, without more [ado] he rode towards the noble king, and he had both those two with him. The king was cheered by his present, and thanked him for it many times.

732-3. His uncle. See note to 696.
737. His sister. See note to 696.

And thocht into the Forest to ly
And occupy it throu thar mycht,
And with travaill and stalwart fycht
705 Chace Douglas out of that countre.   700
Bot otherwayis then yeid the gle
For quhen James had wittering
That strang men had taken herbryng
In the place that he schup him to ly
710 He to the hous went hastily   705
And umbeset it all about.
Quhen thai within hard swilk a rout
About the hous thai rais in hy
And tuk thar ger rycht hastily
715 And schot furth fra thai harnasyt war.   710
Thar fayis thaim met with wapnys bar
And assaylit rycht hardely
And thai defendyt douchtely
With all thar mycht, till at the last
720 Thar fayis pressyt thaim sa fast   715
That thar folk failyt thaim ilkane.
Thomas Randell thar wes tane
And Alexander Stewart alsua
Woundyt in a place or twa.
725 Adam of Gordoun fra the fycht   720
Quhat throu his strenth and his mycht
Eschapyt and ser off thar men,
Bot thai that war arestyt then
War off thar taking wondre wa,
730 Bot neidlingis behovit it be sua.   725

[*Thomas Randolph upbraids the king*]

That nycht the gud lord off Douglas
Maid to Schyr Alysander that was
His emys sone rycht glaidsome cher,
Sua did he als withoutyn wer
735 Till Thomas Randell for that he   730
Wes to the king in ner degre
Off blud, for his sistre him bar,
And on the morne foroutyn mar
Towart the noble king he raid
740 And with him bath thai twa he haid.   735
The king off his present wes blyth
And thankyt him weill fele syth,

And he said to his nephew, 'For a while you have refused your allegiance, but you must be reconciled [to me] now.' (746) Then he roundly answered the king, and said, 'You rebuke me, but rather you should be rebuked. For since you made war on the king of England, you should strive to prove your right in open fighting, and not by cowardice nor cunning.' (753) The king said, 'Well, perhaps it may come to that before too long. But since you speak so forcefully, it is quite right that men should rebuke those proud words, until you know the right and submit to it, as you should.' (759) The king, without further delay, sent him to be in secure custody, where he would be alone, and not free in his own jurisdiction.

761–62. Such a prisoner would normally be made the responsibility of a loyal noble; Randolph was not allowed to go to his own estates on parole. By March 1309 Thomas had been released and was at King Robert's parliament as lord of Nithsdale.

And till his nevo gan he say,
'Thou has ane quhill renyid thi fay,
745 Bot thou reconsalit now mon be.' 740
Then till the king answerit he
And said, 'Ye chasty me, bot ye
Aucht bettre chastyt for to be,
For sene ye werrayit the king
750 Off Ingland, in playne fechtyng 745
Ye suld pres to derenyhe rycht
And nocht with cowardy na with slycht.'
The king said, 'Yeit may-fall it may
Cum or oucht lang to sic assay.
755 Bot sen thou spekys sa rudly 750
It is gret skyll men chasty
Thai proud wordis till that thou knaw
The rycht and bow it as thou aw.'
The king foroutyn mar delaying
760 Send him to be in ferme keping 755
Quhar that he allane suld be,
Nocht all apon his powste fre.

When Thomas Randolph had been taken in the way I have described, and sent to live in safe custody because of the speech that he uttered to the king, the good king, thinking about the harm, injury and mischief that John of Lorn had done to him, mustered his host soon and took the way towards Lorn, with his men well-equipped. (11) But John of Lorn had knowledge of their coming long before he arrived, and gathered men on all sides – there must have been two thousand of them – and sent them to block the route where the king had to go. (17) That was in a dreadful place, that was so narrow and confined that two men could not ride abreast at some parts of the hillside. The lower side was dangerous, for a sheer crag, high and fearsome, reached down to the sea from the pass. (24) On the other side was a mountain,

---

9. Towards Lorn. The date of this expedition, the week 15–22 August 1308, is given by the Verse Chronicle:

[In] 1308 / in the week when the feasts of the Assumption of Our Lady are made / King Robert defeated the folk of Argyll. / This folk, reared in proud words and deeds / willy-nilly obeyed the king's commands. (*Bower6*, 344)

This is three months after the battle of 'Inverurie', which was followed by the ravaging of Buchan in June. Edward Bruce must have departed by mid-June for Galloway. Aberdeen was under siege by about 1 July and about 1 August it fell. This is a tight schedule for an attack on Argyll in mid-August, but it is not impossible. The English reaction on 11 August was to urge local truces with Bruce, which may have suited him; talks for a local truce in the east would leave him free to attack Argyll in the west (dates calculated from reactions at the English court some 10 days later). (*CDS5, 519; Cal. Cl. R.*, 1307–13, 40, 69–70, 75–76; *Cal. Pat. R.*, 1307–13, 81–82)

11. John of Argyll wrote a letter to Edward II:

I have received your letter sent on 11 March last ... When it arrived I was confined to my bed with illness and have been for six months past. Robert Bruce approached these parts by land and sea with 10,000 or 15,000 men, they say. I have no more than 800 men, 500 in my own pay, whom I keep continually to guard the borders of my territory. The barons of Argyll give me no aid. Yet Bruce asked for a truce which I granted him for a short space, and I have got a similar truce until you send me help. I have heard ... that when Bruce came he was boasting and claiming that I had come to his peace, in order to increase his own reputation, so that others would rise more readily in his support. May God forbid this; I certainly do not wish it, and if you hear this from others you are not to believe it, for I shall always be ready to carry out your orders ... I have three castles to keep as

BOOK 10

[Preparations for battle against John of Lorn]

Quhen Thomas Randell on this wis
Wes takyn as Ik her devys
And send to dwell in gud keping
For spek that he spak to the king,
5   The gud king that thocht on the scaith
The dispyt and felny bath
That Jhone off Lorne had till him doyn
His ost assemblyt he then sone
And towart Lorn he tuk the way
10   With his men intill gud aray.
Bot Jhone off Lorn off his cummyng
Lang or he come had wittering,
And men on ilk sid gadryt he
I trow twa thousand thai mycht be
15   And send thaim for to stop the way
Quhar the gud king behovyt away,
And that wes in an evill plas
That sa strayt and sa narow was
That twasum samyn mycht nocht rid
20   In sum place off the hillis sid.
The nethyr halff was peralous
For schor crag hey and hydwous
Raucht to the se doun fra the pas,
On athyr halff the montane was

---

well as a loch 24 miles long, on which I keep and build galleys, with trusty men in each galley. I am not sure of my neighbours in any direction ...

The date of this letter is debated but the placing of *directas* in *litteras vestras vltimo directas xi die mensis Marcii percepimus*, means that the king's letter was dated 11 March. John's was written some six months after that, and could refer either to Bruce going north in September 1307, or to his attack in 1308. As the picture of Bruce with a large force in 1307 is very improbable, I believe that it belongs to September–October 1308, and is a heavily edited version of Bruce's attack in August 1308. The lake is Loch Etive. Barbour ignored the truce, as was his usual practice.

22–23. A sheer crag reached down to the sea from the pass. E has pas, C place, also at 35, 54. Tradition has designated this site as the Pass of Brander whose slopes are too steep to allow three parallel lines of soldiery to stand upright, let alone engage in uphill-downhill struggle. The reasons seem to be (1) the use of 'pass', but this can mean any

so rocky, high and steep that it was hard to get by that way. That mountain was called Ben Cruachan, and I believe that in all Britain a higher hill can't be found. (30) John of Lorn had his following make an ambush there above the way, for, if the king took that way, [John] thought that he would soon be defeated. He took up his position with his galleys on the sea near the pass. But the king, who was found prudent and well-advised in all his enterprises, saw through their trickery, and that he would have to go that way. (40) He divided his men in two and committed to the good lord of Douglas, in whom lodged all virtues, all the archers. This good lord took with him the vigorous Sir Alexander Fraser and a good knight William Wiseman, and with them too Sir Andrew Gray. (48) These held their way with their company, and fleetly climbed the hill, [so that] before those of the other side spied them, they had all taken the height above their foes.

(53) The king and his men held their way and when they had entered the pass, the men of Lorn quickly raised a cry and rushed to tumble on him stones, very large and heavy for the occasion. (59) But they scarcely harmed the king, because he had there in his following men who were fleet and swift, and had light armour on there, so that they vigorously climbed the hill and prevented their enemies carrying out most of their ill-intentions.

---

constricted route, here by crag and sea; and (2) the use of 'on athyr halff' (24), the other side. But this refers to 'the way' (15) on whose lower half was a steep crag (22); on the other side ('halff') of the way was the slope above it. Loch Awe was also was 24 miles long and had three castles, hence has been cast as the place where John kept his galleys in the letter, and in Barbour as the 'sea' whence he had sight of the battle (97–98). But the letter does not say that the three castles were in the lake – indeed it rather implies that they (or all of them) were not. The sea meant salt water, Loch Etive; the lake in the letter was also probably Loch Etive. The battle of Ben Cruachan took place on the northern slope of that hill, below Barran Dubh, watched from Loch Etive.

31. The way. It is not known how the king reached Argyll, but he could have come down the Great Glen to Glencoe and Glen Etive. Unfortunately Barbour gives no hint of where Douglas, who had been in the south, joined him.

45–47. William Wiseman had been Edward I's sheriff of Elgin in 1305, but was active for Bruce in 1308 (note to 9.189), and was at the March 1309 parliament. He is not found later, but if he lived would become a tenant of the earl of Moray. For Sir Andrew Gray, *SP4*, 269–70 and note to 649.

25   Sua combrous hey and stay
        That it was hard to pas that way.
        Crechinben hecht that montane
        I trow nocht that in all Bretane
        Ane heyar hill may fundyn be.
30   Thar Jhone off Lorne gert his menye
        Enbuschyt be abovyn the way,
        For giff the king held thar away
        He thocht he suld sone vencussyt be,
        And himselff held him apon the se
35   Weill ner the pais with his galayis.
        Bot the king that in all assayis
        Wes fundyn wys and avisé
        Persavyt rycht weill thar sutelté,
        And that he neid that gait suld ga.
40   His men departyt he in twa
        And till the gud lord off Douglas
        Quham in herbryd all worschip was
        He taucht the archerys everilkane
        And this gud lord with him has tane
45   Schyr Alysander Fraser the wycht,
        And Wylyam Wysman a gud knycht
        And with thaim syne Schyr Androw Gray.
        Thir with thar mengne held thar way
        And clamb the hill deliverly
50   And or thai off the tother party
        Persavyt thaim thai had ilkane
        The hycht abovyne thar fayis tane.

[*The battle beneath Ben Cruachan*]

        The king and his men held thar way,
        And quhen intill the pas war thai
55   Entryt the folk of Lorne in hy
        Apon the king raysyt the cry
        And schot and tumblit on him stanys
        Rycht gret and hevy for the nanys,
        Bot thai scaith nocht gretly the king
60   For he had thar in his leding
        Men that lycht and deliver war
        And lycht armouris had on thaim thar
        Sua that thai stoutly clamb the hill
        And lettyt thar fayis to fulfill
65   The maist part of thar felny.

(66) And also on the other side James Douglas and his force came and rushed on them with a yell, wounding them with swift arrows. Then with swords finally they rushed among them boldly because the men of Lorn put up stubborn and bold defence like men. (74) But when they saw that they were attacked like this on both sides, and saw well that their enemies had the better of the fight, they took to flight with great speed. (79) But [the king's men] gave chase fiercely, and killed all they could overtake, [while] those who could escape held their way, without pausing, to a stream that ran down by the hillside. (84) It was swift-flowing, deep and wide, so that men couldn't cross it at any point except at a bridge beneath them. To that bridge they went directly, and tried quickly to break it [down]. (89) But those who gave chase, when they saw them stop there, without fear or dread they rushed boldly upon them and defeated them completely, holding the bridge until the king with all the men in his following passed the bridge comfortably. (96) It must have been displeasing to John of Lorn when, from his ships on the sea, he could see his men being killed and chased on the hill, [yet] be unable to help them. (101) For it is a greatly angers a stout and worthy heart to see the enemy carry out his will and to have to suffer the ill [consequences].

The men of Lorn were in just that trouble,

82–86. The stream, the bridge. The River Awe does not flow down the side of Ben Cruachan, but 'beside the hill' may be meant. The bridge is surely one over the same river.

And als apon the tother party
Come James of Douglas and his rout
And schot apon thaim with a schout
And woundyt thaim with arowis fast,
70   And with thar swerdis at the last
Thai ruschyt amang thaim hardely,
For thai of Lorn full manlely
Gret and apert defens gan ma.
Bot quhen thai saw that thai war sua
75   Assaylit apon twa partys
And saw weill that thar ennemys
Had all the fayrer off the fycht
In full gret hy thai tuk the flycht,
And thai a felloun chas gan ma
80   And slew all that thai mycht ourta,
And thai that mycht eschap but delay
Rycht till ane water held thar way
That ran doun be the hillis syd.
It was sa styth and depe and wid
85   That men in na place mycht it pas
Bot at ane bryg that beneuth thaim was.
To that brig held thai straucht the way
And to brek it fast gan assay,
Bot thai that chassyt quhen thai thaim saw
90   Mak arest, but dred or aw
Thai ruschyt apon thaim hardely
And discumfyt thaim uterly,
And held the brig haile quhill the king
With all the folk off his leding
95   Passyt the brig all at thar ese.
To Jhone off Lorne it suld displese
I trow, quhen he his men mycht se
Oute off his schippis fra the se
Be slayne and chassyt in the hill,
100   That he mycht set na help thartill,
For it angrys als gretumly
To gud hartis that ar worthi
To se thar fayis fulfill thar will
As to thaim selff to thole the ill.

[*The taking of Dunstaffnage and the surrender of Alexander of Argyll*]

105   At sic myscheiff war thai of Lorn,

for many had lost their lives and others had fled away. (108)
The king quickly had the booty of the whole country seized,
so that you could see such a great abundance of cattle coming
that it was a wonder to watch. The king, who was strong,
firm and bold, set a sturdy siege to Dunstaffnage, and diligently
attacked the castle to take it. (116) In a short time he had
those inside set in such hardship that, in spite of their [men],
he won it and appointed a good warden in it, delivering to
him both men and food so that he could be there for a long
time, despite all those of that country. (123) Sir Alexander of
Argyll, who saw the king destroy his land, clean to the ground,
sent negotiators to the king, and became his man, without
tarrying, [so that the king] received him to his peace. (128)
But John of Lorn, his son, was still a rebel, as he persisted in
being, and fled with ships on the sea. But those left on land
were all obedient to the king, and he took the hostages from
them all, then went again to Perth to take recreation there in
the open [country].

(136) Lothian was still against him and there was a big strong
peel at Linlithgow,

---

113. Dunstaffnage castle. It is possible that the definitive surrender of
    Dunstaffnage took place at this time, as both Barbour and Fordun state.
    But in the summer of 1309 the king went north to Loch Broom and
    then is found at Dunstaffnage on 20 October, 1309. This seems to have
    have marked the deprivation of the Macdougalls, who both appear in
    Ireland at the end of 1309.

123–28. Alexander of Argyll and John of Lorn. Alexander appears at the
    St Andrews parliament of March 1309 at Robert's peace, which confirms
    Barbour's statement, and disproves Fordun's claims that he led the
    men of Argyll at the battle, and that after giving up Dunstaffnage (in
    1308), he refused homage and retired to England. In October 1308
    John of Argyll had permission to replenish the castle in Loch Awe in
    his charge, suggesting that he was not in possession of Dunstaffnage.
    Perhaps Barbour and Fordun have different parts of the truth. Alexander
    submitted as Barbour states after the battle, i.e. in August 1308, but
    would surely be allowed to keep his castle (otherwise why submit?).
    John was given a truce (as in his letter) to persuade him to follow suit,
    but did not do so and perhaps took over Dunstaffnage in 1309. In
    October 1309 the king expelled them both, probably without a battle.
    Alexander died in 1310. (Barrow, *Bruce*, 179; *F1*, 345; *RotSci*, 58a;
    RRS5, 10. *CDS3,95* belongs to 1310, not 1309)

134. Toward Perth. This is confirmed by Robert I's charters, one of
    which is dated at Perth on 14 October, 1308. If the account of the
    Argyll campaign known to Barbour ended with the king going to Perth,
    this may explain why the taking of that town was placed earlier in the
    poem (9.331–454). (*RRS5, 4*)

For fele the lyvys thar has lorne
And other sum war fled thar way.
The king in hy gert sese the pray
Off all the land, quhar men mycht se
110 Sa gret habundance come of fe
That it war wonder to behauld.
The king that stout wes stark and bauld
Till Dunstaffynch rycht sturdely
A sege set and besily
115 Assaylit the castell it to get,
And in schort tym he has thaim set
In swilk thrang that tharin war than
That magre tharis he it wan,
And ane gud wardane tharin set
120 And betaucht hym bath men and met
Sua that he lang tyme thar mycht be
Magre thaim all off that countre.
Schyr Alexandir off Arghile that saw
The king dystroy up clene and law
125 His land send treyteris to the king
And cum his man but mar duelling,
And he resavit him till his pes,
Bot Jhone off Lorne his sone yeit wes
Rebell as he wes wont to be
130 And fled with schippis on the se,
Bot thai that left apon the land
War to the king all obeysand.
And he thar hostage all has tane
And towart Perth agayne is gane
135 To play him thar into the playne.

[*The plan to take the peel of Linlithgow*]

Yeit Lothyane was him agayne,
And at Lythkow wes than a pele

---

137. A peel. A place fortified by ditch, bank and palisade. Edward I had
built this peel in 1302–3, planning originally that it would have a stone
gatehouse and towers, but soon modifying this to build in timber. With
its subordinate peel at Livingston, it was an important link in the supply
route between Edinburgh and Stirling. The commander from 1310 was
the Gascon Piers Lubaud, but by 1313 he was also constable of Edin-
burgh castle, so would not be at Linlithgow. It is last mentioned as in
his charge on 20 August, 1313, in a writ dated at Windsor, so must
have fallen after the beginning of that month. (*CDS3, 330. Official Guide
to Linlithgow Palace*; H. M. Colvin, *History of the King's Works*, i. 411–15)

well garrisoned by Englishmen, which was a place of refuge
for those who sought to go with armour or provisions from
Edinburgh to Stirling, or back from Stirling; they did the
country much harm. (144) Now you will hear, if you want,
[about] skirmishes and feats, [by] which men tried, in many
ways to take castles and peels. This Linlithgow was one of
them, and I shall tell you how it was taken. (150) In the
country there dwelt one who was a husbandman, and by his
cattle often led hay to the peel. He was called William Bunnock
by name, and was a stalwart man in a fight. (155) He saw the
country so hard pressed that he was both angered and sad by
the great duress whereby it was then controlled and ruled by
Englishmen who troubled people immeasurably. (160) He was
a stout and sturdy fellow, stern and resolute in himself, with
friends living near him, to some of whom he showed his secret,
and according to his plans he got men who could make an
ambush, while he went with his cart to lead hay into the peel.
(168) But his cart would be well manned, for eight armed
men would sit in the body of his cart secretly, concealed by
hay around them, and he himself, stern and resolute, would
walk noncholantly beside the cart. (174) A yeoman, strong
and bold, would drive the cart in front, carrying a hatchet,
sharp to cut, under his belt; and when the gate had been
opened, and they were at it, when [the yeoman] heard him
cry loudly 'call all, call all,' then quickly

150–250. The taking of Linlithgow. This bears a resemblance to the taking
of Edinburgh castle in 1341, when Sir William Douglas hired a ship at
Dundee, putting men in it who feigned to be English merchants. They
went to the Forth, sent word to the castle that they had supplies and
would bring a present the next day, when the gates should be opened;
meanwhile Douglas hid in ambush near the castle. The following day
twelve of them loaded horses with fake goods, covered their armour,
and at the castle persuaded the castle porter to open the gate. When
he did so they killed him, put a staff under the portcullis to prevent it
descending, emptied their goods on the turnpike [to stop the gates
being closed, *Chron le Bel*], then sounded their horns. They engaged
the garrison till Douglas arrived, and soon took the castle. The leaders
were William Fraser, Joachim of Kinbuck, 'and William Bullock who
was then the king of Scotland's sworn man'. (*Wyntoun*6, 138–144;
F1, 365; *F2*, 356; *Chron le Bel*, i. 278–79)

152. Led, as still used in the sense of 'cart in', but the cart drawn by
cattle.

153. William Bunnock, a husbandman, is not otherwise known. The name
may have been borrowed from the taking of Edinburgh in 1341 (note
on 150).

Mekill and stark and stuffyt wele
With Inglismen, and wes reset
140 To thaim that with armuris or met
Fra Edynburgh wald to Strevelyn ga
And fra Strevelyng agane alsua,
And till the countre did gret ill.
Now may ye her giff that ye will
145 Entremellys and juperdyis
That men assayit mony wys
Castellis and peyllis for to ta,
And this Lithquhow wes ane off tha
And I sall tell you how it wes tane.
150 In the contre thar wonnyt ane
That husband wes, and with his fe
Oftsys hay to the peile led he,
Wilyame Bunnok to name he hicht
That stalwart man wes into ficht.   154*
155 He saw sa hard the contre staid   154
That he gret noy and pite had   155*
Throw the gret force that it was then   155
Governyt and led with Inglismen,
That travalyt men out-our mesure.
160 He wes a stout carle and a sture   158
And off himselff dour and hardy,
And had freyndis wonnand him by
And schawyt to sum his prevete,
And apon his convyne gat he
165 Men that mycht ane enbuschement ma   163
Quhill that he with his wayne suld ga
To lede thaim hay into the pele
Bot his wayne suld be stuffyt wele,
For aucht men in the body
170 Off his wayn suld sit prevely   168
And with hay helyt be about,
And himselff that wes dour and stout
Suld be the wayne gang ydilly,
And ane yuman wycht and hardy
175 Befor suld dryve the wayne and ber   173
Ane hachat that war scharp to scher
Under his belt, and quhen the yat
War opynnyt and thai war tharat
And he hard him cry sturdely,
180 'Call all, call all,' than hastyly   178

he should strike with the axe [and cut] in two the leading traces; (182) then those who were within the cart should come out quickly and make a fight until the force that was lying in ambush nearby arrived to take on the struggle.

(187) This was at harvest time, when fair broad fields, were laden all over with corn; for the different crops they bore ripened to become men's food, and the trees all grew together laden with fruits of various kinds. (194) At this sweet time that I describe, those in the peel had cut [their] hay, and had spoken with this Bunnock to lead their hay, because he was near; he agreed without difficulty, and said that early in the morning he would bring a load, better, bigger, and a great deal more than any he had brought earlier that year; that was their firm agreement. (204) For that night he secretly warned those who were to go in the cart, and also those to be in the ambush. They went so quickly there, that they were lying in ambush before daybreak quite near the peel, where they could hear the cry, as soon as there was one, and stayed like that without moving, so that no-one espied them. (213) [Then] this Bunnock quickly took trouble to arrange his group in his cart, and a while before daybreak he had them hidden by the hay; then he set about yoking his cattle, until [the time when] men could see the sun shining. (219) And some of those inside the peel had come out – [it was] their misfortune – to cut their harvest close by.

---

187. Harvest time. This does not fit with leading the hay. Harvest was a conventional time indicator.

He suld stryk with the ax in twa
The soyme, and than in hy suld tha
That war within the wayne cum out
And mak debate quhill that thar rout
185　That suld nerby enbushyt be　　　　183
Cum for to manteyme the mellé.

[The taking of the peel of Linlithgow]

This wes intill the hervyst tyd
Quhen feldis that ar fayr and wid
Chargyt with corne all fully war,
190　For syndry cornys that thai bar　　188
Wox ryp to wyn to mannys fud,
And the treys all chargyt stud
With ser frutis on syndry wys.
In this swete tyme that I devys
195　Thai off the pele had wonnyn hay　193
And with this Bunnok spokyn had thai
To lede thar hay, for he wes ner,
And he assentyt but daunger
And said that he in the mornyng
200　Weile sone a fothyr he suld bring　198
Fayrer and gretar and weile mor
Than he brocht ony that yer befor,
And held thaim cunnand sekyrly.
For that nycht warnyt he prevely
205　Thaim that in the wayne suld ga　203
And that in the buschement suld be alsua,
And thai sa graithly sped thaim thar
That or day thai enbuschyt war
Weile ner the pele quhar thai mycht her
210　The cry als sone as ony wer,　　208
And held thaim sua still but stering
That nane off thaim had persaving.
And this Bunnok fast gan him payne
To dres his menye in his wayne
215　And all a quhile befor the day　213
He had thaim helyt weile with ha
And maid him to yok his fe
Till men the son schynand mycht se,
And sum that war within the pele
220　War ischyt on thar awne unsele　218
To wyn thar hervyst ner tharby.

Then Bunnock with the group that he had enclosed in his cart, went on his way withou delay, and drove his cart to the peel. (226) The porter, who saw him clearly coming near the gate, opened it soon, when Bunnock, without hesitation, had the cart move straight on. (230) And when it was set evenly between the checks of the gate, so that no-one could get by, he shouted, 'Call all, call all,' and then he let the goad drop, and quickly cut the traces in two. Bunnock, with that, struck the porter such a blow that blood and brains both were spilled. (239) And those who were inside the cart jumped out with agility and soon killed the men of the castle who were near [the gate]. Then for a while there was shouting; those lying in ambush nearby leapt out, came with drawn swords and took all the castle, without trouble, and slew those who were inside. (245) And those who had gone out earlier, when they saw the castle lost, fled to safety here and there; some went to Edinburgh, others to Stirling, and some were slain on the road.

(253) In this way Bunnock with his wain took the peel and slew the men, then gave it to the king who rewarded him worthily and had it knocked down to the ground. Then [the king] journeyed over the whole land setting in peace all the country willing to obey him. (261) After a little time had passed, he sent for Thomas Randolph,

---

225–34. In the plan Bunnock walks beside the cart and is to shout 'call all'; the yeoman sits on it and is to cut the traces (172–82). In the execution of the plan, Bunnock is ahead of the cart, leading the cattle, managing them with his goad; once inside the peel he cannot squeeze past; it is he who now has an axe to cut the traces. The yeoman is nowhere to be seen.

233. E and C have 'criyt theyff', but McDiarmid emends to 'heych'.

241. The peel now becomes a castle, so called several times in the next few lines; but there was only a peel at Linlithgow, sometimes called 'castle'.

262. Thomas Randolph very quickly made his peace with Robert I after his capture by the Lyne (9.735–62) for he was one of the barons at the St Andrews parliament of March 1309, when he was called 'lord of Nithsdale'. He was apparently not with the king in the north and Argyll that year, and was perhaps left as royal lieutenant for in 1310 he is called 'lord of Nithsdale and lieutenant of the prince of Scotland from Forth to Orkney'. In April 1312, when Dundee fell, he appears as 'lord of Annandale'. This title of Randolph is not repeated till 1318. (*RRS5*, 6–9, 19–20, 384–85; *Lindores Liber, 10*)

Than Bunnok with the cumpany
That in his wayne closyt he had
Went on his way but mar abaid
225 And callit his wayne towart the pele, 223
And the portar that saw him wele
Cum ner the yet, it opnyt sone,
And then Bunnok foroutyn hone
Gert call the wayne deliverly,
230 And quhen it wes set evynly 228
Betwix the chekis of the yat
Sua that men mycht it spar na gat
He cryit hey, 'Call all, call all,'
And he than lete the gad-wand fall
235 And hewyt in twa the soyme in hy. 233
Bonnok with that deliverly
Roucht till the portar sic a rout
That blud and harnys bath come out,
And thai that war within the wayne
240 Lap out belyff and sone has slayne 238
Men off the castell that war by
Than in ane quhile begouth the cry,
And thai that ner enbuschyt war
Lap out and come with swerdis bar
245 And tuk the casell all but payn 243
And has thaim that war tharin was slayn,
And thai that war went furth beforn
Quhen thai the castell saw forlorn
Thai fled to warand to and fra,
250 And sum till Edinburgh gan ga 248
And sum till Strevilline ar other gane
And sum intill the gat war slayne.

[*A profile of Thomas Randolph, earl of Moray*]

Bonnok on this wis with his wayne
The pele tuk and the men has slane,
255 Syne taucht in till the king in hy 253
That him rewardyt worthely
And gert dryve it doun to the ground,
And syne our all the land gan found
Settand in pes all the countré
260 That at his obeysance wald be. 258
And quhen a litill time wes went
Eftre Thomas Randell he sent

and dealt so well with him that [Thomas] promised to be his man, and the king gave up his anger. To raise his standing he gave Moray to [Thomas], and made him earl thereof; and he gave him in heritage various other broad lands. (270) He knew his worthy vassalage, his great knowledge and judgment, his trusty heart and loyal service, and, for that, trusted him, and made him rich in land and beasts, as was indeed the right [thing]. (276) For, if men [were to] speak truly of him, he was so courageous a knight, so wise, worthy and brave, and of such supreme courage, that much might be said of him. (281) Because I intend to speak of him, to show part of his good deeds, I'll describe to you his appearance and some of his character. (285) He was of moderate stature and well-formed in proportion, with a broad face, pleasant and fair, courteous and debonair in all respects and of assured demeanour. He loved loyalty above everything, always stood diligently against falsehood, treason and felony. (293) He exalted honour and generosity and always supported righteousness. He was caring, even loving, in company, and he always loved good knights, for, to tell the truth, he was full of spirit and made of all [the] virtues. (301) I will praise him here no more, but you shall hear further on that he should be prized supremely for his worthy deeds.

266–67. Between 12 April and 29 October, 1312 he was given the earldom of Moray, with huge bounds and extensive powers. The Isle of Man followed in 1316 and the lordship of Annandale (again) in December 1318. (*RRS5, 378–79, 389*)

And sa weile with him tretit he
That he his man hecht for to be,
265 And the king his ire him forgave   263
And for to hey his state him gave
Murreff and erle tharoff him maid,
And other syndry landis braid
He gave him intill heritage.
270 He knew his worthi vasselage   268
And his gret wyt and his avys
His traist hart and his lele service,
Tharfor in him affyit he
And ryche maid him off land and fe,
275 As it wes certis rycht worthi.   273
For and men spek off him trewly
He wes sua curageous ane knycht
Sa wys, sa worthy and sa wycht
And off sa soverane gret bounté
280 That mekill off him may spokyn be,   278
And for I think off him to rede
And to schaw part off his gud dede
I will discryve now his fassoun
And part off his condicioun.
285 He wes off mesurabill statur   283
And weile porturat at mesur
With braid vesage plesand and fayr,
Curtais at poynt and debonayr
And off rycht sekyr contenyng.
290 Lawté he lovyt atour all thing,   288
Falset tresoun and felony
He stude agayne ay encrely,
He heyit honour ay and larges
And ay mentemyt rychtwysnes.
295 In cumpany solacious   293
He was and tharwith amorous,
And gud knychtis he luffyt ay,
And giff I the suth sall say
He wes fulfilly off bounté
300 As off vertuys all maid was he.   298
I will commend him her no mar
Bot ye sall her weile forthyrmar
That he for his dedis worthy
Suld weile be prisyt soverandly.

(305) When the king was thus reconciled with him and had given him great lordships, [Thomas] became so prudent and wise that he first brought his land into good order, and then sped to the war to help his uncle in his need. (311) With the consent of the king, and with only simple equipment, he went to Edinburgh with good men in his company, and set siege to the castle, which was then remarkably well supplied befittingly with men and victuals, so that it feared no man's might. (319) But this good earl, nonetheless, took on the siege very boldly, and pressed the folk that were inside so that not one dared pass through the gate. They can stay inside and eat their victual as long as they can get any, but I'm sure they will be prevented from getting more in the country[side].

(327) At that time King Edward of England had given the castle in keeping to Sir Piers Lubaud, a Gascon, and when those of the garrison saw the siege set so strictly, they suspected him of treachery, because he had spoken with the king. (334) And because of that suspicion,

---

305–830. The year 1313–14. Edward II had striven to restore his position in Scotland, to little effect, in 1310–11. By about September 1313, with the fall of Linlithgow, the situation in Lothian was for the first time under threat. At 13.736, Barbour explains that, after Bannockburn, the king gave a year for dissenting Scots to come to his peace. The record of this decision, on 6 November, 1314, shows that it was at the end, not (as Barbour says) the beginning, of the year, notice of which must have been given about early November 1313, probably in an assembly at Dundee on 21–24 October 1313. The Scots in Lothian loyal to Edward II took to him a powerful plea for action against his garrisons at Berwick and Roxburgh (unfortunately undated), which seems to have prodded him into reassurances issued on 8 November, but it was surely Bruce's threat against the remaining Anglo-Scots which led to the decision, announced on 28 November, 1313, that Edward II would return to Scotland by midsummer 1314 with an army to end the 'rebellion' of the Scots. To anticipate this invasion, the Scots attacked the castles of Roxburgh, Edinburgh and Stirling about Lent 1314. The invasion was not provoked by the siege of Stirling, though the threat that Stirling, his father's last achievement, would be lost, made it impossible for Edward II to cancel the campaign. The year attributed by Barbour for the surrender of Stirling castle is an error, but the period was borrowed from the year allowed to the remaining Anglo-Scots to shift allegiance.

311. The date at which the siege of Edinburgh began is not known, but it was clearly well before the attack on Roxburgh, 19 February, 1314, perhaps in January 1314. Barbour has nothing on Robert's threatened invasion of England after midsummer, 1313, which yielded much black-mail for truces in the northern English counties lasting till 29 September, 1314. (*L*, 222; *LT*, 203)

[*Moray sets siege to Edinburgh castle*]

305	Quhen the king thus was with him sauch	303
	And gret lordschyppis had him betaucht	
	He wox sa wyse and sa avysé	
	That his land fyrst weill stablyst he	
	And syne he sped him to the wer	
310	Till help his eyme in his myster	308
	And with the consent off the king	
	Bot with a symple aparaling	
	Till Edinburgh he went in hy	
	With gud men intill cumpany,	
315	And set a sege to the castell	313
	That than was warnyst wonder weill	
	With men and vyttalis at all rycht	
	Sua that it dred na mannys mycht.	
	Bot this gud erle nocht-forthi	
320	The sege tuk full apertly	318
	And pressyt the folk that tharin was	
	Sua that nocht ane the yet durst pas.	
	Thai may abid tharin and ete	
	Thair vittaill quhill thai ouch mai get	
325	Bot I trow thai sall lettyt be	323
	To purchas mar in the contré.	

[*The situation in Edinburgh; Douglas's activity*]

	That tyme Edward off Ingland king	
	Had gevyn that castell in keping	
	Till Schyr Perys Lombert a Gascoun,	
330	And quhen thai of his warnysoun	328
	Saw the sege set thar sa stythly	
	Thai mystrowit him off tratoury	
	For that he spokyn had with the king,	
	And for that ilk mystrowing	

---

329. Piers Lubaud, described by the *Vita Edwardi* as a cousin of Piers
Gaveston, was a Gascon who had served Edward II for several years in
Scotland, especially in Lothian garrisons. He was constable of Edinburgh
castle and of Linlithgow peel in March 1312. The story of his imprison-
ment may be true, because he certainly was treated as Robert's subject
after the fall of the castle. The *Vita* claims that Lubaud betrayed the
castle, but Lanercost has no hint of this and Gray, who was imprisoned
in the castle 40 years later, comments on Piers without any such sug-
gestion. Perhaps Francis (535) was a sympathiser with Lubaud. See note
to 766.

they took him and put him in prison, and appointed a con-
stable of their own nationality to lead them, [a man] right
wary, wise and active; and he used knowledge, strength and
cunning to keep his hold on the castle. (341) But now I will
be silent about them, and speak a little while of the brave lord
Douglas, who was then in the Forest, where he [made] many
attacks and showed feats of chivalry, as well by night as by
day, to those that lay in the castles of Roxburgh and Jedworth.
(349) But I will let many of them pass by, for I cannot rehearse
them all, and even if I could, believe me, I would not be up
to it, [for] there would be so much to be [said]; but those
that I know for certain, I shall tell according to my knowledge.
(357) At the time that the good Earl Thomas besieged Edin-
burgh (as the writing says) James Douglas turned all his
thoughts to work out how Roxburgh might be won by stealth
or any contrivance, till he had Simon of Ledhouse, a cunning
and skillful man, make ladders of hempen ropes, with wooden
steps so tied that they would never break. (368) They made a
crook of iron, of their own design, that was strong and square,

---

344. The Forest, of Ettrick. Douglas went there in 1307–08 also (8.425,
    515; 9.1).

361. The date of the taking of Roxburgh was 19–20 February 1314, as
    given at 377 and confirmed by the Verse Chronicle. The king is not
    said to have backed this venture and the later sending of Edward Bruce
    to take over at Roxburgh (499–510) suggests that Douglas acted on his
    own initiative.

363. Simon of Ledhouse is otherwise unknown, but as Ledhouse was
    near Lesmahagow, Sim would probably be a Clydesdale follower of
    Douglas, not a Roxburgh man.

365–72. The ladders (plural in both E and C at 365) are described by
    Lanercost, as used in a failed attack on Berwick, January 1312, ignored
    by Barbour:

> They were of wonderful construction, as I myself, who write these
> lines, saw with my own eyes. For the Scots had made two strong
> ropes as long as the height of the wall, making a knot at one end of
> each cord. They had made a wooden board also, about two and a
> half feet long and six inches broad, strong enough to carry a man,
> and in the extremities of the board they made two holes through
> which the two ropes could be passed; then the cords, having been
> passed through as far as the knots, they had made two other knots
> in the ropes eighteen inches higher, and above these they placed
> another board and so on to the end of the ropes. They had also made
> an iron hook, measuring at least a foot along one limb, and this was
> to lie over the wall, but the other limb, being of the same length,
> hung downwards to the ground, having at its end a round hole wherein
> the point of a lance could be inserted, and two rings on the two sides
> wherein the said ropes could be knotted ... Two men lifted the ropes

335 Thai tuk him and put in presoun,   333
And off thar awine nacioun
Thai maid ane constable thaim to lede
Bath wys and war and wycht off deid,
And he set wyt and strenth and slycht
340 To kep the castell at his mycht.   338
Bot now off thaim I will be still,
And spek a litill quhill I will
Off the douchty lord off Douglas
At that tyme in the Forest was
345 Quhar he mony a juperty   343
And fayr poyntis off chevalry
Servyt als weill be nycht as day
Till thaim that in the castellis lay
Of Roxburch and Jedwort, bot I
350 Will let fele off thaim pas forby   348
For I can noucht rehers thaim all,
And thoucht I couth, weill trow ye sall
That I mycht nocht suffice tharto,
Thar suld mekill be ado,
355 Bot thai that I wate utterly   353
Eftre my wyt rehers will I.

[*Douglas plans to take Roxburgh castle*]

This tyme that the gud erle Thomas
Assegyt as the lettre sayis
Edinburgh, James off Douglas
360 Set all his wit for to purchas   358
How Roxburch throu sutelté
Or ony craft mycht wonnyn be,
Till he gert Syme off the Leidhous
A crafty man and a curious
365 Off hempyn rapis leddris ma   363
With treyn steppis bundyn sua
That brek wald nocht on nakyn wis.
A cruk thai maid at thair divis
Off irne that wes styth and squar

___

and boards with a spear, and placed the iron hook, which was not a
round one, over the wall ... But lest the ropes should lie too close
to the wall, ... they had made fenders round every third step, which
thrust the ropes away from the wall. (*L*, 221; *LT*, 201–2)
Curiously, wooden ladders, not these rope ones, were used at Perth in
January 1313.

so that if it was in an embrasure, and the ladder stretched from it, it would hold firm. (373) This good lord of Douglas, as this was devised and carried out, gathered good men in secret – I'm sure they numbered three score – and on Shrove Tuesday, at the beginning of the night, they took the way to the castle. (380) With black cloaks they concealed the armour that they had on. Without delay they came nearby there, and sent all their horses away from them; they went as a company, in file, on hands and feet when they were near, as much as if they were cattle and oxen that had been left out untethered. (388) There's no doubt it was really dark, yet one of those that lay on the wall said to his companion beside him, 'This man' – and named a nearby husbandman – 'plans to make good cheer, leaving all his oxen out.' (394) The other said, 'There's no doubt he'll make merry tonight, even if they are led away by the Douglas.' They thought the Douglas and his men were oxen, because they went on hands and feet, one by one. (400) The Douglas paid very good heed to all their talk, but soon they went indoors, chatting on their way.

(403) The Douglas men were pleased at that and sped quickly to the wall; soon they set up their ladder that made a clatter when the catch caught fast in the embrasure. (408) One of the watches heard that clearly, and hurried there without delay, but Ledhouse, who had made the ladder,

---

369. Square. See the description in the previous note.
405. *C* has ladders, *E* only ladder; cf. 371. But the story makes it clear that the attackers had only one ladder for the assault, otherwise Ledhouse would never have been alone on the wall signalling to the others to climb (426).

370 That fra it in a kyrneill war 368
And the ledder tharfra straitly
Strekit, it suld stand sekyrly.
This gud lord off Douglas alsone
As this divisit wes and done
375 Gaderyt gud men in preveté 373
Thre scor I trow thai mycht be,
And on the Fasteryngis evyn rycht
In the begynnyng off the nycht
To the castell thai tuk thar way.
380 With blak frogis all helyt thai 378
The armouris that thai on thaim had.
Thai come nerby thar but abad
And send haly thar hors thaim fra,
And thai on raunge in ane route gan ga
385 On handis and fete quhen thai war ner 383
Rycht as thai ky or oxin wer
That war wont to be bondyn left tharout.
It wes rycht myrk withoutyn dout,
The-quhether ane on the wall that lay
390 Besid him till his fere gan say, 388
'This man thinkis to mak gud cher,'
And nemmyt ane husband tharby ner,
'That has left all his oxyn out.'
The tother said, 'It is na dout
395 He sall mak mery tonycht thocht thai 303
Be with the Douglas led away.'
Thai wend the Douglas and his men
Had bene oxin, for thai yeid then
On handis and fete ay ane and ane.
400 The Douglas rycht gud tent has tane 398
Till thar spek, bot all sone thai
Held carpand inwart thar way.

[*The taking of the enclosure of Roxburgh castle*]

Douglas men tharoff war blyth
And to the wall thai sped thaim swith,
405 And sone has up thar ledder set 403
That maid ane clap quhen the cruchet
Wes fixit fast in the kyrneill.
That herd ane off the wachis weill
And buskyt thidderwart but baid,
410 Bot Ledehous that the ledder maid 408

hurried to climb first to the wall[top]. But before he had quite got up, [the man] who had that sector to guard, met him just as he came up, and, because he thought to knock him down, he made no noise, no cry, no sound, but rushed nimbly at him. (418) [Ledhouse] who was at risk of death, made a lunge at him, got him swiftly by the neck, and stabbed him upwards with a knife, until, in his hand, he gave up his life. (423) And when [Ledhouse] saw him lying dead upon the wall, he went speedily and threw the body down to them and said, 'All goes to plan. Hurry up [the ladder] smartly' – and they did so with real speed. (429) But before they came up, someone came who saw Ledhouse standing alone, and knew he was not [one] of their men. (432) Quickly he rushed to him then and attacked him sturdily, but [Ledhouse] slew him at once for he was armed and strong [while] the other was unarmed, I'm sure, and had nothing to stop the blow. (438) [Ledhouse] made that fight up there while Douglas and all his company were climbing up on to the wall. Then they went hastily to the tower.

(443) The folk were then all in the hall at their dancing, singing and other kinds of fun, and making merry on this Shrove Tuesday as is the custom for folk that are safe. (448) They believed they were [safe] at that time, but before they knew [what was happening] right into the hall came Douglas and his men,

---

441. The tower. Roxburgh castle is now a hill with unexcavated mounds, largely destroyed by cannon in the sixteenth century. But it had strong natural defences.

445. Fastern's Even, the beginning of Lent, Shrove Tuesday. In 1314 this fell on 19 February.

447. 'Pouste', translated 'safe'; strictly 'in authority'.

Sped him to clymb fyrst to the wall,
Bot or he wes up gottyn all
He at that ward had in keping
Met him rycht at the up-cummyng,
415 And for he thocht to ding him doun 413
He maid na noys na cry na soun
Bot schot till him deliverly.
And he that wes in juperty
To de a launce he till him maid
420 And gat him be the nek but baid 418
And stekyt him upwart with a knyff
Quhill in his hand he left the lyff.
And quhen he ded sua saw him ly
Up on the wall he went in hy
425 And doun the body kest thaim till 423
And said, 'All gangis as we will,
Spede you upwart deliverly.'
And thai did sua in full gret hy.
Bot or thai wan up thar come ane
430 And saw Ledhous stand him allane 428
And knew he wes nocht off thar men.
In hy he ruschyt till him then
And him assailit sturdely,
Bot he slew him deliverly
435 For he wes armyt and wes wycht, 433
The tother nakyt wes, Ik hicht
And had nocht for to stynt the strak.
Sic melle tharup gan he mak
Quhill Douglas and his mengne all
440 War cummyn up apon the wall, 438
Than in the tour thai went in hy.

[*The taking of the hall at Roxburgh castle; the garrison in the tower*]

The folk wes that tyme halily
Intill the hall at thar daunsing
Syngyng and other wayis playing,
445 And apon Fasteryngis evyn this 443
As custume is to mak joy and blys
Till folk that ar into pousté.
Sua trowyt thai that tyme to be,
Bot or thai wyst rycht in the hall
450 Douglas and his rout cummyn war all 448

and yelled out 'Douglas! Douglas!'; they, who were more [numerous] than he was, heard 'Douglas!' shouted fearsomely, were demoralised at the cry and made no real effort at defence. [The Scots] slew them without mercy till they had gotten the upper hand. (458) The other [side] fled to seek refuge, fearing death utterly. The warden, who was called Guillemin de Fiennes, saw how things went, took himself to the great tower with others of his company, and hastily barred the entry. The rest, who had been left outside, were taken or slain without doubt, unless any jumped over the wall. (468) The Douglas held the hall that night, although his foes were woeful at it. His men went to and fro throughout the castle all that night, till morning when day lightened.

(473) The warden that was in the tower, who was a man of great valour, when he saw that the castle, high and low, was lost, bent his efforts to defend the tower, but those outside fired arrows at him in such an amount that he was impeded by them, (481) but nonetheless till the next day he held the tower stoutly, and then, at an assault, he was wounded so badly in the face that he feared for his life. (486) For that reason he soon negotiated then and surrendered the tower in such a way that he and all that were with him could pass safely into England. Douglas gave them good terms and

---

461. Guillemin de Fiennes was another Gascon and had been Constable of Roxburgh since 1311 when he was knighted. The garrison then consisted of 50 men-at-arms, 18 crossbowmen, 29 hobelars, 61 archers, plus some 20 others who served for less than the year. The number may have shrunk by 1314 but was still large. In 1313 the constable had arrested some Scots loyal to Edward II during a truce, and had fined them 80 merks; they had had to pay the Scots 160 merks for this breach of truce. His garrison robbed merchants who came to Roxburgh (CDS3, 337, 406, index under Filinge). Barbour's account does suggest poor discipline.

479. It is not clear where all the archers could have come from, but this storm of arrows explains away the day's action, and may have been suggested by Fiennes' wound, evidently from an arrow, since Gray claims that Fiennes was killed by an arrow while holding the tower.

489. The fall of Roxburgh is described by (a) Lanercost, and (b) the *Vita Edwardi*:

(a) At the beginning of Lent, the Scots cunningly entered Roxburgh castle at night by ladders, and took all the castle except one tower, in which the warden of the castle, Sir Guillemin de Fiennes, a Gascon, had taken refuge with difficulty and his people with him; but the Scots got possession of that tower soon afterwards, and they knocked to the ground the whole of that beautiful castle, just as they did other castles. (*L*, 223; *LT*, 204)

And cryit on hycht, 'Douglas! Douglas!'
And thai that ma war than he was
Hard 'Douglas!' criyt hidwysly,
Thai war abaysit for the cry
455 And schup rycht na defens to ma, 453
And thai but pite gan thaim sla
Till thay had gottyn the overhand.
The tother fled to sek warand
That out off mesure ded gane dreid.
460 The wardane saw how that it yeid 458
That callyt wes Gilmyn de Fynys,
In the gret toure he gottyn is
And other off his cumpany
And sparryt the entre hastily.
465 The lave that levyt war without 463
War tane or slayne, this is na dout,
Bot giff that ony lap the wall.
The Douglas that nycht held the hall
Allthocht his fayis tharoff war wa,
470 His men was gangand to and fra 468
Throu-out the castell all that nycht
Till on the morn that day wes lycht.

[*Surrender of the tower at Roxburgh castle; slighting of the castle*]

The wardane that was in the tour
That wes a man off gret valour
475 Gilmyn the Fynys, quhen he saw 473
The castell tynt be clene and law
He set his mycht for to defend
The tour, bot thai without him send
Arowys in sa gret quantite
480 That anoyit tharoff wes he, 478
Bot till the tother day nocht-forthi
He held the tour full sturdely,
And than at ane assalt he was
Woundyt sa felly in the face
485 That he wes dredand off his lyff. 483
Tharfor he tretit than beliff
And yauld the tour on sic maner
That he and all that with him wer
Suld saufly pas in Ingland.
490 Douglas held thaim gud conand 488

escorted them to their country. (492) But there [Fiennes]
lived for a very short time, because he soon died from the
wound in his face, and was buried. Douglas seized all the
castle, that was then enclosed by a strong wall; he sent this
Ledhouse to the king, who gave him a very fine reward, and
with great speed sent his brother Sir Edward, a doughty man,
to [Roxburgh] to knock it down, tower, castle and donjon.
(503) He came with a large company, and made [them] work
so hard that tower and wall were knocked down to the ground
in a short time; and he stayed there till all Teviotdale came
to the king's peace, apart from Jedworth and other [parts]
that were near the Englishmen's border.

(511) When Roxburgh had been won like this, Earl Thomas,
who always held bold enterprise as a sovereign achievement,
was lying at the siege of Edinburgh with his company, as I
told you plainly before. (517) But when he heard how Rox-
burgh had been taken by a stratagem, I know he set all his
endeavours in thought and deed to find some stratagem
whereby he could help himself, by cunning mixed with good
chivalry, to win the castle wall through a ruse of some kind,
because he well knew that force would not take it openly while
those within had men and food. (527) Therefore he privately
asked if any man could be found who knew any good strata-
gem to climb the walls secretly,

(b) James Douglas came secretly to the castle by night, and placed
ladders, stealthily brought up, on the wall; and so he climbed the wall
and, leading his companions on the sleeping or heedless guards,
attacked those he found and took the castle. (*VitaEd*, 48)

500. Sent Sir Edward to Roxburgh, 507, and he dwelt there. There is
no other evidence of this expedition, which implies that Edward Bruce
could not have begun a siege of Stirling before March at the earliest.
See note to 820.

509. Jedwort. Jedburgh, where the castle can be visited. The date of its
fall is uncertain, but it was probably at the end of 1314, since on 25
January, 1315 Edward II gave a pardon for all offences to William
Prenderguest, who held it against the Scots; he seems now to be a
refugee. The captor is also unknown. Later references do not show it
in English hands. (*CDS3, 418, 494, 576, 746*)

526. Men and food. A full account for the Edinburgh garrison in 1311-12
names about 200 men (83 men-at-arms, 40 crossbowmen, 40 archers,
29 hobelars), and while it would not be at that strength by 1314, it was
probably still well garrisonned; it had also been provisioned. (*CDS3,
303, 408-10*)

And convoid thaim to thar countré,
Bot thar full schort tyme levyt he
For throu the wound intill the face
He deyt sone and beryit was.

495 Douglas the castell sesyt all 493
That thane wes closyt with stalwart wall,
And send this Leidhous till the king
That maid him full gud rewarding
And hys brother in full gret hy

500 Schyr Edward that wes sa douchty 498
He send thidder to tumbill it doun
Bath tour and castell and doungeoun.
And he come with gret cumpany
And gert travaile sa besyly

505 That tour and wall rycht to the ground 503
War tumblit in a litill stound,
And dwelt thar quhill all Tevidale
Come to the kingis pes all haile
Outane Jedwort and other that ner

510 The Inglismennys boundis wer. 508

[*Moray seeks a means of taking Edinburgh castle*]

Quhen Roxburgh wonnyn was on this wis
The Erle Thomas that hey empris
Set ay on soverane he bounté
At Edynburgh with his mengne

515 Wes lyand at a-sege as I 513
Tauld you befor all opynly.
Bot fra he hard how Roxburgh was
Tane with a trayne, all his purchas
And wyt and besines Ik hycht

520 He set for to purches sum slycht 518
How he mycht help him throu body
Mellyt with hey chevalry
To wyn the wall off the castell
Throu sumkyn slycht, for he wyst weill

525 That na strenth mycht it playnly get 523
Quhill thai within had men and met.
Tharfor prevely speryt he
Giff ony man mycht fundyn be
That couth fynd ony juperty

530 To clymb the wallis prevely 528

and he would be rewarded; for it was his intention to put himself at any risk before that siege came to nothing.

(535) There was there one William Francis, skilled and bold, wise and curious, who had been in the castle in his youth. When he saw the earl set himself especially to find some ruse or wile whereby he could take the castle, he came to him in private and said, (543) 'I think you would be glad if men would find you some stratagem whereby you might get over the walls; assuredly, if you want to start to try in this way, I undertake, for my service, to [let] you know [how] to climb the wall; (550) and I shall be foremost of all where, with a short ladder (I think it could be twelve feet [long]) we may climb up the wall quietly. And if you want to know how I knew this, I'll tell you cheerfully that when I was young, not so long ago, my father was keeper of yon house; (558) I had a roving eye and loved a girl here in the town, and so that I could go to her secretly, without [arousing] suspicion, I made a ladder of ropes for myself, and slid over the wall by it. (564) Then I went down a narrow path that I had spied in the rock, and came often to my destination. And when it drew near to day[time], I kept again to that same way and came in, always without [being] seen. I used that route for a long time, so that I can go right [along]

---

535. William Francis. A William Francis was in charge of Kirkintilloch castle before 1306. This man is likely to be the namesake who received land at Sprouston near Kelso about 1322. (*RMS1*, app. 2, *285, 373*)

552. Twelve-foot ladder. A climber on the north face of Edinburgh castle rock (note to 643), carrying a twelve-foot ladder, would excite much admiration today.

And he suld have his warysoun,
For it wes his entencioun
To put him till all aventur
Or that a sege on him mysfur.

[*The plan suggested by William Francis*]

535   Than wes thar ane Wilyame Francus   533
       Wycht and apert wys and curyus
       That intill hys youtheid had bene
       In the castell. Quhen he has sene
       The erle sua enkerly him set
540   Sum sutelte or wile to get   538
       Quharthrou the castell have mycht he
       He come till him in prevete
       And said, 'Me think ye wald blythly
       That men fand you sum jeperty
545   How ye mycht our the wallis wyn,   543
       And certis giff ye will begyn
       For till assay on sic a wys
       Ik undertak for my service
       To ken you to clymb to the wall,
550   And I sall formast be off all,   548
       Quhar with a schort ledder may we,
       I trow off tuelf fute it may be,
       Clymb to the wall up all quytly,
       And gyff that ye will wyt how I
555   Wate this I sall you blythly say.   553
       Quhen I wes young this hendre day
       My fader wes kepar of yone hous,
       And I wes sumdeill valegeous
       And lovyt a wench her in the toun,
560   And for I but suspicioun   558
       Mycht repayr till hyr prevely
       Off rapys a leddre to me mad I
       And tharwith our the wall I slaid.
       A strait roid that I sperit had
565   Intill the crage syne doun I went   563
       And oftsys come till myn entent,
       And quhen it ner drew to the day
       Ik held agayne that ilk way
       And ay come in but persaving.
570   Ik usyt lang that travaling   568
       Sua that I kan that roid ga rycht

that path even if men have never seen so dark a night. (573)
And if you intend that you will try to pass up that way after
me, I will take you up to the wall, if God preserves us from
the view of those that [keep] watch upon the wall. (578) And
if things go so well for us that we can set our ladder up, if a
man can get on to the wall, he shall defend [the position] if
there is need, while the rest hasten up.' The earl was pleased
with his proposal, and promised him a goodly reward.
(585)[The earl] undertook to go that way, and bade him make
his ladder soon, and keep [everything] quiet until they could
firm up on a [particular] night for their purpose.

(589) Soon afterwards the ladder was made, and then the
earl, without more delay, betook himself secretly one night
with thirty strong and bold men; they held their way on a
dark night that put them to great effort and in great peril
indeed. (596) I know if they could have seen it clearly they
would not have tried that way, even though they had no-one
to stop them, for the rock was high and terrifying and the
climbing [of it] really dangerous, [and] if anyone happened
to slide or fall, he would soon have been smashed up. (603)
The night was dark, as I heard tell, and they soon came to
the foot of the rock, which was high and sheer. Then before
them William Francis climbed in the clefts, always first among
them, and they followed him at the back; (609) with great
difficulty, sometimes to, sometimes fro, they climbed in the
clefts thus until they had climbed half the crag, and there they
found a place broad enough

---

591. A night. The fall of the castle 'with ladders' is dated by the Verse
    Chronicle, 14 March, 1314.
605. The crag. The description is the same as that for the rock-face at
    Ben Cruachan (22).

Thoucht men se nevyr sa myrk the nycht.
And giff ye think ye will assay
To pas up efter me that way
575 Up to the wall I sall you bring, 573
Giff God us savys fra persaving
Off thaim that wachys on the wall.
And giff that us sua fayr may fall
That we our ledder up may set,
580 Giff a man on the wall may get 578
He sall defend and it be ned
Quhill the remanand up thaim sped.'
The erle wes blyth off his carping
And hycht him fayr rewarding
585 And undretuk that gat to ga 583
And bad him sone his ledder ma
And hald him preve quhill thai mycht
Set for thar purpos on a nycht.

[*The climbing of Edinburgh castle rock*]

Sone efter was the ledder made,
590 And than the erle but mar abaid 588
Purvayt him a nycht prevely
With thretty men wycht and hardy,
And in a myrk nycht held thar way
That put thaim till full hard assay
595 And to gret perell sekyrly. 593
I trow mycht thai haiff sene clerly
That gat had nocht bene undretane
Thoucht thai to let thaim had nocht ane,
For the crag wes hey and hidwous
600 And the clymbing rycht peralous, 598
For hapnyt ony to slyd and fall
He suld sone be to-fruschyt all.
The nycht wes myrk as Ik hard say,
And to the fute sone cummyn ar thai
605 Off the crag that wes hey and schor, 603
Than Wilyame Fransoys thaim befor
Clamb in crykes forouth ay
And at the bak him folowyt thai.
With mekill payne quhile to quhile fra
610 Thai clamb into thai crykys sua 608
Quhile halff the crag thai clumbyn had
And thar a place thai fand sa brad

that they could just sit on [it]. They were breathless and
weary, and stayed there to get back their wind. (616) And
just as they were sitting so, above them, upon the wall, the
check-watches assembled together. Now, may God omnipo-
tent help [the Scots], for they are in great peril. (621) For if
they could see them, none of them would escape from that
place alive – they would strike them to death with stones,
[for] they could not help themselves at all. (625) The night
was extraordinarilly dark so that [the watches] caught no sight
of them, but nonetheless there was one of them that chucked
down a stone and said, 'Away, I see you fine', although he
saw them not a bit. (631) Over their heads flew the stone,
and they sat still, each of them lurking [there]. The watches,
when they heard nothing move, all passed together from that
sector, and, chatting, went further on their way. (636) Earl
Thomas and those that sat beside him on the rock very soon
climbed toward the wall hastily, and came there with great
effort and not without much danger and suffering, because it
far was more difficult to climb up from that point than [on
the first part] beneath.

(643) But never mind what difficulty they had, they came
without a halt to the wall that was just about twelve feet in
height. And without being seen or noticed, they set their
ladder to the wall, and first Francis climbed up before them
all, and then Sir Andrew Gray,

---

618. Check-watches. Those who did rounds to check that guards kept
watch.

643. The assault on Edinburgh castle. The description in Lanercost gives
a fuller picture:

> In the evening one day, the besiegers of that castle delivered an assault
> in force upon the south gate, because owing to the position of the
> castle there was no other quarter where an assault could be made.
> Those within gathered together at the gate and offered a stout resist-
> ance. But meanwhile other Scots climbed the rocks on the north side,
> which was very high and fell away steeply from the foot of the wall.
> There they laid ladders to the wall and climbed up in such numbers
> that those within could not withstand them. Thus they threw open
> the gates, admitted their comrades, got possession of the whole castle
> and killed the English. They razed the said castle to the ground.
> (*L*, 223; *LT*, 204)

Barbour has omitted the diversionary assault on the gate, perhaps
because his source did so.

649. Sir Andrew Gray. Although Barbour puts him in the Argyll campaign
of 1308 (47) he is not found among those at the St Andrews parliament
of 1309, nor again until this siege. Much later evidence suggests that

	That thai mycht syt on anerly,	
615	And thai war ayndles and wery	
	And thar abaid thar aynd to ta,	613
	And rycht as thai war syttand sua	
	Rycht aboune thaim up apon the wall	
	The chak-wachys assemblyt all.	
	Now help thaim God that all thing mai	
620	For in full gret perell ar thai!	618
	For mycht thai se thaim thar suld nane	
	Eschape out off that place unslane,	
	To dede with stanys thai suld thaim ding	
	That thai mycht halp thaimselvyn na thing.	
625	Bot wonder myrk wes the nycht	623
	Sua that thai off thaim had na sicht,	
	And nocht-forthi yete wes thar ane	
	Off thaim that swappyt doun a stane	
	And said, 'Away, I se you weile,'	
630	The-quhether he saw thaim nocht a dele.	628
	Out-our thar hedis flaw the stane	
	And thai sat still lurkand ilkane.	
	The wachys quhen thai herd nocht ster	
	Fra that ward samyn all passit er	
635	And carpand held fer by thar way.	633
	The erle Thomas alsone and thai	
	That on the crag thar sat him by	
	Towart the wall clamb hastily	
	And thidder come with mekill mayn	
640	And nocht but gret perell and payn.	638
	For fra thine up wes grevouser	
	To clymb up ne beneth be fer.	

[*The taking of Edinburgh castle*]

	Bot quhatkyn payne sua ever thai had	
	Rycht to the wall thai come but bad	
645	That had weile ner twelf fute of hycht,	643
	And forout persaving or sycht	
	Thai set thar ledder to the wall,	
	And syne Fransoys befor thaim all	
	Clamb up and syne Schyr Androw Gray,	

---

his family lands were in Berwickshire, so he may have returned there
during the truce of 1309. The various charters which he received suggest
that he had a connection with Thomas Randolph. Although not named
in the Declaration of Arbroath, he witnessed two royal charters in 1322;

and then the earl himself was the third man who took [to] the wall. (652) When those down below saw their lord climbing thus up upon the wall, they climbed after [them] all like men possessed. But before they had all come up, those who were [there] to test the watches, heard both movement and whispering, and also the rubbing of armour, and sturdily rushed at them, and they met them right boldly and slew them mercilessly. (662) Then through the castle rose the cry: 'Treason, treason', they shouted loud. Then some of them were so afraid that they fled, and jumped over the wall. But to tell the truth, they didn't all flee, for the constable, who was a tough [man], rushed forth all armed to the cry, and with him many bold and stout [men]. (670) The earl and his men were still fighting with those on the wall, but soon he defeated them all. By then his men had each come up the wall, and he soon took his way down to the castle. (676) He has put himself in great danger, for there were far more men therein than he [had], if [only] they had been in good spirit; but they were frightened. And nonetheless, with drawn weapons the constable and his company met him and his [men] right boldly. (683) There you could see great strife arise, for with weapons of many kinds they laid into [each] other regardless, with [all] their might, until swords that had been fair and bright were all bloody to the hilt. Then cries arose hideously, for those who were struck down or wounded shouted and bellowed with great roaring. (691) The good earl and his company fought in that fight so sturdily

---

he died between 1332 and 1335. (*SP4*, 269–70; *RRS5*, 334, 475, 480; *CDS3*, *1180*)

656. *B1907*, 178 translates 'the officers of the watch'.

684. regardless: literally, in many ways.

650 And syne the erle himselff perfay   648
Was the thrid that the wall can ta.
Quhen thai thar-doune thar lord sua
Saw clumbyne up apon the wall
As woud men thai clamb eftre all,
655 Bot or all up clumbene war thai   653
Thai that war wachys till assay
Hard steryng and preve speking
And alsua fraying off armyng
And on thaim schot full sturdely,
660 And thai met thaim rycht hardely   658
And slew off thaim dispitously.
Than throu the castell rais the cry,
'Tresoun! Tresoun!' thai cryit fast.
Than sum of thaim war sua agast
665 That thai fled and lap our the wall,   663
Bot to sa swyth thai fled nocht all,
For the constabill that wes hardy
All armyt schot furth to the cry
And with him fele hardy and stout.
670 Yeyt wes the erle with his rout   668
Fechtand with thaim apon the wall
Bot sone he discumfit thaim all.
Be that his men war cummyn ilkan
Up to the wall and he has tane
675 His way doun to the castell sone.   673
In gret perell he has him doyn
For thai war fer ma men tharin
And thai had bene of gud covyn
Than he, bot thai effrayit war,
680 And nocht-forthi with wapnys bar   678
The constabill and his cumpany
Met him and his rycht hardely.
Thar mycht men se gret bargane ris,
For with wapnys of mony wis
685 Thai dang on other at thar mycht   683
Quhill swerdis that war fayr and brycht
War till the hiltis all bludy.
Then hydwysly begouth the cry
For thai that fellyt or stekyt war
690 Hidwysly gan cry and rar.   688
The gud erle and his cumpany
Faucht in that fycht sa sturdely

that all their foes were driven back. The constable was slain right there, and, when he fell, the rest fled where they best might to safety – they dared not stay nor make resistance. (698) The earl was dealt with there so hotly that, had it not happened by chance that the constable was slain there, [the earl] would have been in great danger there, but when they fled there was nothing more [to be done] but each man, to save his life, fled forth to live out his days, and some slid down over the [castle] wall.

(706) The earl has taken all the castle, for there was none dared withstand him. I never heard of where in any country, a castle was taken so bravely, except Tyre alone, where Alexander the [Great], who conquered Babylon's tower, leaped from a berfrey on to the wall where he defended himself really bravely among his foes, until his noble chivalry went over the wall with ladders, holding back neither for death nor for fear.

(719) For after they knew for certain that the king was in the town, there was nothing that could hold them back at that time, for all danger was as nothing. They climbed the walls and Aristeus came first to the good king, where he was defending himself with all his might, in such a hard fight, I tell you, that he was down on one knee. (728) He had set his back to a tree, for fear that they should attack him from behind. Aristeus then hastened sturdily and speedily to the battle, and launched on them so boldly that the king was rescued.

---

710. The siege of Troy. From the *Roman d'Alixandre*, branch 2, lines 1965–92.

713. Berfrois. A berfrey, that is a tall tower, a siege tower here; the *beffroi* in northern French towns today. By a false connection with 'bell' comes the modern English 'belfry'

That all thar fayis ruschyt war.
The constable wes slane rycht thar,
695 And fra he fell the ramanand 693
Fled quhar thai best mycht to warand,
Thai durst nocht bid to ma debate.
The erle wes handlyt thar sa hat
That had it nocht hapnyt throu cas
700 That the constable thar slane then was 698
He had bene in gret perell thar,
Bot quhen thai fled thar wes no mar,
Bot ilk man to sauff his lyff
Fled furth his dayis for to dryve,
705 And sum slaid doune out-our the wall. 703

[Comparison with the taking of Tyre by Alexander the Great]

The erle has tane the castell all
For then wes nane durst him withstand.
I hard nevyr quhar in nakin land
Wes castell tane sa hardely
710 Outakyn Tyre all anerly, 708
Quhen Alexandir the conquerour
That conqueryt Babylonys tour
Lap fra a berfrois on the wall
Quhar he amang his fayis all
715 Defendyt him full douchtely 713
Quhill his noble chevalry
With leddris our the wall yeid
That nother left for deid no dreid,
For thai wyst weill that the king
720 Wes in the toune thar wes na thing 718
Intill that tym that stynt thaim moucht,
For all the perell thai set at nocht.
Thai clamb the wall and Aristé
Come fyrst to the gud king quhar he
725 Defendyt him with all his mycht 723
That then sa hard wes set Ik hycht
That he wes fellit on a kne,
He till his bak had set a tre
For dred thai suld behind assaile.
730 Aristé then to the bataile 728
Sped him in all hy sturdely
And dang on thaim sa douchtely
That the king weile reskewit was,

(734) For his men climbed over the wall in various places, sought the king and rescued him with fierce fighting, and won the town forthwith. Apart from this success alone, I never heard, in times past, [of] where a castle was so bravely taken. (741) And of this capture that I am speaking of, the good holy queen, St Margaret, knew in her time through a revelation from Him who knows and understands all things. (745) So, in place of prophecy, she left a merry sign, namely that in her chapel she had well portrayed a castle, a ladder standing up to the wall, with a man climbing on it, and written above him (as old men say) in French: '*Gardez-vous de Francois.*' (753) And from these words, which she had written thus, men expected that Frenchmen would take it; but he who climbed up thus secretly was called Francis – she wrote that as a prophecy which duly came to pass afterwards, just as she said, for taken it was, and *Francois* led them up to that place.

(761) In this way Edinburgh was taken, and all those that were within were taken or slain or jumped the wall. [The Scots] seized all their goods and searched every house. Sir Piers Lubaud, who had been taken, as I said once before, they found sitting in prison, bound with fetters. (769) They brought him to the earl at once and he had him released forthwith; then [Lubaud] became the king's man.

---

747. The chapel of St Margaret in Edinburgh castle remains.

766. Piers Lubaud. Probably he was indeed rescued from a dungeon, for King Robert rewarded him with several estates. But on 8 March, 1316 he is described as 'deceased, recently convicted in our [Robert's] court of betrayal (*prodicio*) of us and our kingdom'. Gray comments on him that 'he became Scots at the faith of Robert Bruce, who afterwards accused him of treason and caused him to be hanged and drawn. It was said that he suspected him because he was too outspoken, believing him nevertheless to be English at heart, on his guard not to give [Bruce] offence.' Perhaps he had betrayed the king's unsuccessful attack on Berwick in January 1316 (which Barbour ignores) and was tried in a parliament at Edinburgh in early March; Barbour ignores his later career. (*S*, 140; *ST*, 52; *VitaEd*, 48; *CDS3*, 254; *RRS5*, 84)

For his men into syndri plas
735 Clamb our the wall and soucht the king 733
And him reskewit with hard fechting
And wane the toun deliverly.
Outane this taking anerly
I herd nevyr in na tym gane
740 Quhar castell wes sa stoutly tane. 738

[*St Margaret's prophecy*]

And off this taking that I mene
Sanct Margaret the gud haly quene
Wyst in hyr tyme throu reveling
Off Him that knawis and wate all thing,
745 Tharfor in sted of prophecy 743
Scho left a taknyng rycht joly,
That is that intill hyr chapele
Scho gert weile portray a castell,
A ledder up to the wall standand
750 And a man up thar-apon climband, 748
And wrat outht him as auld men sais
In Frankis, 'Gardys vous de Francais.'
And for this word scho gert writ sua
Men wend the Frankis-men suld it ta,
755 Bot for Fraunsois hattyn wes he 753
That sua clamb up in preveté
Scho wrat that as in prophecy,
And it fell efterwart sothly
Rycht as scho said, for tane it was
760 And Fraunsoys led thaim up that pas. 758

[*Treatment of Piers Lubaud; rewards of the earl of Moray*]

On this wis Edinburgh wes tane
And thai that war tharin ilkane
Other tane or slane or lap the wall.
Thar gudis haiff thai sesyt all
765 And souch the hous everilkane. 763
Schyr Peris Lubaut that wes tane,
As I said er, befor thai fand
In boyis and hard festnyng sittand.
Thai brocht him till the erle in hy
770 And he gert lous him hastily,
Then he become the kingis man.

They sent word to the king then, and told [him] how the castle was taken; he hurried there with a company of many men, and had tower and wall mined [to collapse] completely to the ground. (778) Then he travelled all over the land taking the country to his peace. The earl was valued highly for this deed, which was so [praise]worthy. (782) The king, who held him so deserving, was pleased and joyful, more than the rest, and to maintain his standing gave him plentiful rents and fair lands. [Moray] achieved such a high reputation that all spoke of his great generosity; he greatly confounded all his foes for he never fled because the fighting was fierce. (790) What more shall I say of his prowess? His great courage and his liberality still – and often – make him famous.

(793) In the time that the enterprises which I explained were accomplished so bravely at these castles, bold Sir Edward Bruce had reduced completely to his disposal all Galloway and Nithsdale, and knocked down all the castles, tower and wall, right into the ditches. (801) Then he heard tell, and knew well, that there was a peel in Rutherglen; he went there with his company and in short time took it. (805) Then he took the road to Dundee which was then held, as I heard, against the king;

784-85. This repeats the theme of 268-69, but Moray is not known to have received further lands before Bannockburn.

796. Edward Bruce. In 1312, perhaps at the Ayr parliament in July, he was made earl of Carrick. Barbour always denies him any title other than 'Sir'.

797. Galloway and Nithsdale. In July 1312 it was reported that the king had held a parliament at Ayr, intending to send Edward Bruce to attack northern England, while he himself attacked Dumfries, Buittle and Caerlaverock. But if this is correct, only the outliers, e.g. Buittle, can have fallen at this time. Six months later Dumfries was surrendered by Dungal Macdowall to Robert Bruce on 7 February, 1313, within a month of the taking of Perth and two months after an assault on Berwick. Caerlaverock must have been lost too because the king attacked Man on 18 May, 1313, taking Rushen castle on 12 June, 1313. There is no evidence that Edward Bruce was active in the south-west in 1313, but he could have been with the king. (*CDS3, 279, 304*; Barrow, *Bruce*, 193)

802. Rutherglen. A minor peel which was already under siege in November 1308; Barbour is the source for associating this siege with Edward Bruce, presumably on his return from Galloway. It must have fallen at this time. (*RotSc1*, 60)

805. Dundee. One of the sad omissions from the poem is any account of the taking of Dundee, which was under siege in February–March 1312; there seems to have been an arrangement that if not relieved it would be surrendered, and an appropriate concluding date would be

Thai send word to the king rycht than
And tauld how the castell wes tane,
And he in hy is thidder gane
775 With mony ane in cumpany 773
And gert myne doun all halily
Bath tour and wall rycht to the grond,
And syne our all the land gan fond
Sesand the countre till his pes.
780 Off this deid that sa worthy wes 778
The erle wes prisyt gretumly,
The king that saw him sa worthi
Wes blyth and joyfull our the lave
And to manteyme his stat him gave
785 Rentis and landis fayr inewch, 783
And he to sa gret worschip dreuch
That all spak off his gret bounté.
Hys fayis gretly stonayit he
For he fled never for force off fycht.
790 Quhat sall I mar say off his mycht? 788
His gret manheid and his bounté
Gerris him yeit renownyt be.

[*Places taken by Sir Edward Bruce; his siege of Stirling castle*]

In this tyme that thir jupertys
Off thir castellis that I devis
795 War eschevyt sa hardely, 793
Schyr Edward the Bruce the hardy
Had all Galloway and Nydysdale
Wonnyn till his liking all haile
And doungyn doun the castellis all
800 Rycht in the dyk bath tour and wall. 798
He hard then say and new it weill
That into Ruglyne wes a pele,
Thidder he went with his menye
And wonnyn it in schort tyme has he,
805 Syne to Dunde he tuk the way 803
That then wes haldyne as Ic herd say
Agayne the king, tharfor in hy

Easter, 26 March, 1312. The king was certainly involved, for he held
a parliament at Inchture, a few miles away, about 7 April, and was at
Dundee (now his) on 12 April. But Edward Bruce was not a witness
to the charter dated at Inchture, so may have been at Dundee with
day-to-day charge of the siege. (*RotSc1*, 108–9; *RRS5*, 17–20)

so boldly he set siege to it, and lay there till it was surrendered. Next he sets out to Stirling, where good Sir Philip Mowbray was warden, a valiant man when put to the test. (813) [He] had the keeping [of] that castle from the English king. He set a close siege to it. They often skirmished robustly, but no great chivalry was done. (818) Sir Edward lay about [the castle] for a pretty long time from [when] the siege began, that's to say from Lent till before St John's mass. (822) The English folk who were inside began to lack victuals then. Then Sir Philip, the valiant man, negotiated, till they had agreed that if, a year from coming Midsummer, it had not been relieved by a force, then without fail he would surrender the castle altogether. They secured that agreement firmly.

810-30. The siege of Stirling. The chronology of Barbour here is most misleading, though it has commanded almost total acceptance. The crucial lines are 820-21 and 826. Supposedly the siege began in Lent, over a year before Bannockburn, i.e. 4 March-15 April, 1313, yet it began after the fall of Roxburgh and Edinburgh in Lent 1314. There was an agreement to surrender the castle on 24 June, 1314, but, although such agreements were quite common, I can find no other example where the period allowed for relief was more than a few months; Barbour's chronology is quite unrealistic. It also clashes with record evidence that Edward II planned from late November 1313 to come to Scotland. He summoned troops in March-April 1314 for a muster in April, then May, and came north in the latter month. Suddeenly, on 27 May, a note of desperation entered renewed orders isssued from Newminster, near Morpeth (Northumberland): the expedition is now, *for the first time*, for the rescue of Stirling castle, which will otherwise have to be surrendered in terms of an agreement entered into by the constable. The army will have to go to strong and morose (*morosis*, marshy?) places, inaccessible to cavalry, so the sheriffs must send their full quotas of infantry – and the earlier figures are repeated – to Wark on Monday 10 June (which was the date of muster announced on 23 December, 1313). The agreement for the surrender of Stirling was told to Edward II by Mowbray at Newminster on 26-27 May; it would have been made about a week, no more than ten days, earlier, in the third week of May. The notice was so remarkably short that incredulous later writers extended it to a whole year, having picked up that other period of notice from King Robert's ultimatum to the Anglo-Scots (see note to 305). (*RotSci*, 118-27)

He set a sege tharto stoutly
And lay thar quhill it yoldyn was.
810 To Strevillyne syne the way he tais   808
Quhar gud Schyr Philip the Mowbray
That wes sa douchty at assay
Wes wardane and had in keping
That castell of the Inglis king.
815 Thartill a sege thai set stythly,   813
Thai bykyrrit oftsys sturdely
Bot gret chevalry done wes nane.
Schyr Edward fra the sege wes tane
A weile lang tyme about it lay,
820 Fra the Lentryne that is to say   818
Quhill forouth the Sanct Jhonys mes.
The Inglis folk that tharin wes
Begouth to failye vitaill be than.
Than Schyr Philip that douchti man
825 Tretyt quhill thai consentit war   823
That gyff at mydsomer the neyst yer
To cum it war nocht with bataile
Reskewyt, then that foroutyn faile
He suld the castell yauld quytly,
830 That connand band thai sickerly.   828

And when this agreement had been made thus, Sir Philip rode to England, and told the king the whole story, how he had a whole twelvemonth (as was written in their reckoning) to rescue Stirling with a force. (7) And when he heard Sir Philip say that Scotsmen had fixed a day to fight, and that he had such an interval to get ready, he was very pleased. (11) [He] said that it was great presumption which had pushed them to such folly, for he expected before that day to be so prepared and in such [good] order, that no power could withstand him there. (16) And when the lords of England heard that this day had been fixed openly, they [too] judged it great folly, and thought they would have it all their [own] way if men waited to fight them. But a fool's thinking is often daft and wise men's intentions don't always pan out as they wish; a little stone, as men say,

---

2. Mowbray rode to England. That Mowbray went to Edward II is confirmed by note to 4 extract (b). We can be pretty sure that they met at Newminster in Yorkshire on 26 or 27 May, 1314. See note to 10.810.

4. The twelve month. The accounts by (a) Lanercost, and (b) the *Vita Edwardi* show that no such lapse of time occurred; (c) Gray however is ambiguous; the wording of his source may also have misled Barbour:

(a) The Scots razed Edinburgh castle to the ground ... Having accomplished this success they marched to Stirling and besieged that castle with their army ... On Tuesday [16 April] Edward Bruce ... invaded England by way of Carlisle with an army, contrary to agreement ... (*L*, 223–24; *LT*, 204–5)

(b) He took two of the king of England's strongest fortresses, namely Edinburgh and Roxburgh ... Robert Bruce next addressed himself to the siege of Stirling castle. The lord Edward [I] laid siege to this castle ... for three months [in 1304] before he could take it . When the warden of the castle saw that the siege had already begun, that their stores were insufficient, that Robert and the Scots lay continually in ambush, he agreed to a truce, on condition that he would either get the king of England to come and defend the castle, or, if he could not persuade the king to do this, he would give up the castle without delay. The request was granted and the truce ratified, and the day of [24 June] was assigned for a term. About the beginning of Lent messengers came to [Edward II] with news of the ... capture of the castles ... the constable of Stirling came too and pointed out to the king how he had been compelled by necessity to enter upon the truce ... (*VitaEd*, 48–49)

(c) After the earl of Atholl had taken the town of Perth ... Robert

[*Criticism of the compact about Stirling castle*]

	And quhen this connand thus wes mad
	Schir Philip intill Ingland raid
	And tauld the king all haile his tale,
	How he a tuelf moneth all hale
5	Had as it wryten wes in thar taile
	To reskew Strevillyne with bataill.
	And quhen he hard Schyr Philip say
	That Scottismen had set a day
	To fecht and that sic space he had
10	To purvay him he wes rycht glaid,
	And said it wes gret sukudry
	That set thaim apon sic foly,
	For he thocht to be or that day
	Sa purvayit and in sic aray
15	That thar suld nane strenth him withstand,
	And quhen the lordis off Ingland
	Herd that this day wes set planly
	Thai jugyt all to gret foly,
	And thoucht to haiff all thar liking
20	Giff men abaid thaim in fechting,
	Bot oft faillys the fulis thocht
	And yeit wys mennys ay cummys nocht
	To sic end as thai wene allwayis.
	A litill stane oft, as men sayis,

---

marched in force before Stirling castle, where ... Mowbray ... made terms with ... Robert Bruce to surrender the castle ... unless he should be relieved, that is unless the English army came within three leagues of the castle within eight days of [24 June] in the summer next to come, he would surrender the castle. The king of England came there for that reason, where [Mowbray] met him three leagues from the castle on [23 June] and told him he need approach no nearer, for he considered himself relieved. (*S*, 141; *ST*, 53)

6. Bataill. Possibly 'by battle'.

13. That day. i.e. 24 June. On 28 November, 1313 Edward II announced his intention to be with an army at Berwick by 24 June, 1314 to deal with his Scottish enemies. On 23 December, 1313 he summoned an army to assemble there on 10 June, 1314. In March 1314 orders were issued for the provisioning of the host. He chose 24 June; the choice of that date by Mowbray for the surrender of the castle was made in the light of Edward II's declared intention, and did not dictate it.

can often cause a big heap to tumble. (26) No man's might can stand against the grace of God, who rules everything; He knows what everything leads to and orders everything at His will and after His ordinance.

(31) When Sir Edward, as I told you, had given so extreme a day for the surrender or rescue of Stirling, he went very soon to the king and told what negotiations he had had and what day he had given them. (37) The king, when he heard the day, said: 'That was unwisely done, *perfay*; I never yet heard of where so long a warning was given to so mighty a king as the king of England is. Because he now has in his hands England, Ireland, and Wales too, yes, and Aquitaine, with all those who live under his lordship, and still a part of Scotland. (47) He is so well provided with treasure, that he can have abundance of mercenaries. [But] we are few against so many. God may assign our destinies right well, but we are placed at risk to lose or win then speedily.' (53) Sir Edward said 'God counsel me! Even if he and all that he can lead come, we shall fight, however many they are.' When the king heard his brother speak thus about the battle so boldly, he honoured him greatly in his heart and said: 'Brother, since it has happened that this thing has been undertaken thus, let's get ready for it manfully; (62) [let] all that love us tenderly and [love] the freedom of this country, equip themselves to be ready at that time with all the power that ever they can

---

31. Sir Edward Bruce. At the note to 10.810 I have indicated the difficulties about Edward's activities. He must have gone to Roxburgh in late February 1314. About 14 March (the day of Edinburgh's fall) Mowbray, cut off from supplies via Edinburgh, sent an agent south to seek supplies for Stirling, authorised by Edward II on 25 March. If the siege began about the end of March, it was probably under King Robert, because Edward Bruce made his unauthorised agreement with Mowbray about mid May, long after he had taken his men on a pillaging expedition in Cumbria on 16 April. He was there for three or more days during which he tried to take Carlisle, perhaps to equal the 'chivalry' of Douglas and Moray. Lanercost says that 'the Scots did all those wrongs at that time because the people of that March had not paid them the tribute which they had pledged themselves to pay on certain days. Although the Scots had hostages from the sons and heirs of the knights of the country in full security for sums agreed, yet they did not refrain from committing the aforesaid wrongs.' One must ask whether this expedition had royal approval – and indeed whether the prominence of Douglas, Moray and Edward Bruce at this time, the king not even visiting Roxburgh or Edinburgh, and perhaps leaving Stirling, signifies a serious bout of royal illness, during which his captains used a pretty free hand. Edward Bruce would be in charge at Stirling only after 19 April.

25   May ger weltyr a mekill wayn,
       Na mannys mycht may stand agayn
       The grace off God that all thing steris,
       He wate quhat till all thing afferis
       And disponys at his liking
30   Efter his ordynance all thing.

[*King Robert criticises his brother*]

       Quhen Schyr Edward, as I you say,
       Had gevyn sa outrageous a day
       To yeld or reskew Strevillyne,
       Rycht to the king he went him syne
35   And tauld quhat tretys he had mad
       And quhat day he thaim gevyn had.
       The king said quhen he hard the day,
       'That wes unwisly doyn, perfay.
       Ik herd never quhar sa lang warnyng
40   Wes gevyn to sa mychty a king
       As is the king off Ingland,
       For he has now intill hand
       Ingland, Ireland and Walis alsua
       And Aquitayngne yeit with all tha,
45   And off Scotland yeit a party
       Dwellis under his senyoury,
       And off tresour sa stuffyt is he
       That he may wageouris haiff plenté,
       And we are quhoyne agayne sa fele.
50   God may rycht weill oure werdys dele,
       Bot we ar set in juperty
       To tyne or wyn then hastely.'
       Schyr Edward said, 'Sa God me rede,
       Thocht he and all that he may led
55   Cum, wes sall fecht, all war thai ma.'
       Quhen the king hard his broder sua
       Spek to the bataile sa hardyly
       He prisyt him in hys hart gretumly
       And said, 'Broder, sen sua is gane
60   That this thing thus is undretane
       Schap we us tharfor manlely,
       And all that luffis us tenderly
       And the fredome off this countré
       Purvay thaim at that time to be
65   Boune with all mycht that ever thai may,

[have], so that if our foes try to rescue Stirling by battle, we shall make them fail in that purpose.

(69) To this they all agreed and bade their men all make themselves ready, to be prepared against that day in the best way that ever they could. (73) Then all from Scotland that were worthy to fight, put all their effort into equipping themselves against that day. They procured weapons and armour, and all that is necessary for a fight. (78) And the mighty king of England prepared himself in such lavish order that I truly have never yet heard tell that English men made more preparations than they did then for battle. (83) And when the time had come near he mustered all his power, and, apart from his own chivalry, which was so huge it was fearsome, he had with him good men of great spirit from many a far country. (89) He had worthy chivalry from France in his company; the count of Hainault was there also, and with him men who were worthy from Gascony and Germany. (94) From the duchy of Britanny he had brave fine-looking men, thoroughly armed, both on foot and hand. He had gathered there the chivalry of the whole [of] England so thoroughly that he left none capable of using a weapon or suitable for fighting in the field. (101) From Wales and Ireland he also had with him a great company ; from Poitou Aquitaine and Bayonne he had a great many of high renown. And from Scotland he still had then

---

91–94. Foreign assistance to Edward II. There would be some Gascon knights in the host but otherwise there is little evidence of foreigners; the count of Hainault served with Edward III against the Scots in 1327, but he was not at Bannockburn. Baston's poem mentions four Germans in the English army. (*Bower* 6, 369)

101–3. Troops from Edward II's other possessions. Almost 5,000 men were summoned from Wales and its Marches. There were elaborate arrangements to secure service from Irish magnates and 4,000 infantry were to be levied; it is not clear how many reached the English army, but the earl of Ulster certainly brought his service. Those named in 103 would be covered by Gascony in 93. Few men can have served from there.

105. Men from Scotland. Sir Alexander Seton was in his army, the earl of Dunbar was not; the Scottish numbers would be very small.

Sua giff that our fayis assay
To reskew Strevilline throu bataill
That we off purpos ger thaim faill.'

[*Both sides prepare for an English invasion; King Edward's resources*]

To this thai all assentyt ar
70 And bad thar men all mak thaim yar
For to be boun agayne that day
On the best wis that ever thai may.
Than all that worthi war to fycht
Off Scotland set all hale thar mycht
75 To purvay thaim agane that day,
Wapynnys and armouris purvayit thai
And all that afferis to fechting.
And in Ingland the mychty king
Purvayit him in sa gret aray
80 That certis hard I never say
That Inglismen mar aparaile
Maid than did than for bataill,
For quhen the tyme wes cummyn ner
He assemblit all his power,
85 And but his awne chevalry
That wes sa gret it wes ferly
He had of mony ser countré
With him gud men of gret bounté.
Of Fraunce worthi chevalry
90 He had intill his cumpany,
The erle off Henaud als wes thar
And with him men that worthi war,
Off Gascoyne and off Almany
And off the duche of Bretayngny
95 He had wycht men and weill farand
Armyt clenly bath fute and hand,
Off Ingland to the chevalry   97*
He had gaderyt sa clenly   98*
That nane left that mycht wapynnys weld   97
100 Or mycht war to fecht in feild,   98
All Walis als with him had he
And off Irland a gret mengne,
Off Pouty Aquitane and Bayoun
He had mony off gret renoune,
105 And off Scotland he had yeit then   103*

a large company of worthy men.
(107) When all these were mustered together, he had with him there of fighters a hundred thousand men and more; forty thousand of them were armed, both head and hand, and horsed. (112) Moreover, of these three thousand were with covered horse in plate and mail, to make the front of the division; and he had fifty thousand archers, apart from hobelars. With men on foot and petty followers who looked after equipment and food he had so many it was terrifying. (120) So many carts went along with them there, that, apart from those that carried equipment and also that were loaded with tents, plate and furnishing for chamber and hall, wine, wax, shot and provisions, eight score were loaded with poultry. (127) They were so many where they rode by, and their divisions were so broad and their wagon train took up so much space that men could see that great host occupy the land widely. (132) Anyone who had been nearby could see then many a worthy and brave man, many a gaily armoured knight, and many a sturdy frisky steed, arrayed in rich attire,

---

109–19. Barbour's breakdown of 100,000 seems to be: 40,000 men-at-arms, of whom 3,000 were heavy cavalry; 50,000 archers (apparently the only infantry); hobelars, who logically would number 10,000. The surprisingly modest figure in this vastly exaggerated reckoning is 3,000 heavy cavalry, which is comparable with the *Vita Edwardi*'s 2,000 cavalry with numerous infantry. Other English chronicles give no figures. But the plans for the expedition are revealing. On 9 March, when the bishop of Durham was instructed to raise 1,000 men, they were to muster at Newcastle on 31 March; on 24 March general orders went out to Wales, the Midlands and the north to raise 10,540 men to be there at 28 April. On 20 April it was announced that more men would be needed and the same English sheriffs had a further 9,500 men to raise for the assembly at Berwick on 19 May. This summons of infantry was repeated on 27 May; again the total was 21,540 men, apart from any Irish. The implication, however, is that men were not appearing in the numbers demanded, and there has been much debate on the true size of the English infantry force. J. E. Morris suggested that it may have numbered 15,000. But according to the pay records, in 1319, when the army summoned was of much the same size as in 1314, there was a show-rate of 25%. In 1322, when some 55,000 infantry were summoned (including 7,000 Irish), plus a man from each vill, there was again a show-rate of about 25% though the men from the vills added significantly to the force. See notes to 17.283 and 18.235. Some men would escape the record, but a generous allowance would raise the show-rate to 33% in 1314, some 7,000 infantry. For cavalry (about 2,000) see note to 466.
120. Carts. Extensive preparations were made for transporting supplies

A gret menye of worthy men.   104*

[*The appearance of the English host*]

     Quhen all thir sammyn assemblit war   105*
     He had of fechtaris with him thar   106*
     Ane hunder thousand men and ma   103
110 And fourty thousand war of tha   104
     Armyt on hors bath heid and hand,
     And of thai yeit war thre thousand
     With helyt hors in plate and mailye
     To mak the front off the batailye,
115 And fyfty thousand off archeris   109
     He had foroutyn hobeleris,
     And men of fute and small rangale
     That yemyt harnays and vittaile
     He had sa fele it wes ferly.
120 Off cartis als thar yeid thaim by   114
     Sa fele that, but all thai that bar
     Harnays and als that chargyt war
     With pailyounys and veschall with-all
     And aparaile of chambyr and hall
125 And wyne and wax schot and vittaile,   119
     Aucht scor wes chargyt with pulaile.
     Thai war sa fele quhar that thai raid
     And thar bataillis war sa braid
     And sua gret roume held thar chare
130 That men that mekill ost mycht se   124
     Ourtak the landis largely.
     Men mycht se than that had bene by
     Mony a worthi man and wycht
     And mony ane armur gayly dycht
135 And mony a sturdy sterand stede   129
     Arayit intill ryche wede,

---

by ship. The *Vita Edwardi* comments that 'the multitude of wagons, if
they had been placed from end to end, would have taken up a space
of 20 leagues', and other narrative sources make similar comments.
Indeed that feature of the army seems to have impressed as much as
the number of men. But there are no orders for carts, until on 6 June,
1314, 13 sheriffs from the Midlands were ordered to send to Berwick:
for 8 July ten units each of a cart (*caretta*) with four horses and one
cart (*carra*) with eight oxen, 82 units for 15 July, 70 units for 22 July
and 24 units for 1 August. Edward expected his force to be in Scotland
for some six weeks. (*VitaEd*, 50; *RotSci*, 127)

126. Pulaile. C: fewale.

many helmets and habergeouns, shields and spears and pen-
nons, and so many handsome knights that it seemed indeed
that in a fight they would vanquish the whole world.
(142) Why should I make my tale longer? They all came to
Berwick; some took their lodging there and some lodged
outside the towns in tents and pavilions. (147) And when the
king saw his host, so great, such good men and so efficient,
he had real pleasure in his mind, and was very confident that
there was not in the world a king who could withstand him.
(152) He thought [he had] won everything into his own hands,
and distributed the lands of Scotland widely among his men
– he was generous with other men's lands! And those who
were of his company threatened all the Scots with big words
– but in spite of that, before they fulfil their purpose holes will
be torn in good cloth! (161) The [English] king, by the advice
of his men, divided his men into ten divisions. There were a
good ten thousand in each, who intended to stand stalwartly
and fight stoutly in the battle, and not leave because of the
enemy's strength. (167) He appointed leaders to each division
who were known to be good commanders. To two famous
earls, those of Gloucester and Hereford, he gave command of
the vanguard with many men at their command mustered in
truly good battle-order. (174) They were so chivalrous that
they believed that if they came to the fight, no force could
withstand their might. And the king, when his army was

143. Berwick. The original summons was to Berwick but on 27 May this
   was shifted to Wark. The king and some of the army were at Berwick
   11–14 June, 1314.
162. Ten divisions of 10,000 each. This is fanciful, though there might
   have been ten divisions of infantry on the march, from S. Wales, N.
   Wales, Durham, Northumberland, Yorkshire, Lincs. Chester + Lancs.
   Shropshire, Notts. + Derby, Warwick + Leics. They would have varied
   in size: 4,000 were summoned from Yorks., 500 from Warwick + Leics.
167. Leaders.
   The earl of Pembroke he sent ahead with a force of knights to seek
   out the ambushes of the Scots and prepare the king's route into
   Scotland ... The earl of Lancaster, Earl Warenne, the earl of Arundel
   and the earl of Warwick did not come, but sent knights equipped to
   do their due service for them in the army ... The earl of Gloucester
   and the earl of Hereford commanded the first line. (*VitaEd.* 50–51)
   About the feast of Whitsun [26 May] the king ... approached the
   borders of Scotland, also the earls of Gloucester, Hereford, Pembroke,
   Angus, Sir Robert Clifford, Sir John Comyn, Sir Henry Beaumont,
   Sir John Segrave, Sir Pain Typtoft, Sir Edmund Mauley, Sir Ingram
   Umfraville with other barons, knights and a splendid and numerous
   army. (*L*, 228; *LT*, 206)

Mony helmys and haberjounys
Scheldis and speris and penounys, 132*
And sa mony a cumbly knycht 132
140 That it semyt that into fycht 133
Thai suld vencus the warld all haile.

[*The dispositions of the English host; the march from Berwick*]

Quhy suld I mak to lang my taile?
To Berwik ar thai cummyn ilkane
And sum tharin has innys tane
145 And sum logyt without the town ys 138
In tentis and in pailyounys.
And quhen the king his ost has sene
So gret and sa gud men and clene
He wes rycht joyfull in his thocht
150 And weile supposyt that thar wes nocht 143
In warld a king mycht him withstand,
Him thocht all wonnyn till his hand,
And largly amang his men
The land of Scotland delt he then,
155 Off other mennys thing larg wes he. 148
And thai that war off his menye
Manausyt the Scottismen hely
With gret wordis, bot nocht-forthi
Or thai cum all to thar entent
160 Howis in haile claith sall be rent. 153
The king throu consaile of his men
His folk delt in bataillis ten,
In ilkane war weile ten thousand
That lete thai stalwartly suld stand
165 In the bataile and stythly fycht 158
And leve nocht for thar fayis mycht.
He set ledaris till ilk bataile
That knawin war of gud governaile,
And till renownyt erlis twa
170 Off Glosyster and Herfurd war tha 163
He gaf the vaward in leding
With mony men at thar bidding
Ordanyt into full gud aray.
Thai war sa chevalrous that thai
175 Trowyt giff thai come to fycht 168
Thar suld na strenth withstand thar mycht.
And the king quhen his mengne wer

divided into various divisions, made orders for his own division and who should be at his bridle. (181) He placed Sir Giles de Argentan on one side to take his reins, and Sir Aymer de Valence, who was distinguished, on the other side, for he trusted in their supreme [and] great spirit above [that of] the remainder. (187) And when the king had ordered in this way his divisions and his command[-structure], as I've told you here, he rose early one morning and set out on the way from Berwick. They covered both hills and valleys as the broad divisions rode, separated, over the fields. (195) The sun was shining bright and clear, and arms that were newly polished, flashed in the sun's rays, in such a way that the whole land was aflame with banners fluttering right freshly and penoncels waving in the wind. (201) So many were they, with divers coats of arms, that it would [require] great skill to describe [them]; for if I wanted to recite all their equipment, their appearance and their bearing, even if I could I'd find it difficult. (206) The king with all that great force rode straight to Edinburgh. They were altogether too many to fight with few folk of a poor land; but where God helps, what can withstand [Him]? (211) When King Robert heard that English men in such splendour and in such numbers had come into his land, he hastily caused a general summons of his men. And they all came willingly to the Torwood, where the king had ordered [them] to make their muster.

181. Giles d'Argentan. Since being at Methven and Loch Tay, d'Argentan had set out for Rhodes to help the Knights of St John. He had been taken prisoner in Greece and was imprisoned at Salonika till Edward II secured his release. Gray and the *Vita Edwardi* confirm that d'Argentan was responsible for the king's rein. (Barrow, *Bruce*, 207)

183. Aymer de Valence, one of the few earls present; Barbour never calls him earl of Pembroke.

191. Berwick. This was the place of muster. According to the *Vita Edwardi* Edward II left Berwick on 18 June, but privy seal letters were dated there until 14 June, and on 18 June at Soutra. The army marched by the latter route to Edinburgh, not along the coast.

200. Penoncels, small penons.

207. Edinburgh, where the castle would be slighted and untenable. The English probably reached Edinburgh about 19–20 June, where there was a short rest. It should be remembered that daylight would last a good 18 hours at this time.

214. The Scottish summons. It is not known when the king issued orders for a muster, nor to what day, though it may be presumed that he anticipated that the English could arrive at least a week before midsummer.

217. The Torwood. See Bannockburn Commentary.

Divisit intill bataillis ser
His awyne bataill ordanyt he
180 And quha suld at his bridill be, 173
Schyr Gilis Argente he set
Apon a half his reyngye to get,
And off Valence Schyr Amery
On other half that wes worthy,
185 For in thar soverane bounté 178
Out-our the lave affyit he.
Quhen the king apon this kyn wys
Had ordanyt as Ik her divis
His bataillis and his stering
190 He rais arly in a mornyng 183
And fra Berwik he tuk the way.
Bath hillis and valis hely thai
As the bataillis that war braid
Departyt our the feldis raid.
195 The sone wes brycht and schynand cler 188
And armouris that burnysyt wer
Sua blomyt with the sonnys beme
That all the land wes in a leme,
Baneris rycht fayrly flawmand
200 And penselys to the wynd wavand 193
Sua fele thar wer of ser quentis
That it war gret slycht for to divise,
And suld I tell all thar affer
Thar contenance and thar maner
205 Thoucht I couth I suld combryt be. 198
The king with all that gret menye
Till Edinbyrgh he raid him rycht,
Thai war all-out to fele to fycht
With few folk of a symple land,
210 Bot quhar God helpys quhat ma withstand? 203

[*Muster of the Scottish army; its size and commanders*]

The King Robert quhen he hard say
That Inglismen in sic aray
And into sua gret quantité
Come in his land, in hy gert he
215 His men be somound generaly, 208
And thai come all full wilfully
To the Torwod quhar that the king
Had ordanyt to mak thar meting.

(219) Sir Edward Bruce, who was worthy, came with a fine great company of good men, well armed and equipped, valiant and eager for the fight. Next Walter Steward of Scotland, who was just a beardless lad, came with a band of noble men, whom all would know by [their] bearing. (227) And the good lord Douglas, too, brought men with him, I tell you, who were well used to fighting; they are less [likely] to be discouraged if they happen to be in a press, and will more quickly see opportunity to defeat their enemy's might than men who are not used to fighting. (235) The earl of Moray too came then, with his well equipped men, in good heart to fight [and] determined to maintain their might; quite apart from many other barons and knights of great repute [who] came sturdily with their men. (242) When they were all assembled, I'm sure they numbered thirty thousand or rather more fighting men, apart from porters and humble folk who guarded equipment and provisions. (247) The king then went round the whole army, looking to their bearing, and saw [that] they [were] of really fine appearance. They were of bold demeanour; the most cowardly in appearance seemed ready to play his part right well. (253) The king, who was well versed in such matters, saw their whole bearing, and saw that they were generally of such demeanour and so hardy, fearless and not cast down. (258) He had great joy in his heart, and thought that men of such determination, if they would put their backs into it, would truly be hard to beat.

---

223. Walter Stewart. In 1306 King Robert had possession of Andrew, son and heir of James Stewart. He must have died in 1306–7, leaving Walter as heir, to succeed his father on the latter's death on 16 July, 1309. James married in 1296, so Walter would be born in 1298 or later, and would still not have possession of the Stewart lands in 1314. Nonetheless he may have led a 'rout of noble men' from Renfrew and Kyle.

244. Thirty thousand. Barrow suggests 5,000–6,000 men, which McDiarmid would reduce to 3,500. The *Vita Edwardi* speaks of 'a great multitude of armed men' whom it later numbers at 40,000. Fordun stresses that King Robert came with 'few men' to the battle. 5,000–6,000 seems reasonable, but the 'probabilities' would not impress a statistician, for there is no sound evidence.

Schir Edward the Bruce the worthi
220 Come with a full gret cumpany 213
Off gud men armyt weill at rycht
Hardy and forsy for to fycht,
Walter Stewart of Scotland syne
That than wes bot a berdles hyne
225 Come with a rout of noble men, 218
That men mycht be contynence ken.
The gud lord of Douglas alsua
Brocht with him men Ik underta
That weile war usit in fechting,
230 Thai sall the les haiff abayimg 223
Giff thaim betid in thrang to be,
Avantage thai sall tittar se
For to stonay thar fayis mycht
Than men that usis nocht to fycht.
235 The erle off Murreff with his men 228
Arayit weile come alsua then
Into gud covyne for to fycht
And gret will for to manteym thar mycht
Outakyn other mony barounys
240 And knychtis that of gret renowne is 233
Come with thar men full stalwartly.
Quhen thai war assemblyt halely
Off fechtand men I trow thai war
Thretty thousand and sumdele mar,
245 Foroutyn cariage and pettaill 238
That yemyt harnayis and vittaill.
Our all the ost than yeid the king
And beheld to thar contenyng
And saw thaim of full fayr affer.
250 Off hardy contenance thai wer, 243
Be liklynes the mast cowart
Semyt full weill to do his part.
The king has sene all thar having
That knew him weile into sic thing,
255 And saw thaim all commounaly 248
Off sic contenance and sa hardy
Forout effray or abaysing.
In his hart had he gret liking
And thoucht that men of sa gret will
260 Giff thai wald set thar will thartill 253
Suld be full hard to wyn perfay.

(262) Each time, as he met them on the way, he welcomed them with cheerful countenance, saying the right words here and there. And they, who saw their lord welcome them in such a gentle and homely [way] – they were joyful and thought that they should put themselves to trying with hard fighting or stalwart affray, to uphold his honour.

(271) The worthy king, when he saw his host all duly gathered, and saw them determined to carry out his wishes with good heart and will, and to uphold their freedom, he was gladdened in many ways, and called [together] all his confidential council.

(278) He said to them: 'Lords, now you see that the English, with great power, have prepared for the fight, because they want to rescue yon castle. So it is good that we decide now how we can prevent them [achieving their] purpose, and so close the ways to them that they do not get by without great obstruction. (286) We have here with us, under our command, about thirty thousand men or more; let us make four divisions of them all, and draw ourselves up in such a way that when our foes come near, we take the way to the New Park, because they must pass there, surely. (293) But if they go beneath us, and pass over the marsh, we shall have the advantage there. Because I believe that it would be very advisable to go on foot to this fighting, armed in only light armour. For if we try to fight on horseback, when our foes are stronger and better horsed than we are, we would be in great danger.

---

288. Four divisions. See note to 311.

296–97. To gang on fute. This is Barbour's 'chivalrous' explanation of the fact that the Scottish army was almost wholly an infantry one, and its commanders had to fight in the same way, as Moray seems to do against Clifford. The *Vita Edwardi* says:

> About 40,000 men [Bruce] brought with him, and split them into three divisions; and not one of them was on horseback, but each was furnished with light arming, which a sword would not easily penetrate. They had axes at their sides and carried lances in their hands. They advanced like dense hedge, and such a crowd could not easily be penetrated. (*VitaEd*, 52)

In fact, when it comes to the battle, the king had '500' men armed on light horse under Sir Robert Keith (13.53–59). Baston's poem (and Baston was there) says: 'The Scottish king ranges and arranges deadly battle lines/They are cavalry and infantry; Oh what a wonderful assembly!' (*Bower6*, 370)

298. In litill armyng. Perhaps 'with little armour on.' See *Vita Edwardi*, in note to 296.

Ay as he met thaim in the way
He welcummyt thaim with glaidsum far
Spekand gud wordis her and thar,
265 And thai that thar lord sa mekly 258
Saw welcum thaim and sa hamly
Joyfull thai war, and thocht that thai
Aucht weill to put thaim till assay
Off hard fechting or stalwart stur
270 For to maynteyme hys honur. 263

[*King Robert proposes the division of his host*]

The worthi king quhen he has sene
Hys ost assemblit all bedene
And saw thaim wilfull to fulfill
His liking with gud hart and will
275 And to maynteyme weill thar franchis 268
He wes rejosyt mony wys
And callyt all his consaile preve
And said thaim, 'Lordis, now ye se
That Inglismen with mekill mycht
280 Has all disponyt thaim for the fycht 273
For thai yone castell wald reskew.
Tharfor is gud we ordane now
How we may let thaim of thar purpos
And sua to thaim the wayis clos
285 That thai pas nocht but gret letting. 278
We haiff her with us at bidding
Weile thretty thousand men and ma,
Mak we four bataillis of tha
And ordane us on sic maner
290 And quhen our fayis cummys ner 283
We to the New Park hald our way,
For thar behovys thaim nede away
Bot giff that thai will beneuth us ga
And our the merrais pass, and sua
295 We sall be at avantage thar. 288
And me think that rycht spedfull war
To gang on fute to this fechting
Armyt bot in litill armyng,
For schup we us on hors to fycht
300 Sen our fayis ar mar off mycht 293
And bettyr horsyt than ar we
We suld into gret perell be,

(303) But if we fight on foot, *perfay*, then we shall always have the advantage, for in the park among the trees horsemen are always disadvantaged, and the streams down below will throw them into confusion.

(309) They all agreed with that opinion, and then, in a short while, they drew up their four divisions. To Earl Thomas they gave command of the vanguard, because they had full confidence in his noble conduct and in his great chivalry. (317) And to uphold his banner, lords who were most valorous were assigned, with their following, to be in his division. (321) The second division was given, to be led, to him who was brave in deeds and esteemed of great chivalry, namely the worthy Sir Edward; I'm sure he will conduct himself so that, no matter how the game goes, his enemies shall have plenty to complain about. (328) Then he gave the third division to Walter Stewart to lead, and to Douglas. bold in action. They were close cousins and therefore [Stewart] was entrusted to him for he was young – but nonetheless I know he will do his duty manfully, and behave so well that he will need no more taking-care-of. (337) The fourth division the noble king took the command of for himself, and had in his company all the men of Carrick, of Argyll and Kintyre, and of the Isles (whose lord was Angus of Islay).

---

305. The Park. This New Park was created by enclosure by Alexander III in the 1260s, and palisaded about 1288. Together with the Old Park, nearer Stirling, and Coxet, it was given by Robert I to Adam Barbour in the 1320s.

307. The sykis. The sluggish streams or pows which flowed through the carse to the Forth.

311. Four divisions. Barbour has perhaps anticipated this arrangement, which would become necessary for the withdrawal to the New Park. The English chronicles are unanimous for three divisions: for *VitaEd* see note to 296.

   Lanercost: They had so arranged their army that two columns went abreast in advance of the third, so that neither should be in advance of the other; and the third followed, in which was Robert. (*L*, 225; *LT*, 207–8)

   Gray: at sunrise the Scots marched out of the wood on foot in three divisions. (*S*,142; *ST*, 55)

Such unanimity is surely more powerful than Barbour's testimony.

339–46. Only the king's division is analysed by Barbour. It is curious that the men of Carrick are there and not with their earl, Edward Bruce. It is also noteworthy that Barbour does not actually say that Angus of Islay was present, only that his men were. 'And but' was formerly read as 'and Bute, all those', but wrongly.

And gyff we fecht on fute perfay
At a vantage we sall be ay,
305 For in the park amang the treys 298
The horsmen alwayis cummerit beis,
And the sykis alssua that ar thar-doun
Sall put thaim to confusioune.'

[*The four divisions and their commanders*]

All thai consentyt till that saw
310 And than intill a litill thraw 303
Thar four bataillis ordanyt thai,
And till the Erle Thomas perfay
Thai gaiff the vaward in leding
For in his noble governyng
315 And in his hey chevalry 308
Thai assoueryt rycht soveranly,
And for to maynteyme his baner
Lordis that off gret worschip wer
Wer assygnyt with thar mengne
320 Intill his bataill for to be. 313
The tother bataill wes gevyn to led
Till him that douchty wes of deid
And prisyt off hey chevalry,
Thar wes Schyr Edward the worthy,
325 I trow he sall maynteyme it sua 318
That howsaever the gamyn ga
His fayis to plenye sall mater haf.
And syne the thrid bataill thai gaff
Till Walter Stewart for to leid
330 And to Douglas douchty of deid 323
Thai war cosyngis in ner degre
Tharfor till him betaucht wes he
For he wes young, bot nocht-forthi
I trow he sall sa manlily
335 Do his devour and wirk sa weill 328
That him sall nede ne mar yemseill.
The ferd bataile the noble king
Tuk till his awne governyng,
And had intill his cumpany
340 The men of Carrik halely 333
And off Arghile and of Kentyr
And off the Ilis quharof wes syr
Angus of Ile, and but all tha

(344) Apart from all those, he also had a great host of armed men from the Lowlands; his division was stalwart and strong. He said that he would take the rear, with the vanguard going in front of him and on either side the other divisions should be placed set back, a little space apart [from the vanguard]. (352) And the king, who was behind them, would see where there was greatest need, and [give] relief [to] them with his banner.

(355) So the king, [a man] skilled and wise, right able at planning, drew up his men for the fighting in good order in every way. And on the next day, Saturday, the king heard his spies say that Englishmen with a great force, had lain at Edinburgh all night. (363) Therefore, without more delay, he took the way to the New Park with all who were in his army, and they lodged themselves there in the Park. (367) And in an open field beside the road, where he thought the Englishmen would have to go if they wanted to move through the Park to the castle, he had many holes dug, a foot in diameter and all as deep as a man's knee, so thickly [placed] that they could be compared to a wax-comb that bees make. (376) All that night he was working, so that before day he had made those holes, and had concealed them with sticks and with green grass, so that they couldn't really be seen.

347–54. This arrangement was for battle, and inappropriate to the time Barbour is describing. It is also contradicted by 455–60, where Edward Bruce and Douglas are to give help where needed.

354. His banner. That is, the men who followed his banner.

371–98. The 'pots'. Baston also records these traps:

A contrivance full of evils is formed for the feet of horses / holes (*concava*) with stakes, so they may not pass without disasters / the people (*plebs*) have dug holes (*foveas*) so that through them cavalry shall stumble / and infantry, if any are seen to pass, will die. (*Bower*6, 370–72)

He off the plane land had alsua
345 Off armyt men a mekill rout, 338
His bataill stalwart wes and stout.
He said the rerward he wald ma
And evyn forrouth him suld ga
The vaward, and on ather hand
350 The tother bataillis suld be gangand 343
Besid on sid a litill space,
And the king that behind thaim was
Suld se quhar thar war mast myster
And releve thar with his baner.

[*The digging of pots by the roadside*]

355 The king thus that wes wycht and wys 348
And rych avisé at divis
Ordanyt his men for the fechting
In gud aray in alkyn thing.
And on the morn on Setterday
360 The king hard his discourouris say 353
That Inglismen with mekill mycht
Had lyin at Edinburgh all nycht.
Tharfor withoutyn mar delay
He till the New Park held his way
365 With all that in his leding war 358
And in the Park thaim herberyt thar,
And in a plane feld be the way
Quhar he thoucht ned behovyd away
The Inglismen, gif that thai wald
370 Throu the Park to the castell hald 363
He gert men mony pottis ma
Off a fute-breid round, and al tha
War dep up till a mannys kne,
Sa thyk that thai mycht liknyt be
375 Till a wax cayme that beis mais. 368
All that nycht travailland he wais
Sua that or day he has maid
Thai pottis, and thaim helit haid
With stykkis and with gres all grene
380 Sua that thai moucht nocht weil be sen. 373

(381) Then on Sunday in the morning, quite soon after sunrise, they heard their mass all together, and many shrived themselves devoutly, [men who] meant to die in that battle or to make their country free then. They prayed to God for their right. (388) None of them dined that day, but for the vigil of St John they fasted each [on] bread and water. The king, when that mass was over, soon went to see the holes, and saw that they were made as he wanted; for some distance on either side, it was well 'potted', as I've said; if their enemies try to ride on horse that way, I'm sure that they cannot well escape without falling. (399) Then he had it announced throughout the host, that all should arm themselves speedily, and prepare themselves as best they could. And when they were all assembled he had them drawn up for the fight, and then had it proclaimed aloud (405) that anyone at all who found that his heart was not firm to stand to win all or die with honour in order to carry on the stalwart struggle, should forthwith depart, and none should remain with him but those who would stand with him to the end, and accept the fate that God would send. (413) Then all answered with a shout and said together in one voice, that none would shirk for fear of death until the great host was beaten.

(417) When the good king heard his men

---

381. Sunday, 23 June, 1314.
394. On either side. C reads 'On athyr syde the way weill braid.' This probably represents the meaning correctly (cf. 367, 'be the way') but the absence of 'the way' from E is noteworthy.

[*Sunday; the Scots prepare for combat with mass and by arming themselves*]

On Sonday than in the mornyng
Weile sone after the sone rising
Thai hard thar mes commounaly
And mony thaim schraiff full devotly
385 That thocht to dey in that melle   378
Or than to mak thar contré fre.
To God for thar rycht prayit thai,
Thar dynit nane of thaim that day
Bot for the vigil off Sanct Jhane
390 Thai fastyt water and breid ilkan.   383
The king quhen that the mes wes don
Went furth to se the pottis sone
And at his liking saw thaim mad,
On ather sid rycht weill braid
395 It wes pittyt as Ik haif tauld.   388
Giff that thar fayis on hors wald hald
Furth in that way I trow thai sall
Nocht weill eschaip foroutyn fall.
Throu-out the ost thar gert he cry
400 That all suld arme thaim hastily   393
And busk thaim on thar best maner,
And quhen thai assemblyt wer
He gert aray thaim for the fycht,
And syne gert cry our-all on hycht
405 That quha-sa-ever he war that fand   398
Hys hart nocht sekyr for to stand
To wyn all or dey with honur
For to maynteyme that stalwart stour
That he betyme suld hald his way,
410 And suld duell with him bot thai   403
That wald stand with him to the end
And tak the ure that God wald send.
Than all answerd with a cry
And with a voce said generaly
415 That nane for dout off deid suld faile   408
Quhill discumfyt war the gret bataile.

[*Disposition of the small folk; preparations for the English advance*]

Quhen the gud king has hard his men

answer him so bravely then, saying that neither fear nor death would lead them to such discouragement that they would shirk the fighting, he rejoiced greatly in his heart. (423) For he thought men of such bearing, so good, so bold, so fine, would uphold their right in battle against men of mighty strength. Then he sent all the small folk and carters, with equipment and provisions in the Park a good way away from him, and had them go [away] from the divisions; they went the way he ordered. (432) There were almost twenty thousand [of them], [and] they took their way to a valley, leaving the king with a goodly company, who nonetheless numbered thirty thousand. I know that they will stand boldly and do their duty as they ought. (438) They stood then, all ranked in a line, ready to give hard battle if anyone wanted to attack them. The king had them all be ready for he knew for a certainty that his enemies lay all night at the Falkirk, and then that they held the way straight towards him, with many men of great power. (447) Therefore he ordered his nephew, the earl of Moray with his following, to keep the road beside the kirk, so that no man [should] pass by that way to fight for the castle. (452) And he said that he himself would keep the entry with his division, if any wanted to attack there. Then his brother Sir Edward, and young Walter, the good Steward, and the lord Douglas also, with their following should pay great attention to which of [the king and Moray] had need of help, and [should] help with those who were with him.

---

427. Pitall. In C poverale. Pitall seems to be rare, but it occurs in relation to supplies (*DOST*), hence I have translated it 'carters'. Sending away the ill-armed had already been reported by Barbour as happening at Loudoun (8.275–78).

444–49. See Bannockburn Commentary.

452–53. The entry. Usually taken to mean the entry to the New Park.

451. For to debate the castell. To fight for the castle. But C has 'For out debat to the castell', to pass to the castle without being challenged, and this may be correct.

455–60. This contradicts the disposition and arrangements outlined at 347–54.

Sa hardely answer him then
Sayand that nother dede na dreid
420   Till sic discomfort suld thaim leid   413
That thai suld eschew the fechting
In hart he had gret rejosing,
For him thocht men off sic covyn
Sa gud and hardy and sa fyne
425   Suld weile in bataill hald thar rycht   418
Agayne men off full mekill mycht.
Syne all the smale folk and pitall
He send with harnays and with vitaill
Intill the Park weill fer him fra
430   And fra the bataillis gert thaim ga   423
And als he bad thai went thar way,
Twenty thousand weile ner war thai.
Thai held thar way till a vale,
The king left with a clene mengne
435   The-quhethir thai war thretty thousand   428
That I trow sall stalwartly stand
And do thar devour as thai aw.
Thai stud than rangyt all on a raw
Redy for to gyff hard bataill
440   Giff ony folk wald thaim assaile.   433
The king gert thaim all buskit be
For he wyst in certanté
That his fayis all nycht lay
At the Fawkyrk, and syne that thai
445   Held towart him the way all straucht   438
With mony men of mekill maucht.
Tharfor till his nevo bad he
The erle off Murreff with his menye
Besid the kyrk to kepe the way
450   That na man pas that gat away   443
For to debate the castell,
And he said himself suld weill
Kepe the entre with his bataill
Giff that ony wald assale,
455   And syne his broder Schyr Edward   448
And young Walter alsua Steward
And the lord of Douglas alsua
With thar mengne gud tent suld ta
Quhilk off thaim had of help myster
460   And help with thaim that with him wer.   453

(461) The king then sent James Douglas and Sir Robert Keith, who was heritable marshall of the host, to watch the approach of the Englishmen. They mounted and rode forth, having well-horsed men with them. (467) Soon they saw the great army, where shining shields had such sheen, and basnets were burnished [so] bright that [they] reflected the sun's great light. (471) They saw so many embroidered banners, standards, pennons and spears, so many knights on horseback, all brilliant in their clothing, so many and such broad divisions, that took so much space as they rode that the largest and boldest host in Christendom, and the greatest, would be cast down to see their enemies in such numbers and so equipped to fight. (482) And when their scouts had sight of their foes, as I tell you, they took the road [back] to the king, and told him in great secrecy [of] the multitude and fine appearance of their enemies, who came in such breadth, and of the great power that they had. (489) Then the king ordered them that they should give no recognition that it was like that, but let them say generally that [the enemy] came in poor order, thus comforting his men. (494) For many a time from one [wrong] word defeat and loss can arise, and through a [good] word, equally well, comfort and determination can arise, causing men to achieve their aim. It did just that here: their comfort and good cheer encouraged them so greatly

---

461–504. Barbour is the only source for this scouting party and the king's deception.

466. Well horsed. Barbour numbered them at 3,000 from a total of 40,000 horsed (110–13). The English cavalry at Bannockburn, made up of knights, esquires and (less well horsed) men-at-arms, would not be included in the summonses for infantry. The magnates obtained letters of protection for some 890 cavalry, and there is good reason to use a multiplier of 2 to obtain the total of some 1,800 serving, close to the *Vita Edwardi*'s 2,000. (For the multiplier see note to 17.283.) Bower is determined on 300,000 cavalry, but his source is Abbot Bernard's poem, which gives *milia ter quoque centum* which just could be 3,100.

[*King Robert has the English host surveyed; spreads a false
account of its strength*]

The king send than James of Douglas
And Schyr Robert the Keyth that was
Marschell off the ost of fe
The Inglismennys come to se,
465 And thai lap on and furth thai raid 458
Weile horsyt men with thaim thai haid,
And sone the gret ost haf thai sene
Quhar scheildis schynand war sa schene
And bassynetis burnyst brycht
470 That gave agayne the sone gret lycht. 463
Thai saw sa fele browdyne baneris
Standaris and pennounys and speris,
And sa fele knychtis apon stedis
All flawmand in thar wedis,
475 And sa fele bataillis and sa braid 468
That tuk sa gret roume as thai raid
That the maist ost and the stoutest
Off Crystyndome and the grettest
Suld be abaysit for to se
480 Thair fayis into sic quantité 473
And sua arayit for to fycht.
Quhen thar discourrouris has had sycht
Off thar fayis as I you say
Towart the king thai tuk thair way,
485 And tauld him intill preveté 478
The multitud and the beauté
Off thair fayis that come sa braid
And off the gret mycht that thai haid.
Than the king bad thaim thai suld ma
490 Na contenance that it war sua 483
Bot lat thaim into commoune say
That thai cum intill evyll aray
To confort his on that wys,
For oftsys throu a word may rys
495 Discomford and tynsaill with-all, 488
And throu a word als weill may fall
Comford may rys and hardyment
May ger men do thar entent.
On the samyn wys it did her,
500 Thar comford and thar hardy cher 493
Comford thaim sa gretumly

that the least bold of the army in behaviour [now] wanted to be foremost to begin the great battle.

(505) In this way the noble king gave his men encouragement, through a bold and cheerful countenance, which he put on in a truly effective way. They thought that there could be no misfortune so great that it would trouble them, provided they could see him before them, [and] which his valour could not relieve them [of]. (513) His valour comforted them so, and the demeanour that he maintained, that the most cowardly was brave. On the other side, very stalwardly, the Englishmen, in such condition as you heard me say previously, came closer with their divisions, banners waving in the wind. (521) And when they had come so near that there was only two miles between the [two sides], they chose a good company of men who were skilled and bold, on fair steeds that were in suitable armour. (526) Three bannerets of very great position were captains of the whole force: the lord Clifford, who was so bold, was chief leader of them all. I believe they were eight hundred armed men. (531) They were all fine young men, anxious for [deeds of] chivalry; they were the best of all the host, in demeanour and equipment. They were the fairest company that you could find, among so many.

(537) They meant to go to the castle, for if they could indeed reach there, they thought it would be rescued. This company set forth on its way, and took the road to Stirling. They avoided the New Park,

---

509–12. They thought that, provided they could see him before them, there could be no misfortune so great that it would trouble them and which his valour could not relieve them of.

522. Two miles. This would place the main host south of Plean, and probably still in the Torwood.

Off thar ost that the leyst hardy
Be contenance wald formast be
For to begyne the gret mellé.

[The English send an advance party to rescue the castle]

505 Apon this wis the noble king   498
     Gaff all his men recomforting
     Throu hardy contenance of cher
     That he maid on sa gud maner.
     Thaim thocht that na myscheiff mycht be
510 Sa gret with-thi thai him mycht se   503
     Befor thaim sua tha thaim suld greve
     That ne his worschip suld thaim releve,
     His worschip confort thaim sua
     And contenance that he gan ma
515 That the mast coward wes hardy.   508
     On other half full sturdely
     The Inglismen in sic aray
     As ye haf herd me forouth say
     Come with thar bataillis approchand
520 The baneris to the wynd wavand,   513
     And quhen thai cummyn war sa ner
     That bot twa myle betwix thaim wer
     Thai chesyt a joly cumpany
     Off men that wicht war and hardy
525 On fayr courseris armyt at rycht,   518
     Four banrentis off mekill mycht
     War capitanys of that route,
     The syr the Clyffurd that wes stout
     Wes off thaim all soverane leidar,
530 Aucht hunder armyt I trow thai war.   523
     Thai war all young men and joly
     Yarnand to do chevalry,
     Off best of all the ost war thai
     Off contenance and off aray.
535 Thai war the fayrest cumpany   528
     That men mycht find of sa mony,
     To the castell thai thocht to far
     For giff that thai weill mycht cum thar
     Thai thocht it suld reskewit be.
540 Forth on thar way held this menye   533
     And towart Strevilline held thar way,
     The New Park all eschewit thai

because they knew well that the king was there, and they went
beneath the New Park, well beneath the kirk, in a body.
(546) Earl Thomas, who was so determined, when he saw
them take to the open thus, went against them in great haste,
with five hundred [men], no more, annoyed and angry in his
mind that they had passed so far by. (552) For the king had
said bluntly to him that a rose had fallen from his chaplet,
because these men had passed where he was set to guard the
way. (556) Therefore he hurried so quickly that he came in
a short time to the open field with his following, because he
meant to redeem his failure or die then. (561) And when the
Englishmen saw him come on without fear or dread, and take
the open [ground] so bravely, they sped against him in haste,
and struck with spurs the strong steeds that carried them
steadily, hard, and fast. (567) And when the earl saw that
company coming so boldly, he said to his [men],

552–55. Rose from the chaplet. In France in 1350 Edward III took Sir
  Eustace Rybemont prisoner. At dinner he said to him: 'I give you the
  prize for the whole battle above everyone.' Then the king took a very
  rich chaplet, richly worked with pearls, put it on his head and then put
  it on the head of Sir Eustace and said, 'I have given you this chaplet
  as a sign of worth, and beg you as much as I can, that you wear it all
  year ...' Moray had failed and diminished his reputation. The story
  requires that Moray was with the king, on account of which McDiarmid
  rejects it as 'traditional fiction'. (*Chron. le Bel*, ii. 181; *B1985*, 90)

561–633. The fight of Moray with Clifford. This is not mentioned in
  Baston's poem, but the other English sources are in substantial agree-
  ment. The *Vita Edwardi* notes only that Gloucester was unhorsed and
  Clifford routed, but this pair of names confirms Gray's two episodes:
  The vanguard, of which the earl of Gloucester had command, entered
  the way inside the Park, where they were soon driven back by the
  Scots who had occupied the way. Here Piers de Mountforth, knight,
  was killed at the hands of Robert Bruce with an axe, as was said. While
  the said vanguard were following this road, Robert, lord of Clifford
  and Henry de Beaumont, with 300 men-at-arms, went round the
  wood on the other side towards the castle, staying on the open ground
  (*beaux chaumps*) ... Moray, who was leader of the Scottish vanguard,
  had heard that his uncle had rebuffed the English vanguard on the
  other side of the wood, thought that he would play his part, went out
  of the wood with his division, and took the open ground towards the
  two lords aforenamed. [*A contretemps between Beaumont, who wishes
  to wait for the Scots, and Sir Thomas Gray*] [Gray] spurred his horse
  between [Beaumont] and Sir William Dayncourt, fighting in the midst
  of the enemy. William was killed, Thomas taken prisoner, his horse
  killed by the lances, he himself taken off on foot by them, who went
  on to defeat utterly the said force of the two lords, some of whom
  fled to the castle, others to the king's army. (*S*, 141; *ST*, 53–54)

For thai wist weill the king wes thar
And newth the New Park gan thai far
545 Weill newth the kyrk intill a rout. 538

[*The advance party is challenged by Moray; his force is surrounded*]

The Erle Thomas that wes sa stout
Quhen he saw thaim sa ta the plane
In gret hy went he thaim agane
With fyve hunder foroutyn ma
550 Anoyit in his hart and wa 543
That thai sa fer wer passit by,
For the king haid said him rudly
That a rose of his chaplete
Was fallyn, for quhar he wes set
555 To kep the way thai men war passit 548
And tharfor he hastyt him sa fast
That cummyn in schort tyme wes he
To the plane feld with his menye,
For he thocht that he suld amend
560 That he trespassit had or than end. 553
And quhen the Inglismen him saw
Cum on foroutyn dyn or aw
And tak sa hardely the plane
In hy thai sped thaim him agane
565 And strak with spuris the stedis stith 558
That bar thaim evyn hard and swith.
And quhen the erle saw that menye
Cum sa stoutly, till his said he

This places the king's single combat before the rebuff of Clifford, but is close to Barbour in many other respects, particularly in naming Dayncourt (580). But it is clear that Clifford came from the main body of the English army, behind the van, still in the [Tor]wood as Clifford departed. (Gray distinguishes the wood from the Park). Lanercost confuses Clifford's force with the vanguard:

> After dinner [? late afternoon] the king's army came next to the Torwood, and hearing that the Scots were in the wood, the king's vanguard, led by Lord Clifford, sought to go round the wood, lest the Scots escape by flight. The Scots, however, allowed this until [Clifford's force] was far distant from their colleagues, and then they showed themselves, and cutting the king's vanguard off from the main and rear divisions, they rushed upon them, killed some and put others to flight. (*L*, 225; *LT*, 207)

563. The plain. This may be the proper name, Plean.

'Don't be afraid of their menace, but set [your] spears before you, and form yourselves up back to back, with all the spears' points out[wards]. (573) In that way we can best defend ourselves if we are surrounded by them.' And they did as he bade them. And the others came on very soon. Before them all there came galloping a knight, bold of heart and hand, who was a very great lord at home – Sir William Daincourt was his name. (581) He galloped on them so boldly, and they met him so sturdily that he and [his] horse were borne down and killed just there, without ransom. He and his valour were greatly bemoaned that day by Englishmen. (587) The rest came on right sturdily, but none of them rushed among them so rashly as he did; with far more deliberation they gathered all in one force, and surrounded them completely, attacking them on every side.

(594) And [the Scots] with spears gave wide wounds to the horses that came near them; those who were riding on these [horses] who were borne down, lost their lives. And others threw spears, darts and knives and weapons of different kinds among those who were fighting, who defended themselves so skilfully, that their foes were astonished. (603) For some would shoot out of their force, stab horses of those who attacked round [them], and bring down men. The Englishmen then threw swords and maces so fiercely among them that there there was a mountain of weapons amidst them, which had been thrown there.

---

571. Literally: 'set all your force back to back'. Barbour does not apply 'schiltrum' to this formation.
598. I have taken 'other' (= others) as subject of 'kest' (600).

'Be nocht abaysit for thar schor,
570 Bot settis speris you befor 563
And bak to bak set all your rout
And all the speris poyntis out,
Suagate us best defend may we
Enveronyt with thaim gif we be.'
575 And as he bad thaim thai haif done, 568
And the tother come on alsone.
Befor thaim all come prikand
A knycht hardy off hart and hand
And a wele gret lord at hame
580 Schyr Gilyame Danecourt wes his nam 573
And prikyt on thaim hardely
And thai met him sturdely
That he and hors wes borne doune
And slayne rycht thar forout ransoun,
585 With Inglismen gretly wes he 578
Menyt that day and his bounté.
The lave come on rycht sturdely
Bot nane off thaim sa hardely
Ruschyt amang thaim as did he,
590 Bot with fer mar maturyté 583
Thai assemblyt all in a rout
And enveround thaim all about
Assailyeand thaim on ilka sid.

[*The fight between Moray's force and the English*]

And thai with speris woundis wyd
595 Gaff till the hors that come thaim ner, 588
And thai that ridand on thaim wer
That doune war borne losyt the lyvis,
And other speris dartis and knyffis
And wapynnys on ser maner
600 Kast amang thaim that fechtand wer 593
That thaim defendyt sa wittily
That thar fayis had gret ferly,
For sum wald schout out of thar rout
And off thaim that assaylyt about
605 Stekyt stedis and bar doun men. 598
The Inglismen sa rudly then
Kest amang thaim swerdis and mas
That ymyd thaim a monteyle was
Off wapynnys that war warpyt thar.

(610) The earl and his [men] were fighting thus at great risk, as I tell you, for they were fewer by a great deal than their enemies and were surrounded all round, where many a blow was struck in real anger. (616) Their foes harassed them right fiercely; they were so beset on both sides that from the great heat that they had from fighting and from the blazing sun their flesh was all wet with sweat. (621) Such a cloud rose from them then from breathing, both by horses and by men, and from dust, that such darkness was in the air above them that it was wonderful to see. (626) They were in great trouble, but nonetheless with great effort they defended themselves manfully, and put both determination and strength and force to drive back in that fight the enemies who harassed them grievously. Unless God helps them soon, they will have their fill of fighting!

(634) But when the noble [and] famous king, with other lords who were with him, saw how the earl took the open field recklessly, James Douglas came to the king just where he was and said, 'Ah, Sir! Saint Mary! The earl of Moray plainly takes the open field with his following. (642) He is in danger unless he is helped soon, because his foes have more [men] than he [has], and are well horsed too. With your leave I will hurry to help him, because he has need [of it]; he is entirely surrounded by enemies.' (648) The king said, 'As Our Lord sees me, you shall not go one foot towards him. If he does well, let him take well.

648–59 This story is extraordinary. In eleven lines the king changes his mind from determined refusal to acquiescence, without any explanation; the Randolph story was that Douglas was refused permission to help; the Douglas story was that he went to help, but in the event chivalrously held back from doing so (12.105–29).

610 The erle and his thus fechtand war   603
At gret myscheiff as I you say,
For quhonnar be full far war thai
Than thar fayis and all about
War inveround, quhar mony rout
615 War roucht full dispitously.   608
Thar fayis demenyt thaim full starkly,
On ather half thai war sa stad
For the rycht gret heyt that thai had
For fechtyn and for sonnys het
620 That all thar flesche of swate wes wete,   613
And sic a stew rais out off thaim then
Off aneding bath of hors and men
And off powdyr that sic myrknes
Intill the ayr abovyne thaim wes
625 That it wes wondre for to se.   618
Thai war in gret perplexite
Bot with gret travaill nocht-forthi
Thai thaim defendyt manlily
And set bath will and strenth and mycht
630 To rusch thar fayis in that fycht   623
That thaim demanyt than angyrly.
Bot gyff God help thaim hastily
Thai sall thar fill have of fechting.

[Douglas proposes to help Moray]

Bot quhen the noble renownyt king
635 With other lordis that war him by   628
Saw how the erle abandounly
Tuk the plane feld, James of Douglas
Come to the king rycht quhar he was
And said, 'A! Schyr, Sanct Mary!
640 The erle off Murref opynly   633
Tays the plane feld with his mengne,
He is in perell bot he be
Sone helpyt for his fayis ar ma
Than he and horsyt weill alsua,
645 And with your leve I will me speid   638
To help him for he has ned,
All umbeveround with his fayis is he.'
The king said, 'Sa our Lord me se,
A fute till him thou sall nocht ga,
650 Giff he weile dois lat him weile ta.   643

Whatever happens to him, win or lose, I shall not change my plans for his [sake].' (653) 'Indeed' said James, 'In no way can I see his enemies overcome him when I can give him help. With your leave, assuredly I will help him, or die in the effort.' (658) 'Do [so], then, and hurry back soon,' the king said, and he held his way. If he comes in time, I'm sure indeed that he will help [Moray] so well that [some] of his enemies will feel it!

---

662. C has 'off his fayis sum sall feill'; presumably E is preferred as the more difficult reading.

Quhatever him happyn, to wyn or los,
I will nocht for him brek purpos.'
'Certis,' said James, 'I may na wis
Se that his fayis him suppris
655 Quhen that I may set help thartill, 648
With your leve sekyrly I will
Help him or dey into the payn.'
'Do than and speid the sone agayn,'
The king said, and he held his way.
660 Gyff he may cum in tyme perfay 653
I trow he sall him help sa weill
That off his fayis sall it feill.

Bannockburn Commentary

In the notes to books 10–13 I have argued that Barbour has misled us over events leading up to the battle, in particular by placing the siege of Stirling in Lent 1313, with a year allowed for its relief. I summarise the true sequence, beginning in October 1313 when an assembly, probably at Dundee, gave the king's enemies a year to swear fealty to him or lose their lands; about the same time the Anglo-Scots of Lothian appealed to Edward II for help and protection, and Edward, perhaps also moved by the threat from Robert I, promised to bring an army to Scotland by 24 June of the next year. This threat prompted the Scots to anticipate, undermining his position further by setting siege to Edinburgh castle; the successful attack on Roxburgh may have been Douglas's private initiative. When Edinburgh fell, the army set siege to Stirling, and, after attacking Cumbria in April 1314, Edward Bruce joined in that enterprise. King Robert withdrew from it, because, and here Barbour is presumably correct, Edward Bruce made an arrangement with the constable, Philip Mowbray, for surrender if not relieved by 24 June. The date of that arrangement was mid-May, because on 27 May it suddenly became known to Edward II, making his way at Newminster to the muster of his army; from this time he was under a new pressure – to relieve Stirling by 24 June. He had also been warned of the unfavourable terrain south of the castle, and probably that the Scots were mustering an army there.

The site of the battle of Bannockburn was the subject of much debate earlier in the present century; our main source must be Barbour's poem, but J. E. Morris's study, *Bannockburn* (1914), showed the importance of taking into account also the English sources. The outcome has been a consensus best represented by Professor Barrow's description, which is supported by a study of the place names of the district and a reconstruction of its landscape in 1314. Here I am concerned mainly to relate the evidence of Barbour to other evidence for events leading to the battle. Much depends on the location of places mentioned by those sources, of which only Stirling and the Bannock Burn are certain beyond the need for discussion.

Barbour tells us first that the Scots were summoned to assemble at the Torwood (11.217); in November 1299, during the siege of Stirling by the Scots, the Guardians, including Bruce, wrote to Edward I from 'the Forest of the Tor', a fact which makes a muster there entirely likely. It has been described as a great wood between Falkirk and Stirling, and more specifically by McDiarmid as 'stretching north to Bannockburn and beyond it to about one mile south of Stirling castle' (*B1985*, 88). In no map from the time of Bleau does it appear to stretch so far north, but always stops at the stream now called the Tor Burn. Nor do the place names between the Tor and Bannock Burns suggest that this area was formerly wooded. On the contrary, in the settlement of a dispute about 1215, the teinds of the chapel of Dunipace were drawn from Carnock, 'Plane' and 'Ochtirbannok', all of which are distinguished from places like Skeoch and Polmaise, owing teinds to St Ninian's kirk.

In 1509 the barony of Ochterbannock was another name for that of Bannockburn; Carnock now survives as 'Bruce's castle' a little to the east of Plean. 'Plane' is Plean, and must be derived from a British word, though *blaen*, 'summit' is impossible and *blen* 'hollow' is not well attested; the name is *lie Plane* in 1365, and by then seems to have been understood as English 'the plain', open, level ground; it appears in the eighteenth century as Plane, Hill o' Plane, Cotts o' Plane, and it may have begun as a district or estate name. Teinds from these places imply open cultivated ground between the Tor Burn and Bannock Burn in 1215 and a century later. The Tor Wood stopped at or about the Tor Burn; on the south it began at, or a little north of, the River Carron.

Next Barbour says that King Robert decided to move to the New Park where there were trees, and to fight on foot (11.291–305). The location of the New Park was worked out by Thomas Miller, in *Transactions of the Stirling Natural History and Archaeological Society*, (1922), 192–237, using later title deeds. He makes one doubtful assertion by including Coxet Hill in the Park, but otherwise his conclusions must command respect, and we can place the Park fairly certainly on the map between St Ninian's and the Bannock Burn.

Barbour describes how on Saturday morning (22 June), knowing that the English were leaving Edinburgh, King Robert, with all in his *leding* moved to the New Park where he camped (11.359–66). This *leding* does not mean the whole

Scottish army; rather it seems to be the king's division (*DOST s. v.* leding (p. 643)). The king then ordered that pots be dug thickly 'in a plane field by the way where he thought' the English would have to go if they tried to move through the Park to the castle (11.367-71). The pots are also mentioned in Baston's poem (*Bower6*, 373); in Barbour and Baston they play no part in the battle and their location is vague, but the intention to close a route northward is clear.

How did the English approach from Falkirk, where they spent Saturday night? If we go back to the earliest maps, two main roads are shown running north to St Ninian's where they join, one from Falkirk, Camelon, Larbert, Torwood, Plean and Bannockburn village, the other following the Carron westwards from Falkirk to Denny, then running due north to St Ninian's. The former is the old A9, the latter the old A80. These are the only roads shown on Roy's map of *c.* 1750. Barbour does not say that the English came through the Torwood but the *Vita* does, and we can be sure that they followed the A9 route thus far. By the end of the eighteenth century maps show that where the Torwood on its northern edge reached the Tor Burn, this road, the A9, forked, and a branch followed the Roman road by West Plean to join the A80 a little south of Snabhead. This Roman road has been generally favoured as Edward II's route because it takes him to the A80 which ran through a corner of the New Park, which the A9 does not do. But there is no evidence that Edward II sought the entry to the Park or took this Roman road.

Now Barbour, in a short passage (11.444-67) gives us further puzzles. The English, having spent a night at 'the Falkirk', moved straight toward Bruce, so he ordered Moray to keep 'the way' beside the kirk, so that none could get by to 'debate' – rescue – the castle. He himself would keep 'the entry' against any who might attack and Edward Bruce, Stewart and Douglas would assist whichever, Moray or the king, had need. The implication is that the 'way' and the 'entry' were alternative lines of English approach. The passage names only one 'kirk', Falkirk, which can scarcely be correct for Moray's position, even if intended by Barbour; we must look for another kirk, and opinion has not hesitated to fix on St Ninian's (never named by Barbour), while identifying 'the entry' with an entry to the New Park, on the A80 south of St Ninian's. But the way beside St Ninian's lay to the north of the New Park, and only two miles from the castle, a very belated stop on any

English approach to the castle. Nor do these seem to be alternative defences, for they are too close.

Of English sources, Gray demands attention because he alone distinguishes between 'the wood' where the Scots had stopped up the narrow roads, 'the Park' where the English vanguard was driven back by the Scots, and 'the wood' which Clifford went round 'on the other side' towards the castle, staying on the good (*beaux*) ground. Moray was in 'the wood', from which he emerged to march his men across the good ground towards Clifford. Clifford was far from the Park, and we must conclude that Gray's 'wood' was the Torwood, especially since Lanercost tells much the same story: that as the English reached the Torwood they learned that there were Scots in it and Clifford rode round it to prevent these from escaping. The motive is much clearer than in Gray, but the circuit of the Torwood is the same.

The Torwood would have to stretch to the Bannock Burn in order to place Moray beside St Ninian's. But the Torwood cannot be put thus to the rack, and either Clifford's men rode three miles across the Plane and the Bannock Burn to St Ninian's to fight Moray where 'the kirk' usually places him or Gray and Lanercost are right in agreeing that the Scots (led by Moray, Gray agrees) emerged from the wood and stopped Clifford either to the east or the north-east of the Torwood. I am in no doubt that this makes a great deal more sense than the identification of Barbour's kirk as St Ninian's. But Barbour does say that Clifford went towards Stirling, eschewing the New Park, going beneath it and 'well beneath' the kirk, taking 'the plain' (11.541–45). Since the New Park is fixed by scholarship, we must conclude that Barbour here and previously identified 'the kirk' as St Ninian's ('well beneath' would make better sense applied to the Park; it was probably demanded by the metre and should not be asked to carry weight). But if Moray from St Ninian's saw Clifford take 'the plain' – Plean – as he left the Torwood, he had ample time to move south, and Clifford could scarcely have come near St Ninian's or the latitude of the Park before the engagement. In other words, Barbour's account is internally inconsistent. When it says that Moray commanded the van (11.312–13) and then places him well to the rear of the king, it is plain unbelievable.

Barbour and Gray agree that Moray commanded the van; it is therefore right to place him in the Torwood while Keith and Douglas rode to reconnoitre the English as they moved north-west out of Falkirk (11.461–81). What, then, are we to make of 'the kirk' in Barbour? Either another kirk was meant, or Barbour has confused this with another time when Moray was placed to keep the way to the castle by St Ninian's – presumably next day. The only possible alternative identity for 'the kirk' is the chapel of Larbert, listed with Dunipace in 1195 as dependent on St Ninian's, but lying to the east of the road north from Falkirk and south of the Torwood; Moray was to keep the southern entry to the Torwood, the A9 route. The 'entry' which the king defended lay across the A80 route to St Ninian's, and the division of Scottish forces reflected uncertainty as to the route by which Edward II would choose to approach Stirling.

Thus the king was with his men in the Park when the English van (12.11–13) approached them and de Bohun pressed ahead to attack and be killed by the king. This encounter is described by Barbour (12.18–59), the *Vita*, and Gray, but only the two latter mention Gloucester with the van. They indicate a fight at this encounter, which Barbour plays down, having the English withdraw with small losses (12.72, 81); later he admits that Edward Bruce's division helped the king's at this time (12.345), so it was presumably nearby. Gloucester and the van, to reach the Park from the Torwood, must have crossed from the A9 route to the A80, presumably by the Roman road and unimpeded by pots, which, therefore, were elsewhere on a route to impede a possible English advance to the Park. Barbour does not tell us where that was, but I suggest that it was further south across the A80 route close to the position by the Torwood which the king abandoned on Saturday 22 June.

The repulse of their van persuaded the English to stick to the A9 route leaving it (as Gray says they did) perhaps near the village of Bannockburn, to cross the Burn by descending into its gorge and then down that and across the stream so that they debouched into the wet carse between the Burn and the Forth. There, in the Carse of Balquhiderock, they spent the night. King Robert was still in the Park with his men, but no account is given of the whereabouts of the other Scottish divisions, until, on the following morning, they all emerged from the Park. They had presumably withdrawn there as the English army advanced to the Bannock Burn.

The site of the battle has been identified by Professor Barrow. The progress of the battle is described differently by the sources and for the archery-encounter the sources are contradictory and the outcome was inconclusive. Barbour has the Scots come forth to take the hard field – open ground (12.422–23). The English van attacked Edward Bruce (12.497–532), and Moray attacked the main English host (12.533–90), followed by Douglas in support (13.1–40); the English archers were dispersed by the marischal's cavalry (13.41–75) whereupon the king's force joined in (13.131–163). The English, frightened by the distant (13.252) appearance of the carriage-men (13.229–52) in what seemed a new army, began to fall back (13.253–81). Gray and the *Vita* are agreed that the Scots came out of the wood – that is, now, the Park – corresponding to Barbour's coming forth to the hard field. Two divisions attacked the English, leaving the third, King Robert's, in reserve (Grey and Lanercost); of the three divisions, the first under Douglas, attacked the English van, killing Gloucester (the *Vita*).

Most commentators have accepted Barbour's four divisions, but, given the English evidence and the low profile of Douglas before 1314, McDiarmid with some justice prefers the English consensus of three. The ghost division is surely that of Douglas. In Barbour on 24 June Edward Bruce was attacked by the English cavalry van, but in the *Vita* (usually dismissed as erring here) Douglas attacked that van. Now Douglas had ridden with the marischal to reconnoitre the English army and when Edward II fled, Douglas left the battle with a cavalry force (13.385–91), passing through the Torwood (where he met Sir Laurence Abernethy 'riding on the muir', 13.555–57) to catch up on, and capture, him. It seems that, despite Barbour's emphasis on the Scots' intention to fight on foot (11.296–309) and the *Vita*'s statement that they were all on foot, the marischal and Douglas were leaders of two small cavalry contingents, the former attached to the king's division, the latter to Edward Bruce's. Edward Bruce is associated thus with Douglas and Stewart at 11.455–57. As Edward Bruce's infantry stood to receive the impact of the English cavalry van, Douglas led a counter-charge of cavalry which contributed to Gloucester's failure and death. Elsewhere on the field the king's cavalry, under Keith, dispersed the English archers.

I do not believe that Barbour misled intentionally, rather that he was misled by sources which told him that on 23 June Edward Bruce, Stewart and Douglas were to help the king or Moray, whichever had need (11.455–60), and that Douglas went to Moray's aid while Edward Bruce helped the king. From this he concluded, doubtless very willingly but wrongly, that Douglas had an independent command.

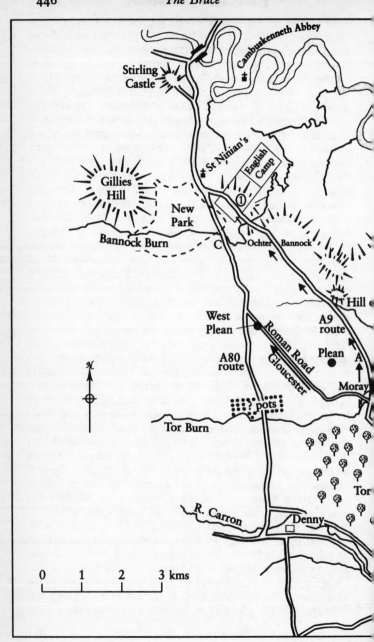

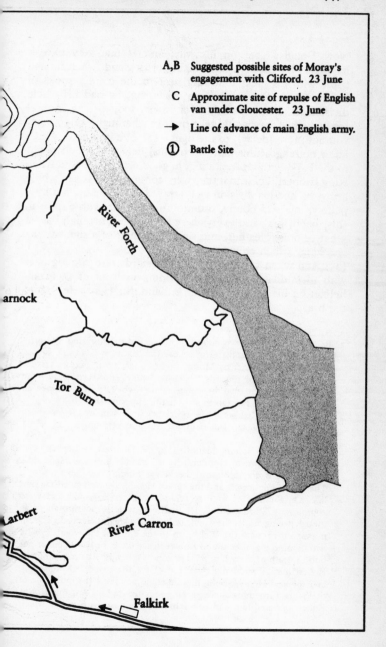

A,B   Suggested possible sites of Moray's engagement with Clifford. 23 June

C   Approximate site of repulse of English van under Gloucester. 23 June

→   Line of advance of main English army.

①   Battle Site

River Forth

arnock

Tor Burn

Larbert

River Carron

Falkirk

Now Douglas goes on his way; and at that very time it happened by chance that the king of England, when he had come with his great following near to the place I spoke of before, where Scotsmen were drawn up, he had his whole division halt, and the other [divisions] too, to take counsel [on] whether they would take quarters that night, or go then, without more [delay], to the fight. (11) The vanguard, which knew nothing of this halt nor of [his] delaying, rode straight to the Park, without hesitating, in good order. (15) And when King [Robert] knew that they were coming so close as a whole army, he had his division well arrayed. He rode upon a little palfrey, low and bonny, ordering his division with an axe in [his] hand; (21) and everywhere he wore on his high basnet a hat of boiled leather, and on top of that, as a sign that he was king, a high crown

(25) And when Gloucester and Hereford were coming near with their division there came riding in front of them all, helmet on his head and spear in hand, Sir Henry de Bohun the brave,

---

2. Barbour makes the two episodes of Bruce–de Bohun and Clifford–Moray contemporaneous; Gray whose father was in Clifford's squad, and was taken prisoner by Moray, says (see his text in note to 11.561) that Clifford moved towards the castle 'while' (*endementiers que*) the English van took the road through the Park – which led to the Bruce-de Bohun encounter (13). On the whole this supports Barbour.

21–22. The leather hat would be necessary since a metal crown would slip on a metal basnet. But cuirbolle was also very tough and would absorb a blow.

29. Sir Henry de Bohun, identified by McDiarmid as nephew (31, 'cousin') of the earl of Hereford; he is certainly found in Hereford's retinue. Here is the account in the *Vita Edwardi*:

The earl of Gloucester and the earl of Hereford commanded the first line. On Sunday ... as they passed by a certain wood and were approaching Stirling castle, lo! the Scots were wandering about as though fleeing, under the wood, and a certain knight, Henry de Bohun, pursued them with the Welsh, up to the entry of the wood. For he had in mind that if he found Robert Bruce there, he would either put him to death or carry him off a prisoner. When he had come thither, Robert himself suddenly came out of the the coverts of the wood, and the said Henry, seeing that he could not resist the multitude of the Scots, turned his horse, seeking to return to his companions. But Robert opposed him and struck him on the head with an axe which

BOOK 12

[*The king prepares his division*]

   Now Douglas furth his wayis tais,
   And in that selff tyme fell throw cais
   That the king off Ingland quhen he
   Was cummyn with his gret menye
5 Ner to the place, as I said ar,
   Quhar Scottismen arayit war,
   He gert arest all his bataill
   And other alsua to tak consaill
   Quhether thai wald herbry thaim that nycht
10 Or than but mar ga to the fycht.
   The vaward that wist na thing
   Off this arest na his dwelling
   Raid to the Park all straucht thar way
   Foroutyn stinting in gud aray,
15 And quhen the king wist that thai wer
   In hale bataill cummand sa ner
   His bataill gert he weill aray.
   He raid apon a litill palfray
   Laucht and joly arayand
20 His bataill with ane ax in hand,
   And on his bassynet he bar
   Ane hat off quyrbolle ay-quhar,
   And thar-upon into taknyng
   Ane hey croune that he wes king.

[*The king kills Henry de Bohun*]

25 And quhen Glosyster and Herfurd wer
   With thar bataill approchand ner
   Befor thaim all thar come ridand
   With helm on heid and sper in hand
   Schyr Henry the Boune the worthi,

---

he carried in his hand. His squire was overcome by the Scots while
he strove to protect or rescue his lord. (*VitaEd*, 51)
This differs greatly from Barbour's version in having the king attack.
Gray is not helpful: 'The vanguard, of which the earl of Gloucester had
command, entered the way within the park, where they were soon
driven back by the Scots who had occupied the way. Here Piers
Mountforth knight was killed by an axe at the hands of Robert Bruce,
it was said.' (*S*,141; *ST*, 53)

who was a valorous and bold knight, cousin to the earl of Hereford, armed in fine good armour. (33) [He] came on his horse almost a bow-shot in front of all the others who were there, and knew the king, because he saw him arraying his men in line thus, and by the crown also that was set upon his basnet, [so] toward him he went with speed. (40) And when the king saw him coming so openly in front of all his comrades, he set his horse towards him at once. (43) And when Sir Henry saw the king come on without dismay, he rode to him full tilt. He thought that he would beat him quite easily, and have him at his will, because he saw him so poorly horsed. (49) They closed together in a direct course; Sir Henry missed the noble king, and he, standing in his stirrups, with an axe that was both hard and good, struck him a blow with such great force that neither hat not helmet could stop the heavy clout that he gave him, so that he cleaved the head to his brains. (57) The hand-axe shaft broke in two and [de Bohun] fell flat to the ground, because his strength had gone. This was the first blow of the fight, [and] was mightily done. And when the king's men saw him, right at the first encounter, without hesitation or trepidation, slay a knight thus with one blow, they took such encouragement from it that they advanced right boldly. When the Englishmen saw them advancing stoutly, they were greatly cast down, especially because the king had slain that good knight so quickly, [so] that they all withdrew,

---

68–86. This is Barbour's account of what, from the other sources, seems to have been a significant skirmish between the English van and Bruce's division. The *Vita Edwardi* follows the passage in the note to 29 with: 'This was the beginning of the troubles. On the same day there was bitter fighting in which the earl of Gloucester was unhorsed and Robert Clifford shamefully put to flight, and also our men long pursued the Scots, [and] many on both sides perished.' The unhorsing of Gloucester can only have been at the park by the king's men; no other source refers to it, and it may be a duplicated report of the same event next day. It is difficult to see when the English pursued the Scots on the Sunday.

30 That was a wycht knycht and a hardy
    And to the erle off Herfurd cusyne,
    Armyt in armys gud and fyne
    Come on a sted a bow-schote ner
    Befor all other that thar wer,
35 And knew the king for that he saw
    Him sua rang his men on raw
    And by the croune that wes set
    Alsua apon his bassynet,
    And towart him he went in hy.
40 And quhen the king sua apertly
    Saw him cum forouth all his feris
    In hy till him the hors he steris.
    And quhen Schyr Henry saw the king
    Cum on foroutyn abaysing
45 Till him he raid in full gret hy,
    He thocht that he suld weill lychtly
    Wyn him and haf him at his will
    Sen he him horsyt saw sa ill.
    Sprent thai samyn intill a ling,
50 Schyr Hanry myssit the noble king
    And he that in his sterapys stud
    With the ax that wes hard and gud
    With sua gret mayne raucht him a dynt
    That nother hat na helm mycht stynt
55 The hevy dusche that he him gave
    That ner the heid till the harnys clave.
    The hand-ax schaft fruschit in twa,
    And he doune to the erd gan ga
    All flatlynys for him faillyt mycht.
60 This wes the fryst strak off the fycht
    That wes perfornyst douchtely,
    And quhen the kingis men sa stoutly
    Saw him rycht at the fyrst meting
    Foroutyn dout or abaysing
65 Have slayne a knycht sua at a strak
    Sic hardyment tharat gan thai tak
    That thai come on rycht hardely.
    Quhen Inglismen saw thaim sa stoutly
    Cum on thai had gret abaysing
70 And specially for that the king
    Sa smartly that gud knycht has slayne
    That thai withdrew thaim everilkane

and not one dared stay to fight, so [much] did they fear the
king's might. (75) And when the king's men saw them with-
draw thus as a whole army, they gave a great shout at them,
and [the English] quickly fled; and [the Scots] who followed
them slew some of those that they overtook, though, to be
truthful, they were few; their horses' hooves took nearly all
away. (83) But no matter how few died there, they were
severely beaten, and rode away with a good deal more shame
by far, than [when] they came from home.

(87) When the king had returned, and made his men give up
the pursuit, the lords of his company, as they dared, blamed
him greatly, for putting himself at risk in meeting so hardy
and strong a knight, equipped as he was then seen [to be];
for they said it could well have been the cause of each of them
losing [everything]. (96) The king made them answer none,
but bemoaned his hand-axe shaft, broken in two by the stroke
in that way. (99) Earl Thomas was still fighting with foes on
both sides and slew a number of them, but he and his men
were weary. Nonetheless they defended themselves manfully
with [their] weapons, until the Douglas came near, hurrying
with [his] great strength. (107) The Englishmen who were
fighting, when they saw the Douglas near at hand, fell back
and made a gap. James Douglas knew that by their withdrawal
they were nearly beaten, [so] then he ordered those who were
with him [to] stand still and push no further forward;

99–164. The conclusion of the fight between Moray's men and Clifford,
with Douglas holding back. Although Barbour limits Moray's force to
500 (ll. 549), the other sources imply that this was the whole of Moray's
division, and I cannot accept McDiarmid's conclusion that Douglas
was part of it (*B1985*, 89). He was in command of cavalry and was, or
was to be, assigned to Edward Bruce's division.

And durst nocht ane abid to fycht
Sa dred thai for the kingis mycht.
75   And quhen the kingis men thaim saw
Sua in hale bataill thaim withdraw
A gret schout till thaim gan thai mak
And thai in hy tuk all the bak,
And thai that folowit thaim has slane
80   Sum off thaim that thai haf ourtane
Bot thai war few forsuth to say
Thar hors fete had ner all away.
Bot how-sa quhoyne deyt thar
Rebutyt foulily thai war
85   And raid thar gait with weill mar schame
Be full fer than thai come fra hame.

[*Douglas admires the struggle of Moray and his men*]

Quhen that the king reparyt was
That gert his men all leve the chas
The lordis off his cumpany
90   Blamyt him as thai durst gretumly
That he him put in aventur
To mete sa styth a knycht and sture
In sic poynt as he than wes sene,
For thai said weill it mycht haiff bene
95   Cause off thar tynsaill everilkan.
The king answer has maid thaim nane
Bot menyt hys handax schaft that sua
Was with the strak brokyn in twa.
The Erle Thomas wes yete fechtand
100 With fayis apon athyr hand
And slew off thaim a quantité,
Bot wery war his men and he
The-quhether with wapynnys sturdely
Thai thaim defendyt manlely
105 Quhill that the Douglas come ner
That sped him on gret maner,
And Inglismen that war fechtand
Quhen thai the Douglas saw ner-hand
Thai wandyst and maid ane opynnyng.
110 James of Douglas be thar relying
Knew that thai war discumfyt ner,
Than bad thaim that with him wer
Stand still and pres na forthyrmar.

(114) 'for those who are fighting yonder' he said, 'are of such great valour, that their foes will very soon be beaten by their might, even if nobody helps them to fight. If we enter the fray now, when they are nearly beaten, men would say that we had driven [the English] back, (122) and so those who have given good service with great effort and hard fighting, would lose a part of their credit. It would be a sin if those who are of such supreme valour should lose their renown. And he, through open and hard fighting, has achieved here something unlikely; he shall have what he has earned.'

(130) The earl, with those who were fighting, when he saw his enemies in such confusion, went upon them with speed and pressed them so very hard with fierce blows, until, finally, they fled and not daring to stay any longer. (136) They left there dead both men and horses, and held their way in real haste, not together but scattered, and those that were overtaken were killed; the rest went to their host again, cast down and sorry at their loss. (142) The earl who had so defended himself, and his men too, who were weary, quickly took off their basnets to get air, for they were hot [and] were all covered in sweat. (147) In truth they seemed men who had tested their strength in fight – and they did so right doughtily. They found that of all their company there was only one yeoman slain; they they praised God and were right glad and happy that they had escaped thus. (154) Then they went towards the king,

'For thai that yonder fechtand ar,'
115 He said, 'ar off sa gret bounté
That thar fayis weill sone sall be
Discumfyt throu thar awne mycht
Thocht na man help thaim for to fycht,
And cum we now to the fechting
120 Quhen thai ar at discumfiting
Men suld say we thaim fruschit had,
And sua suld thai that caus has mad
With gret travaill and hard fechting
Los a part of thar loving,
125 And it war syn to les thar prys
That off sa soverane bounté is.
And he throu plane and hard fechting
Has her eschevyt unlikly thing
He sall haff that he wonnyn has.'

[Moray's victory over Clifford's men]

130 The erle with that that fechtand was
Quhen he hys fayis saw brawland sua
And hy apon thaim gan he ga,
And pressyt thame sa wonder fast
With hard strakys quhill at the last
135 Thai fled that dust abid ne mar.
Bath hors and men slane left thai thar
And held thar way in full gret hy
Nocht all togydder bot syndryly
And thai that war ourtane war slayn,
140 The lave went till thar ost agayne
Off thar tynsall sary and wa.
The erle that had him helpyn sua
And his als that wer wery
Hynt off thar bassynettis in hy
145 Till avent thaim for thai war wate,
Thai war all helyt into swate.
Thai semyt men forsuth Ik hycht
That had fandyt thar force in fycht
And sua did thai full douchtely.
150 Thai fand off all thar cumpany
That thar wes bot a yuman slayne
And lovyt God and wes full fayne
And blyth that thai eschapyt sua.
Towart the king than gan thai ga

and quite soon came to him. He asked them about their
welfare, and looked on them with a cheerful mein because
they had borne themselves so well. Then all pushed with great
eagerness to see the earl of Moray; because of his high repu-
tation and great valour all yearned to do him honour. (163)
They ran so fast to see him there that nearly all were gathered
together. And when the good king saw them assembled like
that before them, he was boyed up and glad that their enemies
had been repelled in that way; he stood still for a little while,
then he spoke his wishes as follows:

[*Lines 171–327 are given in a line-by-line translation*]

(171) 'Lords' he said, 'we ought to praise and love/Almighty
God, who sits above,/Who sends us so fair a start./It is a great
discouragement/ (175) To our foes, who in this way/Have
been twice repulsed so soon/For when the men of their army
hear/And know the truth of the way/That their vanguard,
which was so bold,/ (180) And then yon other fine force/That
I know were the best men/That they could find amongst them
there,/Were repulsed so suddenly,/Then I'm sure and certain
beyond a doubt/ (185) That many a heart will be in trepida-
tion/That earlier seemed of great courage;/And if the heart is
cast down/The body is not worth a jot./Therefore I know that
a good conclusion/ (190) Will follow from our beginning./But
I don't say this to you/So that you will follow my determin-
ation/To fight, for everything is up to you./For if you think it
right that we/ (195) Fight, we shall fight; and if you want/

---

166. Befor thaim. C has Befor him, which may be preferable.

171–91. King Robert offers to withdraw. Gray gives the same discussion
in a different context:

The Scots in the wood thought that they had done well enough for
the day and were all on the point of decamping during the night as
far as Lennox, a stronger country, when Sir Alexander Seton, who
had been at the faith of the English and had come there with King
[Edward] secretly absconded from the English army, went to ... Bruce
in the wood and said to him, 'Sir this is the time if ever you mean
to undertake to recover Scotland; the English have lost heart, are
demoralised and expect nothing but a sudden open assault.' Then he
described their condition, saying to [Bruce] on his head and on pain
of being hanged and drawn, that if he would attack them in the
morning, he would easily discomfit them, without losses. At [Seton's]
instigation the Scots resolved to fight. (S, 142; ST, 55)

Sir Alexander Seton (no relative of Christopher Seton) probably played
this vital role; he is not mentioned in the poem. For him see Barrow,
Bruce, 151, 285; *SP8*, 563–70.

155 And till him weill sone cummyn ar.
He wyttyt at thaim of thar far
And glaidsome cher to thaim mad
For thai sa weile thaim borne had.
Than pressyt into gret daynte
160 The erle off Murreff for to se,
For his hey worschip and gret valour
All yarnyt to do him honour,
Sa fast thai ran to se him thar
That ner all samyn assemblit ar.
165 And quhen the gud king gan thaim se
Befor thaim sua assemblit be
Blyth and glaid that thar fayis wer
Rabutyt apon sic maner
A litill quhill he held him still,
170 Syne on this wys he said his will.

[The king asks his men whether they should stay and fight]

'Lordingis, we aucht to love and luff
Allmychty God that syttis abuff
That sendis us sa fayr begynnyng.
It is a gret discomforting
175 Till our fayis that on this wis
Sa sone has bene rabutyt twis,
For quhen thai off thar ost sall her
And knaw suthly on quhat maner
Thar vaward that wes sa stout,
180 And syne yone othyr joly rout
That I trow off the best men war
That thay mycht get amang thaim thar,
War rebutyt sa sodanly,
I trow and knawis it all clerly
185 That mony ane hart sall waverand be
That semyt er off gret bounté,
And fra the hart be discumfyt
The body is nocht worth a myt,
Tharfor I trow that gud ending
190 Sall folow till our begynnyng.
The-quhether I say nocht this you till
For that ye suld folow my will
To fycht, bot in you all sall be,
For gyff you thinkis spedfull that we
195 Fecht we sall, and giff ye will

Us to leave, to carry out your choice/I shall agree in every way/To do just what you decide./So speak your mind openly.'/ (200) Then with one voice they cried aloud/'Good king, without more delay,/Tomorrow as soon as you see [the light of] day,/Get all ready for the battle/For fear of death we shall not fail,/ (205) Nor shall any effort be refused/Till we have made our country free!'/When the king heard them so bravely/And boldly speak to the fight/In his heart he took great encouragement,/ (210) And said, 'Lords, since you decide so,/Let us prepare it in the morning,/So that we, by sunrise/Have heard mass and prepared well,/Each man in his own squad/ (215) Drawn up outside the tents/In divisions with banners displayed,/And take care that you in no way break array./And as you love me, I beg you/That each man, for his own honour/ (220) Provide himself with a good banner./And when it comes to the fight/Let each man set his heart will and strength/To humble our foes' great pride./They will come arrayed on horse/ (225) And advance on you at no small speed;/Meet them with spears boldly,/And think then of the great ill/That they and theirs have done to us/And are still determined to do/

210–327. Bruce's speech on the eve of battle. It should be remembered that he did not have the advantage of a public address system directed at the army; he spoke to 'lords', each one of whom should have a banner (220), and held land by ward and relief (320). The speech clearly impressed the Scots, for it was also recreated by (a) Baston and (b) Abbot Bernard (placing it on the morning of battle) in verse, also addressed to nobles:

(a) The king speaks; he inspires the more noble of the Scots;/he calls and urges the more powerful to wars;/he surveys and arrays the divisions ready for a fight;/he holds such [enemy] mortals [as] a defeated people;/he encourages and comforts the crowds of people following;/he scoffed and jeered at the compacts of the English./A brave leader taught the fingers of death for wars;/he ordered that none should yield to bold slaves. (*Bower6*, 370)

(b) Oh! nobles. My people who value greatly the freedom for which the kings of Scotland have suffered many struggles, dying in the Lord, let all of them now think on the labours we suffered while we have struggled for eight years now, for [our] right to the kingdom, for the honour of freedom. We have lost brothers, friends, relatives; your relatives and friends are prisoners, and now prelates and clergy are shut up in prison; mother church is safe in no Order; the nobility of the land have died in the blood of war. Armed nobles, whom all you see before [you] have already decreed with impiety the destruction of us, kingdom, people, nor do they believe we can survive. Their glory is in carts and horses, for us hope is in the name of the Lord and victory in war. This is a happy day, the birthday of John the Baptist;

We leve, your liking to fulfill.
I sall consent on alkyn wis
To do rycht as ye will dyvys,
Tharfor sayis off your will planly.'
200   And with a voce than gan thai cry,
'Gud king, foroutyn mar delay
Tomorne alsone as ye se day
Ordane you hale for the bataill,
For doute off dede we sall nocht faill
205   Na na payn sall refusyt be
Quhill we haiff maid our countré fre.'

[*The king's address to his men: the reasons for the fight*]

Quhen the king had hard sa manlily
Thai spak to fechting and sa hardely
In hart gret gladschip can he ta
210   And said, 'Lordingis, sen ye will sua
Schaip we us tharfor in the mornyng
Sua that we be the sone-rysing
Haff herd mes and buskyt weill
Ilk man intill his awn eschell
215   Without the palyounys arayit
In bataillis with baneris displayit,
And luk ye na wis brek aray.
And, as ye luf me, I you pray
That ilk man for his awne honour
220   Purvay him a gud baneour,
And quhen it cummys to the fycht
Ilk man set hart will and mycht
To stynt our fayis mekill prid.
On hors thai will arayit rid
225   And cum on you in full gret hy,
Mete thaim with speris hardely
And think than on the mekill ill
That thai and tharis has done us till,
And ar in will yeit for to do

---

and St Andrew and [St] Thomas who shed his blood, with the saints
of Scotland, will fight today for the honour of the people with Christ
the Lord in front. With him [as] leader you will win, you will make
an end to war. If you weep from the heart for your sins, our royal
power decrees that all offences committed against us are pardoned
for those who now defend [our] ancestral kingdom well.' (*Bower*6,
362–64)

(230) If they have the power to achieve it./And, *certis*, I think indeed that you/Ought to be without timidity,/Worthy, and of great prowess;/For in three ways we have the edge:/(235) The first is, that right is on our side/And God will always fight for the right./The second is, they have come here/Trusting in their great power/To seek us in our own land;/ (240) And have brought here, right to our hands/ Riches in such great plenty/That the poorest of you shall be/Both rich and powerful as well,/If we win, as well may happen./ (245) The third is that for our lives/ And for our children and our wives/ And for our freedom and for our land/We are bound to stand in battle./And they for their power only,/ (250) And because they think scornfully of us/And because they would destroy us all,/Makes them fight; but it may yet happen/That they will rue confronting us./And indeed, I warn you of one thing/ (255) That if it happens that they (God forbid)/Find us faint-hearted in our acts/So that they beat us openly/They will have no mercy on us./And since we know their wicked will/ (260) I think it would suit our skill/To set bravery against cruelty/And make our fighting stand in that way./Therefore I ask and beseech you/That with all the strength that you can muster/ (265) At the beginning you get ready/Without cowardice or holding back/To meet those that reach you first/So stoutly that the hindmost tremble./And think of your great valour/ (270) Your courage, and your doughty deeds/And of the joy that waits for us/If it befalls, as well may be,/

235-49. This has strong echoes of 1 Maccabees, 3.19-22: 'Victory does not depend on numbers, strength comes from Heaven alone. Our enemies come filled with insolence and lawlessness to plunder and kill us, and our wives and children. But we fight for our lives and for our religion. Heaven will crush them before our eyes. You need not be afraid of them.' Maccabees is probably the source for Trokelowe's statement which so strongly parallels Barbour: 'The leaders of the Scots, going through their troops urged them that they would embark on a very just fight for the defence of themselves, their wives, children and possessions, promising them victory by the help of prayers to God.' The Scots said they were ready to live or die for defence of their 'part', *partis*, for which, surely, read *patrie*, 'country'. (*Chron. Trokelowe*, 84)

247. C has 'and for the fredome of our land', which is metrically more regular.

265. Ye pres you. *DOST* gives as a rare meaning for 'press oneself', 'to begin, get ready.' This seems to fit here, and I have translated accordingly.

230 Giff thai haf mycht to cum tharto.
And certis me think weill that ye
Forout abasing aucht to be
Worthy and of gret vasselagis
For we haff thre gret avantagis

235 The fyrst is that we haf the rycht
And for the rycht ay God will fycht.
The tother is that thai cummyn ar
For lyppynyng off thar gret powar
To sek us in our awne land,

240 And has brocht her rycht till our hand
Ryches into sa gret quantité
That the pourest of you sall be
Bath rych and mychty tharwithall
Giff that we wyne, as weill may fall.

245 The thrid is that we for our lyvis
And for our childer and for our wyvis
And for our fredome and for our land
Ar strenyeit in bataill for to stand,
And thai for thar mycht anerly

250 And for thai lat of us heychtly
And for thai wald distroy us all
Mais thaim to fycht, bot yeit may fall
That thai sall rew thar barganyng.
And certis I warne you off a thing

255 That happyn thaim, as God forbed,
Till fynd fantis intill our deid
That thai wyn us opynly
Thai sall off us haf na mercy,
And sen we knaw thar felone will

260 Me think it suld accord to skill
To set stoutnes agayne felony
And mak sa-gat a juperty.
Quharfor I you requer and pray
That with all your mycht that ye may

265 That ye pres you at the begynnyng
But cowardys or abaysing
To mete thaim at sall fyrst assemble
Sa stoutly that the henmaist trymble,
And menys of your gret manheid

270 Your worschip and your douchti deid
And off the joy that we abid
Giff that us fall, as weill may tid,

That we happen to defeat this great host./In your hands,
without fail,/ (275) You bear honour, reputation and riches/
Freedom, wealth and happiness,/If you carry yourselves like
men; /And exactly the opposite/Will befall if you let cowardice/
(280) And wickedness take over your hearts./You could have
lived in serfdom,/But, because you yearned to have freedom/
You are gathered here with me;/So it is needful that you be/
(285) Strong and bold and without fear./I warn you well of
one more thing,/That no more mischief could happen to
us/Than to be taken [prisoner] in their hands,/For they would
kill us, as I well know/ (290) Just as they did my brother
Neil./But when I reflect on your stoutness,/And on the many
daring deeds/That you have done so boldly,/I trust and believe
assuredly/ (295) To have full victory in this fight./For though
our foes have great power,/They are in the wrong, and
pride/And desire for domination/Moves them, nothing more./
(300) Nor need we fear them except in front/For strength of
this place, as you see,/Prevents us from being encircled./And
I pray you also, particularly,/Highborn and low, all together,/
(305) That none of you from greediness/Have an eye on taking
their riches, /Nor yet on taking prisoners,/Until you see them
thrown into such confusion/That the field is plainly
yours,/(310) And then, at your pleasure, you may/Take all the
riches that are there./If you will behave in this way/You will
surely have victory./

---

280. E has 'wykytnes you suppris'. Exceptionally I have preferred C's
reading, 'your hertis suppris'.

303-11. McDiarmid points out that this warning against taking booty
before victory is won is found in the *Roman d'Alixandre,* in the mouth
of Alexander before the battle of Ephesus. The order against taking
prisoners (307) is not in the *Roman*; the context shows that taking
prisoners was akin to plundering, a financial aim of the captor, who
would enjoy the ransom. Men of substance (which could be judged by
the horse and armour) were liable to be taken prisoner, infantry were
not. Bruce's instruction here runs counter to the accepted laws of war
of the time. (*B1985*, 91)

Hap to vencus this gret bataill.
In your handys without faile
275   Ye ber honour price and riches
Fredome welth and blythnes
Giff you contene you manlely,
And the contrar all halily
Sall fall giff ye lat cowardys
280   And wykytnes your hertis suppris.
Ye mycht have lyvyt into threldome,
Bot for ye yarnyt till have fredome
Ye ar assemblyt her with me,
Tharfor is nedfull that ye be
285   Worthy and wycht but abaysing.

[*The king's address to his men: practical advice*]

And I warne you weill off a thing,
That mar myscheff may fall us nane
Than in thar handys to be tane,
For thai suld sla us, I wate weill
290   Rycht as thai did my brothyr Nele.
Bot quhen I mene off your stoutnes
And off the mony gret prowes
That ye haff doyne sa worthely
I traist and trowis sekyrly
295   To haff plane victour in this fycht,
For thoucht our fayis haf mekill mycht
Thai have the wrang, and succudry
And covatys of senyoury
Amovys thaim foroutyn mor.
300   Na us thar dreid thaim bot befor
For strenth off this place as ye se
Sall let us enveronyt to be.
And I pray you als specially
Bath mar and les commonaly
305   That nane of you for gredynes
Haff ey to tak of thar riches
Ne presonaris for to ta
Quhill ye se thaim contraryit sa
That the feld anerly youris be,
310   And than at your liking may ye
Tak all the riches that thar is.
Giff ye will wyrk apon this wis
Ye sall haff victour sekyrly.

I know not what more I can say;/(315) You know well what honour is;/Carry yourselves, then, in such a way/That your honour is always safeguarded./And I promise here, in good faith/If any die in this battle, /(320) His heir, without wardship, relief or tailzie,/Shall possess his land on the next day,/Be he never so young in age./Now get you ready for the fight./God, who is all-powerful, help us!/(325) I advise that we stay armed all night/Prepared for battle, so that we/Are always ready to meet our foes.'

(328) Then they all answered with a shout, 'As you intend, let everything be done.' Then they went soon to their quarters, and prepared themselves for the fighting, then mustered in the evening, and in that way stayed all night, till the morning when it was daylight.

(335) When the Clifford and his whole force were driven back, as I said before, and also their great vanguard was forced to turn tail, and they told of their retreat – they of the vanguard how the king in one blow slew so plainly a knight who was valiant and strong; and how the whole of the king's division, and Sir Edward Bruce also, tried right boldly to attack them, when they all retreated together, and how the [English] lost [some] of their men; (348) and [they] also told [about] Clifford then, how Thomas Randolph took the open [ground] with few folk, and how Sir William Daincourt, the worthy was killed, and how the earl fought manfully, so that, like a hedgehog, all his force had set out spears all round [them],

---

318–22. This concession of succession without payment of relief or without wardship of a minor (without tailzie, entail, makes no sense to me), was granted before Harlaw (1411) and Flodden (1513). There seems to be no earlier example.

348. Randolph 'tuk the plane'. Again this may be the Plain, Plean (11.563).

I wate nocht quhat mar say sall I
315 Bot all wate ye quhat honour is,
Contene you than on sic a wis
That your honour ay savyt be.
And Ik hycht her in leauté
Gyff ony deys in this bataille
320 His ayr but ward releff or taile
On the fyrst day his land sall weld
All be he never sa young off eild.
Now makys you redy for to fycht,
God help us that is maist of mycht.
325 I rede armyt all nycht that we be
Purvayit in bataill sua that we
To mete our fayis ay be boune.'
Than answeryt thai all with a soune,
'As ye dyvys all sall be done.'
330 Than till tha innys went thai sone
And ordanyt thaim for the fechting
Syne assemblyt in the evynnyng,
And suagat all the nycht bad thai
Till on the morn that it wes day.

[*The English prepare: the night before the battle*]

335 Quhen the Cliffurd, as I said ar,
And all his rout rebutyt war
And thar gret vaward alsua
War distrenyeit the bak to ta
And thai had tauld thar rebuting –
340 Thai off the vaward how the king
Slew at a strak sa apertly
A knycht that wycht wes and hardy,
And how all haile the kingis bataill
Schup thaim rycht stoutly till assaill
345 And Schyr Edward the Bruce alsua
Quhen thai all haill the bak gan ta
And how thai lesyt of thar men,
And Cliffurd had tauld alsua then
How Thomas Randell tuk the plane
350 With a few folk and how wes slane
Schyr Gilyame Danecourt the worthi,
And how the erle faucht manly
That as ane hyrchoune all his rout
Gert set out speris all about

and how the [English] were driven back and some of their
good men were slain – (357) the Englishmen were so cast
down and so fearful at that news that in five hundred and
more places you could see [them] gathering together, saying,
'Our lords, for [the sake of] their power, will fight altogether
against the right. (363) But whoever makes war thus wrong-
fully offends God all too thoroughly, and they may take a
nasty fall; and so it may happen that we take [one] here.' And
when their lords discerned the dejection and the huddles that
they held, two and two together, they soon had heralds go
through the army, to make a proclamation, that none should
be cast down; (373) for in skirmishes it often happens that
you win some and lose some, and that in the great battle,
which in no way could fail to happen unless the Scots fled
away, full amends would be made, *perfay*. Therefore they
admonished them to be of high courage and bravery, and to
stand firm in the battle, and take revenge on [the Scots]. (383)
The [heralds] can admonish as they want, and the [men] can
also promise to fulfil all their orders with stout hearts, but
nonetheless, I'm sure that they will be afraid in their hearts.
(388) The [English] king with his confidential council has
taken advice that he would not fight before morning, unless
he was attacked. So they lodged there that night down in the
Carse, and had everyone clean and make ready their equip-
ment before morning, for the battle. And because there were
streams in the Carse,

---

371. The proclamation. English sources make no mention of this, and it
probably came from a Scottish source wishing to emphasise poor English
morale.

392. Down in the Carse. The *Vita Edwardi* comments that after the rout
of Clifford, 'the day being spent, the whole army met at the place where
it was to rest that night'. (*VitaEd.* 51) Lanercost explains that at the
end of the battle, 'whereas the English had shortly before crossed a
great ditch called Bannockburn into which the tide flows, and now
wanted to recross it ...' (*L*, 226; *LT*, 208) It is Gray who describes
this bivouac in more detail (see also note to 406):

[The English army] having already abandoned the way through the
wood, had come to a plain towards the River Forth, beyond Ban-
nockburn, an evil deep boggy stream, where the said ... army
unharnessed and remained all night in discomfort, having lost con-
fidence and being too demoralised by the [events of] the past day.
(*S*, 141–42; *ST*, 56–57)

Unfortunately the French is not without ambiguity. I take Gray to be
saying that the Bannockburn was a boggy stream, and not that the plain
was 'an evil deep bog with streams', for Barbour speaks (406) of the

355 And how that thai war put agayne
     And part off thar gud men slayne -
     The Inglismen sic abasing
     Tuk and sic drede of that tithing
     That in fyve hunder placis and ma
360 Men mycht se samyn routand ga
     Sayand, 'Our lordis for thar mycht
     Will allgate fecht agane the rycht,
     Bot quha-sa werrayis wranguysly
     Thai fend God all to gretumly
365 And thaim may happyn to mysfall,
     And swa may tid that her we sall.'
     And quhen thar lordys had persaving
     Off discomfort and rownnyng
     That thai held samyn twa and twa,
370 Throu-out the ost sone gert thai ga
     Heraldis to mak a crye
     That nane discomfort suld be,
     For in punye is oft hapnyne
     Quhile for to wyn and quhile to tyne,
375 And that into the gret bataill
     That apon na maner may faill
     Bot giff the Scottis fley thar way
     Sall all amendyt be perfay.
     Tharfor thai monest thaim to be
380 Off gret worschip and off bounté
     And stoutly in the bataill stand
     And tak amendis at thar hand.
     Thai may weill monys as thai will
     And thai may hecht als to fulfill
385 With stalwart hart thar bidding all
     Bot nocht-forthi I trow thai sall
     Intill thar hartis dredand be.
     The king with his consaill prevé
     Has tane to rede that he wald nocht
390 Fecht or the morne bot he war socht,
     Tharfor thai herberyd thaim that nycht
     Doune in the Kers, and gert all dycht
     And maid redy thar aparaill
     Agayne the morne for the bataill,
395 And for in the Kers pulis war

English camping in the 'hard field' and Baston's poem places the opening
battle on *arida terra*.

they broke [into] houses and carried thatch to make bridges over which they could pass. (398) And some still say that, when night fell, the folk who were in the castle, knowing all the [English army's] difficulty, went very near, all of them, bearing doors and windows with them, so that before daytime they had bridged the streams, had all passed over, and had taken the hard field on horseback, all ready to give battle, arrayed in their equipment.

(409) When it became day the Scotsmen devoutly heard mass said, then ate a bite and got themselves ready. And when they had all mustered, and were drawn up in their divisions with their broad banners all displayed, they made knights, as was appropriate to men who share in those mysteries. (417) The king made Walter Stewart knight, and James Douglas, who was skilled, and also he made others of great valour, each in their order [of precedence]. When this that I've told you about, was done, they all went forth well in good order, and took the field quite openly; you could see in their forces many a good, vigorous, strong man, filled with the highest courage. (427) On the other side the Englishmen,

---

393-94. Maid redy thar aparaill. This is Barbour's only reference to the English activity overnight. Gray says that the English were under arms all night with their horses bitted, and the *Vita Edwardi* agrees that they 'spent the night sleepless, expecting the Scots rather to attack by night than to await battle by day'. There would be less than six hours of darkness on 23 June.

396-404. The use of thatch to make bridges is curious, unless Barbour meant 'roof timbers'. He hints at doubt about the story that the castle garrison sneaked out doors and window-shutters to make bridges. The use of roofs from one source, doors and windows from another, suggests a poetic invention, perhaps by Barbour's source. The English, with their long train of carts, must have had some timbers with them, and they knew of the marshy ground by Stirling before they entered Scotland.

406. The hard field (and at 459). The placing of this, the English camp, is now generally agreed as lying in the Carse, just below the slope and the New Park. Professor Barrow is inclined to place only the cavalry there, but the sources seem to claim that the whole army was together. The Scots too are said to have been on the hard field (449).

410. Mass was said. Bower claims that men were shriven, heard mass and took communion before the battle; he is probably following Bernard's poem which briefly says that very early in the morning masses were said. It is striking how little emphasis Barbour places on this celebration. See note to 477. The *Vita Edwardi* says that at this point Bruce gave his men bread and wine.

415-18. The making of knights before a battle was usual, a morale-builder

Housis thai brak and thak bar
To mak briggis quhar thaim mycht pas,
And sum sayis that yeit the folk that was
In the castell quhen nycht gan fall
400 For that thai knew the myscheiff all
Thai went full ner all that thai war
And duris and wyndowys with thaim bar,
Swa that thai had befor the day
Briggyt the pulis swa that thai
405 War passyt our everilkane,
And the hard feld on hors has tane 406*
All reddy for till gif batale 407*
Arayit intill thar apparaill. 406

[*The Scottish and English preparations on the morning*]

The Scottismen quhen it wes day
410 Thar mes devotly gert thai say 408
Syne tuk a sop and maid thaim yar,
And quhen thai all assemblyt war
And in thar bataillis all purvayit
With thar braid baneris all displayit
415 Thai maid knychtis, as it afferis 413
To men that usys thai mysteris.
The king maid Walter Stewart knycht
And James of Douglas that wes wycht,
And other als of gret bounté
420 He maid ilkane in thar degré. 418
Quhen this wes doyne that I you say
Thai went all furth in gud aray
And tuk the plane full apertly,
Mony gud man wicht and hardy
425 That war fulfillyt of gret bounté 423
Intill thai routis men mycht se.
The Inglismen on other party

to show that glory was to be won in victory. The English commander
did this before Stirling Bridge in 1297.

423. The plane. This is Barbour's brief mention of the Scots leaving the
New Park to take the hard field, where they would be visible to the
English. The shift of position is noted by Gray: 'at sunrise on the
morrow the Scots marched out of the wood in three divisions of
infantry'; and by the *Vita Edwardi*: 'when he learned that the English
force had occupied the field, he led his whole army out of the wood
... in three divisions.'

who shone as brightly as [if they were] angels, were not ordered in this way, for all their divisions were together in a schiltrum; but whether it was through the extreme narrowness of the place that they were in to await the fight, or was to overawe I do not know; (435) but it seemed that they were one and all in a schiltrum, apart from the vanguard alone, which were drawn up by themselves in a large force. Anyone who had come by would have seen there those folk spread over a great broad area, where many a shining shield, much burnished bright armour, many a man of great valour and many a bright brilliant banner could be seen in that great schiltrum.

(447) And when the king of England saw Scotsmen dare to take the hard field thus so openly and on foot, he was astonished, and said, 'What, are yon Scots going to fight?' (452) 'Yes indeed, Sir,' said a knight called Sir Ingram Umfraville, who continued, 'Forsooth, Sir, now I see quite the most astonishing sight that ever I saw, when, in order to fight, the Scotsmen have undertaken to give battle against the might of England on open hard ground. (460) But if you'll listen to my advice, you will easily beat them.

431, 435, 446. See also 13.175, 15.360. A schiltrum. This has often been used of habitual Scottish infantry tactics, because it occurs in Guisborough of the Scots at the battle of Falkirk (1298): after most of the cavalry fled, a few stayed to regroup (evidently) the archers (who had been in line between circles of pikemen), into circles 'which they call schiltrums'. Guisborough does not use 'schiltrum' of the four circles (surely meaning crescents) of pikemen. The force of the word is that the dispersed had been brought close together, as in Barbour where the word is used only of the English, and where there is an implied contrast between 'battaillis', divisions, and a schiltrum. Gray also uses the word, the Scots at Bannockburn advancing *de tot aleyn en schiltrome* and attacking the English *bataillis*. I take it that *aleyn* here means 'aligned', 'all in one line', not broken up, hence 'in schiltrum'. Finally Trokelowe says that 'the Scots resolutely awaited the attack; they were all on foot, picked men, enthusiastic, armed with sharp axes and other weapons, and with a density of shields fitted before them, they formed an impenetrable force.' (*Chron. Trokeleowe*, 84) Other than close order, no particular formation, weapon or tactic is meant by the word schiltrum. See *DOST* and, under 'sheltron', *NED*.

437. The vanguard. At 495–502 this is a cavalry force. (a) Lanercost and (b) Trokelowe give different versions, with a force of archers in front which probably did not advance on the Scots. Barbour has ignored this vanguard until he describes its disperal, 13.47ff. (see note to that):

(a) When both sides had made themselves ready, the archers of England came out in front of the line, with whom the Scottish archers engaged, and some were wounded, some killed, on both sides, but the English archers quickly drove off the others. (*L*, 225; *LT*, 207)

That as angelis schane brychtly
War nocht arayit on sic maner
430 For all thar bataillis samyn wer   428
In a schilthrum, but quhether it was
Throu the gret straitnes of the place
That thai war in to bid fechting
Or that it was for abaysing
435 I wate nocht, bot in a schiltrum   433
It semyt thai war all and sum,
Outane the avaward anerly
That rycht with a gret cumpany
Be thaimselvyn arayit war.
440 Quha had bene by mycht have sene thar   438
That folk ourtak a mekill feild
On breid quhar mony a schynand scheld
And mony a burnyst brycht armur
And mony man off gret valour
445 And mony a brycht baner and schene   443
Mycht in that gret schiltrum be sene.

[*Umfraville's advice to Edward II rejected*]

And quhen the king of Ingland
Swa the Scottis saw tak on hand
Takand the hard feyld sa opynly
450 And apon fute he had ferly   448
And said, 'Quhat, will yone Scottis fycht?'
'Ya sekyrly, schir,' said a knycht,
Schyr Ingrame the Umfravill hat he,
And said, 'Forsuth now, schyr, I se
455 It is the mast ferlyfull sycht   453
That evyre I saw quhen for to fycht
The Scottismen has tane on hald
Agayne the mycht of Ingland
In plane hard feld to giff bataile.
460 Bot and ye will trow my consaill   458
Ye sall discomfy thaim lychtly.

(b) The English leaders put infantry with bows and lances in the front
line; they placed the knights behind, divided into wings (*alis divisis*).
(*Chron. Trokelowe*, 84)

452–76. This Umfraville episode has all the characteristics of a literary
topos. The tactic proposed was a commonplace, and is best known in
the claim that it was used by Duke William at Hastings in 1066.

Pull back suddenly from here, with divisions and with pennons, until we pass our tents, and you will see quite quickly that they will break rank, despite their lords, and scatter to take our equipment. (468) And when we see them scattered like that, gallop on them fiercely and we will have them quite easily, for then none will be closely arrayed to fight who could withstand your great impact.' (473) The king said, 'Indeed I will not do that. For nobody is going to say that I shall avoid battle, or [that I] withdrew for such a rabble.' When what I've just reported was said, the Scotsman all together knelt down to pray to God; they made a short prayer there to God to help them in that fight. (482) And when the English king had sight of them kneeling, he said at once, 'Yon folk are kneeling to ask mercy.' Sir Ingram said, 'You are right this time; they ask mercy, but not from you. They ask God [for mercy] for their sins. I'll tell you something for a fact, that yon men will win all, or die; none will flee for fear of death.' (491) Then the king said, 'So be it.' And then without further delay, they had the bugle-call for the attack. On either side you could see many a gallant and brave man all ready to do some chivalry.

(497) Thus they were ready on either side. And Englishmen of great pride who were in their vanguard held their way straight to the division that Sir Edward commanded and led. (500) They spurred their horses

---

477–90. The Scots kneel for a short prayer. According to Bower, (after quoting Bernard's poem which mentions mass) just before the battle Maurice, abbot of Inchaffray said mass at a prominent spot and put forward a 'short and effective statement on freedom and the defence of their right'. Then he walked in front of the army with a crucifix, urging the men to prayer. They knelt (here Bower perhaps uses Barbour) and the English thought they were surrendering, but Umfraville disabused them. Barbour (like Abbot Bernard) has chosen to ignore Maurice, but the story is much the same. (*Bower*6, 362–66) Lanercost claims that after the archers on both sides had engaged, the two armies approached each other and then the Scots knelt to pray before their final advance. This seems a highly improbable Franciscan explanation of divine favour to the Scots in the battle. The kneeling in prayer clearly impressed all who were there.

Withdrawys you hyne sodandly
With bataillis and with penounys
Quhill that we pas our palyounys,
465 And ye sall se alsone that thai 463
Magre thar lordys sall brek aray
And scaile thaim our harnays to ta.
And quhen we se thaim scalit sua
Prik we than on thaim hardely
470 And we sall haf thaim wele lychtly 468
For than sall nane be knyt to fycht
That may withstand your mekill mycht.'
'I will nocht,' said the king, 'perfay
Do sa, for thar sall na man say
475 That I sall eschew the bataill 473
Na withdraw me for sic rangaile.'
Quhen this wes said that er said I
The Scottismen commounaly
Knelyt all doune to God to pray
480 And a schort prayer thar maid thai 478
To God to help thaim in that fycht,
And quhen the Inglis king had sycht
Off thaim kneland he said in hy,
'Yone folk knelis to ask mercy.'
485 Schyr Ingrahame said, 'Ye say suth now, 483
Thai ask mercy bot nane at you,
For thar trespas to God thai cry.
I tell you a thing sekyrly,
That yone men will all wyn or de,
490 For doute of dede thai sall nocht fle.' 488
'Now be it sa,' than said the king,
And than but langer delaying
Thai gert trump till the assemblé.
On ather sid men mycht than se
495 Mony a wycht man and worthi 493
Redy to do chevalry.

[*The English attack Edward Bruce's division*]

Thus war thai boune on ather sid,
And Inglismen with mekill prid
That war intill thar avaward
500 To the bataill that Schyr Edward 498
Governyt and led held straucht thar way
The hors with spuris hardnyt thai

and galloped at them boldly, and [the Scots] met them hardily so that at their meeting there was such a smashing of spears that men could hear it far away. (508) At their encounter, not a doubt, many a steed was impaled, and many a good man borne down and killed; and many a valiant deed was done there bravely, for they assaulted each other stoutly with many [kinds of] weapons. (514) Some of the horses that were stabbed reared and fell right roughly. But the rest, nonetheless, who could get to the encounter, did not hold back because of that hindrance, but attacked very strongly. (520) And [the Scots] met them sturdily, with spears that were cutting-sharp, and axes that were well ground, with which many a blow was struck. The fight there was so hard and fierce that many a worthy and brave man was felled in that struggle, and had no strength to rise again. (528) The Scotsmen battled hard to overthrow their enemy's great power. I'm sure they will refuse no effort or danger until their enemies are in really great danger.

(533) And when the earl of Moray saw their vanguard so stoutly take the way straight to Sir Edward, who met them with very great force, he held his way with his banner

---

497–590. This passage essentially narrates an attack by the English van on Edward Bruce's division, and only a little later, by Moray on the English main force. Lanercost, after describing a skirmish of archers (mentioned by no other source) and the Scots at prayer, essentially confirms Barbour's version:

> They had so arranged their army that two divisions went in front of their third, one beside the other so that neither was in front of the other, and the third, in which was Robert, followed. Indeed when the two armies made contact with one another, and the great horses of the English charged on the spears of the Scots, as it were on a dense wood, there arose a great and dreadful noise ... (*L*, 225; *LT*, 207–8)

Gray has nothing on the phases of the battle, remarking only that the Scots attacked on foot, the English mounting hastily,

> for they were not accustomed to dismount to fight on foot ... The Scots came all in line in schiltrum, and attacked the English divisions, which were crushed [together], which could in no way move towards them, until their horses were impaled on spears. (*S*, 142; *ST*, 55–56)

This translation is stilted to preserve the original, for it has been suggested that Gray says that the Scots were crushed together; I do not agree. The English charge in Lanercost corresponds to the attack on Edward Bruce in Barbour. But Lanercost and Gray agree that from the English point of view the two Scottish divisions seemed as one. For the account of the *Vita Edwardi*, which is the only source to say that the Scots attacked first, see note to 13.1.

And prikyt apon thaim sturdely,
And thai met thaim rycht hardely
505   Sua that at thar assemble thar   503
Sic a fruschyng of speris war
That fer away men mycht it her.
At that meting foroutyn wer
War stedis stekyt mony ane
510   And mony gude man borne doune and slayne,   508
And mony ane hardyment douchtely
Was thar eschevyt, for hardely
Thai dang on other with wapnys ser.
Sum of the hors that stekyt wer
515   Ruschyt and relyt rycht rudlye,   513
Bot the remanand nocht-forthi
That mycht cum to the assembling
For that led maid na stinting
Bot assemblyt full hardely,
520   And thai met thaim full sturdely   518
With speris that wer scharp to scher
And axys that weile groundyn wer
Quhar-with was roucht mony a rout.
The fechting wes thar sa fell and stout
525   That mony a worthi man and wicht   523
Throu fors wes fellyt in that fycht
That had na mycht to rys agane.
The Scottismen fast gan thaim payn
Thar fayis mekill mycht to rus,
530   I trow thai sall na payn refuse   528
Na perell quhill thar fayis be
Set in weill hard perplexité.

[Moray's men attack the main English host]

And quhen the erle of Murref swa
Thar vaward saw sa stoutly ga
535   The way to Schyr Edward all straucht   533
That met thaim with full mekill maucht,
He held hys way with his baner

521–22. The *Vita Edwardi* remarks that not one of the Scots was horsed,
'but each was provided with light armour which a sword would not
readily penetrate; they had axes at their sides and carried spears in their
hands'. (*VitaEd.* 52) The resistance to penetration suggests a quilted
or leather coat or jacket. For Trokelowe's comments on the Scots' arms
see next note.

to the great army, where there were together the nine divisions of such breadth, which had so many banners with them, and with such a quantity of men, that it was remarkable to see. (543) The good earl took the way there with his division in good order, and attacked so strongly that if you had come by you would have heard a great crash of the spears that broke, for their enemies attacked fast, galloping on steeds with great arrogance, as if to ride down the earl and all his company. (552) But [the latter] met them so firmly that they bore many of them down to the earth, for many a horse was impaled there, and many good men felled under their feet had no chance of getting up again. (557) There you could see a remorseless battle, some defending, some attacking, and many a royal knock-out thwack dealt there on both sides, until blood burst through the mail-coat and went streaming down to the earth. (563) The earl of Moray and his men carried themselves so valiantly then that they won more and more ground from their enemies, although [the enemy] was ten or more to [their] one, I'm sure, so that it even seemed that they were lost among so huge a host, like [men] plunged into the sea. (571) And when the Englishmen saw the earl and all his men together fight so stoutly and fearlessly, as if they were not discouraged, they pressed the [Scots] with all their might. And, with bright spears and swords and axes that cut pretty sharply, the [latter] met them there, face to face. (579) There you could see a fierce engagement, and many men of great valour

To the gret rout quhar samyn wer
The nyne bataillis that war sa braid,
540   That sa fele baneris with thaim haid   538
And of men sa gret quantité
That it war wonder for to se.
The gud erle thidder tuk the way
With his battaill in gud aray
545   And assemblit sa hardily   543
That men mycht her that had bene by
A gret frusch of the speris that brast,
For thar fayis assemblyt fast
That on stedis with mekill prid
550   Come prikand as thai wald our-rid   548
The erle and all his cumpany,
Bot thai met thaim sa sturdely
That mony of thaim till erd thai bar,
For mony a sted was stekyt thar
555   And mony gud man fellyt under fet   553
That had na hap to rys up yete.
Thar mycht men se a hard bataill
And sum defend and sum assaile
And mony a reale romble rid
560   Be roucht thar apon ather sid   558
Quhill throu the byrnys bryst the blud
That till erd doune stremand yhude.
The erle of Murreff and his men
Sa stoutly thaim contenyt then
565   That thai wan place ay mar and mar   563
On thar fayis the-quhether thai war
Ay ten far ane or may perfay,
Sua that it semyt weill that thai
War tynt amang sa gret menye
570   As thai war plungyt in the se.   568
And quhen the Inglismen has sene
The erle and all his men bedene
Faucht sa stoutly but effraying
Rycht as thai had nane abasing
575   Thaim pressyt thai with all thar mycht   573
And thai with speris and swerdis brycht
And axis that rycht scharply schar
Ymyddis the vesag met thaim thar.
Thar mycht men se a stalwart stour
580   And mony men of gret valour   578

with spears, maces, knives and other weapons, give up their lives, so that many fell down dead; the grass grew red with the blood. (585) The earl, who was valiant and bold, and his men, fought so manfully that anyone who saw them on that day would, I am sure, have said that they did their duty well, so that their foes felt it.

With speris mas and knyffis
And other wapynnys wyssyll thar lyvis
Sua that mony fell doune all dede,
The greys woux with the blud all reid
585 The erle that wycht wes and worthi 583
And his men faucht sa manlyly
That quha-sa had sene thaim that day
I trow forsuth that thai suld say
That thai suld do thar devor wele
590 Swa that thar fayis suld it fele. 588

When these first two divisions had engaged, as I said to you before, the Steward, Walter that is, and also the good lord of Douglas, in one division, when they saw the earl, without fear or dread, with his company, encounter all the [English] folk so sturdily, they held their way to help him with their division, in good array, (11) and clashed so strongly a little way beside the earl, that the enemy certainly felt their arrival, for with strong steel weapons they launched [themselves] on [the English] with all their might. Their foes received [their attack] well, I'm sure, with swords, spears and maces. (18) The battle was so fierce there, [with] such a huge spilling of blood, that pools [of it] formed on the earth. The Scotsmen bore themselves so well, made such great slaughter there and deprived so many of their lives, that the whole field was left bloody. (25) At that time the three divisions were fighting there pretty closely side by side. You could hear many a blow there, and weapons falling on armour, and see knights and horses fall, with lots of rich and flamboyant clothes trampled basely underfoot; some kept on [saddle], some [fell and] lost their lives. (33) They fought like that for a long while, [so] that you could hear no noise there;

1-24. Barbour here engages the division of the Steward and Douglas. With McDiarmid I doubt that this division existed. (*B1985*, 89) The *Vita Edwardi* states that the Scots had three divisions, and advanced like a thick hedge, not easily broken:

When matters were such that the two sides met, James Douglas, who commanded the first division of the Scots, attacked the earl of Gloucester's force fiercely. The earl withstood him vigorously, penetrated their formation once and again, and would have achieved a triumph if he had had faithful companions. But, lo! Suddenly the Scots make a rush, the earl's horse is killed and the earl falls to the ground. He lacked a defender and burdened by the excessive weight of his body [armour] he could not easily get up, but among the five hundred whom he had brought to the battle at his own expense, he alone was killed ... Some said [*Gloucester died as the result of a dispute with Hereford over who should lead the English van*]. While they disputed ... and the Scottish division was approaching fiercely ... Gloucester flung himself forward out of line (*inordinate*) wanting to achieve the glory of the first encounter, but, lo!, the earl is met by the advancing Scots and his horse immediately killed ... he was shamefully killed. (*VitaEd.* 52–53)

[*Douglas's division attacks*]

Quhen thir twa fyrst bataillis wer
Assemblyt as I said you er,
The Stewart Walter that than was
And the gud lord als of Douglas
5 In a bataill, quhen that thai saw
The erle foroutyn dred or aw
Assembill with his cumpany
On all that folk sa sturdely
For till help him thai held thar way
10 And thar bataill in gud aray,
And assemblyt sa hardely
Besid the erle a litill by
That thar fayis feld thar cummyn wele,
For with wapynnys stalwart of stele
15 Thai dang apon with all thar mycht.
Thar fayis resavyt weile Ik hycht
With swerdis speris and with mase,
The bataill thar sa feloune was
And sua rycht gret spilling of blud
20 That on the erd the flousis stud.
The Scottismen sa weill thaim bar
And sua gret slauchter maid thai thar
And fra sa fele the lyvis revyt
That all the feld bludy wes levyt.
25 That tyme thar thre bataillis wer
All syd be sid fechtand weill ner,
Thar mycht men her mony dynt
And wapynnys apon armuris stynt,
And se tumble knychtis and stedis
30 And mony rich and reale wedis
Defoullyt foully under fete,
Sum held on loft sum tynt the suet.
A lang quhill thus fechtand thai war
That men na noyis mycht her thar,

There can be no doubt that Gloucester was in the English van, which
Barbour states (12.499–500) advanced against Edward Bruce's division;
see note to 469. Douglas probably served under Edward Bruce, see
Bannockburn Commentary.

men heard nothing but grunts and blows, that struck fire as you do striking a flint. (37) They fought each other so intently that they made neither shout nor yell, but struck each other with all their might, with weapons that were burnished bright. The arrows, too, flew so thickly there, that those who saw them could well have said that they made a horrible shower, for wherever they fell, I promise you, they left tokens behind them that needed medical treatment.

(47) The English archers fired so fast that if their shooting had persisted, it would have gone hard for the Scotsmen. But King Robert, who knew well what a danger their archers were, [with] their hard and right hurtful shooting, ordered out of the fray his marischal, with a great company, (55) five hundred armed in steel, who were well horsed on light steeds, to gallop among the archers and so attack them with spears, that they would have no opportunity to fire. This marischal that I tell of, who was called Sir Robert Keith, as I've told you before, when he saw the divisions encounter and clash together thus, and saw the archers firing boldly, with [the men] of all his company rode quickly against them, and came upon them at a flank; (69) [he] rode among them so forcefully, spearing them so relentlessly, knocking [them] down and slaying them in such numbers without mercy, that one and all they scattered; from that time on none gathered to try such firing.

41–49. The English archers. Lanercost, I suggest, was correct in placing the exchange between the archers on both sides before the battle began. He says that the English archers were advanced before the [cavalry] line, and Trokelowe says this even more strongly. See note to 12.437. That is surely required also by Barbour's version, for the Scottish cavalry could not have attacked them behind the English cavalry. Lanercost claims that the Scots, Barbour that the English, were driven off. But bickering by archers seems to have been a usual preliminary to battle, and would be broken off when the main forces advanced, leaving each group of archers to claim withdrawal by the other. It has been remarked that Edward II seems not to have favoured large archery contingents in his armies.

53–75. The Scottish light horse. The English sources comment on the Scots fighting on foot. Barbour had earlier reported the king's decision to fight the battle on foot (11.297), and the appearance of 'light horse' 'ordered in front of the fray' is unexplained. Certainly there was a Scottish cavalry force, see Bannockburn Commentary.

35 Men hard nocht bot granys and dintis
That slew fyr as men slayis on flyntis,
Thai faucht ilk ane sa egerly
That thai maid nother moyis na cry
Bot dang on other at thar mycht
40 With wapnys that war burnyst brycht.
The arowys als sua thyk thar flaw
That thai mycht say wele that thaim saw
That thai a hidwys schour gan ma,
For quhar thai fell Ik undreta
45 Thai left efter thaim taknyng
That sall ned as I trow leching.

[Sir Robert Keith's cavalry disperses the English archers]

The Inglis archeris schot sa fast
That mycht thar schot haff ony last
It had bene hard to Scottismen
50 Bot King Robert that wele gan ken
That thar archeris war peralous
And thar schot rycht hard and grevous
Ordanyt forouth the assemblé
Hys marschell with a gret menye,
55 Fyve hunder armyt into stele
That on lycht hors war horsyt welle,
For to pryk amang the archeris
And sua assaile thaim with thar speris
That thai na layser haiff to schut.
60 This marschell that Ik off mute
That Schyr Robert of Keyth was cauld
As Ik befor her has you tauld
Quhen he saw the bataillis sua
Assembill and togidder ga
65 And saw the archeris schoyt stoutly,
With all thaim off his cumpany
In hy apon thaim gan he rid
And ourtuk thaim at a sid,
And ruschyt amang thaim sa rudly
70 Stekand thaim sa dispitously
And in sic fusoun berand doun
And slayand thaim foroutyn ransoun
That thai thaim scalyt everilkane,
And fra that tyme furth thar wes nane
75 That assemblyt schot to ma.

(76) When the Scottish archers saw that they had been driven back like that, they grew bold, shot eagerly with all their might among the horsemen who rode there, and made terrible wounds among them, slaying a very great many of them. (82) They behaved boldly and well, for, after the enemy's archers were scattered, as I said to you before, who were more numerous than they were by a large number, so that they did not fear their firing, they grew so bold that they thought they would completely defeat their enemies.

(89) The marischal and his company were still, as I said before, among the archers where they made space with spears where they rode, and slew all that they could overtake. They could do this quite easily because they had no blows to stop nor [had they] to withstand a knock. And unarmed men have little power to fight against those with armour. [The English archers] scattered in such a way that some pulled back in great haste to their great division, and some fled altogether. (103) But the folk who were behind them and who had no space for their own men who had still to reach the [place of] conflict, soon came bang up against the archers whom they met fleeing, and who were then made so frightened that they clean lost heart; I'm sure that they will not harm the Scots much that day with firing. (112) And good King Robert, who was always filled with a generous spirit, saw how his three divisions were engaged so strongly there, bore themselves so well in the fighting,

---

99–111. Barbour attributes the confusion in the English ranks to the withdrawal of the archers. The point (104–5) that the rear ranks could not struggle through to the battle is made by both (a) Gray and (b) Lanercost:

(a) [see passage in note to 12.497] ... the English divisions which were crushed [together], which could in no way move towards them until their horses were impaled on spears. The troops in the English rear fell back upon the ditch of Bannockburn falling over one another. The English divisions, thrown into confusion by the thrust of spears upon the horses, began to flee. (S, 142; ST, 56)

(b) [see passage in note to 12.497] when the two armies made contact with each other and the great horses of the English charged on the spears of the Scots, as it were on a dense wood, there arose a great and dreadful noise of spears broken and of destriers wounded to death; so they remained for a while in peace. The English who followed could not reach the Scots on account of the leading division being interposed, nor could they help themselves at all, and so there remained nothing but to take to flight. (L, 225–26; LT, 208)

Quhen Scottis archeris saw that thai sua
War rebutyt thai woux hardy
And with all thar mycht schot egrely
Amang the horsmen that thar raid
80 And woundis wid to thaim thai maid
And slew of thaim a full gret dele.
Thai bar thaim hardely and wele
For, fra thar fayis archeris war
Scalyt as I said till you ar
85 That ma na thai war be gret thing
Sua that thai dred nocht thar schoting
Thai woux sa hardy that thaim thocht
Thai suld set all thar fayis at nocht.

[The king addresses his division and commits it to the battle]

The merschell and his cumpany
90 Wes yeit, as till you er said I,
Amang the archeris quhar thai maid
With speris roume quhar that thai raid
And slew all that thai mycht ourta,
And thai wele lychtly mycht do sua
95 For thai had nocht a strak to stynt
Na for to hald agayne a dynt,
And agayne armyt men to fycht
May nakyt men have litill mycht.
Thai scalyt thaim on sic maner
100 That sum to thar gret bataill wer
Withdrawyn thaim in full gret hy
And sum war fled all utrely,
Bot the folk that behind thaim was,
That for thar awne folk had na space
105 Yheyt to cum to the assembling
In agayn smertly gan thai ding
The archeris that thai met fleand
That then war maid sa recreand
That thar hartis war tynt clenly,
110 I trow thai sall nocht scaith gretly
The Scottismen with schot that day.
And the gud King Robert that ay
Wes fillyt off full gret bounte
Saw how that his bataillis thre
115 Sa hardely assemblyt thar
And sa weill in the fycht thaim bar

and pressed so hard on their foes that he thought none was losing heart, and how the archers had scattered then, he was very cheerful, and said to his men, (121) 'Lords, now be careful that you are worthy, bold, and of good skills at this fight; and struggle so hard that nothing will withstand you. (126) Our men are fighting so freshly that they have thrown the enemy into such disorder that if the [enemy] are pressed a little harder, you'll see that they'll soon be defeated.' When this was said, they held their way and fought on one field so stoutly that when they came upon their foes, [these] were drastically pushed back.

(135) There you could see men fighting for dear life, and men who were worthy and brave do many a courageous act, fighting as though they were in a rage, for when the Scots especially saw their foes standing against them in battle so sturdily, with all their might and main they laid into [them] like men out of their wits. (144) Where they could strike with a full stroke, there no armour could withstand their blow. They cut down those they could overtake, and gave such blows with axes that they split heads and helmets. Their foes met them right boldly and whacked them doughtily with weapons that were of strong steel. (152) The battle was well-fought there. There was such a din of blows, [such] as weapons landing on armour, such a great breaking of spears, such pressure and such pushing, such snarling and groaning,

---

112–61. Barbour commits the king's division to the battle. Although the English sources agree that there were three Scottish divisions, and some mention the initial advance of two of them, no English source confirms the engagement of the third division.

And sua fast on thair fayis gan ding
That him thocht nane had abaysing
And how the archeris war scalyt then,
120 He was all blyth and till his men
He said, 'Lordingis, now luk that ye
Worthy and off gud covyn be
At thys assemblé and hardy,
And assembill sa sturdely
125 That na thing may befor you stand.
Our men ar sa freschly fechtand
That thai thar fayis has contrayit sua
That be thai pressyt, Ik underta,
A litill fastyr, ye sall se
130 That thai discumfyt sone sall be.'
Quhen this wes said thai held thar way
And on ane feld assemblyt thai
Sa stoutly that at thar cummyng
Thar fayis war ruschyt a gret thing.

[*A further description of the fighting*]

135 Thar mycht men se men felly fycht
And men that worthi war and wycht
Do mony worthi vasselage,
Thai faucht as thai war in a rage,
For quhen the Scottis ynkirly
140 Saw thar fayis sa sturdely
Stand into bataill thaim agayn
With all thar mycht and all thar mayn
Thai layid on as men out of wit
And quhar thai with full strak mycht hyt
145 Thar mycht na armur stynt thar strak.
Thai to-fruschyt that thai mycht ourtak
And with axis sic duschys gave
That thai helmys and hedis clave,
And thar fayis rycht hardely
150 Met thaim and dang on thaim douchtely
With wapnys that war styth of stele.
Thar wes the bataill strikyn wele.
Sa gret dyn thar wes of dyntis
As wapnys apon armur styntis,
155 And off speris sa gret bresting
And sic thrang and sic thrysting,
Sic gyrnyng granyng and sa gret

so much noise as they struck the others, and shouted rallying cries on each side, giving and receiving great wounds, that it was horrible to hear. (162) At that all four divisions were fighting altogether on one front. Ah! Mighty God! how bravely Sir Edward Bruce and his men bore themselves among their foes then, (167) fighting in such good spirit, so hardy, worthy and distinguished, that [the English] vanguard was defeated and, in spite of their [men], left the ground going for safety to the great host, which had got into so much trouble that they were dismayed, for the Scots relentlessly attacked them, who were then all in one schiltrum. (176) Whoever chanced to fall in that fighting, I don't think he would get up again! There you could see valiant deeds of many kinds accomplished boldly, and many brave and strong [men] soon lying dead underfoot, where all the field was red with blood; the arms and coats of arms that they wore were so besmirched with blood there, that they could not be made out. (186) Ah! Mighty God! Anyone who could see Walter Stewart and his following, and the good Douglas, who was so brave, fighting then in that mighty encounter, would say that those who pressed their foes' might so hard in that fight, defeating them wherever they went, were worthy of all honour. (194) There you could see many a steed fleeing riderless without a lord. Ah! Lord! [Anyone] who then paid attention to the good earl of Moray and his [men] who gave such mighty blows, and fought so hard in that battle, undergoing such toil and trouble

---

162–224. Barbour runs again through his other three Scottish divisions – Edward Bruce, Douglas, Moray – but adds nothing specific. This is vivid padding.

A noyis as thai gan other beit
And ensenyeys on ilka sid
160 Gevand and takand woundis wid,
That it wes hydwys for to her.
All four thar bataillis with that wer
Fechtand in a frount halyly.
A! mycht God! how douchtely
165 Schyr Edward the Bruce and his men
Amang thar fayis contenyt thaim then
Fechtand in sa gud covyn
Sa hardy worthy and sa fyne
That thar vaward ruschyt was
170 And maugré tharis left the place,
And till thar gret rout to warand
Thai went that tane had apon hand
Sa gret anoy that thai war effrayit
For Scottis that thaim hard assayit
175 That than war in a schiltrum all.
Quha hapnyt into that fycht to fall
I trow agane he suld nocht rys.
Thar mycht men se on mony wys
Hardimentis eschevyt douchtely,
180 And mony that wycht war and hardy
Sone liand undre fete all dede
Quhar all the feld off blud wes red,
Armys and quyntys that thai bar
With blud war sa defoulyt thar
185 That thai mycht nocht descroyit be.
A! mychty God! quha than mycht se
That Stewart Walter and his rout
And the gud Douglas that wes sa stout
Fechtand into that stalwart stour,
190 He suld say that till all honour
Thai war worthi that in that fycht
Sa fast pressyt thar fayis mycht
That thaim ruschyt quhar thai yeid.
Thar men mycht se mony a steid
195 Fleand on stray that lord had nane.
A! Lord! quha then gud tent had tane
Till the gud erle of Murreff
And his that sua gret routis geff
And faucht sa fast in that battaill
200 Tholand sic paynys and travaill

that they and theirs made such an affray that whereever they came they made a way. (203) Then men could hear rallying cries, and Scotsmen shouting boldly, 'On them, on them, on them! They yield!' With that they attacked so hard, killing all they could overcome, and the Scottish archers also shot so swiftly among them, harassing them so grievously (210) that, what with those who were fighting against them, raining such mighty blows on them, pressing them so fiercely, and what with the arrows that made so many wicked wounds upon them, persistently slaying their horses also, they gave a little ground. (218) They feared dying then so greatly that their discipline got worse and worse, for those who were fighting against them set boldness, strength and will, and heart and courage too, with all their might and all their main, to put them utterly to flight.

(225) At this point that I am telling of just now, when that battle was being fought in this way, where on each side they were fighting vigorously, yeomen and boys and men on foot who had been left in the Park to guard the provisions, when they knew without doubt that their lords were fighting their enemies in desperate combat, (234) made one of themselves, [of those] who were there, chieftain of them all, and fastened sheets that were fairly broad in place of banners upon long poles and spears, saying that they meant to see the fight, and help their lords to their utmost.

225–64. According to Barbour, Bruce on Sunday sent the small folk and carters (20,000 in number) with equipment and victuals into the Park well away from him, and they took their way to a valley (11.427–31). However, they now reappear as 15,000 in the Park, and are given a fairly decisive role in breaking English morale, although they never actually reach the battle. The traditional association of their 'valley' with Coxet Hill seems unlikely. In a late chronicle largely derived from Bower we are told that 'the king instructed the carriage men, varlets and boys, that when they saw the armies engaged they should go with standards made from sheets and clothes, and preceded by trumpets, from the neighbouring wood, [mounted] on carriage horses, so that when the English saw them they would think they were an army twice the size of the army they were fighting with. The king and his men quickly mount and attack the enemy, and the carriage men came out of the wood as was ordained ... Victory went to the Scots.' (*Extracta e Variis Cronicis Scocie* (1842), 140–41) This may be an elaboration of Barbour, of no independent value. At 496–500 the king also had victual and 'men enough' at Cambuskenneth abbey – possibly cavalry supplies. Probably the carters did choose a leader (the most interesting feature of the story) late on, intent on sharing in the loot, but too late to fight.

That thai and tharis maid sic debat
That quhar thai come thai maid thaim gat.
Than mycht men her ensenyeis cry
And Scottismen cry hardely,
205   'On thaim, on thaim, on thaim, thai faile.'
With that sa hard thai gan assaile
And slew all that thai mycht ourta,
And the Scottis archeris alsua
Schot amang thaim sa deliverly
210   Engrevand thaim sa gretumly
That quhat for thaim that with thaim faucht
That sua gret routis to thaim raucht
And pressyt thaim full egrely
And quhat for arowis that felly
215   Mony gret woundis gan thaim ma
And slew fast off thar hors alsua,
That thai wandyst a litill wei.
Thai dred sa gretly then to dey
That thar covyn wes wer and wer,
220   For thaim that fechtand with thaim wer
Set hardyment and strenth and will
And hart and corage als thar-till
And all thar mayne and all thar mycht
To put thaim fully to flycht.

[*The men guarding supplies in the Park choose a leader and move towards the battle, dismaying the English*]

225   In this tyme that I tell off her
At that bataill on this maner
Wes strykyn quhar on ather party
Thai war fechtand enforcely,
Yomen and swanys and pitaill
230   That in the Park to yeme vittaill
War left, quhen thai wist but lesing
That thar lordis with fell fechting
On thar fayis assemblyt wer,
Ane off thaimselvyn that war thar
235   Capitane off thaim all thai maid,
And schetis that war sumdele brad
Thai festnyt in steid of baneris
Apon lang treys and speris,
And said that thai wald se the fycht
240   And help thar lordis at thar mycht.

(241) When all had agreed to this, they gathered in one body – they were fifteen thousand or more – and then at great speed they went with their banners all in one force, as if they had been strong brave men. (247) They came with all that gathering to just where they could see the battle, then all together they gave a cry, 'Kill! kill! On them now!' and with that they were coming, although they were still far away. (253) The Englishmen who were giving ground by force of pressure, as I said before, when they saw coming towards them such a company, shouting like that, [a company] which they thought was at least as numerous as that fighting against them there, and which they had not seen before, [well,] you can believe without a doubt, that they were so badly disheartened, that the best, the bravest, who were in their army that day, wished that they were [somewhere else] with their honour. (265) King Robert saw from their pulling-back that they were close to defeat, and had his battle cry shouted, then with those of his company pressed his enemies so hard that they were so apprehensive that they gave ground more and more, for all the Scotsmen who were there, when they saw them escaping from the fighting, laid into them with all their might. (275) They scattered in sundry groups and were close to defeat; some of them fled openly, but those who were brave and bold, whom shame prevented from fleeing, kept up the struggle at great cost, standing firm in the fight.

Quhen her-till all assentyt wer
In a rout thai assemblit er
Fyften thousand thai war or ma,
And than in gret hy gan thai ga
245 With thar baneris all in a rout
As thai had men bene styth and stout.
Thai come with all that assemblé
Rycht quhill thai mycht the bataill se,
Than all at anys thai gave a cry,
250 'Sla! sla! apon thaim hastily!'
And thar-withall cumand war thai,
Bot thai war wele fer yete away.
And Inglismen that ruschyt war
Throuch fors of fycht as I said ar
255 Quhen thai saw cummand with sic a cry
Towart thaim sic a cumpany
That thaim thocht wele als mony war
As that wes fechtand with thaim thar
And thai befor had nocht thaim sene,
260 Than wit ye weill withoutyn wene
Thai war abaysit sa gretumly
That the best and the mast hardy
That war intill thar ost that day
Wald with thar mensk haf bene away.

[The king presses the enemy harder and some flee]

265 The King Robert be thar relyng
Saw thai war ner at discomfiting
And his ensenye gan hely cry,
Than with thaim off his cumpany
His fayis he pressyt sa fast that thai
270 War intill sa gret effray
That thai left place ay mar and mar,
For the Scottismen that thar war
Quhen thai saw thaim eschew the fycht
Dang on thaim with all thar mycht
275 That thai scalyt thaim in troplys ser
And till discomfitur war ner
And sum off thaim fled all planly,
Bot thai that wycht war and hardy
That schame lettyt to ta the flycht
280 At gret myscheiff mantemyt the fycht
And stythly in the stour gan stand.

(282) When the king of England saw his men fleeing in various places, and saw the enemy's army that had grown so brave and bold that all his folk were altogether so dismayed that they lacked strength to withstand their foes in the encounter, (289) he was so greatly discouraged that he and his company [of] five hundred fully armed [men] in a mighty rush all took to flight and made towards the castle. (294) Yet I've heard some men say that Sir Aymer de Valence, when he saw the field almost lost, led the king away from the fighting by his rein against his will, and when Sir Giles d'Argentan saw the king and his company making to flee so speedily thus, he came swiftly right to the king and said, (303) 'Sir, since you mean to go [on] your way like this, [I] bid you good day, for I mean to [go] back; assuredly I never yet fled, and I choose to stay here and die, rather than to live in shame [by] flight. (309) Without another [word] he turned his bridle,

---

290–98. Edward II leaves the battlefield. At 11.180–86 Barbour notes that Edward II appointed Giles d'Argentan and Aymer de Valence to be responsible for his reins on either side; the duty was to get the king out of difficulty and danger. The *Vita Edwardi* confirms that d'Argentan was in command of the king's rein. (*VitaEd.* 53)

(a) Gray (b) Trokelowe (confirming Edward's courage) and (c) the *Vita Edwardi* comment on Edward's departure:

(a) [*continuing from note to 99*] Those who had been appointed to [look after] the king's rein seeing the debacle, led the king off the field by the reins, towards the castle, despite his going much vexed at his departure. As the Scottish knights, who were on foot, took in their hands the covering of the king's destrier, to have him stopped, he struck out so vigorously behind him with a mace, that no-one whom he struck was not knocked to the ground. (*S*, 142; *ST*, 56)

(b) The king, taking the ruin and flight of his men with a bitter spirit, and despising the fear of death from a strength of rage, swallowing a more bitter spirit, rushed fiercely against the enemy like a lion which had lost its whelps, and in the way of a bold knight, spilled the blood of many with a flashing sword. But the groups of knights (*militares acies*), considering that he was placed in such peril, could scarcely drag him out, undefeated and pretty reluctant, from such danger. And pulling back thus, compelled by his men, he began [his] flight, awaiting a better fortune and promising that at a time of retribution he would dearly repay the injuries done to him. (*Chron. Trokelowe*, 86)

(c) [*continuing from note to 99*] When those who were with our king saw that [Gloucester's] division was broken and his companions ready to flee, they said that it would be dangerous to delay any longer, but safer for the king to withdraw. At their remarks the king left the field and went towards the castle. Moreover when the king's banner was seen to leave, the whole army quickly dispersed. (*VitaEd*, 54)

295. Valence. According to Lanercost, Pembroke left the army on foot

[*King Edward abandons the battle, but Sir Giles d'Argentan fights on and is killed*]

    And quhen the king of Ingland
    Saw his men fley in syndry place,
    And saw his fayis rout that was
285 Worthyn sa wycht and sa hardy
    That all his folk war halyly
    Sa stonayit that thai had na mycht
    To stynt thar fayis in the fycht,
    He was abaysyt sa gretumly
290 That he and his cumpany
    Fyve hunder armyt all at rycht
    Intill a frusch all tok the flycht
    And to the castell held thar way,
    And yeit haiff Ik hard som men say
295 That off Valence Schir Aymer
    Quhen he the feld saw vencusyt ner
    Be the reyngye led away the king
    Agayne his will fra the fechting.
    And quhen Schyr Gylis the Argenté
300 Saw the king thus and his menye
    Schap thaim to fley sa spedyly,
    He come rycht to the king in hy
    And said, 'Schyr, sen it is sua
    That ye thusgat your gat will ga
305 Havys gud day for agayne will I,
    Yeit fled I never sekyrly
    And I cheys her to bid and dey
    Than for to lyve schamly and fley.'
    His bridill but mar abad

---

and saved himself with the fleeing Welsh; Melsa, that he was among those fleeing to Dunbar; Trokelowe comments that 'after the death of many, he scarcely escaped the peril of death,' and the London annals say he fled barefoot.

299–319. The death of d'Argentan. According to Gray:

As those who had his rein drew him thus always forward, Giles d'Argentan, a famous knight ... said to the king, 'Sir, your rein was committed to me. You are now in safety. See, there is your castle where your body could be safe. I am not accustomed to flee nor will I do so now. I commend you to God.' Then setting spurs to his horse, he returned to the fray, where he was killed. (*S*, 142–43; *ST*, 56–57) But the *Vita* claims that he had hurried to help Gloucester and died with him, 'thinking it more honourable to die with so great a man than to escape death by flight'.

rode back and galloped at Sir Edward Bruce's force, which was so stout and unyielding, as though he had no fear of anything, shouting 'Argentan'. (315) They met him so with spears, and set so many spears upon him, that he and his horse were so pressed that both fell to earth and he was killed in that very place. There was great sorrow at his death, [for] in truth he was the third best knight who lived in his time known to men; he achieved many a fine feat of arms. (324) He fought three campaigns against the Saracens, and in each of those campaigns he defeated two Saracens. His great valour came to an end [in this battle].

(328) When Sir Aymer had fled with the king, there was none who dared remain, but [all] fled scattering in every direction, their foes pressing them hard. (332) Truth to tell, they were so terrified, and they fled in fear so fast, that a very great part of them fled to the River Forth and there most of them were drowned; Bannockburn between [its] banks was so filled with men and horse that men could then pass dry-foot over it on drowned horses and men. (341) Lads, boys and rabble, when they saw the [English] force defeated, ran among them and killed them like men who could put up no defence – it was dreadful to see. (346) I never heard of where in any country people were placed in such a dilemna; on one side they had their foes, killing them without mercy,

---

321-27. D'Argentan's reputation. Bower reports a response to Edward II by his chief herald, called 'King Robert', that d'Argentan was one of the three best knights of that time, with Emperor Henry VII and King Robert I; the herald mentioned d'Argentan defeating two Saracens in each of three encounters – but Bower could have got this from Barbour. (*Bower7*, 52–57)

335. The Forth. Other sources do not mention deaths there.

337-55. Death in Bannockburn. For deaths see below on 397. Barbour is confirmed here by (a) Lanercost and (b) the *Vita Edwardi*:

(a) Another misfortune befell the English in that whereas they had shortly before crossed a big ditch into which the tide flows, called Bannockburn, and now wished to recross it in confusion, many nobles and others fell into it with their horses, in the press, and [while] some escaped with great difficulty, many could never extricate themselves from the ditch. (*L*, 226; *LT*, 208)

(b) While our folk fled, following in the steps of the king, lo! a certain ditch caught many, and a great part of our men died in it. (*VitaEd*, 54)

310 He turnyt and agayne he rade
     And on Edward the Bruys rout
     That wes sa sturdy and sa stout
     As drede off nakyn thing had he
     He prikyt, cryand, 'the Argenté,'
315 And thai with speris sua him met
     And sua fele speris on him set
     That he and hors war chargyt sua
     That bathe till the erd gan ga
     And in that place thar slane wes he.
320 Off hys deid wes rycht gret pité,
     He wes the thrid best knycht perfay
     That men wyst lyvand in his day,
     He did mony a fayr journé.
     On Saryzynys thre derenyeys faucht he
325 And intill ilk derenye off tha
     He vencussyt Saryzynnys twa.
     His gret worschip tuk thar ending.

[*The English army scatters; many are drowned in Bannock-
burn or are killed by Scots*]

     And fra Schyr Aymer with the king
     Was fled wes nane that durst abid
330 Bot fled scalyt on ilka sid,
     And thar fayis thaim pressyt fast.
     Thai war to say suth sua agast
     And fled sa fast rycht effrayitly
     That off thaim a full gret party
335 Fled to the water of Forth and thar
     The mast part off thaim drownyt war,
     And Bannokburne betwix the brays
     Off men and hors sua stekyt wais
     That apon drownyt hors and men
340 Men mycht pas dry out-our it then.
     And laddis swanys and rangaill
     Quhen thai saw vencussyt the bataill
     Ran amang thaim and sua gan sla
     As folk that na defens mycht ma
345 That war pitté for to se.
     Ik herd never quhar in na contré
     Folk at sa gret myscheiff war stad,
     On ane sid thai thar fayis bad
     That slew thaim doun foroutyn mercy,

and on the other side they had Bannockburn which was so difficult to pass because of [its] mud and depth so that none could ride over it. (354) They had to stay, despite themselves, so that some were slain and some drowned; none who ever came there could escape, although many got away who fled elsewhere, as I shall explain.

(359) The king with those he had with him rode in a group to the castle, and wanted to get inside, for they did not know what way [to take] to get away, but Philip Mowbray said to [the king], 'The castle, sir, is at your disposal, but if you come into it you will see that you will soon be besieged, and no-one from England will undertake to relieve you, and without relief no castle can be held for long, as you well know. (371) So take courage, rally your men around you very strongly, and take your way around the Park, in as close order as you can [manage], for I'm sure that none who chases you will have strength to fight with so many [men].' (377) They did what he advised, going soon beneath the castle, holding close by the Round Table, and then they went round the Park, holding speedily toward Linlithgow. (382) But I know that they will quickly be convoyed by such folk as they would prefer (I'm sure) [to be] quite elsewhere, for Sir James lord of Douglas came to the king and asked [for] the pursuit, [which] he gave him without hesitation. (388) But he had far too few horse, having fewer than sixty in his force,

---

359–76. The king at the castle. Barbour does not claim that Edward was refused entry, but the *Vita* is unsure:

> The king, coming to the castle and thinking to have refuge there, was repulsed like an enemy; the drawbridge was raised and the gate closed. Therefore the keeper of the castle was thought by many to be not innocent of betrayal, and yet he was seen that day armed in formation, as if to fight for the king. I neither absolve the keeper nor accuse him of betrayal ... If the king had been admitted, he would never have escaped without capture. (*VitaEd*, 54)

377–81. Edward's flight. Gray remarks that 'the king's destrier was wounded and could go no further, [so] he was remounted on a courser which was led all around the Torwood and through the plains of Lothian.' According to Lanercost, the king's flight was 'guided by a certain knight of Scotland who knew through what districts they could escape,' but this seems an unlikely embellishment about men who had travelled in the other direction only two days before.

393. The account of Douglas's pursuit begins at 551.

350   And thai had on the tother party
    Bannokburne that sua cumbyrsum was
    For slyk and depnes for to pas
    That thar mycht nane out-our it rid,
    Thaim worthit maugré tharis abid
355   Sua that sum slayne sum drownyt war,
    Mycht nane eschap that ever come thar
    The-quhether mony gat away
    That ellisquhair fled as I sall say.

[*Edward II goes by Stirling castle, round the Park to Linlithgow; Douglas pursues with too small a force*]

    The king with thaim he with him had
360   In a rout till the castell rad
    And wald haiff bene tharin, for thai
    Wyst nocht quhat gat to get away,
    Bot Philip the Mowbra said him till,
    'The castell, Schyr, is at your will,
365   But cum ye in it ye sall se
    That ye sall sone assegyt be
    And thar sall nane of Ingland
    To mak you rescours tak on hand
    And but rescours may na castell
370   Be haldyn lang, ye wate this wele.
    Tharfor confort you and rely
    Your men about you rycht starkly
    And haldis about the Park your way
    Knyt als sadly as ye may,
375   For I trow that nane sall haff mycht
    That chassys with sa fele to fycht.'
    And his consaill thai haiff doyne
    And beneuth the castell went thai sone
    Rycht be the Rond Table away,
380   And syne the Park enveround thai
    And towart Lythkow held in hy.
    Bot I trow thai sall hastily
    Be conveyit with sic folk that thai
    I trow mycht suffre wele away,
385   For Schyr James lord of Douglas
    Come to the king and askyt the chace
    And he gaff him it but abaid,
    Bot all to few of hors he haid,
    He haid nocht in his rout sexty

although he hurried speedily to take the way after the [English] king. Now let him go on his way, and after this we shall tell properly what happened to him in the pursuit.

(395) When the great army had been defeated in this way, as I have descibed, with thirty thousand at least dead or drowned in that very place, [while] some had been taken prisoner and others had fled on their way. (401) The earl of Hereford left the encounter with a large company, taking the way straight to Bothwell, which was then in the faith of the English, held as a place of war, [with] Sir Walter fitz Gilbert as captain having it in keeping. (408) The earl of Hereford sped there and was taken in over the wall, with fifty of his men; they were placed separately in houses so that they had no control [of the place]; the rest went towards England, but I warrant that three-quarters of that group were taken or killed and the rest got home with great difficulty. (417) Sir Maurice Berkeley too departed from the great army with a big force of Welshmen; wherever they went men could distinguish them because they were pretty well completely naked or had linen clothing and no more. They held their way at a pretty pace,

---

397. Thirty thousand dead. The full number of dead cannot be known. See the discussion of casualties in J. R. S. Phillips, *Aymer de Valence*, 75, where also he suggests that Pembroke and his men fought a 'prolonged rearguard action to cover [Edward's] retreat ... to Dunbar'.

401. Hereford. Lanercost has the fullest account of this event:
[*Hereford, Angus, Sir John Segrave, Sir Antony Lucy and Sir Ingram Umfraville with a great crowd, fled towards Carlisle.*] They were captured on the way at Bothwell castle for the sheriff, keeper of the castle, who up to that time had held the castle for the needs of the king of England, seeing that his [countrymen] had prevailed in battle, allowed the more noble of those who had come there to enter the castle as though to get a safe refuge, and when they had entered, took them prisoner, and thus wickedly deceived them. [*continued at note to 413*]

403. The great donjon at Bothwell would be complete but it is not clear how much of the enclosure had been walled. This castle had been given to Aymer de Valence but resumed by Edward II. Its garrison in 1312 numbered 30 men-at-arms and 29 archers. (*L*, 417–18)

406. Sir Walter Gilbertson, whom Lanercost calls a Scot, was certainly in Scotland before 1296, but he seems to have come from a Homildon in Northumberland. Walter was ancestor of the Hamilton family. (*SP4*, 340–42)

413. The rest. Lanercost continues from note to 401: 'Many also were taken wandering around outside the castle and in the countryside and many were killed; it was said also that certain knights were taken by women. None of them got back to England unless in a miserable state.' (*L*, 228; *LT*, 210)

390 The-quhether he sped him hastely
The way eftyr the king to ta.
Now lat him on his wayis ga
And eftre this we sall weill tell
Quhat him intill the chace befell.

[*Capture of Hereford at Bothwell; escape of Sir Maurice
Berkeley; flight of many to Stirling castle; King Robert fears an
English recovery*]

395 Quhen the gret battaill on this wis
Was discumfyt as Ik devys
Quhar thretty thousand wele war ded
Or drownyt in that ilk sted,
And sum war intill handis tane
400 And other sum thar gate war gane.
The erle of Herfurd fra the mellé
Departyt with a gret mengne
And straucht to Bothwell tok the wai
That than in the Inglismennys fay
405 Was, and haldyn as place of wer,
Schyr Walter Gilbertson wes ther
Capitane and it had in ward.
The erle of Herfurd thidderward
Held and wes tane in our the wall
410 And fyfty of his men withall,
And set in housis sindryly
Sua that thai had thar na mastry.
The lave went towart Ingland
Bot off that rout I tak on hand
415 The thre partis war slane or tane,
The lave with gret payn hame ar gan.
Schyr Maurice alsua the Berclay
Fra the gret bataill held hys way
With a gret rout off Walis-men,
420 Quharever thai yeid men mycht thaim ken
For thai wele ner all nakyt war
Or lynnyn clathys had but mar.
Thai held thar way in full gret hy

---

417. Sir Maurice Berkeley. The *Vita*, written by a west-countryman who
knew Berkeley, mentions Maurice among the prisoners who were ran-
somed. It seems that his father, Thomas, and his sons, Thomas and
Maurice, were taken prisoner, and that the *Vita* errs here. (Phillips,
Aymer de Valence, 75)

but before they came to England many of their company were
taken [prisoner], and many of them too were slain. (427) [The
English] fled also in divers other ways, but such a company
fled to the castle of Stirling that was near-by that it was
remarkable to behold, for the rocks about the castle were all
covered here and there by those who fled thither for safety
because of the strength of the place; (435) because those who
fled [to] under the castle were so numerous, King Robert,
who was prudent, maintained his good men near by him for
fear that they should rise again.

(440) To tell you the truth, this was the reason why the king
of England escaped home to his own country. When the field
had been so cleared of Englishmen that none remained, the
Scotsmen soon appropriated everything of theirs that they
could find, like silver, gold, clothes and armour, with plate
and everything else that they could lay their hands on. (450)
They found such great wealth there that many a man was
made powerful by the riches that they took there. When what
I have described had been done, the king sent a great company
up to the rock to attack those who had fled from the great
army; they surrendered without a struggle [to the Scots], were
taken in captivity hot-foot and then [the Scots] went on their
way to the king. (460) They spent the whole of that day from
the end of the fighting in taking spoils and riches, and when
those who had been killed in the battle had been stripped
naked,

437–42. This passage shows King Robert's caution and uncertainty, but
the remark about Edward's escape is an exculpation of Douglas.

Bot mony off thar cumpany
425 Or thai till Ingland come war tane
And mony als off thaim war slayne.
Thair fled als other wayis ser,
Bot to the castell that wes ner
Off Strevilline fled sic a mengye
430 That it war wonder for to se,
For the craggis all helyt war
About the castell her and thar
Off thaim that for strenth of that sted
Thidderwart to warand fled,
435 And for thai war sa fele that thar
Fled under the castell war
The King Robert that wes wytty
Held his gud men ner him by
For dred that ris agayne suld thai.

[*Looting of the enemy; the dead knights; the treachery of the earl of Atholl*]

440 This was the caus forsuth to say
Quharthrouch the king of Ingland
Eschapyt hame intill his land
Quhen that the feld sa clene wes maid
Off Inglismen that nane abaid
445 The Scottismen sone tuk in hand
Off tharis all that ever thai fand,
As silver gold clathis and armyng   447*
With veschall and all other thing   448*
That ever thai mycht lay on thare hand.   449*
450 So gret a riches thair thai fand   450*
That mony man mychty wes maid   447
Off the riches that thai thar haid.
Quhen this wes doyne that her say I
The king send a gret cumpany
455 Up to the crag thaim till assaile   451
That war fled fra the gret battaill,
And thai thaim yauld foroutyn debate,
And in hand has tane thaim fute-hate
Syne to the king thai went thar way.
460 Thai dispendyt haly that day   456
In spulyeing and riches takyng
Fra end wa's maid off the fechting
And quhen thai nakyt spulyeit war

it was a terrible sight to see so many lying dead together. (467) Two hundred pairs of red spurs were taken from dead knights; the earl of Gloucester was dead there, whom men called Sir Gilbert Clare, Giles d'Argentan too, Payne Tiptoft and various others whose names I cannot recount. (474) On the side of the Scotsmen two worthy knights were killed: William Vipont was one of them and the other Sir Walter Ross, whom Sir Edward, the king's brother, loved and held in such esteem that he loved him as though [he were] himself. (481) When he knew that he was dead, he was so miserable and at a loss that he said, in a sad mood, that he would rather that the day was undone than that he had died like that. (486) Apart from [Ross] men had not seen [an occasion] when he made lamentation for any man, and the cause of his love was that he loved [Ross's] sister as his mistress and held his own wife, Dame Isabel, in great distaste. (492) For that reason so great a coolness arose between him and Earl David of Atholl,

---

469. Gloucester. See note to 1; the *Vita Edwardi* suggests that Gloucester died early on. But Trokelowe, in a vivid account says that Gloucester, seeing many killed, urged his companions to attack and then set an example himself 'in the heat of anger' but was killed after a shift in the 'weight' of the battle. 'Seeing him thus killed, all the rest of the army, struck with fear, fled, leaving their lord dead on the field.' This probably places his death too late. An anonymous English poem on the battle says that he was betrayed by Bartholomew, a retainer. (*Chron. Trokelowe*, 85)

473. The unknown dead. Barbour nowhere names among the dead the man who figures so prominently elsewhere in his narrative, Sir Robert Clifford.

476. Sir William Vipont. He was active as a patriot by 1299, and supported Robert I from at least late 1308.

477. Sir Walter Ross was a younger son of William, earl of Ross, studying at Cambridge (i.e. for the church) in 1306 but a knight when given the lands of Glenken in Galloway by Edward Bruce (either as lord of Galloway before 1313, or as earl of Carrick thereafter). He left no children.

486–87. Apart from him. But at 15.236–38 Barbour makes the same comment of Edward and Neil Fleming, evidence that the two passages were composed some time apart.

489. His sister. Edward Bruce must have been almost 40 by 1314. On 1 June, 1317, a papal dispensation for his marriage to Isabella, daughter of William, earl of Ross was granted; this marriage had been arranged by common friends of the two families as settlement of 'wars' between the families. Despite the late date of the dispensation, it is likely that Edward and Isabella were married late in 1308 as part of the deal to secure Ross's submission to King Robert. (Theiner, *Vetera Monumenta Hibernorum et Scotorum*, no. 414)

491. Dame Isabell. Isabella of Atholl was sister to Earl David, but she

That war slane in the bataill thar
465 It wes forsuth a gret ferly 461
To se samyn sa fele dede ly.
Twa hundyr payr off spuris reid
War tane of knychtis that war deid,
The erle of Glosyster ded wes thar
470 That men callyt Schyr Gilbert of Clar, 464
And Gylis de Argenté alsua
And Payn Typtot and other ma
That thar namys nocht tell can I.
And apon Scottismennys party
475 Thar wes slane worthi knychtis twa, 471
Wilyame the Vepoynt wes ane of tha
And Schyr Walter of Ross ane other
That Schyr Edward the kingis brother
Luffyt and had in sic daynte
480 That as himselff him luffyt he. 476
And quhen he wyst that he wes ded
He wes sa wa and will of reide
That he said makand ivill cher
That him war lever that journay wer
485 Undone than he sua ded had bene. 481
Outakyn him men has nocht sene
Quhar he for ony man maid menyng,
And the caus wes of his luffing
That he his sister paramouris
490 Luffyt, and held all at rebouris 486
His awyne wyff dame Ysabell.
And tharfor sa gret distance fell
Betwix him and the erle Davi

---

cannot have been married to Edward Bruce, for she lived on till at least
1326 and had a son Alexander Bruce, nephew of Robert I, who had
no right to the Scottish throne, i.e. an illegitimate son of Edward Bruce.
He seems to have been adult in the 1320s and was therefore born long
before the dispensation granted in 1317. Isabella of Atholl was perhaps
affianced to Edward in or by 1306 and discarded by him for the Ross
marriage. I suspect, purely on the analogy of other cases, that Edward,
who had no surviving children from his marriage to the Ross lady, was
resisting pressure in 1314 to divorce her and legitimate his Atholl son
by marrying Dame Isabella.

493–94. David de Strathbogie, earl of Atholl, was son of Earl John
executed in 1306 for supporting Robert I. He was active as a commander
for Edward II until January 1312 when he was at the York parliament,
was commissioned to negotiate with Scottish commissioners over a
truce and set out on 29 January, 1312 for Roxburgh to do so. Thereafter

brother of [the latter], that on St John's night, when both the kings were ready to fight, he took the king's provisions at Cambuskenneth, had Sir William Airth closely assaulted and killed him and plenty of other men. (501) For that he was subsequently banished to England, and all his land was seized as forfeit to the king, who then did what he chose with it.

(505) When the field had been despoiled and left all bare, as I told you before, the king and all his company, cheerful, joyful, happy, merry at the grace which had befallen them, took their ways towards their quarters for rest, because they were weary. (512) But the king was somewhat saddened for Earl Gilbert de Clare, who had been killed on the battlefield, because he was closely related to him; he had him carried then to a kirk and guarded all that night. In the morning the king rose at daylight as was his wont. (520) Then an English knight happened by chance to wander here and there so that no man laid a hand on him; he had hidden his armour in a bush and waited until he saw the king come out early in the morning. (526) Then he went to him quickly. He was called Sir Marmaduke Tweng. He went directly to the king, and greeted him upon his knee. 'Welcome, Sir Marmaduke,' said [the king], 'to whom are you prisoner?' 'To none,' he said, 'but I surrender to you here, to be at your disposal.'

---

he disappears and is not named among those at the Scottish parliament at Inchture in April 1312. He appears with the king at Inverness in October 1312 but probably deserted to him in the spring of 1312. He was rewarded not only with his earldom, but also with the office of constable, stripped from Sir Gilbert Hay.

495. St John's night is strictly the night of 24–25 June; Barbour clearly means the eve, 23–24 June.

496–500. It is not clear why the king had victuals at Cambuskenneth abbey, but possible that they were feed for the horses, for which Atholl, as constable, would be responsible. Sir William Airth does not occur in sources for the early part of Robert's reign; Airth is on the Forth near Falkirk.

512. Gilbert de Clare, earl of Gloucester and Robert I married daughters of Richard, earl of Ulster. Barbour correctly does not say that Gloucester was buried at Stirling; his body (and that of Clifford) was returned to England and he lies in Tewksbury abbey.

527. Sir Marmaduke Tweng, a Yorkshire baron, had already been a prisoner of the Scots, in 1299.

Off Athole, brother to this lady
495   That he apon Saynct Jhonys nycht,   491
Quhen bath the kingis war boun to fycht,
In Cammyskynnell the kingis vittaill
He tuk and sadly gert assaile
Schyr Wilyam off Herth and him slew
500   And with him men ma then ynew.   496
Tharfor syne intil Ingland
He wes bannyst and all his land
Wes sesyt as forfaut to the king
That did tharoff syne his liking.

[*The burial of Gloucester; the surrender of Sir Marmaduke Tweng and of Stirling castle*]

505   Quhen the feld as I tauld you ar   501
Was dispulyeit and left all bar
The king and all his cumpany
Blyth and joyfull glaid and mery
Off the grace that thaim fallin was
510   Towart thar innys thar wayis tays   506
To rest thaim, for thai wery war.
Bot for the erle Gilbert of Clar
That slane wes in the bataill-place
The king sumdele anoyit was
515   For till him wele ner sib wes he,   511
Than till a kirk he gert him be
Brocht and walkyt all that nycht.
But on the morn quhen day wes lycht
The king rais as his willis was.
520   Than ane Inglis knycht throu cas   516
Hapnyt that he yeid waverand
Swa that na man laid on him hand,
In a busk he hyd hys armyng
And waytyt quhill he saw the king
525   In the morne cum furth arly   521
Till him than is he went in hy,
Schyr Marmeduk the Tweingue he hycht.
He raykyt till the king all rycht
And halyst him apon his kne.
530   'Welcum, Schyr Marmeduk,' said he,   526
To quhat man art thou presoner?'
'To nane,' he said, 'bot to you her
I yeld me at your will to be.'

'And I accept you, sir,' he said. (535) Then he had him treated courteously, staying long in his company, then sending him to England well equipped and free of ransom, and gave him great gifts as well. A worthy man who would do this could make himself highly esteemed. (542) When Marmaduke had surrendered in this way that I told you, Sir Philip Mowbray came next and surrendered the castle to the king, having kept his agreement well, and the king dealt with him so that he remained in [the king's] household, holding loyally to his allegiance until the very last day of his life.

(551) Now we shall tell of the lord Douglas, how he followed the chase. He had too few in his company, but he sped in great haste, and as he rode through the Torwood, he met riding on the moor Sir Laurence Abernethy, who came with four score men in his company to help the Englishmen, for he was then still an English man; (561) but when he heard how [things] were he left the Englishmen's peace and right there swore to be loyal and true to the lord Douglas. Then both followed the chase, and before the king of England had passed Linlithgow, they and all the folk who were with them came so close that they could pretty well shout [in derision] among them, (570) but they felt they were too few to fight with the large force that [the English] had there, for they numbered five hundred men at arms. They rode in close order together,

---

544. Sir Philip Mowbray who subsequently fought in Ireland, witnessed a few charters, including one of Edward Bruce, king of Ireland, and was given the lands of North Tyndale (Northumberland) by Robert I; all seem to be before 1319. For his fate see note to 18.159. His heir was his daughter. (*RRS5*, 401, 505, 651, 665)

551. Douglas's pursuit of Edward II. It is some 65 miles (105 kilometres) from Stirling to Dunbar. The English sources do not mention Douglas. Gray confirms Barbour in outline, suggesting even more English panic:
The king ... turned his steps towards Dunbar and coming there took ship. He landed with his following at the port of Berwick. Others having no ship came by land. The knights shed their armour and fled without it; the Scots continually pursued from behind, and the pursuit lasted fifty miles. Many of our men died and many too were taken prisoner, for the inhabitants of the land, who had previously feigned peace, now slaughtered our men everywhere. (*VitaEd*, 55)

557. Sir Laurence Abernethy was perhaps a son of Sir Alexander, a prominent commander for Edward II, e.g. as Guardian between Forth and Mounth in 1311-12, but who disappears from record, probably dead, after the fall of Dundee in March 1312. Sir Laurence had land in Roxburghshire (in an English pale?) and was given land in Berwickshire by Robert I. (*CDS5*, 575; *B1985*, 94)

'And I ressave the, schyr,' said he.
535   Than gert he tret him curtasly,   531
He dwelt lang in his cumpany,
And syne till Ingland him send he
Arayit weile but ransoun fre
And geff him gret gyftis tharto.
540   A worthi man that sua wald do   536
Mycht mak him gretly for to prise.
Quhen Marmeduk apon this wis
Was yoldyn, as Ik to you say,
Than come Schyr Philip the Mowbra
545   And to the king yauld the castell,   541
His cunnand has he haldyn well,
And with him tretyt sua the king
That he belevyt of his dwelling
And held him lely his fay
550   Quhill the last end off his lyf-day.   546

[*Douglas is joined by Sir Laurence Abernethy; they follow King
Edward to Winchburgh*]

Now will we of the lord of Douglas
Tell how that he folowit the chas.
He had to quhone in his cumpany
Bot he sped him in full gret hy,
555   And as he throuch the Torwod fur   551
Sa met he ridand on the mur
Schyr Laurence off Abyrnethy
That with four scor in cumpany
Come for till help the Inglismen
560   For he was Inglisman yet then,   556
Bot quhen he hard how that it wes
He left the Inglis-mennys pes
And to the lord Douglas rycht thar
For to be lele and trew he swar.
565   And than thai bath folowit the chas,   561
And or the king off Ingland was
Passyt Lythkow thai come sa ner
With all the folk that with thaim wer
That weill amang thaim schout thai mycht,
570   Bot thai thocht thaim to few to fycht   566
With the gret rout that thai had thar
For fyve hunder armyt thai war.
Togidder sarraly raid thai

always with tight reins, and were prudently led for it seemed that they were always ready to defend themselves to the utmost if they were attacked in a fight. (579) The lord Douglas and his men, although he could not attempt then to fight with them in the open, accompanied them so closely that he kept picking off the hindmost, [so that] none could be a penny-stone's throw behind his companions without being quickly killed or swiftly taken [captive], [for] none would bring him help, however much he loved him. (589) In this way he escorted the king and all his following until they all came to Winchburgh.

(592) Then all of them dismounted to rest their weary horses, and Douglas and his company also rested close beside them. (596) They were so numerous without a doubt, so thoroughly equipped with arms, so arrayed for a fight, and he was so few, and without reinforcement, that he would not fight them in open attack, but continually rode beside them, constantly awaiting his opportunity. (603) They rested for a little there, then mounted and set forth [with] him always close by them, not letting them have enough leisure to make water [even] once. If any were so placed that he was left any space behind, he was forthwith taken prisoner. (611) They convoyed them in just this way until the king and his force were come to the castle of Dunbar,

And held thaim apon bridill ay,
575   Thai wat governyt wittily   571
For it semyt ay thai war redy
For to defend thaim at thar mycht
Giff thai assailyt war in fycht.
And the lord Douglas and his men,
580   How that he wald nocht schaip him then   576
For to fecht with thaim all planly,
He convoyit thaim sa narowly
That of the henmaist ay tuk he,
Mycht nane behin his falowis be
585   A pennystane cast na he in hy   581
Was dede, or tane deliverly
That nane rescours wald till him ma
All-thocht he luvyt him never sua.
On this maner convoyit he
590   Quhill that the king and his menye   586
To Wenchburg all cummyn ar.

*[Both sides rest at Winchburgh; they ride on till King Edward
takes a boat at Dunbar]*

Than lychtyt all that thai war
To bayt thar hors that wer wery,
And Douglas and his cumpany
595   Baytyt alsua besid thaim ner.   591
Thai war sa fele withoutyn wer
And in armys sa clenly dycht
And sua arayit for to fycht,
And he sa quhoyne and but supleyng
600   That he wald nocht in plane fechting   596
Assaile thaim, bot ay raid thaim by
Waytand hys poynt ay ythandly.
A litill quhill thai baytyt thar
And syne lap on and furth thai far
605   And he was alwayis by thaim ner,   601
He leyt thaim nocht haff sic layser
As anys water for to ma,
And giff ony stad war sa
That he behind left ony space
610   Sesyt alsone in hand he was.   606
Thai convoyit thaim on sic a wis
Quhill that the king and his rout is
Cummyn to the castell of Dunbar

where he and some of his followers were right well received,
because Earl Patrick was still an English man then. (617) He
had them well refreshed with food and drink, then had a boat
procured and sent the king by sea to Bamburgh, in his own
country. They left their horses all running wild, but I'm sure
they were all captured pretty quickly. (623) The remainder
who had been left outside [the castle] mustered themselves
into one force and took their way straight to Berwick as a
company, but, if we tell the truth, they were in a very tight
situation before they came there, but in spite of that they
reached Berwick safely and were received into the town there,
otherwise they would have been in great difficulty. (632) And
when the lord of Douglas saw that all his effort had been in
vain, he went back towards the king.

(635) This king escaped in this way. Lo! How fortune fades
[when] she smiles upon a man at one time, and then assaults
him another time; at no time does she stand still. (640) She
had set this mighty king of England at the top on her wheel,
when he came riding out of his country with so marvellous a
host of men at arms, archers, footmen and hobelars, as I
recounted previously, (647) and then in one night and one
day she put him under such heavy pressure

---

616. Earl Patrick of Dunbar. This episode is well known to (a) Gray and
(b) Lanercost:

  (a) The king ... travelled to Dunbar where Earl Patrick ... received
  him honourably, and delivered his castle to him, even emptying the
  place and [evacuating] all his men, so that there could be no doubt
  or suspicion that he would do anything other than his duty to his lord
  – for at that time he was his *homager*. (*S*, 143; *ST*, 57)

  (b) The king, Sir Hugh Despenser and Sir Henry Beaumont ... with
  many knights and infantry, led by a certain knight of Scotland who
  knew by what parts they could escape, fled like miserable people
  towards the castle of Dunbar, to their perpetual shame. Some of the
  more laggardly were killed while fleeing by Scots who pursued them
  hotly. [*LT prints* * ... * *here, surely wrongly*] At Dunbar the king with
  some more favoured by him embarked in a skiff in the sea for Berwick,
  abandoning all the others to their fate, *but these holding bravely
  together came safe and sound through the ambushes into England. *
  (*L*, 227–28; *LT*, 208–9)

Earl Patrick had succeeded in 1308, and struggled to uphold the English
cause in Lothian, suffering plundering from both sides. His English
lands were held forfeit as from 24 June, 1314, and his earldom was
confirmed to him by Robert I; he died at a great age in 1368. (*SP3*,
264–69) The battered remains of Dunbar castle are ready to follow the
rest into the North Sea.

Quhar he and sum of his menye war
615 Resavyt rycht weill, for yete than 611
The Erle Patrik was Inglisman,
That gert with mete and drynk alsua
Refresche thaim weill, and syne gert ta
A bate and send the king by se
620 To Baumburgh in his awne contre. 616
Thar hors thar left thai all on stray
Bot sesyt I trow weill sone war thai.
The lave that levyt thar-without
Addressyt thaim intill a rout
625 And till Berwik held straucht thar way 621
In route, bot, and we suth say,
Stad thai war full narowly
Or thai come thar, bot nocht-forthi
Thai come to Berwik weill and thar
630 Into the toune ressavyt war, 626
Ellys at gret myscheff had thai bene.
And quhen the lord off Douglas has sene
That he had losyt all hys payne
Towart the king he went agane.

[Reflections on the kings' failure and success; destruction of Stirling castle]

635 The king eschapyt on this wis. 631
Lo! quhat fading in fortoun is
That will apon a man quhill smyle
And prik on him syne a nothyr quhill,
In na tym stable can scho stand.
640 This mychty king off Ingland 636
Scho had set on hyr quheill on hycht
Quham with sa ferlyfull a mycht
Off men off armys and archeris
And off futemen and hobeleris
645 He come ridand out off his land 641
As I befor has borne on hand,
And in a nycht syne and a day
Scho set him in sa hard assay

---

620. Bamburgh. All English sources say Berwick, and it may be that the
king rode back from Bamburgh to Berwick, for he seems to have been
there from 27 June for two weeks.

636. The wheel of fortune was a favourite moralising tool for medieval
chroniclers.

that he had no choice but to take his road home with a few men in a boat. (653) But King Robert should not bemoan the turning of this same wheel, because the wheel rose up to the top on his side [at the same time as] the other [king] revolved downwards, for [with] two opponents set against [each] other on a wheel, you can well see [that] when one is up, the other is down, and if it happens that fortune birls the wheel round, what was previously at the top must descend down, and what was previously low at the bottom must contrariwise rise aloft. (663) That's how it happened for those two kings: when King Robert was so placed that he was in terrible difficulty, the other [king] was in his majesty, and when King Edward's might collapsed, King Robert was on top; now such [good] fortune befell him that he was on top and [had matters] at his will. (671) He was still lying at Stirling, and the great lords that he found dead on the field he had buried honourably in a holy place, and then the rest who had died there were buried in great pits. (677) Next he had the castle and the towers mined [and reduced] right down to the ground and then he sent Sir Edward to Bothwell with a great company, for words had been sent him from there that the rich earl of Hereford and other mighty [lords] were there.

(684) He negotiated with Sir Walter so that he handed over the earl, the castle and the rest to Sir Edward, and he sent the earl to the king who had him well guarded.

---

680. As after the taking of Roxburgh castle (10.500–2), it is Edward Bruce who is sent by the king to deal with this newly won castle.

	That he with few men in a bate	
650	Wes fayne for till hald hame his gate.	646
	Bot off this ilk quhelys turnyng	
	King Robert suld mak na murnyng	
	For on his syd the quheyle on hycht	
	Rais quhen the tother doun gan lycht,	
655	For twa contraris yhe may wit wele	651*
	Set agane othir on a quhele	652*
	Quhen ane is hye the tothir is law,	653*
	And gif it fall that fortoune thraw	654*
	The quheill about, it that on hicht	655*
660	Was ere it most doune lycht,	656*
	And it that undre lawch was ar	651
	Mon lepe on loft in the contrar.	
	Sa fure it off thir kingis twa,	
	Quhen the King Robert stad was sua	
665	That in gret myscheiff wes he	655
	The tother was in his majesté,	
	And quhen the King Edwardis mycht	
	Wes lawyt King Robert wes on hycht,	
	And now sic fortoun fell him till	
670	That he wes hey and at his will.	660
	At Strevillyne wes he yeyt liand,	
	And the gret lordis that he fand	
	Dede in the feld he gert bery	
	In haly place honorabilly,	
675	And the lave syne that dede war thar	665
	Into gret pyttis erdyt war thar	
	The castell and the towris syne	
	Rycht till the ground gert he myn,	
	And syne to Bothwell send he	
680	Schyr Edward with a gret menye	670
	For thar wes thine send him word	
	That the rich erle off Herford	
	And other mychty als wer ther.	

[*Surrender of Bothwell castle; exchange of prisoners; Robert Stewart and the date of compiling this book*]

	Sua tretyt he with Schyr Walter	
685	That erle and castell and the lave	675
	In Schyr Edwardis hand he gave,	
	And till the king the erle send he	
	That gert him rycht weill yemyt be	

Eventually they negotiated [a settlement] whereby he would go home to England free without paying a ransom, and that he should be exchanged for Bishop Robert, who had gone blind, [for] the queen whom they had taken to prison as I explained before, and [for] her daughter, Dame Marjory. (697) The earl was exchanged for these three, and when they had returned home free, the king married off his daughter, who was fair and also his heir apparent, to Walter Stewart; (702) very soon they begat of their bed, by Our Lord's grace, a male child, who was called Robert after his good grandfather, and later was king, having the government of the country after his worthy uncle David [II] who reigned for forty-two years. (709) At the time of the compiling of this book, this Robert was king, and five years of his reign had passed, in the year of grace 1375, and the sixtieth year of his age, and that was forty-six winters, no more, after the good King Robert had died. (718) God grant that those who are come of his offspring [may] maintain the land, protect the people in security and maintain justice and loyalty as well as he did in his time.

(723) King Robert was now right at the top, for each day then his might increased, his men grew rich and his country had an abundance of corn, cattle and all other kinds of wealth; mirth, happiness and blythness were general in the land,

---

689. The agreement over prisoners does seem to have been limited to Hertford, though e.g. Angus did return to England, presumably ransomed. Ingram Umfraville did not.

693. Robert Wishart, bishop of Glasgow, a prisoner since 1306. See note to 4.13. He died in 1316.

694. The queen had not been harshly treated at least since her early captivity. Marjory Bruce, of course, was not her daughter, but daughter of Robert's first wife.

705–17. This passage is examined by McDiarmid. (*B1985*, 94) David II reigned for 41 years and 8 months, so Barbour is rounding up. Five years of Robert II's reign ended on 21 February 1375/6. '1375' ended on 24 March, 1376. The other dates are unhelpful because we do not know when Robert II was born – the date 2 March, 1316 is found for the first time in an editorial note of 1759 to Bower's *Scotichronicon*. And for the time since Robert I's death E has 'v and fourty', C, probably correctly, 'sex yher and fourty'; 46 winters since June 1329 gives the spring of 1375, whereas McDiarmid's dating of March 1376 surely requires 47 winters to have passed. The best we can do is '25 March, 1375–24 March, 1376'.

725–30. Abundance. In fact the years 1315–18 were marked by bad weather, poor harvests and dreadful want.

Quhill at the last thai tretyt sua
690 That he till Ingland hame suld ga 680
Foroutyn paying of raunsoune fre,
And that for him suld changyt be
Bischap Robert that blynd was mad
And the queyne that thai takyn had
695 In presoune as befor said I 685
And hyr douchter Dame Marjory.
The erle was changyt for thir thre,
And quhen thai cummyn war hame all fre
The king his douchter that was far
700 And wes als aperand ayr 690
With Walter Stewart gan he wed
And thai wele sone gat of thar bed
A knav child throu our Lordis grace,
That eftre his gud eldfader was
705 Callyt Robert and syne wes king, 695
And had the land in governyng
Eftyr his worthy eyme Davy
That regnyt twa yer and fourty.
And in the tyme of the compiling
710 Off this buk this Robert wes king, 700
And off hys kynrik passit was
Fyve yer, and wes the yer of grace
A thousand thre hunder sevynty
And fyve, and off his eld sexty,
715 And that wes efter that the gud king 705
Robert wes broucht till his ending
Sex and fourty winter but mar.
God grant that thai that cummyn ar
Off his ofspring manteyme the land
720 And hald the folk weill to warand 710
And manteyme rycht and leawté
Als wele as in his tyme did he.

[*The king's territorial settlement; an attack on Northumberland*]

King Robert now wes wele at hycht
For ilk day than grew his mycht,
725 His men woux rich and his contré 715
Haboundyt weill of corne and fe
And off alkyn other ryches,
Myrth and solace and blythnes
War in the land commonaly

for each man was cheerful and happy. (731) After the great encounter the king, by advice of his inner council had a proclamation [made] in sundry towns that anyone who claimed to have a right to hold land or feu in Scotland should come and claim it within twelve months, and do what was appropriate for it to the king; (739) if they did not come in that year, then they should know that without doubt none would be heard thereafter. After this had been accomplished, the king, who was [a man] of great generosity and active, had a host summoned soon afterwards, took them into England, overrunning all Northumberland, burning houses and seizing booty, and then took their way home again. (749) I let this pass briefly for no proven chivalry was done there worth speaking about here. The king often went into England in this way to enrich his men, who had an abundance of riches then.

731–41. Claims to lands. Placed after Bannockburn, this refers to the judgment in parliament at Cambuskenneth on 6 November, 1314 (a document which survives in the original), that

all who died in war or elsewhere against the faith and peace of the king, or who on the said day had not come into his peace and faith, *although often called and lawfully awaited*, be disinherited for ever of their lands and holdings and of all their other estate within the kingdom of Scotland and be held as enemies of the king and kingdom, deprived of all vindication of heritable right or of any other right hereafter for themselves or their heirs for ever. (My italics)

There is no word of a year's grace, because that had now elapsed. Despite Barbour, the first warning of this process must have been given a year earlier, I suggest at a council or parliament at Dundee in October 1313. It should be noted that the legislation empowered the king to forfeit, but that he rarely did so; Donald, earl of Mar returned in 1327 and received his earldom back.

746. Overrunning Northumberland. Barbour has ignored all the Scottish incursions to northern England before 1314; he is not clear whether the king was involved in this one, and there seem to have been two incursions, according to Lanercost:

About [1 August] Sir Edward Bruce, Sir James Douglas, John de Soulis and other nobles of Scotland with knights and a large army, invaded England by way of Berwick and devastated by fire virtually the whole of Northumberland, except the castles, during a time of truce. Then they crossed further into the bishopric of Durham, but there they did not burn much because the men of the bishopric paid them off from burning by a large sum of money. But the Scots took away booty in cattle, and men whom they could take prisoner, and so they crossed further into the earldom of Richmond, and perpetrated the same things there without anyone resisting. But almost all fled southwards or hid in the woods, except those who found refuge in

730   For ilk man blyth war and joly.   720
       The king eftre the gret journé
       Throu rede off his consaill prevé
       In ser townys gert cry on hycht
       That quha-sa clemyt till haf rycht
735   To hald in Scotland land or fe,   725
       That in thai twelf moneth suld he
       Cum and clam yt and tharfor do
       To the king that pertenyt tharto,
       And giff thai come nocht in that yer
740   Than suld thai wit withoutyn wer   730
       That hard thareftre nane suld be.
       The king that wes of gret bounté
       And besines, quhen this wes done
       Ane ost gert summound eftre sone
745   And went thaim intill Ingland   735
       And our-raid all Northummyrland,
       And brynt housis and tuk tharpray
       And syne went hame agane thar way.
       I lat it schortly pas forby
750   For thar wes done na chevalry   740
       Provyt that is to spek of her.
       The king went oft on this maner
       In Ingland for to rich his men
       That in riches haboundyt then.

castles. [*They went beyond Richmond*] Reuniting their forces they re-
turned by Swaledale and other valleys and by Stainmoor, from where
they carried off a huge booty in cattle. They also burned the towns
of Brough, Appleby and Kirkoswald, and other towns here and there
on their travels, and trampled down the crops by themselves and their
animals as much as they could. So ... they entered Scotland having
many prisoners from whom they could extort money at will ...
Meantime [*i.e. about December*] the Scots occupied South and North
Tyndale ... and places towards Newcastle, and Tyndale did homage
to the king of Scotland, and he fiercely attacked Gillesland and other
parts of England around. (*L*, 228–29; *LT*, 210–12)
There is another account of Bannockburn and this invasion (not naming
King Robert) in the recently published English verse *Castleford's
Chronicle*, ed. C. D. Eckhardt, ii, 1054–57.

Sir Edward, earl of Carrick, who was stronger than a leopard
and had no desire to live in peace, felt that Scotland was too
small for both him and his brother; therefore he formed a
purpose that he would become king of Ireland. (8) To that
end he sent and negotiated with the Irishry of Ireland who,
in good faith, undertook to make him king of all Ireland,
provided that he could overcome by hard fighting the Eng-
lishmen who dwelt in the land then, while they would help
with all their might. (16) He, hearing them make this promise,
was very pleased in his heart, and, with the king's consent,
assembled to himself men of great courage; then he took ship
at Ayr in the following month of May, [and] took his way
straight to Ireland. (23) He had in his company there Earl
Thomas, who was a fine [man], good Sir Philip Mowbray
who was staunch under great pressure, Sir John Soules a good
knight, and Sir John Stewart, a brave [one]; also Ramsay of
Auchterhouse, who was brave and chivalrous, Sir Fergus
Ardrossan and many another knight. (33) They arrived safely
in Larne Lough without opposition or attack,

1. The Irish campaign of Edward Bruce in 1315 (with Moray very
   prominent) is the subject of 14.1 to 15.265, followed by the siege of
   Carrickfergus in 1316. In the following notes I have suggested several
   revisions of the accepted chronology and topography; to understand
   these it is important to know that Edward Bruce advanced south twice
   in 1315. His first campaign began after he landed, reached Ardee in
   Meath and withdrew to the battle of Connor (Co. Antrim) in Septem-
   ber. The second began in November 1315, reached into Leinster with
   ravaging in Cos. Kildare and Leix in January 1316, and withdrew to
   Ulster in February 1316. Barbour describes the first campaign, with
   undoubted elements of the second in his narrative.

4. Edward Bruce's discomfort with his brother is mentioned by Fordun:
   Edward ... entered Ireland with a mighty hand in 1315, and having
   been set up as king there he destroyed the whole of Ulster and
   committed countless murders ... The cause of this war was this.
   Edward was a very mettlesome and high-spirited man and would not
   dwell together with his brother in peace, unless he had half the
   kingdom for himself; and for this reason this war was stirred up in
   Ireland. (*F1*, 347–48; *F2*, 340)

24. His company. The Laud annals add John Menteith, John Campbell,
    Thomas Randolph [?Moray's son], John *de Bosco*, John Bisset. As Bisset
    was Irish, *de Bosco* may have been so too.

33. 'Wolringis fyrth' is now represented by Oldersfleet in Larne Lough.
    The Laud annals say the Edward put in at 'Clandonne', either Glendun

BOOK 14

[*Edward Bruce goes to Ireland*]

The erle off Carrik Schyr Edward,
That stoutar wes than a libard
And had na will to be in pes,
Thocht that Scotland to litill wes
5   Till his brother and him alsua,
Tharfor to purpos gan he ta
That he off Irland wald be king.
Tharfor he send and had tretyng
With the Irschery off Irland,
10   That in thar leawte tuk on hand
Off all Irland to mak him king
With-thi that he with hard fechting
Mycht ourcum the Inglismen
That in the land war wonnand then,
15   And thai suld help with all thar mycht.
And he that hard thaim mak sic hycht
Intill his hart had gret liking
And with the consent of the king
Gadryt him men off gret bounté
20   And at Ayr syne schippyt he
Intill the neyst moneth of Mai,
Till Irland held he straucht his wai.
He had thar in his cumpany
The Erle Thomas that wes worthi
25   And gud Schyr Philip the Mowbray
That sekyr wes in hard assay,
Schyr Jhone the Soullis ane gud knycht
And Schyr Jhone Stewart that wes wycht
The Ramsay als of Ouchterhous
30   That wes wycht and chevalrous
And Schyr Fergus off Ardrossane
And other knychtis mony ane.
In Wolringis Fyrth aryvyt thai
Sauffly but bargan or assay

---

in Antrim (Bisset country), or a 'Clondumales' (now Drumalys) which was near Oldersfleet, and then that the Scots entered Ireland on 26 May, 'next to Carrickfergus' in Belfast Lough, perhaps close enough to Larne. In early May Edward may have first tried and failed to persuade the head of the Bissets to join him (cf. 47).

and sent home all their ships. They have undertaken a great
project when with so few as they were there – six thousand
men, no more – they prepared to conquer all Ireland, where
they would see many thousands come armed to fight against
them. (42) But although few, they were brave, and without
fear or dread took the way in two divisions, towards Carrick-
fergus, to see it.

(46) But the lords of that country, Mandeville, Bisset and
Logan, assembled every one of their men – the Savages were
there too – and when they were all gathered, they numbered
almost twenty thousand. (52) When they learned that such a
company had arrived in their country, with all the folk that
they had there, they went towards them in great haste. As
soon as Sir Edward knew for a fact that they were coming
close to him, he had his men arm themselves well. (58) Earl
Thomas had the vanguard and Sir Edward was in the rear.
Their enemies approached to fight and they met them without
flinching. (63) There you could see a great mellee for Earl
Thomas and his company laid into their foes so doughtily
that in a short time men could see lying a hundred who were
all bloody, for hobbies who were stabbed there reared and
thrashed and made a lot of space, throwing those riding on
them. (71) Sir Edward's company then attacked so hardily
that they drove back all their foes. Anyone who chanced to
fall in that fight was in danger of [not] rising.

46–81. This battle before the Scots arrive at Carrickfergus is not men-
  tioned in Irish sources, although Laud is probably referring to it when
  it says that the Scots 'took Ulster and expelled Sir Thomas Mandeville
  and other loyal men from their own land'.
47–49. Mandeville, Bisset, Logan, Savage. In September 1315 a corre-
  spondent told Edward II that Bisset-men and Logans had helped
  Edward on his arrival. Only Mandeville remained resolutely opposed
  to the Scots.
68. Hobby was a small horse. The word is used only here and at 500.

35 And send thar schippis hame ilkan.
A gret thing have thai undretane
That with sa quhoyne as thai war thar
That war sex thousand men but mar
Schup to werray all Irland,
40 Quhar thai sall se mony thousand
Cum armyt on thaim for to fycht,
But thocht thai quhone war thai war wicht,
And forout drede or effray
In twa bataillis tuk thar way
45 Towart Cragfergus it to se.

[*The Scots defeat the lords of Ulster*]

Bot the lordis of that countre
Mandveill, Besat and Logane
Thar men assemblyt everilkane,
The Savagis wes alsua thar,
50 And quhen thai assemblit war
That war wele ner twenty thousand.
Quhen thai wyst that intill thar land
Sic a menye aryvyt war
With all the folk that thai had thar
55 Thai went towart thaim in gret hi,
And fra Schyr Edward wist suthly
That ner till him cummand war thai
His men he gert thaim wele aray,
The avaward had the Erle Thomas
60 And the rerward Schyr Edward was.
Thar fayis approchyt to the fechting
And thai met thaim but abaysing.
Thar mycht men se a gret melle,
For Erle Thomas and his menye
65 Dang on thar fayis sa douchtely
That in schort tym men mycht se ly
Ane hunder that all blody war,
For hobynys that war stekyt thar
Relyt and flang and gret rowme mad
70 And kest thaim that apon thaim rad,
And Schyr Edwardis cumpany
Assemblyt syne sa hardely
That thai thar fayis ruschyt all.
Quha hapnyt in that fycht to fall
75 It wes perell off his rysing.

The Scotsmen in that fighting bore themselves so boldly and well that their foes were driven back [until] they took entirely to flight. (80) In that battle there was taken or killed all the flower of Ulster. The earl of Moray had great praise there, for his very bold chivalry encouraged all his company. That was a really excellent beginning, for immediately after their arrival, in open battle they defeated their enemies, who were still four to one. (90) Next they went to Carrickfergus and took lodging in the town. The castle was then well [and] recently provisioned with victuals and [garrisoned] with men; they set siege to it at once. (94) Many a sally was made very boldly while the siege lay there, until eventually they made a truce, when the folk of Ulster had come entirely to his peace, because Sir Edward meant to undertake to ride forth further into the country.

(101) There came to him and made fealty some of the kings of that country, a good ten or twelve, as I heard say; but they kept their faith to him only a short time, for two of them, Macduilechain and another called Macartan, surrounded by two thousand men with spears and by as many [again] of their archers,

---

89. Carrickfergus castle belonged to the earl of Ulster; it still stands.

96. Truce. This may be of June 1315; it is not mentioned in any Irish source, but it seems likely that Edward Bruce regarded the taking or at least neutralising of this castle as a high priority, since it controlled or threatened his shortest line of communication with Scotland.

97–98. The annalist Clyn says that 'the Scots landed in Ulster and virtually all the Irish of the land adhered to them the whole time that they were in Ulster', a view confirmed by letters from Dublin to Edward II saying that Ulster 'received the Scots willingly'. Other annalists (Clonmacnoise, Connacht, Loch Cé) later sought to portray the Scots as ravaging Ulster, but it seems clear that the ravaging began only after they crossed from Ulster into Uriel.

100. To ride further. But Edward seems to have delayed about a month at Carrickfergus, allowing the government time to assemble forces. The Laud annals say that after becoming king, Edward took Greencastle, left men there, and then took Dundalk. The bishop of Down fled to Dublin, suggesting that Edward had gone by Downpatrick.

101–7. The Irish chiefs. *B1985, 95* and other secondary works give an identification of these, but it derives from a nineteenth-century forged treatise ('The Battle of Faughart'), and is worthless. Of Barbour's two who turned against him, Makartane is certainly Mac Cartan (Mac-Artáin) whose lands were in south Down. The other, Makgullane, was identified by Orpen as Mac Duilechain of Clanbrassil (Co. Down) whose loyalty was noted by Edward II in 1318; but he may be Mac-Quillan (Mac Uighilin), who had the Rout, north Antrim around

The Scottismen in that fechting
Sua apertly and wele thaim bar
That thar fayis sua ruschyt war
That thai haly the flycht has tane.
80   In that bataill wes tane or slane
All hale the flur off Ulsyster.
The Erle off Murreff gret price had ther,
For his worthi chevalry
Comfort all his cumpany.
85   This wes a full fayr begynnyng,
For newlingis at thar aryving
In plane bataill thai discomfyt thar
Thar fayis that four ay for ane war,
Syne to Cragfergus ar thai gane
90   And in the toune has innys tane.
The castell weill wes stuffyt then
Off new with vittaill and with men,
Thartill thai set a sege in hy.
Mony eschewe full apertly
95   Wes maid quhill thar the sege lay
Quhill trewys at the last tuk thai,
Quhen that the folk off Hulsyster
Till his pes haly cummyn wer,
For Schyr Edward wald tak on hand
100   To rid furth forthyr in the land.

[*Defeat of two Irish kings; the Lieutenant assembles an army
at Dundalk*]

Off the kingis off that countre
Thar come till him and maide fewté
Weill ten or twelf as Ik hard say,
Bot thai held him schort quhile thar fay,
105   For twa off thaim, ane Makgullane
And ane other hat Makartane,
Withset a pase intill his way
Quhar him behovyt ned away
With twa thousand off men with speris
110   And als mony of thar archeris,

_____

Portrush, and had probably sent help to King Robert in February 1307.
The battle at the pass is mentioned only by Barbour, and should be
placed in June 1315 since Moray participated (119), and he was not
with Bruce when he marched south in November 1315.

a place on his way where he had of necessity to go, and all the cattle of the land were brought there to safety. (113) Men call that place Innermallan; in all Ireland there is none narrower. For they thought that Sir Edward, whom they watched, would not go in their direction, but he soon pushed on his way, and went straight towards the pass. (119) Sir Thomas, the earl of Moray, who always placed himself first in attacks, alighted on foot with his following, and boldly took the pass. (123) Those Irish kings of whom I spoke previously, with all the folk who were with them, opposed him very sturdily, but he attacked so with his company, that despite their [men] they won the pass; many of their foes were slain there. (129) They chased them all through the wood, and seized their booty in such quantities that all the folk of their host were refreshed for a good week or more. (133) At Kilnasaggart Sir Edward lay, and very soon heard tell there that a gathering of lords of that country had been made at Dundalk. They were assembled in a host there. There was first Sir Richard Clare,

113. E has Innermallane but added in a gap left by the original scribe; C has Enderwillane and the 1571 edition Endnellane. The name occurs twice in record, in 1282 as Imberdoilan (*CDI2*, 432) and in 1343 as Emberdullam (probably a misreading of Emberdullan; Grace, *Annals*, 136). In both cases it was a pass from Ulster towards the south, controlled by MacCartan. I have failed to find a surviving linked name on the modern map. It has long been identified with the Moiry pass between Newry and Dundalk, by the old (Jonesborough) road, which would indeed bring Bruce to Kilnasaggart (133). The suggested link with Castlewellan arose from the reading Enderwillane, and is to be rejected.

122, 127. pass; again C reads 'plas', but 'pass' makes better sense.

132–33. Barbour does not justify those modern authorities who say that Edward spent a week at Kilnasaggart.

138–48. These names, which pose many problems, are largely repeated at 512–16 (Fitz Thomas replaced by Fitz Warin) as being at Connor at the end of the first campaign. and two are mentioned in connection with the battle of Connor at 15.75–76: 'Clare' fled, which shows that he has here been confused with Richard de Burgh, earl of Ulster; Fitz Warin, an Ulster baron, was taken prisoner, as indeed he was at Connor. It seems that the resemblances of names, 'Richard' and 'Fitz Thomas/Warin' have linked Clare, Butler, Birminghan, Verdoun and the earls of Kildare and Desmond, to the earl of Ulster and Fitz Warin. But this does not mean that for 'Sir Richard Clare' we should read 'Ulster' throughout. In fact the group named at 138–48, apart from Butler, took no part against Edward Bruce's first campaign, but were active in defence of Leinster in January 1316, during the second campaign. Maurice Fitz Thomas occurs in his own name (146) and as the earl of Desmond (141), a title conferred in 1329; the earldom of Kildare

And all the catell of the land
War drawyn thidder to warand.
Men callys that plase Innermallane,
In all Irland straytar is nane.
115   For Schyr Edward that kepyt thai,
Thai thoucht he suld nocht thar away,
Bot he his viage sone has tane
And straught towart the pas is gane.
The erle off Murreff Schyr Thomas
120   That put him fyrst ay till assayis
Lychtyt on fute with his menye
And apertly the pase tuk he.
Thir Ersch kingis that I spak off ar
With all the folk that with thame war
125   Met him rycht sturdely, bot he
Assaylyt sua with his menye
That maugre tharis thai wan the pas.
Slayne off thar fayis fele thar was,
Throu-out the wod thaim chasyt thai
130   And sesyt in sic fusoune the pray
That all the folk off thar ost war
Refreschyt weill ane wouk or mar.
At Kilsagart Schyr Edward lay,
And wele sone he has hard say
135   That at Dundalk wes assemblé
Made off the lordis off that countre.
In ost thai war assemblyt thar,
Thar wes fyrst Schyr Richard of Clar

---

was created for John Fitz Thomas FitzGerald in May 1316. Barbour is here using a source written after 1329. He or the source wrongly made Richard de Clare Lieutenant or Warden of Ireland; Butler was head of the Irish administration as Justiciar (1315–16); his successor Roger Mortimer had the title of Lieutenant (1317–18); all these seem to be confused in the list in 138–48, probably because a source spoke of 'justiciar', 'warden', 'lieutenant', without name, and he misidentified these. The Wardoune is Miles Verdon, the Breman John Birmingham. None of these men was at Dundalk before it was taken, but they were called on by Edward II in July 1315 to cooperate in resisting Bruce and replied to him later that year. Some, including Clare, were involved in the army which was defeated at Skerries (or Ardscull) on 26 January, 1316, but not Verdon nor Birmingham, who were at the final defeat of Edward Bruce, at Faughart in October 1318. The list seems to be eclectic, but best fits the period when the government strove desperately to cope with Bruce's second campaign in Leinster in January–February 1316.

who was Lieutenant of the king of England in all Ireland.
(141) The earl of Desmond was also there, the earl of Kildare,
de Birmingham and de Verdon, who were lords of great
reputation. Butler was also there, and Sir Maurice Fitz-
Thomas. These came with their men and were indeed a really
mighty host.

(149) When Sir Edward knew for a fact that such a chivalry
was there, he had his host armed in haste and took the way
towards [the enemy], taking lodging near the town. But be-
cause he knew for a certainty that there were a lot of men in
the town, he armed his divisions then and stood arrayed in
division, to hold them if they should attack. (159) When Sir
Richard Clare and other lords who were there learned that
the Scotsmen with their divisions had come so near, they
consulted [and decided] that they would not fight that night,
because it was late, but that on the morrow, in the morning
very soon after sunrise, all who were there would issue forth;
(168) for that reason they did no more that night but both
sides made camp. That night the Scottish company were very
well guarded, in good order, and on the morrow, when [the]
day was light, they drew themselves up in two divisions; they
stood with banners all displayed, fully ready for battle. (176)
Those who were inside the town when the sun had risen,
shining brightly, sent fifty of those who were within [the town]
to see the demeanour

(*Note to ll. 138–48 appears on pp. 526–7*)

49–215. A battle at Dundalk. According to the Laud annals, 'on 29 June
the Scots came to Dundalk and took the town, despoiling and burning
it, and killing those who resisted them. The greater part of Uriel is
burned by the Scots.' This perhaps confirms a battle the scale of which
is greatly exaggerated here, probably by Barbour's source. On 15 Sep-
tember, 1315 Moray sailed to Scotland; on 13 November Edward Bruce
left Carrickfergus; 'to him came the earl of Moray with 500 men likewise
to the parts of Dundalk, and some gave them the right hand.' This
second visit may explain confusion between the first and second cam-
paigns in Barbour's narrative.

That in all Irland lufftenande
140   Was off the king off Ingland
The erle of Desmond wes thar
And the erle alsua of Kildar,
The Breman and the Wardoune
That war lordis of gret renoune,
145   The Butler alsua thar was
And Schyr Morys le fys Thomas,
Thai with thar men ar cummyn thar,
A rycht gret ost forsuth thai war.

[*The two sides prepare for battle*]

And quhen Schyr Edward wyst suthly
150   That thar wes swilk chevalry
His ost in hy he gert aray
And thidderwartis tuk the way
And ner the toune tuk his herbery,
Bot for he wyst all witterly
155   That in the toune war mony men
His bataillis he arayit then,
And stud arayt in bataill
To kep thaim gif thai wald assaile,
And quhen that Schyr Rychard of Clar
160   And other lordis that thar war
Wyst that the Scottis men sa ner
With thar bataillis cummyn wer,
Thai tuk to consaile that that nycht
For it wes layt thai wald nocht fycht
165   Bot on the morne in the mornyng
Weile sone aftre the sone-rysing
Thai suld isch furth all that thar war,
Tharfor that nycht thai did no mar
Bot herbryit thaim on athyr party.
170   That nycht the Scottis cumpany
War wachyt rycht weill all at rycht,
And on the morn quhen day wes lycht
In twa bataillis thai thaim arayit,
Thai stud with baneris all displayit
175   For the bataill all redy boun.
And thai that war within the toun
Quhen sone wes rysyn schenand cler
Send furth of thaim that within wer
Fyfty to se the contenyng

of the Scotsmen and their arrival. They rode forth and soon
saw them, then returned without delay. (183) When they had
dismounted together, they told their lords who were there
that the Scotsmen appeared to be worthy and of great valour,
'but without doubt they are not half a dinner [compared] to
us here.' (189) At this news the lords rejoiced and took great
comfort, causing men to proclaim through the city that all
should arm themselves quickly.

(193) When they were armed and equipped and all drawn up
for the fight, they went forth in good order; soon they engaged
with their enemy, who resisted them right strongly. The fight
began there fiercely, for each side put all their might into
defeating their foes in the struggle, and laid into the others
forcibly. (202) The hard-fought engagement lasted a long
time, so that men could not make out or see who most had
the upper hand. From soon after sun-rise until after mid-
morning the fighting continued in this uncertainty; but then
Sir Edward, who was bold, with all those of his company,
attacked them so fiercely that they couldn't withstand the
fighting any more. (212) All in a rush they took to flight and
[the Scots] followed swiftly; into the town all together they
entered, both intermixed. (216) There you could see dreadful
slaughter, for the right noble Earl Thomas, who followed the
chase with his force, made such a slaughter in the town,

---

191. City. Dundalk had no episcopal seat so this description is erroneous.

180   Off Scottismen and thar cummyng,
        And thai raid furth and saw thaim sone,
        Syne come agayne withoutyn hone.
        And quhen thai samyn lychtyt war
        Thai tauld thar lordis that wer thar
185   That Scottismen semyt to be
        Worthi and off gret bounté,
        'Bot thai ar nocht withoutyn wer
        Half-dell a dyner till us her.'
        The lordys had off this tithing
190   Gret joy and gret reconforting
        And gert men throu the cite cry
        That all suld arm thaim hastily.

[*The Scots are victorious and take Dundalk; drunkenness in the army*]

        Quhen thai war armyt and purvayit
        And for the fycht all hale arayit
195   Thai went thaim furth in gud aray,
        Sone with thar fayis assemblyt thai
        That kepyt thaim rycht hardely.
        The stour begouth thar cruelly
        For athyr part set all thar mycht
200   To rusche thar fayis in the fycht
        And with all mycht on other dang.
        The stalwart stour lestyt wele lang
        That men mycht nocht persave na se
        Qyha maist at thar above suld be,
205   For fra sone eftre the sone-rissing
        Quhill eftre mydmorne the fechting
        Lestyt intill swilk a dout.
        Bot than Schyr Edward that wes stout
        With all thaim of his cumpany
210   Schot apon thaim sa sturdely
        That thai mycht thole no mar the fycht,
        All in a frusche thai tuk the flycht
        And thai folowyt full egrely,
        Into the toun all commonaly
215   Thai entryt bath intermelle.
        Thar men mycht felloune slauchter se,
        For the rycht noble erle Thomas
        That with his rout folowyt the chas
        Maid swilk a slauchter in the toun

such a dreadfull killing, that the streets were all bloody with
slain men lying there; the lords had got quite away! (224)
When the town had been taken as I tell you, by dint of much
fighting, and all their enemies had fled or been killed, they all
lodged themselves in the town where there was such profusion
of food and so great an abundance of wine the the good earl
had a great fear that [some] of their men would get drunk
and in their drunken state start brawling. (233) So he made
an issue of wine to each man so that he would be content,
and they all had enough, *perfay*. That night they were very
relaxed and much cheered by the great honour that accrued
to them through their valour. (239) After this fight they stayed
there in Dundalk for no more than three days; then took their
way southwards. Earl Thomas was always to the fore. As they
rode through the country it was remarkable that they could
see so many men upon the hills. (246) When the earl would
boldly ride up to them with his banner, they would one and
all take to flight so that not one remained to fight. [The Scots]
rode on their way southwards until they came to a great forest
which was called Kilross as I heard tell, and they all made
camp there.

(254) All this time Richard Clare, who was the king's Lieut-
enant,

---

240. 'But mar', E, but C says three days 'and mar'.

241. Took their way southwards. Here Barbour omits Edward's ravaging
as far south as Rathmore (Co. Meath), in an advance on Dublin, which
turned back as the earl of Ulster approached with troops from the west.

252. Kilrose. The identity of this place has been sought (though there is
no appropriate Kilrose) to fit with the following skirmish in the first
campaign: 'the earl lay at Ardee beside Slieve Brey, while Edward Bruce
with his Ulstermen and Scots lay at Inishkeen, and the next day the
earl followed them up and encamped at Louth. Then William Burke
went out to catch Edward and his Scots unawares and a few on each
side were killed.' (*Ann. Connacht*, 233) However, the most likely modern
form of Kilrose is Kilrush, of which there are several in Ireland. This
one was probably Kilrush, 4 miles, 6 kilometres south-east of Kildare,
where Edward Bruce was in January 1316. Thence he went south
to Castledermot, Athy and Reban, before defeating the Justiciar at
Ardscull/Skerries on 25 January, 1316; Kilrush is less than 2 miles from
Ardscull.

254-309. This battle is usually equated with the skirmish described in
the note to 252. But it is in my view more likely to be the battle of
Skerries, of which (a) Laud and (b) a report to Edward II say:
(a) Then Bruce came to Skerries beside Ardscull in Leinster. There
met him there in battle Sir Edmund Butler, Justiciar of Ireland, and
Sir John Fitz Thomas and Sir Arnold Poer, and other magnates of

220   And sua felloune occisioun
        That the rewys all bludy war
        Off slayne men that war lyand thar,
        The lordis war gottyn all away.
        And quhen the toun as I you say
225   Wes throu gret force of fechting tane
        And all thar fayis fled or slayne
        Thai herbryit thaim all in the toun
        Quhar off vitaill wes sic fusoun
        And sua gret haboundance of wyne
230   That the gud erle had doutyne
        That off thar men suld drunkyn be
        And mak in drunkynnes sum melle.
        Tharfor he maid of wyne levere
        Till ilk man that he payit suld be,
235   And thai had all yneuch perfay.
        That nycht rycht weill at ese war thai
        And rycht blyth of the gret honour
        That thaim befell for thar valour.
        Eftyr this fycht thai sojornyt thar
240   Into Dundalk thre dayis but mar,
        Syne tuk thai southwartis thar way.
        The Erle Thomas wes forouth ay
        And as thai raid throu the countré
        Thai mycht apon the hillis se
245   Sua mony men it wes ferly,
        And quhen the erle wald sturdely
        Dres him to thaim with his baner
        Thai wald fle all that evir thai wer
        Sua that in fycht nocht ane abad.
250   And thai southwart thar wayis raid
        Quhill till a gret forest come thai,
        Kylrose it hat as Ik hard say,
        And thai tuk all thar herbery thar.

[*The Lieutenant is defeated in another battle*]

        In all this tyme Rychard of Clar
255   That wes the kingis luftenand

_____

Leinster and Munster, so that one of these lords with his force would
suffice to defeat the same Edward and his army. But discord arose
among them; confused, they left the field to the said Edward ... On
the Scottish side Sir Fergus Ardrossan and Sir Walter Moray and

had assembled a great host of all the baronage of Ireland. They were [in] five divisions, great and broad, seeking Sir Edward and his men [who] had come very near to him then. (261) He soon got knowledge that they were coming against him and were so near. He drew up his men against them, and had them stoutly take to the open [ground]; then the earl came there to see and he sent Sir Philip Mowbray, and Sir John Stewart went also. (268) They take their way ahead to reconnoitre, [and] saw the host coming to hand, which was, at a guess, fifty thousand. They rode back to Sir Edward then, and said that there were indeed many men. (273) He said in response, 'The more they are, the greater honour we shall have for ourselves if we bear ourselves manfully. We are placed here at risk to win honour or to die. We are too far from home to flee, so let each man be brave. (280) Yon are the sweepings of the country, and they will flee quickly, I'm sure, if men attack them courageously.' Then they all said that they would do their best. With that the divisions came approaching near to them, ready to fight, and [the Scots], who numbered ten thousand worthy men, met them with great determination. (288) The Scots were all on foot then, [the enemy] well equipped on horses, some [men] all protected in iron and steel. (291) But Scotsmen pierced their armour with spears at the encounter, impaled horses and struck men down.

---

many others were killed, their bodies buried at Athy in the Dominicans' church.

(b) [*Further names include Maurice Fitz Thomas*] The Justiciar and the bannerets and their retinues which were men-at-arms, hobelars and followers (*pitaill*), more than enough if they had had good fortune, had an encounter with the enemy on hard field between Kildare and Castle Dermot near a town called Ardscull ... and by mischance the field remained with the enemy. But they lost some of their important men and our men lost only one man.

There is another possibility: that Kilrose is a transcription error for Kenlis (Kells), where Edward Bruce on his second campaign, defeated Roger Mortimer, later Lieutenant (cf. 255), in early December 1315. Laud's description is quite like Barbour's battle at Kilrose:

A second conflict at Kells in Meath ... The Scots crossed from Kells in Meath, to whom came ... Mortimer with a large army, with almost 15,000, not loyal among themselves, as is believed, nor allied with [Mortimer]. They took to flight around the third hour, turning their backs, especially the Lacys, leaving [Mortimer] alone with a few men who had to flee to Dublin, Sir Walter Cusack to Trim, leaving the district and the town of Kells to the Scots.

265–267. Came there to see. This seems to mean that Earl Thomas went

Off the barnagis of Irland
A gret ost he assemblyt had,
Thai war fyve bataillis gret and braid
That soucht Schir Edward and his men,
260   Weill ner him war thai cummyn then.
He gat sone wittring that thai wer
Cummand on him and war sa ner.
His men he dressyt thaim agayn
And gert thaim stoutly ta the playn
265   And syne the erle thar come to se
And Schyr Philip the Mowbray send he,
And Schyr Jhone Stewart went alsua.
Furth to discover thar way thai ta,
Thai saw the ost sone cum at hand
270   Thai war to ges fyfty thousand,
Hame till Schyr Edward raid thai then
And said weill thai war mony men.
He said agayne, 'The ma thai be
The mar honour all-out haff we
275   Giff that we ber us manlyly.
We ar set her in juperty
To wyn honour or for to dey,
We ar to fer fra hame to fley
Tharfor lat ilk man worthi be.
280   Yone ar gadryngis of this countre
And thai sall fley I trow lychly
And men assaile thaim manlyly.'
All said than that thai weile suld do,
With that approchand ner thaim to
285   The bataillis come redy to fycht,
And thai met thaim with mekill mycht
That war ten thousand worthi men.
The Scottismen all on fute war then,
And thai on stedys trappyt weile
290   Sum helyt all in irne and stele,
Bot Scottismen at thar meting
With speris persyt thar armyng
And stekyt hors and men doun bar.

---

ahead to see the enemy, and that 'he' (Edward Bruce) sent the two
others to do so also.

290. Protected in iron and steel. The line seems to describe the men,
not their horses. But it is very improbable that either would have plate
armour in Ireland at this date; the mail hauberk was still universal.

It was a tough battle then, there. (295) I can't tell [of] all their smiting, nor who struck down which other in the fight, but in a short while, I assure you, those of Ireland had been so resisted that they did not dare to stay there any longer, but fled, scattered, every one of them, leaving on the battlefield a great many of their good men dead. (303) The field was wholly covered by weapons, arms and dead men. That great army had been forcibly driven off, but Sir Edward allowed no man to give chase, but they went back with the prisoners they had taken to the wood where their armour had been left. (310) That night they made merry [with] good cheer and praised God for his grace. This good knight, who was so worthy, could well be compared to Judas Maccabeus who in a fight avoided no host of men as long as he had one against ten.

(317) Thus, as I said, Richard Clare and his great host were driven back. But in spite of that he was busily collecting men about him, for he meant to regain his good fortune. It angered him very very greatly that he had been defeated twice in battle by a small company. (325) The Scotsmen who were riding to the forest to take their rest, lay there for all [of] two nights, enjoying life, relaxing and playing.

(329) Then they rode towards O'Dempsy, an Irish king who had made an oath of fealty to Sir Edward, for before that he had begged him to see his land and [there] would be no lack of food

---

302. Good men, i.e. leading men.

309. This is the first mention that the Scots had fought without 'harnes', meaning armour. Since they were engaged when their horses were also elsewhere (288), it seems that in the skirmish which lies behind Barbour's account, the Scots were caught away from their camp, almost wholly unprepared.

317–66. Long ago Orpen (*Ireland under the Normans*, iv, 164–74) showed that O'Dempsy, whose lands of Clanmalier lay in Leix and Offaly, can scarcely have been by the Bann in 1315. Edward Bruce was in Leix in his second campaign, after the battle of Skerries on 26 January, 1316, at which time this episode is to be placed.

332. 'For forouth that'. Logically before O'Dempsy swore fealty, but that hardly makes sense. Perhaps before the Scots marched south. I suspect that Barbour was faced by an ambiguous *antea* in his source.

A feloun fechting wes than thar,
295   I can nocht tell thar strakys all
Na quha in fycht gert other fall
Bot in schort tyme Ik underta
Thai of Irland war contraryit sua
That thai durst than abyd no mar
300   Bot fled scalyt all that thai war,
And levyt in the bataill sted
Weill mony off thar gud men dede,
Off wapnys, armyng and of ded men
The feld was haly strowyt then.
305   That gret ost rudly ruschyt was
Bot Schyr Edward let na man chas
Bot with presonaris that thai had tane
Thai till the woud agayne ar gane
Quhar that thar harnys levyt war.
310   That nycht thai maid thar men gud cher
And lovyt God fast off his grace.
This gud knycht that sa worthi was
Till Judas Machabeus mycht
Be lyknyt weill that into fycht
315   Forsuk na multitud off men
Quhill he had ane aganys ten.

[*The Scots go to O'Dempsy, who gives them quarters; he seeks
to starve and drown them*]

Thus as I said Rychard of Clar
And his gret ost rebutyt war,
Bot he about him nocht-forthi
320   Wes gaderand men ay ythenly
For he thocht yete to covyr his cast.
It angyrryt him rycht ferly fast
That twys intill batell wes he
Discomfyt with a few mengne.
325   And Scottismen that to the forest
War ridyn for to mak thar rest
All thai twa nychtis thar thai lay
And maid thaim myrth solace and play.
Towart Ydymsy syne thai raid,
330   Ane Yrsche king that aith had maid
To Schyr Edward of fewte,
For forouth that him prayit he
To se his land and na vittaill

or anything else that could help him. Sir Edward trusted in
his promise and rode straight there with his force. (337)
[O'Dempsy] had them pass [by] a great river and in a very
fair place which was down by a burn he had them make their
camp, and said that he would go to have men bring victuals
to them. He went off without staying any longer, because he
meant to betray them. (344) He had brought them to such a
place where all the cattle were withdrawn [from them] by a
good two days' [travel] or more, so that they could get nothing
worth eating in that land. He meant to enfeeble them with
hunger and then bring their enemies against them. (351) This
false traitor had caused his men to dam up the outlet of a
lough a little above where he had lodged Sir Edward and his
men, and let it out in the night. The water then came down
on Sir Edward's men with such force that they were in danger
of drowning, for before they knew it, they were afloat. (360)
They got away with great difficulty and by God's grace kept
their lives, but [some] of their armour was lost. He made no
great feast for them, *perfay*, but nonetheless they had their
fill, for although they got no food, I can tell you they were
good and wet.

(367) They were placed in great distress because they so lacked
meat, for they were placed between two rivers and could cross
neither of them. The Bann, which is an arm of the sea [and]
which can't be crossed on horseback, was between them and
Ulster.

---

339. 'Bourne', a burn, E. C has a 'brym' or loughside, but a stream
makes better sense in the upshot.

354. The lough; Lough Beg, just north of Lough Neagh is usually
suggested. But the Bann flowed unstoppably through it, and in any
case, a lough in or near O'Dempsy country is required. A small lough,
such as that (now drained) shown on the Elizabethan map of Leix and
Offaly north-west of Killeigh and less than ten miles from Clanmalier,
is more likely. See A. Smyth, *Celtic Leinster*.

367–82. Crossing the Bann. We now return to the first campaign and
Edward's withdrawal north, in July–August 1315. There is debate about
how Bruce and the earl reached the mouth of the Bann – east or west
of Lough Neagh. The earl surely went by the east, and Bruce may have
gone west, through Tyrone. But Irish sources say the earl followed
Bruce. Thomas Dun (376) was a Scottish sea-captain (in English terms,
a pirate) active in the Irish sea and involved in the Scottish attempt to
hold the Isle of Man; in September 1315 his ship and three others
attacked Holyhead, effectively confirming Barbour's 'four ships' (381).
Irish sources make no mention of this rescue, which would occur (if
Barbour has correctly placed it here) after the withdrawal of the earl
(contd p. 540)

Na nocht that mycht thaim help suld faile.
335   Schyr Edward trowit in his hycht
And with his rout raid thidder rycht
A gret ryver he gert him pas
And in a rycht fayr place that was
Lauch by a bourne he gert thaim ta
340   Thar herbery, and said he wald ga
To ger men vittaill to thaim bring,
He held hys way but mar dwelling.
For he betrais thaim wes his thocht,
In sic a place he has them broucht
345   Quharof twa journais wele and mar
All the cattell withdrawyn war,
Swa that thai in that land mycht get
Na thing that worth war for til ete,
With hungyr he thocht thaim to feblis
350   Syne bring on thaim thar ennemys.
This fals traytouris men had maid
A litill outh quhar he herbryit had
Schyr Edward and the Scottismen
The ischow off a louch to den
355   And leyt it out into the nycht.
The water than with a swilk a mycht
On Schyr Edwardis men com doun
That thai in perell war to droun
For or thai wist on flot war thai.
360   With mekill payn thai gat away
And held thar lyff as God gaff grace,
Bot off thar harnayis tynt thar was.
He maid thaim na gud fest perfay
And nocht-forthi yneuch had thai,
365   For thoucht thaim faillyt of the mete
I warn you wele thai war wele wet.

*[The Scots are rescued; they camp near an enemy army, seize
its foragers and make a surprise attack]*

In gret distres thar war thai stad
For gret defaut off mete thai hade,
And thai betwix reveris twa
370   War set and mycht pas nane off tha,
The Bane that is ane arme of the se
That with hors may nocht passyt be
Wes betwix thaim and Hulsyster.

(374) They would have been in great danger there but for a sea-pirate who was called Thomas Dun, [who] heard that the army was placed in such straits and [who] sailed up the Bann till he came very close to where they lay. They knew him well and were greatly cheered. (381) Then with four ships that he had captured he set them all across the Bann. When they came to populated land they found enough victuals and meat, and made camp in a wood. No-one of the land knew where they were; they relaxed and made good cheer. (388) At that time, close beside them, Sir Richard Clare and other great [men] of Ireland were camped with a great host in a forest side. Each day they had men ride [out] to bring them victuals of various kinds from the town of Connor which was good ten miles from them. Each day as they came and went, they came so near the Scots' host that there were only two miles between them. (399) When Earl Thomas perceived them coming and going, he got him a goodly company of three hundred on horse, bold and brave. There was Sir Philip Mowbray,

---

of Ulster from Coleraine as described most fully in the *Annals of Inisfallen*:

> The Scots had retreated secretly ... through Armagh to Es Craíbe on the River Bann. [*The earl of Ulster decides to pursue them only with his own men*] This he did, for he pursued the Scots to Coleraine on the Bann. The latter became alarmed at his approach and burned the whole town except [the Dominican Friary] and moreover they destroyed the bridge to deprive him of a suitable passage as he was about to cross over. [*There were only two fords, and these passable only at time of drought*] The earl thus remained on the opposite bank without interference from the enemy waiting for the water level to fall or a shortage of food among his foes. One of these came about because it was reported that in the Scottish camp four quarters of a sheep fetched 2s. sterling. On account of this dearth however, the people of the countryside, especially O'Neill, O'Cathain, O'Flaind did not fail to provide for them [the Scots] as best they could. When the earl saw this he retreated to Antrim, desiring to procure plentiful supplies for his army.

The Annals of Loch Cé say that O'Neill guided Bruce's retreat to Coleraine. Es Craibe is just south of Coleraine, which is about 38 miles north of Antrim. The annals of Connacht add an explanation for the earl's weakness at Coleraine – that Feidlim O'Conchobair of Connacht deserted him after talking to Edward Bruce. They also comment that the earl and Edward, between them, 'left neither wood nor lea nor corn nor crop nor steading nor barn nor church, but fired and burned them all'. (*Ann. Connacht*, 233–5)

388–446. The events described here are not located precisely, and may

Thai had bene in gret perell ther
375 Ne war a scowmar of the se,
Thomas of Downe hattyn wes he,
Hard that the ost sa straytly than
Wes stad, and salyt up the Ban
Quhill he come wele ner quhar thai lay,
380 Thai knew him weil and blyth war thai,
Than with four schippys that he had tane
He set our the Ban ilkane.
And quhen thai come in biggit land
Vittaill and mete yneuch thai fand
385 And in a wod thaim herberyt thai,
Nane of the land wist quhar thai lay,
Thai esyt thaim and maid gud cher.
Intill that tym besid thaim ner
With a gret ost Schyr Richard of Clar
390 And othyr gret of Irland war
Herberyt in a forest syde,
And ilk day thai gert men rid
To bring vittaill on ser manerys
To thaim fra the toun off Coigneris
395 That wele ten gret myle wes thaim fra.
Ilk day as thai wald cum and ga
Thai come the Scottis ost sa ner
That bot twa myle betwix thaim wer,
And quhen the Erle Thomas persaving
400 Had off thar cummyng and thar ganging
He gat him a gud cumpany,
Thre hunder on hors wycht and hardy,
Thar wes Schyr Philip the Mowbray

seem to be close to Coleraine (383–85) but Laud says that 'the earl
withdrew to Connor, seeing which the said Bruce cautiously crossed
the said river [Bann] following him, whom he put to flight with several
on the side of the earl, George de Rupe being wounded and others
killed [two names given], and also many were killed on Bruce's side.
Sir William de Burgh was taken prisoner on 10 September, and the
earl was overthrown next to Connor.' This is usually taken to refer as
a whole to the battle of Connor, but I suspect that only the last sentence
does so, the earlier part referring to what is described in 388–446. Bruce
followed the earl, to whom, in 394–95, victuals were being brought ten
miles from Connor, an episcopal see and presumably manor. This
would fit with the earl's stay at Antrim, some seven miles south of
Connor, where, according to Inisfallen, many men (3,000 supposedly)
deserted him under Walter son of Sir Walter 'Cattus' de Burgh.
389. Clare, again wrongly for the earl of Ulster.

also Sir John Stewart with Sir Alan Stewart, Sir Robert Boyd and others. (407) They rode to meet the victuallers who were coming from Connor with their victuals, holding the way to their host. They assaulted them so suddenly that they were all dismayed so that they dropped all their weapons and piteously cried for mercy. (414) [The Scots] took them into their mercy and so thoroughly cleaned them up that not one of them escaped. The earl got information about them, that [some] of their host would come out of the wood-side in the evening and ride [to meet] their victuals. (421) He thought then of an exploit, causing all his followers deck themselves in the prisoners' clothing, take their pennons with them too, wait till the night was near and then ride toward the host. (427) Some of the [enemy's] great host saw them coming, and thought that these were indeed their victuallers, so they rode towards them dispersed, because they had no fear that these were their foes, and also they were very hungry, so they came higgledy-piggledy. (434) When they were near, the earl and all that were with him in great speed assaulted them with unsheathed weapons, shouting aloud their rallying cries; then they, seeing their foes so suddenly attack them were so fearful that they had no heart to encourage them but went to the host, [while the Scots] gave chase and killed many [so] that all the fields were strewn [with corpses]; more than a thousand dead lay there. (445) They chased them right up to their host, then took their way back.

---

423. 'Aray' translated 'clothing' but probably also meaning 'armour'.

And Schyr Jhone Stewart als perfay
405 And Schyr Alan Stewart alsua
Schyr Robert Boid and other ma.
Thai raid to mete the vittaleris
That with thar vittaill fra Coigneris
Come haldand to thar ost the way.
410 Sua sudanly on thaim schot thai
That thai war sua abaysyt all
That thai leyt all thar wapnys fall
And mercy petously gan cry,
And thai tuk thaim in thar mercy
415 And has thaim up sa clenly tane
That off thaim all eschapyt nane.
The erle of thaim gat wittering
That off thar ost in the evynnyng
Wald cum out at the woddis sid
420 And agaynys thar vittail rid.
He thocht than on ane juperty,
And gert his menye halily
Dycht thaim in the presoneris aray,
Thair pennounys als with thaim tuk thai,
425 And quhill the nycht wes ner thai bad
And syne towart the ost thai raid.
Sum of thar mekill ost has sene
Thar come and wend thai had bene
Thar vittalouris, tharfor thai raid
430 Agaynys thaim scalyt, for thai haid
Na dred that thai thar fayis war
And thaim hungryt alsua weill sar,
Tharfor thai come abandounly.
And quhen thai ner war in gret hi
435 The erle and all that with him war
Ruschyt on thaim with wapnys bar
And thar ensenyeis hey gan cry.
Than thai that saw sua sodanly
Thar fayis dyng on thaim war sa rad
440 That thai na hart to help thaim had
Bot to the ost thar way gan ta,
And thai chassyt and sua fele gan sla
That all the feldys strowyt war,
Ma than a thousand ded war thar.
445 Rycht till thar ost thai gan thaim chas
And syne agane thar wayis tais.

(447) In this way the victual was taken and many of the Irishmen slain. Then the earl with his company brought all the prisoners and victuals speedily to Sir Edward, who was very pleased by their arrival. That night they were merry and cheerful and were entirely at ease. (455) They were all under secure watch, [while] their foes on the other hand, when they heard how their men had been killed and how their victuals had been taken, consulted [and decided] that they would hold their way towards Connor, and take lodging in the city. (462) They did this in great haste, riding by night to the city. They found there an abundance of victual and made right good cheer, for they were entirely confident in the town. In the morning they sent [men] to discover where the Scotsmen had lodged themselves, but [the men] were met as well, taken and brought each one right to the [Scottish] army. (471) The earl of Moray very gently asked one of their company where there host was and what they meant to do; he said that if he should find that he had told him the truth, he should go home quit of ransom. (477) 'Indeed,' said he, 'I'll tell you; they expect tomorrow, when it's day, to seek you with all their following, if they can get knowledge of where you are. They have wickedly caused be proclaimed through the country that all men, on pain of life, [must] be in the city tonight. (485) Truly they will be so numerous that you won't [be able to] deal with them in any way.' *'Pardieu'* said [the earl], 'that's as may be.'

447–554. Preliminaries to the battle of Connor. These episodes are known from no other source; the prominence of Moray in these actions is noteworthy.

461. City. This is correct, for Connor was seat of the bishop of Connor.

[The Lieutenant and his army occupy Connor and plan to attack the Scots]

On this wis wes that vittaill tane
And of the Irche-men mony slane.
The erle syne with his cumpany
450 Presoneris and vittalis halily
Thai broucht till Schyr Edward alswith
And he wes of thar cummyn blyth.
That nycht thai maid thaim mery cher
For rycht all at thar eys thai wer,
455 Thai war ay walkyt sekyrly.
And thar fayis on the tother party
Quhen thai hard how thar men war slane
And how thar vittalis als wes tane
Thai tuk to consaill that thai wald
460 Thair wayis towart Coigneris hald
And herbery in the cite ta,
And than in gret hy thai haf don sua
And raid be nycht to the cité,
Thai fand thar of vittalis gret plente
465 And maid thaim rycht mery cher
For all traist in the toun thai wer.
Apon the morne thai send to spy
Quhar Scottismen had tane herbery,
Bot thai war withall als tane
470 And brocht rycht till the ost ilkane.
The erle of Murreff rycht mekly
Speryt at ane of thar cumpany
Quhar thar ost wes and quhat thai thocht
To do, and said him gif he moucht
475 Fynd that till him the suth said he
He suld gang hame but ransoun fre.
He said, 'Forsuth I sall you say,
Thai think to-morn, quhen it is day,
To sek you with all thar menye
480 Giff thai may get wit quhar ye be.
Thai haff gert throu the countre cry
Off payne of lyve full felounly
That all the men of this countre
Tonycht into the cyté be,
485 And trewly thai sall be sa fele
That ye sall na wis with thaim dele.'
'De pardew,' said he, 'weill may be.'

With that he went to Sir Edward and told him the whole of this tale.

(490) They took counsel then altogether that they would ride to the city that very night, so that they should be with all their force between the town and those who were to come [from] outside. (495) They did just as they had planned; they soon came before the town and only half a mile on the road from the city they halted. When the day dawned light, fifty nimble men on hobbies came to a little hill which was only a short distance from the town, and saw Sir Edward's camp; they were astonished at the sight, (505) that so few dared at all undertake such a great enterprise as to come so boldly against all the great chivalry of Ireland to await battle. (510) And so it was, without doubt, for there were gathered against them there, with Richard Clare the Warden, the Butler, with the two earls of Desmond and Kildare, Birmingham, Verdon, and Fitz-Warin, Sir Pascal Florentine who was a knight of Lombardy and was full of chivalry. (519) The Mandevilles were there also, Bissets, Logans and various others; Savages too, and there was also a man called Sir Nicholas Kilkenny. With these lords, there were so many then that for each of the Scotsmen I believe they were five or more. (526) When their scouts had seen the Scottish host like that, they went in haste

---

512–22. For these names see note to 138–46. Sir Paschal, the Lombard knight is presumably Bindo the Lombard who seized the cattle of the Bissets and drove them to Carrickfergus to feed the castle garrison. (*Irish Hist. Studies*, x, 99–100) Mandevilles, Bissets, Logans and Savages were tenants of the earl of Ulster who according to Barbour (46–9) had opposed Edward Bruce at his first landing. All but the Mandevilles were later pardoned by Edward II for aiding the Scots, but their misconduct probably occurred after the battle of Connor.

To Schyr Edward with that yeid he
And tauld him utrely this tale.

[The Scots move camp; the enemy scouts survey them, and decide to attack; Moray ambushes the enemy]

490   Than haf thai tane for consale hale
       That thai wald rid to the cite
       That ilk nycht sua that thai mycht be
       Betwix the toune with all thar rout
       And thaim that war to cum with-out.
495   Als thai devisyt thai haf done,
       Befor the toune thai come alsone
       And bot halfindall a myle of way
       Fra the cité arest tuk thai.
       And quhen the day wes dawyn lycht
500   Fyfty on hobynys that war wycht
       Come till a litill hill that was
       Bot fra the toun a litill space
       And saw Schyr Edwardis herbery,
       And off the sycht had gret ferly
505   That sua quhone durst on ony wis
       Undretak sa hey enprys
       As for to cum sa hardely
       Apon all the chevalry
       Off Irland for to bid battaill.
510   And sua it wes withoutyn faill,
       For agane thaim war gadryt thar
       With the wardane Richard of Clar
       The Butler and erlis twa,
       Off Desmound and Kildar war tha,
515   Bryman, Werdoune and fis Waryne
       And Schyr Paschall the Florentine
       That wes a knycht of Lumbardy
       And wes full of chevalry.
       The Maundveillis war thar alsua
520   Besatis Loganys and other ma
       Savages als, and yeit wes ane
       Hat Schyr Nycholl of Kylkenane,
       And with thir lordis sa fele wes then
       That for ane of the Scottismen
525   I trow that thai war fyve or ma.
       Quhen thir discourouris seyne had sua
       The Scottis ost thai went in hy

and told their lords fully how they had come near to [the enemy]; there was no need to seek them afar. (531) When Earl Thomas saw that those men had been on the hill, he took with him a good company on horse, perhaps a hundred in number, and they took their way to the hill. (536) They lay in ambush in a declivity, and in a short time they saw coming riding from the city a company intending to reconnoitre to the hill. [The Scots] were pleased at that, and kept still until [the enemy] came near to them, then in a rush all who were there burst upon them boldly. (544) Seeing those folk come on so suddenly, they were dismayed. Although some of them stayed there to fight stoutly, others took to their heels. In a very short time those who stayed behind were so defeated that they fled altogether on their way. (552) [The Scots] chased them right to the gate, killing a great part of them, then returned to their host.

And tauld thair lordis opynly
How thai to thaim war cummyn ner
530 To sek thaim fer wes na myster.
And quhen the erle Thomas had sene
That thai men at the hill had bene
He tuk with him a gud menye
On hors, ane hunder thai mycht be,
535 And till the hill thai tuk thar way.
In a slak thaim enbuschyt thai
And in schort tyme fra the cité
Thai saw cum ridand a mengne
For to discur to the hill.
540 Then war thai blyth and held thaim still
Quhill thai war cummyn to thaim ner,
Than in a frusche all that thai wer
Thai schot apon thaim hardely,
And thai that saw sa sudandly
545 That folk cum on abaysit war.
And nocht-forthi sum of thaim thar
Abad stoutly to ma debate,
And other sum ar fled thar gate,
And into wele schort tym war thai
550 That maid arest contraryit sua
That thai fled halyly thar gat,
And thai thaim chassyt rycht to the yat
And a gret part off thaim has slayn,
And syne went till thar ost agayn.

When those within saw their men killed like that, and driven home again, they were cast down and in great haste shouted aloud, 'To arms!' Then all of them armed themselves and made ready for the battle. They came out, all well equipped, to the battle, banner displayed, prepared to the best of their ability to attack their foes in tough fighting. (11) When Sir Philip Mowbray saw them come out in such good order, he went to Sir Edward Bruce and said, 'Sir, it would be a good idea to prepare some deception which will do something to help us in this battle. (17) Our men are few, but they are willing to do more than they can achieve. Therefore I suggest that our carts, without any man or boy, should be drawn up by themselves, so that they look like far more than we [are]. (23) Let us stand our banners before them; yon folk coming out of Connor, when they can see our banners there, will believe for a certainty that we are there, and will ride thither in great haste. (28) Let us come on them from the flank, and we shall have the advantage, for, when they have come to our carriage, they will be impeded and we can lay into them with all our might and do everything we can.'

1–85. The battle of Connor. Laud's *Et Dominus Willelmus de Burgo captus fuit decimo die Septembris et Comes confectus est iuxta Coyners* may date the taking of de Burgh to 10 September, but not the battle. Certainly 1 September seems more likely to be correct; see (b). Compare Barbour's account with that in (a) Inisfallen and (b) a letter of October 1315 from John le Poer to Edward II:

(a) With a view to heartening his men, the earl eventually turned back [from Antrim] to Connor to oppose the Scots, and there they and their Irish supporters suddenly charged him and his forces about midday before they were armed or prepared for battle. They wounded and took prisoner William de Burgh along with many other nobles whom they transported to Scotland. The earl himself and his men took flight since none would stand by him. (*Ann. Inisfallen*, 418–21)

(b) The Scots were driven from those parts [Uriel] and chased into Ulster. And then I went in the company of the said earl [of Ulster] to Ulster to do what good I could ... and stayed in those parts for five weeks and more and in this time they lost part of their folk, but then later, by chance, on Monday after John's Beheading last, O'Neill and the other Irish of Ulster and your said enemies [the Scots] attacked us suddenly at Connor, finding us in the open there by default of our scouts (*aggentz*) who ought to have warned us, [and] in whom we trusted. Some of the earl's company fought them, and in the fight Sir

BOOK 15

[The Scots win a great battle at Connor]

Quhen thai within has sene sua slayn
Thar men and chassyt hame agayn
Thai war all wa, and in gret hy
'Till armys!' hely gan thai cry.
5   Than armyt thaim all that thai war
And for the bataill maid thaim yar
Thai ischyt out all wele arayit
Into the bataill baner displayit
Bowne on thar best wis till assaile
10   Thar fayis into fell bataill.
And quhen Schyr Philip the Mowbra
Saw thaim ische in sa gud aray
Till Schyr Edward the Bruys went he
And said, 'Schyr, it is gud that we
15   Schap for sum slycht that may availe
To help us into this bataill.
Our men ar quhoyne, bot thai haf will
To do mar than thai may fulfill,
Tharfor I rede our cariage
20   Foroutyn ony man or page
Be thaimselvyn arayit be
And thai sall seyme fer ma than we,
Set we befor thaim our baneris,
Yone folk that cummys out of Coigneris
25   Quhen thai our baneris thar may se
Sall trow traistly that thar ar we
And thidder in gret hy sall thai rid.
Cum we than on thaim at a sid
And we sall be at avantag,
30   For fra thai in our cariag
Be entryt thai sall combryt be,
And than with all our mycht may we
Lay on and do all that we may.'

John Siward and Sir John du Boys were killed on their side and a
large part of their folk died as I heard, but the place remained theirs
at the end . . . Sir William de Burgh was wounded and sent to Scotland.
The date in (b) is Monday 1 September. The versions in (a) and (b)
share essentials; Barbour does not even suggest a surprise attack by the
Scots. On Siward see below on 80–85.

(34) They did exactly what he had ordered. The [men] who came out of Connor addressed themselves towards the banners, quickly striking their horses with spurs, rushing suddenly among [the banners]. (39) The barrels that were there soon impeded them [as they] were riding. Then the earl with his force rode up and attacked closely, [while] Sir Edward, a little nearby, fought so very boldly that many a doomed man fell underfoot; the field soon grew wet with blood. (47) They fought there with such great fierceness, and struck such blows on each other with stick, with stone and with [blow] returned, as each side could land on the other, that it was dreadful to see. (52) They kept up that great engagement, so knight-like on both sides, giving and taking violent blows, that it was past prime before men could see who might have the upper hand. But soon after prime was past the Scotsmen attacked so hard and assaulted them impetuously, as [if] each man was a champion, [so] that all their foes took to flight. (62) None of them was so brave that he dared wait for his fellow, but each fled in their different ways.

(65) The majority fled to the town. Earl Thomas and his force pursued so fiercely with drawn swords, that [they] were all mixed among them and came into the town all together. (70) Then the slaughter was so ghastly that all the streets ran with blood. Those that they overtook [were] all done to death so that there were almost as many dead as on the battlefield.

---

61. Flight. Irish sources are agreed that the earl of Ulster withdrew hastily to Connacht.

All as he ordanyt done haf thai,
35   And thai that come out of Coigneris
Addressyt thaim to the baneris
And smate with spuris the hors in hy
And ruschit thaim sudandly.
The barell-ferraris that war thar
40   Cumbryt thaim fast that ridand war,
And than the erle with his bataill
Come on and sadly gan assaill,
And Schyr Edward a litill by
Assemblit sua rycht hardely
45   That mony a fey fell undre fete,
The feld wox sone of blud all wete.
With sa gret felny thar thai faucht
And sic routis till other raucht
With stok with stane and with retrete
50   As ather part gan other bet
That it wes hidwys for to se.
Thai mantemyt that gret mellé
Sa knychtlik apon ather sid
Giffand and takand routis rid
55   That pryme wes passyt or men mycht se
Quha mast at thar abov mycht be,
Bot sone eftre that prime wes past
The Scottismen dang on sa fast
And schot on thaim at abandoun
60   As ilk man war a campioun
That all thar fayis tuk the flycht,
Wes nane of thaim that wes sa wicht
That evyr durst abid his fer
Bot ilk man fled thar wayis ser.

[*Slaughter in Connor; the prisoners and wounded*]

65   To the toun fled the mast party,
And Erle Thomas sa egrely
And his route chassyt with swerdis bar
That amang thame mellyt war
That all togidder come in the toun.
70   Than wes the slauchter sa felloune
That all the ruys ran of blud,
Thaim that thai gat to ded all yhud
Sua that than thar weill ner wer dede
Als fele as in the bataill-stede.

(75) Fitz-Warin was taken there, but Richard Clare was so frightened that he fled to the south country. I'm sure that all that month he will have no stomach for fighting. Sir John Stewart, a noble knight, was wounded in the body there, by a spear which pierced right sharply. (83) He went subsequently to Montpelier and lay recovering there for a long time but eventually he was healed. Then Sir Edward and his company took their lodging in the town. That night they were cheerful and happy because of the victory which they had had there. (90) On the morrow, without delaying, Sir Edward had men go to survey all the victuals of that city. They found such a profusion there of corn, flour, wax and wine, that they were astonished at it; Sir Edward had it all carried to Carrickfergus. (98) Then he and his men went there, pressing the siege very stalwardly until Palm Sunday had passed. Then both sides took a truce until the Tuesday in Easter week, so that they could spend that holy time in penance and prayer. (105) But on the eve of Easter right to the castle, during the night, came fifteen ships from Dublin, fully laden with armed men – I'm pretty sure they numbered four thousand;

---

75. Fitz Warin was later pardoned by Edward II for aid to the Scots. Barbour does not mention William de Burgh as prisoner.

80–85. Sir John Stewart was brother of Walter Stewart; he was probably the Siward whose death was erroneously reported to Edward II (above (b) in note on 1). It is incredible that as a wounded man he travelled, even by sea, to Montpellier in Provence, and this must represent misreading of an account in which he was cured by a Montpellier-trained doctor. Sir John Stewart was with the king, Moray, Douglas and others in the Park of Duns on 9 July, 1316, when Moray made a gift to Newbattle abbey.

97. Carrickfergus. According to Laud, Edward Bruce did besiege Carrickfergus immediately after his first campaign (September 1315), and later (October–early November) English sailors came at night, killed forty Scots and stole their tents, 'and the lords there fought and meanwhile they killed several Scots, at which time Richard Lan of Ofervill was killed by a certain Irishman'. Then, on 8 April, 1316, Sir Thomas Mandeville with men from Drogheda 'came to Carrickfergus and fought a battle with the Scots, put them to flight and killed almost thirty of them. Afterwards, on the eve of Easter [10 April] Sir Thomas and his men attacked the Scots, killed several of them about the gates (*circa kalendas*), and Sir Thomas was killed there in his own land for his own right.' It is likely that Mandeville came with ships (107) and Barbour agrees that he commanded the relieving force, even though he was constable of Carrickfergus, commanding the besieged. He must have slipped out to secure relief.

75   The fys Warine wes takyn thar,
Bot sua rad wes Richard of Clar
That he fled to the south countre,
All that moneth I trow that he
Sall haf na gud will for to fycht.

80   Schyr Jhone Stewart a noble knycht
Wes woundyt throu the body thar
With a sper that scharply schar,
Bot to Monpeller went he syne
And lay thar lang intill helyne

85   And at the last helyt wes he.
Schyr Edward than with his menye
Tuk in the toun thar herbery,
That nycht thai blyth war and joly
For the victour that thai had thar.

[Siege of Carrickfergus castle; a truce is broken by ships from Dublin]

90   And on the morn foroutyn mar
Schyr Edward gert men gang and se
All the vittaill of that cite,
And thai fand sic foysoun tharin
Off corne and flour and wax and wyn

95   That thai had of it gret ferly,
And Schyr Edward gert halily
Intill Cragfergus it caryit be,
Syne thidder went his men and he
And held the sege full stalwartly

100   Quhill Palme Sonday wes passit by.
Than quhill the Twysday in Pays wouk
On ather half thai trewys touk
Sua that thai mycht that haly tid
In pennance and in prayer bid.

105   Bot apon the Pasche evyn rycht
To the castell into the nycht
Fra Devillyne schippis come fyften
Chargyt with armyt men bedene,
Four thousand trow I weill thai war,

100–1. Palm Sunday was 4 April, 1316, Tuesday in Easter week was 13 April, 1316.
101–2. The Laud annals do not mention this truce, but it is likely enough.
105. Pasche evyn. 10 April, 1316. This confuses the arrival on 8 April with the garrison's assault on 10 April (note on 97).

they entered the castle. (111) Old Sir Thomas Mandeville was captain of that company. They went into the castle secretly for they had managed to spy that many of Sir Edward's men were then scattered in the country. (117) For that reason they meant to sally out in the morning, without delaying longer, and to surprise [the Scots] suddenly, for they believed that they would lie trusting in the truce that they had taken. But I know that dishonesty will always have a bad and unpleasant conclusion.

(124) Sir Edward knew nothing of [all] this, having no thought of betrayal, but despite the truce he did not fail to set watches on the castle; each night he had men watch it carefully, and Neil Fleming watched that night with sixty worthy and bold men. (131) As soon as day grew clear those who were in the castle armed themselves, got ready, then lowered the draw-bridge and sallied forth in large numbers. When Neil Fleming saw them, he hastily sent a man to the king and said to those near him,(139) 'Now I promise you, men will see who dares to die for the sake of his lord. Now carry yourselves well, for assuredly I will fight against their whole company. By fighting we shall hold them until our master is armed.' (145) With those words, they fought; they were far too few, *perfay,* to fight with such a large force. (148) But nonetheless with all their might they laid into [their foes] so boldly

113-14. They entered secretly. This may be a version of the attack in September 1315. Barbour ignores Mandeville's first battle with the Scots. It is unlikely that he was able to enter the castle secretly, even with relaxed Scottish guards.

129. Neil Fleming. He is not described as a knight, and may have been of humble birth, whence the surprise at Edward Bruce's sorrow at 231-42.

137. The king. This is Barbour's first acknowledgment that Edward Bruce was 'king of Ireland'.

139-44. This reported speech was made among a company every one of whom was killed (155).

110 In the castell thai entryt ar.
The Maundveill auld Schyr Thomas
Capitane of that menye was.
Intill the castell prively
Thai entryt for thai had gert spy
115 That mony of Schyr Edwardis men
War scalyt in the contre then,
Tharfor thai thocht in the mornyng
Till isch but langer delaying
And to suppris thaim suddanly,
120 For thai thocht thai suld traistly
For the trewys that takyn war,
Bot I trow falset evermar
Sall have unfayr and evill ending.

[The new force attacks the besieging Scots; Sir Neil Fleming wounded]

Schyr Edward wist of this nathing
125 For off tresoun had he na thoucht,
Bot for the trew he levyt nocht
To set wachis to the castell,
Ilk nycht he gert men walk it wele
And Nele Flemyng wachit that nycht
130 With sexty men worthi and wycht.
And als sone as the day wes cler
Thai that within the castell wer
Had armyt thaim and maid thaim boun
And sone thar brig avalit down
135 And ischit intill gret plente,
And quhen Nele Flemyng gan thaim se
He send ane to the king in hy
And said to thaim that war him by,
'Now sall men se, Ik undretak,
140 Quha dar dey for his lordis sak.
Now ber you weill, for sekyrly
With all this mengne fecht will I,
Intill bargane thaim hald sall we
Quhill that our maister armyt be.'
145 With that word assemblyt thai,
Thai war to few all-out perfay
With sic a gret rout for to fycht,
Bot nocht-forthi with all thar mycht
Thai dang on thaim sa hardely

that all the enemy were greatly astonished that [the Scots] were all of such courage as if they had no fear of death. But their ruthless enemies attacked so that no valour could prevail. (155) Then they were slain, one and all, so completely that not one escaped. The man who went to the king to warn him about their sally, warned him with great speed.

(160) Sir Edward was commonly called the king of Ireland. When he heard that such a thing was happening, he got his gear in very great haste; there were twelve brave men in his chamber who armed themselves with speed, then went through the middle of the town with his banner. (168) His enemies, who had divided their men into three, were coming very close. Mandeville, with a great company, held his way down right through the town, the rest kept on either side of the town to meet those who were fleeing; they thought that all that they found there would die without ransom, every one. (176) But the game went quite otherwise, for Sir Edward with his banner and his twelve men that I mentioned before, attacked all that force so strongly that it was extraordinary. (181) For Gib Harper went in front of him, who was the doughtiest in his deeds then living in his position, made such way with an axe that he felled the first to the ground, and a moment afterwards recognised Mandeville among three by his armour, and struck him such a blow that he fell to the earth at once.

160–61. Edward as king of Ireland. This couplet is extraordinarily un-related to what goes before and after, but, by its placing among events of 1316, it has been seen as evidence that Edward became king then. But all the Irish annals place that event in 1315, and (in *The British Isles, 1100–1500*, ed. R. R. Davies), I have argued that it occurred in June 1315, soon after his landing. The point is important since it bears on the Scots' ambitions in coming to Ireland. Barbour once calls Edward earl of Carrick (14.1), and the omission of his kingship up to this point, *and afterwards*, does not date his assumption of it; on the contrary, it is another scrap of evidence that events of 1315 and 1316 are intermingled in Barbour's narrative.

181–83. Gib Harper occurs again at 18.97 with a reference to his excellence in his estate which can only mean that he was a fine minstrel. At the battle of Faughart he wore the surcoat with arms of Edward Bruce and his body was taken for that of Edward, according to Barbour. See note to 18.94.

186. Off thre, E.; I have kept this reading but am not convinced that it makes as good sense as C's 'And eftir'.

150   That all thar fayis had gret ferly
         That thai war all of swilk manheid
         As thai na drede had of thar dede.
         Bot thar fayis sa gane assaile
         That na worschip thar mycht availe,
155   Than thai war slayne up everilkane
         Sa clene that thar eschapyt nane
         And the man that went to the king
         For to warne him of thar isching
         Warnyt him in full gret hy.

[*Edward Bruce defeats the men from the castle; Neil Fleming dies*]

160   Schyr Edward wes commonaly
         Callyt the king of Irland.
         And quhen he hard sic thing on hand
         In full gret hast he gat his ger,
         Twelff wycht men in his chawmer wer
165   That armyt thaim in full gret hy,
         Syne with his baner hardily
         The myddis of the toun he tays.
         Weill ner cummand war his fayis
         That had delt all thar men in thre,
170   The Maundvell with a gret menye
         Rycht throu the toun the way held doun,
         The lave on athyr sid the toun
         Held to mete thaim that fleand war,
         Thai thoucht that all that thai fand thar
175   Suld dey but ransoune everilkane.
         Bot uthyr-wayis the gle is gane,
         For Schyr Edward with his baner
         And his twelff I tauld you of er
         On all that route sua hardely
180   Assemblyt that it wes ferly,
         For Gib Harpar befor him yeid
         That wes the douchteast in deid
         That than wes livand off his state,
         And with ane ax maid him sic gat
185   That he the fyrst fellyt to ground,
         And off thre in a litill stound
         The Maundveill be his armyng
         He knew and roucht him sic a swyng
         That he till erd yeid hastily.

(190) Sir Edward who was nearby him turned him over, and in that very place took his life with a knife. With that Fergus Ardrossan, who was a very courageous knight, attacked with sixty or more men. (196) They pressed their foes so, that they, having seen their lord killed, lost heart and wanted to be back [in the castle]. All the time, as the Scotsmen could be armed, they came to the encounter and laid into their foes so, that they all turned tail, and [the Scots] chased them to the gate. (204) It was a hard fight and bitter struggle there. Sir Edward killed by his own hand there a knight who was called the best and most generous in all Ireland; by surname he was called Mandeville, [but] I can't say what his first name was. (210) His men were pressed so hard that those in the donjon dared neither open the gate nor let down the drawbridge. Sir Edward, I promise, pursued those fleeing to safety there so hard that, *perfay*, of all those who sallied against him that day, not one escaped, [for] they were either taken or slain. (219) For Macnacill then came to the fight with two hundred spear-men, killing all that they could overtake. This Macnacill won four or five of their ships by a trap and killed all the men [on them]. (225) When this fighting came to an end Neil Fleming was still alive. Sir Edward went to see him; his dead followers lay around him all in a heap, on both sides, and he, in mortal pain, [was] about to die. Sir Edward was moved by his [fate] and mourned him deeply,

---

193. Sir Fergus Ardrossan. According to Laud (note to 14.254), he was killed at the battle of Skerries in January 1316. He is not named in Scotland after the Irish war. I think it unlikely that Laud is wrong here, and suggest that either his son and namesake is meant or his participation belongs to the fight at Carrickfergus in October–November 1315 (above note to 97).

206–9. According to a Dublin annal John brother of Sir Thomas Mandeville was killed.

222. Maknakill. On 12 March, 1315 John of Argyll was to receive to Edward II's peace Donald of Islay, Guthred his brother, John Macnakild and Sir Patrick Graham. Graham was son-in-law of John of Argyll and had lands near Inverness. For reasons given in the note to 305, this may have been John Macnakild's brother or son.

190	Schyr Edward that wes ner him by
	Reversyt him and with a knyff
	Rycht in that place him reft the liff.
	With that off Ardrossane Fergus
	That wes a knycht rycht curageous
195	Assemblyt with sexty and ma,
	Thai pressyt than thar fayis sua
	That thai that saw thar lord slayne
	Tynt hart and wald haf bene again,
	And ay as Scottismen mycht be
200	Armyt thai come to the melle
	And dang apon thar fayis sua
	That thai all the bak gan ta,
	And thai thaim chassyt to the yat,
	Thar wes hard fycht and gret debat.
205	Thar slew Schyr Edward with his hand
	A knycht that of all Irland
	Was callit best and of maist bounté,
	To surname Maundveill had he,
	His awne name I can nocht say,
210	Bot his folk to sa hard assay
	War set as thai of the doungeoun
	Durst opyn na yhat na brig lat doun.
	And Schyr Edwarde, Ik tak on hand,
	Soucht thaim that fled thar to warand
215	Sa felly that of all perfay
	That ischyt apon him that day
	Thar eschapyt never ane
	That thai ne war other tane or slayn,
	For to the fycht Maknakill then
220	Come with twa hundreth spermen
	And thai slew all thai mycht to-wyn.
	This ilk Maknakill with a gyn
	Wan off thar schippis four or fyve
	And haly reft the men thar lif.
225	Quhen end wes maid of this fechting
	Yeit then wes lyffand Nele Fleming.
	Schyr Edward went him for to se,
	About him slayne lay his menye
	All in a lump on athyr hand
230	And he redy to dey throwand.
	Schyr Edward had of him pité
	And him full gretly menyt he

lamenting his great courage and his valour in doughty deeds. (235) He mourned so much that they were astonished, for in the usual way he was not accustomed to lament anything, nor would he listen to men making lamentations. He stood by there until [Neil] had died, then he took him to a holy place and had him buried with ceremony [and] great solemnity.

(243) That's how Mandeville sallied forth, but for sure deceit and guile will always come to an ill conclusion, as was obvious from this sally. They came out in time of truce, and in such a [holy] time as Easter day, when God rose to save mankind from the stain of old Adam's sin. (251) For that, great misfortune befell them, [so] that each, as you heard me say, was killed or taken there and those who were in the castle were so alarmed at that time, being unable to see where help could [come from] to relieve them, that they negotiated and shortly thereafter surrendered the castle freely to [Sir Edward], to save their life and limb, and he kept his word to them as was right. (262) He took the castle into his hands, provisioned it well and appointed a good warden to guard it, and he rested there for a time.

(266) We shall speak no more about him now, but we'll go to King Robert, whom we have left long unspoken of. When he had convoyed his brother Edward and his followers to the sea,

---

236–38. This echoes the comment in 13.486–87.

254–61. Carrickfergus castle. Following on note to 97, a truce was made for a month at midsummer 1316, while the castle was besieged by sea by Thomas Dun; its constable went to see Edward Bruce at Coleraine. According to Laud, at this time also Edward Bruce came to the castle demanding its surrender; the garrison agreed, asking that 30 men be sent to receive it. When they entered, the garrison imprisoned them. This breach of the laws of war seems unwise; in any case we should surely read three for 30. In *RRS5*, 379 I discussed the chronology of these events, but it has since been pointed out to me that before the fall of Carrickfergus, Dublin heard that King Robert had arrived to help Edward Bruce (Laud annals); this may be correct, the king crossing in late July 1316. In September 1316 Dublin heard that the castle had surrendered with grant of life and limb to the garrison; Robert and Edward would then return to Scotland (note to 16.6). On the siege *Irish Historical Studies*, x, 94–100.

And regratyt his gret manheid
And his worschip and douchty deid,
235 Sic mayn he maid men had gret ferly
For he wes nocht custummabilly
Wont for to meyne men ony thing
Na wald nocht her men mak menyng.
He stud tharby till he wes ded
240 And syne had him till haly sted
And him with worschip gert he be
Erdyt with gret solemnité.

[*Surrender of Carrickfergus castle*]

On this wis ischit Maundvill,
Bot sekyrly falset and gyle
245 Sall allwayis haif ane ivill ending
As weill is sene be this isching,
In tyme of trewys ischit thai
And in sic tyme as on Pasche day
Quhen God rais for to sauf mankin
250 Fra wem of auld Adamys syne,
Tharfor sa gret myschaunce thaim fell
That ilkane as ye hard me tell
War slayne up or takyn thar.
And thai that in the castell war
255 War set intill sic fray that hour
For thai couth se quhar na succour
Suld cum to releyff, and thai
Tretyt and till a schort day
The castell till him yauld fre
260 To sauff thaim lyff and lym, and he
Held thaim full weill his cunnand.
The castell tuk he in his hand
And vyttalyt weill and has set
A gud wardane it for to get,
265 And a quhill tharin restyt he.

[*King Robert sails to the Isles, is drawn between the Tarberts; submission of the Islesmen*]

Off him no mar now spek will we
Bot to King Robert will we gang
That we haff left unspokyn of lang.
Quhen he had convoyit to the se

he prepared to journey to the Isles with his ships. He took his son-in-law, Walter Stewart, with him, and a great following with him, and other men of great nobility. (276) They held their way to the Tarbert in galleys ordered for their journey. But there they had to draw there ships there, and it was a mile between the seas, [which] was all sheltered by trees. (281) The king had his ships dragged there, and because the wind was blowing strongly upon their backs, [in the direction] they wanted to go, he had men take stays and masts, raise them up in the ships, tie sails to the yards and go beside [the ships] pulling [them]. (288) The wind that was blowing helped them, so that in a little time their fleet had been completely drawn over. When those who were in the Isles heard how the good king had had his ships go there with sails, over between the two Tarberts, they were all utterly dejected. (296) For they knew by an old prophecy that whoever should have ships go between those seas with sails would so win the Isles for himself that no-one could withstand him by force. Therefore they all came to the king [and] none withstood his commands, apart from John of Lorn alone. (304) But quite soon after he was taken and handed over to the king. Those who were in his following, who had broken faith to the king, were all dead and utterly destroyed.

273–74. Walter Stewart. He had not married Marjory Bruce in April 1315, but this implies that he did so very soon afterwards.

276. The Tarbert. There are several places of this name in the Western Isles, all at narrow necks of land. It means 'draw across', 'porterage', which Barbour seems to know as he calls it 'the Tarbert'. But in 290 he speaks of 'the two Tarberts', which must refer to the sea-lochs at either end. On 8 May, 1315 a royal charter implies that the king was then at Tarbert, Loch Fyne, perhaps collecting ships for Edward's Irish expedition; he may have returned there after Edward sailed, as Barbour states. (*RRS5*, 136–37, 353) Tarbert is the site of the only castle building which can be confidently attributed to King Robert; it is almost lost in nettles, but is important evidence of his abiding interest in the western seaboard.

296–300. It was reported that Magnus of Norway was drawn between the Tarberts in 1098, in order to include Kintyre in the islands ceded to him. But sailing across land occurs elsewhere in folk-lore.

298. None withstood his bidding. It is curious that Barbour does not say that they did homage to him.

305–310. John of Lorn. This person cannot be John of Argyll, who died of natural causes on pilgrimage to Canterbury in 1317 and was buried in London at Edward II's expense. The name John is not common at this time among known West Highlanders, but in March 1315 John Macnakild and Macdonalds were considering submitting to Edward II

270   His brodyr Edward and his menye
        With schippes he maid him yar   271*
        Intill the Ilis for till fare   272*
        Walter Steward with him tuk he   273*
        His mawch and with him gret menyhe   274*
275   And other men off gret noblay.   271
        To Tarbart thai held thar way
        In galayis ordanyt for thar far,
        Bot thaim worthyt draw thar schippis thar,
        And a myle wes betwix the seys
280   Bot that wes lownyt all with treis.   276
        The king his schippis thar gert draw,
        And for the wynd couth stoutly blaw
        Apon thar bak as thai wald ga
        He gert men rapys and mastis ta
285   And set thaim in the schippis hey   281
        And sayllis to the toppis tey
        And gert men gang tharby drawand,
        The wyind thaim helpyt that wes blawand
        Sua that in a litill space
290   Thar flote all our-drawin was.   286
        And quhen thai that in the Ilis war
        Hard how the gud king had thar
        Gert his schippis with saillis ga
        Out-our betwix the Tarbartis twa
295   Thai war abaysit sa uterly   291
        For thai wyst throu auld prophecy
        That he that suld ger schippis sua
        Betwix thai seis with saillis ga
        Suld wyne the Ilis sua till hand
300   That nane with strenth suld him withstand.   296
        Tharfor thai come all to the king,
        Wes nane withstud his bidding
        Outakyn Jhone of Lorne allane,
        Bot weill sone eftre wes he tane
305   And present rycht to the king,   301
        And thai that war of his leding
        That till the king had brokyn fay
        War all dede and distroyit away.

---

via John of Argyll (note to 222). This desertion may have prompted
the king's expedition to Argyll and the imprisonment of the unreliable
John, while his son or brother was 'encouraged' to serve Edward Bruce
in Ireland (note to 222).

(309) The king took this John of Lorn and sent him on to Dumbarton, to be kept in prison there for a time; then he was sent to Loch Leven where he was kept in captivity for a long time; I believe that he died there. (315) When all the Isles, greater and small, had been brought to his will, the king dwelt all that season there, at the hunt, sport and relaxation. (319) When the king subdued the Isles in the way I've told here, the good Sir James Douglas was staying in [Ettrick] Forest, bravely defending the land. At that time there lived in Berwick a Gascon, Edmund de Caillou. who was a knight of great fame and lord of a great seigneurie in Gascony, his own country. (329) He was then in charge of Berwick, made a secret muster [which] gave him a great company of staunch men splendidly armed. He looted for himself all the lower part of Teviotdale and a good part of the Merse, then went hastily towards Berwick. (337) Sir Adam Gordon, who had then become a Scottish man, saw them driving off their cattle thus, and believed that they were only a few, for he saw only the hurrying small groups and those who seized the booty. (343) Then he took the way in great haste to Sir James Douglas, telling [him] how Englishmen had taken their prey and then had gone

---

317–18. The king did not stay in Argyll in 1315.

325. Edmund de Caillou, correctly Raymond de Caillou, who was a king's serjeant in the garrison of Linlithgow peel in 1312. (*CDS3*, 411)

329. Berwick. The keeper in 1316 was Sir Maurice Berkeley. It is noteworthy that the Barbour gives no account of the unsuccessful assault on Carlisle in July 1315, nor of the failed surprise attack by sea on Berwick on 13 January, 1316, when, according to Lanercost, Douglas was lucky to escape in a small boat.

331. A great company. On 18 February, 1316 a petition to Edward II narrates that on 14 February a great part of the garrison of Berwick, though without a knight and against the warden's orders, made a foray to near Melrose, because they were starving. They took many prisoners and cattle but were defeated on their return, losing 20 men-at-arms and 60 foot, among whom five were named, one of them Raymond Caillou. Another petition tells of the same foray and names the Scottish leaders as Douglas, Sir William de Soules and Sir Henry Balliol. On their return they were attacked at a ford eight leagues from Berwick; they lost most horses and all provisions. Barbour does not mention a ford, but his account is in agreement with these petitions. Gray mentions briefly the killing by Douglas of a number of Gascons from the Berwick garrison, at Scaithmoor (near Coldstream). (*CDS3*, 470)

337. Sir Adam Gordon. A Berwickshire laird who had followed his

This Jhone of Lorne the king has tane
310 And send him furth to Dunbertane   306
A quhill in presoun thar to be,
Syne to Louchlevyn send wes he
Quhar he wes quhill in festnyng,
I trow he maid tharin ending.
315 The king quhen all the Ilis war   311
Brocht till his liking les and mar,
All that sesoun thar dwellyt he
At huntyng gamyn and at gle.

[*Edmund de Caillou plunders the Merse*]

Quhill the king apon this maner
320 Dauntyt the Ilis as I tell her   316
The gud Schyr James of Douglas
Intill the Forest dwelland was
Defendand worthely the land.
That tyme in Berwik wes dwelland
325 Edmound de Cailow a Gascoun   321
That wes a knycht of gret renoune
And intill Gascoune his contré
Lord off gret senyoury wes he.
He had Berwik in keping
330 And maid a privé gadering   326
And gat him a gret cumpany
Of wycht men armyt jolily,
And the nethyr end of Tevidale
He prayit doun till him all hale
335 And of the Mers a gret party,   331
Syne towart Berwik went in hy.
Schyr Adam of Gordoun that than
Wes becummyn Scottisman
Saw thaim dryf sua away thar fe
340 And wend thai had bene quhone for he   336
Saw bot the fleand scaill perfay   337*
And thaim that sesyt in the pray.   338*
Than till Schyr James of Douglas   339*
Into gret hye the way he tais   340*
345 And tauld how Inglismen thair pray   341*
Had tane and syne went thar way   342*

---

lord, the earl of Dunbar, from the English allegiance to the Scottish in
1314.

towards Berwick with all their cattle. He said they were few, and [that] if [Douglas] would hurry up, he would very easily reach them and rescue all the cows.

(351) Sir James very quickly agreed to follow them, and set out with only the men that he had there, meeting [Caillou] by the road without any more [men]. They followed them in a great hurry and rapidly came quite near to them, for before they could see them properly they came very close with their company. (359) Then both the forrayers and the small groups gathered all together into a schiltrum, making a pretty fair company. They had the cattle driven in front of them by boys and servants who had no capacity to stand in the field to fight. (365) The rest took a fixed position behind [the cattle]. Douglas saw their whole mass, saw that they were in a good state, and that they were now so many that there were two of them to one of his. (370) 'Lords,' he said, 'since it seems that we have pursued in such a way that we have now come so near that we can't avoid a fight unless we take miserably to flight, let each man remember his sweetheart and how often he has been in great danger [but] emerged unscaithed. (378) Let's try to do just that today and take our position beside this ford, for they will come swiftly to fight against us. Let us have determination, strength and energy to meet them right forcefully.' (384) With those words he displayed his banner swiftly, for his foes were approaching, who, when they saw that [his men] were so few,

	Toward Berwik with all thar fee,	343*
	And said thai quheyn war and gif he	344*
	Wald sped him he suld weill lichtly	337
350	Wyn thaim and reskew all the ky.	338

[*Douglas pursues, catches and kills Caillou*]

	Schyr James rycht soyne gaf his assent	
	Till follow thame and furth is went	
	Bot with the men that he had thair	
	And met hym by the gat but mair.	
355	Thai followit thame in full gret hy	343
	And com weill neir thame hastely	
	For or thai mycht thame fully se	
	Thai come weill ner with thair menye,	
	And than bath the forreouris and the scaill	
360	Intill a childrome knyt all haill	348
	And wes a rycht fair cumpany.	
	Befor thame gert thai driff the ky	
	With knavis and swanys that na mycht	
	Had for to stand in feld and fycht,	
365	The lave behynd thaim maid a stale.	353
	The Douglas saw thar lump all hale	
	And saw thaim of sa gud covyn	
	And saw thai war sa mony syne	
	That thai for ane of his war twa.	
370	'Lordingis,' he said, 'sen it is sua	358
	That we haf chassyt of sic maner	
	That we now cummyn ar sa ner	
	That we may nocht eschew the fycht	
	Bot gif we fouly ta the flycht,	
375	Lat ilkane on his lemman mene	363
	And how he mony tyme has bene	
	On gret thrang and weill cummyn away.	
	Think we to do rycht sua today,	
	And tak we of this furd her-by	
380	Our avantage for in gret hy	368
	Thai sall cum on us for to fycht.	
	Set we than will and strenth and mycht	
	For to mete thaim rycht hardely.'	
	And with that word full hastily	
385	He displayit his baner	373
	For his fayis war cummand ner	
	That quhen thai saw he wes sa quhoyne	

imagined that they would soon be done with [the Scots] and attacked very forcibly. You could see men fighting desperately there, making a merciless mellee, giving and taking many blows. (393) Douglas was very hard pressed there, but his great courage so inspired his men that no man thought of cowardice, but [they] fought so hard with all their might that they slew many of their foes. Though they were a great many more than [the Scots], yet fate dealt [with] them such that Edmund de Caillou was killed right in that place of battle. (403) When he was killed all the rest were plainly beaten soon; those who pursued killed some [of them] and turned the prey back. In truth this was the hardest fighting that the good lord of Douglas was ever in with so small a following. (410) For, had it not been [for] his great valour, killing their chieftain in the fight, his men would all have been consigned to death. It was his custom always, whenever he came to [be] hard pressed, to press himself to kill the [enemy's] chieftain, and good luck befell him when he did so, giving him victory many a time. (418) When Sir Edmund had died in this way, the good lord Douglas took his way to the Forest. His foes feared him greatly; news of this deed spread far [and wide] so that men spoke quite commonly about it in England near thereby.

---

425. Sir Robert Neville, son of Sir Randolf Neville of Raby; he had been taken prisoner at Bannockburn.

425–529. The fight between Neville and Douglas is mentioned by (a) Gray and (b) the *Gesta Edwardi de Carnarvon*:

(a) Another time there happened a disaster on the Borders at Berwick, by treachery of the false traitors of the Borders, where was slain Robert Neville, which Robert had shortly before killed Richard Fitz Marmaduke, cousin of Robert Bruce, on the old bridge of Durham because of a quarrel between them arising out of jealousy which should be reckoned the greater lord. [*To win royal pardon, Neville took service with the king*] (*S*, 143; *ST*, 58)

(b) 1319. On 6 June Sir Robert Neville was killed by the Scots at Berwick, and many of his company were taken prisoner while the rest took to flight. In the preceding December he killed Richard Marmaduke, steward of the bishop of Durham on the bridge of Durham, claiming he was a foul traitor to the king and kingdom. (*Gesta in Chronicles of ... Edward I and Edward II*, ed. Stubbs, ii, 56)

The date given by the *Gesta* is certainly correct; the petition ascribed to 1316, which shows that Robert's brothers were taken prisoner and held to ransom is not dated and could perfectly well be of 1319 or 1320. (*CDS3*, 527) Gray places this fight correctly after that at Lintalee (16.337–492) of early 1317; Barbour has misplaced it perhaps because it referred to Berwick and therefore, he felt, should be placed before its fall in 1318. (*CP9*, 498–99)

Thocht thai suld with thaim sone haf done
And assemblit full hardely.
390 Thar men mycht se men fecht felly 378
And a rycht cruell mellé mak
And mony strakys giff and tak.
The Douglas thar weill hard wes stad,
Bot the gret hardyment that he hade
395 Comfort hys men on sic a wys 383
That na man thocht on cowardys
Bot faucht sa fast with all thar mayn
That thai fele of thar fayis has slayn,
And thoucht thai be weill fer war ma
400 Than thai, yeit ure demanyt thaim sua 388
That Edmound de Cailow wes ded
Rycht in that ilk fechtyn-stede,
And all the lave fra he wes done
War planly discomfyt sone,
405 And thai that chassyt sum has slayn 393
And turnyt the prayis all agayn.
The hardast fycht forsuth this wes
That ever the gud lord off Douglas
Wes in as off sa few mengne,
410 For nocht had bene his gret bounte 398
That slew thar chyftane in that fycht
His men had all to dede bene dycht.
He had intill custoume alway
Quhenever he come till hard assay
415 To preys him the chiftane to sla, 403
And her fell hap that he did sua,
That gert him haff victour fele sys.
Quhen Schyr Edmound apon this wis
Wes dede the gud lord of Douglas
420 To the Forest his wayis tays. 408
His fayis gretly gan him dred,
The word sprang weile fer of his deid
Sua that in Ingland ner tharby
Men spak of it commonaly.

(425) Sir Robert Neville lived at Berwick at that time, close
to the March where the lord Douglas was staying in the Forest,
and had great hatred for [Douglas], for he saw him so manfully
increasing his territory more and more. (432) He heard the
folk who were with him speaking about the power of the lord
Douglas, how valiant he was in fighting, and how often fortune
smiled on him. Very soon he was furious at this and said,
'What are you thinking about? Is there nobody of any merit
except him alone? (429) You esteem him as though he had
no equal, but I promise before you here that if ever he comes
into this land, he will find me near at hand. And if ever I can
see his banner displayed for war, I will attack him, be assured,
however bold you think he is.' (447) Word of this promise
was soon carried to Sir James Douglas, who said, 'If he wants
to keep his promise, I shall do [something] so that he will get
sight of me and my company, and before very long, very close
to him.' (453) Then he collected his retinue, good men of
great valour, and took the way one night in good order to the
March, so that early in the morning, with all his company,
he was before Berwick, and there he made [his] men display
his broad banner. (461) He sent some of his followers to burn
two or three villages, ordering them to hurry soon against [the
villages], so that they would be at hand, ready to fight, if need
arose.

426. Dwelt at Berwick. This is erroneous.
447. This avow. According to Bain, Neville was known as 'the peacock
of the north'; I have not found the evidence for this.

[*The challenge of Sir Robert Neville is taken up by Douglas*]

425	Schir Robert Nevile that tid	413
	Wonnyt at Berwik ner besid	
	The march quhar the lord Douglas	
	In the forest repayrand was	
	And had at him gret invy,	
430	For he saw him sa manlyly	418
	Mak ay his boundis mar and mar.	
	He hard the folk that with him war	
	Spek off the lord Douglas mycht	
	And how he forsye wes in fycht	
435	And how him fell oft fayr fortoun.	423
	He wrethyt tharat all-soun	
	And said, 'Quhat wene ye, is thar nane	
	That ever is worth bot he allane.	
	Ye set him as he wer but per,	
440	Bot Ik avow befor you her	428
	Giff ever he cum intill this land	
	He sall fynd me ner at his hand,	
	And gif Ik ever his baner	
	May se displayit apon wer	
445	I sall assembill on him but dout	433
	All-thocht yhe hald him never sa stout.'	
	Of this avow sone bodword was	
	Brocht to Schyr James of Douglas	
	That said, 'Gif he will hald his hycht	
450	I sall do sa he sall haiff sycht	438
	Off me and my cumpany	
	Yeyt or oucht lang wele ner him by.'	
	Hys retenew than gaderyt he	
	That war gud men of gret bounté,	
455	And till the march in gud aray	443
	Apon a nycht he tuk the way	
	Sua that into the mornyng arly	
	He wes with all his cumpany	
	Befor Berwik and thar he maid	
460	Men to display his baner brad,	448
	And of his menye sum sent he	
	For to bryn townys twa or thre,	
	And bad thaim sone agayne thaim sped	
	Sua that on hand giff thar come ned	
465	Thai mycht be for the fycht redy.	453

(466) Neville, who knew for a fact that Douglas had come so close, and saw his banner standing all unfurled, with the folk who were with [Neville] then (and he had a great company there, because at that time he had all the good [folk] of that country with him, so that he had there with him at that time many more than the Scots were), held his way up to a hill, and said, (476) 'Lords, it was my intention to make an end of the mighty trouble that Douglas creates for us every day. But I think it sensible that we wait until his men have dispersed through the country, to seize booty, then we can rush on them fiercely and will have them at our mercy.' (484) They all gave their agreement to this, and stayed waiting on the hill. The men of the land quickly gathered and drew quickly to him. Then Douglas, who was brave, thought it would be foolish to wait any longer [and] rode toward the hill; (491) when Neville saw that they were not [going to] set forth to forray but pressed toward [his men] with their force, he knew then that they meant to fight and said to his following, (496) 'Lords, now let's go forth. The flower of this country is here [with us], and we are more [numerous] than them as well. Let's attack them forcefully, for Douglas with yon peasantry will have no strength [equal to] ours, *perfay*' (502) Then they met up in a rush. You could hear the spears breaking, each man assaulting another hard; blood burst out from deep wounds. They fought hard on either side, for both sides strove

[*Neville waits then attacks Douglas's force*]

        The Nevill that wyst witterly
        That Douglas cummyn wes sa ner
        And saw all braid stand his baner,
        Than with the folk that with him war
470   And he had a gret menye thar   458
        For all the gud off that countre
        Intill that tyme with him had he
        Sua that he thar with him had then
        Wele may then war the Scottismen,
475   He held his way up till a hill   463
        And said, 'Lordingis, it war my will
        To mak end off the gret deray
        That Douglas mayis us ilk day,
        Bot me think it spedfull that we
480   Abid quhill his men scalit be   468
        Throu the countre to tak thar pray,
        Than fersly schout on thaim we may
        And we sall haf thaim at our will.'
        Than all thai gaf assent thar-till
485   And on the hill abaid howand.   473
        The men fast gaderyt of the land
        And drew till him in full gret hy.
        The Douglas then that wes worthi
        Thoucht it wes foly mar to bid,
490   Towart the hill than gan he rid,   478
        And quhen the Nevill saw that thai
        Wald nocht pas furth to the forray
        Bot pressyt to thaim with thar mycht
        He wyst weill than that thai wald fycht
495   And till his mengye gan he say,   483
        'Lordingis, now hald we furth our way,
        Her is the flour of the countré
        And may then thai alsua ar we,
        Assembill we then hardely,
500   For Douglas with yone yhumanry   488
        Sall haf na mycht till us perfay.'
        Then in a frusch assemblyt thai,
        Than mycht men her the speris brast
        And ilkane ding on other fast,
505   And blude bryst out at woundis wid.   493
        Thai faucht fast apon athyr sid
        For athyr party gan thaim payn

to drive their enemies back again.

(509) The lords Neville and Douglas met together right in the crush where the fighting was fiercest. Then there was a great battle between them; they fought fiercely with all their might, each striking mighty blows at the other. (515) But Douglas was the stronger, I know, and also more accustomed to fighting; he had set his heart and will to free himself of his enemy, until at last by a violent [blow delivered] with great strength he killed Neville. (521) Then he shouted his rallying cry and rushed so hard with all his following on the rest that in a short while you could see their foes take to flight, and they pursuing them with all their might. (527) In the chase Sir Ralph Neville, the baron of Hilton and others of great power were taken [prisoner]. Many were killed in the battle who had been [thought] worthy in their time. (532) When the field had been swept clean, so that everyone of their foes had been killed, driven off or taken [prisoner], then he had the whole land forrayed, seizing whatever they found, burning the villages in their way then coming home whole and sound. (539) He divided the booty among his followers, according to their merits, keeping nothing for himself. Such acts should cause men to love their lord, as they certainly did. He always treated them so wisely and also with such great love, giving such praise to their deeds that he made the most cowardly braver than a leopard;

527-28. Sir Ralph Neville was Sir Robert's brother and was certainly taken; the baron of Hiltoun may be a Sir Robert Hilton, a witness in 1310. Hilton could be the place of that name near Berwick. (*B1909*, 458)

To put thar fayis on bak agayn.

[Douglas fights with and kills Neville; division of the spoils]

	The lordis off Nevill and Douglas	
510	Quhen at the fechting fellast was	498
	Met togidder rycht in the preys,	
	Betwix thaim than gret bargane wes.	
	Thai faucht felly with all thar maucht,	
	Gret routis ather othyr raucht,	
515	Bot Douglas starkar wes Ik hycht	503
	And mar usyt alsua to fycht,	
	And he set hart and will alsua	
	For to deliver him of his fa	
	Quhill at the last with mekill mayn	
520	Off fors the Nevill has he slayn,	508
	Then his ensenye hey gan cry	
	And the lave sa hardely	
	He ruschyt with his menye	
	That intill schort tym men mycht se	
525	Thar fayis tak thaim to the flycht	513
	And thai thaim chassyt with all thar mycht	
	Schir Rauff Nevill in the chas	
	And the baron of Hiltoun was	
	Takyn and other of mekill mycht.	
530	Thar wes fele slayne into that fycht	518
	That worthi in thar tym had bene.	
	And quhen the feld wes clengit clen	
	Sua that thar fayis everilkane	
	War slayne or chassyt awai or tan	
535	Than gert he forray all the land	523
	And sesyt all that ever thai fand	
	And brynt townys in thar way,	
	Syne hale and fer cummyn ar thai.	
	The prayis amang his menye	
540	Eftre thar meritis delt he	528
	And held na thing till his behuff.	
	Sic dedis aucht to ger men luff	
	Thar lord, and sua thai did perfay.	
	He tretyt thaim sa wisly ay	
545	And with sa mekill luff alsua	533
	And sic avansement wald ma	
	Off thar deid that the mast cowart	
	He maid stoutar then a libart,	

(549) by warm treatment like that he made his men strong and of great courage.

(551) When Neville had been thus brought to the ground, and old Sir Edmund de Caillou, fear of the lord Douglas, and his reputation was so spread throughout the marches of England that those who dwelt therein feared him like the devil [out] of hell. (558) Even now I have heard it often said that he was so greatly feared then that when women wanted to scold their children, they would consign them with a very angry face to the Black Douglas, for in their story, he was more dreadful than was any devil in hell. (563) Because of his great valour and courage he was so feared by his foes that they were terrified by the mention of his name. He can stay at ease at home now for a while, for I'm sure he won't be troubled by enemies for some time. (569) Now let him stay in the Forest, we shall speak no more of him. But we propose to speak further of worthy Sir Edward who was still lying at Carrickfergus with all his chivalry.

562a–b. These two lines are found only in MS C and are usually rejected as inauthentic.

With cherysing thusgat maid he
550 His men wycht and of gret bounté.   538

[*The reputation of Douglas*]

Quhen Nevill thus was brocht to ground
And of Cailow auld Schyr Edmound,
The drede of the lord of Douglas
And his renoune sa scalit was
555 Throu-out the marchis of Ingland   543
That all that war tharin wonnand
Dred him as the fell devill of hell,
And yeit haf Ik hard otfsys tell
That he sa gretly dred wes than
560 That quhen wivys wald childer ban   548
Thai wald rycht with ane angry face
Betech thaim to the blak Douglas.
562a For with thair taill he wes mair fell   ⋆
562b Than wes ony devill in hell.   ⋆
Throu his gret worschip and bounté
Sua with his fayis dred wes he
565 That thaim growyt to her his name.   553
He may at ese now dwell at hame
A quhill for I trow he sall nocht
With fayis all a quhile be socht.
Now lat him in the Forest be,
570 Off him spek now no mar will we,   558
Bot off Schyr Edward the worthi
That with all his chevalry
Wes at Cragfergus yeit liand
To spek mar we will tak on hand.

As I told you before, when Sir Edward had thrice defeated
Richard Clare and all the baronage of Ireland by his worthy
courage and with all his mighy men had come back to Car-
rickfergus then, Thomas, the good earl of Moray, took leave
to go to Scotland. (9) He gave him leave with reluctance and
then charged him [to speak] to the king, to beg him specially
that he would come to Ireland to see him; for if they were
both in that land they would find no-one able to withstand
them. (15) The earl went on his way to his ships and sailed
well over the sea. (18) He arrived soon in Scotland, then went
quickly to the king, who received him gladly, asking after his
brother's fortunes and about the expeditions they had there;
he told him everything without embellishment. (24) When
the king had stopped his questioning, [the earl] delivered his
message to the good king, who said he would cheerfully see
his brother, and also the state of that country and of their
war. (29) Then he gathered a large company, making two
lords of high repute, one Walter Stewart, the other James
Douglas, wardens in his absence to look after the country
well. (35) Then he took his way to the sea, taking ship at
Loch Ryan in Galloway with his whole following; he soon
arrived at Carrickfergus. (39) Sir Edward was pleased by his
coming,

6–14. Moray goes to Scotland. This is placed after the fall of Carrickfergus
    in September 1316. probably wrongly, since Moray returned in March
    1316 and seems to have remained in Scotland till January, 1317. Both
    Moray and Edward Bruce were at Cupar, Fife, on 30 September 1316,
    when Edward consented to a very formal confirmation by Robert I of
    Moray's endowments, including the Isle of Man; probably Edward had
    taken exception to that recent grant. On 1 November, 1316 the Laud
    annals report a slaughter of Scots in Ulster by John Logan and Sir
    Hugh Bisset. This may have been the event which prompted Robert I
    to agree to go to Ireland. As late as November 1316 the Scots had been
    negotiating a truce or peace with English emissaries at Jedburgh. See
    the discussion in *RRS5*, 378–79.

31–33. Wardens. There is no documentary reference to Guardians in the
    king's absence, and it is much more likely that the statement at 338 is
    correct: Douglas had been appointed Warden of the Marches. The
    association of Walter Stewart with him as an equal is unlikely, and
    should be seen as Barbour's determination to promote Walter's image.

BOOK 16

[*King Robert goes to Ireland*]

Quhen Schyr Edward, as Ik said ar,
Had discomfyt Richard of Clar
And of Irland all the barnage
Thris throu his worthi vasselag
5   And syne with all his men of mayn
Till Cragfergus wes cummyn agayn,
The gud erle of Murreff Thomas
Tuk leyff in Scotland for to pas,
And he him levyt with a gruching,
10   And syne him chargyt to the king
To pray him specialli that he
Cum intill Irland him to se,
For war thai bath into that land
Thai suld fynd nane suld thaim withstand.
15   The erle furth thane his way has tane
And till his schipping is he gayn
And sayllyt weill out-our the se.
Intill Scotland sone aryvit he,
Syne till the king he went in hy,
20   And he resavyt him glaidsumly
And speryt of his brodyr fayr
And of journayis that thai had thar,
And he him tauld all but lesing.
Quhen the king left had the spering
25   His charge to the gud king tauld he,
And he said he wald blythly se
Hys brother and se the affer
Off that cuntre and off thar wer.
A gret mengye then gaderyt he,
30   And twa lordys of gret bounté
The tane the Stewart Walter was
The tother James of Douglas
Wardanys in his absence maid he
For to maynteyme wele the countré,
35   Syne to the se he tuk the way
And at Lochriane in Galloway
He schippyt with all his menye,
To Cragfergus sone cummyn is he.
Schyr Edward of his come wes blyth

went down to meet him at once, welcoming him with warmth, as he did to all who were with [the king], especially Earl Thomas of Moray, who was his nephew. (45) Then they went to the castle there and had a big feast and festivities. They stayed there for three days enjoying themselves.

(49) King Robert arrived in Ireland in this way, and when he had stayed in Carrickfergus for three days, they consulted [and decided] that with all their men they would hold their way through all Ireland, from one end to the other. (56) Then Sir Edward, the king's brother, rode ahead in the vanguard; the king himself took up the rear, having in his company the worthy Earl Thomas. They took their way southward, soon passing Innermallan. (63) This was in the month of May, when birds sing on each branch, mixing their notes with harmonious sound, because of the softness of that sweet season; leaves sprout on branches, blooms grow brightly beside them and fields are decked with fine-scented flowers of many colours; everything becomes happy and joyful. (72) When this good king took his way to ride southward, as I said before, the warden at that time, Richard Clare, knew that the king had arrived thus, and knew that he planned to take

---

38. To Carrickfergus. Clyn places Robert's arrival about Christmas 1316 (which is probably correct), in Annals of Connacht and related annals, early in 1317, remarking that he had many galloglasses with him.

52. Three days. Laud annals say that 'about the feast of *Carniprivium* the Scots came to Slane [west of Drogheda in Meath] with 20,000 armed men, and the army of Ulster with them, and they laid the whole country waste before them.' *Carniprivium* can mean different dates, here possibly 30 January, 6 February, or 20 February, 1317. They would have left Carrickfergus about a week earlier, and must have been there for something like three weeks.

62. Inderwillane in C; E has a blank. For this pass see the note to 14.113.

63. Month of May. It is a topos that a great enterprise began in May. Cf. 5.1-13. The true date was January–February 1317.

74. Richard Clare, the Warden. It is usual to understand this as confusion with Richard de Burgh earl of Ulster who was arrested by Dubliners on 21 February and was not freed until 8 May, 1317. Orpen thought that he was arrested because he was suspected of complicity with Bruce (the suspicion is likely enough), having laid the ambush described by Barbour (85-95) and yet fled to Dublin (211-20), which scarcely suggests collusion. The battle is placed by Barbour before Drogheda and Dublin were passed (265 66), when the earl of Ulster was at his manor (Ratoath), though there is no evidence to support the idea that Bruce attacked him there. It seems to me more likely that the earl was arrested because he had failed to join in resisting Bruce (as the annal's wording suggests), and that the government leader was the Justiciar, Butler, who

40 And went doun to mete him swyth
And welcummyt him with glaidsome cher,
Sa did he all that with him wer
And specially the erle Thomas
Off Murreff that his nevo was,
45 Syne till the castell went thai yar
And maid thaim mekill fest and far.
Thai sojournyt that dayis thre
And that in myrth and jolyté.

[*The Scots march south and an ambush is prepared for them*]

King Robert apon this kyn wis
50 Intill Irland aryvit is,
And quhen in Cragfergus had he
With his men sojournyt dayis thre
Thai tuk to consaill that thai wald
With thar folk thar wayis hald
55 Throu all Irland fra end till other.
Schyr Edward than the kingis brother
Befor in the avaward raid,
The king himselff the rerward maid
That had intill his cumpany
60 The erle Thomas that wes worthi.
Thar wayis southwart haff thai tane
And sone ar passyt Inderwillane.
This wes in the moneth of May
Quhen byrdis syngis in ilk spray
65 Melland thar notis with seymly soune
For softnes of the swet sesoun,
And levys off the branchys spredis
And blomys brycht besid tham bredis
And feldis ar strowyt with flouris
70 Well saverand of ser colouris
And all thing worthis blyth and gay,
Quhen that this gud king tuk his way
To rid southwart as I said ar.
The wardane than Richard of Clar
75 Wyst the king wes aryvyt sua
And wyst that he schup him to ta

was in Dublin on 24 January, but subsequently abandoned the city,
retreating south to Cork by 27 February I would place the ambush
around mid-February and somewhere between Slane and Dublin. See
note on 148.

his way to the south country. He assembled from all Ireland burgesses and chivalry, hobelars and peasantry, until he had nearly forty thousand men. (82) But he still wouldn't undertake to fight in the field with his foes, instead thinking up a stratagem whereby he with all his great company, would lie in ambush in a wood quite secretly beside the road by which their enemies would pass; [he would] allow the van to pass far by and then attack boldly upon the rear with all their men. (92) They did then as they had planned. They lay in ambush in a wood, the Scottish host rode near by them but they made no showing of themselves.

(96) Sir Edward rode well ahead with those who were of his company, paying no heed to the rear. When Sir Edward had passed by, Sir Richard Clare in haste sent light yeomen, who could shoot well, to harrass the rear on foot. Two of those who had been sent harrassed them at the side of the wood there shooting among the Scotsmen. (106) The king, who had a good five thousand brave and hardy men with him then, saw those two shooting among them so recklessly and coming so close. (110) He knew very well, without [any] doubt, that they had support close at hand, so he issued an order that no man should be so bold as to gallop to them, but [should] always ride in close order ready for battle, to defend themselves if men sought to attack.

His way towart the south contré,
And of all Irland assemblit he
Bath burges and chevalry
80   And hobilleris and yhumanry
Quhill he had ner fourty thousand.
Bot he wald nocht yet tak on hand
With all his fayis in feld to fycht
Bot he umbethocht him of ane slycht,
85   That he with all his gret menye
Wald in a wod enbuschit be
All prively besid the way
Quhar that thar fayis suld away,
And lat the avaward pas fer by
90   And syne assembill hardely
On the rerward with all thar men.
Thai did as thai divisyt then,
In ane wod thai enbuschit wer,
The Scottis ost raid by thaim ner
95   Bot thai na schawing of thaim maid.

[*The ambush of King Robert's men; the folly of Colin Campbell*]

Schyr Edward weill fer forouth rad
With thaim that war of his menye,
To the rerward na tent tuk he,
And Schyr Richard of Clar in hy
100   Quhen Schyr Edward wes passyt by
Send lycht yomen that weill couth schout
To bykkyr the rerward apon fute.
Then twa of thaim that send furth war
At the wod sid thaim bykkerit thar
105   And schot amang the Scottismen.
The king that had thar with him then
Weill fyve thousand wicht and worthi
Saw thai twa sa abandounly
Schut amang thaim and cum sa ner.
110   He wist rycht weill withoutyn wer
That thai rycht ner suppowall had,
Tharfor a bidding has he mad
That na man sall be sa hardy
To prik at thaim, bot sarraly
115   Rid redy ay into bataill
To defend gif men wald assail,

(117) 'For I'm sure,' he said, 'that very soon we shall have to cope with more.' (119) But Sir Colin Campbell, who was nearby where those two yeomen were shooting boldly among them, galloped against them at full speed, soon overtaking one of them, [whom] he quickly killed with his spear. (125) The other turned and shot again, killing his horse with one shot. With that the king came hastily, and in his annoyance gave Sir Colin such a bash with a truncheon in his fist, that he slumped on his saddle-bow. (132) The king ordered him to be smartly pulled down, but other lords who were near him, calmed the king somewhat. He said, 'The breaking of orders can lead to defeat. Do you think that yon wretches would dare attack so near us in our formation, unless they had support nearby? (140) I know very well, without [any] doubt, that we shall have [much] to do very soon; so let each man look to being prepared.' (143) At that a good thirty and more archers came and so harrassed that they hurt [some] of the king's men. The king then had his archers shoot to drive them back. With that they entered open ground and saw standing, drawn up against them in four divisions, forty thousand. (151) The king said, 'Now lords, show who is to be valiant in this fight. On them, without more delay.'

(154) They rode so stoutly against them, and attacked so fiercely, that a great part of their foes lay [slain] on the ground at the encounter.

---

119. Sir Colin Campbell. Son of Sir Neil, he had a grant of Lochaw from Robert I on 10 February 1315. (*SPi*, 325)

148–215. This battle may have followed the ambush as Barbour describes. The Scottish van under Edward Bruce must have been many miles ahead if the enemy could redeploy its forces from a wood into four field divisions – even if, as is likely, they were 1,000 rather than 40,000 – between Edward's passing and Robert's arrival. The harassment by archers makes sense as a device to slow the king and win time for deployment. But in April 1317, when the Scots were at Cashel, Butler as Justiciar, gathered a force of 780 men, followed the enemy and made an attack on them before disbanding his force. This is the only encounter between the Scots and the government for which there is non-Barbour evidence; I wonder if the battle in Barbour was this engagement, shifted by him to explain why the Warden fled to Dublin after a minor skirmish at the ambush.

'For we sall sone, Ik undreta,'
He said, 'haf for to do with ma.'
Bot Schyr Colyne Cambell, that ner
120 Was by quhar thai twa yhumen wer
Schoutand amang thaim hardily,
Prykyt on thaim in full gret hy
And sone the tane has our-tane
And with the sper him sone has slane,
125 The tother turnyt and schot agayne
And at the schot his hors has slane.
With that the king come hastily
And intill his malancoly
With a trounsoun intill hys new
130 To Schyr Colyne sic dusche he geve
That he dynnyt on his arsoun,
Than bad he smertly tit him doun.
Bot other lordis that war him by
Ameyssyt the king into party,
135 And he said, 'Breking of bidding
Mycht caus all our discumfiting.
Weyne ye yone ribaldis durst assaill
Us sa ner intill our bataill
Bot giff thai had suppowaill ner.
140 I wate rycht weill withoutyn wer
That we sall haf to do in hy,
Tharfor luk ilk man be redy.'
With that weill neir thretty or ma
Off bowmen come and bykyrit sua
145 That thai hurt off the kingis men.
The king has gert his archeris then
Schoute for to put thai men agayn.
With that thai entryt in a playn
And saw arayit agayn thaim stand
150 In four bataillis fourty thousand.
The king said, 'Now, lordingis, lat se
Quha worthy in this fycht sall be,
On thaim foroutyn mar abaid.'

[*The fight and victory of King Robert*]

Sa stoutly than on thaim thai raid
155 And assemblyt sa hardely
That off thar fayis a gret party
War laid at erd at thar meting.

There was such a breaking of spears as each [side] rode against
the other, that it made a truly great crashing [noise]. (161)
Horses came charging there, head to head, so that many fell
dead to the ground. As each [man] ran against another many
a bold and worthy man was struck down dead to the ground;
red blood gushed out of many a wound in such great profusion
that the streams ran red with blood. (169) Those who were
wrathful and angry struck others so hardily with drawn and
sharp weapons, that many a brave man died there. For those
who were hardy and brave, fighting face-to-face with their
enemies, pushed to be foremost [in the fight]. (176) You could
see fierce fighting and a cruel struggle there. I'm sure that
such hard fighting was not seen in the whole Irish war;
although Sir Edward doubtless had nineteen great victories
in less than three years, and in various of those battles he
defeated twenty thousand men and more, [their] horse with
trappings right to the feet. (186) But at all times he was still
[only] one to five when he was least [in numbers]. But in this
engagement the king always had eight of his enemies to one,
but he bore himself so [well] then that his good deeds and
generosity so encouraged all his followers [and] the shakiest
was bold. For where he saw the thickest press he rode so
hardily against them that he always made space around him.
(197) Earl Thomas the worthy was always close to him,
fighting as though he were in a fury, so that, by their great
valour,

---

182. Edward Bruce was in Ireland May, 1315–October 1318, almost three
    and a half years.

185. Trappyt hors. Horse with mail or plate protection; but such covering
    to the feet seems impossible for the period.

197. Earl Thomas, Moray, who is again specified in this Irish context.
    Also at 699.

Thar wes off speris sic bristing
As ather apon other raid
160   That it a wele gret frusch has maid,
Hors come thar fruschand heid for heid
Sua that fele on the ground felle deid.
Mony a wycht and worthi man
As ather apon other ran
165   War duschyt dede doun to the ground,
The red blud out off mony a wound
Ruschyt in sa gret foysoun than
That off the blud the stremys ran.
And thai that wraith war and angry
170   Dang on other sa hardily
With wapnys that war brycht and bar
That mony a gud man deyit thar,
For thai that hardy war and wycht
And frontlynys with thar fayis gan fycht
175   Pressyt thaim formast for to be.
Thar mycht men cruell bargane se
And hard bataill. Ik tak on hand
In all the wer off Irland
Sa hard a fechting wes nocht sene,
180   The-quhether of gret victours nynteyne
Schyr Edward has withoutyn wer,
And into les than in thre yer,
And in syndry bataillis of tha
Vencussyt thretty thousand and ma
185   With trappyt hors rycht to the fete,
Bot in all tymys he wes yete
Ay ane for fyve quhen lest wes he.
Bot the king into this mellé
Had alwayis aucht of his fa-men
190   For ane, bot he sua bar him then
That his gud deid and his bounté
Confortyt sua all his menye
That the mast coward hardy wes,
For quhar he saw the thikkest pres
195   Sa hardely on thaim he raid
That thar about him roume he maid,
And Erle Thomas the worthi
Wes in all tyme ner him by
And faucht as he war in a rage,
200   Sua that for thar gret vasselage

their men took such courage that they would avoid no danger, but exposed themselves [to danger] so stoutly, assaulting them so hardily, that all their foes were terrified. (206) And [the Scots] who perceived well from the bearing [of the Irish] that they were avoiding the fight somewhat, then pushed on with all their might and pressed them, striking so hard that eventually they turned [to flee]. (211) [The Scots], seeing them take to flight, pressed them then with all their might, and slew many as they were fleeing. The king's men gave such chase that every one of them was scattered. Richard of Clare took the way to Dublin in a mighty hurry, with other lords who fled with him, supplying both castles and towns that were in their possession. (221) They were so soundly beaten there that, as I believe, Richard Clare will have no desire to put his strength to the test in battle, nor to fight in force, as long as King Robert and his company are staying in that country. (227) They replenished strong-points like that, and the king who was so estimable, saw right many slain on the field. He saw one of those who was taken [prisoner] there and was decked out splendidly crying with great tenderness, and asked him why he made such a face. (234) He said to [the king], 'Sir, it's not surprising that I'm crying. I see many here [who've] lost their life-blood, the flower of all northern Ireland, [men] who were stoutest of heart and deed, and most feared in a tight corner.' (240) The king said, 'You're wrong, *perfay*; you've more reason to laugh, because you've escaped death.'

---

219. Supplying castles and towns, and see also 227. These statements have no relevance to the following narrative, but in Barbour's source they probably excused the Scots' failure to win Irish strongholds.

237. North Ireland. In Barbour Ireland excludes Ulster; this means Louth and Meath.

Thar men sic gret hardyment gan tak
That thai na perell wald forsak
Bot thaim abandound sa stoutly
And dang apon thaim sa hardely
205 That all thar fayis affrayit war.
And thai that saw weill be thar far
That thai eschewyt sumdele the fycht
Than dang thai on with all thar mycht
And pressit thame dyngand so fast   209*
210 That thai the bak gaf at the last,   210*
And thai that saw thaim tak the flicht   211*
Pressit thame than with all thare mycht   212*
And in thar fleyng fele gan sla.   209
The kingis men has chassyt sua
215 That thai war scalyt everilkane.   211
Rychard off Clar the way has tane
To Devillyne into full gret hy
With other lordys that fled him by
And warnysyt bath castellis and townys
220 That war in thar possessiounys.   216
Thai war sa felly fleyit thar
That I trow Schyr Richard off Clar
Sall haiff na will to faynd his mycht
In bataill na in fors to fycht
225 Quhill King Robert and his menye   221
Is dwelland in that cuntré.
Thai stuffyt strenthis on this wis,
And the king that wes to pris
Saw in the feld rycht mony slane,
230 And ane of thaim that thar wes tane   226
That wes arayit jolyly
He saw greyt wonder tenderly,
And askyt him quhy he maid sic cher.
He said him, 'Schyr, withoutyn wer
235 It is na wonder thocht I gret.   231
I se fele her lossyt the suet,
The flour of all north Irland
That hardyast war of thar hand
And mast doutyt in hard assay.'
240 The king said, 'Thou dois wrang perfay,   236
Thou has mar caus myrthis to ma
For thou the dede eschapyt sua.'

(243) Richard Clare and all his men were defeated like this by a few men, as I told you. When bold Edward Bruce heard that the king had fought like that against so many men, and in his absence, you couldn't see an angrier man. (250) But the good king said then to him that it was his own folly, for he rode so carelessly so far in advance, with no vanguard made to the men behind; for, he said, anyone who wants to ride in the van in war, should never press far out of sight from his rearward, because great danger could arise therefrom. (259) We shall speak no more about this battle. The king and all those with him rode forwards in better order and closer together than they had done previously. They rode openly through all the land, finding that no-one stood in their way. They even rode before Drogheda and then before Dublin also, but they found no-one to give battle. (268) Then they went southward in the land holding their way right to Limerick, which is the southernmost town to be found in Ireland. They lay there for two or three days, then prepared to travel again. (274) And when they were all ready, the king heard a woman cry. He quickly asked what that was. 'It's a laundry-woman, Sir,' someone said, 'who is taken in childbirth now, and will have to remain behind us here, so she's making that awful noise.' (281) The king said, 'It would indeed be a pity to leave her at that crisis; for there is no man, I'm sure,

266. Dublin. Barbour avoids explaining why the Scots made no effort to take Dublin.

269-96. Limerick. The Scots had ravaged in Leinster before reaching Limerick in early April 1317. The city refused to surrender. It was not, of course, the southernmost town in Ireland. It is not clear how long the Scots remained in the vicinity. But Barbour says nothing of the reasons why the Bruces struck into Munster, nor of their actions there. He mentions Limerick because in his source this was the location of the laundress story.

[*Edward Bruce upbraided; the Scots' journey, and the wait for the laundress*]

Richard off Clar on this maner
And all his folk discomfyt wer
245 With few folk, as I to you tauld,   241
And quhen Edward the Bruys the bauld
Wyst at the king had fochtyn sua
With sa fele folk, and he tharfra,
Mycht na man se a waer man.
250 Bot the gud king said till him than   246
That it wes his awne foly
For he raid sua unwittely
Sa far befor, and na vaward
Maid to thaim of the rerward,
255 For he said quha on wer wald rid   251
In a vaward he suld na tid
Pas fra his rerward fer of sycht
For gret perell sua fall thar mycht.
Off this fycht will we spek no mar,
260 Bot the king and all that thar war   256
Raid furthwartis in bettyr aray
And nerar togidder than er did thai.
Throu all the land playnly thai raid,
Thai fand nane that thaim obstakill maid.
265 Thai raid evyn forouth Drochindra   261
And forouth Devillyne syne alsua
And to giff battaill nane thai fand,
Syne went thai southwart in the land
And rycht till Lynrike held thar way
270 That is the southmaist toun perfay   266
That in Irland may fundyn be.
Thar lay thai dayis twa or thre
And buskyt syne agayn to far,
And quhen that thai all redy war
275 The king has hard a woman cry,   271
He askyt quhat that wes in hy.
'It is the laynder, schyr,' said ane,
'That hyr child-ill rycht now has tane
And mon leve now behind us her,
280 Tharfor scho makys yone ivill cher.'   276
The king said, 'Certis, it war pité
That scho in that poynt left suld be,
For certis I trow thar is no man

who won't have pity on a woman then.' He halted the whole army then, and soon had a tent pitched; [he] had her go in hastily and other women to be with her, [and] waited until she had been delivered, then rode forth on his way; and before ever he set forth, he gave orders how she was to be transported. (293) It was a very great kindness that such a king, so mighty, had his men wait in this way, for a mere poor laundry-woman. They took their way northwards again, and thus passed through all Ireland, through Connaught right to Dublin, through all Meath, then Uriel, and Munster and Leinster then wholly through Ulster to Carrickfergus, without a battle, for there was no-one who dared attack them.

(305) Then all the kings of the Irishry came to Sir Edward and did their homage to him, except for one or two. They came to Carrickfergus again – on all that way there was no battle unless there were any skirmishes not to be spoken of here. (313) Then every one of the Irish kings went home to their own parts, undertaking to be obedient in all things to the bidding of Sir Edward, whom they called their king. (318) He was well set now, [and] in a good way, to conquer the land altogether, for he had on his side the Irish and Ulster, and was so far on with his war that he had passed through all Ireland from end to end, by his own strength.

299–304. This confused list does give a general idea of the distance travelled by this expedition. For a full account see e.g. A. Cosgrove, *New History of Ireland*, ii. Fordun sums the expedition up. 'In the year 1316 King Robert went to Ireland to the southern parts thereof, to afford his brother succour and help. But in this march many died of hunger and the rest lived on horse-flesh. The king however at once returned and left his brother there.'

305–17. The Irish kings. No statement could be further from the facts of relentless strife among the native Irish, seeking to use the Scots against the government and each other. Note that Barbour does not himself recognise Edward as king. He was accepted as king in Ulster, but even the Remonstrance of the Irish to the pope against the English makes only incidental mention of him. (*Bower*6, 400–1)

That he ne will rew a woman than.'
285 His ost all thar arestyt he 281
And gert a tent sone stentit be
And gert hyr gang in hastily,
And other wemen to be hyr by.
Quhill scho wes deliver he bad
290 And syne furth on his wayis raid, 286
And how scho furth suld caryit be
Or ever he furth fur ordanyt he.
This wes a full gret curtasy
That swilk a king and sa mychty
295 Gert his men dwell on this maner 291
Bot for a pouer lauender.
Agayne northwart thai tuk thar way
Throu all Irland than perfay,
Throu all Connach rycht to Devillyne,
300 And throu all Myth and Irell syne 296
And Monester and Lenester,
And syne haly throu Ulsister,
To Cragfergus foroutyn bataill,
For thar wes nane durst thaim assaill.

[Edward Bruce and the Irish kings; his failings]

305 The kingis off Irchery 301
Come to Schyr Edward halily
And thar manredyn gan him ma
Bot giff that it war ane or twa.
Till Cragfergus thai come again,
310 In all that way wes nane bargain 306
Bot giff that ony poynye wer
That is nocht for to spek of her.
The Irsche kingis than everilkane
Hame till thar awne repayr ar gane,
315 And undretuk in allkyn thing 311
For till obey to the bidding
Off Schyr Edward that thar king callit thay.
He wes now weill set in gud way
To conquer the land halyly,
320 For he had apon his party 316
The Irschery and Ulsyster,
And he wes sa furth on his wer
That he wes passyt throu Irland
Fra end till uthyr throu strenth of hand.

(325) If he could have controlled himself by discretion, and not been too self-indulgent but governed his actions with moderation, it was doubtless very probable that he could have conquered the whole land of Ireland, every bit. (331) But his excessive arrogance and stubbornness, which was more than hardy, distorted his resolve, *perfay*, as I shall tell you afterwards. (335) Now we leave the noble king here, all at ease and comfort, and turn to the lord Douglas, who had been left to keep the Borders. (339) He had wrights who were adept brought, and in the haugh of Lintalee he had them make a fair manor, and when the houses had been built, he had himself very well provisioned there, because he meant to have a house-warming, to make good cheer with his men. (346) At Richmond there dwelt at hat time an earl called Sir Thomas. He had a [great] dislike of the Douglas, and said that if he could see [Douglas's] banner displayed in war, he would quickly attack it. (351) He heard how Douglas intended to be at Lintalee to have a feast. He also knew well that the king and a great company had left the country, [with] Thomas earl of Moray. (358) For that reason he thought the country was

325–34. Edward Bruce. When he left Ayr (15.20), Edward had been at an assembly which recognised him as heir presumptive to the Scottish throne, calling him 'an energetic man and abundantly experienced in martial acts for the defence of the right and liberty of the kingdom of Scotland'. Two years later the Irish Remonstrance to the pope calls him 'pious and prudent, humble and chaste, exceedingly temperate, in all things sedate and moderate, and possessing power mightily to snatch us [Irish] from the house of bondage'. He had not one of these qualities listed by the Irish.

338. Keep the marches. This probably describes Douglas's commission accurately.

339–42. Lintalee is on the Jed Water, only a few miles from the Border (NT646182). The houses built by wrights would be of timber. There are earthworks there defending the promontory above Linthaugh, which is bordered by the Jed Water. See RCAHMS, *Inventory of Roxburghshire*, no. 438.

346–47. Richmond. The earl, according to Barbour, was Richmond, i.e. John of Britanny. This is wrong, for Edmund, earl of Arundel was captain and Warden of the March for six months, Christmas 1317–24 June 1317, at a fee of £3,000 (Soc. Antiq. London, MS 120, 88). He led a foray to Jedforest, mentioned in a petition of May 1317, in which Sir Thomas Richmond, the central figure of this episode, was killed. He had been constable of Norham castle, and in July 1314 was warden of Cockermouth castle. It is probable that Barbour deliberately wrote Arundel out, but kept the 'earl' to establish the importance of the foray,

325	Couth he haf governyt him throu skill	321
	And folowyt nocht to fast his will	
	Bot with mesur haf led his dede	
	It wes weill lik withoutyn drede	
	That he mycht haiff conqueryt weill	
330	The land of Irland ilkadele,	326
	Bot his outrageous sucquedry	
	And will that wes mar than hardy	
	Off purpose lettyt him perfay,	
	As Ik herefter sall you say,	

[*Douglas at Lintalee; Sir Thomas Richmond proposes to cut down Jedworth Forest*]

335	Now leve we her the noble king	331
	All at his ese and his liking,	
	And spek we of the lord of Douglas	
	That left to kep the marches was.	
	He gert set wrychtis that war sleye	
340	And in the halche of Lintaile	336
	He gert thaim mak a fayr maner,	
	And quhen the housis biggit wer	
	He gert purvay him rycht weill thar	
	For he thoucht to mak ane infar	
345	And to mak gud cher till his men.	341
	In Rychmound wes wonnand then	
	Ane erle that men callit Schyr Thomas,	
	He had invy at the Douglas	
	And said gif that he his baner	
350	Mycht se displayit apon wer	346
	That sone assemblé on it suld he.	
	He hard how the Douglas thocht to be	
	At Lyntailey and fest to ma,	
	And he had wittering weill alsua	
355	That the king and a gret menye	351
	War passyt than of the countré	
	And the erle of Murref Thomas,	
	Tharfor he thocht the countré was	

which was evidently intended to be a serious attack on southern Scotland by land and (543–666) sea. Undoubtedly it sought to exploit the absence of the king, Edward Bruce and Moray, but its specific direction, Jed-forest, may reflect knowledge gained during a visit to Jedburgh by an English embassy in late November 1316. (Soc. Antiq. London, MS 120, 27, 29)

weak in men to withstand those who [might] seek them with
determination. At the time he had control of the Marches and
power [there]. (363) He collected men about him then until
he had almost ten thousand; he had wood axes taken with
him, for he meant to get his men to hew down Jedworth
Forest so clean, that no tree could be seen therein. (369) They
held forth on their way, but the good lord Douglas always
had spies out in every direction, and had good information
that they meant to ride and come upon him suddenly. He
collected as quickly as he could those he could [reach] of his
following. (376) I'm sure that he had with him fifty good,
brave men, fully armed [and] well equipped; he also had a
large company of archers mustered with him. (381) There
was a place there on the way by which he well knew they
would go, with woods on both side; the entry was pretty broad
and wide, [but] it narrowed continually like a shield, until at
one place, the way was not a so much as a chucky-stone's
throw in breadth.

352–492. This foray is described by (a) Gray and (b) an entry in the
Wardrobe book for 10 Ed. II. Also in a chronicle which dates the event
to 23 April, given below, note to 370.
   (a) At the same time [*as Edward Bruce was in Ireland*] the king of
   England sent the earl of Arundel as commander on the March of
   Scotland who was repulsed at Lintalee in the forest of Jedworth by
   James Douglas, and Thomas Richmond was killed. The said earl
   retreated south without doing any more. (*S*, 143; *ST*, 58)
   (b) To Thomas Grey, soldier at arms, by gift of the king, in recom-
   pense for one horse of his, *Arselli*, which died in the king's service at
   Lyntanlye in Scotland in the company of the earl of Arundel, warden
   of the March, in the month of March, present year ... 20 marks.
   (Soc. Antiq. London, MS 120, 102)
The date, March, conflicts with that given by the chronicle of 23 April;
I have failed to find a meaning for *Arselli*.
370. Douglas's preparations. There is a unique account of the Lintalee
skirmish in Harleian MS 655, edited by Joseph Stevenson:
   About the feast of St Gregory [23 April] the earl of Arundel, Warden
   of Northumbria and the March appointed by the king, having collected
   an army of 30,000 men, along with the earl of Atholl, Henry de
   Beaumont and other magnates, at a time when the Scots magnates
   were fighting in Ireland, entered Scotland which was virtually destitute
   of men, and set out for Lintalee where James Douglas was staying in
   a certain fortified place (*municio*) with 200 men. Hearing of their
   coming, Douglas took to flight, leaving the place empty, which a noble
   freebooter (*schavaldus nobilis*), called Elias the clerk, with 30 compan-
   ions entered, and satiated himself splendidly with the many victuals
   he found there. But James, having ascertained the sloth of the English,

Febill of men for to withstand
360 Men that thame soucht with stalwart hand, 356
And of the marchis than had he
The governaile and the pousté.
He gaderyt folk about him then
Quhill he wes ner ten thousand men,
365 And wod-axys gert with him tak 361
For he thocht he his men wald mak
To hew Jedwort Forrest sa clene
That na tre suld tharin be sene.
Thai held thaim forthwart on thar way,
370 Bot the gud lord Douglas that ay 366
Had spyis out on ilka sid
Had gud wittering that thai wald rid
And cum apon him suddanly.
Than gaderyt he rycht hastily
375 Thaim that he moucht of his menye, 371
I trow that than with him had he
Fyfty that worthy war and wicht
At all poynt armyt weill and dycht,
And off archeris a gret menye
380 Assemblyt als with him had he. 376
A place thar was thar in the way
Quhar he thocht weill thai suld away
That had wod apon athyr sid,
The entre wes weill large and wid
385 And as a scheild it narowit ay 381
Quhill at intill a place the way
Wes nocht a pennystane cast of breid.

---

who made little effort to approach that place, recovered his boldness
and entered the fortified place; he cut off the head of Elias and stuck
the face inhumanly into the anus, and killed the remaining men by
the sword. Then he violently attacked the army of the English which
conducted itself very carelessly, and killed Sir Thomas Richmond, a
certain noble who resisted bravely. (*Illust. of Scott. Hist.* 3–4)
Atholl was certainly in Arundel's following (Soc. Antiq. London MS
120, 88, 94). This passage was not known to Barbour, for it clearly
distinguishes the earl from Richmond; cutting down the forest and
Richmond's fur hat do not appear in it. But a common source, probably
at more than one remove from each, seems certain. Barbour places
Douglas's attack and the death of Richmond before the death of Elias,
the chronicle after. But Barbour hints at Douglas's initial flight in
370–75, and the broad outline of the chronicle is probably correct,
making it likely that Barbour inverted events in order to excise Douglas's
flight, but retaining the final fearful withdrawal of the English.

(388) The lord Douglas went thither when he knew that they were coming close, and in a hollow on one side put all his archers in an ambush, ordering them to keep themselves all concealed until they heard him give the call, when they should shoot briskly among their foes, holding them there until he had passed through them, and then they should go forward with him. (398) Then he knitted together young birch-trees which were growing thickly nearby on both sides of the way, in such a way that men could not readily ride through them. (402) When this had been done, he waited on the other side of the way, and Richmond came riding in the first squad. The lord Douglas saw him well, and had his men keep very still until they came close at hand to them and entered the narrow way. Then with a shout they rushed on them, yelling aloud, 'Douglas! Douglas!' (412) Then Richmond, a really fine man, when he heard the shout rise like that and saw Douglas's banner openly [displayed] turned himself towards it speedily. They came on so boldly that they made good way through [the English], bearing down to the ground all that they met. (419) Richmond was born down there; Douglas stopped above him, turned him over and then with a knife on that very spot killed him dead. He wore a hat on his helmet [which] Douglas took with him there as proof, because it was furred. Then [he] took their way in haste until they had entered the wood.

The lord of Douglas thidder yeid
Quhen he wyst thai war ner cummand,
390   And a-lauch on the ta hand   386
All his archeris enbuschit he
And bad thaim hald thaim all prevé
Quhill that thai hard him rays the cry,
And than suld schut hardely
395   Amang thar fayis and sow thaim sar   391
Quhill that he throu thaim passyt war,
And syne with him furth hald suld thai.
Than byrkis on athyr sid the way
That young and thik war growand ner
400   He knyt togidder on sic maner   396
That men moucht nocht weill throu thaim rid.

[*Douglas defeats and kills Richmond, then drives off Elias the
clerk from Lintalee*]

Quhen this wes done he gan abid
Apon the tother half the way,
And Richmound in gud aray
405   Come ridand in the fyrst escheill.   401
The lord Douglas has sene him weill
And gert his men all hald thaim still
Quhill at thar hand thai come thaim till
And entryt in the narow way,
410   Than with a schout on thaim schot thai   406
And criyt on hycht, 'Douglas! Douglas!'
The Richmound than that worthi was
Quhen he has hard sua rais the cry
And Douglas baner saw planly
415   He dressyt thidderwart in hy   411
And thai come on sa hardily
That thai throu thaim maid thaim the way,
All that thai met till erd bar thai.
The Richmound borne doun thar was,
420   On him arestyt the Douglas   416
And him reversyt and with a knyff
Rycht in that place reft him the lyff.
Ane hat apon his helm he bar
And that tuk with him Douglas thar
425   In taknyng, for it furryt was,   421
And syne in hy thar wayis tays
Quhill in the wod thai entryt war.

The archers had done a good job there, for they shot well and boldly. (430) The English force was put in great fear, for Douglas suddenly, with all those of his company, were among their force before they knew [it], and broke through them nearly everywhere. [He] had almost completely finished his deed before they could gather their wits to help themselves. (437) When they saw their lord slain, they picked him up and turned back to withdraw from the shooting. Then they assembled in open ground, and because their lord was dead, they prepared to make camp all that night in that very place. (444) Douglas, who was a brave man, got information that a clerk, Elias, with a good three hundred of the enemy had gone straight to Lintalee and had made camp for their host. [So] he went thither in haste with all [the men] of his company, finding Elias at food with all his force around him. (453) There [the Scots] came upon them stoutly and dealt with them remorselessly with swords that cut sharply. They were killed so grievously that almost none of them escaped; they dealt with them in such quantity with slashing swords and with knives that nearly all lost their lives. (461) They had a cruel final course, for that last mouthful was too much! Those who managed to escape went right to their army and told how their men had been killed so thoroughly that almost none escaped. (467) When [the men] of the army heard how Douglas had fared with them, had killed their advance party, assaulted all of themselves,

---

445. Elias may have been a renegade clerk. He does not appear in printed record sources, but schavaldours like him were active on the Borders as a result of the breakdown of order in Northumberland, for example the John de Espeley and companions who occupied the nunnery of Eccles at this very time. (PRO C47/22/12(19))

446. Three hundred. In the chronicle 30.

The archeris weill has borne thaim thar
For weill and hardily schot thai.
The Inglis rout in gret affray   426
War set, for Douglas suddanly
With all thaim of his cumpany
Or ever thai wyst wes in thar rout
And thyrlyt thaim weill ner throchout,
And had almast all doyn his deid   431
Or thai to help thaim couth tak heid.
And quhen thai saw thar lord slayn
Thai tuk him up and turnyt agayn
To draw thaim fra the schot away,
Than in a plane assemblit thai   436
And for thar lord that thar wes dede
Thai schup thaim in that ilk sted
For to tak herbery all that nycht.
And than the Douglas that wes wicht
Gat wytteryng ane clerk Elys   441
With weill thre hunder ennymys
All straucht to Lintaile war gayn
And herbery for thar ost had tane.
Than thidder is he went in hy
With all thaim of his cumpany   446
And fand clerk Elys at the mete
And his round about him set,
And thai come on thaim stoutly thar
And with swerdis that scharply schar
Thai servyt thaim full egrely.   451
Slayn war thai full grevously
That wele ner eschapyt nane,
Thai servyt thaim on sa gret wane
With scherand swerdis and with knyffis
That weile ner all left the lyvys.   456
Thai had a felloun efter mes,
That sourchargis to chargand wes.
Thai that eschapyt thar throu cas
Rycht till the ost the wayis tais
And tauld how that thar men war slayn   461
Sa clene that ner eschapyt nane.
And quhen thai of thar ost had herd
How that the Douglas with thaim ferd
That had thar herbryouris slane
And ruschyt all thaim self agayn   466

Line numbers in left margin: 430, 435, 440, 445, 450, 455, 460, 465, 470

and killed their lord in the middle of their force, not one of them all was stout enough to have more will to attack Douglas then; so they consulted, decided to go homewards and went [in that direction]; they hurried so on the way that they soon came into England. (479) They left the forest still standing [for] then they had no will to cut it down, especially while the Douglas was so close at hand, their neighbour. He, seeing them turn back realised that their lord had been killed, and knew it also from the hat that he had taken; for one of the prisoners said truthfully to him that Richmond was commonly in the habit of wearing that furred hat. (490) Then Douglas was even more pleased than before because he knew for a fact that his deadly enemy, Richmond, had been felled to the ground.

(493) In this way Sir James Douglas defended the land worthily by his valour and great daring. I'm sure that this feat of war had been undertaken so boldly, accomplished so hardily [that] he defeated without a doubt folk who numbered a good ten thousand with no more than fifty armed men. (502) I can also tell you of two other feats which were accomplished well with fifty men; without any doubt they were done so very bravely that they were esteemed as sovereign, above all other war-exploits accomplished in their time. This was the first to be brought well to a conclusion so stoutly with fifty [men]. (511) The second happened in Galloway,

And slew thar lord in-myd thar rout,
Thar wes nane of thaim all sa stout
That mar will than had till assaile
The Douglas, tharfor to consaill
475 Thai yeid and to purpose has tane   471
To wend hamwart, and hamwart ar gan
And sped thaim sua apon thar way
That in Ingland sone cummyn ar thai.
The forest left thai standand still,
480 To hew it than thai had na will   476
Specially quhill the Douglas
Sua ner-hand by thar nychtbur was.
And he that saw thaim torne agayn
Persavyt weill thar lord wes slayn
485 And be the hat that he had tane   481
He wist alsua weill, for ane
That takyn wes said him suthly
That Rychmound commounly
Wes wount that furryt hat to wer.
490 Than Douglas blythar wes than er   486
For he wist weill that Rychmound
His felloun fa wes brocht to the ground.

[*A comparison of Douglas's exploits*]

Schyr James of Douglas on this wis
Throu his worschip and his empris
495 Defendyt worthely the land.   491
This poynt of wer, I tak on hand,
Wes undretane full apertly
And eschevyt rycht hardely,
For he stonayit foroutyn wer
500 That folk that well ten thousand wer   496
With fyfty armyt men but ma.
I can als tell you other twa
Poyntis that wele eschevit wer
With fyfty men, and but wer
505 Thai war done sua rycht hardely   501*
That thai war prisit soveranly   502*
Atour all othir poyntis of wer   503*
That in that tym eschevit wer   504*
This wes the fyrst that sua stoutly   501
510 Wes brocht till end wele with fifty   502
Into Galloway the tother fell

when, as you heard me telling previously Sir Edward Bruce
with fifty [men] defeated Sir Aymer de St John, and fifteen
hundred men (when counted). (516) The third happened in
Eskdale when Sir John de Soulis was in charge of all that
area, blocking the way with fifty men to Sir Andrew Harclay,
who had three hundred finely horsed men in [his] company.
(523) This Sir John defeated them all sturdily in an open
engagement by courage and superior skill, taking Sir Andrew
prisoner. I shall not go over the whole means, for anyone who
likes can hear young women, when they are at play, sing [of]
it among themselves every day. (531) These were the three
worthy feats which I believe will be prized for evermore, as
long as men can remember them. (534) It is entirely right
without doubt that for evermore the names of those who were
so worthy in their own time that men still take pleasure in
their valour and great skill, should endure in the future in
praises, where He who is king of Heaven, should bring them
up to Heaven's bliss, where praise lasts for ever!

(543) At this time, when Richmond was brought to the ground
in this way, men from the coast of England who lived on the
Humber or nearby, gathered a great company and went in
ships to the sea;

---

512. Previously told. At 9.541–647.

516–26. The capture of Sir Andrew Harclay, sheriff of Cumberland from
1310, who had valiantly and successfully defended Carlisle in a siege
by Robert I in July–August 1315, occurred in the half-year before 19
April, 1316. His ransom was over 1,000 marks. Sir John de Soules was
younger brother of William de Soules (19.11), and came to Scotland
from France in November 1314 to ransom kinsmen taken by the Scots
at Bannockburn. But he adhered to Robert I, and was given sundry
Dumfries-shire lands. He was killed at Dundalk in 1318 (18.110–13)
(*CDS3, 514, 515*, redated in *CDS5*)

543–666. This attack on Fife was part of an expedition planned by
Arundel, and was probably intended to coincide with his attack on
Lothian which came adrift at Lintalee, but it must have sailed after his
force withdrew. According to the account in the Wardrobe book it
attacked right up the east coast:

> To Roger le Katour master of the king's ship called *la Bliche de
> Westminstre* and his four colleagues masters of four ships, sent with
> their ships on the orders of the earl of Arundel, then Warden and
> captain of the Scottish March, from Newcastle-on-Tyne to Berwick,
> Dundee and Aberdeen and elsewhere on the coast of Scotland, to
> attack the Scots, the king's enemies, for the wages of himself, four
> masters, five constables, and 323 accompanying armed sailors ... in
> the five ships ... from 13 May [1317], which day they first sailed
> towards those parts, to 11 June, when they returned, (30 days) at 6d.

Quhen as ye forouth herd me tell
Schyr Edward the Bruys with fifty
Vencussyt of Sanct Jhon Schyr Amery
515   And fyften hunder men be tale.   507
The thrid fell intill Esdaill
Quhen that Schyr Jhone the Soullis was
The governour of all that place,
That to Schyr Androw Hardclay
520   With fifty men withset the way   512
That had thar in his cumpany
Thre hunder horsyt jolyly.
This Schyr Jhone intill playn mellé
Throu soverane hardiment and bounté
525   Vencussyt thaim sturdely ilkan   517
And Schyr Andrew in hand has tane,
I will nocht rehers the maner
For quha-sa likis thai may her
Young wemen quhen thai will play
530   Syng it amang thaim ilk day.   522
Thir war the worthi poyntis thre
That I trow evermar sall be
Prissyt quhile men may on thaim mene.
It is well worth foroutyn wene
535   That thar namys for evermar,   527
That in thar tym sua worthi war
That men till her yeit has daynté,
For thar worschip and thar bounté
Be lestand ay furth in loving,
540   Quhar He that is of hevynnys king   532
Bring thaim he up till hevynnys blis
Quhar allwayis lestand loving is.

[*English ships come to Fife; the Scots let them land*]

In this tym that the Richmound
Was on this maner brocht to ground
545   Men off the cost off Ingland   537
That dwelt on Humbre or nerhand
Gaderyt thaim a gret mengne
And went in schippes to the se,

------

per day for each master and constable, 3d per day for each sailor,
£128.12s. (Soc. Antiq. London, MS 120, p. 56)
Sailors killed in Fife or elsewhere would not appear among the 323
paid.

[they] went towards Scotland speedily and came quickly to the Firth [of Forth]. (551) They thought they would have everthing at their mercy, for they knew very well that the king was then far out of the country, and many of great courage with him. So they came to the Firth, and sailed up it until they landed beside Inverkeithing, on the west side towards Dunfermline, [when] they began to plunder hard. (560) The earl of Fife and the sheriff saw the ships approaching their coast; they mustered to defend the land and held their way always in parallel with the ships as they sailed, meaning to prevent them from landing. (566) When the men on the ships saw them with such demeanour [and] in such order, they said among themselves that [the Scots] would not prevent them from landing, then sped to the land so that they came there with great speed and arrived very determinedly. (573) The Scotsmen saw them coming and were so intimidated by them that they rode [away] from them all together, allowing them to make a landing without hindrance. They dared not fight with them and so withdrew altogether despite numbering almost five hundred.

(580) When they were riding away like that, and began to prepare no defence, the good bishop of Dunkeld, whom men called William Sinclair, came with a force in good order – I'm sure they were sixty horse. He himself was splendidly armed and rode upon a fine horse. (588) He had a robe over his armour then,

---

560. The earl of Fife. For the return of Earl Duncan from England in 1315 see *RRS5*, 354–60. The sheriff was probably Sir David Wemyss or Sir David Barclay.

582–83. William Sinclair, bishop of Dunkeld, a younger brother of the laird of Roslin, had been elected to the see in 1309, but, because of English pressure, was not confirmed till May 1312. His see had detached portions on the Forth, including Aberdour, Inverkeithing, Inchcolm and Cramond, which would explain his presence here.

	And towart Scotland went in hy	
550	And in the Fyrth come hastely.	542
	Thai wend till haiff all thar liking	
	For thai wist weile that the king	
	Wes then fer out of the countré,	
	With him mony of gret bounté,	
555	Tharfor into the Fyrth come thai	547
	And endlang it up held thai	
	Quhill thai besid Ennerkething	
	On west half towart Dunferlyng	
	Tuk land and fast begouth to ryve.	
560	The erle of Fyff and the schyrreff	552
	Saw to thar cost schippis approchand	
	Thai gaderyt to defend thar land	
	And a-forgayn the schippis ay	
	As thai saillyt thai held thar way	
565	And thocht to let thaim land to tak.	557
	And quhen the schipmen saw thaim mak	
	Swilk contenance in sic aray	
	Thai said amang thaim all that thai	
	Wald nocht let for thaim land to ta,	
570	Than to the land thai sped thaim sua	562
	That thai come thar in full gret hy	
	And aryvyt full hardely.	
	The Scottismen saw thar cummyng	
	And had of thaim sic abasing	
575	That thai all samyn raid thaim fra	567
	And the land letles lete thaim ta.	
	Thai durst nocht fecht with thaim, forthi	
	Thai withdrew thaim all halily	
	The-quhethyr thai war fyve hunder ner.	

[The bishop of Dunkeld drives the English to their ships]

580	Quhen thai away thus ridand wer	572
	And na defens begouth to schape,	
	Off Dunkeldyn the gud byschap	
	That men callyt Wilyam the Sanctecler	
	Come with a rout in gud maner.	
585	I trow on hors thai war sexty,	577
	Himselff was armyt jolyly	
	And raid apon a stalwart sted,	
	A chemer for till hele his wed	
	Apon his armour had he then	

to hide what he wore, and his men were also well armed. He
met the earl with the sheriff retreating with their great follow-
ing, and pretty quickly asked them what hurry made them go
back so hastily. (595) They said their foes had made a landing
with stalwart bearing in such numbers that they felt they were
altogether too many, themselves too few to deal with them.
When the bishop heard it was like this, he said, 'The king
ought to esteem you, who are making such a good job of
protecting the land in his absence. (603) Indeed, if he gave
you your just deserts he would soon chop the gilt spurs from
you right at the heel; that's what justice requires men to do
with cowards. Whoever loves his lord and his country [let
him] turn back now with me.' (609) With that he threw off
his cloak, seized a stalwart spear and rode swiftly to his foes.
All turned with him without exception for he had so reproved
them that none of them deserted him. (615) He rode sturdily
in front of them, and they followed him in ranks until they
came approaching near to their foes who had landed. Some
were grouped in good order and some had gone to plunder.
(621) When the good bishop saw them he said, 'Lords, without
fear or dread let us gallop boldly upon them, and we shall
have them easily. If they see us coming without fear, provided
that we don't hesitate here, they will be defeated very soon.
Now do [your] best, for men shall see who loves the king's
honour today.' (630) Then all together in good order they
galloped sturdily

590 And armyt weill als war his men. 582
The erle and the schyrreff met he
Awaywart with thar gret menye,
And askyt thaim weill sone quhat hy
Maid thaim to turne sa hastily.

595 Thai said thar fayis with stalwart hand 587
Had in sic foysoun takyn the land
That thai thocht thaim all out to fele
And thaim to few with thaim to dele.
Quhen the bischap hard it wes sua

600 He said, 'The king aucht weill to ma 592
Off you, that takys sa wele on hand
In his absence to wer his land.
Certis giff he gert serff you weill
The gilt spuris rycht be the hele

605 He suld in hy ger hew you fra, 597
Rycht wald with cowartis men did sua.
Quha luffis his lord or his cuntre
Turne smertly now agayne with me.'
With that he kest of his chemer

610 And hynt in hand a stalwart sper 602
And raid towart his fayis in hy,
All turnyt with him halyly
For he had thaim reprovyt sua
That off thaim all nane fled him fra.

615 He raid befor thaim sturdely 607
And thai him folowyt sarraly
Quhill that thai come ner approchand
To thar fayis that had tane land,
And sum war knyt in gud aray

620 And sum war went to the foray. 612
The gud bischap quhen he thaim saw
He said, 'Lordingis, but drede or aw
Pryk we apon thaim hardely
And we sall haf thaim wele lychtly.

625 Se thai us cum but abaysing 617
Sua that we mak her na stinting
Thai sall weill sone discumfyt be.
Now dois weill, for men sall se
Quha luffis the kingis mensk today.'

630 Than all togidder in gud aray 622
Thai prekyt apon thaim sturdely,
The byschap that wes rycht hardy

against [the English]. The bishop, a very hardy, big strong man, rode always at their head. Then they met in a violent encounter, and those who felt such a sharp pain at the first meeting of spears, gave ground wanting to get away. (638) They went quickly towards their ships, and [the Scots] came chasing them fiercely, slaying them so mercilessly that all the fields were scattered with Englishmen who had been killed there. (643) Those who were still not killed pressed to [reach] the sea again. The Scotsmen who chased like that, killed all whom they could overtake. Nonetheless those who still fled hurried so to their ships and went in such number into some barges, [with] their enemies chasing them, that they overturned and the men on board drowned. (653) One Englishman there, *perfay*, did [a feat of] great strength, as I heard tell, for when he had been chased to the boat, he seized with both arms a Scotsman who had dealt with him, and for good or ill just threw him over his back, went with him to his boat and threw him in, despite all [the man's] efforts. (662) This was a truly great feat indeed. The Englishmen who got away went quickly to their ships and sailed home, angry and disappointed that they had been driven off like that.

(667) When the shipmen had been defeated in this way, the bishop who bore himself so well that he inspired everone who was there, was still on the battlefield where nearly five hundred were dead, apart from those who were drowned.

---

649. Barge. The record (above note to 543) makes no mention of a barge; it might have been a ship's boat.

And mekill and stark raid forouth ay.
Than in a frusche assemblit thai,
635 And thai that at the fryst meting 627
Feld off the speris sa sar sowing
Wandyst and wald haiff bene away,
Towart thar schippis in hy held thai,
And thai thaim chassyt fellounly
640 And slew thaim sua dispitously 632
That all the feldis strowyt war
Off Inglismen that slane war thar,
And thai yeyt that held unslayne
Pressyt to the se agayne,
645 And Scottismen that chassyt sua 637
Slew all that ever thai mycht ourta.
Bot thai that fled yeit nocht-forthi
Sua to thar schippis gan thaim hy,
And in sum barge sua fele gan ga
650 And thar fayis hastyt thaim sua 642
That thai our-tumblyt and the men
That war tharin war drownyt then.
Thar did ane Inglisman perfay
A weill gret strenth as Ik hard say,
655 For quhen he chassyt wes till his bat 647
A Scottisman that him handlyt hat
He hynt than be the armys twa,
And, war him wele or war him wa,
He evyn apon his bak him slang
660 And with him to the bat gan gang 652
And kest him in all mawgré his,
This wes a wele gret strenth i-wis.
The Inglismen that wan away
To thar schippis in hy went thai
665 And saylyt hame angry and wa 657
That thai had bene rebutyt sua.

[*The bishop is praised; the king returns from Ireland*]

Quhen that the schipmen on this wis
War discumfyt as I devys
The byschap that sa weill him bar
670 That he all hartyt that thar war 662
Was yeyt into the fechtyn-sted
Quhar that fyve hunder ner war ded
Foroutyn thaim that drownyt war,

When the field had been looted bare, they all went home to their dwellings. (676) It was good fortune for the bishop who by his renown and his valour achieved so great a victory; the king from that day onwards, therefore, loved, honoured and esteemed him, holding him in such favour that he called him his own bishop. (683) Thus they defended the country on both sides of the Firth of Forth while the king was out of the country; [he] then, as I have already described, had made his journey through all Ireland and had ridden to Carrickfergus. (689) When his brother, as he was king, had all the Irish at his obedience and all Ulster too, he prepared to take his way home. He left with his brother a large part of his men who were most hardy and renowned for all chivalry, then he went to the sea. (697) When they had taken leave on each side, he went quickly to sail. He had earl Thomas with him; they hoisted sail without delay and arrived without danger in the land of Galloway.

688–96. Carrickfergus. The Bruces arrived back in Ulster on 1 May, 1317. King Robert sailed home about 22 May; nothing is heard of Edward Bruce for a further 16 months, but it is presumed that he remained in Ulster.

And quhen the feld was spulyeit bar
675   Thai went all hame to thar repar.   667
To the byschap is fallyn fayr
That throu his price and his bounte
Wes eschevyt swilk a journé.
The king tharfor ay fra that day
680   Him luffyt and prisyt and honoryt ay   672
And held him in suylk daynte
That his awne bischop him callit he.
Thus thai defendyt the countré
Apon bath halffis the Scottis se
685   Quhill that the king wes out off land   677
That than as Ik haf borne on hand
Throu all Irland his cours had maid
And agane to Cragfergus raid.
And quhen his broder as he war king
690   Had all the Irschery at bidding   682
And haly Ulsistre alsua
He buskyt hame his way to ta.
Off his men that war mast hardy
And prisyt mast of chevalry
695   With his broder gret part left he,   687
And syne is went him to the se.
Quhen thar levys on ather party
Wes tane he went to schip him in hy,
The Erle Thomas with him he had,
700   Thai raissyt sayllis but abaid   692
And in land off Galloway
Forout perell aryvyt thai.

The lords of the land were pleased when they learned that he had returned, and went to him in great haste; he received them kindly and made a feast [with] joyful cheer. They were so wonderfully happy at his arrival that no words can express it; they made great feasting and welcome for him. Wherever he rode the whole country turned out with pleasure to see him. (11) There was great happiness in the land. All had been won to his authority then; from the valley of the Reid to Orkney none of Scotland was outside his allegiance except Berwick alone. At that time there dwelt in it one who was captain of the town. He was suspicious of all Scotsmen, treating them very badly. He always had a very ill will towards them and kept them firmly under control. (22) Then it happened one day that Sym Spalding, a burgess, thought that it was a very bitter thing to be repulsed always like that. So he conceived in his heart that he would secretly make an agreement with the marischal, whose cousin he had married as his wife, and he quickly did what he had planned.

---

1. Barbour brings together the taking of Berwick in April 1318 and Edward II's siege of the town in September 1319, with the Chapter of Myton necessarily occurring within the latter; but the following account in book 18 of Edward Bruce's death (October 1318) is displaced chronologically to provide a better literary effect. This book-division does make sense!

13. Red Swyre is in Northumberland, which had become no-man's land.

15. Berwick. The English effort to replenish Berwick in 1316–18 is shown by many entries in the Wardrobe books for 10 and 11 Ed. II, Soc. Antiq. London, MSS 120, 121. Although no printed source refers to the fact, the Scots besieged Berwick from September to November 1317 (King Robert was in Lothian), for two ships with men-at-arms were sent on 2 October from Whitby and York to Berwick 'for the rescue of the town besieged by the Scots' and remained till early December (MS 121, 38, 39, 83, 84). For a graphic account of these months see RRS5, 140–43. It is said that there was a truce between English and Scots in the early months of 1318, but I can find no evidence of this. On the contrary, on 18 March, 1318 Edward II issued many letters for his own mission and the Scots to negotiate at Berwick to 'begin' a truce or peace, and the embassy would reach Berwick in early April (not March as in RRS5, 144). The Scots must have indicated a willingness to treat, and the taking of Berwick would seem like bad faith. But it was not a breach of faith or law.

23. Simon Spalding. A Simon of Saltoun, de Camera, was tronar and

BOOK 17

[*Only Berwick remains in English hands; a burgess offers to
betray it*]

    The lordis off the land war fayne
    Quhen thai wist he wes cummyn agan
    And till him went in full gret hy,
    And he ressavit thaim hamlyly
5   And maid thaim fest and glaidsum cher,
    And thai sa wonderly blyth wer
    Off his come that na man mycht say,
    Gret fest and fayr till him maid thai.
    Quharever he raid all the countré
10   Gaderyt in daynté him to se,
    Gret glaidschip than wes in the land.
    All than wes wonnyn till his hand,
    Fra the Red Swyre to Orknay
    Wes nocht off Scotland fra his fay
15   Outakyn Berwik it allane.
    That tym tharin wonnyt ane
    That capitane wes of the toun,
    All Scottismen in suspicioun
    He had and tretyt thaim tycht ill.
20   He had ay to thaim hevy will
    And held thaim fast at undre ay,
    Quhill that it fell apon a day
    That a burges Syme of Spalding
    Thocht that it wes rycht angry thing
25   Suagate ay to rebutyt be.
    Tharfor intill his hart thocht he
    That he wald slely mak covyne
    With the marchall, quhays cosyne
    He had weddyt till his wiff,
30   And as he thocht he did belyff.

---

clerk of customs of Berwick from 1317, and is here confused with Peter
Spalding, his name in all other sources, who is listed among the Berwick
garrison in 1312. Lanercost calls him 'a certain Englishman living in
the town, who, being bribed by a great sum of money received from
them and by the promise of land, allowed them to scale the wall and
enter by that part of the wall where he was stationed as guard and
sentry.' The *Annales Paulini* add the name of John Drory as accomplice.
See further note to 56. (*L*, 234–35; *LT*, 219–20)

(31) He sent letters to [the marischal] speedily by a trusted man very secretly, giving him a time to come one night with ladders and good brave men to the Cow Gate clandestinely, bidding him to keep his tryst exactly, and he would meet them at the wall because his watch would fall there that night.

(39) When the marischal saw the letter, he reflected for a while, for he knew that by himself he would not be sufficiently strong or powerful to pull off so big an exploit; and if he took help from one [person] another would be offended. (46) Therefore he went straight to the king, showing him, [confidentially to] the two of them, the letter and the bidding too. When the king heard that this plan had been put forward with such certainty that he felt there was no deceit in it, he said to [the marischal],(52) 'Indeed you have behaved very wisely in telling me first, for if you had revealed yourself to my nephew, Earl Thomas, that would have annoyed the lord Douglas; and *vice versa*. But I shall arrange [things] in such a way that you will follow your plan and have no problem with them. (61) You shall pay good heed to the day, and with whoever you can get shall be in ambush in the evening, in Duns Park – but be secret. And I shall have Earl Thomas and the Lord Douglas also, each with a company of men, be there to do what you instruct.' (69) Without more delay the marischal then took [his] leave, went on his way

---

28–9. The marischal. Sir Robert Keith. Sir William Keith of Galston, mentioned favourably at 150, was his cousin, and a possible source for information on the taking of Berwick. William's sister may have married Spalding.

35. The Cow Port. In the middle of the north wall of the town.

56. Douglas. Gray claims that Berwick was taken by Douglas with the assistance of Earl Patrick. The Harleian MS. 655 chronicle gives details: [*About 1 August 1317 the burgesses obtained keeping of the town from Edward II*] When he heard this James Douglas [became] very excited and hoped that entry to the town by some betrayal would be easily open to him; in the course of time, James, as was said, so corrupted a certain Peter Spalding, a serjeant employed by the townsmen in its defence, by himself and his men, on the promise of £800, that, when an opportune moment arrived about [25 March] he let the Scots in at the part of the wall committed to his keeping. (*Illust. of Scott. Hist.* 5)

64. Duns Park. The king was there in June–July 1315, probably preparing to attack Berwick. (*CDS3, 440; RRS5, 99*)

Lettrys till him he send in hy
With a traist man all prively,
And set him tym to cum a nycht
With leddrys and with gud men wicht
35 Till the kow yet all prively,
And bad him hald his trist trewly
And he suld mete thaim at the wall,
For his walk thar that nycht suld fall.

[*The marischal shows the letter to the king, who seeks to avoid
jealousy between Douglas and Moray*]

Quhen the marchell the lettre saw
40 He umbethocht him than a thraw,
For he wist be himselvyn he
Mycht nocht off mycht no power be
For till escheyff sa gret a thing,
And giff he tuk till his helping
45 Ane, other suld wrethit be.
Tharfor rycht to the king yeid he
And schawyt him betwix thaim twa
The letter and the charge alsua.
Quhen that the king hard that this trane
50 Spokyn wes intill certayne
That him thocht tharin na fantis
He said him, 'Certis thou wrocht as wis
That has discoveryt the fryst to me,
For giff thou had discoveryt the
55 To my nevo the Erle Thomas
Thou suld disples the lord Douglas,
And him alsua in the contrer,
Bot I sall wyrk on sic maner
That thou at thine entent sall be
60 And haff of nane of thaim mawgré.
Thou sall tak kep weill to the day,
And with thaim that thou purches may
At evyn thou sall enbuschit be
In Duns Park, bot be prevé,
65 And I sall ger the Erle Thomas
And the lord alsua of Douglas
Ather with a soume of men
Be thar to do as thou sall ken.'
The marchell but mar delay
70 Tuk leve and held furth on his way

and kept the conversation confidential and quiet up to the day that had been fixed for him. Then he took [some] of the best [men] of Lothian with him to his tryst, because he was then sheriff thereof.

(76) He came at evening very quietly to Duns Park with his following. Then soon afterwards Earl Thomas came with a goodly company, who had met with the lord Douglas. They were a right fine company when they had met together there. When the marischal had revealed the agreement, line by line, to both the lords, they went forth on their way; they left their horses far from the town. (87) To cut it short, they acted in such a way then that, without being seen by any man apart from Sym Spalding alone, who had brought the deed about, they set ladders to the wall, and all came up undiscovered; they kept themselves secretly in a corner until the night should be over. (95) [They] ordered that the larger part of their men should go in orderly fashion with their lords and hold a place, [while] all the remainder should disperse through the town and take prisoner or kill the men they could overcome. (101) But they soon broke these orders, for as soon as day dawned, two-thirds of their men and more went all over the place through the town. They were so greedy for booty that they ran as if they were demented, seizing houses and killing men. (108) The [Berwick folk] who saw their enemies come upon them so suddenly, raised a cry throughout the town

---

75. Sheriff of Lothian. Probably Edinburgh is meant.

79–80. Moray and Douglas. No other source gives Moray a role, and it is striking that these two play little part (138–39) in the taking of the town in Barbour's narrative. In *RRS5*, 144 there is a serious error: the charter no. 136 is dated at Kelso not Colquhoun. The evidence suggests that Moray was at sieges in Northumberland; Douglas played a leading part in the taking of Berwick.

90. That deed. The date was the night of 2 April, 1318 according to Lanercost. Fordun gives 5 kal. April, 28 March.

107. Slew men. There is a rather different emphasis in (a) Lanercost, note to 23 cont. and (b) the chronicle above, note to 56, cont.:

(a) After the Scots had entered and obtained full possession of the town, they drove out all the English, almost naked and despoiled of their property; nonethless they killed few or none at their entry, except those who resisted them. (*L*, 235; *LT*, 220)

(b) At dawn, with the gates opened, they had James Douglas, who was waiting outside, come in. This James entered the town with such lightness and joy in his heart that he claimed that he had come into the city more cheerfully and affectionately than even paradise. For they despoiled all that they found, and killed those resisting them, throwing the rest into prison. (*Illust. of Scott. Hist.* 5)

And held his spek prevé and still
Quhill the day that wes set him till.
Than of the best of Lothiane
He with hym till his tryst has tane
75 For schyrreff tharoff than wes he.

[*The Scots take the wall of Berwick, but discipline breaks down*]

To Duns Park with his menye
He come at evyn prively,
And syne with a gud cumpany
Sone eftyr come the Erle Thomas
80 That wes met with the lord Douglas.
A rycht fayr cumpany thai war
Quhen thai war met togidder thar,
And quhen the marchell the covyn
To bath the lordis lyne be lyne
85 Had tauld, thai went furth on thar way.
Fer fra the toun thar hors left thai,
To mak it schort sua wrocht thai then
That but seyng off ony men
Outane Sym of Spaldyn allane
90 That gert that deid be undertane
Thai set thar leddrys to the wall,
And but persaving come up all
And held thaim in a nuk prevé
Quhill that the nycht suld passit be,
95 And ordanyt that the maist party
Off thar men suld gang sarraly
With thar lordis and hald a stale,
And the remanand suld all hale
Skaill throu the toun and tak or sla
100 The men that thai mycht ourta.
Bot sone this ordynance brak thai,
For alsone as it dawyt day
The twa partis off thar men and ma
All scalyt throu the toun gan ga.
105 Sa gredy war thai to the gud
That thai ran rycht as thai war woud
And sesyt housis and slew men,
And thai that saw thar fayis then
Cum apon thaim sa suddanly
110 Throu-out the toun thai raissyt the cry

and rushed together here and there. And each time as they
attacked they would stop and put up resistance. (114) If they
had been warned, I know well, they would have sold their
deaths dearly, for they were good men and were far more
[numerous] than those who pursued them, but they were so
dispersed that in no way could they be mustered. (120) There
were two or three big engagements, but the Scotsmen always
fought so well that their enemies were pushed back and finally
so overwhelmed that they one and all turned tail. (125) Some
reached the castle but not all, some slid over the wall, some
were taken [prisoner] at close quarters, and some were killed
in the fighting. (129) They struggled like this until it was
almost noon-day, then those who were in the castle, with
others who had fled there to them, [making] a very large
company, when they saw the banners standing thus plainly,
supported by few, opened the gates soon and issued boldly
against them. (138) Then the worthy Earl Thomas, and the
good lord Douglas too, with the few men who were with
them, met them stoutly with all sorts of weapons. Anyone
who had been near could have seen men fighting boldly.

(144) The Englishmen fought without sparing and with all
their might struggled to drive the Scotsmen back. (147) I
believe they would have done so, *perfay*, for [the Scots] were
fewer than them, had it not been for a new-made knight, who
was called by name Sir William, hailed as of Keith and Galston

---

119. Assemblyt. I have translated as 'mustered', but the sense could be
     'attacked'.

126. Some slid over the wall. Of the town's garrison 24 men-at-arms, 13
     hobelars, 29 balistars and 19 foot archers escaped to Edward II's court.
     See also note to 200. (Soc. Antiq. London MS 121, 64)

150. Sir William Keith of Galston. It is not known how the family acquired
     Galston in Ayrshire. He was a cousin of the marischal, Sir Robert Keith,
     and occurs at 20.501, 601, again in association with Douglas. (*SP6*, 29)

And schot togidder her and thar,
As ay as thai assemblyt war
Thai wald abid and mak debate.
Had thai bene warnyt wele I wate
115   Thai suld haiff sauld thar dedis der
For thai war gud men and thai wer
Fer ma than thai were that thaim socht,
Bot thai war scalyt that thai mocht
On na maner assemblyt be.
120   Thar war gret melleys twa or thre,
Bot Scottismen sa weile thaim bar
That thar fayis ay ruschyt war
And contraryit at the last war sua
That thai haly the bak gan ta,
125   Sum gat the castell bot nocht all
And sum ar slydyn our the wall
And sum war intill handis tane
And sum war intill bargane slane.
On this wis thaim contenyt thai
130   Quhill it wes ner none of the day,
Than thai that in the castell war
And other that fled to thaim thar
That war a rycht gret cumpany
Quhen thai the baneris saw simply
135   Standand and stuffyt with a quhone
Thar yattis haff thai opnyt sone
And ischit on thaim hardely.
Than the Erle Thomas that wes worthi
And the gud lord als of Douglas
140   With the few folk that with thaim was
Met thaim stoutly with wapnys ser.
Thar mycht men se that had bene ner
Men abandoune thaim hardely.

[The town of Berwick falls]

The Inglismen faucht cruelly
145   And with all mychtis gan thaim payn
To rusche the Scottis men agayn.
I trow thai had done sua perfay
For thai war fewar fer than thai
Giff it na had bene a new-mad knycht
150   That till his name Schyr Wilyam hycht,
Off Keyth and off Gallistoun

by differencing of surname, (153) who bore himself so very well that day, putting himself to such great efforts, striking such blows around him, that he pressed where he saw the thickest throng so mightily and fought so forcefully that he made a way for his following. (160) Those who were near by him kept laying into their foes so boldly that they turned tail to a man and went to the castle. They went in at great risk, because they were so hard pressed there that they lost many of the last[-comers]. (167) But those who got in, nonetheless, barred the gates hastily and ran to the walls in haste, for they were not all secure then.

(171) The town was taken like this, by great valour and much initiative, and all the goods that they found there were smartly seized. They found victuals in great profusion, and everything that was for provisioning a town they kept from destruction, then sent word to the king. He was delighted at that news and hurried thither very speedily. (181) As he rode through the country men gathered to him until he had a great force of worthy men. (184) The folk who then dwelt in the Merse, Teviotdale, also in the whole Forest and the east end of Lothian, went to Berwick before the king came, with so stalwart an intent that no-one who dwelt at that time beyond the Tweed dared put in an appearance.

---

180. He sped. But he arrived after the fall of the castle (203). The sequence here is distorted by Barbour's six-day siege (199) which in fact took eleven weeks. Thus King Robert is excluded from the siege, though he dated a charter at Berwick on 12 April. The Harl. 655 chronicle, note to 192, is more reliable.

181-91. Barbour seems to say that the king collected a force as he progressed but that his arrival was anticipated by many inhabitants of the Border hurrying to Berwick to secure it. This duplication may represent two different versions in Barbour's sources. The king issued a proclamation in all towns that anyone with enough substance able and willing to stay in Berwick should go there to receive either a built-on plot, or a plot and 100s. This text fits autumn 1318 well, and is probably what lies behind Barbour's migrant Borderers. (*RRS5*, 560)

He hycht throu difference of sournoune,
That bar him sa rycht weill that day
And put him till sua hard assay
155 And sic dyntis about him dang
That quhar he saw the thikkest thrang
He pressyt with sa mekill mycht
And sua enforslye gan fycht
That he maid till his mengne way,
160 And thai that ner war by him ay
Dang on thar fayis sua hardely
That thai haff tane the bak in hy
And till the castell held the way,
And at gret myscheiff entryt thai
165 For thai war pressyt thar sa fast
That thai fele lesyt of the last.
Bot thai that entryt nocht-forthi
Sparyt thar yattis hastily
And in hy to the wallis ran
170 For thai war nocht all sekyr than.

[*Men flock to Berwick; the castle holds out but eventually surrenders*]

The toun wes takyn on this wis
Throu gret worschip and hey empris,
And all the gud that thai thar fand
Wes sesyt smertly intill hand.
175 Vittaill they fand in gret foysoun
And all that fell to stuff off toun
That kepyt thai fra destroying,
And syn has word send to the king,
And he wes off that tything blyth
180 And sped him thidderwart swith
And as he throu the cuntre raid
Men gaderyt till him quhill he haid
A mekill rout of worthi men,
And the folk that war wonnand then
185 Intill the Mers and Tevidaill
And in the Forest als all hale
And the est end off Lothiane
Befor that the king come ar gane
To Berwik with sa stalwart hand
190 That nane that wes that tyme wonnand
On yond half Tweid durst weil apper.

(192) Those who were in the castle, when they saw their foes gathered in such numbers before them, and [when] they had no hope of being rescued, were cast down to a great extent. But they held the castle for five days sturdily nonetheless, then surrendered it on the sixth day and finally went [back] to their country.

(201) Thus the castle and the town were brought to the Scotsmen's possession; and soon after the king came riding with his force to Berwick, and in the castle he was lodged honourably and well, [with] all his lords near him. The rest went generally to lodge in the town. (210) Then the king took the advice that he should not break down the wall, but should supply the castle and the town, both, well with men, victuals and every other kind of equipment that might help or else be needed to hold a castle or town in war. (217) Walter Steward of Scotland, who was then young and handsome, the king's son-in-law, had such a strong-determination and such a desire to be near at hand to the Marches, that he took Berwick under his care

---

192–99. The castle held out for six days. This is the delay found in the English siege of 1319 (325) and is incorrect: Gray correctly placed the surrender of the castle at the end of June, after 11 weeks. The Wardrobe book shows Edward II sending messengers to it on 11 June and 7 July (p. 60); in May and June no fewer than 10 ships were sent with provisions and a total of 470 men from London, King's Lynn and Newcastle, to attempt the relief of the castle (p. 83). The Harl. 655 chronicle continues from note to 107 (b):

> When King Robert came, they attacked the castle with machines and other instruments, those inside resisting manfully, and when they made little advance, the king of Scotland, realising he could not continue the support (*munitio*) for long, quickly gave up the attack on the castle, which was to be reduced by want and hunger, saying to his men that he was unwilling to ruin himself. The besieged, thereupon suffering from hunger and sending in vain to the king of England, gave up all hope of relief and surrendered the castle, saving life and limb to all within it. They handed over to death the said Peter Spalding, hated by them for asking for the money promised him, after setting up a plot against him [*machinata contra eum prodicione*] for the death of the king of Scotland. The king raised the walls and bulwarks a lot and repaired the castle well. (*Illust. of Scott. Hist.* 5)

Spalding does not occur among those rewarded by the king, suggesting that he was indeed killed, but the chronicle is unclear by whom: 'they' = the garrison; but he asked the Scots for his money.

200. The garrison was evidently allowed to depart. But it must have been kept together, because in early August 1319 it mustered for the invasion

And thai that in the castell wer
Quhen thai thar fayis in sic plente
Saw forouth thaim assemblyt be
195   And had na hop of reskewing
Thai war abaysit in gret thing,
Bot thai the castell nocht-forthi
Held thai fyve dayis sturdely
Syne yauld it on the sext day,
200   And till thar countre syne went thai.

[*The king plans to hold Berwick; Walter Stewart given command there; the garrison and its arms*]

Thus wes the castell and the toun
Till Scottis mennys possessioun
Brocht, and sone eftre he king
Come ridand with his gadering
205   To Berwik, and in the castell
He wes herbrid bath fayr and weill
And all his lordis him by,
The remanand commonaly
Till herbry till the toun ar gane.
210   The king has then to consaill tan
That he wald nocht brek doun the wall
Bot castell and the toun witthall
Stuff weill with men and with vittaill
And alkyn other apparaill
215   That mycht availe or ellis myster
To hald castell or toun off wer,
And Walter Stewart of Scotland
That than wes young and avenand
And sone-in-laucht wes to the king
220   Haid sa gret will and sic yarnyng
Ner-hand the marchis for to be
That Berwik to yemsell tuk he,

---

of Scotland at 19 arbelasters and 120 foot archers. By 10 September
this had changed to 44 arbelasters and 98 archers. In April 1320 10
disabled archers of the garrison were sent to religious houses. (PRO
E101/378/4 fo. 35r; BL Add. MS 17632, fo. 4)

217–24. Walter Stewart. This (and 233–38) is preparing the ground for
Barbour's version of the 1319 siege, when he claims that Stewart
commanded in the town. In royal charters dated at Berwick (12 April,
1318, 25 March, 1319) Stewart is a witness, otherwise only at the Scone
parliament (December 1318).

and received from the king the town [with] castle and donjon.
(225) The king had men of great nobility ride into England to
loot, [and they] brought out a great quantity of cattle; he gave
a truce to some countries for victuals, which he had brought
smartly in great profusion to the town so that both town and
castle were well provided for a year or more. (233) The good
Steward of Scotland then sent for his friends and his men until
he had with him, apart from archers, spearmen and crossbow-
men, five hundred strong and worthy men who bore ancestral
arms. (239) He also had John Crab a Fleming who was of
such great skill in designing and making apparatus to defend
and to attack a war-castle or a city, that none more able could
be found. He had engines and cranes made and provided
Greek fire also; he provided plenty of springalds and shots of
different kinds that suited defending a castle. (250) But he
had no engines for 'bangs' for in Scotland at that time the use
of them had doubtless not been seen yet. (253) When the town
had been provided for in the way I describe here, the noble
king took his way riding towards Lothian. Walter Stewart, who
was brave, remained with his force in Berwick, and gave firm
orders for apparatus for defence in case men attacked.
(261) When the king of England had been told how with
determination Berwick had been taken, and then provided for

225-27. Ride into England. Barbour does not say who (?Moray) led this
raid far into Yorkshire, after reprisals on Hartlepool. Richmond was
probably ransomed, Ripon paid 1,000 marks, Fountains abbey paid up,
Knaresborough was ravaged and the forest thereof searched for towns-
folk and their cattle; then the force crossed the Pennines and returned
by an unknown route, having achieved a combination of devastation
and blackmail; according to Lanercost the expedition brought back 'a
herd of cattle beyond counting'. The purpose was doubtless to reduce
English capacity in the north, and raise money and provisions for
Berwick, as Barbour (229-32) implies. See the forthcoming work by
Colm McNamee.

228. Trewit, in C. E has 'tholyt', meaning either 'took toll [tribute] from'
or 'spared'. McDairmid also suggests 'tretyt' as an emendation, meaning
that he negotiated with foreign countries; this is far-fetched. (*B1985*, 64,
101)

239. John Crab, a Fleming, see note to 434.

245-50. In this list, engine seems to mean mangonel and trebuchet (heavy
catapults), Greek fire was a combustible substance to which no further
reference is made, springald was a large crossbow; for guns cf. 19.399.

261. For the English siege of Berwick in 1319 there is an account in J.
R. Maddicott, *Thomas of Lancaster*, ch. 7, which did not have the benefit
of the account in *Anonimalle Chronicle, 1307-33*, ed. W. R. Childs and
J. Taylor, (1991) 96.

And resavit of the king the toun
And the castell and the dongeoun.
225 The king gert men of gret noblay
Ryd intill Ingland for to pray
That brocht out gret plente of fe,
And sum contreis trewyt he
For vittaill, that in gret foysoun
230 He gert bring smertly to the toun
Sua that bath castell and toun war
Well stuffyt for a yer and mar.
The gud Stewart off Scotland then
Send for his frendis and his men
235 Quhill he had with him, but archeris
And but burdouris and awblasteris,
Fyve hunder men wycht and worthi
That bar armys of awncestry.
Jhone Crab a Flemyng als had he
240 That wes of sa gret sutelté
Till ordane and mak apparaill
For to defend and till assaill
Castell of wer or than cité
That nane sleyar mycht fundyn be.
245 He gert engynys and cranys ma
And purvayit Grec fyr alsua,
Spryngaldis and schot on ser maneris
That to defend castellis afferis
He purvayit intill full gret wane,
250 Bot gynnys for crakys had he nane
For in Scotland yeit than but wene
The us of thaim had nocht bene sene.
Quhen the toun apon this wis
Was stuffyt as Ik her divis
255 The nobill king his way has tane
And riddyn towart Lowthiane,
And Walter Stewart that wes stout
Be-left at Berwik with his rout
And ordanyt fast for apparaill
260 To defend giff men wald assail.

[Edward II comes to besiege Berwick with land and sea forces]

Quhen to the king of Ingland
Was tauld how that with stalwart hand
Berwik wes tane and stuffyt syn

with men, victuals and arms, he was greatly angered, had his council meet hastily and took the advice that he should lead his army there and with all the resources that he could muster lay siege to the town; (271) and [that he should] have them so strongly entrenched that as long as they chose to remain [there] they should be that much the safer. If the men of the country wished to attack them with a large force of men, fighting them at their trenches, [the English] would be at a great advantage, though all Scots would be very foolish to attack in warfare so strong a force in his trenches. (281) When he had taken counsel to this effect, he had his army mustered all together from far and near. He had a great host with him then. Earl Thomas of Lancaster, who later became a saint, as men say, was there in his company, and also all the earls in England who were capable of fighting and very powerful barons too, he had with him for that siege. (292) He had ships bring by sea shot and other gear with a generous provision of victuals. He came to Berwick with all his following,

271. Gert dik thame. It is clear from what follows that it is the English who were protected by trenches, but this 'plan' seems to be far from the truth. The *Vita Edwardi* implies that attack on Berwick was decided when the army was near there; although there were ditchers, carpenters and other tradesmen with the army, siege engines and trench-diggers were sent for *after* the siege began (BL, Add. MS. 17362, fo. 20v, 23; *CDS3,663*). The most extraordinary (and unremarked) feature of this expedition is that large supplies were brought by ship from England and sent back still laden at the end of the siege. Seven ships from London brought timber for a peel, and another brought a 'wooden peel of the king', none of which left the ships. Edward II was well aware that no Scottish castle was tenable, and that he would have to provide his own fortifications when he advanced into Scotland, as he clearly intended to do. (BL, Add. MS 17362, fos. 25–27)

283–84. A great host. Edward II summoned 22,600 infantry plus 2,000 from the earl of Lancaster, rather more than in 1314, but from the northern counties and Wales only; protections were issued for about 700 cavalry. Maddicott, *Lancaster*, 244 relies on *CDS3, 668* (which does not include cavalry), showing 8080 men paid (1,040 hobelars, the rest infantry); these figures are those mustering at Newcastle before Scotland was entered. Working from a clearer version of this account (PRO E101/15/27), I have calculated that the infantry paid for service from 10 September, i.e. early in the siege, was about 5,500, including 436 hobelars. Phillips (*Aymer de Valence*, 184) using the Wardrobe book E101/378/4, puts the total at about 12,600 plus 1,400 cavalry. This, I think, accepts the hopelessly overstated figures for troops leaving their home counties. Again I have taken the figures paid from 10 September in this source, showing 5,467 infantry including 456 hobelars, and cavalry of 1,340. The two records therefore are in close agreement about

       With men and vittaill and armyn

265   He wes anoyit gretumly

       And gert assermbill all halely

       His consaill, and has tane to reid

       That he hys ost will thidder leid

       And with all mycht that he mycht get

270   To the toune ane assege set,

       And gert dyk thaim sa stalwartly

       That quhill thaim likyt thar to ly

       Thai suld fer out the traister be.

       And gif the men of the contré

275   With strenth of men wald thaim assaill

       At thar dykis into bataill

       Thai suld avantage have gretly,

       Thocht all Scottis for gret foly

       War till assaill into fechting

280   At hys dykis sa stark a thing.

       Quhen this consaill on this maner

       Wes tane he gert bath fer and ner

       Hys ost haly assemblyt be,

       Ane gret folk than with him had he.

285   Off Longcastell the Erle Thomas

       That syne wes sanct as men sayis

       In his cumpany wes thar

       And all the erllys that als war

       In Ingland worthi for to fycht,

290   And baronys als of mekill mycht

       With him to that assege had he,

       And gert his schippis by the se

       Bring schot and other apparaill

       And gret warnysone of vittaill.

295   To Berwik with all his menye

---

the infantry, and show that while some 8,080 turned up in late August, on 10 September this had shrunk to 5,500, a quarter of the 22,600 summoned. One thousand, two hundred of the shrinkage, however, was deliberate: Harcla brought 980 archers and 354 hobelars from Cumberland up to 9 September, but from 10 September his contingent numbered 32 and 38 respectively; presumably the 1,200 were sent to Carlisle to cut off Moray's retreat from Yorkshire. Some further allowance at Berwick (?500–1,000) must be made for Lancaster's contingent, which was not paid by the king.

285–89. Lancaster, the earls and barons. This was the first and last campaign of Lancaster with Edward II. Arundel, Hereford, Pembroke, Warenne and major barons all served. On Lancaster see note to 852.

with forces arrayed, assigning to the great lords, each one
severally, a field for their quarters. (299) Then you could see
tents of various kinds being quickly erected, so numerous that
they made a town there bigger than were both town and castle.
Then, on the other side, on the sea, the ships came in such
numbers, with victuals, arms and men, [so] that the whole
harbour was filled then. (307) When those who were in the
town saw their foes come sturdily by land and sea in such
numbers, they prepared like bold and worthy men to defend
their place, [so] that they would put themselves at risk of
death or of driving their enemies back. (314) For their captain
treated them [very] affectionately, and moreover the greater
part of those who bore arms with him were of his blood and
near kin to him, or else were his allies. Men could see [that
they were] of such morale and of such excellent bearing that
none of them was discouraged. (323) In daytime they were
well armed and by night kept a good watch. They stayed like
that for a good six days during which there was no major
engagement.

(327) At this time of which I'm speaking,

295-96. The army arrived before Berwick on 7 September, 1319.

303-6. According to the *Vita Edwardi*, 'By sea the sailors in charge of the
Cinque Ports fleet watched the entrances and exits so that no-one at
all could get out.' But the *Vita* is poorly informed about the land siege.

314-19. The captain was Walter Stewart. Barbour does not give the name
of any of his supposed relatives; the Stewarts of Bonkill were close to
Berwick.

325. Six days. This would place the assault on 13 September, the day of
the second attack. But Barbour is describing the first attack on 8
September.

327. The main English narratives are in (a) Lanercost and (b) Anonimalle:
(a) [Edward II and Lancaster] entered Scotland about the feast of the
Assumption [15 August] and positioned themselves to assault the town
of Berwick; they almost scaled the wall at the first assault, and when
many of those on the wall saw this, they fled to the castle, but
afterwards, when the English acted more slackly, those inside re-
covered their courage and defended themselves manfully, manning
the walls better than before and burning the sow which had been
brought to the wall to undermine it. (*L*, 239; *LT*, 226)
(b) [The English] arrived at Berwick with trumpets blowing and spent
the night in great joy and pleasure and music, in contempt of their
Scottish enemies who were inside the town. But the Scots shouted
at our people foully and hideously and climbed on to the walls and
defended it honourably against the English. On the day of the
Assumption of Our Lady [15 August] the king and the lords of the
land and their folk launched a great attack on the town but could

With his bataillis arayit come he,
And till gret lordis ilkane sindry
Ordanyt a feld for thar herbry.
Than men mycht sone se pailyounys
300 Be stentyt of syndry fassounys
That thai a toune all sone maid thar
Mar than bath toun and castell war.
On other half syne on the se
The schippis come in sic plenté
305 With vittaill armyng and with men
That all the havyn wes stoppyt then.
And quhen thai that war in the toun
Saw thar fayis in sic foysoun
Be land and se cum sturdely,
310 Thai as wycht men and rycht worthi
Schup thaim to defend thar steid
That thai in aventur of deid
Suld put thaim or than rusch agane
Thar fayis, for thar capitane
315 Tretyt thaim sa luflely,
And thar-with-all the mast party
Off thaim that armyt with him wer
War of his blud and sib him ner,
Or ellis war his elye.
320 Off sic confort men mycht thaim se
And of sa rycht far contenyng
As nane of thaim had abaysing.
On dayis armyt weill war thai
And on the nycht wele walkyt ay,
325 Weill sex dayis sua thai abaid
That na full gret bargane haid.

[*The English assault the town by land*]

Intill this tyme that I tell her

---

accomplish nothing. The king had siege engines sent up from North-
ampton and Bamburgh, and had them drawn up against the walls of
the said town of Berwick, and caused much injury to those who were
inside the town. Those on the seaward side had moored their ships
to the walls of the said town and delivered a much more vigorous
assault than they had previously done, and [the Scots] fought most
bitterly with the king's fleet on the seaward side. The English defended
themselves so honourably against their Scottish enemies that these
had neither the resources nor the stamina to hold their ground. The

when they were without fighting, the Englishmen had so
enclosed their army with trenches which they maid, that they
were greatly strengthened. Then with all hands busy, they got
ready with their gear to attack [the folk] of the town. (335)
On the eve of the feast which men call the nativity of our lady
Mary, who bore the birth that bought [us] all, early in the
morning, men could see the English host arming itself with
speed, displaying banners bravely and mustering at their ban-
ners with implements of various kinds, like scaffolds, ladders,
covering, pikes, hoes, and long slings. (345) Each lord and
his section was assigned [the place] where he would attack.
Those within, when they saw that company range themselves
thus in battle-order, they went in haste to their sectors, which
were thoroughly provided with stones, shot and other things
needed for the defence; in that position they awaited their
foes who were to attack them. (355) When those outside were
ready, they quickly sounded the assault, and each man with
his gear went to attack where he should be. Archers had been
assigned to shoot at each embrasure that was there. (361)
When they were ready in this way, they went swiftly toward
the town, filling ditches very hurriedly, then going to the wall
boldly with ladders that they had. But those who were above
on the wall made such strong defence that they often made
ladders and the men on them tumble flat to the ground. (370)
Then in a short spell you could see

English were at this time on the point of conquering the town easily
without making a further attack, if certain lords of the land had not
been [*verb missing*].

These two sources share an error of date, evidently the Assumption (15
August) for the Nativity (8 September). It is clear that there were two
attacks, and that the first, on 8 September, achieved little for lack of
assault towers. This agrees with Barbour's version (355-490), also in
including an attack by ships, when the engineer was taken prisoner
(434, 468).

335. Our Lady's eve. 7 September, 1319. This was the date of arrival,
not of assault.

That thai withoutyn bargayne wer
The Inglismen sa clossyt had
330 Thar ost with dykis that thai maid
That thai war strenthit gretumly.
Syne with all handis besely
Thai schup thaim with thair apparaill
Thaim of the toun for till assaill,
335 And of our ladys evyn Mary
That bar the byrth that all gan by
That men callis hyr nativité
Sone in the mornyng men mycht se
The Inglis ost arme thaim in hy
340 And display baneris sturdely,
And assembill to thar baneris
With instrumentis of ser maneris
As scaffoldis leddris and covering
Pikkys, howis and with staff-slyng.
345 Till ilk lord and his bataill
Wes ordanyt quhar he suld assaill.
And thai within, quhen that thai saw
That mengne raung thaim sua on raw
Till thar wardis thai went in hy
350 That war stuffyt rycht stalwartly
With stanys and schot and other thing
That nedyt to thar defending,
And into sic maner abaid
Thair fayis that till assail thaim maid.
355 Quhen thai without war all redy
Thai trumpyt till asalt in hy,
And ilk man with his apparaill
Quhar he suld be went till assaill,
Till ilk kyrnell that war thar
360 Archeris to schut assignyt war,
And quhen on this wys thai war boun
Thai went in hy towart the toun
And fillyt the dykis hastily,
Syne to the wall rycht hardely
365 Thai went with leddris that thai haid.
Bot thai sa gret defend has maid
That war abovyne apon the wall
That oft leddris and men with-all
Thai gert fall flatlingis to the ground,
370 That men mycht se in a litill stound

men assaulting very boldly, setting up ladders doughtily, and some attacking on ladders. But those who were on the wall there exposed themselves to any danger till their foes had been knocked down. (377) In great peril they defended their town, for, to be perfectly frank, the walls of the town were then so low that a man with a spear [on the ground] could hit another above in the face. The shooting there was so intense that it was remarkable to watch. (384) Walter Stewart with a following kept riding about to see where there was the greatest necessity for help, and where men pressed hardest he gave succour to his [own men] who needed it. The great force which was outside had surrounded the town, so that no part of it was accessible. (392) You could see the attackers there risk themselves very bravely and the defenders struggled doughtily with all their might to turn back their foes by force. (397) They continued like this till after noon of the day had passed. (399) Then those who were in the ships, ordered a well-rigged ship to come with all her gear right [up] to the wall in order to attack. They drew their boat with a lot of armed men in it to the middle [of things], having a bridge to let fall down from their boat on to the wall. (407) They rowed in barges beside her and exerted themselves hard to tow her by the Brighouse to the wall; they all set themselves to that purpose. They brought her till she came very close;

379–80. The low walls. Repeated at 729–32. Presumably a deduction from the later heightening of the walls by Robert I (939–40). Edward I had begun the construction of a stone wall around the town in 1296, but it is by no means certain that it lacked a stone wall before that.

384–85. Walter Stewart rode about. This is the first occurrence of a tactic which is repeated twice by Barbour during the siege. I suspect that in his sources there was only an account of Walter's final circuit, leading to the defence of the Mary gate.

409. The Brighouse. In 1316 Robert I tried to take Berwick 'by land and sea on the waterside between the Brighouse and the castle, where the wall was not yet built' (Lanercost). Here the English row past the Brighouse to the wall. The Brighouse was surely not part of a drawbridge arrangement (*B1909*, 468) but the northern end of the (presumably dismantled) bridge over the Tweed.

Men assailand hardely
Dressand up leddris douchtely
And sum on leddris pressand war.
Bot thai that on the wall war thar
375 Till all perellis gan abandoun
Thaim till thar fayis war dongyn doun.
At gret myscheff defendyt thai
Thar toun, for, giff we suth sall say,
The wallis of the toun than wer
380 Sa law that a man with a sper
Mycht stryk ane other up in the face,
And the schot alsa thik thar was
That it war wondre for to se.
Walter Stewart with a menye
385 Raid ay about for to se quhar
That for to help mast myster war,
And quhar men presit mast he maid
Succour till his that myster haid.
The mekill folk that wes without
390 Haid enveronyt the toun about
Sua that na part of it wes fre.
Thar mycht men the assailiaris se
Abandoun thaim rycht hardely,
And the defendouris douchtely
395 With all thar mychtis gan thaim payn
To put thar fayis with force agayn.

[The assault by sea; it fails, and an engineer is taken prisoner]

On this wis thaim contenyt thai
Quhill none wes passit off the day,
Than thai that in the schippis wer
400 Ordanyt a schip with full gret fer
To cum with all hyr apparaill
Rycht to the wall for till assaill.
Till myd-mast up thar bat thai drew
With armyt men tharin inew,
405 A brig thai had for to lat fall
Rycht fra the bat apon the wall,
With bargis by hir gan thai row
And pressyt thaim rycht fast to tow
Hyr by the brighous to the wall,
410 On that entent thai set thaim all.
Thai brocht hyr quhill scho come well ner,

then you could see in their different ways, some men defend-
ing, some attacking, intently [and] with great effort. (415) The
[folk] of the town bore themselves so well, dealing with the
shipmen so that there was no way that they could bring the
ship close enough to the wall so that their drop-bridge could
come close to it, whatever they did, good or ill, as long as
she was left on the shore; then in a little space men could see
that those in her were in a far worse condition than they were
before. (425) When the tide had so ebbed that men could go
dry-shod to her, a very large force issued out of the town to
her and quickly set fire to her. In a short while they had done
[enough] to have her burned [up] by fire. (432) Some who
were in her were killed, some fled and got away. They took
an engineer who was the best at that craft that men knew
[of], far or near; then they went [back] into the town. (438)
They were fortunate that they got in so quickly, for a very
large company came up by the sea when they saw the ship
was burning. But before they arrived, the others had gone
through the gate and barred it right fast. (445) Those [English]
folk attacked hard that day, [while] those within defended
always in such a way that those who were assaulting with
great force there could in no way achieve their aim. When
evensong-time was near, the men outside who were tired,
some very badly wounded, saw those inside defend themselves
like this, and saw that it was not [going to be] easy to take

---

426. Dry must be an exaggeration.

434. An engineer. This man was taken at the ship (468), but was very
gifted with siege engines. He is nowhere named but surely was none
other than John Crab, the Fleming (above 239) who was also a shipman
and an engineer, and of whom Edward II complained bitterly to the
Count of Flanders after the siege. Both were the most gifted at their
craft, according to Barbour. The unnamed engineer was threatened
into manning an engine (why, if Crab was nearby?) which demolished
the sow (662–701) and immediately thereafter Crab, who had had a
crane placed on the walls and prepared bundles of faggots (607–24),
used these (702–5) to burn the sow (in Lanercost it is burned).

There were two sources for these events, in one of which the engineer
was named Crab and the sow burned, in the other anonymous and the
sow smashed. The former represents an early and correct version of
events; the latter is a distorted version recorded after Crab changed
sides in 1333 and helped Edward III to take Berwick; it is likely to have
come from the account of the wars collected and written (?for Moray)
after 1329, the 'chronicles' of Robert I. Lines 465–70 show that Barbour
put these two versions together.

441. Up by the sea. Meaning 'on the sea' or 'beside the sea' ?

Than mycht men se on seir maner
Sum men defend and sum assaill
Full besyly with gret travaill.
415 Within sa stoutly thai thaim bar
That the schipmen sa handlyt war
That thai the schip on na maner
Mycht ger to cum the wall sa ner
That thar fall-brig mycht neych thartill
420 For oucht thai mycht gud or ill,
Quhill that scho ebbyt on the grund,
Than mycht men in a litill stound
Se thaim be fer of wer covyn
Than thai war er that war hyr in.
425 And quhen the se wes ebbyt sua
That men all dry mycht till hyr ga,
Out off the toun ischit in hy
Till hyr a weill gret cumpany
And fyr till hyr has keyndlyt son.
430 Into schort tyme sua haif thai done
That thai in fyr has gert hyr bryn
And sum war slayn that war hyr in
And sum fled and away ar gane.
Ane engynour thar haif thai tane
435 That wes sleast of that myster
That men wist ony fer or ner,
Intill the toun syne entryt thai.
It fell thaim happily perfay
That thai gat in sa hastily
440 For thar come a gret cumpany
In full gret hy up by the se
Quhen thai the schip saw brynnand be,
Bot or thai come, the tother war past
The yat and barryt it rycht fast.
445 That folk assaylyt fast that day,
And thai within defendyt ay
On sic a wis that thai that war
With gret enforce assailland thar
Mycht do thar will on na maner.
450 And quhen that evynsang tym wes ner
The folk without that war wery
And sum woundyt full cruelly
Saw thaim within defend thaim sua,
And saw it wes nocht eyth to ta

the town as long as such a defence was made by those who
had it under control. (457) [When] the host saw that their
ship had been burned, some of those in it lost, their folk
wounded and tired, they had the retreat sounded in haste.
After the shipmen were driven back, they did not allow the
other [ships] to attack any more, for they had all expected
that they would take the town by [that] ship. (465) Men say
that more ships than this tried to take the town at that time;
but because only one was burned, and the engineer was taken
in it, I previously made mention of one ship alone.

(471) When they had sounded the retreat, those men who
had suffered heavily withdrew altogether from the wall; they
all gave up the assault. (475) Those inside who were weary,
and many of them badly wounded, were heartened and cheer-
ful when they saw their foes withdraw like that. Because they
knew that in fact they were going to their tents, [the Scots]
set good watches on their wall, then they all went to their
quarters and, wearied, took their ease. (484) Others who were
badly wounded, had good leeches, I know, to help them as
best they could. Both sides were tired, [and] that night they
did no more, *perfay*. They were quiet for five days after that,
neither doing much harm to the other.

(491) Now let us leave the folk lying quietly here, as I have
described, and turn the direction of our discourse to Sir
Robert, the doughty king,

465-70. Men say. This passage is surely second thoughts arising from a
conflict in the sources.

489. Five days. Five days from 8 September indicates 13 September for
the second assault. See notes to 325 and 594.

494-588. The Chapter of Mytoun. The *Vita Edwardi* has a long story,
found elsewhere, that Douglas planned this expedition in order to
capture the English queen at York, that a spy was captured and betrayed
the plot; the archbishop sent the queen to safety at Nottingham and
on the next day fought the Scots. (*VitaEd*, 95-96)

455 The toun quhill sic defens wes mad,
     And thai that intill stering had
     The ost saw that thar schip war brynt
     And of thaim that tharin wes tynt,
     And thar folk woundyt and wery,
460 Thai gert blaw the retreit in hy.
     Fra the schipmen rebotyt war
     Thai lete the tother assaill no mar,
     For throu the schip thai wend ilkan
     That thai the toun wele suld haf tane.
465 Men sayis that ma schippis than sua
     Pressyt that tym the toun to ta,
     Bot for that thar wes brynt bot ane
     And the engynour tharin wes tane
     Her-befor mencioun maid I
470 Bot off a schip allanerly.

[*The English withdraw from the walls; King Robert invades
England, ravaging*]

     Quhen that thai blawyn had the retret
     Thar folk that tholyt had paynys gret
     Withdrew thaim haly fra the wall,
     The assalt have thai left all.
475 And thai within that wery war
     And mony of thaim woundyt sar
     War blyth and glaid quhen that thai saw
     Thar fayis on that wis thaim withdraw,
     And fra thai wyst suthly that thai
480 Held to thar pailyounys thar way
     Set gud wachys to thar wall,
     Syne till thar innys went thai all
     And essyt thaim that wery war,
     And other that had woundis sar
485 Had gud lechys forsuth Ik hycht
     That helpyt thaim as thai best mycht.
     On athyr sid wery war thai,
     That nycht thai did no mar perfay.
     Fyve dayis eftyr thai war still
490 That nane till other did mekill ill.
     Now leve we thir folk her lyand
     All still as Ik have borne on hand
     And turne the cours of our carping
     To Schyr Robert the douchty king,

who gathered a host [from] both far and near, when he discovered without doubt that the king of England had besieged Berwick with a firm grip, where Walter Stewart was. (500) He formed a plan with his men that he would not so soon attack the king of England in battle, especially at his trenches, for that could well be foolish. (505) Therefore he ordered two lords, one the earl of Moray, the other the lord Douglas, to go with fifteen thousand men to England, to burn and kill, and make such destruction there that those who were besieging the town, when they heard of the harrying, would go [back] to England, (514) so fearful and alarmed for their children and their wives, who, they feared, could lose their lives and their goods too, which they dreaded would be carted off, that they would leave the siege quickly, going to rescue hastily their goods, their friends and their land. (522) Therefore, as I have explained, he sent those lords forth swiftly, and they took their way rapidly burning and killing in England, doing such great harm there, as they plundered the country, that it was heart-breaking for any who wished it well to see, for they destroyed everything as they went.

(531) They rode so long, destroying like that as they went to and fro, that they came to Ripon and destroyed that town altogether. Then they took up quarters at Boroughbridge

509. To burn and slay, repeated at 525–30. Lanercost agrees, but destruction seems to have begun when the Scots could no longer move secretly. The *Flores Historiarum* say that the Scots were led clandestinely by difficult ways to near York by a traitor, Sir Edmund Darel, in pursuance of an intention to capture the records of the bench and exchequer (!) and the queen, who fled to Nottingham. Gray says that the Scots entered England by Carlisle, and they seem to have done so about the beginning of September or end of August, so the expedition was not prompted by the siege of Berwick and may well have been planned for the purpose given by the *Flores*.

535. Boroughbridge and Mytoun. The battle took place on 12 September, 1319. (a) Lanercost and (b) the *Vita Edwardi* describe the armies:

(a) Moray ... and Douglas not daring to encounter the king of England and the earl, entered England with an army, burning the land and taking booty, and so went to Boroughbridge. When the citizens of York heard of this, without knowledge of the country folk, led by the archbishop of York ... with a great number of priests ... met the Scots after dinner one day next the village of Myton, 12 miles north of York, but they came like men unused to war, all scattered through the fields, not in one body. (*L*, 239; *LT*, 226)

(b) [The men from York] came out stealthily to take the enemy by surprise ... but they were warned and did not flee, for when they saw (*contd p. 644*)

495   That assemblyt bath fer and ner
       Ane ost quhen that he wist but wer
       That the king sua of Ingland
       Had assegyt with stalwart hand
       Berwik quhar Walter Stewart was.
500   To purpose with his men he tais
       That he wald nocht sua sone assaile
       The king of Ingland with bataill
       And at his dykis specially,
       For that moucht weill turne to foly.
505   Tharfor he ordanyt lordis twa,
       The erle of Murreff wes ane of tha
       The tother wes the lord of Douglas
       With fyften thousand men to pas
       In Ingland for to bryn and sla
510   And sua gret ryote thar to ma
       That thai that lay segeand the toun
       Quhen thai hard the destructioun
       That thai suld intill Ingland ma,
       Suld be sua dredand and sua wa
515   For thar childer and for thar wiffis
       That thai suld drede to lese the lyvis,
       And thar gudis alsua that thai
       Suld dreid than suld be had away,
       Thai suld leve thar sege in hy
520   And wend to reskew hastily
       Thar gud thar frendis and thar land.
       Tharfor, as Ik haf born on hand,
       Thir lordis send he furth in hy
       And thai thar way tuk hastily
525   And in Ingland gert bryn and sla,
       And wrocht tharin sa mekill wa
       As thai forrayit the countre
       That it wes pite for to se
       Till thaim that wald it ony gud,
530   For thai destroyit all as thai yhud.

[*The battle at Myton-on-Swale*]

       Sua lang thai raid destroyand sua
       As thai traversyt to and fra
       That thai ar cummyn to Repoun
       And destroyit haly that toun,
535   At Borowbrig syne thar herbry

and at nearby Myton. (537) When the men of that country
saw their land being so destroyed, they gathered in great haste,
archers, burghers and yeomanry, priests, clerks, monks, friars,
husbandmen and men of all crafts, until they had gathered
together a good twenty thousand men and more; they had
very good arms a-plenty. (546) They made the archbishop of
York their captain, and decided that they would attack in
open battle the Scotsmen who were then far fewer than they
were. (551) Then he displayed his banner, and other bishops
who were there also had banners unfurled. They set forth all
in one army the direct way toward Myton. When the Scotsmen
heard news that they were coming near to them, they got
ready in their best fashion and divided themselves into two
forces. (560) Douglas took the vanguard, and Earl Thomas
took the rear, for he was commander of the army. Drawn up
like that in good order, they went towards their foes. When
each could see the other, both sides pressed [forward] to fight.
(567) The Englishmen came on in close order with good,
hardy bearing, in one front, with a banner, until their enemies
came so close that they could easily make out their faces.
There could well have been three spear-lengths between them,
I'm sure, when such panic seized them that suddenly, without
more ado, they all turned tail and fled. (576) When the
Scotsmen saw them all fleeing [on] their way in such a funk,
they swiftly threw themselves upon them

---

our men advancing in disorder, they said, 'These are not soldiers but
huntsmen; they won't do much.' So the Scots set fire to a large
amount of hay gathered in that place, and the smoke arose, spread
widely in the air, making it difficult for our men to see, so that they
found prepared for battle those whom they thought had fled. They
were indeed men chosen from the whole of Scotland for their ability
to fight, ready for every task. Our men however were untrained in
the art of war, readier to flee than fight. (*VitaEd*, 96)

552. Other bishops. Only the bishop of Ely, royal treasurer.

556–75. The Scottish army in two divisions. Again Barbour seems to have
tailored information to provide Douglas with an independent command.
The Scots probably remained in one division under Moray (562), as
Lanercost biblically describes:

When the Scots saw men rushing to fight against them, they came
together (*conglobati*) in one schiltron, and having done so, all together,
they gave a mighty shout, terrifying the English, who, when they heard
it, at once turned to flight.

Thai tuk and at Mytoun tharby.
And quhen the men of that countre
Saw thar land sua destroyit be
Thai gaderyt into full gret hy
540 Archeris burges and yhumanry
Preystis clerkys monkis and freris
Husbandis and men of all maneris
Quhill that thai samyn assemblit war
Wele twenty thousand men and mar,
545 Rycht gud armys inew thai had.
The archebyschop of York thai mad
Thar capitane, and to consaill
Has tane that thai in plane bataill
Wald assaill the Scottismen
550 That fewar than thai war then.
Than he displayit his baner
And other byschappis that thar wer
Gert display thar baneris alsua,
All in a rout furth gan thai ga
555 Towart Mytoun the redy way.
And quhen the Scottismen hard say
Thai war to thaim cummand ner
Thai buskyt thaim on thar best maner
And delyt thaim in bataillis twa,
560 Douglas the avaward gan ma,
The rerward maid Erle Thomas
For chyftane of the ost he was
And sua ordanyt in gud aray
Towart thar fayis thai held thar way.
565 Quhen athyr had on other sycht
Thai pressyt on bath half to the fycht.
The Inglismen come rycht sadly
With gud contenance and hardy
Rycht in a frusch with thar baner
570 Quhill thar fayis come sa ner
That thai thar visag mycht se,
Thre sper lenth I trow weill mycht be
Betwix thaim, quhen sic abasing
Tuk thaim that but mar in a swyng
575 Thai gaff the bak all and to-ga.
Quhen the Scottismen had sene thaim sua
Effrayitly fle all thar way
In gret hy apon thaim schot thai

and killed and took prisoner a large number. The rest fled in a panic as best they could to find a refuge. (582) They were pursued so closely that nearly a thousand died there; of these a good three hundred were priests, who died in that pursuit. So that encounter was called the Chapter of Myton, because so many priests were killed there.

(589) When these folk had been defeated like that, and the Scots had given up the pursuit, they went further in the land, slaying, destroying and burning, [while] those who were at the siege, before the fifth day had passed, had made various apparatus to go to the attack afterwards. (597) They made a sow of great timbers that had a strong covering above, with plenty of armed men inside; also implements for mining. Moreover they made various scaffolds which were markedly higher than the wall, and ordered also that the town should be well attacked from the sea. (605) Those inside, seeing them so busy making so much equipment, on the advice of Crab, who was smart, had a crane raised up high, running on wheels so that they could bring it close to where there was need for help. (611) They also took pitch and tar, flax, oakum, brimstone, and dry timber which would burn well; they mixed each with the others and made great faggots of them, bound by broad iron bands. The quantity of those faggots could have been measured at a great tun.

576–83. The flight. Lanercost's version continues:

> So the Scots divided their schiltrum in which they were united, mounted their horses and followed the English, killing clergy and laity, so that about 4,000 died ... and about 1,000, it was said, were drowned in the River Swale. If night had not fallen scarcely one Englishmen would have escaped; many were taken alive, carried off to Scotland and afterwards ransomed for a fat sum. (*L*, 239; *LT*, 226–27)

594. The fifth day. The assault would follow on the sixth day (by inclusive reckoning 13 September), at dawn (634).

601–2. Scaffaldis. These would be siege towers or berfrays, but they do not occur later in the narrative.

618. E has 'townys', C 'tunnys'. The tun was a barrel for transport of liquid, and since taxation of wine was per tun, it tended to grow larger with time. Something between 700 and 1,000 litres (about 1.5 m high by 1m diam.) has been suggested for the fourteenth century; a 'great tun' does not seem to have been an official measure, so Barbour probably meant 'of the largest size'.

And slew and tuk a gret party,
580   The laiff fled full effrayitly
As thai best moucht to sek warand.
Thai chassyt sa ner at hand
That ner a thousand deyt thar.
Off thaim yet thre hunder war
585   Preystis that deyt in that chas,
Tharfor that bargane callit was
The chaptur of Mytone for thar
Slayn sa mony prestis war.

[*The men in Berwick prepare engines, the English a sow; a second English assault*]

Quhen this folk thus discomfyt was
590   And Scottismen had left the chas
Thai went thaim forthward in the land
Slayand sua and destroyand,
And thai that at the sege lay
Or it wes passyt the fyft day
595   Had maid thaim syndry apparal
To gang eftsonys till assaill.
Off gret gestis a sow thai maid
That stalwart heildyne aboun it had
With armyt men inew tharin
600   And instrumentis for to myne,
Syndry scaffaldis thai maid withall
That war weill heyar than the wall,
And ordanyt als that be the se
The toun suld weill assaillyt be.
605   Thai within that saw thaim sua
Sua gret apparaill schap to ma
Throu Crabys consaill that wes sley
A crane thai haiff gert dres up hey
Rynnand on quheillis that thai mycht bring
610   It quhar that nede war of helping,
And pyk and ter als haiff thai tane
And lynt and herdis and brynstane
And dry treyis that weill wald brin
And mellyt ather other in,
615   And gret fagaldis tharoff thai maid
Gyrdyt with irne bandis braid,
The fagaldis weill mycht mesuryt be
Till a gret townys quantité.

(619) With their crane they meant to use those faggots burning
in a fire, and if the sow came to the wall to let it fall upon
her, burning, holding it there with a strong chain until all that
was there was consumed. (625) They ordered and made ready,
secure, engines for projectiles, then put each man at his [place]
of duty. (628) Sir Walter, the good Steward, had to ride about
to see where there was most uncertainty, giving help there
with his following. When they had set themselves for defence
to this extent, the English host sounded the assault at dawn
on the eve of [the Exaltation of the] Cross. (636) Then men
could see that great host with much equipment coming sturd-
ily; they surrounded the town rapidly, and attacked with such
a good will, for they bent all their efforts to it, that they pressed
hard against the town. (642) But [the Scots], risking death
or terrible wounds, defended themselves so well there that
they slung ladders to the ground, striking their foes so hard
with stones that they left many lying [there], some dead, some
hurt, some passed out.

(649) But [the English] who were still on foot pulled them
away quickly, and not disheartened by that, went stoutly on
the attack. Those above [continued to] defend, putting [the
English] under great pressure until many of them were
wounded; they made such a fine defence there that they
checked the enemy's power. (658) They fought like that until
it was nearly noon in the day, when those outside, in good
order, pushed their sow toward the wall.

626–31. They ordained. This is the second occurrence of this tactic. Note
that 'those within' (605) decided what the commander was to do.

634. Rude Evyn, the day before the feast of the Exaltation of the Cross,
i.e. 13 September.

635. The attack. The only English source to confirm that there were two
assaults is Anonimalle. The second was clearly the more serious and is
that described by Lanercost. See note to 327.

Thai fagaldis brynnand in a baill
620 With thar cran thocht thai till availl,
And gyff the sow come to the wall
To let it brynnand on hyr fall
And with stark chenyeis hald it thar
Quhill all war brynt up that thar war.

625 Engynys alsua for to cast
Thai ordanyt and maid redy fast
And set ilk man syne till his ward,
And Schyr Walter the gud Steward
With armyt men suld rid about
630 And se quhar that thar war mast dout
And succour thar with his menye.
And quhen thai in sic degre
Had maid thaim for defending,
On the Rud Evyn in the dawing
635 The Inglis ost blew till assaill.
Than mycht men with ser apparaill
Se that gret ost cum sturdely,
The toun enveround thai in hy
And assaillyt with sua gret will
640 For all thar mycht thai set thartill
That thaim pressyt fast on the toun.
Bot thai that gan thaim abandoun
To dede or than to woundis sar
Sa weill has thaim defendit thar
645 That leddrys to the ground thai slang,
And with stanys sa fast thai dang
Thar fayis that fele thar left liand
Sum dede sum hurt and sum swonand.
Bot thai that held on feyt in hy
650 Drew thaim away deliverly
And scounryt nocht for that thing
Bot went stoutly till assailling,
And thai aboun defendyt ay
And set thaim to sa hard assay
655 Quhill that fele of thaim woundyt war,
And thai sa gret defens maid thar
That thai styntit thar fayis mycht.
Apon sic maner gan thai fycht
Quhill it wes ner none of the day,
660 Than thai without on gret aray
Pressyt thar sowe towart the wall.

(662) Those inside very quickly called [up] the engineer who had been taken [prisoner], and threatened him powerfully, swearing that he would die unless he proved such skill against the sow that he smashed her to bits. (668) He, perceiving clearly that he was pretty close to death unless he did what they wanted, decided to do all he could. [The mangonel] that was placed opposite the sow was very swiftly tensed. (674) Quickly he pulled out the chock, and smartly the stone flew out, going away over the sow, falling a little way behind her; then those who were in her shouted loudly, 'On to the wall, for it's all ours, no doubt!' (681) Then at once the engineer had the machine tensed as fast as possible and the stone flew out smartly. It flew out, whizzing with a roar, and fell right in front of the sow. Then their hearts began to sink, but they still pushed the sow with all their might toward the wall, and set her close to it. (690) The engineer then had the machine tensed speedily and slung out the stone, which sailed into the air, and then, with its great weight, crashed down in a line right by the wall, hitting the sow in such a way, that it broke in bits with that hit the largest beam, which was strongest for warding off a blow. (699) The men ran out pretty fast, and those on the wall shouted that their sow had farrowed there. John Crab, who had his gear all ready, set fire to the faggots,

---

662–705. Destruction of the sow by the engineer and Crab. See note to 434.

672. Bendit wes scho. 'She' must be an engine, but this has somehow dropped out. I have translated 'bendit' as 'tensed', for the word suggests that the engine worked by bending (i.e. tensing) wood; that would be a mangonel, not a trebuchet, which propelled the missile by a counterweight.

[*The Scots force the engineer to destroy the sow*]

And thai within sone gert call
The engynour that takyn was,
And gret mannance till him mais
665 And swour that he suld dey bot he
Provyt on the sow sic sutelté
That he to-fruschyt hir ilk-dele,
And he that has persavyt wele
That the dede wes weill ner him till
670 Bot giff he mycht fulfill thar will
Thocht that he at his mycht wald do.
Bendyt in gret hy than wes scho
That till the sow wes evyn set,
In hy he gert draw the cleket
675 And smertly swappyt out a stane.
Evyn our the sow the stane is gane
And behind it a litill wey
It fell, and than thai cryit hey
That war in hyr, 'Furth to the wall,
680 For dredles it is ouris all.'
The gynour than deliverly
Gert bend the gyn in full gret hy
And the stane smertly swappyt out,
It flaw out quhetherand with a rout
685 And fell rycht evyn befor the sow.
Thar hartis than begouth to grow,
Bot yeyt than with thar mychtis all
Thai pressyt the sow towart the wall
And has hyr set tharto juntly.
690 The gynour than gert bend in hy
The gyne and wappyt out the stane
That evyn towart the lyft is gane
And with gret wecht syne duschit down
Rycht be the wall in a randoun,
695 And hyt the sow in sic maner
That it that wes the mast summer
And starkest for to stynt a strak
In sunder with that dusche it brak.
The men ran out in full gret hy,
700 And on the wallis thai gan cry
That thar sow wes feryt thar.
Jhone Crab that had his ger all yar
In his fagaldis has set the fyr

threw them over the wall and burned the sow to the bare framework. (706) With all this, the folk outside were attacking hard in a determined struggle, [while] those inside manfully defended their position with great energy, at great risk of death.

(711) The shipmen with a lot of equipment came to the attack in their ships with top-castles well manned by bold men well armed in steel. (715) Their boats were drawn up pretty high on their masts and made fast, and [they] pressed toward the wall with all that equipment, but the engineer struck the long-boat with a stone, and the men who had gone in her, some dead, some stunned, sank, turning over and over. (722) From that time on no-one dared undertake to advance to the wall with ships. But the rest were all attacking on every side so determinedly that it was, in truth, astonishing that those men made such a defence, given the great difficulties that they had. (729) For their walls were then so low that a man could strike another in the face upwards with a spear, as was previously told to you. Many of them were badly wounded, and the rest were labouring so hard that none had leisure to rest, their adversaries pressed so.

(737) They were placed in such a tight situation inside that their warden, who had a hundred men, armed, bold and brave, in company with him, riding about to see where

---

705. Burned the sow. The intention to hold the sow fast by chains (623) is forgotten.

713. Topcastle. The platform at the top of the mast.

715–721. Boats. I find it difficult to understand what is meant here. Are the ship's boats are held vertical by being lashed to the mast? But the ship's boat was drawing the ship, for it was hit and the men rowing therein killed. Sisam suggested that a boatful of men was hoisted to the top of the mast and was smashed (719) by a stone from the mangonel.

737. The warden's perambulation occurs here for the third time, but on this occasion to some purpose.

And our the wall syne gan thaim wyr
705 And brynt the sow till brundis bar.
With all thys fast assailyeand war
The folk without with felloun fycht,
And thai within with mekill mycht
Defendyt manlily thar steid
710 Into gret aventur off deid.

[An attack by a ship is repulsed]

The schipmen with gret apparaill
Come with thar schippis till assail
With top-castell warnyst weill
Off wicht men armyt into steill,
715 Thar batis up apon thar mast
Drawyn weill hey and festnyt fast,
And pressyt with that gret atour
Towart the wall, bot the gynour
Hyt in the aspyne with a stane,
720 That the men that tharin war gane
Sum ded sum dosnyt come doun wynland.
Fra thyne furth durst nane tak on hand
With schippis to preys thaim to the wall,
Bot the lave war assailyeand all
725 On ilk sid sa egrely
That certis it wes gret ferly
That that folk sic defens has maid
With the gret myscheiff that thai had,
For thar wallis sa law than wer
730 That a man rycht weill with a sper
Mycht stryk ane other up in the face
As her-befor said to you was,
And fele of thaim war woundit sar,
And the laiff sa fast travaillyt war
735 That nane had tyme rest for to ma,
Thar adversouris assaillyt sua.

[The Steward's defence of the Mary gate]

Thai war within sa straitly stad
That thar wardane, that with him had
Ane hunder men in cumpany
740 Armyt that wicht war and hardy
And raid about for to se quhar

his folk were hardest pressed, to relieve those in need, came at various times to different places where some of the defenders were quite dead, others sorely wounded, so that he had to leave part of his company there; (749) as a result, when he had made a tour round, of all the men that he had, only one was left with him – he had left them all to relieve where he saw need. (754) The folk who were attacking at the Mary-gate had cut down the outwork and made a fire at the draw-bridge, burning it down and crowding in large numbers right to the gate, to set a fire. (760) Then those inside quickly had one [man] go to the warden to tell [him] how hard pressed they were. When Sir Walter Stewart heard how men were dealing so pressingly with them, he then caused come from the castle all the armed men who were there, because no-one attacked there on that day, and went speedily with that force to the Mary-gate, sending [some] to the wall and seeing all the dangers. (771) He suddenly realised that unless a great [deal of] help was quickly given there, they would burn up the gate, which they could not prevent from the wall. (775) For that reason he quickly set his purpose upon a great exploit, causing the gate to be opened wide and the fire which he found at it scattered by a force of men. (780) He put himself at very great risk, for those who were attacking there pressed on him with drawn weapons, and he defended himself with all his might. You could see a fierce sight there

---

755. The Mary gate was on the west side of the walls, north of the castle.
756–57. The English seized the outwork and so were able to cross the drawbridge. *B1909*, 470 is surely right to argue that it would be foolish to burn the drawbridge, which in any case would be raised. 'Burned it down' means 'burned [the tackle to bring] it down'.

That his folk hardest presyt war
To releve thaim that had myster,
Come sindry tymys in placis ser
745   Quhar sum of the defendouris war
All dede and other woundyt sar,
Sua that he of his cumpany
Behuffyt for to leve thar party,
Sua that be he a cours had maid
750   About, of all the men he haid
Thar wes levyt with him bot ane
That he ne had left thaim everilkan
To releve quhar he saw myster.
And the folk that assailland wer
755   At Mary yat tohewyn haid
The barrais and a fyr had maid
At the drawbrig and brynt it doun,
And war thringand in gret foysoun
Rycht to the yat a fyr to ma.
760   Than thai within gert smertly ga
Ane to the wardane for to say
How thai war set in hard assay,
And quhen Schyr Walter Stewart herd
How men sa straitly with thaim ferd
765   He gert cum of the castell then
All that thar war off armyt men,
For thar that day assaillyt nane,
And with that rout in hy is gane
To Mary yate and to the wall
770   He send and saw the myscheff all,
And umbethocht him suddanly
Bot giff gret help war set in hy
Tharto, thai suld bryn up the yet
That fra the wall thai suld nocht let.
775   Tharfor apon gret hardyment
He suddanly set his entent,
And gert all wyd set up the yat
And the fyr that he fand tharat
With strenth of men he put away.
780   He set him to full hard assay,
For thai that war assailyeand thar
Pressyt on him with wapnys bar
And he defendyt with his mycht.
Thar mycht men se a felloun sycht

of stabbing, thrusting and striking. (786) They put up a stout
defence there, for they held the gate with a large force of men,
[making a] stand there despite their foes, until night caused
both sides to leave [off] fighting.

(791) Those of the [English] army all withdrew from the
assault when night fell. They left the attack dispirited and
went swiftly to their camp, setting their watches hastily. (797)
The rest relaxed as best they could, for they had great need
of rest. That night they spoke among themselves of those
inside, astonished that they had made so stout a defence
against the great assault upon them. (803) Those inside, on
the other side, when they saw their enemies withdraw so
completely, were all cheered and swiftly set watches then went
to their quarters. Only a few of them were slain, but many
were very badly wounded, and the rest were desperately weary.
(811) It was a bold assault, *perfay*, and certainly I never heard
tell of a few men making a greater defence who were under
such heavy attack. (815) One thing that happened there was
astonishing; I'll tell you about it. That is, that on that day
when all there were most [heavily] attacked and the shot too
was thickest, women with child and small children gathered
up arrows in armfulls, carrying them to those who were on
the wall, and not one who was there was killed nor yet
wounded; that was more

785   Off stabing, stocking and striking,
       Thair maid thai sturdy defending
       For with gret strenth of men the yat
       Thai defendyt and stud tharat
       Mawgré thar fayis, quhill the nycht
790   Gert thaim on bath half leve the fycht.

[*The assault ends, but the garrison prepares for another*]

       Thai off the ost quhen nycht gan fall
       Fra the assalt withdrew thaim all.
       Woundyt and wery and forbeft
       With mad cher the assalt thai left
795   And till thar innys went in hy
       And set thar wachis hastily,
       The lave thaim esyt as thai mycht best
       For thai had gret myster of rest.
       That nycht thai spak commonaly
800   Off thaim within and had ferly
       That thai sua stout defens had maid
       Agayne the gret assalt thai haid.
       And thai within on other party
       Quhen thai thar fayis sa hastily
805   Saw withdraw thaim thai war all blyth,
       And has ordanyt thar wachis swith
       And syne ar till thar innys gane.
       Thar wes bot full few of thaim slane
       Bot fele war woundyt utterly,
810   The lave our mesur war wery.
       It was ane hard assault perfay,
       And certis I herd never say
       Quhar quheyn mar defence had maid
       That sua rycht hard assailling haid,
815   And off a thing that thar befell
       Ik haff ferly that I sall tell,
       That is that intill all that day
       Quhen all thar mast assailyeit thai
       And the schot thikkerst wes withall
820   Women with child and childer small
       In armfullis gaderyt up and bar
       Till thaim that on the wallis war
       Arrowes, and nocht ane slayne wes thar
       Na yeit woundyt, and that wes mar

a miracle of God Almighty [than man's doing, for] I can attribute it to nothing else.

(827) They were quiet that night on both sides, and in the morning, no later, there came news from England to [the men] of the host, telling how at Myton by Boroughbridge their men had been killed and borne down, and that Scotsmen were still riding throughout the land, burning and destroying. (835) When the king heard this recital, he assembled all his council, to see whether it would be better for him to lie inactive around the town and attack until it was taken, or to go then into England and rescue his land and men. (842) His council was in bitter disagreement then, for the southerners wanted him to remain there until he had taken the town and the castle too. But the northerners would not agree, fearing to lose their friends and the greater part of their goods through the ruthlessness of the Scotsmen; (850) they wanted him to let the siege be and to ride to rescue the land. I understand that Earl Thomas of Lancaster was one of those who advised the king to go home. (855) Because [King Edward] inclined more to the south-country folk than to the wishes of the northerners, [Earl Thomas] took that so ill

---

828. The morn. 14 September, 1319. For confirmation see note to 858.

842. Disagreement. There is much evidence that the English camp was riven with rumour, suspicion and dispute, with Edward II making foolish promises of reward to his supporters and of punishing those responsible for Gaveston's death in 1312. The *Vita Edwardi* reports that Lancaster was supposedly paid £40,000 by Robert I to hold his men back from the attack on Berwick. Lanercost, though acknowledging two possible courses of action, claims that the king wished to follow both:

> When the king heard that the Scots were perpetrating such [ills (in Yorkshire)] he wanted to send part of the army to deal with the Scots still in England, and maintain the siege with the rest of his folk; but by the advice of magnates who were unwilling to split up and not to fight with the Scots, he raised the siege and turned his army to England hoping to meet the Scots [*who therefore returned by the west coast*] (*L*, 239; *LT*, 227)

852. Lancaster, son of Edmund earl of Lancaster, brother of Edward I.

858. Lancaster departs first. This is generally accepted, though it depends wholly on Barbour. (a) A letter written soon after by Hugh Despenser, and (b) the *Vita Edwardi* give a different account:

> (a) Before the king had been [at Berwick] eight days, news came to him that the Scots had entered the land of England with the prompting and assistance of the earl of Lancaster. The earl acted in such a way that the king took himself off with all his army, to the great shame and grievous damage of us all. For that reason we very much doubt

825   The myrakill of God almichty
        And to noucht ellis it set can I.

[*The English debate whether to continue, but withdraw; the
fate of Thomas, earl of Lancaster; the return of the Scottish
army*]

        On athyr syd that nycht thai war
        All still, and on the morn but mar
        Thar come tythandis out off Ingland
830   To thaim of the ost, that bar on hand
        How that by Borowbrig at Mytoun
        Thar men war slayn and dongyn doun,
        And at the Scottismen throu the land
        Raid yeit brynnand and destroyand.
835   And quhen the king had hard this tale
        His consaile he assemblyt haile
        To se quhether fayr war him till
        To ly about the toun all still
        And assailye quhill it wonnyn war,
840   Or than in Ingland for to fayr
        And reskew his land and his men.
        His consaill fast discordyt then,
        For sotheroun men wald that he mad
        Arest thar quhill he wonnyn haid
845   The toun and the castell alsua,
        Bot northyn men wald na thing sua
        That dred thar frendis for to tyn
        And mast part of thar gudis syne
        Throu Scottis mennys cruelte,
850   Thai wald he lete the sege be
        And raid for to reskew his land.
        Off Longcastell I tak on hand
        The Erle Thomas wes ane of tha
        That consaillyt the king hame to ga,
855   And for that mar inclynyt he
        To the folk of the south countre
        Na to the northyn mennys will,
        He tuk it to sa mekill ill

---

if matters will end so happily for our side as is necessary. (Maddicott,
Lancaster, 249)
(b) Word [of Mytoun] came to the king and to our army and at once
by the advice of I don't know who, the siege was completely raised.
For the king was trying to meet the fleeing Scots by one way, and

that he had his gear bundled up in haste and took his way home to England with his whole contingent, which made up nearly a third of the [English] host. (863) He took his road home without leave; because of that [great] disputes arose later between him and the king that lasted on until Andrew Harclay, who had been directed against him by the king, took him eventually to Pontefract and on a hill beside the town struck off his head without mercy. (871) Then he was drawn and hanged and with him a pretty fine company. Men said after this that Thomas, who had been made a martyr like this, was a saint and did miracles, but [that] envy then had them hidden, (877) but whether he was holy or not, he was slain at Pontefract like that. Then the king of England, when he saw [Thomas] prepared to depart so openly, decided it was dangerous to lie there with the rest of his force, so he packed his equipment and went home to England. (886) The Scotsmen who were destroying in England, soon got news of the departure [from] this great siege. Therefore they took the way westward, going home by Carlisle with prey, with prisoners, and [with] other booty of various kinds. (893) The lords went to the king and the rest took their ways, each man going to his home.

---

the earl of Lancaster by another. But the Scots ... took [a third route]. (*VitaEd.* 97)

The eighth day would be 14 September ... But if Lancaster had deserted the king, Despenser would surely have said so. The king left Berwick on 17 September and Lancaster was still at court on 16 September. He may have wanted to move rapidly towards his estates at Pontefract while the king proposed, in a letter of 18 September, to chase the Scots. But it was the king who decided to give up the siege, and the claim by Barbour that Lancaster forced this by withdrawing his troops is very doubtful. He probably withdrew after the decision, and the claim that his troops were a third of the English army (861) is certainly a great exaggeration; a tenth is possible. The fragile relations between Thomas and Edward II never recovered from this fiasco.

866–70. Andrew Harcla had been ransomed from the Scots; in March 1322 he led men from Carlisle against Earl Thomas who had rebelled, and, after years of accusing Edward II of being in league with, or failing to oppose, Robert Bruce, had himself sought an alliance with King Robert, whom he proposed to visit. He was caught and defeated by Harcla at Boroughbridge, and given a summary trial at his own castle of Pontefract. Harcla was made earl of Carlisle but in January 1323 made an agreement with Robert I which was adjudged treasonable by the English; Harcla too was executed.

871. Hanged after beheading! In fact he was to be hanged, drawn and beheaded, but the two former were remitted because of his royal blood –

That he gert turs his ger in hy
860 And with his bataill halily
That off the ost ner thrid part was
Till Ingland hame his way he tais.
But leve he hame has tane his gat,
Tharfor fell efter sic debat
865 Betwix him and the king that ay
Lastyt quhill Andrew Hardclay
That throu the king wes on him set
Tuk him rycht in Pomfret,
And on ane hill beside the toun
870 Strak off his hede but ransoun,
Tharfor syne hyngyt and drawyn wes he
And with him a weill gret menye.
Men said syne efter this Thomas
That on this wis maid marter was
875 Was saynct and myrakillis did,
Bot envy syne gert thaim be hid,
Bot quhether he haly wes or nane
At Pomfret thus was he slane.
And syne the king of Ingland
880 Quhen that he saw him tak on hand
To pas his way sa opynly,
Him thocht it wes perell to ly
Thar with the lave of his menye
Hys harnays tharfor tursit he
885 And intill Ingland hame gan he far.
The Scottismen that destroyand war
In Ingland sone hard tell tithing
Off this gret sege departing,
Tharfor thai tuk westwart the way
890 And till Carlele hame went ar thai
With prayis and with presoneris
And other gudis on ser maneris.
The lordis to the king ar gain,
And the lave has thar wayis tain
895 Ilk man till his repayr agayne.

---

so there *was* 'ransoune' (870). Six of his adherents were sentenced with
him. The execution was on 22 March, 1322.

875. Saint. Miracles were ascribed to the tomb of Earl Thomas within
six weeks of his death and in 1327 the English Commons asked for his
canonisation; his memory remained popular even thereafter.

879. Syne. Barbour thus places Edward II's departure from Berwick after
the death of Earl Thomas.

The king was indeed very pleased that they had come back whole and sound, and that they prospered in such a way that they had defeated their enemies, rescuing, without loss of men, those who had been besieged in Berwick right up to the ditch. (903) When the king had asked news of how they had fared in England, and they had told him all their doings, [and] how the English were defeated, he was delighted in his heart, and held a feast for them with sport and entertainment.

(909) Berwick and those inside it were rescued in this way by manliness and by skill. He was worthy to be a prince who was able to bring so important an enterprise to a good conclusion with sense [and] without loss. (915) Then he took the way to Berwick, and when he heard there how it had been defended so very boldly, he praised those who were there greatly. (919) He commended Walter Stewart's great merits above the others, for the great defence he had made at the gate, where men had burned the bridge, as you heard me describe. It was indeed right to esteem him who put up a defence so stoutly at an open gate with hand-to-hand fighting. (927) Had he lived until he had been of mature years, without doubt his reputation would have spread far. But death, who always watches to thwart with all her power [both] the strong and the weak, was very envious of his worthiness, [so] that all his bold deeds ended thus in the flower of his youth, as I shall tell you later. (936) When the king had been there for a little while,

---

930-35. Barbour here inserts a brief preview of his obituary of Walter Stewart, 19.205-28.

The king i-wys was wondre fayn
That thay war cummyn hale and fer,
And that thai sped on sic maner
That thai thar fayis discomfyt hade
900   And but tynsaill of men has maid
Rescours to thaim that in Berwik
War assegyt rycht till thar dyk.
And quhen the king had speryt tithand
How thai had farne in Ingland
905   And thai had tauld him all hale thar far
How Inglismen discumfyt war,
Rycht blyth intill his hart wes he
And maid them fest with gamyn and gle.

[*Praise of Walter Stewart; help is to be sent to Edward Bruce*]

Berwik wes on this maner
910   Reskewyt and thai that tharin wer
Throu manheid and throu sutelté.
He wes worthi a prynce to be
That couth with wit sa hey a thing
But gret tynsaill bring till ending.
915   Till Berwik syne the way he tays
And quhen he hard thar how it ways
Defendyt rycht sua apertly,
He lovyt thaim that war thar gretly.
Walter Stewart his gret bounté
920   Out-our the laiff commendyt he
For the rycht gret defens he maid
At the yat quhar men brynt had
The brig as ye herd me dyvis,
And certis he wes weill to pris
925   That sa stoutly with plane fechting
At opyn yate maid defending.
Mycht he haff levyt quhill he had bene
Off perfyt eild, withoutyn wene
His renoun suld have strekyt fer,
930   Bot dede that walkis ay to mer
With all hyr mycht waik and worthy
Had at his worschip sic invi
That in the flour of his youtheid
So endyt all his douchti deid,
935   As I sall tell you forthermar.
Quhen the king had a quhill bene thar

he sent far and near for masons who were most skilled in that trade and had the wall around the town of Berwick be raised everwhere by ten feet. (941) Soon then he took his way toward Lothian with his company, then speedily he had both armed men and yeomanry collected to go to Ireland to help his brother there.

939–40. The walls of Berwick. There was taxation for the keeping of the town of Berwick, probably in early 1320; money was still being spent on the walls in 1328–29. (*RRS5, 565, 547*)

943–46. In fact the Irish war had ended in 1318; in 1319 a second invasion of northern England drove the English government to agree to a two-year truce in December 1319, a truce which Barbour ignores.

He send for maysonys fer and ner
That sleast war off that myster
And gert weill ten fute hey the wall
940   About Berwykis toune our-all,
And syne towart Louthyane
With his menye his gat is gane.
And syne he gert ordane in hy
Bath armyt men and yhumenry
945   Intill Irland in hy to fayr
To help his brother that wes thar.

But he, always irritated by inaction, always wanting to be busy, a day before the arrival of those who had been sent him by the king, took his way to go southwards, despite all those who were with him. (7) For he had in that land no more than two thousand men, I believe, apart from the kings of the Irish who rode with him in great contingents. (11) He took the way toward Dundalk, and when Richard Clare heard news that he was coming with so small a following, he gathered all the armed men from all Ireland that he could, so that he had there with him then twenty thousand horse with trappings, apart from those [men] who were on foot, and held northwards on his way. (20) When Sir Edward heard tell that they had come near to him,

---

1. He. Edward Bruce. The time is October 1318.

3–4. A day before reinforcements from the king arrived. The 'day' should not be taken literally. With this passage compare three different versions, by (a) Lanercost (b) the annals of Clonmacnoise and (c) Gray:

(a) Within 15 days after [29 September, Edward Bruce] came to the town on Dundalk with his Irish adherents and a great army of Scots which had newly come to Ireland to help him to invade and destroy that land and the king of England's men, as best they could. (Contd at note to 99) (*L*, 238; *LT*, 225)

(b) Edward Bruce, seeing the English encamp before his face and fearing [that] his brother Robert ... would acquire and get the glory of that victory which he made himself believe he would get of the English, [whom] he was sure he would be able to overthrow without the assistance of the said brother ... attacked. (*Ann. Clonmacnoise*, 281–82)

(c) Edward Bruce was defeated and slain at Dundalk by the English of that country; through over-confidence he would not wait for reinforcements which had arrived lately and were not more than six leagues distant. (*S*, 143; *ST*, 57)

The argument for Lanercost is that Edward had lain low for 16 months, awaiting help, and would not leave when it was just about to arrive. But both versions may be correct, for among those killed in Edward's army were two Hebridean 'kings', MacRuairidh and MacDonald, who are unlikely to have been hanging around Carrickfergus for months; there may have been timely reinforcements from the Isles, while Lowland reinforcements arrived from Loch Ryan after Edward had marched – and the weight of independent sources surely confirms this belatedness in Barbour.

A more important question is one which has, to my knowledge, never been asked: did King Robert take men to Ireland in 1318 to help his

BOOK 18

[*Edward Bruce marches toward Dundalk; he debates whether to fight*]

	Bot he that rest anoyit ay
	And wald in travaill be alway,
	A day forouth thar aryving
	That war send till him fra the king,
5	He tuk his way southwart to far
	Magré thaim all that with him war,
	For he had nocht than in that land
	Of all men I trow twa thousand,
	Outane the kingis off Irchery
10	That in gret routis raid him by.
	Towart Dundalk he tuk the way,
	And quhen Richard of Clar hard say
	That he come with sa few menye
	All that he mycht assemblit he
15	Off all Irland off armyt men,
	Sua that he had thar with him then
	Off trappyt hors twenty thousand
	But thai that war on fute gangand,
	And held furth northward on his way.
20	And quhen Schyr Edward has hard say
	That cummyn ner till him wes he

brother? Clonmacnoise is generally reliable; the silence of other Irish sources (e.g. Laud) is understandable if Robert got no further than Carrickfergus and its environs. *Bower 6*, 413 adds a phrase to Fordun's version which is surely conclusive: 'his brother King Robert would have come to him with a great army if he had waited until the next day.' The silence of Barbour has clearly discredited these sources, but unfairly. Barbour echoes them in making John Stewart report that 'men sayis' the leader of reinforcements is 'my brother' (33), i.e. the uncharacteristically anonymous Walter Stewart, who is also unnamed at the later mention of the reinforcements (188–91). Barbour was unsure who the leader was, but knew it was someone's brother. And finally, there is no trace of any writ or charter being issued by King Robert between 27 July and 3 December, 1318. In these circumstances I believe that King Robert went to Carrickfergus about the middle of October 1318.

12. Richard Clare had been killed in a domestic war on 10 May, 1318. The Justiciar in October was the archbishop of Dublin; the commander at the battle of Faughart was John Birmingham; the archbishop of Armagh was present.

15-19. The army was largely of local, Louth, levies.

he sent scouts to see him – they were Soulis, the Steward and also Sir Philip Mowbray. When they had seen them coming they went back to make their report, saying that they were indeed very numerous. (28) Quickly Sir Edward answered them saying that he would fight that day, [even] though they were treble or quadruple [the number]. (31) Sir John Stewart said, 'Now, I advise you, don't fight in such a hurry. Men say my brother is coming nearby with fifteen thousand men; if they were combined with you, you could stay to fight more confidently.' (37) Sir Edward glowered angrily and said swiftly to Soulis, 'What do you say?' 'Sir', he said, '*perfay*, I agree with what my companion said.' Then he spoke to Sir Philip. 'Sir,' said he, 'as God sees me, I think it no folly to wait for your men, hurrying to ride [to us]. (45) For we are few and our foes are many; God may deal our fates very well, but it would be remarkable if our force could overcome so many in battle.' Then with great anger, 'Alas', [Edward] said, 'I never thought to hear that from you! Now let whoever wants to, help, but rest assured [that] I will fight, today, without more delay. (53) Let no man say while I'm alive that superior numbers would make me flee! God forbid that anyone should blame us for defending our noble name.' 'Well, let it be so.' said they, 'We shall take whatever God sends.'

(59) When the kings of the Irish heard it said, and knew for a fact, that their king meant to fight with so few against a force of such great power,

---

31. Sir John Stewart. Barbour sent him to Montpellier at 15.83. The Laud annals report the presence of Sir Alan Stewart and his three brothers, but not Sir John; see note to 38.

34.15,000, E. C has 1,500.

38 The Soules, also so called at 23, but at 110 he is Sir John, who had been in Ireland in 1315 (14.27), captured Harclay in Eskdale in 1316 (16.516) and was to die at Dundalk (110) of which there is record confirmation. The Walter de Soules of the Laud annals is therefore an error (no such de Soules is known), which bears on the reliability of Sir 'Alan' Stewart (note to 31).

56. C has 'That we defoul'.

He send discouriouris him to se,
The Soullis and the Stewart war thai
And Schyr Philip the Mowbray,
25 And quhen thai sene had thar cummyng
Thai went agayne to tell tithing,
And said weill thai war mony men.
In hy Schyr Edward answerd then
And said that he suld fecht that day
30 Thoucht tribill and quatribill war thai.
Schyr Jhone Stewart said, 'Sekyrly
I reid nocht ye fecht on sic hy,
Men sayis my brother is cummand
With fyften thousand men ner-hand,
35 And war thai knyt with you ye mycht
The traistlyer abid to fycht.'
Schyr Edward lukyt all angrely
And till the Soullis said in hy,
'Quhat sayis thou?' 'Schyr,' he said, 'Perfay
40 As my falow has said I say.'
And than to Schyr Philip said he.
'Schyr,' said he, 'sa our Lord me se
Me think na foly for to bid
Your men that spedis thaim to rid,
45 For we ar few, our fayis ar fele,
God may rycht weill our werdis dele,
Bot it war wondre that our mycht
Suld our-cum sa fele in fycht.'
Than with gret ire 'Allace,' said he,
50 I wend never till her that of the.
Now help quha will for sekyrly
This day but mar baid fecht will I,
Sall na man say quhill I may drey
That strenth of men sall ger me fley.
55 God scheld that ony suld us blam
Gif we defend our noble nam.'
'Now be it swagat than,' quod thai,
'We sall tak that God will purvai.'

[The Irish kings promise to remain and watch the fight]

And quhen the kingis of Irchery
60 Herd say and wyst sekyrly
That thar king with sa quhone wald fycht
Agane folk of sa mekill mycht

they came to him very quickly and advised him gently to wait for his men, [while] they would keep their enemies busy all that day, and on the morrow also, with the raids they would make. (69) But their advice had no effect; whatever came, he would have battle. When they saw he was so determined to fight, they said, 'You may well go to fight with yon great company; but we discharge ourselves completely – none of us will stand to fight. (76) So don't rely on our strength, for our tactics are [those] of this land, to follow and to fight while fleeing, and not to stand in open encounter until one side is defeated.' (81) He said, 'Since that is your custom, I ask no more of you than this, that is, that you and your followers should be arrayed all together, standing a distance away, without leaving, and see our fight to the end.' They said that they would indeed do so, and then went toward their men who numbered nearly forty thousand.

(90) Edward, with those who were with him, who weren't fully two thousand, drew themselves up to stand stalwartly against forty thousand and more. (94) That day Sir Edward would not wear his coat of arms; but Gib Harper, whom men held also [to be] without an equal in his position, on that day wore all Sir Edward's apparel. They waited for the fight in this way, their enemies came in great haste all ready to engage [them] and they met them boldly.

---

89. E: 20,000. C has 40,000.

94–97. Gib was a harper, see note to 15.183. Barbour does not explain Edward's refusal to wear his surcoat, so much at variance with his determination to defend his noble name (56). Probably the source made no mention of such a refusal and it was introduced to explain why Gib was wearing the coat, so that his head was cut off in mistake for Edward's (165–70). The combination of 'Harper' and wearing his lord's coat indicates that Gib was Edward's herald. By Barbour's time the common origin of the two occupations had been quite lost.

Thai come till him in full gret hy
And consaillyt him full tenderly
65 For till abid his men, and thai
Suld hald thar fayis all that day
Doand, and on the morn alsua
With thar ronnyngis that thai suld ma.
Bot thar mycht na consail availe,
70 He wald algat hav bataile.
And quhen thai saw he wes sa thra
To fycht, thai said, 'Ye ma well ga
To fycht with yone gret cumpany,
Bot we acquyt us uterly
75 That nane of us will stand to fycht.
Assuris nocht tharfor in our mycht,
For our maner is of this land
To folow and fecht fleand
And nocht to stand in plane melle
80 Quhill the ta part discomfyt be.'
He said, 'Sen that your custum is
Ik ask at you no mar bot this,
That is that ye and your menye
Wald all togidder arayit be
85 And stand on fer but departing
And se our fycht and the ending.'
Thai said weill that thai suld do sua,
And syne towart thar men gan thai ga
That war weill twenty thousand ner.

[*The defeat and death of Edward Bruce; Philip Mowbray's fate*]

90 Edward with thaim that with him wer
That war nocht fully twa thousand
Arayit thaim stalwartly to stand
Agayne fourty thousand and ma.
Schyr Edward that day wald nocht ta
95 His cot-armour, bot Gib Harper
That men held as withoutyn per
Off his estate, had on that day
All hale Schyr Edwardis aray.
The fycht abad thai on this wis,
100 And in gret hy thar ennymys
Come till assemblé all redy
And thai met thaim hardely.

(103) To tell the truth they were so few that they were pushed back by their enemies, [while] those who struggled most to stand [firm] were killed dead, and the remainder fled to the Irish for help. (108) Sir Edward, [a man] of such courage, was dead, as were John Stewart and John Soules too, and others also of their company. They were so quickly defeated that few were killed in the field, for the rest took their ways to the Irish kings, who were there and hovering in one whole force. (117) John Thomasson who was leader of [the men] of Carrick who were there when he saw the defeat, withdrew to an Irish king of his acquaintance, who received him in fidelity. (123) When John had come to that king, he saw led from the fighting the brave Sir Philip Mowbray, who had been knocked senseless in the fight. He was led by the arms by two men, upon the causeway that was between them and the town, [and] stretched in a long straight line. (131) They held their way toward the town, and when they were half-way along the causeway, Sir Philip recovered from his dizziness and saw that he had been taken and was led by the two like that. (136) He soon threw one away from himself, and then swiftly the other; then he drew his sword swiftly and took his way to the fight along the causeway, which was then filled in great numbers with men going to the town. (143) On meeting them, he made them such payment where he went, that he caused a good hundred men

---

99–107. The battle. On 14 October, 1318. The account in 'The battle of Faughart' is a worthless forgery. This brief account can only be compared with the accounts in the Laud annals (note to 108) and in Lanercost, continued from note to 3:

By the help of God, almost all [Edward's army] was killed, except those who escaped by flight. Since they had three divisions, each was so far distant from the others that the first was dealt with before the second arrived, and the second before the third, in which Edward was, could give help, but that third was routed just like the two preceding. Edward fell at the same time, was beheaded after death, his body divided into four parts, and those parts sent to the four principal towns of Ireland. (*L*, 238; *LT*, 225–26)

108. Death of Edward Bruce. According to the Laud annals:

[The mayor and about 20 men came to the battle from Drogheda], with whom came John Maupas to the said battle. They engaged and the English penetrated the first division, and John Maupas killed the said Sir Edward Bruce manfully in that battle, with great honour, [but] this John was found dead on the body of the said Edward; almost all the Scots were killed, about 2,000, and few escaped, apart from Sir Philip Mowbray who was wounded to death [the two Lacys], and a few others who were with them scarcely escaped. This happened between Dundalk and Faughart.

Bot thai sa few war, south to say,
That ruschyt with thar fayis war thai,
105 And thai that pressyt mast to stand
War slane doun, and the remanand
Fled till the Irche to succour.
Schyr Edward that had sic valour
Wes dede and Jhone Stewart alsua
110 And Jhone the Soullis als with tha
And other als off thar cumpany.
Thai war vancussyt sa suddanly
That few intill the place war slane,
For the lave has thar wayis tane
115 Till the Irsche kingis that war thar
And in hale bataill howand wer.
Jhone Thomas-sone that wes leder
Off thaim of Carrik that thar wer
Quhen he saw the discumfiting
120 Withdrew him till ane Irsch king
That off his aquentance had he,
And he resavit him in leawté.
And quhen Jhone cummyn wes to that king
He saw be led fra the fechting
125 Schyr Philyp the Mowbray the wicht
That had bene dosnyt into the fycht,
And with armys led wes he
With twa men apon a causé
That wes betwix thaim and the toun
130 And strekyt lang in a randown.
Towart the toun thai held thar way,
And quhen in myd-causé war thai
Schyr Philip of his desynes
Ourcome, and persavit he wes
135 Tane and led suagat with twa.
The tane he swappyt sone him fra
And syne the tother in gret hy,
And drew the swerd deliverly
And till the fycht his wayis tays
140 Endlang the causé that than was
Fillyt intill gret foysoun
Off men that than went till the toun,
And he that met thaim agayn gan ma
Sic payment quhar he gan ga
145 That weile a hundre men gert he

leave the causeway, despite their [companions]. As John Thomasson, who saw all his achievement, said truthfully, he went straight towards the battle.

(150) John Thomasson, who well realised that they had been completely defeated, shouted to him as quickly as possible, and said, 'Come here, none of them is alive, for they are all dead.' Then [Mowbray] stood still for a while and saw that they had all been deprived of life, then went close toward [Thomasson]. (158) This John then behaved so sensibly that all those who then fled thither, although they lost [some] of their gear, came sound and safe to Carrickfergus. (162) Those who were at the fighting looked for Sir Edward to get his head among the folk who lay there dead, and found Gib Harper in his gear; because his arms were so noble, they struck off his head, then had it salted in a box and sent it to England as a present to King Edward. (171) They believed that it was Sir Edward's but they were deceived about the head by the armour, which was splendid, although Sir Edward died there. (175) This is how these noble men were lost there through stubbornness, a sin and a great sorrow. For if their outstanding courage been led with intelligence and moderation, unless a greater misfortune had befallen them, it would have been a very difficult task to lead them to disaster. (183) But a great unbridled pride

---

147. John Thomson. He 'said' what happened, but Barbour does not say that it was said to him. This comes from Barbour's source.

149. 'The bataill' I have translated as 'the battle' but it could be 'the army' meaning Edward Bruce's force. The result is the same.

159. The fate of Mowbray is left unresolved; the Laud annals name him as dying of wounds here (note to 108) but a fragmentary English letter of Jan. 1319 says that he is active in Scotland. (*RRS5*, 146. But this could be a mistake for another Mowbray, Roger or Alexander.) Barbour in the following passage twice describes the escape of the Scots to Carrickfergus, probably a swift and disorderly retreat. Thomson is unlikely to have lingered to watch the fate of his companions.

163. Edward Bruce's head, see note to 224.

Leve maugré tharis the causé.
As Jhone Thomas-sone said suthly
That saw his deid all halily
Towart the bataill evyn he yeid.

[*The body of Edward Bruce*]

150 Jhone Thomas-sone that tuk gud heid
That thai war vencussyt all planly
Cryit on him in full gret hy
And said, 'Cum her for thar is nane
On lyve for thai ar dede ilkane.'
155 Than stud he still a quhill and saw
That thai war all doune of daw,
Syne went towart him saraly.
This Jhone wrocht syne sa wittely
That all that thidder fled than wer
160 Thocht that thai lossyt of thar ger
Come till Cragfergus hale and fer.
And thai that at the fechting wer
Socht Schyr Edward to get his heid
Amang the folk that thar wes dede
165 And fand Gib Harper in his ger,
And for sa gud hys armys wer
Thai strak hys hed of and syn it
Thai have gert salt intill a kyt
And send it intill Ingland
170 Till the King Edward in presand.
Thai wend Schyr Edwardis it had bene,
Bot for the armyng that wes schene
Thai of the heid dissavyt wer
All thocht Schyr Edward deyt ther.

[*A verdict on Edward Bruce; the belated reinforcements*]

175 On this wis war thai noble men
For wilfulnes all lesyt then,
And that wes syne and gret pité
For had thar outrageous bounté
Bene led with wyt and with mesur,
180 Bot gif the mar mysaventur
Be fallyn thaim, it suld rycht hard thing
Be to lede thaim till outraying,
Bot gret outrageous surquedry

led them to buy their valour dearly. Those who fled from the
encounter hastened toward the sea and came to Carrickfergus.
Those who were on the way to Sir Edward, sent from the
king, when they heard of the defeat, went back to Carrick-
fergus, [though] that was not without difficulty. (193) For
many times that day they were attacked by Irishmen, but they
held together closely always, defending themselves so intelli-
gently that they often escaped by strength, and often, too, by
guile; (199) for often they gave [bribes] to them to allow them
to pass unharmed on their way – and thus they came to
Carrickfergus. They took boats and ships and sailed at once
to Scotland, all arriving there safely. (205) When [the folk]
of Scotland got word of the defeat of Sir Edward, they grieved
tenderly for him generally throughout the land; those who
were killed with him there were also lamented sorrowfully.

(211) As I said before, Edward Bruce was defeated in this
way, and when the field had been swept clean so that no
resistance could be seen, the warden then, Richard Clare, and
all the folk who were with him, took the way toward Dundalk,
so that they they had no encounter with the Irish at that time,
but hurried to the town. (221) Then they sent on to the king
who ruled over England the head of Gib Harper in a box.
John Maupas took it to the king.

---

211. As I said before. E has 'her' = 'here', C has 'air' = 'before'. I have
   kept E's reading but have assumed that 'er' 'before' was meant.
224. John Maupas and Bruce's head. For Maupas see note to 108.
   According to the Laud annals 'Sir John Birmingham took the head of
   Edward to the lord king of England, to whom the king then gave the
   earldom of Louth ... and the barony of Ardee.'

Gert thaim all deir thar worschip by.
185 And thai that fled fra the mellé
Sped thaim in hy towart the se
And to Cragfergus cummyn ar thai,
And thai that war into the way
To Schyr Edward send fra the king
190 Quhen thai hard the discumfiting
To Cragfergus thai went agayne.
And that wes nocht foroutyn payn,
For thai war mony tyme that day
Assailyeit with Irschery, bot thai
195 Ay held togidder sarraly
And defendyt sa wittely
That thai eschapyt oft throu mycht
And mony tyme alsua throu slycht,
For oft of tharis to thaim gaff thai
200 To lat thaim scaithles pas thar way,
And till Cragfergus come thai sua
That batis and schyppis gan thai ta
And saylyt till Scotland in hy
And thar aryvyt all saufly.
205 Quhen thai of Scotland had wittering
Off Schyr Edwardis vencussing
Thai menyt him full tenderly
Our all the land commounaly,
And thai that with him slayn war thar
210 Full tenderly als menyt war.

[*Edward Bruce's head; Edward II plans to invade Scotland*]

Edward the Bruys as I said her
Wes discumfyt on this maner
And quhen the feld wes clengit clene
Sua that na resistens wes sene
215 The wardane than Schyr Richard of Clar
And all the folk that with him war
Towart Dundalk has tane the way
Sua that rycht na debat maid thai
At that tym with the Irschery,
220 Bot to the toun thai held in hy,
And syne had send furth to the king
That had Ingland in governyng
Gib Harperis heid in a kyt.
Jhone Maupas till the king had it

He accepted it with joy; he was very pleased at that present, for he was so glad that he had been delivered of a great enemy. (229) His heart so [swelled with] pride that he formed an intention to ride with a great army into Scotland, to take revenge with a strong hand for the vexation, trouble and harm which had been done to him there. (235) He gathered a right great host, and had his ships come by the sea with a great stock of victuals, because he meant to destroy Scotland so completely on this occasion that no-one would remain alive there. With his folk thoroughly equipped he took the way towards Scotland.

(243) When King Robert knew that he was coming against him with such a company, he collected his men [from] far and near, until so many had come [or] also were coming to him, that he was pretty sure that he would be alright. (249) He had all the cattle from every single place in Lothian, and had them sent to strongpoints, appointing men to defend these. He lay quietly at Culross with his army, for he meant to try to cause his foes to lose strength by starvation and by long marches, then, when he had weakened their strength, he would engage in a fight with them. (259) He meant to act in this way, [when] English men in superior numbers

---

229–31. The invasion of 1322. This took place not after the death of Edward Bruce, but after a two year truce (ending Christmas 1321) and the death of Thomas of Lancaster (1322) who had sought an alliance with Robert I. Robert invaded northern England in June 1322 while Edward was preparing his invasion of Scotland. There is a full account of this campaign in N. Fryde, *Tyranny and Fall of Edward II*, ch. 9.

235. A great host. Edward took extraordinary measures to raise this army, demanding a foot-soldier from every vill to serve for forty days (the total thus demanded is not calculable), in addition to levies from almost all counties, who were to bring sixteen days' food with them. These demands for levies, including 7,000 from Ireland and 10,000 from Wales, total 54,800 (plus the men from the vills), in addition to which 11,000 were to be at Carlisle, presumably to stop Robert invading England by the west. The Wardrobe book, BL, MS Stowe 553, gives details of the numbers paid. I have extracted the figures of those who were in Scotland, not the initial muster. About 1,200 men-at-arms served, and 20,000 infantry (including 1,500 hobelars), made up of 13,100 levies plus 6,900 sent by the vills. The Irish sent 282 infantry, the Welsh 6,627. Twenty-four per cent of infantry summoned (i.e. men from the vills discounted) served, or 1 in 4.2.

237. Victual. There were large purveyances to feed the army; the Wardrobe alone controlled supplies worth £15,500.

242. Toward Scotland. Edward II set out from Newcastle (where his

225   And he ressavyt it in daynté,
       Rycht blyth off that present wes he
       For he wes glaid that he wes sua
       Deliveryt off a felloun fa.
       In hart tharoff he tuk sic prid
230   That he tuk purpos for to rid
       With a gret ost in Scotland
       For to veng him with stalwart hand
       Off tray of travaill and of tene
       That done tharin till him had bene,
235   And a rycht gret ost gaderit he
       And gert his schippis be the se
       Cum with gret foysoun of vittaill,
       For at that tyme he wald him taile
       To dystroy up sa clene the land
240   That nane suld leve tharin levand,
       And with his folk in gret aray
       Towart Scotland he tuk the way.

[*King Robert withdraws; the English starve at Edinburgh*]

       And quhen King Robert wist that he
       Come on him with sic a mengne
245   He gaderyt his men bath fer and ner
       Quhill sa fele till him cummyn wer,
       And war als for to cum him to,
       That him thocht he rycht weill suld do.
       He gert withdraw all the catell
250   Off Lowthiane everilkdeill,
       And till strenthis gert thaim be send
       And ordanyt men thaim to defend,
       And with his ost all still he lay
       At Culros, for he wald assay
255   To gert hys fayis throu fasting
       Be feblyst and throu lang walking,
       And fra he feblist had thar mycht
       Assembill than with thaim to fycht.
       He thocht to wyrk apon this wis,
260   And Inglismen with gret maistrys

---

troops had rioted against the townsmen) on 10 August, and travelling by the Soutra road, reached Crichton, near Dalkeith, on 18 August and Musselburgh the next day.

254. Culross, on the northern shore of the Forth; it had a Cistercian abbey.

came to Lothian with their host, soon going to Edinburgh,
where they stayed for three days. (264) Their ships, which
were on the sea, had winds continuously contrary to them,
so that in no way could they bring their supplies to the Firth
to relieve the king. (269) [The men] of the host, lacking food,
when they saw that they could not get their victuals [brought]
to them by sea, sent out a large company to forage [in] all
Lothian; but they found no cattle, apart from a bull which
was lame, [and] which they found in Tranent's corn[fields].
(277) They brought him back to their host, and when the
Earl Warenne saw that bull coming alone like that, he asked
if they got no more. They all said to him, 'No.' 'Then in
truth,' said he, 'I'm quite sure that this is the dearest beef
that I've ever seen up to now; for a fact, it cost a thousand
pounds and more.' (286) When the king and those who were
of his council saw that they could get no cattle to eat for their
host, they turned back to England.

(291) They planned to camp at Melrose, and sent ahead a
company of nearly three hundred armed men. But the lord
Douglas who was then nearby in the Forest, knew of their
coming and how [many] they were, and with those of his
company

262-3. Three days at Edinburgh. A week in fact. Edward was at Mus-
selburgh on 19 and 26 August, in between at Leith. The castle of
Edinburgh was, of course, uninhabitable.

264. The ships. Some supplies did arrive on 20 August. But in letters
written on his return Edward explained that he had entered Scotland,
'the better to harass our enemies, but we found in our way neither man
nor beast'. The failure of supplies to arrive was attributable to the
Flemings, who 'had come to the aid of our enemies, the Scots, and
put to sea with the fleet just when our fleet was nearing Scotland, and
took ships with goods on them, so that none dared come to us'. Fourteen
ships were destroyed by storms.

275. Bull, E. In C 'cow' here and later.

289. Fasting. Many chronicles (e.g. *Flores Historiarum*, iii, 210 and see
note to 291) comment on the starvation of this army on its return.

290. They returned to England. The whole campaign had lacked any
strategic purpose, other than to bring King Robert to battle – a risk he
was wise enough not to repeat. Fordun comments:

1322. King Edward entered Scotland on 12 August with a large army
of cavalry and infantry and a large multitude of ships, and came to
the town of Edinburgh seeking battle with King Robert. But [he]
prudently declining a military engagement, promptly removed the
animals on which they might feed, from the [English] army, which,
pressed by famine, returned frustrated after a fortnight to its own
country, having first looted and reduced to desolation the monasteries

Come with thar ost in Lowthian
And sone till Edynburgh ar gan,
And thar abaid thai dayis thre.
Thar schippys that war on the se
265   Had the wynd contrar to thaim ay
Sua that apon na maner thai
Had power to the Fyrth to bring
Thar vittailis to releve the king,
And thai of the ost that faillyt met
270   Quhen thai saw that thai mycht nocht get
Thar vittaillis till thaim be the se
Thai send furth rycht a gret menye
For to forray all Lowthiane,
Bot cataill haf thai fundyn nane
275   Outakyn a bule that wes haltand
That in Tranentis corne thai fand.
That brocht thai till thar ost agayne,
And quhen the erle of Warayne
Saw that bule anerly cum swa
280   He askyt giff thai gat na ma,
And thai haff said all till him nay.
Than said he, 'Certis I dar say
This is the derrest best that I
Saw ever yeit, for sekyrly
285   It cost a thousand pound and mar.'
And quhen the king and thai that war
Off his consaill saw thai mycht get
Na cattell till thar ost till ete
That than of fasting had gret payn
290   Till Ingland turnyt thai agayn.

[*The retreating English advance party attacked by Douglas at Melrose*]

At Melros schup thai for to ly
And send befor a cumpany
Thre hunder ner of armyt men.
Bot the lord Douglas that wes then
295   Besyd intill the Forest ner
Wyst of thar come and quhat thai wer,
And with thaim of his cumpany

---

of Holyrood and Melrose. [*They killed the prior, a monk and two lay brothers, and wounded others, at Melrose, and burned Dryburgh abbey to the ground.*] (*F1*, 349–50; *F2*, 342)

he lay in wait secretly in ambush in Melrose. (300) He sent a right sturdy friar out of the gate to watch their arrival, telling him to keep himself concealed until he saw them all coming, right at the corner there of the wall, and then to shout aloud, 'Douglas! Douglas!' (306) The friar then set out on his way, a sturdy, strong and bold [man]; his great hood concealed altogether the armour that he had on him. (310) He rode upon a stalwart horse having a spear in his hand, [and] stayed like that until he saw them coming near. When the foremost had passed the corner, he shouted, 'Douglas! Douglas!' then makes a charge at them all, bearing down remorselessly and Douglas with his company issued against them with a shout. (320) When they saw so great a force come upon them so suddenly, they were wholly demoralised and turned tail without hesitating. The Scotsmen rode among them and killed all whom they could overtake, making a great slaughter there. (327) Those who escaped with their lives went back to their host and told them what kind of welcome Douglas had given them at their encounter, in convoying them roughly back and denying them camping in open ground.

(333) The king of England and his men, seeing their camp-makers come back repulsed like that, were cast down in their spirits and concluded that it would be very foolish

---

291–332. The assault at Melrose. This is noted by Gray who also says that the army was forced to retreat for lack of food:

at which time the king's hobelars foraging at Melrose were defeated by James Douglas; none dared to leave the host to seek victuals by foray. The English were so harassed and worn with warfare that before their arrival at Newcastle there was such a murrain in the host from lack of food, that of necessity they had to disband. (*L*, 149; *LT*, 69)

294. Douglas. Notably, he was not with the Scottish host at Culross.

Into Melros all prevely
He howyt in a buschement,
300 And a rycht sturdy frer he sent
Without the yate thar come to se,
And bad him hald him all prevé
Quhill that he saw thaim cummand all
Rycht to the coynye thar of the wall,
305 And than cry hey, 'Douglas! Douglas!'
The frer than furth his wayis tais
That wes all stout derff and hardy,
Hys mekill hud helyt haly
The armur that he on him had,
310 Apon a stalwart hors he rad
And in his hand he had a sper,
And abaid apon that maner
Quhill that he saw thaim cummand ner,
And quhen the formest passyt wer
315 The coynye he criyt 'Douglas! Douglas!'
Than till thaim all a cours he mas
And bar ane doun deliverly,
And Douglas and his cumpany
Ischyt apon thaim with a schout,
320 And quhen thai saw sa gret a rout
Cum apon thaim sa suddanly
Thai war abaysyt gretumly
And gaf the bak but mar abaid.
The Scottis men amang thaim raid
325 And slew all that thai mycht our-ta,
A gret martyrdome thar gan thai ma,
And thai that eschapyt unslayne
Ar till thar gret ost went agayne
And tauld thaim quhatkyn welcummyng
330 Douglas thaim maid at thar meting
That convoyit thaim agayn rudly
And warnyt planly herbery.

[*King Robert invades England; the English army awaits him at Byland*]

The king of Ingland and his men
That saw thar herbriouris then
335 Cum rebutyt on that maner
Anoyit in thar hart thai wer,
And thocht that it war gret foly

to take quarters in the woods. For that reason they made camp in open ground by Dryburgh, then went back home on the road to England. (342) When King Robert heard tell that they were returning home again, and how their camp-makers had been killed, he quickly gathered his host and went south over the Firth of Forth, taking his way to England. (348) When his host had assembled, he had eighty thousand men and more, [which] he divided into eight divisions, ten thousand to each division. Then he went on to England, following the English king very fast with his whole army until eventually he came closing in to Byland, where the king of England was lying at that time with his men. (358) King Robert, who had intelligence then that [King Edward] lay there with a strong force, made a forced march on him one night so that by morning when day came they had come into open country, just a short distance from Byland. (364) But between them and it there was a rocky brae, stretching some distance, with a broad path to go up it. There was no other way for them to go to Byland abbey except by a very roundabout [road]. (370) When the great English force heard that King Robert was so near,

---

339. Dryburgh. For the burning of this abbey see note to 290 .

345–51. Gathered his host. But at 253 the host was at Culross. The divisions of 10,000 each recall the English host at Bannockburn. Lanercost comments that it came from both sides of the Forth, from the Isles and Bute, and entered England on 30 September.

353. Followed fast. According to Lanercost the king stayed for five days near Carlisle, then went into England:

> towards Blakehoumor, since he had never gone there before nor destroyed that region, because of difficulty of access, and since he had learned for a certainty from scouts that the king of England was there. [*Edward II ordered Harclay to muster men to help him*] The Scots burned villages and manors in Blakehoumor, devastating everything as much as they could, taking men prisoner and animals as booty. The earl of Richmond, sent by the English king with his men to reconnoitre the Scottish army from a certain hill between the abbey of Byland and the abbey of Rievaulx, met them unexpectedly and fought them suddenly, trying with his men to impede by throwing stones their ascent by a certain narrow and steep pass on the hill. But the Scots climbed up against them fiercely and fearlessly; many English escaped by flight and many were taken prisoner with the aforesaid earl. (*L*, 247; *LT*, 240)

366. Path. The word meant a steep road or track. The account given here and in Lanercost (above note to 353), is broadly confirmed by the *Gesta Edwardi*:

> King Robert with an army ... followed the English into England so swiftly and secretly that he would have almost taken the unwise and

Intill the wod to tak herbery,
Tharfor by Dryburgh in the playn
340 Thai herbryit thaim and syne again
Ar went till Ingland thar way.
And quhen the King Robert hard say
That thai war turnyt hame agayn
And how thar herbriouris war slayn,
345 In hy his ost assemblit he
And went south our the Scottis se
And till Ingland his wayis tais.
Quhen his ost assemblyt ways
Auchty thousand he wes and ma
350 And aucht batallis he maid of tha,
In ilk bataill war ten thousand,
Syne went he furth till Ingland
And intill hale rout folowit sa fast
The Inglis king, quhill at the last
355 He come approchand to Biland
Quhar at that tyme thar wes lyand
The king of Ingland with his men.
King Robert that had witteryng then
That he lay thar with mekill mycht
360 Tranountyt sua on him a nycht
That be the morn that it wes day
Cummyn in a plane feld war thai
Fra Biland bot a litill space,
Bot betwix thaim and it thar was
365 A craggy bra strekyt weill lang
And a gret peth up for to gang,
Other wayis mycht thai nocht away
To pas to Bilandis abbay
Bot gif thai passyt fer about.
370 And quhen the mekill Inglis rout
Hard that the King Robert wes sa ner,

---

unprepared king in the monastery of Byland, had not the love of
Christ spared him; for on the top of a hill above the monastery of
Byland, where the English army was drawn up, the Scots climbed up
among the trees in the middle of a wood, and in their first encounter
the English were scattered, [*Richmond and others were taken prisoner*]
and the king fled swiftly from Byland.

368. Byland abbey. As in Lanercost and the *Gesta*, but this seems to be
an error. Barrow, *Bruce*, 371,n. 45 and *B1985*, 103, from the identification
of Blakehoumor, place the battle near [Old] Byland. There is no doubt
that Edward II went from Rievaulx to Byland abbey before the battle.

the majority of those who were there went to the path and
took the brae, meaning to put up their defence there. They
had their banners displayed there and their divisions drawn
up in breadth, thinking to defend the pass well. (378) When
King Robert saw that they meant to defend themselves there,
he sent for his council and asked what had best be done.
(382) The lord Douglas answered him, saying, 'Sir, I under-
take that in a short while I shall do [enough] to win yon place
openly or then make all that company come down here to
you in this open [ground]. The king then said back to him,
'do so, where God speed you.'

(390) Then [Douglas] went forth on his way putting the
boldest of the host in his company and going to the pass.
(394) Thomas, the good earl of Moray, left his division and
speedily, with only four men in his company came to the force
of the lord Douglas, and, before he entered the pass took a
position in front of them all, for he wanted men to see him.
(401) And when Sir James Douglas saw that he had come
thus, he esteemed him greatly for it, and welcomed him very
kindly, then they both fell in step together. When the Eng-
lishmen saw them do that, they dismounted and advanced
against them. (408) Two knights, who were bold in their
deeds, one called Thomas Ughtred, the other Sir Ralph Cob-
ham, came down in front of all their company.

---

396. Four men, E. C has 'thre'.

398–405. In E before Douglas entered the 'pas' (pass), Moray took the
'pas' (pace) in front of them all, and at 405 they both took the 'pas'.
But what does this really signify? That Douglas usurped the leadership
of the attack, that Moray placed himself at its head, that Douglas
protested ('welcummyt him hamlily') and that they finally shared the
leadership together?

406. The battle was on 14 October, 1322. One of the English commanders
was Aymer de Valence, earl of Pembroke, but Barbour does not remark
on this.

409–10. Ralph Cobham, see *CP3*, 338; Thomas Ughtred of Scarborough,
was taken prisoner by Sir William Abernethy. (*CDS5, 684*; *CP12/2*,
158–59) BL, Stowe MS 553, fo. 60v shows that with three esquires he
served with Edward II in Scotland (4 August–12 September 1322), then
was at Newcastle with 20 hobelars to keep the Marches for 28 days
from 5 October. He must have gone from there to Byland where he
was captured.

The mast part of thaim that thar wer
Went to the peth and tuk the bra,
Thai thocht thar defens to ma,
375   Thar baneris thar thai gert display
And thar bataillis on braid aray,
And thocht weill to defend the pas.
Quhen the King Robert persavit was
That thai thocht thar thaim to defend
380   Efter his consaill has he send
And askyt quhat wes best to do.
The lord Douglas answeryt thar-to
And said, 'Schyr, I will underta
That in schort tyme I sall do sa
385   That I sall wyn yon pas planly,
Or than ger all yon cumpany
Cum doun to you her to this plane.'
The king said than till him agayn,
'Do than, quhar mychty God the speid.'

[*Douglas and Moray attack uphill at Byland; defence by two English knights*]

390   Than he furth on his wayis yeid,
And of the ost the mast hardy
Put thaim intill his cumpany
And held thar way towart the pas.
The gud erle of Murreff Thomas
395   Left his bataill and in gret hy
Bot with four men of his cumpany
Come till the lordis rout of Douglas
And or he entryt in the pas
Befor thaim all the pas tuk he
400   For he wald that men suld him se.
And quhen Schyr James off Douglas
Saw that he suagat cummyn was
He prisyt him tharoff gretly
And welcummyt him hamlyly,
405   And syne the pas thai samyn ta.
Quhen Inglis men saw thaim do sua
Thai lychtyt and agayn thaim yeid,
Twa knychtis rycht douchty of deid,
Thomas Ouchtre ane had to name
410   The tother Schyr Rauf of Cobhame,
Come doun befor all thar menye,

They were both full of great courage, meeting their foes very manfully, but they were strongly pressed. (415) There you could see men attacking very strongly, [others] defending themselves by fighting stoutly and arrows flying in great numbers, [while] those who were above tumbled stones down on [the Scots] from the high [ground]. (420) But they, having set both determination and force to win the path, pressed them so that Sir Ralph Cobham took the way to his horse in haste, and left Sir Thomas defending the pass manfully with great energy until he was so overcome that he was taken [prisoner] by a hard struggle. (428) Because of that, from then until his death he was renowned for the best fight put up by a knight in all England. For this same Sir Ralph Cobham had the name in all England of the best knight of that land; and because Sir Thomas stayed fighting when Sir Ralph withdrew, as we said before, he was esteemed above [Sir Ralph].

(437) They were fighting like that in the pass; when King Robert, who was wise and intelligent in his deeds, saw that his men were so very boldly taking the path against their foes, and saw those foes defend themselves thus, he had all the Irish who were in his company from Argyll and also from the Isles, hurry swiftly to the brae. (447) He bade them leave the path altogether, and climb up the high rocks, hastening to seize the heights. Then you could see them go boldly climbing up any way to the heights,

---

423. E has Cobham go to his horse, C to his host.

426. 'Supprisit' usually means 'surprised, attacked suddenly', but I have taken it here rather as 'overcame'.

443-45. The Irschery here means Scottish Gaels. Barbour again comments on the presence of Islesmen, and is confirmed by Lanercost.

Thai war bath full of gret bounté
And met thar fayis manlely,
Bot thai war pressyt rycht gretumly.
415 Thar mycht men se rycht weill assaile
And men defend with stout bataill
And arowes fley in gret foysoun
And thai that owe war tumbill doun
Stanys apon thaim fra the hycht,
420 Bot thai that set bath will and mycht
To wyn the peth thaim pressyt sua
That Schyr Rauff of Cobhame gan ta
The way up till hys hors in hy,
And left Schyr Thomas manlily
425 Defendand with gret mycht the pas
Quhill that he sua supprisit was
That he wes tane throu hard fechting.
And tharfor syne in his ending
He wes renownyt for best of hand
430 Off a knycht off all Ingland,
For this ilk Schyr Rauf of Cobhame
Intill all Ingland he had name
For the best knycht of all that land,
And for Schyr Thomas dwelt fechtand
435 Quhar Schyr Rauff as befor said we
Withdrew him, prisit our him was he.

[*The king's men take the heights, take prisoners and defeat the
English*]

Thus war thai fechtand in the pas,
And quhen the King Robert that was
Wys in his deid and averty
440 Saw his men sa rycht douchtely
The peth apon thar fayis ta
And saw his fayis defend thaim sa,
Than gert he all the Irschery
That war intill his cumpany
445 Off Arghile and the Ilis alsua
Speid thaim in gret hy to the bra,
And bad thaim leif the peth haly
And clym up in the craggis hy
And speid thaim fast the hycht to ta.
450 Than mycht men se thaim stoutly ga
And clymb all-gait up to the hycht

not yielding at all at the strength of their enemies. (453) Despite their foes, they bore themselves so [well] that they got to the top of the brae. Then men could see them fighting fiercely, attacking their foes sturdily. Those who had gone to the pass reached the summit in spite of their enemies. Then they fought with all their might; you could see men fighting desperately. (461) There was a dangerous combat there, for a knight called Sir John Brittany who was dismounted above the brae, put up a stout defence with his men. Scotsmen attacked them so, and fought so desperately with them, that they were demoralised so that those who could fled away. (469) Sir John Brittany was taken there, and a great many of his folk were slain. Two knights of France were taken there; the lord of Sully was one of them, the other was the marshall Brittany, who was a very great lord at home. Of the rest, some died and some were taken [prisoner], all the remainder fleeing. (477) When the king of England who was still based at Byland, saw his men openly defeated, he departed in great haste, fleeing forth with his whole force. Scotsmen chased him hard, I know, and took many [prisoners] in the pursuit. The king [Edward] got clean away with the majority of his followers. (486) Walter Stewart, who always put a high price on distinguished chivalry, with a company of five hundred,

---

462. Sir John Brittany was earl of Richmond. He had been Guardian of Scotland in 1305 and again in 1307, when Valence resigned. The dislike of Robert I may date back to that period. He had served on the Scottish campaign (10 August–10 September, 1322), with a retinue of the earl of Angus, a banneret, 13 knights and 47 men-at-arms. (BL, Stowe MS 553, fo. 61v. See *CP10*, 814–18)

472-73. Sir Henry de Sully was Butler of Philip V of France. The marshall Bretayn was presumably one of Robert and William Bercham, who with Elyas Anillage, French knights, were taken prisoner by Douglas at Byland. See note to 543.

475-76. Some dead. BL, MS Stowe 553: Roger Mauduyt took 18 men-at-arms [m/a] and 77 hobelars to Byland; next day he had 18 m/a and 64 hobelars (fo. 56v); Henry Percy took 56 m/a (eight knights) and 60 hobelars, left with 43 m/a (six knights) and 48 hobelars (fo. 57); Ralph Neville took 40 m/a (seven knights) and 80 hobelars, left with 36 m/a (six knights) and 80 hobelars (fo. 57). The lost m/a stood a better chance of being prisoners.

478-85. Edward II's escape was from Rievaulx abbey (see note to 499) to Bridlington and eventually by ship to York, as BL, Stowe MS 553, fo. 61 confirms: Hugh Despenser served with 47 men-at-arms till the day of the battle, 14 October, 'the day the king left Rievaulx for southern parts'. See note to 499.

And leve nocht for thar fayis mycht,
Magre thar fayis thai bar thaim sua
That thai ar gottyn aboun the bra.
455   Than mycht men se thaim fecht felly
And rusch thar fayis sturdely,
And thai that till the pas war gane
Magre thar fayis the hycht has tane.
Than laid thai on with all thar mycht,
460   Thar mycht men se men felly fycht.
Thar wes a peralous bargane,
For a knycht Schyr Jhone the Bretane
That lychtyt wes aboune the bra
And his men gret defens gan ma,
465   And Scottismen sua gan assaill
And gave thaim sa felloun bataill
That thai war set in sic affray
That thai that mycht fley fled away,
Schyr Jhone the Bretane thar wes tane
470   And rycht fele off his folk war slane.
Off Fraunce thar tane wes knychtis twa,
The lord the Sule wes ane of tha,
The tother wes the merschell Bretayn
That wes a wele gret lord at hame,
475   The lave sum ded war and sum tane
And the remanand fled ilkane.
And quhen the king of Ingland
That yeit at Biland wes liand
Saw his men discumfyt planely
480   He tuk his way in full gret hy
And furthwart fled with all his mycht,
Scottismen chassyt fast, Ik hycht,
And in the chas has mony tane,
The king quitly away is gane
485   And the mast part of his menye.

[*Walter Stewart attacks up to York; John of Brittany a
prisoner*]

Stewart Walter that gret bounté
Set ay on hey chevalry
With fyve hunder in cumpany

486–94. The purpose of this expedition to York may have been to seize
the town by surprise; it is not mentioned by any English source.

gave chase to the gates of York, slaying some of their men
there and staying nearly till night-time to see if any would
issue to fight. (493) When he saw none would come out, he
turned back with all his force and hurried back to the host
which had taken quarters in the abbey of Byland and nearby
Rievaulx. They divided up the king of England's gear, which
he had left at Byland, among those who were there; (502)
they ransacked everything through their hands, and rejoiced
merrily [over it]. When the king had taken up lodging, they
brought the prisoners to him, all unarmed as is appropriate.
(507) When he saw John Brittany he showed him great in-
dignation, for [John] was accustomed to speak haughtily and
too maliciously at home; [the king] ordered that [John] be
taken quickly away and see that he was closely imprisoned,
saying that if he had not been such a wretch, he would have
bought his disgraceful words dearly; and [John] miserably
begged him for mercy. (517) They led him out forthwith and
kept him close until they had come home to their own country.
Long afterwards he was ransomed, paying twenty thousand
pounds as I have heard various men say.

(523) When the king had spoken thus, the French knights
whom men had taken

499–503. The loot. Lanercost probably places this taking of plunder
correctly, Barbour wrongly; the king, having gone from Rievaulx to
Byland abbey before the battle, returned to Rievaulx presumably to
save this wealth, but had to flee further:

When [the defeat at Byland] became known to the king of England,
who was then in Rievaulx abbey, he, being ever chicken-hearted and
luckless in war ... now took to flight in England, leaving behind him
in the monastery in his haste silver plate and much treasure. Then
the Scots, arriving immediately after, seized it all and plundered the
monastery. (Contd at note to 552)

But the Scots seem to have reached Rievaulx on Edward's heels because
John Thorpe, archer, when paid on 1 March, 1323 was said to have
been 'following the body of the lord king from the conflict had with
Scots at Rievaulx on 14 October'. (Stowe MS 553, fo. 68v) That Edward
was nearly taken at Bannockburn was bad enough; narrrowly to escape
the same fate inside his own kingdom, while fleeing a raiding party,
suggests an incompetence beyond the ordinary.

520–21. Long after ransomed. He was freed between May and September
1324, after much urging by Edward II, who is said to have asked
parliament (unsuccessfully) for a tax for the purpose. According to
Flores Historiarum, his ransom was 14,000 marks, offered by Edward
II, of which King Robert sent 2,000 each to Charles IV and the pope.
On 27 September, 1324 the pope thanked Moray, who had recently

Till Yorkis yettis the chas gan ma
490 And thar sum of thar men gan sla
And abade thar quhill ner the nycht
To se giff ony wald ische to fycht,
And quhen he saw nane wald cum out
He turnyt agane with all his rout
495 And till his ost he went in hy
That tane had than thar herbery
Intill the abbay off Biland
And Ryfuowis that was by ner-hand.
Thai delt amang thaim that war ther
500 The king off Inglandis ger
That he had levyt in Biland,
All gert thai lep out our thar hand,
And maid thaim all glaid and mery.
And quhen the king had tane herbery
505 Thai brocht till him the prisoneris
All unarmyt as it afferis,
And quhen he saw Jhone of Bretangne
He had at him rycht gret engaigne,
For he wes wont to spek hychtly
510 At hame and our dispitusly,
And bad have him away in hy
And luk he kepyt war straitly,
And said war it nocht that he war
Sic a catyve he suld by sar
515 Hys wordys that war sua angry,
And he humbly cryit him mercy.
Thai led him furth foroutyn mar
And kepyt him wele quhill thai war
Cummyn hame till thar awne countré,
520 Lang eftre syne ransonyt wes he
For twenty thousand pund to pay
As Ik haff hard syndry men say.

[*French knights released without ransom; the expedition returns
to Scotland*

Quhen that the king this spek had maid
The Frankys knychtis men takyn had

---

been (perhaps still was) in France, for lending 3,000 marks to Rich-
mond; it looks as though he was the medium for sending the pope his
douceur. See the note in *CP10*, 817.

were brought right there, before the king, [who] gave them a
fair welcome and said, 'I know very well that you came to see
the fighting here because of your great reputation and valour.
(530) Because, since you were in the country, your strength,
your reputation and your stoutness would not allow you to
avoid the fight. Since that cause led you to it, and not hatred
nor ill-will, you will be accepted as friends [here] where you
will always be welcome.' (537) They kneeled and thanked him
greatly, and he had them treated courteously, keeping them
with him for a long time, and doing them honour [with]
generosity. When they longed for their own land, he sent them
to the king of France as a present, quit and free of ransom,
giving them great gifts. (545) He received his friends like that
courteously and kindly, and stoutly repelled his enemies. He
stayed all that night at Byland; they were delighted at their
victory. In the morning, without delay, they took their way
forth. (552) They travelled so far at that time, burning, slaying
and destroying, damaging their enemies by their might, until
they came to the Wolds, then they took their way home
northwards, destroying on their journey the vale of Beauvoir
very widely. (559) Then with prisoners and cattle, riches and
many a fair jewel they took their way home to Scotland,

---

543. Ransom free. Henry de Sully was made a member of Edward II's
council at a fee of £400 p.a. on 29 September 1322 at Durham, and
seems not to have been in Scotland with the king; he left for Compostella
by Edward's leave on 9 June, 1323, immediately after the truce of
Bishopthorpe was made. He had been used by King Robert as an
intermediary to the English council in 1323, and we have graphic letters
to and from him, in one of which he mentions Richmond's (not Sully's,
B1985, 104) ransom. His ransom was not remitted for Edward II promised
him 1,000 marks 'in aid of his ransom', and indeed gave him
a further 1,000 marks as a gift towards his lost horses and arms. If Sully
was taken by a Scottish lord, the king was perhaps entitled to only a
third of his ransom, and may have remitted that. Curiously MS Stowe
553 mentions the funeral of John barber of Henry Sully! The three
French knights mentioned in the note to 472 and their valets were
redeemed by the king from Douglas for 4,400 merks, which, I suggest,
represents two-thirds of a valuation of 6,600 merks, 6,000 for the knights,
600 for the valets, of which the king could claim one third. He sent the
knights back to France without ransom, to curry favour with Charles IV.
(BL, Stowe MS 553, fo. 8v, 9v, 22v, 65r, 69; *RRS5, 222, 448*)

552–58. They travelled so far. This great raid into the East Riding, which
had hitherto escaped Scottish ministrations, is described by Lanercost:
[From Rievaulx the Scots] marched on to the Wolds, taking [the earl
of Richmond] with them, laying waste that country nearly as far as
the town of Beverley, which was held to ransom to escape being

525	War brocht rycht thar befor the king,
	And he maid thaim fayr welcummyng
	And said, 'I wate rycht weill that ye
	For your gret worschip and bounté
	Come for to se the fechting her.
530	For sen ye in the countré wer
	Your strenth your worschyp and your mycht
	Wald nocht lat you eschew the fycht,
	And sen that caus you led thartill
	And nother wreyth na ivill will
535	As frendis ye sall resavyt be,
	Quhar all tyme welcum her be ye.'
	Thai knelyt and thankyt him gretly,
	And he gert tret thaim curtasly
	And lang quhill with thaim had he
540	And did thaim honour and bounté,
	And quhen thai yarnyt to thar land
	To the king of Fraunce in presand
	He send thaim quit but ransoun fre
	And gret gyftis to thaim gaff he.
545	His frendis thusgat curtasly
	He couth ressave and hamely,
	And his fayis stoutly stonay.
	At Biland all that nycht he lay,
	For thar victour all blyth thai war,
550	And on the morn foroutyn mar
	Thai haff forthwart tane thar way.
	Sa fer at that tyme travaillyt thai
	Brynnand slayand and destroyand
	Thar fayis with all thar mycht noyand
555	Quhill till the Wald cummyn war thai,
	Syne northwart tuk hame thar way
	And destroyit in thar repayr
	The vale all planly off Beauewar.
	And syne with presoneris and catell
560	Riches and mony fayr jowell
	To Scotland tuk thai hame thar way

burned by them in the same way as they had destroyed other towns. (*L*, 247–48; *LT*, 240)

There is also evidence that the religious and other communities ransomed themselves; nine Scottish horsemen and eighteen horses were billeted by agreement at Bridlington priory. Destruction may have been less serious than Barbour implies. See Colm McNamee, *The Wars of the Bruces*.

happy, content, joyful and pleased. Each man went to his own home, praising God that things had gone so well that they had defeated the king of England in his own country by valour, by force of numbers and by the bravery of their lords.

Bath blyth and glaid joyfull and gay,
And ilk man went to thar repayr
And lovyt God thaim fell sa fayr
565 That thai the king off Ingland
Throu worschip and throu strenth of hand
And throu thar lordis gret bounte
Discumfyt in his awne countré.

Then the land was in peace for a while, but greed, which never stops setting men after wickedness to help them achieve lordship, caused lords of very good reputation make a wicked conspiracy against Robert, the brave king. (8) They meant to bring [his life] to an end and to enjoy the kingdom after his death, reigning in his place. Sir William, the lord Soulis, had the greatest disgrace from that project, for he was the principal in it, in agreeing to that infamy. (15) He had brought various [others] to be with him: Gilbert Malherbe [and] John Logy, these were the knights I mention here, also Richard Brown, a squire. Good Sir David Brechin was also accused eventually for this business, as I shall tell you later on. But all of them were exposed by a lady, as I heard, before they could carry out their intentions. (25) For she told everything to the king, their aims and their plans, how he would have been dead

---

1. Pes. The two-year truce of December 1319 was followed in April–May 1320 by a diplomatic offensive at Avignon, when three letters, from the king (lost), four bishops (lost) and the barons (the 'Declaration of Arbroath') sought to abate papal hostility to the Scots.

5–14. Lords of renown. Barbour curiously says that the lords meant to enjoy the kingdom after Robert's death; not until 28 does he say that Soules, the principal conspirator (13) was to reign.

11. Sir William Soules was son of Sir Nicholas Soules and his wife, a daughter of Alexander Comyn, earl of Buchan (see note to 23 also). William returned to Scotland after Bannockburn, served King Robert militarily, and is found as Butler of Scotland (a family honour) in 1319–20.

16–19. The conspirators. Fordun gives the same names, as does Gray (omitting Broune). The chronicle edited by Stevenson claims that 'William Soules, Patrick Graham, David Wemyss, Philip Mowbray, Alexander Mowbray, Murdoch Menteith and several other Scottish nobles, conspired against King Robert'. 'Philip Mowbray' may be an error for 'Roger', but it is possible that Philip was still alive and was executed in 1320; Alexander Mowbray did flee to England at the end of 1320. (CDS3, 723, 729)

22–23. Revealed by a lady. Fordun says that Soules and the countess of Strathearn were convicted and sentenced to perpetual imprisonment. The countess is usually taken to have been Agnes, wife of the Earl Malise who was deprived when taken at Perth in January 1313; she was a daughter of Alexander Comyn, earl of Buchan (d. 1289), therefore aunt to William de Soules, and would undoubtedly be hostile to the

BOOK 19

[*The conspiracy against King Robert; its discovery*]

Than wes the land a quhile in pes,
Bot covatys, that can nocht ces
To set men apon felony
To ger thaim cum to senyoury,

5   Gert lordis off full gret renoune
Mak a fell conjuracioun
Agayn Robert the douchty king,
Thai thocht till bring him till ending
And to bruk eftre his dede

10   The kynrik and to ryng in hys steid.
The lord the Soullis, Schyr Wilyam,
Off that purches had mast defame,
For principale tharoff was he
Off assent of that cruelté.

15   He had gottyn with him sindry,
Gilbert Maleherbe, Jhone of Logy
Thir war knychtis that I tell her
And Richard Broun als a squyer,
And gud Schyr Davy off Breichyn

20   Wes off this deid arettyt syne
As I sall tell you forthermar.
Bot thai ilkane discoveryt war
Throu a lady as I hard say
Or till thar purpos cum mycht thai,

25   For scho tauld all to the king
Thar purpose and thar ordanyng,
And how that he suld haf bene ded

Bruces. (*CP12/1*, 384) However Gray states that 'this conspiracy was discovered by Murdoch Menteith who himself became earl [of Menteith] afterwards. He had lived long in England in loyalty to the king, and returned home in order to uncover this conspiracy.' and Stevenson's chronicle goes on (from note to 22) that the conspirators 'were accused by Murdoch; some were drawn and hanged and Alexander Mowbray fled to England. As a result Murdoch was made earl of Menteith.' Murdoch does not appear in English records, but it should be remembered that Edward Balliol was brought up in Edward II's court, and could have known Murdoch, the younger brother of Earl Alan, a prisoner with his son in England.

and [how] Soulis would reign in his place, and told him the exact evidence that this intention was a matter of truth. (31) When the king knew that it was so, he took such firm steps that he had every one of them taken [prisoner]. Where the lord Soulis was taken he had three hundred and sixty squires clad in his livery at that time in his company, apart from splendidly [clad] knights. (39) He was taken at Berwick. Then men could see all his following [looking] sad and sorry, but, truth to tell, the king let them all go [free] on their way, and held those whom he had taken.

(44) The lord Soulis soon after made a full admission of the whole plan. There was fixed a parliament for that [business] and that company was brought to it. The lord Soulis there admitted the whole matter in open parliament. For that he was soon after sent to repent at Dumbarton, and died in that stone tower. (53) Sir Gilbert Malherbe, Logy and Richard Brown, these three were there condemned openly by an assize. For that they were all drawn and hanged and beheaded as well, as men had adjudged them to be. (59) And good Sir David Brechin

---

28. Soules reign in his stead. The other sources do not know what the conspiracy was about and this explanation does not ring true, because Soules was not executed; pleading guilty is unlikely to have saved his life, considering the fate of Brechin. The various conspirators had no Soules connection but look like Balliol supporters; the conspiracy was surely intended to restore the Balliol line.

35–39. Three hundred and sixty squires and knights at Berwick. Nothing like this is reported by the other sources, but presumably Soules had mustered a gang of men-at-arms at Berwick.

46. Parliament. According to Fordun, at Scone at the beginning of August; this should have been summoned about 20 June but the conspiracy could have been discovered thereafter.

48–58. The fate of the conspirators. (a) Fordun has the fullest account but (b) Gray adds to it:

(a) Soules ... and the countess ... convicted of *lèse majesté*, by conspiring against the said king, received a sentence of perpetual imprisonment. [Brechin, Malherbe, Logy, Broune] convicted of this conspiracy, first dragged by horses, were punished by beheading. Sir Eustace Maxwell, Walter de Barclay, sheriff of Aberdeen, and Patrick Graham knights, Hamelin Troup and Eustace Rattray, esquires, were accused of the same crime but were found not guilty. (*F1*, 348–49; *F2*, 341)

(b) Bruce caused William Soules to be arrested and had him confined in the castle of Dumbarton for punishment in prison, accusing him of having conspired with other great men ... for [the king's] undoing, which the said William confessed by his acknowledgment. [Brechin, Logie, Malherbe] were hanged and drawn in Perth.

And Soullis ryng intill his steid,
And tauld him werray taknyng
30   This purches wes suthfast thing.
And quhen the king wist it wes sua
Sa sutell purches gan he ma
That he gert tak thaim everilkan,
And quhar the lord Soullis was tane
35   Thre hunder and sexty had he
Off squyeris cled in his lyvere
At that tyme in his cumpany
Outane knychtis that war joly.
Into Berwik takyn wes he
40   That mycht all his mengne se
Sary and wa, bot suth to say
The king lete thaim all pas thar way
And held thaim at he takyn had.

[*The trial in parliament; the fate of the conspirators*]

The lord Soullis sone eftre maid
45   Plane granting of all that purchas.
A parlement set tharfor thar was
And brocht thidder this mengne war.
The lord the Soullis has grantyt thar
The deid into plane parleament,
50   Tharfor sone eftre he wes sent
Till his pennance to Dunbertane
And deit thar in a tour off stane.
Schyr Gilbert Maleherbe and Logy
And Richard Broune thir thre planly
55   War with a sys thar ourtane,
Tharfor thai drawyn war ilkane
And hangyt and hedyt tharto
As men had dempt thaim for to do.
And gud Schyr Davy off Breichyn

Apart from Maxwell, those found not guilty belong to the north-east,
formerly Comyn land. Since Barbour makes no mention of Roger
Mowbray, I omit the passages from other sources which describe how,
since he had died, his body was brought to stand trial, and condemned,
but the king remitted the sentence and allowed it to be buried. The
sentence allowed him to treat Mowbray's lands as forfeit.
59. Sir David Brechin, who been taken prisoner earlier (note to 9.286), at
the time of the siege of Dundee, spring, 1312. (*CDS*5, 575*d*) In October
1314 his wife was still trying to ransom him, but the threat of forfeiture

they had accused very directly, next, and he admitted that revelation of that business had been made to him, but [that] he gave no consent to it. (64) Because he concealed their intention and did not reveal it to the king of whom he held all his lands and [to whom] he had sworn his fealty, he was adjudged to be drawn and hanged. As they drew him to be hanged, the people pressed very hard to see him in his misfortune, a great sadness to behold.

(73) Sir Ingram Umfraville, who was then with the king as a Scots' man, when he saw that miserable [sight] said, 'Lords, why do you push to see in misfortune such a knight, so worthy, so brave that I have seen more [men] press to see him for his truly sovereign qualities than do now to see him here.' (82) When those words had been spoken, he kept quiet in sad spirits till men had done their will of [Brechin], then with the king's leave he brought him honourably to burial. (87) Afterwards he said to the king, 'I beg you grant me one favour; that is that you will give me leave to do what I want with all my land that lies in Scotland.' Soon then, the king said to him, 'I shall certainly agree that it be so, but tell me, what disturbs you?' (95) He said again, 'Sir, grant mercy and I shall tell you openly what [it is]. My heart does not allow me to be any longer with you, living in this country. Therefore, so that it will not grieve you,

---

probably persuaded him to change sides in November. He seems to have received his lands back, but in August 1317 was thought by Edward II to be returning to English allegiance. Barbour may have glamorised Brechin here, to justify Umfraville's outburst. It is possible that Soules revealed knowledge of the plot, but claimed non-participation, and hence was not executed. Brechin was clearly unreliable and may have been deeply involved, as the other sources suggest by not distinguishing him among the conspirators.

73. Umfraville had been taken prisoner at Bannockburn; along with Henry Percy he was co-heir of the Balliols of Red castle, and Robert I gave him Percy's half of the inheritance. Like Brechin, Soulis, Roger Mowbray, Patrick Graham, and David Wemyss, he was one of the accused barons named as having sent the Declaration of Arbroath.

60   Thai gert chalance rycht straitly syne,
And he grauntyt that off that thing
Was wele maid till him discovering
Bot he thartill gaf na consent,
And for he helyt thar entent
65   And discoveryt it nocht to the king
That he held of all his halding
And maid till him his fewté
Jugyt till hang and draw wes he.
And as thai drew him for to hing
70   The pepill ferly fast gan thring
Him and his myscheyff for to se
That to behald wes gret pité.

[*Sir Ingram Umfraville's reaction and decision to leave Scotland*]

Schyr Ingrahame the Umfravill that than
Wes with the king as Scottisman,
75   Quhen he that gret myscheiff gan se
He said, 'Lordingis, quharto pres ye
To se at myscheiff sic a knycht
That wes sa worthi and sa wicht
That Ik haff sene ma pres to se
80   Him him for his rycht soverane bounte
Than now doys for to se him her.'
And quhen thir wordis spokyn wer
With sary cher he held him still
Quhill men had done of him thar will,
85   And syne with the leve of the king
He brocht him menskly till erding.
And syne to the king said he,
'A thing I pray you graunt me,
That is that ye off all my land
90   That is intill Scotland liand
Wald giff me leve to do my will.'
The king that sone has said him till,
'I will wele graunt that it sua be,
Bot tell me quhat amovis the.'
95   He said agane, 'Schyr, graunt mercy
And I sall tell you planely,
Myne hart giffis me na mar to be
With you dwelland in this countré,
Tharfor bot that it nocht you greve

I beg you sincerely for your leave [to depart]. (101) For when so very worthy a knight, [one] so chivalrous, so brave, so famed for [his] valour, and so charged with all manly qualities as good Sir David Brechin was put to so disgraceful a death, in truth my heart will not allow me stay, not for any reason.' (109) Then the king said, 'If that is what you want, you can go whenever you like, and you will have good leave to do your pleasure with your land.' [Umfraville] thanked him warmly, and disposed of his land very speedily as he thought best. (116) Then he took his leave for evermore from the king, a generous man, before all those who were with him; he went to England to the king who gave him a very warm welcome, asking him for news of the north. (122) He told him everything, without embroidery, how those knights had been destroyed and everything I told you before. Also about the king's courtesy, who generously allowed him to do what he wanted with his land. (128) At that time messengers were sent from the king of Scotland, to treat of peace, if they could attain it, as they had been often sent before when they could not achieve their end. (133) The good king had an intention, since God had sent him so fair a grace that he had won all his land to his authority by strength of arms, that he would make peace in his time, and secure all the lands so that his heir would have peace after him, if men maintained their loyalty.

---

119. Umfraville went to England. As early as 20 April, 1320 he had a safeconduct from Edward II to go overseas through England – could it be that he was originally intended to carry the Declaration of Arbroath? He was with Edward II, who gave him gifts, in December 1320, when he claimed that he had never left Edward's allegiance. But he seems to have gone to France and no more is heard of him. (*CDS3, 694, 721*) Alexander Mowbray may have gone south with him.

100   I pray you hartly of your leve.
          For quhar sua rycht worthi a knycht
          And sa chevalrous and sa wicht
          And sa renownyt off worschip syne
          As gud Schyr David off Brechyn
105   And sa fullfyllyt off all manheid
          Was put to sa velanys a ded,
          Myn hart forsuth may nocht gif me
          To dwell for na thing that may be.'
          The king said, 'Sen that thou will sua
110   Quhenever the likys thou may ga,
          And thou sall haiff gud leve tharto
          Thi liking off thi land to do.'
          And he thankyt him gretumly
          And off his land in full gret hy
115   As hym thocht best disponyt he,
          Syne at the king of gret bounte
          Befor all thaim that with him war
          He tuk his leve for evermar,
          And went in Ingland to the king
120   That maid him rycht fayr welcummyng
          And askyt him of the north tithing.
          And he him tauld all but lesing
          How thai knychtis destroyit war
          And as I tauld till you ar,
125   And off the kingis curtassy
          That levyt him debonarly
          To do off his land his liking.
          In that tyme wes send fra the king
          Off Scotland messyngeris to trete
130   Off pes giff that thai mycht it get,
          As thai befor oft-sys war send
          How that thai coutht nocht bring till end.
          For the gud king had in entent,
          Sen God sa fayr grace had him lent
135   That he had wonnyn all his land
          Throu strenth off armys till his hand,
          That he pes in his tyme wald ma
          And all landis stabill sua
          That his ayr eftre him suld be
140   In pes, gif men held lawté.

(141) At this time, when Umfraville came to the king of
England as I explained to you a while ago, he found there
the Scots' messengers negotiating about peace and respite.
The king knew that Sir Ingram was able, and asked his advice
on the matter, what he suggested he should do. (149) For,
he said, he felt it would be a poor [thing] to make peace with
his enemy, King Robert Bruce, until he had been revenged
on him. Sir Ingram answered him, saying, 'He dealt so court-
eously with me, that there is no way I could give advice to
his disadvantage.' (156) 'You must, [I] require it,' said the
king, 'give your advice on this matter here.' 'Sir,' said [Um-
fraville], 'since you require that I speak, know for a fact that,
despite all your great chivalry, you do not have the power to
deal with him. (162) His men have grown so bold through
long experience of heavy fighting [and] have been trained in
this business, that each yeoman is so bold in himself that he
is worth a knight. (167) But if you mean to bring your war
to your aim and good pleasure, take a long truce with him.
In that [situation] most of his forces, who are just simple
yeomanry, will be forced generally to earn their bread by their
labours. (174) Some of them will have to [work] unceasingly
with plough and harrow, and [at] various other trades, to earn
their crust.

(177) Thus their arms will grow old, will deteriorate, be
destroyed or sold, and many who are now skilled in warfare
will die during a long truce, [with] others arising in their place
who will know little of such skills.

---

144. Scottish messengers. These did not come to the English court.
145. Pes and rest. Diplomatic texts often spoke of attaining peace or a
     truce. 'Rest' may have meant 'truce' here; I have translated 'respite'.
147. Askyt consale. Clearly Umfraville cannot have given advice in 1323,
     when the long truce was made. But he may have been been consulted
     in December 1320–January 1321 when serious negotiations, involving
     an embassy from Philip V, were in hand, and a long truce was eventually
     (1321) proposed. In 1323, on 30 May, at Bishopthorpe, when the truce
     was made, Edward II asked his secret council for their opinion of it.
     Henry Beaumont, heir to the Comyn earls of Buchan, 'with an excessive
     motion and irreverent mind answered often that he would not advise
     him on this matter'. Edward ordered him to leave, and Beaumont
     replied that 'it would please him more to be absent than present'.

[*Sir Ingram Umfraville advises a long truce, which is made*]

Intill this tyme that Umfravill
As I bar you on hand er quhill
Come till the king of Ingland
The Scottis messingeris thar he fand
145 Of pes and rest to haiff tretis.
The king wist Schyr Ingrahame wes wis
And askyt consaile tharto
Quhat he wald rede him for to do,
For he said him thocht hard to ma
150 Pes with the King Robert his fa
Quhill that he off him vengit war.
Schyr Ingrahame maid till him answar
And said, 'He delt sa curtasly
With me that on na wis suld I
155 Giff consaill till his nethring.'
'The behovis nedwayis,' said the king,
'To this thing her say thine avis.'
'Schyr,' said he, 'sen your willis is
That I say, wit ye sekyrly
160 For all your gret chevalry
To dele with him yhe haf na mycht.
His men all worthyn ar sa wicht
For lang usage of fechting
That has bene nuryst in swilk thing
165 That ilk yowman is sa wicht
Off his that he is worth a knycht.
Bot, and ye think your wer to bring
To your purpos and your liking,
Lang trewys with him tak ye.
170 Than sall the mast off his menye
That ar bot simple yumanry
Be dystrenyit commonaly
To wyn thar mete with thar travaill,
And sum of thaim nedis but faill
175 With pluch and harow for to get
And other ser crafftis thar mete,
Sua that thar armyng sall worth auld
And sall be rottyn stroyit and sauld,
And fele that now of wer ar sley
180 Intill the lang trew sall dey
And other in thar sted sall rys
That sall conn litill of that mastrys.

When they have grown rusty like that, then you can turn your
war against them, and, as I expect, will sweetly bring your
plans to a good conclusion.' (187) They all agreed to this,
and thereafter a truce was made between the two kings,
reckoned to last for thirteen years; it was proclaimed on the
Marches. (192) Scotsmen kept it strictly, but at sea English-
men iniquitously destroyed merchant ships which were sailing
from Scotland to Flanders with cargo, destroying them all
and taking their goods for themselves. (199) The king sent
often asking for redress, but none of it was redressed though
he always waited [while he] asked. For his part, he had the
truce maintained firmly upon the Marches, and made men
keep it strictly.

(205) At this time, when the truce was being kept on the
Marches, as I said before, Walter Stewart, the worthy [man],
took a serious illness at Bathgate. His sickness kept worsening
more and more, until men realised from his appearance that
the time approached to pay the debt which no man can escape
discharging. (213) Shriven and very penitent too, when every-
thing that a Christian man needs to have, had been done in
all particulars, he gave up his spirit as a good Christian man.
(217) Then you could hear folk weeping and wailing, many
a knight and many a lady openly showing great distress;
whoever they were, they all did it, all men bemoaning him in
common, for he was a worthy [man] among his contempo-
raries. (223) When they had made their mourning for a long
time,

---

185. 'Richt weill' I have translated somewhat loosely as 'sweetly'.
188. Truce. The truce of Bishopthorpe, beside York, 30 May, 1323.
   Moray led the Scottish delegation.
195–96. Shipping. There is much scattered evidence of Flemish trade
   with Scotland; the English government particularly objected to the trade
   in arms. For an example in 1317 see *RRS5, 126.*
205–28. Death of Walter Stewart. He last witnesses a royal charter at
   Stirling on 31 March, 1327; Bower, who calls him 'a noble warrior',
   says he died on 9 April. Paisley abbey was a Stewart foundation.

And quhen thai disusyt er
Than may ye move on thaim your wer
185 And sall rycht well as I suppos 185*
Bring your entent to gud purpos.' 186*
Till this assentyt thai ilkane, 185
And eftre sone war trewis tane
Betwix the twa kingis that wer
190 Tailyeit to lest for thretten yer 188
And on the marchis gert thaim cry.
The Scottismenn kepyt thaim lelely,
Bot the Inglismen apon the se
Distroyit throu gret inyquyté
195 Marchand schippis that sailand war 193
Fra Scotland till Flaundris with war,
And destroyit everilkane
And to thar oys the gud has tane.
The king send oft till ask redres,
200 Bot nocht off it redressyt wes 198
And he abaid all tyme askand,
The trew on his half gert he stand
Apon the marchis stabilly
And gert men kep thaim lelely.

[The death of Walter the Steward]

205 In this tyme that trewis war 203
Lestend on marchis as I said ar
Schyr Walter Stewart that worthi was
At Bathgat a gret seknes tas.
His ivill ay woux mar and mar
210 Quhill men persavit be his far 208
That him worthit nede to pay the det
That na man to pay may let,
Schryvyn and als repentit weill
Quhen all wes doyn him ilkdeill
215 That Crystyn man nedyt till have 213
As gud Crystyn the gast he gave.
Then men mycht her men gret and cry
And mony a knycht and mony a lady
Mak in apert rycht evill cher,
220 Sa did thai all that ever thai war, 218
All men him menyt commounly
For off his eild he wes worthy.
Quhen thai lang quhill thar dule had maid

they took his corpse to Paisley, and there he was buried with
great ceremony and deep mourning. May God in his might
bring his soul where joy lasts [and] never ceases.

(229) After his death, as I said before, [in] the truce which
had been made to last thirteen years, when two and a half
years of them had passed, as I believe, King Robert saw that
men were not willing to give redress for ships that had been
taken, [nor] for the men who had been killed, but continued
their evil ways whenever they met them on the sea. (239) He
sent and formally cancelled and publicly gave up the truce.
In revenge for this trespass [he chose] Thomas, the good earl
of Moray, Donald earl of Mar, James Douglas with those two
and James Stewart, who was leader, after his good brother's
death, of all his brother's men in war; (248) [he] had them
prepare to go with many men to England, to burn and slay,
and they set out for England.

232-33. Two and a half years. May 1323–early 1327, three and a half
years.

240. Gave up formally. In fact he broke the truce by attacking England
on 1 February, 1327; thereafter it was reaffirmed but negotiations for
peace failed at York soon after 10 June, 1327 and Robert seems to have
decided to renew the war against the weak and unpopular regime of
Queen Isabella, governing in the name of Edward III. The English
complained of the treachery of the Scots in invading, so a formal
renunciation seems unlikely. The ensuing campaigns are described in
R. G. Nicholson, *Edward III and the Scots*, and in Barrow, *Bruce*.

243. Donald, earl of Mar had refused to come back to Scotland in 1314.
He returned at the end of 1326, to persuade King Robert to intervene
to save Edward II – which may explain the attack on England on 1 Feb-
ruary, 1327. He is mentioned once (351) in the account of this campaign.

245. James Stewart, of Durisdeer, a shadowy figure who died without
issue. Not mentioned further.

251. They held forth to England. The chronicler Jean le Bel served with
the English army, and describes the Scots as follows:

The Scots are hardily bold and strong, and labour a lot in war, and
at this time they didn't fear the English ... When they want to enter
the kingdom of England, they drive their host 20 or 32 leagues along,
by day and night, at which people can be greatly astonished if they
don't know their custom. It's certain that when they want to go and
invade England, they are all on horse ... apart from the rabble
(*ribaudaille*) who follow on foot; i.e. knights and esquires mounted
on good stout runcins, and the other folk of the land all on little
hackneys. And they drive no carts for the various mountains which
have to be passed in this country, and so they have no purveyance of
bread or wine, for their custom is such in war, and their sobriety so
great, that they last for a good long time on half-cooked flesh without
bread, and good river water, without wine, and also do not have pots

The cors to Paslay haiff thai haid,
225 And thar with gret solempnyte 223
And with gret dule erdyt wes he,
God for his mycht his saule bring
Quhar joy ay lestis but ending.

[*The truce is given up; Moray and Douglas harry Weardale*]

Efftre his dede as I said ar
230 The trewys that sua takyn war 228
For till haff lestyt thretten yer,
Quhen twa yer of thaim passyt wer
And ane halff as I trow allsua
The King Robert saw men wald nocht ma
235 Redres of schippys that war tane 233
And off the men als that war slane,
Bot contynowyt thar mavtyé
Quhenever thai met thaim on the se.
He sent and acquit him planly
240 And gave the trewis up opynly, 238
And in the vengeance of this trespas
The gud erle of Murreff Thomas
And Donald erle of Mar alsua
And James of Douglas with thai twa,
245 And James Stewart that ledar wes 243
Efter his gud brotheris disceis
Off all his bruderys men in wer,
He gert apon thar best maner
With mony men bowne thaim to ga
250 In Ingland for to bryn and sla, 248
And thai held furth till Ingland.

---

or cauldrons, for they cook their meat in the hide of the beast, even when they have skinned it. They know they they will find a great abundance of beasts in the country they are going to, so they carry no other supplies, except that each carries between the saddle and horse-cloth, a big flat stone, and fixed behind a bag full of meal, for the purpose that when they have eaten so much badly cooked meat that their stomachs seem weak and feeble, they throw this flat stone on the fire, mix a little of their meal with water when the stone is hot, and make a little cake of it ... and eat it to settle their stomachs. So it's not surprising that they make greater journeys than other folk who are all on horseback, apart from the rabble, and have no cart or other harness, as you've heard. (*Chron. le Bel*, i, 51–52)

Pity the horse with a stone under the saddle.

They numbered ten thousand good men, [who] burned and
slew on their way; they destroyed their foes remorselessly.
(255) They advanced like that southwards until they reached
Weardale. [By] that time Edward of Caernarvon, the king,
had died and been buried in his tomb, and his son, Edward,
who was young had been crowned king in England, having
the surname of Windsor. (262) He had previously been in
France with his mother, dame Isabel, and was married, as I
heard, to a young lady, fair of face, who was daughter to the
count of Hainault; he brought with him men of great spirit
from that country. Sir John Hainault was their leader, [a man]
very sage and bold in war. (271) At the time when the
Scotsmen were in Weardale, as I said to you before, the
newly-made king was at York, [where he] heard about the
destruction which Scotsmen were making in his country. He
mustered a great army, [numbering] nearly fifty thousand.
(278) Then he went northwards in the land with that company
as one force; he was eighteen years old at that time. One day
the Scots harried all 'Cockdale' from end to end, then rode
back to Weardale.

(284) Their scouts who had sight of the Englishmen coming,
reported it to their lords then. Then the lord Douglas rode
out directly

---

256. Weardale. The Scottish army invaded England in mid-July, appar-
ently by the west. They ravaged south-east into Co. Durham and were
at Bishop Aukland on the Wear by 19 July. Edward II died in September.

264. Was married. Edward III was betrothed to Philippa of Hainault,
but they were not married until 24 January, 1328.

269. Sir John Hainault had led the mercenaries who helped Queen Isabella
to overthrow Edward II. He now brought another party to York, where
on 7 June there was a disastrous riot between them and English archers,
leaving dead on both sides. See note to 462.

273. York. Edward III was at York on 23 May, 1327 and remained there
for five weeks.

277. The English army. There is no reliable evidence as to the size of
the army. It was certainly not a large host.

280. Eighteen. Edward III was born in November 1312, so was 14 in
July 1327.

281. Cokdale. While the Scots were in Weardale between 19 and 30 July,
according to Gray, 'Archibald Douglas [brother of James] having over-
run with forragers almost all the [county] of Durham and brought in
much booty to their army, fell in at Darlington with a great body of
common folk marching towards the English army and killed them nearly
all.' There is a Cockfield between Bishop Aukland and Barnard Castle,
which probably represents the Cockdale name. It cannot be Coquetdale.

283. Weardale. The Scots and English had lost knowledge of each others'

Thai war of gud men ten thousand,
Thai brynt and slew intill thar way,
Thar fayis fast destroyit thai
255 And suagat southwart gan thai far   253
To Wardaill quhill thai cummyn war.
That tyme Edward off Carnaverane
The king wes ded and laid in stane,
And Edward his sone that wes ying
260 In Ingland crownyt wes to king   258
And surname off Wyndyssor.
He had in France bene thar-befor
With his moder Dame Ysabell,
And wes weddyt as Ik herd tell
265 With a young lady fayr of face   263
That the erlis douchter was
Off Hennaud, and off that cuntré
Brocht with him men of gret bounté,
Schyr Jhone the Hennaud wes thar leder
270 That was wys and wycht in wer.   268
And that tyme that Scottismen wer
At Wardaile, as I said you er,
Intill York wes the new-maid king,
And herd tell of the destroying
275 That Scottismen maid in his countré.   273
A gret ost till him gaderyt he,
He wes wele ner fyfty thousand,
Than held he northwart in the land
In haill battaill with that mengne,
280 Auchtene yer auld that tyme wes he.   278
The Scottismen a day Cokdaile
Fra end till end had heryit haile
And till Wardaile again thai raid.

*[Edward III's army approaches; Douglas prepares an ambush;
the skirmish by the Wear]*

Thar discourriouris that sycht has haid
285 Off cummyn of the Inglismen   283
To thar lordis thai tauld it then.
Than the lord Douglas in a ling

---

whereabouts. The English army was blundering about in the Tyne
valley in the last half of July. On 28 July they discovered that the Scots
were at Stanhope in the Wear valley, Co. Durham and the two armies
had sight of each other the following day.

to see them coming, and saw that those who came riding in good order formed seven divisions. (291) When he had surveyed those folk, he rode back towards his army. The earl asked if he had seen the English army. 'Yes, sir, without a doubt.' 'What [size] are they?' 'Sir, many men.' The earl swore his oath then. 'We shall fight them, even if they turned out to be even more [numerous] than they are.' (299) 'Sir, God be praised,' [Douglas] responded, 'that we have such a commander who dares to undertake such serious business. But, by St Bride, it won't be like that if my advice is listened to. For we shall not fight in any way except from an advantageous [position]. I think it isn't foolish for an inferior force to seize an advantage against more [men] when they can.' (309) As they were speaking like this, they saw riding straight towards them over a high ridge, a broad division, having many banners displayed. Another came close after, and so in the same way they came till seven broad divisions had crossed over that high ridge. (317) The Scotsmen were then lying on the north side of the Wear, towards Scotland. The dale was long, I know; on either side there was a hill [running] down rather steeply to the water. (322) The Scotsmen, in good order, all equipped in their best,

---

300. A capitayn. Moray was in command.

309. The English army approaches. From Blanchland they marched across the moor, and, according to Lanercost, who ignores the shift of the armies to Stanhope Park (490–91),

Had [Edward III] attacked them at once with his army he must have beaten them as was commonly said by all men afterwards. Daily they lost both men and horses through lack of supplies, although they had gathered some booty in the country round about, but the affair was put off for eight days in accord with the bad advice of certain magnates of the army, the king always lying between them and Scotland, until one night the Scots, warned, it is said, by an Englishman of the king's army that the king intended to attack them the following day, slipped quietly from the park, and marching round the king's army, held their way to Scotland. (*L*, 259; *LT*, 257)

317–18. The north side. There has been much debate on this, because, as Le Bel and Gray show, the English came from Haydon Bridge to the north and no source says they crossed the river Wear. McDiarmid argues that since Stanhope Park was on the north side of the Wear, the Scots had always been on that side, as Barbour says – a powerful argument if correct about the Park. Le Bel is clear that the river remained between the two armies at both Stanhope and Stanhope Park, ruling out the Scots crossing the river when they moved to the Park. There are important notes on this puzzle in Barrow, *Bruce*, 373,n. 83, and *B1985*, 106. Gray describes the situation:

Raid furth to se thar cummyng
And saw that sevyn bataillis war thai
290   That cum ridand in gud aray,   288
Quhen he that folk behaldyn had
Towart his ost agayn he rad.
The erle speryt gif he had sene
That ost. 'Ya, schyr,' he said, 'but wene.'
295   'Quhat folk ar thai?' 'Schyr, mony men.'   293
The erle his ayth has sworn then,
'We sall fecht with thaim thocht thai war
Yeit ma eftsonys than thai ar.'
'Schyr, lovyt be God,' he said agayn,
300   'That we haiff sic a capitayn   298
That sua gret thing dar undreta,
Bot, be saynct Bryd, it beis nocht sua
Giff my consaill may trowyt be,
For fecht on na maner sall we
305   Bot it be at our avantage,   303
For methink it war na outrage
To fewar folk aganys ma
Avantage quhen thai ma to ta.'
As thai war on this wis spekand
310   Our ane hey rig thai saw ridand   308
Towart thaim evyn a battaill braid,
Baneris displayit inew thai haid,
And a nothyr come eftre ner
And rycht apon the samyn maner
315   Thai come quhill sevin bataillis braid   313
Out-our that hey rig passyt haid.
The Scottismen war than liand
On north halff Wer towart Scotland.
The dale wes strekyt weill Ik hycht,
320   On athyr sid thar wes ane hycht   318
And till the water doune sumdeill stay.
The Scottismen in gud aray
On thar best wis buskyt ilkane

This great host of the English found their enemies ready beside
Stanhope, in three divisions, on a fine plain. They were not many
folk, three captains only, the earls of Moray and Mar and James
Douglas. [Edward III] camped opposite them on the River Wear for
three days, and on the fourth night the Scots moved themselves,
shifting a small league from there, in[to] the Park of Stanhope, where
they waited for six days before this great army of English, Germans,
and Hainaulters. (*S*, 154; *ST*, 81)

stood in the strong [position] they had taken, which was about a quarter of a mile from the river Wear; they stood there awaiting battle. (328) Englishmen on the other side came riding downward, until they had come as close to the river Wear as their enemies were on the other side. (332) Then they halted right there, sending out a thousand archers, with bows uncovered and in their hands; they had them take a good drink of wine, and ordered them to harass the Scots' host with random [fire] and get them to come down towards [the archers], for if they could get them to break ranks, they thought they would have them at their mercy. (341) They sent armed men down with [the archers] to defend them at the water. (343) The lord Douglas saw their display, and he had lie in waiting men who were very well horsed and armed, a large company secretly behind the divisions, to await their arrival, [so that] when he made a signal to them they would come galloping hard and kill with spears who[ever] they could overcome. (351) Donald of Mar was their commander and Archibald Douglas with him.

(353) The lord Douglas rode toward them, having a gown over his armour, crossing always up again to draw them near his division. Those who had drunk of the wine came on rushing in a line until they came so close to the force that many arrows fell among them. (361) Robert Ogle, a good squire came galloping then on a courser, shouting back to the archers,

---

361. Robert Ogle was in the Norham garrison in 1322 and at Newcastle in 1329. (*CDS3*, *787*, *992*)

Stud in a strenth that thai had tane,
325 And that wes fra the water of Wer 323
A quartar of a myle weill ner,
Thar stud thai battaill till abid,
And Inglismen on athyr sid
Come ridand dounwart quhill thai wer
330 To Weris water cummyn als ner 328
As on other halff thar fayis war.
Than haf thai maid a rest rycht thar
And send out archerys a thousand
With hudis off and bowys in hand
335 And gert thaim drink weill of the wyn, 333
And bad thaim gang to bykker syne
The Scottis ost in abandoun
And ger thaim cum apon thaim doun,
For mycht thai ger thaim brek aray
340 To haiff thaim at thar will thocht thai. 338
Armyt men doune with thaim thai send
Thaim at the water to defend.
The lord Douglas has sene thar fer,
And men that rycht weill horsyt wer
345 And armyt a gret cumpany 343
Behind the bataillis prevely
He gert howe to bid thar cummyng,
And quhen he maid to thaim taknyng
Thai suld cum prekand fast and sla
350 With sperys that thai mycht ourta, 348
Donald off Mar thar chiftane was
And Archebald with hym of Douglas.

[*Douglas drives back the English; the two sides encamp;
novelties seen*]

The lord Douglas towart thaim raid,
A gowne on his armur he haid,
355 And traversyt all wayis up agayn 353
Thaim ner his bataillis for to trayn,
And thai that drunkyn had off the wyne
Come ay up lingand in a lyne
Quhill thai the battaill come sa ner
360 That arowis fell amang thaim ser. 358
Robert off Ogill a gud squyer
Come prikand than on a courser
And on the archeris criyt agane,

'You don't know who is leading you astray now! It's the lord Douglas who will teach you some of his tricks!' When they heard talk of Douglas, the bravest was frightened and turned back altogether. (370) Then he made his signal swiftly, and the folk who lay in ambush galloped upon them so stoutly there that they slew a good three hundred of them, chasing all the rest back home to the water. (376) Sir William Erskine, who had been newly made a knight that day, well horsed and equipped, with others who were there, chased so far forward that his horse bore him among the main body of English men, and by force he was taken [prisoner] then. But pretty soon an exchange was made of him for another who had been taken. (385) After those English archers had been killed, their men rode to their host again. So too did the lord Douglas. When he had returned, they could see among their foes that their tents were soon pitched. Then they soon perceived that [the enemy] would make camp that night, planning to do no more that day, so they too made camp. (395) They quickly pitched pavilions; they also had tents and shelters nearby, all laid out in a row. They saw two novelties that day which had not existed previously in Scotland: crests for helmets was one, which they thought very beautiful and also remarkable to view; the other was bangs of war which they had never heard before. (405) They were astonished at these two things. That night they stayed determinedly awake;

---

376. Sir William Erskine, member of a family which grew in importance under David II and Robert II; his son, Robert, would appreciate this mention. (*SP*5, 591–96)

400. Crests. According to the chronicle of the Monk of Westminster, in the 1388 parliament it was enacted that 'all the liveries called crests used since the first year of [Edward III, i.e. 1327] shall be forbidden.'

403. Crakys off wer. Probably very primitive artillery.

'Ye wate nocht quha mays you that trayn,
That is the lord Douglas that will 363
Off his playis ken sum you till,'
And quhen thai herd spek of Douglas
The hardyest effrayit was
And agayn turnyt halely.
His takyn maid he than in hy, 368
And the folk that enbuschit war
Sa stoutly prekyt on thaim thar
That weile thre hunder haiff thai slane
And till the water hame agane
All the remanand gan thai chas. 373
Schyr Wilyam off Erskyn that was
Newlyngis makyn knycht that day 375*
Weill horsit intill gud aray 376*
Chasyt with other that thar war 375
Sa fer furth that hys hors him bar 376
Amang the lump of Inglismen,
And with strang hand wes takyn then,
Bot off him wele sone chang wes maid
For other that men takyn haid.
Fra thir Inglis archeris wes slane 381
Thar folk raid till thar ost agane,
And rycht sua did the lord off Douglas.
And quhen that he reparyt was
Thai mycht amang thar fayis se
Thar pailyounys sone stentyt be, 386
And thai persavyt sone in hy
That thai that nycht wald tak herbery
And schup to do no mar that day,
Tharfor thaim alsua herbryit thay
And stent pailyounys in hy, 391
Tentis and lugis als tharby
Thai gert mak and set all on raw.
Twa novelryis that day thai saw
That forouth in Scotland had bene nane,
Tymmeris for helmys war the tane 396
That thaim thoucht thane off gret bewté
And alsua wondyr for to se,
The tother crakys war off wer
That thai befor herd never er,
Off thir twa thingis thai had ferly. 401
That nycht thai walkyt stalwartly,

365
370
375
380
385
390
395
400
405

most of them lay in arms until daylight of the following morning.

(409) The English men considered in what way they could get the Scots to leave their advantageous [position], for they realised it would be silly and foolhardy to go up to them to attack them in their stronghold in open assault. (415) For that reason they sent a thousand good men, horsed [and] armed both foot and hand, to lie in ambush in a valley behind their foes, and they prepared their divisions as if they meant to take the fight upon [the Scots]. (421) For they believed that the Scots had such determination that they could not remain immobile, because they knew that they had such courage that because of it they would leave [their] stronghold and advantage to meet [the English] in the open. Then their ambush would burst all together upon them from behind; they thought that in this way they would make [the Scots] sorry for their game. (430) They sent their ambush out, which concealed itself in secrecy. In the morning, fairly early in this host they sounded a loud blast and had their broad divisions form up, then all arrayed to fight they held right [down] toward the water. (437) The Scotsmen, seeing them do this, made themselves ready in their best fashion and arrayed openly as [one] division, with banners displayed in the wind. They left their strongpoint, and openly came down to meet [the English] boldly in as good an order as they could, just as their foes had expected. (445) But the lord Douglas, who was always careful, setting out watches here and there, got to know of their ambush.

409–84. This encounter is not mentioned in Lanercost or Gray (above notes to 309, 317). Nor can it be found in Le Bel who, while admitting skirmishing, is clear that the Scots refused to engage with the English army. Barbour is probably describing a very small skirmish.

The mast part off thaim armyt lay
Quhill on the morn that it wes day.

[*Douglas foils an English ambush*]

The Inglismen thaim umbethocht
410 Apon quhat maner that thai moucht 406
Ger Scottis leve thar avantage,
For thaim thocht foly and outrage
To gang up till thaim till assaill
Thaim at thar strenth in plane battaill,
415 Tharfor of gud men a thousand 411
Armyt on hors bath fute and hand
Thai send behind thar fayis to be
Enbuschit intill a vale,
And schup thar bataillis as thai wald
420 Apon thaim till the fechtyn hald, 416
For thai thocht Scottismen sic will
Had that thai mycht nocht hald thaim still,
For thai knew thaim off sic curage
That thar-throuch strenth and avantage
425 Thai suld leve and mete them planly. 421
Than suld thar buschement halily
Behind brek on thaim at the bak,
Sa thocht thai wele thai suld thaim mak
For to repent thaim off thar play.
430 Thar enbuschment furth send haiff thai 426
That thaim enbuschit prevely,
And on the morn sum-dele arly
Intill this ost hey trumpyt thai
And gert thar braid bataillis aray,
435 And all arayit for to fycht 431
Thai held towart the water rycht.
Scottismen that saw thaim do swa
Boune on thar best wis gan thaim ma
And in bataill planly arayit
440 With baneris till the wynd displayit 436
Thai left thar strenth, and all planly
Come doune to mete thaim hardely
In als gud maner as thai moucht
Rycht as thar fayis befor had thocht.
445 Bot the lord Douglas that ay was war 441
And set out wachis her and thar
Gat wyt off thar enbuschement,

Then at oncce he went in great haste in front of the divisions and firmly ordered each man to turn round at once, just where he stood, and, having been turned [thus] he ordered them to go back up to their stronghold, [and] that they should not delay there. (454) They did as he had ordered until they came to their strongpoint again, then they turned with doughtiness and stood ready to give battle if their foes sought to attack them. When the Englishmen saw them go back up like that toward their strongpoint, they shouted aloud, 'They flee [on] their way!' (462) Sir John Hainault said, '*Perfay*, yon flight is just feigned. I see their armed men and their banners behind, so that they [need] only turn there where they were standing, [to] be arrayed to fight if any press them with force. (469) They have seen our ambush and gone back to their strength. Yon folk are commanded intelligently, and he who leads them is worthy by his commonsense, valour and wisdom to govern the Roman Empire.' (475) That's how that worthy knight spoke on that day; those lying in ambush, when they saw that they had been spotted thus, went back toward their army. The divisions of Englishmen, when they saw that they had then failed in their plan, went to their camp and quickly [took up] quarters. Those on the other side did exactly the same, having no more combat that day.

(485) When that day had passed, they made fires in great numbers as soon as night had fallen. Then the good lord Douglas

---

462. Sir John Hainault. According to the *Récits d'un Bourgeois de Valenciennes*, ed. Kervyn de Lettenhove (1877), 147, which has a brief account of the campaign, 'there were several skirmishes, and Sir John Hainault was taken prisoner there by the Scots, who put him to ransom, which he paid.' No other account mentions this. I owe the reference to Dr Graeme Small.

Than intill gret hy is he went
Befor the bataillis and stoutly
450   He bad ilk man turn him in hy   446
Rycht as he stud, and turnyt sua
Up till thar strenth he bad thaim ga
Sua that na let thar thai maid,
And thai did as he biddyn haid
455   Quhill till thar strenth thai come agayne,   451
Than turnyt thai thaim with mekill mayn
And stud redy to giff battaill
Giff thar fayis wald thaim assaill.
Quhen Inglismen had sene thaim sua
460   Towart thar strenth agayne up ga   456
Thai criyt hey, 'Thai fley thar way.'
Schyr Jhone Hennaud said, 'Perfay
Yone fleyng is rycht degysé,
Thar armyt men behind I se
465   And thar baneris, sua that thaim thar   461
Bot turne thaim as thai standand ar
And be arayit for to fycht
Giff ony presyt thaim with mycht.
Thai haiff sene our enbuschement
470   And agane till thar strenth ar went.   466
Yone folk ar governyt wittily,
And he that ledis is worthi
For avisé worschip and wysdome
To governe the empyr off Rome.'
475   Thus spak that worthi knycht that day,   471
And the enbuschement fra that thai
Saw that thai sua discoveryt war
Towart thar ost agane thai fair,
And the bataillis off Inglismen
480   Quhen thai saw thai had faillyt then   476
Off thar purpos to thar herbery
Thai went and logit thaim in hy.
On other halff rycht sua did thai,
Thai maid na mar debat that day.

[*The Scots camp in a walled park; the English follow*]

485   Quhen thai that day ourdrevyn had   481
Fyris in gret foysoun thai maid
Alsone as the nycht fallyn was.
And than the gud lord off Douglas,

who had espied a place by there, two miles away, where the Scots' host could most securely make camp and also defend themselves better that in any other place in [the district] – (494) a park that was wholly surrounded by a wall [and] nearly full of trees, but with a large open [space] in it – thither the lord Douglas meant to bring their army by night. (500) Therefore, without more ado they stoked their fires building them up, and set out all together, coming to the park without [any] loss; they quartered themselves by the river and as near to it as they had been before. (507) In the morning, when it was day[light] the English host saw that the Scotsmen had gone, were astonished and had scouts quickly gallop to see where they had gone. (512) By their fires they discovered that they had had their whole host make camp in the park of Weardale. For that reason their host got ready with all speed, rode just opposite to them, having their tents pitched on the other side of the river Wear, as close [to them] as they had been pitched previously. (520) They lay like that on both sides for eight days, the Englishmen not daring to attack the Scotsmen in open battle because of the strength of the ground that they had [taken up] there. (524) Each day there was made boldly jousting of arms and skirmishing; men were taken [prisoner] on both sides. Those who were taken one day were exchanged on a later one. But no other deeds were done worth remembering until it happened upon the seventh day

---

501. The fires. Le Bel comments on the Scottish fires.
502-3. The move to the park, though noted by several chroniclers, is not dated. Le Bel exaggerates the period spent in Weardale, and Barbour the time spent in the Park. Gray says 'on the fourth night', which would be 2 or 3 August, 1327.
513. Park of Weardale. Stanhope Park.
531. The seventh day. This is impossible; the Scots were not in the Park for more than a few days. It is possible that Barbour's source spoke of the 'second' day, and that this was misread as 'sevynd'; hence 'eight days' in 520.

That had spyit a place tharby
490 Twa myile thin that quhar mar traistly 486
The Scottis ost mycht herbery ta
And defend thaim better alsua
Than ellys in ony place tharby,
It wes a park all halily
495 Wes envyround about with wall, 491
It wes ner full of treys all
Bot a gret plane intill it was,
Thidder thocht the lord of Douglas
Be nychtyrtale thar ost to bring.
500 Tharfor foroutyn mar dwelling 496
Thai bet thar fyris and maid thaim mar,
And syne all samyn furtht thai far
And till the park foroutyn tynseill
Thai come and herbryit thaim weill
505 Upon the water and als ner 501
Till it as thai beforouth wer.
And on the morn quhen it wes day
The Inglis ost myssyt away
The Scottismen and had ferly,
510 And gert discourriouris hastily 506
Pryk to se quhar thai war away,
And be thar fyris persavyt thai
That thai in the park of Werdale
Had gert herbry thar ost all hale.
515 Tharfor thar ost but mar abaid 511
Buskyt, and evyn anent thaim raid
And on athyr halff the water of Wer
Gert stent thar palyounys als ner
As thar befor stentyt war thai.
520 Aucht dayis on baith halff sua thai lay 516
That Inglismen durst nocht assaill
The Scottismen with plane battaill
For strenth of erd that thai had thar.
Thar wes ilk day justyn of wer
525 And scrymyn maid full apertly 521
And men tane on athyr party,
And thai that war tane on a day
On ane other changyt war thai,
Bot other dedis nane war done
530 That gretly is apon to mone, 526
Till it fell on the sevynd day

the lord Douglas had espied a way whereby he could ride round them, coming upon the further side.

(535) In the evening he got ready taking with him a goodly following, five hundred on horse, bold and hardy. In the night, very secretly and noiselessly, he rode far enough until he had almost gone round their host and [then] quietly rode toward them on the further side. (543) He had half the men who were with him carry [their] swords unsheathed in their hands, ordering them to cut in two the ropes, so that they would make the tents collapse on those who were in them. (548) Then the rest who were following were to stab down forcibly with spears. When they heard his horn, they were to make their way at once to the river. When what I've just explained had been said, they rode hard toward their foes, who had no watches on that side. (555) As they were approaching near, an Englishman, who lay warming himself by a fire, said to his companion, 'I don't know what is going to happen to us here but I have a terrible foreboding – I'm terrified of the Black Douglas .' And [Douglas] who heard him, said, *'Perfay*, you will have good reason to, if I [have anything to do with it].'(563) With that, with all his company he charged them boldly, cutting down proud pavilions [while] they stabbed men mercilessly with spears which cut sharp. Very soon noise and shouting arose;

535–616. The attack on the English camp. Le Bel notices this, and Gray (cont. from note to 317) says, 'They did no feats of arms except that the Scots under James Douglas rode one night into the lines at one end of the camp, slew a large number of people of the earls, and withdrew without loss.' This was four nights before the Scots departed – an exaggeration. Other English chronicles say that the attack was possible because of betrayal on the English side, that Douglas hoped to seize Edward III but failed, and that Douglas's chaplain was killed outside the king's tent. Le Bel mentions the king's tent as do the *Anonimalle Chronicle* (ed. Childs and Taylor, 136–38) and Lanercost (cont from note to 309):

> Sir James Douglas, like a valiant and bold knight, one night when they were in the Park, with a few men with him stealthily entered a great part of the king's army, coming almost to the king's tent. But in returning he showed who he was, killed many who were taken by surprise, and escaped unhurt. When the king heard that the Scots had left, he was so vexed that he wept ... (*L*, 260; *LT*, 258)

Gray also mentions Edward III's tears. One other English chronicler, Knighton, supports the story of a quiet infiltration, by recounting that when challenged by an English sentry, Douglas made a reply in

The lord Douglas had spyit a way
How that he mycht about thaim rid
And com on the ferrer sid.

[Douglas rides round the English camp and surprises it on the far side]

535 And at evyn purvayit him he   531
     And tuk with him a gud mengne
     Fyve hunder on hors wicht and hardy,
     And in the nycht all prevely
     Forout noyis sa fer he raid
540 Quhill that he ner enveronyt had   536
     Thar ost and on the ferrar sid
     Towart thaim slely gan he rid.
     And the men that with him war
     He gert in hand have swerdis bar
545 And bad thaim hew rapis in twa   541
     That thai the palyounys mycht ma
     To fall on thaim that in thaim war,
     Than suld the lave that folowit thar
     Stab doune with speris sturdely,
550 And quhen thai hard his horne in hy   546
     To the water hald doune thar way.
     Quhen this wes said that Ik her say
     Towart thar fayis fast thai raid
     That on that sid na wachis haid.
555 And as thai ner war approchand   551
     Ane Inglisman that lay bekand
     Him be a fyr said till his fer,
     'I wat nocht quhat may tyd us her
     Bot rycht a gret growyng me tais,
560 For I dred sar for the blak Douglas,'   556
     And he that hard him said, 'Perfay
     Thou sall haiff caus gif that I may.'
     With that with all him cumpany
     He ruschyt in on thaim hardely
565 And pailyounys doune he bar,   561
     With sperys that scharply schar
     Thai stekyt men dispitously.
     The noys weill sone rais and cry,

---

an English accent. Barbour does not contradict this version of the exploit.

they stabbed, thrust and slew, and eagerly cut down tents. (571) They made a relentless slaughter there, [where] those who were lying unarmed had no chance to make a defence, and they slew them without pity. They taught them what a great folly it was to lie near their enemies without keeping a good watch. (578) The Scotsmen were killing their enemies there like this until the shout arose widely through the great [English] host [so] that [first one] lord [then] another was astir. When Douglas understood that they were arming themselves generally, he blew his horn to call back his men, ordering them to hold their way toward the river, which they did. (587) He remained last [of all] to see that none of his [men] should be left [behind]. As he stayed waiting like that, a man with a club in his hand came and struck him such mighty blows that, if it had not been for his great strength and his supreme manliness, he would have died in that place. (595) But he, never afraid even though he was often hard pressed, with great strength and great courage fought the other to death. His men, who had ridden at full speed down to the river, missed their lord when they got there. (602) They were very fearful for him then, each one asking another for news, but still they heard nothing about him. Then they decided among themselves that they would go up to seek him. (607) As they [stood] in this funk, they heard the tooting of his horn. Recognising it swiftly they were delighted at his arrival and asked him about his delay.

And thai stabbyt stekyt and slew
570 And pailyounys doun yarne thai drew. 566
A felloune slauchter maid thai thar
For thai that liand nakit war
Had na power defens to ma
And thai but pité gan thaim sla.
575 Thai gert thaim weill wyt that foly 571
Wes ner thar fayis for to ly
Bot giff thai traistly wachit war.
The Scottismen war slayand thar
Thar fayis on this wis quhill the cry
580 Ras throu the ost commonaly 576
That lord and other war on ster,
And quhen the Douglas wyst thai wer
Armand thaim all commonaly
He blew his horn for to rely
585 His men and bad thaim hald thar way 581
Towart the water and sua did thai,
And he abaid henmast to se
That nane of hys suld levyt be.
And as he bade sua howand
590 Sua come thane ane with a club in hand 586
And sua gret a rout till him raucht
That had nocht bene his mekill maucht
And his rycht soverane manheid
Intill that place he had bene dede,
595 Bot he that na tyme wes effrayit 591
Thocht he weill oft wes hard assayit
Throu mekill strenth and gret manheid
Has brocht the tother to the ded.
His men that till the water doun
600 War ridyne intill a raundoun 596
Myssyt thar lord quhen thai come thar,
Than war thai dredand for him sar,
Ilkan at other speryt tithing
Bot yeit off him thai hard na thing.
605 Than gan thai consaill samyn ta 601
That thai to sek him up wald ga,
And as thai war in sic effray
A tutilling off his horne hard thai
And thai that has it knawyn swith
610 War of his cummyn wonder blyth 606
And speryt at him of his abaid.

He told [them] how a fellow who met him boldly on the way dealt him such a fierce blow with his club, that, if fate had not helped him a lot he would have been in great danger there.

(617) They held their way speaking about this, until they came to their host which waited for them armed [and] on foot, to help them if they needed it. As soon as the lord Douglas had met with the earl of Moray the earl asked him for news of how he had fared on his expedition. (625) 'Sir,' he said, 'we have drawn blood.' The earl, who was a very courageous [man], said, 'If we had gone together, we could have defeated them all.' 'That might have turned out well,' said [Douglas], 'but surely we were sufficient to put ourselves at yon risk, for if they had defeated [those of] us who went yonder, it would have dismayed all those who are here.' (635) The earl said, 'Since it seems that we can't attack our fierce enemy's might by stratagem, let us do it in open battle!' The lord Douglas said, 'By St Bride, it would be very stupid for us to fight at this time with such a host, which grows stronger every day and has plenty of food as well. (644) Moreover we are in their country here, where no help can reach us. It's hard to rescue us here, nor can we forage to get food – we have to eat whatever we have here. So let's do to our enemy lying here in front of us what I heard some years ago

And he tauld how a carle him maid
With a club sic felloun pay
That met him stoutly in the way
615   That had nocht fortoun helpit the mar   611
He had bene in gret perell thar.

[Douglas and Moray debate; the fable of the fox and the fisherman]

Thusgat spekand thai held thar way
Quhill till thar ost cummyn ar thai
That on fute armyt thaim abaid
620   For till help giff thai myster haid,   616
And alsone as the lord Douglas
Met with the erle off Murreff was
The erle speryt at thaim tithing
How thai had farne in thar outing.
625   'Schyr,' said he, 'we haf drawyn blud.'   621
The erle that wes of mekill mude
Said, 'And we all had thidder gayne
We haid discumfyt thaim ilkan.'
'That mycht haff fallyn weill,' said he,
630   'Bot sekyrly ynew war we   626
To put us in yone aventur,
For had thai maid discumfitur
On us that yonder passyt wer
It suld all stonay that ar her.'
635   The erle said, 'Sen that it sua is   631
That we may nocht with jupertys
Our feloune fayis fors assaill
We sall do it in plane battaill.'
The lord Douglas said, 'Be saynct Brid
640   It war gret foly at this tid   636
Till us with swilk ane ost to fycht
That growys ilk day off mycht
And has vittaill tharwith plenté,
And in thar countre her ar we
645   Quhar thar may cum us na succourys,   641
Hard is to mak us her rescours
Na we ne may ferrar mete to get,
Swilk as we haiff her we mon et.
Do we with our fayis tharfor
650   That ar her liand us befor   646
As Ik herd tell this othyr yer

a fox did with a fisherman.' (653) 'What did the fox do?' said the earl. [Douglas] said, 'A fisherman once lay beside a river to get his nets which he had set [there]. He had made a small shelter there and within it a bed with a little fire; there was a door, nothing more. (661) One night he got up to look at his nets and stayed quite a long time. When he had done his task he went back toward his hut, and by the light of the little fire burning bright in the shelter he saw a fox in his hut, gnawing hard at a salmon. (669) Then he hurried to the door drawing a sword swiftly, and said, 'Thief, [try to] get out of this.' The fox, in a great quandary, looked around to find some hole, but could see no way out except where the man stood sturdily. (676) Then he saw a grey mantle lying near him upon the bed, and drew it with his teeth on top of the fire; when the man saw his mantle lying burning there, he ran quickly to rescue it. The fox then got out like a flash and held his way to his lair. (684) The man thought himself badly deceived, that he had lost his salmon like that and had his mantle burned too, [while] the fox got clean away.

(688) This example I can apply easily to yon folk and ourselves here: we are the fox and they the fisherman who bars the way before us. (692) They believe that we can't get away

---

652. The fox and the fisher. This fable has not been traced. Presumably it comes from Barbour's source. But its implication is that the Scots were hemmed in (by the Park wall?) with only one route of escape, and as Mackenzie noted, there are signs that the Scots were surrounded, notably a letter of the bishop of Ely (who was there) in June 1328, referring to the time that the Scots were 'surrounded and besieged' (*circumdati et obsessi*) in Stanhope Park. (*CDS3, 957*)

That a fox did with a fyscher.'
'How did the fox?' the erle gan say.
He said, 'A fyscher quhilum lay

655 Besid a ryver for to get   651
Hys nettis that he had thar set.
A litill loge tharby he maid,
And thar-within a bed he haid
And a litill fyr alsua,

660 A dure thar wes foroutyn ma.   656
A nycht, his nettis for to se
He rase and thar wele lang dwelt he,
And quhen he had doyne his deid
Towart his loge agayn he yeid,

665 And with licht of the litill fyr   661
That in the loge wes brynnand schyr
Intill his luge a fox he saw
That fast on ane salmound gan gnaw.
Than till the dur he went in hy

670 And drew his swerd deliverly   666
And said, 'Reiffar thou mon her out.'
The fox that wes in full gret dout
Lukyt about sum hole to se,
Bot nane eschew persave couth he

675 Bot quhar the man stud sturdely.   671
A lauchtane mantell than him by
Liand apon the bed he saw,
And with his teth he gan it draw
Out-our the fyr, and quhen the man

680 Saw his mantill ly brinnand than   676
To red it ran he hastily.
The fox gat out than in gret hy
And held his way his warand till.
The man leyt him begilyt ill

685 That he his gud salmound had tynt   681
And alsua his mantill brynt,
And the fox scaithles gat away.

[Douglas proposes a method of withdrawal]

This ensample weill I may say
Be yone ost and us that ar her,

690 We ar the fox and thai the fyscher   686
That stekis forouth us the way.
Thai wene we may na-gat away

except by where they are camped, but, *perdé* it will not be quite how they expect. For I have had a way [out] discovered for us, [and] even if it is a bit wet, we shall not lose a single page of ours. (698) Our enemies, because of [our] modest surprise attack, imagine that we shall be so rash that we will undertake plainly to give them open battle. (702) But this time their expectation will be wrong, for tomorrow, all day, we shall make merry here as [best] we can, getting ready for the night-[time] [when] we shall make our fires [burn] bright, blow our horns and sound busy, as if all the world was our own, until night is well fallen. (710) Then with all our equipment we shall take our way rapidly homeward. We shall be guided carefully until we, presently lying enclosed here, are out of danger from them. Then we shall be able to do what we want and they will think themselves badly misled after they discover we have gone.' (718) They all agreed to this and made good cheer all that night until the morning when it was daylight.

(721) In the morning, secretly, they packed their [arms and] equipment and got ready so that by the evening they were wholly prepared. Their foes, who lay opposite them, had their men who had died taken to a holy place in carts. (727) They were all that day carrying in carts men who had been killed there. You could easily see that there were a lot [for they] took so long to be carried. Both the hosts were peaceful all that day,

---

706–7. Fires and blowing horns, repeated at 735. This is a replay of the means whereby the Scots escaped to Stanhope Park (501), and must compete with Le Bel's version in which the English were very wary the night the Scots left, with large camp fires. The latter commands more confidence than the rerun of a good thing in Barbour.

Bot rycht quhar thai ly, bot perdé
All as thai think it sall nocht be,
695 For I haff gert se us a gait 691
Suppos that it be sumdele wate,
A page off ouris we sall nocht tyne.
Our fayis for this small tranountyn
Wenys weill we sall prid us sua
700 That we planely on hand sall ta 696
To giff thaim opynly battaill.
Bot at this tyme thar thocht sall faill,
For we to-morne her all the day
Sall mak als mery as we may,
705 And mak us boune agayn the nycht, 701
And than ger mak our fyris lycht
And blaw our hornys and mak far
As all the warld our awne war
Quhill that the nycht weill fallin be.
710 And than with all our harnays we 706
Sall tak our way hamwart in hy,
And we sall gyit be graithly
Quhill we be out off thar daunger
That lyis now enclossyt her.
715 Than sall we all be at our will 711
And thai sall lete thaim trumpyt ill
Fra thai wyt weill we be away.'
To this haly assentyt thai,
And maid thaim gud cher all that nycht
720 Quhill on the morn that day wes lycht. 716

[*The Scots withdraw secretly by night, leaving fires burning;
the English give up the chase*]

Apon the morn all prevely
Thai tursit harnays and maid redy
Sua that or evyn all boun war thai,
And thar fayis that agane thaim lay
725 Gert haiff thar men that thar war ded 721
In cartis till ane haly sted.
All that day cariand thai war
With cartis men that slayn war thar,
That thai war fele mycht men well se
730 That in carying sa lang suld be. 726
The ostis baith all that day wer

and when night approached the Scots' folk who lay in the park had a feast and partied, blew horns and made fires, making them burn brightly and broadly so that that night their fires were bigger than they had ever been before. (739) When night had fallen completely, they rode on their way very secretly with every bit of their equipment. Soon they entered a moss that was good long mile broad; they went over that moss on foot, leading their horse by hand. (746) It was a very difficult route, but they made hurdles of branches in the wood, which they had with them, and they bridged streams with these, thus getting their horses away, in such a way that all who were there came safe and sound over [the moss], losing very little of their gear except for any pack-horse left lying in the moss. (756) When all had come as I described over the moss that was so broad, they were mightily relieved and rode forth on their way homeward. In the morning, when it was daylight, the Englishmen saw the camp where the Scotsmen used to lie – all empty. (763) They were very puzzled then and sent various of their men out to discover where [the Scots] had gone away, until eventually they found their tracks which took them to the great moss, so awful to wade [through] that none of them dared to risk it, but [they] went back to their host. (771) [They] told how [the Scots] had gone where no man had ever gone before. When the Englishmen heard this had [happened] they quickly decided

---

741. They rode. The Scots cleared off on the night of 6–7 August, 1327.

746. 'Summer' I have taken as sumter, pack-horse, but 'left lyand' suggests that it may here mean the load rather than the beast.

764–65. Sundry men. One of these was Jean le Bel, by his account.

In pes, and quhen the nycht wes ner
The Scottis folk that liand war
Intill the park maid fest and far
735 And blew hornys and fyris maid   731
And gert thaim mak brycht and braid,
Sua at that nycht thar fyris war mar
Than ony tym befor thai war.
And quhen the nycht wes fallin weill
740 With all the harnayis ilka-dele   736
All prevely thai raid thar way.
Sone in a mos entryt ar thai
That had wele twa myle lang of breid,
Out-our that mos on fute thai yeid
745 And in thar hand thar hors leid thai.   741
It wes rycht a noyus way
Bot flaikkis in the wod thai maid   no no.
Of wandis and thame with thame had   no no.
And sykis thairwith briggit thay,   no no.
750 And sua had weill thair hors away   no no.
On sic wyse that all that thair weir   743
Come weill out-our it hale and fer,
And tynt bot litill off thar ger
Bot giff it war ony summer
755 That in the mos wes left liand.   747
Quhen all as Ik haff born on hand
Out-our that mos that wes sa braid
War cummyn a gret glaidschip thai haid
And raid furth hamwart on thar way.
760 And on the morn quhen it wes day   752
The Inglismen saw the herbery
Quhar Scottismen war wont to ly
All void. Thai wondryt gretly then
And send furth syndry off thar men
765 To spy quhar thai war gayn away   757
Quhill at the last thar trais fand thai
That till the mekill mos thaim haid
That wes sua hidwous for to waid
That awntyr thaim tharto durst nane,
770 Bot till thar ost agayne ar gayn   762
And tauld how that thai passyt war
Quhar never man passit ar.
Quhen Inglismen hard it wes sua
In hy to consaill gan thai ta

that they would follow [the Scots] no further. They dispersed their host immediately and each man rode home.

(778) King Robert who had information that his men lay in the park thus and of the danger they were in there, assembled a host in haste and sent out ten thousand hardy and brave men, with two earls, those of March and Angus, to relieve the army in Weardale; and if they could manage so well that they could [bring] the [two forces] together, they meant to attack the enemy. (789) Thus it happened that on the same day as the moss was crossed as you heard me tell, the scouts who were riding ahead of the host, got sight of another army. They were brave and bold men, who [prepared] for a passage of arms at their meeting. (796) They shouted their rallying cries aloud there, and [the others] realised from their cries that they were friends and of one allegiance. Then you could see them cheerful and happy then, telling [the news] quickly to their lords. The hosts met together next [and] there was a right homely welcoming made among those great lords there; they were delighted at their meeting. (805) Earl Patrick and his following had large supplies of victuals with them, and they provided very well for their friends from them, for, truth to tell, while they were lying in Weardale, they had [starved for] want of food, but they were relieved there abundantly. (812) They went toward Scotland relieved and happy, came home [safely] and then dispersed, each man on his own way.

781–800. The relief force. Gray also describes this, naming the same leaders, and placing its size at 5,000. He confirms that it met Moray and Douglas's force on the day they left Stanhope Park (789).

784. Earls of March and Angus. The former was Patrick, earl of Dunbar (cf. 805), the latter, as Gray says, John Stewart of Bonkill, senior member of that family, who first appears as earl in documents a week after the king's death and would certainly owe the title to Robert I. The ancient line of earls was represented by the d'Umfravilles of Prudhoe, an English family who continued to use the title in Edward III's court.

775 That thai wald folow thaim no mar, 767
Thar ost rycht than thai scalit thar
And ilk man till his awn raid.

[*King Robert sends a relief force; the two Scottish forces meet; the king rejoices*]

And King Robert that wittering haid
At his men in the park sua lay
780 And at quhat myscheiff thar war thai, 772
Ane ost assemblyt he in hy
And ten thousand men wicht and hardy
He has send furth with erllis twa
Off the Marche and Angus war tha
785 The ost in Werdale to releve, 777
And giff thai mycht sa weill escheve
That samyn mycht be thai and thai
Thai thocht thar fayis till assay.
Sua fell that on the samyn day
790 That the mos, as ye hard me say, 782
Wes passyt, the discourrouris that thar
Ridand befor the ost war
Off athyr ost has gottyn sycht,
And thai that worthy war and wicht
795 At thar metyng justyt of wer, 787
Ensenyeys hey thai criyt ther.
And be thar cry persavyt thai
That thai war frendys and at a fay,
Than mycht men se thaim glaid and blyth
800 And tauld it to thar lordis swith. 792
The ostis bath met samyn syne,
Thar wes rycht hamly welcummyn
Maid amang thai gret lordis thar,
Off thar metyng joyfull thai war.
805 The erle Patrik and his menye 797
Had vittaillis with thaim gret plenté
And tharwith weill relevyt thai
Thar frendis, for the suth to say
Quhill thai in Wardale liand war
810 Thai had gret defaut off mete, bot thar 802
Thai war relevyt with gret plenté.
Towart Scotland with gamyn and gle
Thai went and hame wele cummyn ar thai
And scalyt syne ilk man thar way.

The lords went to the king who made them warmly welcome, for he was very pleased at their arrival; and because they had escaped from such hazards without losses they were all high-spirited and made merry.

815   The lordis ar went to the king   807
       That has maid thaim fair welcumyng,
       For off thar come rycht glaid wes he,
       And that thai sic perplexité
       Forout tynsaill eschapyt haid
820   All war thai blyth and mery maid.   812

Soon after earl Thomas had come back like that from Wear-
dale, the king assembled all his forces, leaving none who were
fit to fight. He gathered a great host then, and divided his
army into three parts. (7) One part went to Norham unhin-
dered, and there a close siege was set, holding [the garrison]
in right at their ditch. (10) The second part went to Alnwick
and set a siege there; and while [they] lay at these sieges at
the castles I've just mentioned, open assaults were often made
there and many a fair chivalry was achieved with great courage.
(17) The king left his men before those castles, as I explained,
and held his way with the third host from park to park, for
his recreation, hunting as though it was all his own [property].
(22) To those who were with him there he gave the lands of
Northumberland that lay there nearest to Scotland in fee and
heritage, and they payed the fee for sealing.
(26) He rode like this, destroying, until the king of England,
on the advice of Mortimer and of his mother, who at that
time were his guides (for he was then young), sent messengers
to King Robert to treat of peace. (33) They so expedited
[matters] that they agreed as follows: to make a perpetual
peace then and [with it] a marriage

---

7. Norham. This siege began probably late in August. The king was at
   Melrose on 14 August, 1327.
10. Alnwick. Gray states that Moray with Douglas
    besieged the lord Percy in Alnwick, where there were great jousts of
    war by formal agreement. But these lords did not keep up the siege
    but marched to King Robert at the siege of Norham. At which time
    Percy, with the men of the Marches made a raid upon the side of
    Teviotdale, staying scarcely ten leagues distant. No sooner was James
    Douglas informed of this than he suddenly betook himself with his
    men between Percy and his castle of Alnwick, making [Percy] retreat
    by night towards Newcastle, so demoralised were the English in time
    of war. (S, 155; ST, 82)
19. Third host. There is no other evidence of this hunting sequence and
    it seems unlikely given the king's poor health.
23. Northumberland. Robert I had given Northumberland fiefs earlier.
    One example from this time is known, appropriately to the king's
    standard-bearer, dated 4 September, 1327. (RRS5, 324)
33. Messengers to King Robert. According to Gray, William de Denum
    came to him at Norham. The basis of agreement was laid down by the
    king at Berwick on 18 October, 1327. The final peace was sealed at
    Edinburgh on 17 March, 1328. (RRS5, 326, 342-45)

BOOK 20

[King Robert in Northumberland]

Sone eftre that the erle Thomas
Fra Wardaill thus reparyt was
The king assemblyt all his mycht
And left nane that wes worth to fycht,
5   A gret ost than assemblit he
And delt his ost in partis thre.
A part to Norame went but let
And a stark assege has set
And held thaim in rycht at thar dyk,
10   The tother part till Anwyk
Is went and thar a sege set thai,
And quhill that thir assegis lay
At thir castellis I spak off ar,
Apert eschewys oft maid thar war
15   And mony fayr chevalry
Eschevyt war full douchtely.
The king at thai castellis liand
Left his folk, as I bar on hand
And with the thrid ost held hys way
20   Fra park to park hym for to play
Huntand as all hys awn war,
And till thaim that war with him thar
The landis off Northummyrland
That neyst to Scotland war liand
25   In fe and heritage gave he,
And thai payit for the selys fe.

[The peace with England]

On this wys raid he destroyand
Quhill that the king of Ingland
Throu consaill of the Mortymar
30   And his moder that that tym war
Ledaris of him that than young wes
To King Robert to tret off pes
Send messyngeris, and sua sped thai
That thai assentyt on this way
35   Than a perpetuale pes to tak,
And thai a mariage suld mak

between King Robert's son, David, who then was scarcely five years [old] and lady Joan of the Tower, who was later of great bravery. (41) She was sister to the young king who ruled over England and [she] was then seven years old. They gave up in that treaty various letters and muniments which the English side had at that time, making any [point] against Scotland, and all the claim they might have to Scotland in any way. (50) King Robert, [in compensation] for many damages that he had done to the men of England in the war, was to pay full twenty thousand pounds of silver in good money. (55) When men had agreed these points, and with seals and oaths had made assurance of friendship and peace, which would never cease for any cause, they arranged for the marriage to be at Berwick and fixed the day when it was to be, then each man went to his country. Thus peace was made where war had been, and so the sieges were raised.

(65) King Robert ordered the silver to be paid and he also had good arrangements made against the day for the banquet when his son David was to be married; he also appointed Earl Thomas and the good lord Douglas to be organisers of that feast in his place. (73) For an illness afflicted him so badly that in no way could he be there. His disease arose from catching a chill, for as a result of exposure when he was in his great tribulations

---

37. David, born 5 March, 1324 at Dunfermline; his twin, John, did not survive. He was therefore four years old when the peace was made and when married.

39. Dame Joan, born in the Tower of London, 5 July, 1321. She was approaching seven in March 1328. The description of her great 'valour' is puzzling. It is likely that lines 39 and 40 should be reversed and that 40 refers to David II.

48. All claim. Edward III's letters recognising Scottish independence were actually issued at York on 1 March, before the treaty was made; but they would be handed over only as part of the treaty. It was essential that formally King Robert be recognised as an equal before a treaty was made with him. (*RRS5, 343*)

65–66. The silver, i.e. £20,000. In fact the king held a parliament at the end of February 1328 which granted him a tenth of rents for three years, the 'contribution of the peace'. The last instalment was paid in November 1331, whereupon David II was at last crowned, the first Scottish king to be so.

72. The feast. Because financial records survive from the end of the reign, the wedding at Berwick on 17 July, 1328 is well documented; the cost was well above £1,500. The guests managed to knock down a church-yard wall.

Off the King Robertis sone Davy
That than bot fyve yer had scarsly
And off Dame Jhone als off the Tour
40   That syne wes of full gret valour,
Systre scho wes to the ying king
That had Ingland in governyng,
That than of eild had sevyn yer.
And monymentis and lettrys ser
45   That thai of Ingland that tyme had
That oucht agayn Scotland maid
Intill that tretys up thai gaff,
And all the clame that thai mycht haff
Intill Scotland on ony maner,
50   And King Robert for scaithis ser
That he to thaim off Ingland
Had done off wer with stalwart hand
Full twenty thousand pund suld pay
Off silver into gud monay.
55   Quhen men thir thingis forspokyn had
And with selis and athis maid
Festnyng off frendschip and of pes
That never for na chaunc suld ces,
The mariage syne ordanyt thai
60   To be at Berwik and the day
Thai haff set quhen that this suld be,
Syne went ilk man till his countré.
Thus maid wes pes quhar wer wais ar
And thus the segis raissyt war.

[*The marriage of the king's son, David*]

65   The King Robert ordanyt to pay
The silver, and agane the day
He gert wele for the mangery
Ordane quhen that his sone Davy
Suld weddyt be, and Erle Thomas
70   And the gud lord of Douglas
Intill his steid ordanyt he
Devisouris of that fest to be,
For a malice him tuk sa sar
That he on na wis mycht be thar.
75   His malice off enfundeying
Begouth, for throuch his cald lying
Quhen in his gret myscheiff wes he

that serious illness came upon him. (79) He lay at Cardross
all that time, and when the day appointed for the wedding
approached, the earl and lord Douglas came with much pomp
to Berwick, bringing the young David there with them. The
queen and Mortimer came from the other side, with great
royal ceremony; they brought the young lady of great beauty
there with rich display. (90) The wedding took place right
there with great feasting and solemnity; you could see joy and
gladness there, for they had very long festivities there [when]
English and Scots were together in joy and relaxation, with
no harsh words between them. (97) They kept the festivities
[going] for a good long while, and when they prepared to
depart, the queen left her daughter there with great riches
and royal ceremony. I'm sure that for a long time no lady
was conducted home so richly. (103) The earl and the lord
Douglas received her honourably as was certainly appropriate,
for she was afterwards the best and fairest lady that you needed
to see. After this great ceremony, when both sides had taken
their leave, the queen went home to England, having Mortimer
with her. (112) The earl and those who were left, when they
had convoyed her a little, rode back toward Berwick, and
then, with all their company, went speedily toward the king,
taking with them the young David and also the young lady,
Dame Joan.

---

79. Cardross. Not the modern village of that name, but a lost village on
the bank of the Leven opposite Dumbarton, now swallowed up in that
town. The king built a manor there early in the 1320s; it gave him ease
of transport by water, a sign of his disability.

97. A long time. The duration is not documented, but there were
negotiations with Queen Isabella in which she tried to secure the
restoration of the Disinherited, offering the Westminster stone in return.
Moray seems to have agreed to the 'restoration' of four Disinherited,
against the king's firm policy.

102. Till hous. I have accepted Skeat's translation with some misgiving;
DOST gives nothing for 'till hous'. I wonder if the sense is 'was given
as endowment'? Joan was to be given lands worth £2,000 annually by
Robert I.

116. Toward the king. They probably reached him at Glasgow about 28
July, 1328.

Him fell that hard perplexité.
At Cardros all that tyme he lay,
80 And quhen ner cummyn wes the day
That ordanyt for the weddyn was
The erle and the lord of Douglas
Come to Berwik with mekill far
And brocht young Davy with thaim thar,
85 And the queyn and the Mortymer
On other part cummyn wer
With gret affer and reawté,
The young lady of gret bewté
Thidder thai brocht with rich affer.
90 The weddyn haf thai makyt thar
With gret fest and solempnyté,
Thar mycht men myrth and glaidschip se
For rycht gret fest thai maid thar
And Inglismen and Scottis war
95 Togidder in joy and solace,
Na fellouné betwix thaim was.
The fest a wele lang tym held thai,
And quhen thai buskyt to far away
The queyn has left hyr douchter thar
100 With gret riches and reale far,
I trow that lang quhile na lady
Wes gevyn till hous sa richely,
And the erle and the lord Douglas
Hyr in daynté ressavyt has
105 As it war worthi sekyrly
For scho wes syne the best lady
And the fayrest that men thurft se.
Eftre this gret solemnyté
Quhen of bath half levys war tane
110 The queyn till Ingland hame is gane
And had with hyr Mortymar.
The erle and thai that levyt war
Quhen thai a quhill hyr convoyit had
Towart Berwik again thai raid,
115 And syne with all thar cumpany
Towart the king thai went in hy,
And had with thaim the young Davy
And Dame Jhone als that young lady.

(119) The king gave them a warm welcoming, [then] afterwards, without any long delay, he had a parliament summoned [to which] many men went. For he meant in his lifetime to crown his young son and [the latter's] wife, [which] he did at that parliament. (126) With great pomp and ceremony King David was crowned there, and all the lords who were there, and also [those] of the community made homage and fealty to him. (131)After they had been crowned, King Robert had it ordained there [that] if it happened that his son David should die without an heir male begotten of the body, Robert Stewart, whom his daughter Marjory bore, should be king and enjoy all the royal [dignity]. (138) All the lords swore that this tailzie should be kept loyally, and affirmed it with [their] seals there. If it happened that King Robert should pass to God while [David and Robert Stewart] were young, Thomas the good earl of Moray with the lord Douglas also, should have control of them until they had wisdom to control their affairs and then they should take the lordship. (148) They made their oaths to this [effect] and all the lords that were there swore oaths to those two Guardians, to obey them in loyalty if they should chance to be Guardians.

(153) When all this business had been dealt with thus and affirmed with assurance, the king went to Cardross where the sickness gripped him so seriously, and afflicted him

---

120. Parliament. No parliament was held between the peace treaty and the king's death.

127. David was certainly not crowned before his father's death – even King Robert failed to live long enough to enjoy the coronation granted him by the pope a week after his death.

130. Homage and fealty. Both Bower and Wyntoun (but not Fordun) mention homage and fealty to David and Robert Stewart at the Cambuskenneth parliament of 1326, but this may be confusion with an oath to observe the tailzie of the throne. They were certainly sworn at David II's coronation in November 1331.

131–47. This is a reasonable account of the decisions taken in the Cambuskenneth parliament of July 1326, when the tailzie of 1318 was renewed but probably (no text survives) explicitly taking account of the birth and survival of David. However the association of Douglas with Moray is misleading. Moray would become Guardian if David succeeded young, or if David died and Robert succeeded young. Douglas would be Guardian only if Moray died. The use of 'they' in 147 for David and Robert is confusing; both would not become kings together. (*RRS5, 301*)

[*Coronation of David, settlement of the succession*]

The king maid thaim fair welcumyng

120 And efter but langer delaying

He has gert set a parleament

And thidder witth mony men is went,

For he thocht he wald in his lyff

Croun his young sone and his wyff

125 And at that parleament sua did he.

With gret fayr and solemnyté

The King Davy wes crownyt thar,

And all the lordis that thar war   127*

And als off the comynyté   128*

130 Maid him manredyn and fewté.   129*

And forouth that thai crownyt war   130*

The King Robert gert ordane thar,   128

Giff it fell that his sone Davy

Deyit but ayr male off his body

135 Gottyn, Robert Stewart suld be   131

Kyng and bruk all the realté

That hys douchter bar Marjory,

And at this tailye suld lelely

Be haldyn all the lordis swar

140 And it with selys affermyt thar.   136

And gyff it hapnyt Robert the king

To pas to God quhill thai war ying,

The gud erle of Murreff, Thomas,

And the lord alsua off Douglas

145 Suld haiff thaim into governyng   141

Quhill thai had wyt to ster thar thing,

And than the lordschip suld thai ta.

Her-till thar athys gan thai ma

And all the lordis that thar war

150 To thir twa wardanys athis swar   146

Till obey thaim in lawte

Giff thaim hapnyt wardanys to be.

[*The king's illness and last will*]

Quhen all this thing thus tretit wes

And affermyt with sekyrnes

155 The king to Cardros went in hy,   151

And thar him tuk sa fellely

The seknes and him travailit sua

so that he knew he had to face the end of this life common to all [men], that is, death, when God sends it. (161) So he soon sent his letters for the lords of his country, and they came he had ordered. Then he made his testament before both lords and prelates, giving silver in large amounts for the weal of his soul to religious [bodies] of different orders. (169) He provided for his soul's weal. When this had been done altogether, he said, 'Lords, it has come to this with me, that there remains only one thing [for me], which is [to meet] fearlessly the death which each man has to face [when the time comes]. (175) I thank God for giving me time in this life to repent, for because of me and my war-making there has been much spilling of blood in which many innocent men were slain; therefore I accept this sickness and pain as reward for my transgressions. (183) When I was in prosperity my heart was firmly fixed on being saved from my sins [by] the struggle against God's enemies.

---

166. To religious orders. King Robert had made modest gifts to religious houses, notably Melrose abbey, during his lifetime, though his foundation of a priory at Glendochart was not completed. He probably left sums to various houses, though they do not show in the surviving accounts.

171–244. The king's heart. The fashionable posthumous separation of heart from body had been forbidden by the pope, but a dispensation for having done this to Robert's body was obtained (dated 6 August, 1331). Remarkably, the accounts do not show a penny being paid to Douglas for this enterprise. Barbour's account of the king's speech should be compared with that of Le Bel:

When he saw that he must die, he commanded all the barons of his kingdom whom he trusted most, before him ... [*he commended David to them, to be crowned and married*] After he called the *gentil* knight, Sir William Douglas, and said to him before all the others: '... You know that I had much to do in my time, and suffered much to maintain the rights of this kingdom. When I had the most to do, I made a vow which I have not fulfilled, which troubles me. I vowed that, if I could ever achieve the completion of my war, whereby I could govern this kingdom in peace, I would go to make war on the enemies of Our Lord, and the opponents of the Christian faith overseas, with my loyal following. My heart wanted this, but Our Lord would not agree to it. [*I must die*] and since my body cannot go or accomplish what my heart has so much desired, I want to send my heart for my body, to acquit myself and my vow. Because I know no-one in my whole kingdom more worthy ... nor more talented to carry out this vow in my place, I wish and ask you, my special knight and friend, as much and as lovingly as I can, that you set yourself to make this journey, for love of me and to acquit my soul to Our Lord. I believe so much in your nobility and loyalty that, if you undertake it, you will never

That he wyst him behovyt to ma
Off all this liff the commoun end
160 That is the dede quhen God will send, 156
Tharfor his lettrys sone send he
For the lordis off his countre
And thai come as thai biddyng had.
His testament than has he maid
165 Befor bath lordis and prelatis, 161
And to religioun of ser statis
For hele of his saule gaf he
Silver in gret quantite.
He ordanyt for his saule weill,
170 And quhen this done wes ilkadele 166
He said, 'Lordingis, sua is it gayn
With me that thar is nocht bot ane,
That is the dede withoutyn drede
That ilk man mon thole off nede.
175 And I thank God that has me sent 171
Space in this lyve me to repent,
For throuch me and my werraying
Off blud has bene rycht gret spilling
Quhar mony sakles men war slayn,
180 Tharfor this seknes and this payn 176
I tak in thank for my trespas.
And myn hart fichyt sekyrly was
Quhen I wes in prosperité
Off my synnys to sauffyt be
185 To travaill apon Goddis fayis, 181

---

fail; so, if you will promise me it, I shall die more easy. But let it be in the way that I shall tell you. As soon as I am dead, I want you to take my heart and have it well embalmed, take as much of my treasure as seems good to you, to pay for the journey for you and for all those you want to take with you, and take my heart to the Holy Sepulchre, where Our Lord was raised, since my body cannot go there; do it fittingly (*grandement*) and provide yourself with all things and with sufficient company as is appropriate to your standing. And everywhere that you go, let everyone know that you carry as a messenger the heart of the king of Scotland, since his body cannot go there.' [*All wept; when Douglas recovered he accepted. The king asked for his promise and Douglas gave it. The king said*] 'Now, God be thanked, for I die more at peace than before, when I know that the finest of my kingdom and the best will do what I could not do.' (*Chron Le Bel*, i, 83–85)

185. Against God's enemies. Barbour makes no mention of the Holy Land. The papal absolution in 1331 says that the king in his last will

Since he takes me to him now, so that [my] body can in no way fulfil what the heart called for, I wish that the heart, wherein that resolve was conceived, be sent thither. (191) So I ask you all that you choose from among you one who is honest, wise and brave, and a noble knight in his deeds, to carry my heart against God's enemies when body and soul have parted. For I want it brought there worthily, since God does not will that I have the power to go there.'

(200) Then their hearts were all so heavy that none could prevent himself weeping. He bade them give up their grieving, for, he said, it would not [bring him] relief, and would greatly afflict themselves. He begged them to do speedily the thing that they were charged to do. (207) Then they went out in a sad frame of mind. Among themselves they thought it best that the worthy lord Douglas who possessed both wisdom and valour, should take this burden in hand; they were all agreed on this. (213) Then they went quickly to the king and told him that they thought truly that the doughty lord Douglas was best fitted for that burden. When the king heard that they had thus chosen to take his heart the one whom he most wanted to have it, he said, (220) 'As God himself will save me, I hold myself very well content that you have chosen him, for his generosity and his bravery made me yearn ever since I thought to do this business, that he should carry it with him there.

and testament asked that the heart be removed 'and be born in battle against Saracens'. Edward III issued letters of protection for Douglas with King Robert's heart, 'going to the Holy Land to the help of Christians against Saracens' and letters of commendation to Alfonso of Castille of Douglas going on the same mission. The date is 1 September, 1329. It seems that the King asked that his heart be born against Saracens, and that this was understood to mean the Holy Land. Le Bel noticeably changes the rhetoric, turning a wish that it fight against Saracens into a wish that it be taken to the Holy Sepulchre, and by implication be buried there, which is how Froissart embroiders the story. Bower is explicit that the king bequeathed his heart to be sent to Jerusalem and buried at the Holy Sepulchre, and this is accepted by A. Macquarrie, *Scotland and the Crusades* (1985), 73–75. But that is a peaceful mission, not one calling for Douglas and his posse.

And sen he now me till him tayis
Sua that the body may na wys
Fullfill that the hart gan devis
I wald the hart war thidder sent
190   Quharin consavyt wes that entent.   186
Tharfor I pray you everilkan
That ye amang you ches me ane
That be honest wis and wicht
And off his hand a noble knycht
195   On Goddis fayis my hart to ber   191
Quhen saule and cors disseveryt er,
For I wald it war worthily
Brocht thar, sen God will nocht that I
Haiff power thidderwart to ga.'

[*Douglas is chosen to take the king's heart against God's enemies*]

200   Than war thar hartis all sa wa   196
That nane mycht hald him fra greting.
He bad thaim leve thar sorowing
For it he said mycht not releve
And mycht thaim rycht gretly engreve,
205   And prayit thaim in hy to do   201
The thing that thai war chargit to.
Than went thai furth with drery mode,
Amang thaim thai thocht it gode
That the worthi lord of Douglas
210   Quham in bath wit and worschip was   206*
Suld tak this travaill apon hand,   207*
Heir-till thai war all accordand,   208*
Syne till the king thai went in hy   209*
And tald hym at thai thocht trewly   210*
215   That the douchty lord Douglas   211*
Best schapyn for that travaill was.   206
And quhen the king hard that thai sua
Had ordanyt him his hart to ta
That he mast yarnyt suld it haff
220   He said, 'Sa God himself me saiff   210
Ik hald me rycht weill payit that yhe
Haff chosyn him, for his bounté
And his worschip set in my yarnyng
Ay sen I thocht to do this thing
225   That he it with him thar suld ber,   215

(226) And since you are all agreed, it is all the more to my liking. Let us see now what he says about it.' When the good lord Douglas knew that the king had spoken thus, he came and kneeled to the king, and thanked him as follows: (233) 'I thank you warmly, lord,' said he, 'for the many great and generous gifts that you have many-a-time bestowed on me since I first entered your service. But above everything else I give thanks that you want me to take in my care so precious and valuable a thing as your heart, which shines with every virtue and prowess. (242) For you, Sir, I will cheerfully make this journey, if God will give me leisure and time to live that long.' The king thanked him tenderly. There was no-one in that company who did not weep in grief; their anguish was moving to see.

(249) When the lord Douglas had undertaken in this way so great a venture as to carry the king's heart in war against the enemies of God, he was esteemed [highly] for his enterprise. The king's infirmity got worse and worse until eventually sombre death approached relentlessly. (257) When he had secured for himself all that was proper for a good Christian man, in true repentance he gave up his spirit which God could take to Heaven to be among his chosen people in joy, peace and choirs of angels. (263) And when his people knew that he had died, sorrow rose from home to home. You could see men tear their hair, frequently knights weeping copiously,

---

254-60. The king died at Cardross on 7 June, 1329, aged 53.

And sen ye all assentit er
It is the mar likand to me.
Lat se now quhat thar-till sayis he.'
And quhen the gud lord of Douglas
230   Wist that thing thus spokyn was   220
He come and knelit to the king
And on this wis maid him thanking.
'I thank you gretly lord,' said he,
'Off the mony larges and gret bounté
235   That yhe haff done me fel-sys   225
Sen fyrst I come to your service,
Bot our all thing I mak thanking
That ye sa dyng and worthy thing
As your hart that enlumynyt wes
240   Off all bounté and all prowes   230
Will that I in my yemsall tak.
For you, schyr, I will blythly mak
This travaill, gif God will me gif
Layser and space sua lang to lyff.'
245   The king him thankyt tendrely,   235
Than wes nane in that cumpany
That thai na wepyt for pité,
Thar cher anoyis wes to se.

[The death of King Robert; his burial at Dunfermline]

Quhen the lord Douglas on this wis
250   Had undretane sa hey empris   240
As the guid kyngis hart to ber
On Goddis fayis apon wer
Prissyt for his empris wes he.
And the kingis infirmyté
255   Woux mar and mar quhill at the last   245
The dulfull dede approchit fast,
And quhen he had gert till him do
All that gud Crystyn man fell to
With verray repentance he gaf
260   The gast, that God till hevyn haiff   250
Amang his chossyn folk to be
In joy solace and angell gle.
And fra his folk wist he wes ded
The sorow rais fra steid to steid,
265   Thar mycht men se men ryve thar har   255
And commounly knychtis gret full sar

striking their fists together and tearing their clothes like mad-men, mourning his seemly generosity, his wisdom, strength and his honesty, [but] above all the warm companionship which in his courtesy he often [shared with] them. (273) 'Alas!' they said, 'all our defence, he who was all our comfort, our wisdom, and who led us all, has been brought to an end now. His valour and his mighty strength made all who were with him so brave that they could never be defeated as long as they saw him before them. (281) Alas! What shall we do or say? For as long as he lived we were feared by all our foes, and in many different countries the fame of our valour spread, and all because of [one] person – him.' (287) With such words they made their laments; and certainly it was no wonder, for a better ruler than him could be found in no country. I hope that no-one [now] alive could describe the lamentation that those people made for their lord. (294) When they had grieved for a long time like that, and he had been cleanly disembo-welled, then very richly embalmed and the worthy lord Douglas had received his heart respectfully as had been agreed, they took him to Dunfermline with great ceremony and sol-emnity, and then buried him with dignity in a fine tomb in the [abbey-]choir. (304) Bishops and prelates who were there absolved him, when the service had been done as they could best devise, then on the next day, sad and sorry they went [upon] their way.

---

301. The date of the funeral is given only by Froissart, as 7 November 1327! Seventh November, 1329 seems much too late. Dunfermline abbey was the cult centre of Scottish kingship for a century after the canonisation of St Margaret in *c.* 1250. Alexander III and his first wife, and Robert I and his queen were buried there. In the early 19th century a skeleton with the breastbone cut was discovered near the altar-site, and is generally accepted as that of King Robert; casts were made of the skull, which has disappeared.

303. A fair tomb. The king had ordered this in marble from Paris, and it was erected over the grave after his death. The costs are detailed in the royal accounts. Bower gives two epitaphs of which the first, and shorter, is of some interest, since it may come from a contemporary source: Here lies the unconquered Robert, blessed king./Who reads his deeds lives again all the battles he fought./By probity he brought to freedom/the kingdom of Scots; now he dwells in the Heaven's heights.

And thar newffys oft samyn dryve
And as woud men thar clathis ryve,
Regratand his worthi bounte
270   His wyt his strenth his honeste   260
And our-all the gret cumpany
That he maid thaim oft curtasly.
'All our defens,' thai said, 'allace
And he that all our comford was
275   Our wit and all our governyng   265
Allace is brocht her till ending.
His worschip and his mekill mycht
Maid all that war with him sa wycht
That thai mycht never abaysit be
280   Quhill forouth thaim thai mycht him se.   270
Allace! what sall we do or say,
For on lyff quhill he lestyt ay
With all our nychtbouris dred war we,
And intill mony ser countre
285   Off our worschip sprang the renoun   275
And that wes all for his persoune.'
With swilk wordis thai maid thar mayn
And sekyrly wounder wes nane,
For better governour than he
290   Mycht in na countre fundyn be.   280
I hop that nane that is on lyve
The lamentacioun suld discryve
That that folk for thar lard maid.
And quhen thai lang thus sorowit had,
295   And he debowaillyt wes clenly   285
And bawmyt syne richly,
And the worthi lord of Douglas
His hart as it forspokyn was
Has ressavyt in gret daynté
300   With gret fayr and solemnyté,   290
Thai haiff had hym to Dunferlyne
And him solemply erdyt syne
In a fayr tumb intill the quer.
Byschappys and prelatis that thar wer
305   Assoilyeit him quhen the service   295
Was done as thai couth best devis
And syne on the tother day
Sary and wa ar went thar way.

(309) When the good king had been buried, Sir Thomas, the earl of Moray, took the whole land under his control, [and] all obeyed his commands. The good lord Douglas then had a case of fine silver made, cunningly enamelled; he [put] the king's heart in it and wore it always round his neck, then prepared himself thoroughly to travel. (319) He made his testament, laying down how his land should be managed by friends until his return, and everything that concerned him in whatever way before his departure he [also] regulated with such good foresight and so sensibly that nothing needed changing. (327) When he had taken his leave, he went to Berwick to take ship, and with a noble company of knights and squires put to sea there. He sailed a long way onward, steering between Cornwall and Britanny, leaving the Groin of Spain to the north and held their course until they came to Seville the Great. (337) He and his men were greatly troubled by sea-storms, but although they had a difficult time, they arrived hail and safe. The arrived at great Seville, and after a short while they each led their horses to land and took up quarters in the town. (345) He bore himself lavishly for he had a fine company and plenty of gold to spend. King Alfonso sent for him and received him very courteously, offering him in great plenty

---

310. Moray became Guardian. Probably immediately, in terms of the tailzie of 1326, without any election.

328-36. Douglas's voyage. He was still at Douglas on 1 February, 1330, when he reached an agreement with the abbot of Newbattle. Le Bel has a long and circumstantial account of Douglas sailing to Sluys in Flanders, for news and to collect more companions to go to the Holy Land. He stayed there for 12 days, not setting foot on land, and keeping royal state, with a knight bachelor [? William Sinclair], six knights and 20 squires; his furnishings were lavish. He heard that the king of Spain was warring with the Saracen king of Granada and decided to improve the journey by going there, then afterwards do what he had undertaken. So he went by sea arriving at Valence le grand.

Neither Barbour nor Le Bel suggests that Douglas broke his journey to go to Santiago, although he sailed close by it. Le Bel's port of arrival, distinguishing Valencia from French Valence and Portuguese Valencia, is surely correct. Barbour's Seville 'le graund' is not a port, and competes with no other Sevilles; Seville probably figured later in the story. The English letters of 1 September, 1329 show that Douglas in Scotland was already bound for Spain, but as a stage to the Holy Land. Le Bel's story of the decision at Sluys is to be rejected, though a stay there is probably correct. In 1329 Alfonso XI of Castille was actively seeking the support of other European kings for a war against the Moors of Granada.

348. Alsone E; all soyne, C; emended here. Alfonso XI of Castille.

[*Douglas goes to Seville with the king's heart*]

	Quhen that the gud king beryit was	
310	The erle of Mureff, Schyr Thomas,	300
	Tuk all the land in governyng,	
	All obeyit till his bidding,	
	And the gud lord of Douglas syne	
	Gert mak a cas of silver fyne	
315	Ennamylyt throu sutelté,	305
	Tharin the kingis hart did he	
	And ay about his hals it bar	
	And fast him bownyt for to far.	
	His testament divisyt he	
320	And ordanyt how his land suld be	310
	Governyt quhill his gayn-cummyng	
	Off frendis, and all other thing	
	That till him pertenyt ony wis	
	With sik forsych and sa wys	
325	Or his furth-passing ordanyt he	315
	That na thing mycht amendyt be.	
	And quhen that he his leve had tane	
	To schip to Berwik is he gane,	
	And with a noble cumpany	
330	Off knychtis and off squyery	320
	He put him thar to the se.	
	A lang way furthwart saylit he,	
	For betwix Cornwaill and Bretaynne	
	He sayllyt, and left the Grunye of Spainye	
335	On northalff him, and held thar way	325
	Quhill to Sabill the Graunt com thai,	
	Bot gretly war his men and he	
	Travaillyt with tempestis of the se,	
	Bot thocht thai gretly travaillit war	
340	Hale and fer ar thai cummyn thar.	330
	Thai aryvyt at Gret Sabill	
	And eftre in a litill quhill	
	Thar hors to land thai drew ilkane	
	And in the toun has herbry tane,	
345	He hym contenyt rychly	335
	For he had a fayr cumpany	
	And gold ynewch for to dispend.	
	The King Alfons him eftre send	
	And hym rycht weill ressavyt he	
350	And perofferyt him in gret plenté	340

gold and treasure, horses and armour, (352) but he would take none of them because he said he embarked on that journey to pass on his pilgrimage to God's foes, so that his troubles could afterwards be for the good of his soul. (357) Since he knew that [Alfonso] was at war with Saracens, he [said he] would stay there and serve him loyally to [the best of] his ability. The king thanked him courteously and entrusted to him good men who were experienced in the war of that land and in its methods. Then he went to his quarters when the king had left him.

(366) He stayed there for a good long [time]. Knights who had come from distant lands came in great haste to see him, honouring him very greatly. The English knights who were there above all [other] men honoured him most sovereignly and kept him company. (373) Among those foreigners there was a knight who was thought so remarkably brave that he was esteemed as one of the good [fighting men] in Christendom. His face was so very badly cut that it was disfigured almost all over. (379) Before he had seen the lord Douglas he thought that [Douglas's] face had been scarred but [Douglas] had never been wounded there. When he saw it unscarred, he said that he was astonished that such a worthy knight, famous for his great bounty, could be unscarred on his face. (387) [Douglas] answered him gently, and said, 'Praise God, I always had hands to protect my head.' (390) Whoever pays attention to this answer will see comprehension in it

---

366. A good long time. Douglas must have arrived in mid-1330, and was killed in August 1330.

Gold and tresour hors and armyng,
Bot he wald tak tharoff na thing
For he said he tuk that vaiage
To pas intill pilgramage
355 On Goddis fayis, that his travaill   345
Mycht till his saule hele availl,
And sen he wyst that he had wer
With Saryzynys he wald dwell thar
And serve him at hys mycht lely.
360 The king him thankyt curtasly   350
And betaucht him gud men that war
Weill knawyn of that landis wer
And the maner tharoff alsua,
Syne till his innys gan he ga
365 Quhen that the king him levit had.   355

[The repute of Douglas in Spain]

A weill gret sojourne thar he mad,
Knychtis that come of fer countre
Come in gret hy him for to se
And honouryt him full gretumly,
370 And out-our all men fer soveranly   360
The Inglis knychtis that war thar
Honour and company him bar.
Amang thai strangeris was a knycht
That wes haldyn sa worthi and wicht
375 That for ane of the gud wes he   365
Prissyt off the Cristianté,
Sa fast till-hewyn was his face
That it our-all ner wemmyt was.
Or he the lord Douglas had sene
380 He wend his face had wemmyt bene   370
Bot never a hurt tharin had he.
Quhen he unwemmyt gan it se
He said that he had gret ferly
That swilk a knycht and sa worthi
385 And prissyt of sa gret bounté   375
Mycht in the face unemmyt be,
And he answerd tharto mekly
And said, 'Love God, all tym had I
Handis my hed for to wer.'
390 Quha wald tak kep to this answer   380
Suld se in it understanding

that, if he who had asked had had hands for defence, his face, which was so disfigured in many places through lack of defence, would perhaps have remained sound and hail. (397) The good knights who were near at this time, thought very highly of this answer, for it was made with mild words and showed very good understanding.

(401) They rermained quietly like this until they heard word through the country that the high king of Banu Marin with many a brave Saracen had entered the land of Spain to conquer the whole country. On the other side the king of Spain swiftly gathered his host, dividing it into three divisions. (410) He gave the vanguard to Douglas to lead and command – all the foreigners were with him – and he had the Grand Master of St James take the second division. He took the rearward himself. They went forth in this order to meet their foes who came against them very sturdily, arrayed for battle, ready to attack. (420) Douglas, the worthy man, when he had made a fine charge to those under his command to do well and not to fear death because heaven's bliss would be their reward if they died in God's service, like good and experienced warriors

---

403. Balmeryne. The emir of Banu Marin (Morocco) sent help to the Moorish king of Granada, who was being attacked by Alfonso XI; the name here is influenced by Scottish Balmerino.

407–500. The battle and Douglas's death. It is common ground that this event was linked to a battle at the Muslim camp at Turón, during the siege of Teba, in August 1330. Essentially Barbour places Douglas at a battle in command of one division, where he drives back the enemy, but, seeking to rescue Sinclair who is surrounded, is himself cut off and killed. Le Bel also describes a battle in which Douglas places himself on a flank. He thinks that he sees the army move, and, anxious to be the first to fight, charges the enemy; but the army did not move, Douglas was surrounded and killed. A Spanish source, the *Gran Cronica de Alfonso XI*, supports Le Bel; 'One day at the river there was a big battle in which a foreign count died, who had left his country to serve God and try his strength in battle against the enemies of the Cross. This is what he did on this occasion, although he died through his own fault, because, leaving the Christian lines he inopportunely attacked the Moors in a way that he should not have done ... the next day the Moors were defeated.' Thus Douglas was killed by a tactical mistake on the day before the battle. Fordun dates his death 26 August, 1330 in a version which describes a victory by the king and Douglas over the Sultan; after dividing the booty the king retired, another Sultan emerged to challenge Douglas, and 'James, in his fearlessness dashingly charged them with his men' and was killed along with William Sinclair and Robert Logan. Bower repeats this but adds 37 lines of Latin verse in praise of Douglas, verse which gives the date, 25 August, 1330 and adds 'at Teba'. Although

That, and he that maid that asking
Had handis to wer, hys face
That for faute of defence sa was
395 To-fruschyt intill placis ser 385
Suld have may-fall left hale and fer.
The gud knychtis that than war by
Pryssyt hys answer gretumly,
For it wes maid with mek speking
400 And had rycht hey understanding. 390

[Douglas does battle with the Saracens]

Apon this maner still thai lay
Quhill throu the countré thai hard say
That the hey king of Balmeryne
With mony a mody Saryzine
405 Was entryt intill the land off Spanye 395
All hale the countré to manye.
The king off Spaynye on other party
Gaderyt his ost deliverly
And delt hym intill bataillis thre,
410 And to the lord Douglas gaff he 400
The avaward to led and ster,
All hale the strangeris with him wer,
And the gret maister off Saynct Jak
The tother bataill gert he tak,
415 The rerward maid himselvyn thar. 405
Thusgat divisyt furth thai far
To mete thar fayis that in bataill
Arayit redy till assaill
Come agayn thaim full sturdely.
420 The Douglas that wes sa worthi 410
Quhen he to thaim of his leding
Had maid a fayr monesting
To do weill and na deid to dred,
For hevynnys blys suld be thar mede
425 Gyff that thai deyt in Goddis service 415
Than as gud werrayouris and wis,

Fordun has mistaken the day, his source was pretty surely the verses
from which Bower quotes. Fordun (?mistakenly) places the death after,
instead of before, the battle. See the discussions in A. Macquarrie,
Scotland and the Crusades, 75–80 and *Scott. Hist. Rev.* lxix (1990), 84–90,
which stresses that it was widely thought that Douglas had been let
down by Alfonso's army.

he stoutly joined battle with [the Saracens]. (428) You could see fierce fighting there, for they were all brave and hardy who were on the Christian side; they fought so hard with all their might that many of the Saracens were killed, although they struck down many Christians there with merciless falchions. (435) But eventually the lord Douglas and the great force that were with him pressed the Saracens so hard that they one and all fled. [The Christians] gave chase with all their might and slew many in the pursuit. (441) Lord Douglas and a few men chased so far that he had passed all the folk who were then in pursuit. He had with him then not more than ten of all the men who were [in his command] there. When he saw that all had returned, he then turned toward his host. And when the Saracens saw that the pursuers had turned back, they rallied with great power.

(451) As the good lord Douglas was going back as I described before he saw, very close beside him where Sir William Sinclair had been surrounded by a great force. (455) He was aroused and said, 'Alas! Yon worthy knight will soon be dead unless he is helped, and our valour bids us hurry to help him, since we are so near to him. God knows that our purpose is to live and die in His service; we shall do His will in everything. (464) No danger will be shunned until [either] he is saved from yon danger or we are all killed with him.' With that they swiftly struck their horses with spurs

---

433. Falchion. A sword with a curved blade, i.e. as used by Muslim forces.

454. Sir William Sinclair. Probably in anticipation of Douglas's expedition, the king not long before his death gave William a pension of £40 annually, and £20 to his brother John Sinclair who also died in Spain. Their father, Henry, laird of Roslin, was still alive and on 27 December, 1328 had been given 40 mks annually until the king gave him land worth that or £400 sterling.

With thaim stoutly assemblit he.
Thar mycht men felloun fechtyn se,
For thai war all wicht and worthi
430 That war on the Cristyn party 420
And faucht sa fast with all thar mayne
That Saryzynys war mony slayne,
The-quhether with mony fele fachoun
Mony a Cristyn dang thai doun,
435 Bot at the last the lord Douglas 425
And the gret rout that with him was
Pressyt the Saryzynys sua
That thai haly the bak gan ta,
And thai chassyt with all thar mayn
440 And mony in the chas has slayn. 430
Sa fer chassyt the lord of Douglas
With few, that he passyt was
All the folk that war chassand then,
He had nocht with him our ten
445 Off all men that war with him thar. 435
Quhen he saw all reparyt war
Towart hys ost than turnyt he,
And quhen the Saryzynys gan se
That the chasseris turnyt agayn
450 Thai relyit with mekill mayn. 440

[Douglas seeks to rescue another knight and is killed]

And as the gud lord of Douglas
As I said er, reparand was
Sa saw he rycht besid thaim ner
Quhar that Schyr Wilyam the Sanctecler
455 With a gret rout enveround was. 445
He was anoyit and said, 'Allace!
Yone worthy knycht will sone be ded
Bot he haff help, and our manheid
Biddys us help him in gret hy
460 Sen that we ar sa ner him by, 450
And God wate weill our entent is
To lyve or de in hys service,
Hys will in all thing do sall we.
Sall na perell eschewyt be
465 Quhill he be put out of yone payn 455
Or than we all be with him slayn.'
With that with spuris spedely

and in a rush soon rode among the Saracens, making space around them. (471) They laid in hard with all their might and consigned many of them to death. So few never made a greater defence against so many as they did. As long as they could [fight] they fought. But no valour could avail there that time, for each was slain there since the Saracens were so numerous that they were almost twenty to one. (480) The good lord Douglas was killed there, Sir William Sinclair also, and two other worthy knights, one called Sir Robert Logan, the other Sir Walter Logan; may our Lord in his great power receive their souls to heaven's bliss.

(487) The good lord Douglas died thus; the Saracens stayed no more in that place but held their way leaving those knights dead there. (491) Some of the lord Douglas's men who had found their lord dead there nearly went mad from grief and sorrow. They grieved like that over him for a long while and then carried him back with great lamentation. They found the king's heart there and took it back with them, going towards their quarters with weeping and sadness; their sorrow was moving to hear.

(501) When good Sir William Keith who had been all that day in his quarters – for he was in such sad plight that he did not come to the combat bacause his arm was broken in two – when he saw those men making such lamentation, asked quickly what it was [about].

483–84. Robert and Walter Logan; presumably of the Logans of Hartside, Lanarkshire. Fordun names Robert Logan.

501. Sir William Keith, presumably the laird of Galston to whom Barbour gave a role at the taking of Berwick (17.151, there is no William in the main Keith line). He was probably one source for the events in Spain.

Thai strak the hors and in gret hy
Amang the Saryzynys thai raid
470   And roume about thaim haf thai maid,   460
Thai dang on fast with all thar mycht
And fele off thaim to ded has dycht.
Grettar defens maid never sa quhone
Agayne sa fele as thai haf done,
475   Quhill thai mycht last thai gaf battaill   465
Bot mycht na worschip thar availl
That thai ilkan war slayn doun thar,
For Saryzynys sa mony war
That thai war twenty ner for ane.
480   The gud lord Douglas thar was slane   470
And Schyr Wilyam the Sanct Cler alsua
And other worthy knychtis twa,
Schyr Robert Logane hat the tane
And the tother Schyr Walter Logane,
485   Quhar our Lord for his mekill mycht   475
Thar saulis haff till his hevynnys hycht.
The gud lord Douglas thus wes ded,
And Sarazynys in that sted
Abaid no mar bot held thar way,
490   Thai knychtis dede thar levyt thai.   480
Sum off the lord Douglas men
That thar lord ded has fundyn then
Yeid weill ner woud for dule and wa,
Lang quhill our him thai sorowit sua
495   And syne with gret dule hame him bar.   485
The kingis hart haiff thai fundyn thar
And that hame with thaim haf thai tane,
And ar towart thar innys gane
With gretyng and with ivill cher,
500   Thar sorow wes angry for till her.   490

[*Sorrow at Douglas's death; his love of loyalty, compared to
that of Fabricius*]

And quhen of Keth gud Schyr Wilyam
That all that day had bene at hame,
For at sua gret malice wes he
That he come nocht to the journé
505   For his arme brokyn wes in twa,   495
Quhen he that folk sic dule saw ma
He askyt quhat it wes in hy

(508) They told him everything frankly, how their doughty lord had been killed by Saracens who had rallied. When he learned the circumstances, he grieved more than all the others, being so badly cast down that all who were near him were surprised. But to tell of their grieving vexes [much] and helps little. (517) Men can well understand, even if no-one tells them, how moving, sad and how traumatic it is to those who were of his following to lose such a lord as he. For he was sweet and gentle, a good [friend in] his friends' business, fierce in repulsing his enemies by his great chivalry. (525) Although he was [a man] of little display, but one who loved loyalty above everything, he rejected treason so strongly that no traitor could be near him, of whom he knew, without him being well punished for his fault. (531) I believe that the true Fabricius, who was sent with a great company from Rome to fight against Pyrrhus loved treason no less than he [did]. However when Pyrrhus had inflicted a massive defeat on him and his company, in which he escaped by luck and many of his men were killed, and he gathered an army again, (541) a great master of medicine who treated Pyrrhus, offered to Fabricius to slay Pyrrhus by treason, for he would give him a deadly poison in his next potion. (547) Fabricius who was astonished that he made such an offer to him, said, 'Indeed! Rome is sufficiently powerful to defeat her enemies completely by strength of arms in battle,

---

531-71. Fabricius and Pyrrhus. This story is referred to in Cicero *De Officiis*, III,22, but that is not the source here. The ultimate source is clearly Eutropius *Breviarium Historiae Romanae*, II, 14, whence Fordun when moralising on the death of Malcolm II (in 1035; *F1*, 185) tells how Pyrrhus offered Fabricius a fourth of his kingdom to change sides but was rejected, and how a year later, when Fabricius was leading an army against Pyrrhus, the latter's doctor offered to poison him but was rejected and, after Fabricius defeated Pyrrhus (cf. 570, implying before), was sent back to his lord, who spoke in praise of Fabricius. All this is in Eutropius and in Higden's *Polychronicon*. Now Barbour omits the bribe story, instead giving a first defeat of Fabricius by Pyrrhus (535-39), not in Fordun nor in Eutropius. This is a misunderstanding of Higden's *Pyrrhus prelio primo Romanos vicit*, where Fabricius is not mentioned, (in Eutropius II, 12 Laevinius is the heavily defeated general). Higden, *Polychronicon*, (iv, 20-24) not Fordun, is Barbour's source.

And thai him tauld all opynly
How that thar douchty lord wes slayn
510   With Sarazynys that releyt agayn,   500
And quhen he wyst that it was sua
Out-our all othyr him was wa
And maid sa wondyr yvill cher
That all wondryt that by him wer.

515   Bot to tell off thar sorowing   505
It noyis and helpis litill thing,
Men may weill wyt thoucht nane thaim tell
How angry for sorow and how fell
Is to tyne sic a lord as he
520   To thaim that war off his mengne,   510
For he wes swete and debonar
And weill couth trete hys frendis far,
And his fayis rycht fellounly
Stonay throu his chevalry
525   The-quhether off litill affer wes he.   515
Our all thing luffit he lawté,
At tresoun growyt he sa gretly
That na traytour mycht be him by
That he mycht wyt that he ne suld be
530   Weill punyst off his cruelté.   520
I trow the lele Fabricius
That fra Rome to werray Pyrrus
Wes send with a gret mengne
Luffyt tresoun na les than he,
535   The-quhether quhen Pirrus had   525
On him and on his mengne maid
Ane outrageous discumfitour
Quhar he eschapyt throu aventour
And mony off his men war slayne,
540   And he had gadryt ost agayne,   530
A gret maistre off medicyne
That had Pyrrus in governyne
Perofferyt to Fabricius
In tresoun to sla Pyrrus,
545   For intill his neyst potioun   535
He suld giff him dedly pusoun.
Fabricius that wonder had
Off that peroffre that he him maid
Said, 'Certis, Rome is welle off mycht
550   Throu strenth off armys into fycht   540

and in no way does she stoop to treason. (553) And because you would do this treachery, to get your reward you will go to Pyrrhus and he can do whatever his heart tells him to do about this.' Then he sent this master quickly to Pyrrhus and had him tell the whole story openly from beginning to end. (560) When Pyrrhus had heard it all, he said, 'Was there ever a man that conducted himself towards his enemy out of loyalty as Fabricius does to me here? It is as difficult to cause him be turned from the way of righteousness or to consent to wickedness as to turn back the sun running its course all visibly at midday.' (569) He spoke thus about Fabricius who later defeated this same Pyrrhus in open battle by hard fighting. (572) His honest loyalty made me bring in this example here, for he had the highest esteem for his loyalty. The lord Douglas had just the same, [a man] honest, true and worthy, who died as we said before; everyone grieved for him, strangers and those close to him.

(579) When his men had mourned him for a long time, they disembowelled him and then had him boiled so that the flesh could be completely removed from [his] bones. The flesh was buried there in a holy place with great ceremony. The bones they took with them and then went to their ships. (587) When they had left the king [of Castille] who was sad at their grief, they went to sea, had favourable winds, made their course to England and arrived there safely;

---

585. The bones. In the verses on him preserved in Bower, is the line *Ossibus omissis opus ostentatur obesum*, 'By lost bones the labour is shown wasted away.' If Douglas's bones are meant, I would take *omissis* to mean 'dead' rather than 'lost'. (*Bower7*, 68–69)

To vencus thar fayis, thocht thai
Consent to treusoun be na way,
And for thou wald do sic trewsoun
Thou sall to et a warysoun
Ga to Pyrrus and lat him do   545
Quhatever him lyis on hart tharto.'
Than till Pyrrus he send in hy
This maistré and gert opynly
Fra end till end tell him this tale.
Quhen Pyrrus had it hard all hale   550
He said, 'Wes ever man that sua
For leawté bar him till his fa
As her Fabricius dois to me.
It is als ill to ger him be
Turnyt fra way of rychtwisnes   555
Or ellis consent to wikkitnes
As at midday to turne agayn
The sone that rynnys his cours playn.'
Thus said he off Fabricius,
That syne vencussyt this ilk Pyrrus   560
In plane bataill throu hard fechting.
His honest leawté gert me bring
In this ensample her, for he
Had soverane price off leawté,
And sua had the lord of Douglas   565
That honest lele and worthy was
That wes ded as befor said we,
All menyt him strang and prevé.

[*The body of Douglas brought home and buried*]

Quhen his men lang had mad murnyn,
Thai debowalyt him and syne   570
Gert seth him sua that mycht be tane
The flesch all haly fra the bane
And the carioune thar in haly place
Erdyt with rycht gret worschip was.
The banys have tha with thaim tane   575
And syne ar to thar schippis gane
Quhen thai war levit off the king
That had dule for thar sorowing.
To se thai went, gud wind thai had,
Thar cours till Ingland haiff thai maid   580
And thar sauffly aryvyt thai,

then they took the road to Scotland, arriving there speedily. (594) The bones were interred in the kirk of Douglas, with mourning and much sorrow. Sir Archibald his son then had a rich tomb made of alabaster, fair and beautiful, as was appropriate for such a worthy.

(601) When Sir William Keith had brought his bones home in this fashion, and the good king's heart as well, and men had had richly made his burial with proper ceremony, the earl of Moray, who at that time had complete charge of Scotland, had the king's heart buried with great solemnity at the abbey of Melrose, where men pray always that he and his have paradise. (612) When what I describe had been done, the good earl governed the land, and protected the poor well. He maintained the law so well and kept peace in the country so [firmly] that it was never so [contented] since his time, as I heard old men say. But then, alas! he was poisoned; to see his death was very sad. (621) These lords died in this way. May he who is high Lord of everything bring them up to his great bliss and grant grace that their offspring govern the land well and strive to follow, all their lives, the great bounty of their noble elders. The one God in trinity bring us up to heaven's bliss, where there is everlasting happiness!

---

599. Douglas's tomb. This still lies locked in the surviving chancel of St Bride's kirk at Douglas, a monument in the care of Historic Scotland who reveal the whereabouts of the key.

609–10. The king's heart. In a letter of 11 May, 1329 to his son, the king underlined his devotion to Melrose abbey 'where we have laid down that our heart be buried'. This was rejected as a forgery but more recently has been accepted as genuine. (*RRS5, 380*) Something wrapped in lead, probably Bruce's heart, was unearthed in the abbey in the 1930s and 1996, and reburied on both occasions.

619–20. Moray's death. Bower accuses an English friar of poisoning him. The symptoms reported – flushed, swollen and presumably nauseous – suggest rather cancer of the liver. Moray died at Musselburgh on 20 July, 1332. This perfunctory *obit* ends the poem.

Syne towart Scotland held thar way
And thar ar cummyn in full gret hy,
And the banys honorabilly
595 Intill the kyrk off Douglas war 585
Erdyt with dule and mekill car.
Schyr Archebald his sone gert syn
Off alabast bath fair and fyne
Ordane a tumbe sa richly
600 As it behovyt to sua worthy. 590

[*The death of Moray*]

Quhen that on this wis Schyr Wilyam
Off Keth had brocht his banys hame
And the gud kingis hart alsua,
And men had richly gert ma
605 With fayr effer his sepultur, 595
The erle off Murreff that had the cur
That tyme off Scotland halely
With gret worschyp has gert bery
The kingis hart at the abbay
610 Off Melros, quhar men prayis ay 600
That he and his have paradys.
Quhen this wes done that I devys
The gud erle governyt the land
And held the power weill to warand,
615 The lawe sa weill mantemyt he 605
And held in pes sua the countré
That it wes never or his day
Sa weill, as Ik hard auld men say.
Bot syne, allace! pusonyt wes he,
620 To se his dede wes gret pité. 610
Thir lordis deyt apon this wis.
He that hey Lord off all thing is
Up till his mekill blis thaim bring
And graunt his grace that thar ofspring
625 Leid weill the land, and ententyve 615
Be to folow in all thar lyve
Thar nobill eldrys gret bounte.
Quhar afauld God in trinyte
Bring us hey till his mekill blis
630 Quhar alwayis lestand liking is. 620

APPENDIX

JEAN LE BEL'S ACCOUNT OF THE WEARDALE
ENCOUNTERS (WITH REFERENCES TO EQUIVALENT
PASSAGES IN *The Bruce*).

As soon as [the Scots] saw us, they came out of their camp,
all on foot, and drew up three good divisions carefully on the
slope of the mountain where they were camped. Below this
mountain flowed a strong and broad river full of great rocks
and stones, which we could not cross without great harm
because of these. And moreover if we had crossed the river,
there was no space between it and their force where we could
draw up our divisions.

They had their first two divisions placed on two rocky
outcrops where we could not well climb to attack them, and
they could shower us with stones if we had crossed the river
so that we could not get back. When the lords of our army
saw their disposition, they made us all dismount on foot and
take off our spurs, and form three divisions ... [*The young
Edward III was brought in front of his men to encourage them to
fight well*] A little after, the divisions were ordered to advance
towards the enemy, in good order and at a slow pace. That
was done; each division advanced a great *bonnier*, forward, to
the slope of the mountain, doing this to see if the enemies
would leave the rocks and to see how they would behave.
(19.328) But they could not see that they would move at all,
and we were so near one to another that we well knew part
of their arms, and they ours, therefore we were told to stop
to hold counsel, and (19.341) some of our fellows mounted
on coursers were sent out to skirmish and to reconnoitre the
crossing of the river, and to see their dispositions more closely.
Also they were told through heralds that if they would cross
the river to come and fight in the open, we would pull back
and leave them space to draw up their force, either immediately
or tomorrow morning; and if this didn't please them, that they
should do the same [for us] ... They answered that they would
do neither, but the king and his council could see that they
were in his kingdom and had burned and ravaged it; if he
disliked that let him come and amend it, for they would stay
there as long as pleassed them ...

[*The two armies camped for the night of 1 August, the English in great discomfort, while the Scots left some men where they had been drawn up, the rest camping with great fires.*]

Next day when the lords had heard mass, each man was armed, the divisions drawn up like the day before. When the enemy saw this, they came and drew up on their piece of ground as on the day before, and the two armies remained thus all day till afternoon; the Scots made no sign of coming towards us and also we could not go to attack without very great loss. Several of the fellows who had horses to help them crossed the river, and some on foot, to skirmish, and also they dispersed some of their host who ran about skirmishing, so that there were dead, wounded and prisoners on both sides.

After midday the lords let it be known that each should go to his quarters, for we were there for nothing; we did so very willingly, because we saw very well that there was nothing else we could do. We stayed like that for three days, and the Scots on the other side, not departing from their mountain. All the time there was skirmishing from both sides ... the Scots made such big fires usually at midnight, that it was a great wonder, and made so much noise blowing horns and shouting at the same time, that it seemed to us all hell was there, with the devils gathered there. [*The English hoped to keep the Scots there starving, for lack of bread, wine and salt, as prisoners revealed*] They had plenty of beasts which they had taken from the countryside, so could eat them ... without bread or salt ...

On the fourth day, when we woke up in the morning and we looked at the mountain where the enemy was camped, we saw nothing, for the Scots had not been there since midnight. [*The lords sent scouts to find them, which they did*] (19.485) on another mountain, camped at two short leagues from the mountain they had left. They were on the river, in a stronger position than before, camped in a wood to be better concealed and to come and go as they wanted more secretly. As soon as they were found there [*we decamped, carried everything to another mountain across from them*] and were drawn up ready as though to go against them, but as soon as they saw us coming, they came out of their quarters and came to camp just opposite, close to the river opposite us, but never seeking to come towards us; we could not go towards them without being altogether lost, either dead or captured in difficult circumstances.

We lodged like that opposite them, staying 18 days altogether [*sending heralds, offering space if they would cross to fight; this was refused.*] (19.809) All this time they had no bread, wine, salt, tanned leather nor supplies to make hose or shoes, so they made shoes of raw leather with its bristles; we ... were not too comfortable, for we didn't know where to camp, nor with what to cov⟨ ⟩, nor where to go to forage, apart from in the heath. And you can guess that we greatly missed our tents, our carts and our tools which we had bought to make things easier, but which we had left in a wood without a guard, where we could not get them back because we had forgotten where it was.

We were like that for a month open to such difficulty and in such discomfort, as you heard, that all our supplies had run out, to our great want. [*Comment on the high prices paid for food and drink by the English*]

(19.535) The first night that our lords were lodged on this mountain, Sir William Douglas, who was very brave, bold and enterprising, about midnight took 200 men-at-arms and crossed this river a good way away from our army so that he was not spotted. He threw himself on the English army very courageously, shouting 'Douglas, Douglas, you will all die, English lords!' and they killed, he and his company, more than 300, and spurred as far as before the king's tent, always shouting 'Douglas, Douglas!' They cut 2 or 3 cords of the king's tent.

In the way I have described, we stayed 22 days on these two mountains before the Scots, those who wished to skirmish always skirmishing, and almost every day one side gathered against the other once or twice. Often when we were stood down and disarmed we would hear 'to arms, the Scots have crossed.' so that we had to arms ourselves and then find out what section this was in. Then we had to guard ourselves each night by constables on the field in three places on three sides of the host, after Sir William Douglas made that attack ... [*Fear of night attack. The army exhausted by keeping watch. The Hainaulters exhausted by keeping watch against the Scots and against the English archers who hated them after the melee at York*] On the last day of the 18, a young knight was taken skirmishing, who was very unwilling to tell our lords of the state of their army, except that he said that their lords had agreed among themselves in the morning that at vespers each man should be armed, and each should follow the banner of Sir William Douglas, wherever he chose to go, and that each should keep this a secret. But the lords did not know for certain what he had in mind. The English lords took counsel together and said that perhaps the Scots might easily come to break our army on two sides, risking life and limb, for they could not endure their famine any longer. So our lords ordered that each of our two divisions be arrayed in three places before our camp, and that (cf. 19.735) we should make big fires in the mid of each place, whereby each could see the other more clearly, and that each should spend the night armed in his place to await the decree of God, and to be closer together, and that the boys should stay at the camp to guard the horses. [*The night passed like this*]

When break of day two Scottish renegades came upon one of the watches on the field, were taken and brought before the lords and the king's council. 'Sirs, why are you watching here? You keep watch for nothing because, on our heads, the Scots have been gone since before midnight, and are now 3 or 5 leagues distant; they took us with them for a league to prevent us from telling you, and then gave us leave to come and tell you.' When the lords heard this, they took counsel and saw that they had been deceived; they said that chasing after the Scots would not profit them, because they could not meet them. [*For fear of a trick they kept the renegades, and made the army stand to till prime, then stood it down*]

Meanwhile some of the fellows, and me with them, mounted on our runcins, crossed the river and climbed along the awkward and steep slope of the mountain, and went to the Scots' camp. (19.763) We found more than 500 good, fat beasts, already dead, which the Scots had killed because they could not take them with them, and they did not want to leave them alive for the English. We found more than 400 undressed-leather pots, hanging over the fire and full of meat and water to be boiled, and more than 1,000 spits of meat to be roasted, and more than 10,000 old shoes all worn, made of untreated leather, which they had left. We found five poor prisoners whom the Scots had left in this wood, all naked, tied to trees for spite, two of them with broken limbs. But we were unable to speak to them, and at once we released them and let them go, then returned to our camp [*to find that the host was being marched home.*]

Chron. Le Bel, i, 64–73.

THE DECLARATION OF ARBROATH,

A LETTER FROM THE SCOTTISH MAGNATES TO JOHN
XXII. ARBROATH ABBEY, 6 APRIL, 1320

To the most holy father and lord in Christ, the lord John, by
divine providence supreme pontiff of the holy Roman and
universal church, his humble and devout sons, Duncan earl
of Fife, Thomas Randolph earl of Moray lord of Man and
Annandale, Patrick Dunbar earl of March, Malise earl of
Strathearn, Malcolm earl of Lennox, William earl of Ross,
Magnus earl of Caithness and Orkney, and William earl of
Sutherland; Walter Steward of Scotland, William Soules butler
of Scotland, James lord of Douglas, Roger Mowbray, David
lord of Brechin, David Graham, Ingram Umfraville, John
Menteith guardian of the earldom of Menteith, Alexander
Fraser, Gilbert Hay constable of Scotland, Robert Keith ma-
rischal of Scotland, Henry Sinclair, John Graham, David
Lindsay, William Oliphant, Patrick Graham, John Fenton,
William Abernethy, David Wemyss, William Muschet, Fergus
Ardrossan, Eustace Maxwell, William Ramsay, William
Mowat, Alan Murray, Donald Campbell, John Cameron,
Reginald Cheyne, Alexander Seton, Andrew Seton, Andrew
Leslie, and Alexander Straiton, and the other barons and
freeholders and the whole community of the realm of Scotland
send all manner of filial reverence, with devout kisses of his
blessed feet.

Most holy father and lord, we know, and we gather from
the deeds and books of the ancients, that among other distin-
guished nations our own nation, namely of Scots, has been
marked by many distinctions. It journeyed from Greater Scy-
thia by the Tyrrhenian Sea and the Pillars of Hercules, and
dwelt for a long span of time in Spain among the most savage
peoples, but nowhere could it be subjugated by any people,
however barbarous. From there it came twelve hundred years
after the people of Israel crossed the Red Sea and, having first
driven out the Britons and altogether destroyed the Picts, it
acquired, with many victories and untold efforts, the places
which it now holds, although often assailed by Norwegians,
Danes and English. As the histories of old times bear witness,
it has held them free of all servitude ever since. In their
kingdom one hundred and thirteen kings of their own royal

stock have reigned, the line unbroken by a single foreigner. Their high qualities and merits, if they were not otherwise manifest, shine out sufficiently from this: that the King of kings and Lord of lords, our lord Jesus Christ, after His passion and resurrection called them, even though settled in the uttermost ends of the earth, almost the first to His most holy faith. Nor did He wish to confirm them in that faith by anyone but by the first apostle by calling (though second or third in rank), namely the most gentle Andrew, the blessed Peter's brother, whom He wished to protect them as their patron for ever.

The most holy fathers your predecessors gave careful heed to these things and strengthened this same kingdom and people, as being the special charge of the blessed Peter's brother by many favours and numerous privileges. Thus our people under their protection did heretofore live in freedom and peace until that mighty prince Edward, king of the English, father of the present one, when our kingdom had no head and our people harboured no malice or treachery and were then unused to wars or attacks, came in the guise of friend and ally to invade them as an enemy. His wrongs, killings, violence, pillage, arson, imprisonment of prelates, burning down of monasteries, despoiling and killing of religious, and yet other innumerable outrages, sparing neither sex nor age, religion nor order, no-one could fully describe or fully understand unless experience had taught him.

But from these countless evils we have been set free, by the help of Him who, though He afflicts yet heals and restores, by our most valiant prince, king and lord, the lord Robert, who, that his people and heritage might be delivered out of the hands of enemies, bore cheerfully toil and fatigue, hunger and danger, like another Maccabeus or Joshua. Divine providence, the succession to his right according to our laws and customs which we shall maintain to the death, and the due consent and assent of us all, have made him our prince and king. We are bound to him for the maintaining of our freedom both by his right and merits, as to him by whom salvation has been wrought unto our people, and by him, come what may, we mean to stand. Yet if he should give up what he has begun, seeking to make us or our kingdom subject to the king of England or to the English, we would strive at once to drive him out as our enemy and a subverter of his own right and ours, and we would make some other man who was able to defend us our king. For as long as a hundred of us remain alive, we will never on any conditions be subjected to the lordship of the English. For we fight not for glory nor riches nor honours, but for freedom alone, which no good man gives up except with his life.

Therefore it is, reverend father and lord, that we beseech your holiness with our most earnest prayers and suppliant hearts, that, recalling with a sincere heart and pious mind that, since with Him whose vice-regent on earth you are there is neither weighing nor distinction of Jew and Greek, Scotsman or Englishman, you will look with paternal eyes on the troubles and anxieties brought by the English upon us and upon the church of God; that you will deign to admonish and exhort the king of the English, who ought to be satisfied with what he has, since England used to be enough for seven kings or more, to leave in peace us Scots, who live in this poor little Scotland, beyond which there is no dwelling place at all, and who desire nothing but our own. We are willing to discharge fully to him (due regard having been paid to our standing) whatever will bring about peace for us. It truly concerns you to do this, holy father, who sees the savagery of the heathen raging against Christians, as the sins of Christians have indeed deserved, and the frontiers of Christians being pressed inward day by day; and you must see how much it will tarnish the memory of your holiness if (God forbid it) the church suffers eclipse or scandal in any branch of it during your time. Then rouse the Christian princes who for false reasons pretend that they cannot go to the help of the Holy Land because of wars they have with their neighbours. The truer reason that prevents them is that in warring on their smaller neighbours they anticipate a readier return and weaker resistance. But He from whom nothing is hidden well knows how cheerfully we and our lord the king would go there if the king of the English would leave us in peace. We profess and testify this to you as the vicar of Christ and to all Christendom.

But if your holiness, giving too much credence to the tales of the English, will not give sincere belief to all this, nor refrain from favouring them to our confusion, then the slaughter of bodies, the perdition of souls, and all the other misfortunes that will follow, inflicted by them on us and by us on them, will, we believe, be imputed by the Most High to you. Therefore we are and will be ready, and in these [letters] we are bound, to obey you as His vicar in all things as obedient sons; to Him as supreme king and judge we commit the maintenance of our cause, casting our cares upon Him and firmly trusting that he will inspire courage in us and bring our enemies to nothing.

May the Most High preserve you to His holy church, in holiness and health for many days to come. Given at the monastery of Arbroath in Scotland, on the sixth day of the month of April in the year of grace thirteen hundred and twenty and the fifteenth year of the reign of our aforesaid king.

Index

Index of introduction, translation and notes. In the case of 'Robert I' only the translation is indexed. In the case of chroniclers, only the introduction is indexed. A king or queen is indexed by name; an earl usually by earldom.